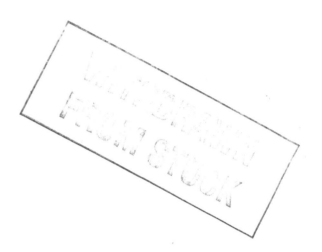

HANDBOOK OF GENTRIFICATION STUDIES

Handbook of Gentrification Studies

Edited by

Loretta Lees

Professor of Human Geography, University of Leicester, UK

with

Martin Phillips

Professor of Human Geography, University of Leicester, UK

EE Edward Elgar
PUBLISHING

Cheltenham, UK • Northampton, MA, USA

Published by
Edward Elgar Publishing Limited
The Lypiatts
15 Lansdown Road
Cheltenham
Glos GL50 2JA
UK

Edward Elgar Publishing, Inc.
William Pratt House
9 Dewey Court
Northampton
Massachusetts 01060
USA

A catalogue record for this book
is available from the British Library

Library of Congress Control Number: 2017959500

This book is available electronically in the **Elgar**online
Social and Political Science subject collection
DOI 10.4337/9781785361746

ISBN 978 1 78536 173 9 (cased)
ISBN 978 1 78536 174 6 (eBook)

Typeset by Servis Filmsetting Ltd, Stockport, Cheshire
Printed by CPI Group (UK) Ltd, Croydon CR0 4YY

Contents

Figures

Tables

Contributors

Editor
Loretta Lees (FAcSS, FRSA) is Professor of Human Geography in the School of Geography, Geology and the Environment at the University of Leicester, UK, where she is Co-director of the Critical and Creative Geographies Research Group. She is internationally known for her research on gentrification/urban regeneration, global urbanism, urban policy, urban public space, architecture and urban social theory (see her TEDxBrixton talk https://www.youtube.com/watch?v=gMz1x5_yF2Q). Since 2009 she has co-organised *The Urban Salon: A London forum for architecture, cities and international urbanism* (see http://www.theurbansalon.org/) and since 2016 the Leicester Urban Observatory (www.leicesterurbanobservatorywordpress.com/). She is the (co) author/(co)editor of eleven books including *Gentrification* (2008, Routledge) and *The Gentrification Reader* (2010, Routledge) with Tom Slater and Elvin Wyly, and *Planetary Gentrification* (2016, Polity) and *Global Gentrifications: Uneven Development and Displacement* (2015, Policy Press) with Hyun Bang Shin and Ernesto López-Morales. Her scholar-activist work on gentrification can be seen in https://justspace.org.uk/2014/06/19/staying-put-an-anti-gentrification-handbook-for-council-estates-in-london/

With
Martin Phillips is Professor of Human Geography in the School of Geography, Geology and the Environment at the University of Leicester, UK, where he is Co-director of the Critical and Creative Geographies Research Group. His research interests include rural social and cultural geographies, including those related to rural gentrification and rural class analysis. This research includes the comparative study of rural gentrification in France, the United Kingdom and the United States. His recent work also includes research on the environmental dimensions of rural gentrification, rural energy geographies, and climate change mitigation and adaptation in rural communities.

Contributors
Sandra Annunziata is a Lecturer in Urbanism and Urban Theory in the Department of Architecture, University of Roma Tre, Rome, Italy, and in European Urbanism in the Cornell in Rome Study Abroad Program of the College of Architecture, Art, and Planning, Cornell University. She was recently a Marie Curie Fellow at the University of Leicester where she completed a two-year, EU-funded project with Loretta Lees on anti-gentrification policies and practices in three southern European cities – Rome, Madrid and Athens. The research involved working with groups resisting gentrification in all three cities. She has guest edited a special issue of *UrbanisticaTre* on anti-gentrification practices in European cities.

Eduardo Ascensão is a postdoctoral researcher at the Centro de Estudos Geográficos, University of Lisbon, Portugal. An anthropologist and urban geographer, his research is on urban informality, housing and postcolonialism in Portuguese-speaking countries. He has published in the *International Journal of Urban and Regional Research*, *CITY* and the edited volume *Global Gentrifications*, amongst others.

Michaela Benson is a Reader in Sociology at Goldsmiths, University of London, UK. She is known for her contributions to the sociology of migration and her research on class, home, identity and belonging. She is the author of *The British in Rural France* (2011, Manchester University Press), co-author of *The Middle Classes and the City* (2015, Palgrave), and co-editor of the volumes *Lifestyle Migration* (2009, Ashgate), and *Understanding Lifestyle Migration* (2015, Palgrave).

Willem Boterman is an Assistant Professor in Urban Geography at the University of Amsterdam, the Netherlands. His PhD thesis was on middle-class families in Amsterdam. His current research focuses on class, school choice and the links between school segregation and residential segregation.

Susannah Bunce is an Assistant Professor in the Department of Human Geography and City Studies, University of Toronto, Scarborough, Canada. She recently completed a comparative study of urban community land trust organizations in Canada, the United States, and the United Kingdom.

Agustín Cocola-Gant is a post-doctoral researcher at the Centre of Geographical Studies, University of Lisbon, Portugal. His research focuses on the political economy of cities and pays particular attention to gentrification, displacement, tourism, architectural heritage and historical urban geography. His current project examines the relationship between tourism and gentrification, in particular exploring the social impacts caused by the growth of tourism in residential urban areas. He is author of the book *El barrio Gótico de Barcelona. Planificación del pasado e imagen de marca* (2011, second edition 2014) in which he explores the recreation of a historic area fuelled by the desire to display an idealised Catalan past and promote Barcelona as a tourist destination.

Mark Davidson is an Associate Professor of Geography at Clark University, USA. He is an urban geographer whose research interests span gentrification, urban policy, sustainability, mega-events and social theory. His current research is examining the impacts of municipal bankruptcies in the United States and includes an attempt to re-theorise critical urban theory. He has held fellowships at the Nelson A. Rockefeller Center for Public Policy and Social Science, Dartmouth College, and the Urban Research Centre, University of Western Sydney.

Freek de Haan is a researcher in the Department of Geography, Planning and Environment at the Nijmegen School of Management, Radboud University, the Netherlands. As part of a European-funded project (JPI Urban Europe, *beyondgentrification.com*), his research investigates gentrification processes in Arnhem, Vienna and Istanbul, applying relational and practice approaches to themes of demographics, planning, commerce and real estate. Apart from research, he is active in senior citizen education (HOVO Rotterdam), directing collective experiments in technical democracy *Young@Mind: Invisible Rotterdam* (2015–2016) and *Young@Mind: Unhuman Rotterdam* (2017).

Geoffrey DeVerteuil is a Senior Lecturer in the School of Geography and Planning at Cardiff University, UK. His research is at the intersection of inequality, its spatial expressions and its management within cities. He is interested more specifically in inequality as it manifests itself in terms of mental health, substance abuse treatment, homelessness, precarious migrants and the voluntary sector. More recently, he has focused on the nexus of gentrification, service hubs, immigration and cosmopolitanism/parochialism in global cities such as London and Los Angeles.

Petra Doan is Professor of Urban and Regional Planning at Florida State University, USA. She has published on international planning as well as planning for marginalised communities, with a special focus on lesbian, gay, bisexual, and transgendered individuals. Several of her papers explore transgendered perceptions of cities and public spaces and others examine the development of LGBTQ spaces in urban areas. In 2011 her edited book, *Querying Planning: Challenging Heteronormative Assumptions and Reframing Planning Practice*, was published by Ashgate. In Spring 2015 Routledge published her second edited volume, *Planning and LGBTQ Communities: The Need for Inclusive Queer Spaces.*

Melissa Fernández Arrigoitia is an urban sociologist and Lecturer in Urban Futures at the University of Lancaster, UK. Her interdisciplinary work focuses primarily on housing and critical and feminist geographies of the home. She has pursued a range of questions regarding urban belonging and exclusion in the UK, Europe, Latin America, South Asia and the Caribbean; including the construction of urban 'others' during a contested social housing demolition process in Puerto Rico. Her most recent strands of investigation have looked at housing as contested objects of 'value' that are being mobilised with and through 'crisis' to re-produce traditional and alternative notions of home and urban citizenship. This includes a long-term ethnography into the production of alternative home futures and collaborative, community-led practices, notably senior co-housing, in London. She co-edited (with Katherine Brickell and Alexander Vasudevan) *Geographies of Forced Eviction: Dispossession, Violence, Insecurity* (2017, Palgrave).

Shenjing He is Associate Professor in the Department of Urban Planning and Design at The University of Hong Kong, China. Her primary research interests focus on urban redevelopment/gentrification, housing differentiation and socio-spatial inequality, rural-urban migration and urban poverty. Shenjing has published more than 80 journal articles and book chapters in English and Chinese. She is the co-author/co-editor of *Urban Poverty in China* (2010, Edward Elgar), *Locating Right to the City in the Global South* (2013, Routledge), *Urban Living: Mobility, Sociability, and Wellbeing* (2016, Springer), and *Changing China: Migration, Communities and Governance in Cities* (2016, Routledge). She is the Chinese editor of *Urban Studies.*

Cody Hochstenbach is a PhD candidate in Urban Geography at the University of Amsterdam, the Netherlands. His PhD thesis investigates gentrification and socio-spatial inequalities from a demographic and life-course perspective. Other research focuses on urban policies, and on the intergenerational transmission of inequalities.

Phil Hubbard is Professor of Urban Studies in the Department of Geography, King's College London, UK. His research examines processes of social exclusion and displacement in the city, with a focus on marginal and disadvantaged groups, including sex workers, asylum seekers, working class populations and ethnic minority groups. He is the author of nine books, including *Key Ideas in Geography – City* (2018, second edition,

Routledge) and *The Battle for the High Street* (2017, Palgrave), which explores the gentrification of local shopping streets.

Tone Huse is a Post Doctoral Fellow at the Tik Centre for Technology, Innovation and Culture, University of Oslo, Norway. Her research concerns the geographies and materialities of politics, how policy is made and what its effects are. Tone has studied this through various projects, spanning political activists' use of public space, gentrification, postcolonial urbanism, and urban climate politics. She is the author of *Everyday Life in the Gentrifying City* (2014, Ashgate) and is currently working on issues concerning the economisation of nature.

Emma Jackson is a Senior Lecturer in Sociology at Goldsmiths, University of London, UK. Her research explores the relationship between everyday practices of belonging and the production of spaces and places in cities. She is author of *Young Homeless People and Urban Space: Fixed in Mobility* (2015, Routledge), co-author of *Go Home? The Politics of Immigration Controversies* (2017, Manchester University Press), and *The Middle Classes and the City: A Study of Paris and London* (2015, Palgrave), and co-editor of *Stories of Cosmopolitan Belonging: Emotion and Location* (2014, Routledge).

Juliet Kahne was awarded an MA in Cities and a PhD in Geography from King's College London, supervised by Loretta Lees, on the topic of gentrification in Brighton and Los Angeles respectively. She works for Projects for Public Spaces in New York City. Juliet has participated in numerous community-focused urban research projects, from monitoring community recovery in the Lower Ninth Ward in New Orleans after Hurricane Katrina, to collaborating on an evaluation of a city-led regeneration scheme in one of London's economically struggling outer boroughs. Her work has focused on exploring and understanding communities through ethnographic methods.

Chloe Kinton is a Research Associate in the Department of Geography at Loughborough University, UK. Her research interests include rural gentrification, (de-)studentification and geographies of higher education.

Antonia Layard is Professor of Law at the University of Bristol, UK. Her research is in law and geography where she has explored how law, legality and maps construct space, place and 'the local'. Her book *Law, Place and Maps: Balancing Protection and Exclusion* will be published by Glasshouse Press, Routledge, in 2018. She has particular interests in 'urban law', and the legal provisions and practices involved in largescale regeneration and infrastructure projects. She has published on community-led housing, creative place-making, property, public space, plus housing and localism. She has a special interest in thinking through the legalities of fighting gentrification.

Ernesto López-Morales is an Associate Professor in the Department of Urban Planning, University of Chile, and Associate Researcher in the Centre of Studies of Conflict and Social Cohesion (COES), Chile. His research topics cover land and housing markets, gentrification, public urban infrastructure and land value capture, social contestation and activism, and social self-management of housing production, especially in Latin American cities. He has co-edited *Global Gentrifications: Uneven Development and Displacement* (2015, Policy Press) and co-authored *Planetary Gentrification* (2016, Polity Press), besides several recent papers and book chapters.

Hamil Pearsall is an Assistant Professor in the Geography and Urban Studies Department, Temple University, USA. Her research bridges several themes in human-environment and human geography: the social dimension of sustainability, environmental justice and health, and community resilience to environmental and economic stressors. Her recent work has focused on environmental gentrification, the role of vacant land in urban greening efforts, and the impact of environmental justice on urban sustainability planning.

Andy Pratt is Professor of Cultural Economy and Director of the Centre for Culture and the Creative Industries, City, University of London, UK. Andy is an internationally acclaimed expert on the topic of the cultural industries and cities. His research has three strands. The first focuses on the social and economic dynamics of clustering and knowledge exchange. The second strand concerns the definition and measurement of employment in the cultural, or creative, industries. The third concerns cultural governance and policy making at the national, regional and urban scales. Andy is Editor-in-Chief of *City, Culture and Society*.

Patrick Rérat is a Professor in Geography of Mobilities in the Institute of Geography and Sustainability, University of Lausanne, Switzerland. His research explores urban changes through the lenses of various forms of spatial mobilities such as residential mobility, internal migration and everyday mobility. His recent papers have addressed gentrification, reurbanization, the real estate market, housing choices, the migration trajectories of young graduates, as well as 'everyday practices' and spatial capital. He is also an expert for several institutions in planning and a member of the Council for the Organisation of the Territory, a Swiss extra-parliamentary committee.

Clara Rivas-Alonso is a PhD student in Geography at the University of Leicester, UK. Her PhD is an investigation into everyday practices and perceptions of resistance in a neighbourhood in Istanbul under threat from state-led gentrification – Okmeydani. With a masters degree in postcolonial theory she is interested in the more invisible solidarities that escape institutional attempts at rent extraction. She argues that the current global urban condition calls for more innovative methods of resistance.

Bahar Sakızlıoğlu completed her PhD in 2014 at the Urban and Regional Research Center, University of Utrecht, the Netherlands. Her PhD was about the displacement experiences of disadvantaged groups in gentrifying neighbourhoods in Amsterdam and Istanbul. Among her main research interests are displacement, gentrification, accumulation by dispossession, and gendered geographies of gentrification. She has written papers on the politics of displacement and the experiences of disadvantaged people living in gentrifying neighbourhoods. Bahar currently holds an H2020 Marie Curie Research Fellowship in the School of Geography, Geology and the Environment at the University of Leicester, UK, and is researching the mutual construction of gender and space in gentrifying neighbourhoods in Istanbul and Amsterdam.

Hyun Bang Shin is Associate Professor of Geography and Urban Studies at the London School of Economics and Political Science, UK. His research centres on critical analysis of the political economic dynamics of urbanisation, the politics of redevelopment and displacement, gentrification, housing, the right to the city, and mega-events as urban spectacles, with particular attention to Asian cities. He has recently co-edited *Global*

Gentrifications: Uneven Development and Displacement (2015, Policy Press) and co-authored *Planetary Gentrification* (2016, Polity Press). He is also working on a monograph *Making China Urban* (Routledge), and is co-editing *Contesting Urban Space in East Asia* (Palgrave Macmillan) and *The Political Economy of Mega Projects in Asia: Globalization and Urban Transformation* (Routledge).

Tom Slater is a Reader in Urban Geography at the University of Edinburgh, UK. He has research interests in the institutional arrangements producing and reinforcing urban inequalities, and in the ways in which marginalised urban dwellers organise against injustices visited upon them. He has written extensively on gentrification (notably the co-authored/edited books, *Gentrification* [2008, Routledge] and *The Gentrification Reader* [2010, Routledge]), displacement from urban space, territorial stigmatisation, welfare reform, and social movements. Since 2010 he has delivered lectures in 18 different countries on these issues, and his work has been translated into 10 different languages and circulates widely to inform struggles for urban social justice.

Darren Smith is Professor of Human Geography and Associate Dean of Enterprise at Loughborough University, UK. His research interests include rural gentrification, studentification, regeneration, and population change and sub-national family migration. He is Co-editor of *Population, Space and Place*, and Associate Editor of *Journal of Rural Studies*. He is Chair of the Organising Committee of the International Conference on Population Geographies (ICPG), Steering Group Member of the IGU Population Commission, and was formerly Chair of the Population Geography Research Group of RGS-IBG (2006–2013).

Jess Steele (OBE) has 25 years' experience as a local community activist and entrepreneur in Deptford, London and Hastings in the UK, and at national level as Deputy Chief Executive of the British Urban Regeneration Association and Director of Innovation at DTA/Locality, including leading the development and delivery of the Meanwhile Project, the Campaign Against Delinquent Ownership, and the national Community Organisers Programme. She is a part-time PhD student in the School of Geography, Geology and the Environment, University of Leicester, UK, working with Loretta Lees. As Director of Jericho Road Solutions, she provides coaching to neighbourhood groups and community businesses, as well as working with government, funders, corporates and academics on national initiatives to make neighbourhood work easier.

Zhao Zhang is currently an independent scholar based in Mainland China. He received his PhD from University College Dublin, Ireland. He has worked for University College Dublin, The University of Hong Kong and The University of Hong Kong-Shenzhen Institute of Research and Innovation. His research interests lie in scrutinising housing inequalities, urban redevelopment and grassroots resistance to urban social injustice in Mainland China and beyond from the perspective of cultural and political economy. He is also dedicated to examining the impacts of urban housing, fiscal and financial policies on urban residents.

Preface and acknowledgements

The debates over gentrification will no doubt continue, as will resistance to gentrification, but we also need alternatives to this socially unjust process to be placed on the table. It is alternatives that should be at the forefront of gentrification scholars' work now, even if I recognise that this is no mean feat. Cities, communities and policy makers need to be persuaded of the value of alternatives in order to displace the gentrification blueprint worldwide. Proving the negative impacts of gentrification remains important but resistance without the elaboration of feasible alternatives is simply not enough.

Special thanks to Matthew Pitman at Edward Elgar for inviting me to collate this Handbook and for his patience with my delivery. Thanks to all the contributors for their excellent chapters, your input is much appreciated. Thanks to my colleague at Leicester, Martin Phillips, for helping review some of the chapters and to my PhD student Clara Rivas-Alonso for her help in formatting chapters.

Loretta Lees
August 2017

1. Introduction: towards a C21st global gentrification studies
Loretta Lees

This *Handbook* surveys the contemporary state of play of the gentrification studies literature, a body of work that now dominates both the sub-discipline of urban geography and also urban studies more generally. It does not set out to rehearse previous debates on the definition of 'gentrification' nor does it rehearse the well-worn battlegrounds over explanations (on these see Lees, Slater and Wyly, 2008, 2010); rather this book is a collection of chapters by both long-standing and up-and-coming researchers on gentrification that represents the latest in global thinking on this process. It provides critical reviews and appraisals of the current state of, and future development of, conceptual and theoretical approaches, as well as empirical knowledge and understanding in gentrification studies. It also seeks to encourage dialogue across disciplinary boundaries, for the contributors sit in and work across geography, sociology, anthropology, planning, policy, law, and so on.

The book is divided into 5 parts: Part 1 looks at recent attempts to extend and rethink gentrification as a planetary process and condition, drawing on the 'new' comparative urbanism; and a more 'earthly' take that replaces old style complementarity in gentrification studies with relationalism. Part 2 reviews the key/core concepts that have dominated gentrification studies to date, including class, landscape, rent gaps, and displacement; adding spatial capital to this list, updating them conceptually and globalizing them. Part 3 looks at other social cleavages in addition to social class, including sexualities, age, ethnicity and gender, providing ideas on future research trajectories. The cross-cutting of social cleavages in addition to social class needs fresh and deeper empirical investigation; this book seeks to instigate such an agenda. Part 4 looks at some of the different types of gentrification, including slum gentrification, new-build gentrification, public housing gentrification, tourism gentrification, retail gentrification, gentle/soft gentrification, environmental/green gentrification, the cultural economy and gentrification, and wilderness/rural gentrification. These types of gentrification all deserve attention in their own right but can also be read together. Part 5 contains chapters on living and resisting gentrification. Unlike in most gentrification books, this part takes seriously the complexities of living with gentrification, resistance to gentrification (all types and levels of resistance) but also key to this resistance – possible alternatives to gentrification. Here readers will find some of the most comprehensive reviews of resistance in the literature to date and real attempts to find alternatives to gentrification. Although the key users of the book are likely to be advanced undergraduates, post-graduate students, and international scholars of gentrification, the chapters also have real purchase for policy makers, planners, housing activists, and indeed everyday people for whom gentrification is an issue.

It is now over 50 years since the British sociologist Ruth Glass coined the term 'gentrification' in 1964. In 2014, University College London held an event to celebrate her contributions (see https://www.mixcloud.com/UCLurbanlab/playlists/ruth-glass-and-london-aspects-of-change-1964-2014/). Yet still, few people have taken the time to read the bulk of Ruth Glass's other work, beyond that little paragraph where she coined the term 'gentrification' (Glass, 1964). Her wider work deserves much more attention; indeed her writings could be seen on a par with those of Jane Jacobs (1961) in New York City. In fact, Glass was a much better predictor of future urbanism than Jacobs was. Indeed, her writings are quite prescient in places. Lees, Shin and López-Morales (2016) discuss her 'prescient comparative urbanism' but there are many other instances too. Glass's research and commentary on social mixing is especially insightful and echoes the findings of Bridge, Butler and Lees (2011) in their discussion of mixed communities policy, which has produced social segregation in the form of gentrification. In her discussion of a new high-rise council estate completed in 1950, Churchill Gardens in Pimlico, London, she was critical of the kind of social balance that today's planners want – a mixed population. She says that this mix 'has given rise to social tensions and anxieties on a moderate, yet still noticeable, scale' (Centre for Urban Studies, 1964: 282). Although she found a genuine neighbourliness in Pimlico flats, she also found a social divide amongst the tenants and undercurrents of resentment. She states: 'Neither "social balance" nor practical collaboration has led to the ideal pattern of perfect "social mixing"' (Centre for Urban Studies, 1964: 282). Indeed, in a footnote (9 on p.289) she says that a dislike of social mixture in Churchill Gardens actually played a part in the decisions of people to move out! She asserts that ideas about social balance and mixing in planning 'are over simplified, and indeed unrealistic. Social solidarity and segmentation inevitably co-exist' (p.282). She is surely correct when saying that 'the aim of "neighbourhood unity" has been much stressed in planning literature; its achievement has even sometimes been regarded as the ultimate yardstick of success, by comparison with which mundane aims, such as the provision of good homes in proximity to workplaces and services, has been seen as subsidiary' (p.283). Here we find some important earlier empirical work to input into longstanding debates around gentrification and social mixing (see Lees, 2008). Perhaps policy makers should (re)visit Glass's work, for she said many of the things that those gentrification scholars critical of (new) urban renewal and mixed communities policy are now saying.

Glass predicts the future of London amazingly well: 'any district in or near London, however dingy or unfashionable before, is likely to become expensive; and London may quite soon be a city which illustrates the principle of the survival of the fittest – the financially fittest, who can still afford to live and work there' (Glass, 1964: xx). She talks about the lodging-house districts, adjacent to expanding middle class areas, 'where all sorts of people who have to keep, or want to obtain, a foothold in central London, are crammed together – and frequently have to pay exorbitant rents for the privilege' (p.xx). We only have to look at the massively expanding and increasingly expensive private rental sector in London today to see this being played out again. She also recognized the emergence of new middle-class fractions before Daniel Bell's (1973) *Coming of Postindustrial Society* or David Ley (1996) who wrote about a cultural new class – 'there has been some reshuffling of social groups, mainly again among the middle classes' (Glass, 1964: xvi). Her wider work really does deserve our attention in gentrification studies and beyond.

Since Glass coined the term 'gentrification' half a century ago in London, academic writing on gentrification has exploded and gentrification studies has become a field in its own right. Figure 1.1 shows that academic writing on gentrification has more than trebled between 1979 and 2016. I have tried to represent the current state of the field in

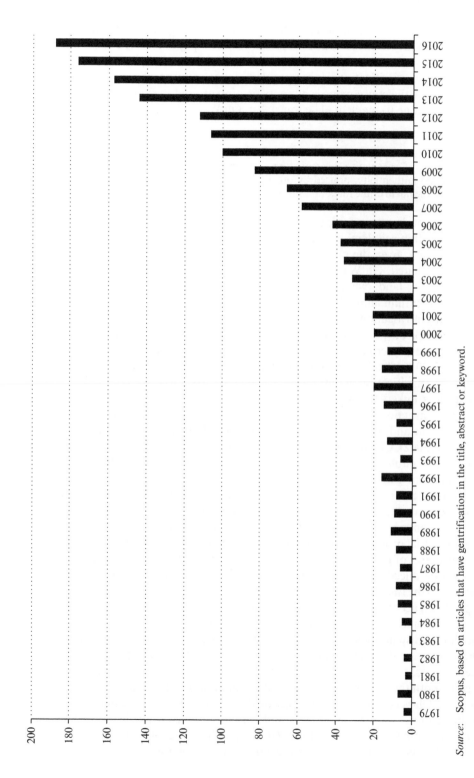

Source: Scopus, based on articles that have gentrification in the title, abstract or keyword.

Figure 1.1   Articles on gentrification 1979–2016

this *Handbook*. There is recognition now that the process is playing out globally and that solutions are urgently needed. In 2016 the *Guardian* newspaper asserted 'Gentrification is a global problem. It's time we found a better solution' (https://www.theguardian.com/cities/2016/sep/29/gentrification-global-problem-better-solution-oliver-wainwright). It set out to examine the consequences of gentrification around the world and interrogate what was being done to tackle it. The journalist, Oli Wainwright, described the process well:

> Gentrification is a slippery and divisive word, vilified by many for the displacement of the poor, the influx of speculative investors, the proliferation of chain stores, the destruction of neighbourhood authenticity; praised by others for the improvement in school standards and public safety, the fall in crime rates, and the arrival of bike lanes, street markets and better parks.

The series did not, however, look at the burgeoning body of work on global gentrifications. Gentrification scholarship still struggles to get into the public and policy realms, it is a difficult task given the predominantly negative evidence base most gentrification scholars have collated. Oli Wainwright asserted a solution to gentrification could be a tax on the value of land, 'which would capture the value of improvements for the local community, rather than lining the pockets of investors'. But this fails to recognize the role of the state in gentrification or different land ownership regimes worldwide.

Academic work on global gentrifications has shown how gentrification is a central ingredient in the reproduction of capitalism worldwide (see Lees, Shin and López-Morales, 2015, 2016; also López-Morales, Shin and Lees, 2016; Shin, López-Morales and Lees, 2016, on gentrification in Latin America and East Asia respectively). Contemporary gentrification is linked to variegated neoliberalisms operating around the world and involves the destruction of state redistribution and provision of welfare while creating new forms of state and elite policy to promote capital mobility and consumption (Brenner and Theodore, 2002). Chapter 16 in this *Handbook* by *Melissa Fernández Arrigoitia* on the gentrification of public housing shows the relationship between the destruction of this form of welfare and gentrification well. The expansion of free market rules to a worldwide scale has turned cities into reserves of rent extraction (Logan and Molotch, 2007), but things have escalated to the point where the secondary circuit of real estate (urban, rural and real estate anywhere in between) has taken over or is at least equal to the primary circuit of industrial production. The ascendance of the secondary circuit of real estate has escalated processes of gentrification around the planet resulting in what Harvey (1990: 77) calls 'market-produced zoning of ability to pay'. This is what Ruth Glass also identified in her reference to the financially fittest having best access to London. The built environment then is produced according to the supposed demands of affluent users, and this displaces indigenous inhabitants and low-income users (see Chapter 9 by *Zhao Zhang* and *Shenjing He*, who discuss displacement and also accumulation by dispossession). Chapter 8 on rent gaps shows the elite discourses circulating on rent gaps and details how rents gaps are produced (that is, socially constructed); here, *Tom Slater* underlines the importance of investigating both the production and indeed consumption of planetary rent gaps.

Since Ruth Glass coined the term 'gentrification' in London it has entered the public lexicon in countries around the world and this has triggered academic debate over whether a term coined in London in the 1960s has purchase outside of London in the 21st century. In Chapter 2, *Hyun Bang Shin* and *Ernesto López-Morales* address these debates and focus on why 'gentrification' cannot be so easily dismissed as a term for processes around the globe. It is interesting that academics are much less bothered by the use of the term 'suburbanization' around the world, than they are with the term 'gentrification'. There seems to be something about the term 'gentrification' that provokes negative reaction from many quarters, both from those in their ivory towers and from activists on the ground. Yet as Ley and Teo (2014) have said of Hong Kong, even if the term is not widely circulated in media and public discourses, its ontological presence can be identified through careful scrutiny of how urban neighbourhoods are targeted for capital (re)investment involving displacement of local inhabitants. Theirs is strong affirmation for investigating gentrification even in those cities (and countries) where the term (and thus the process) seemingly does not even exist. Waley (2016) talks usefully of making a claim for gentrification to be understood from the Global East. Chapter 19 by *Juliet Kahne* shows that gentrification is also happening in another city where one would not expect it to exist, in the most archetypal *suburban* city in the Global North – Los Angeles, one of the few North American cities which has long *not* been associated with gentrification. Indeed, spatial capital (see *Patrick Rérat*'s useful discussion in Chapter 7) in terms of commuting, connections, quality of life and environmental concerns has (re)emerged as a significant factor not only in LA but in gentrification globally.

The different chapters in this book evaluate the state of play in the gentrification studies literature. These scholarly contributions think through gentrification in both developed and developing countries, even if we are uncomfortable with such terms; for as the chapters show, developing world entities such as informal housing or slums exist in developed world cities too (see *Eduardo Ascensão* on slum gentrification in Chapter 14). For a number of the contributors, English is not their first language and their linguistic competences mean that they are able to draw on non-English literatures on gentrification. This immersion in non-English literatures is most welcome and it will no doubt enrich the gentrification studies literature. Indeed in Chapter 4 I continue to make the case for comparative research on gentrification across the globe, taking on board ideas from the 'new' comparative urbanism, pushing back at those who reject gentrification as a process in their specific locational and research contexts. Importantly I argue that there is much theoretical, conceptual and especially methodological work yet to be done. I also balance the neglect and marginalization that I have long been interested in: that of people being socially cleansed from cities and communities worldwide by gentrification, with the neglect and marginalization of cities in the Global South in (northern) urban theory that 'new' comparative urbanists are focused on.

This collection is also the first to take seriously the incorporation of what could be considered gentrification's 'other[s]' (Phillips, 2004), such as rural/wilderness gentrification as opposed to inner city gentrification (see Chapter 22 by *Darren Smith, Martin Phillips* and *Chloe Kinton*), retail gentrification as opposed to residential gentrification (see Chapter 18 by *Phil Hubbard*), and what might be seen as 'add on gentrifications' such as tourism gentrification (see Chapter 17 by *Agustín Cocola-Gant*), and green/environmental gentrification (see Chapter 20 by *Hamil Pearsall*). The blurring of the urban and the rural is to be found in different ways in all of these gentrification types. This blurring (discussed in literatures on planetary urbanization and planetary gentrification (see Brenner and Schmid, 2012, 2014; Lees, Shin and López-Morales, 2016)) is a new window of opportunity now for (re)conceptualizations of these processes. Of course, Glass's (1964) use of the term 'gentrification' was itself a complex mix of urban and rural – as Hamnett (2003) points out, it was 'rooted in the intricacies of traditional English rural class structure' (p. 2401). The term is ironic in that it makes fun of the snobbish pretensions of affluent middle-class households who desire a rural, traditional way of life (or at least a commodified version of it – as seen in the uptake of Aga stoves, wood burning stoves, and fired earth tiles) (Lees, Slater and Wyly, 2008). Gentrification and rustification are intimately connected. A recent article in *The New York Times* (Smith, 2017) exemplifies this when it talks about 'wilderness chic' in a restaurant called Raymonds in St. John's, Newfoundland, Canada, where:

> the moose is garnished with flecks of pickled winter chanterelles, dark, bitter cress leaves and crisp, celadon-green caribou moss. A dab of aioli, flavoured with powered young pine needles, sits in the middle, and the whole thing is drizzled with sunflower oil and white birch syrup.

The journalist talks about the pairing of rural and sophisticated, local and cosmopolitan. The owner even has a trapper who brings him beaver, which is then cooked in a pouch and served on brussel sprout leaves. The wilderness is brought to town and made urbane.

In between urban gentrification and rural gentrification there is also 'suburban gentrification', which is not covered in this book in any detail. In fact, very little has been written on this to date (but see Leaf, 2002; Huang, 2010; and Hudalah, Winarso and Woltjer, 2016). Lees (2003) discussed the suburban mindsets and tastes of super-gentrifiers in New York City, likewise those moving to the suburbs from the city or between suburbs in the Global North now desire what have been seen to be more urban characteristics associated with inner city gentrification. In the US, as in other places, the notion of the sterile, homogenous suburb that long acted as the counterpoint to inner city gentrification is being broken down. Many moving to and living in the suburbs are now seeking walkable villages with a creative vibe and shorter commutes. In another recent *New York Times* article (Foster, 2017), a family moved from the more stereotypical Long Island suburbs to Katona in Westchester County, an hour from New York City. The mother said:

> It was so down to earth, I didn't need to put on a full face of make up to bring my kids to school. I met a lot of artists and could talk about politics and travel.

Such comments could well have been from pioneer gentrifiers in New York City (NYC) itself, instead they were from suburban upstate New York. In the newspaper article, creative cities guru Richard Florida is interviewed and comments that he knew someone who 'evaluated suburban towns based on the availability of fresh mozzarella'; such a food metaphor would have been made for NYC neighbourhoods undergoing gentrification in the 1970s and 1980s. He said: 'Do you want to see pick up trucks or Volvo SUVS? . . . Trump bumper stickers or resist signs?'. These used to be the choices that Anglo-American gentrifiers made between inner city living and suburban living. In the Global North, the traditional notions of suburb versus inner city and their cultural identifiers have broken down, showing the mainstreaming of a culture of gentrification and planetary urbanization. In other parts of the world, the Anglo-American inner city/suburb dichotomy never existed in the first place or not in the same way (Lees, Shin and López-Morales, 2016). *Martin Phillips* says in Chapter 6 that gentrification landscapes urban and rural, material and symbolic, or lived, are a defining, if often taken for granted, feature of gentrification.

It is clear that the classic landscapes from the gentrification studies literature are both dated and not necessarily useful outside of the Anglo-American context.

The *Handbook* looks at a number of different types of gentrification, thinking through what is or is not distinctive about these types. These types overlap of course, for new-build gentrification (see Chapter 15 by *Mark Davidson*) can take place in urban or rural contexts, and certainly is taking place in cities as wide apart as London, Istanbul, Beijing and Santiago. New-build gentrification is evident in slum gentrification and it is the gentrification that replaces public housing. But there are other types of gentrification that are not in the book: super-gentrification (Lees, 2003), for example, does not appear. But this process is continuing in neighbourhoods like Brooklyn Heights in New York City. Some longtime residents are trying to stay in place and protect their real estate investment. For example, the Dean of CUNY Law School and a partner in a law firm recently sold their house in Brooklyn Heights for $5.65 million and moved into a condo elsewhere in the neighbourhood. The ex-chairman of the Brooklyn Academy of Music's board of trustees sold his Brooklyn Heights Historic District home to his son for $4.5 million in 2017. Companies are now buying up property in Brooklyn Heights, even Donald Trump's son-in-law, Jared Kushner, has become involved in profit-making in the neighbourhood. His company Kushner Cos recently did a makeover of the most expensive house in Brooklyn Heights, which had been a law school dorm that the company bought for $7.4 million. The landmark Greek Revival style row house now has an elevator, central air conditioning and five bedrooms that are all suites. Alas the new owner who bought the property for $12.9 million in 2017 does not think it is good enough and is planning to remodel it inside and out! The new owner is the Vice President of AJ Wealth in Lower Manhattan. Yet these sums seem miniscule when we look at the 'hyper-gentrification' happening in areas of London where the top 1%, multi-millionaires and billionaires are buying properties at £20 million ($26.4 million) plus (see Weber and Burrows, 2016). Classic gentrification texts on the role of the 'new' middle classes in gentrification seem somewhat outdated now in the context of super-gentrification and hyper-gentrification; and indeed in contexts outside of the Global North where class is constructed differently. In fact, as *Michaela Benson* and *Emma Jackson* state in Chapter 5, the different social and political histories framing class globally need due attention. I would also add political economic histories and applaud their emphasis on class as relational, situational and in progress. Likewise, *Bahar Sakizlioğlu* also argues, in Chapter 13, that we need to return to looking at gender in gentrification studies, updating our conceptualizations and deepening and expanding our empirical work. A female gentrifier in Istanbul may or may not share the attributes of a female gentrifier in Toronto or Paris.

In an increasingly cosmopolitan world, immigration and ethnicity are topics that gentrification researchers have continued to under-examine. Chapter 12 by *Tone Huse* makes a renewed case for why it is important to research gentrification and ethnicity; in particular, how gentrification can reorder or amplify ethnic segregation. While in Chapter 25, *Geoffrey DeVerteuil* argues that immigration adds to the complexity of race and gentrification, as some immigrants are racialized while others are not. DeVerteuil shows how immigrants can be a barrier to gentrification, displaced by gentrification or gentri-fiers themselves. This complex position of being both victim and cause of gentrification can also be found in *Andy Pratt*'s discussion of artists and gentrification in Chapter 21. He wants us to separate out artists and cultural producers from cultural consumers such as the creative class and hipsters. It is the interaction of immigrants or artists with capital that seems to be the crux of the issue. As *Petra Doan* says in Chapter 10, the complex ways in which capital and sexual orientation interact remain incompletely understood. The same could be said about age/generation too (see Chapter 11 by *Cody Hochstenbach* and *Willem Boterman* who place age centre stage).

Freek de Haan, in Chapter 3, would like gentrification scholars to let go of what he calls 'familiar unifying yet legislative concepts and narratives' in gentrification studies. But this is already happening, because a closer look at gentrification globally forces us to unlearn much of what we have learnt. Narratives based on the Anglo-American post-industrial city are not good at explaining gentrification in 21st century Mumbai! *De Haan* wants to 'slow down conclusions on gentrification's actual presence or absence in order to extract new possibilities from situations of empirical and ethical ambiguity'. I am not sure we need to slow down to do this and the ontological multiplicity that he seeks is, I would argue, already present. Few would now argue that there is a single 'elephant of gentrification' (Hamnett, 1991).

The day before submitting this book I was in the US listening to Maine Public Radio when a two-hour debate came up on gentrification in Portland Maine, a small city I wrote about some time ago (Lees, 2006), in which rents have risen by 40% in the last five years. Fair Rent Portland was seeking a referendum on rent stabilization to protect working class citizens, this is different to NYC's failed rent control. According to a statement from Fair Rent Portland, 'rent stabilization will allow renters to feel secure in their homes, begin to build up financial reserves, and make long-term economic plans. It will ensure that the children of renters can remain in a single district, that vulnerable citizens with mental or physical health conditions can heal without having to face eviction, and that local businesses will have the workforce that they need to grow'. Who could argue against that? Oakland, California, has adopted a similar plan, fixing the amount landlords can raise rent to the Consumer Price Index. Indeed worldwide, from the new tax on foreign buyers in Vancouver, Canada (an extra 15% on the purchase price of a property) to the new Milieuschutz Law (social environment protection) in Berlin, policy makers are looking for ways to control gentrification. Importantly, this *Handbook* includes, in Chapter 23 by *Sandra Annunziata* and *Clara Rivas-Alonso*, a very detailed and much needed survey of the growing literature on resistance to gentrification. In the summer of 2017, in Barcelona and Majorca, protest groups including Arran Paisos Catalans and Endavant Ciutat Vella rallied against tourism gentrification, saying 'Tourism kills the city. Tourists go home. You are not welcome.' Their charge, like that in Chapter 17, is that tourism is making their city too expensive: that people are renting out flats to tourists, forcing residents out. More widely that the situation is forcing people to work in the tourism industry with long hours and low wages. The extreme end of this is the 'dead city' of Venice, which has few real city residents and where most property is turned over to tourists. In Chapter 26, *Antonia Layard* shows that property and planning law (in this case in England) has been used to facilitate gentrification, but it also can be used to counter gentrification. Of course, property and planning law is different in different countries and even cities; as such, context is very important here. The use of law in resisting gentrification needs much more investigation by gentrification scholars (see Hubbard and Lees, 2018).

Much less has been written about alternatives to gentrification; in this *Handbook*, two chapters have been devoted to this. Chapter 24 by *Susannah Bunce* outlines the utility of community land trusts and eco villages. The strength of these initiatives, she argues, lies in their ability to galvanize public interest in and raise necessary discussions about community owned and stewarded land and housing as alternative modes of property ownership. It is interesting that social housing is not put forward as an alternative to gentrification; indeed, as Chapter 16 shows, social/public housing is being gentrified worldwide. This reflects the central role of the state today in both promoting and pushing gentrification forwards and both the destruction of, and lack of building of, social housing; something that, as Ruth Glass (1964) also said, has ruined the prospects for rational urban development: '. . . municipal housing has never yet been viewed as a social service intended for, and progressively extended to, all citizens irrespective of their circumstances' (p.286). The alternatives to gentrification, as Chapter 24 and Chapter 27 show, now seem to be individual- or community-led initiatives. The state is no longer trusted to take a role. Chapter 27, written by *Jess Steele*, a gentrification scholar and regeneration specialist, puts self-renovating neighbourhoods on the table. As such, this final chapter perfectly bookends this volume, for it really directs gentrification scholars to the hard work we have yet to do on developing alternatives to the gentrification blueprint that has come to dominate cities, places and spaces worldwide.

REFERENCES

Bell, D. (1973) *The Coming of Postindustrial Society,* New York: Basic Books.

Brenner, N. and Schmid, C. (2012) 'Planetary urbanization', in Gandy, M. (ed) *Urban Constellations*, Berlin: Jovis, pp. 10–13.

Brenner, N. and Schmid, C. (2014) 'The "urban age" in question', *International Journal of Urban and Regional Research*, 38(3), 731–755.

Brenner, N. and Theodore, N. (2002) 'Cities and the geographies of "actually existing neoliberalism"', *Antipode*, 34(3), 349–379.

Bridge, G., Butler, T. and Lees, L. (eds) (2011) *Mixed Communities: Gentrification by Stealth?*, Bristol: Policy Press. (Republished 2012 by University of Chicago Press.)

Centre for Urban Studies (ed) (1964) *London: Aspects of Change*, London: MacKibbon and Kee.

Foster, B. (2017) 'Exchanging suburbs', *The New York Times*, July 30, p. 10.

Glass, R. (1964) 'Introduction: aspects of change', in Centre for Urban Studies (ed) *London: Aspects of Change*, London: MacKibbon and Kee.

Hamnett, C. (2003) 'Gentrification and the middle-class remaking of inner London, 1961–2001', *Urban Studies*, 40(12), 2401–2426.

Harvey, D. (1990) *The Condition of Postmodernity*, Oxford: Blackwell.

Huang, W. (2010) 'Immigration and gentrification – a case study of cultural restructuring in Flushing, Queens', *Diversities*, 12(1), 56–69.

Hubbard, P. and Lees, L. (2018) 'The right to community?: Legal geographies of resistance on London's final gentrification frontiers', *CITY: Critical Analysis of Urban Trends, Culture, Theory, Policy, Action.*

Hudalah, D., Winarso, H. and Woltjer, J. (2016) 'Gentrifying the peri-urban: Land use conflicts and institutional dynamics at the frontier of an Indonesian metropolis', *Urban Studies*, 53(3), 593–608.

Jacobs, J. (1961) *The Death and Life of Great American Cities*, New York: Random House.

Lees, L. (2008) 'Gentrification and social mixing: towards an urban renaissance?', *Urban Studies*, 45(12), 2449–2470.

Lees, L. (2006) 'Gentrifying down the urban hierarchy: "the cascade effect" in Portland, Maine, USA', in Bell, D. and Jayne, M. (eds) *Small Cities: Urban Experience Beyond the Metropolis*, London: Routledge, pp. 91–104.

Lees, L., Shin, H. and López-Morales, E. (eds) (2015) *Global Gentrifications: Uneven Development and Displacement*, Bristol: Policy Press.

Lees, L., Shin, H. and López-Morales, E. (2016) *Planetary Gentrification*, Cambridge: Polity Press.

Lees, L., Slater, T. and Wyly, E. (2008) *Gentrification*, New York: Routledge.

Lees, L., Slater, T. and Wyly, E. (eds) (2010) *The Gentrification Reader*, London: Routledge.

Ley, D. (1996) *The New Middle Class and the Remaking of the Central City*, Oxford: Oxford University Press.

Ley, D. and Teo, S. (2014) 'Gentrification in Hong Kong? Epistemology vs. ontology', *International Journal of Urban and Regional Research*, 38(4), 1286–1303.

Logan, J. and Molotch, H. (2007) *Urban Fortunes: The Political Economy of Place,* Berkeley and Los Angeles: University of California Press.

López-Morales, E., Shin, H. and Lees, L. [guest editors] (special issue) (2016) 'Latin American gentrifications', *Urban Geography*, 37(8).

Phillips, M. (2004) 'Other geographies of gentrification', *Progress in Human Geography*, 28(1), 5–30.

Shin, H., Lees, L. and López-Morales, E. [guest editors] (special issue) (2016) 'Locating gentrification in the Global East', *Urban Studies*, 53(3).

Smith, C. (2017) 'Classical training meets wilderness chic', *The New York Times*, July 23, p. 6.

Waley, P. (2016) 'Speaking gentrification in the languages of the Global East', *Urban Studies*, 53(3), 615–625.

Weber, R. and Burrows, R. (2016) 'Life in an alpha territory: Discontinuity and conflict in an elite London "village"', *Urban Studies*, 52(13), 2349–2365.

PART 1

RETHINKING GENTRIFICATION (THEORY)

2. Beyond Anglo-American gentrification theory
Hyun Bang Shin and Ernesto López-Morales

2.1 INTRODUCTION

Has gentrification 'gone global'? Has it diffused from its usual suspects (for example, London and New York City) to other non-Anglo-American cities that are more peripheral to global capitalism? What is the meaning of gentrification as a 'global urban strategy' (Smith 2002)? Does it mean gentrification as a neoliberal urban policy colonizing cities outside the core of global capitalism? Or, does it mean that the dominant epistemological horizon has expanded to be more inclusive of non-Anglo-American cities that have seen (historic) endogenous urban processes akin to gentrification? And, what do scholars in the Global North understand about gentrification processes taking place in emergent cities in the Global South, some of which they may not even locate on their world map?

In this chapter, we discuss what it means to study gentrification beyond the Anglo-American domain, emphasizing the possibility of gentrification mutating across time and space, in the same way any other social phenomenon associated with the changing nature of capitalism goes through mutation. We also question here why academia should maintain the Anglo-American cultural region as a necessary comparative framework to talk about gentrification elsewhere. Gentrification is now embedded in urbanization processes that bring together politics, culture, society and ideology. Such urbanization is uneven and place-specific, thus displaying multiple trajectories, hence there is a need to provincialize (c.f. Chakrabarty 2000; cr Lees 2012) gentrification as we know it (namely, the rise of gentrification in plural forms or in other words, *provincial* gentrifications). However, we argue this must be done without losing the most critical aspects of gentrification that need to be investigated, namely the class remaking of urban space involving displacement. For us, gentrification is a reflection of broader political economic processes that result in the unequal and uneven production of urban(izing) space, entailing power struggles between haves and have-nots, be they disputes over the upgrading of small neighbourhoods or larger clashes related to social displacement experienced at the metropolitan or even regional scale.

In this chapter, we focus on four key issues. Firstly, we discuss the epistemology of comparative gentrification studies, explaining what it means to think of gentrification in pluralistic perspectives. In doing so, we remain conscious of how gentrification reflects the more fundamental shift in politics and economics through active circuits of (real estate) capital and policies, which are often dominated by national and transnational economic elites, in spite of widespread dispossession of people across the Global South; thus, we call for *planetary* thinking of gentrification (Lees et al. 2016). Secondly, related to the first point, we discuss the linguistics of gentrification, questioning the extent to which gentrification can be a useful conceptual tool to analyze urban processes in places where gentrification as an expression cannot be easily translated into local expressions. Thirdly, we ascertain the importance of scrutinizing the role of the state and the workings of political elites, for they collectively play a pivotal role in (re-)imagining city-making and deciding how resources are to be allocated in terms of production and consumption. Fourthly, we further elaborate on the state question in gentrification research. The state in the Global South has been of greater significance in gentrification processes because of the vulgar nature of capitalism lacking a historical compromise between dominant and subordinate classes. Finally, we conclude the chapter by thinking about what possibilities there are for seeing social conflicts through the lens of gentrification and how anti-gentrification struggles could be positioned in a broader scheme of societal transformation and defending the right to the city in a manner that is far more socially just than what the current stages of capitalism allow for.

2.2   AN EPISTEMOLOGY OF COMPARATIVE GENTRIFICATION STUDIES

Some urban researchers have been struggling to come to terms with the suitability of a gentrification framework as a useful lens to analyze processes of urban restructuring outside of the Global North. Some still see gentrification (somehow unimaginatively) as associated only with specific spatio-temporal contexts, not susceptible to transfer to elsewhere outside the usual suspects. These sceptics have mechanically interpreted London and New York City as the only emblems of gentrification. This is an extreme perspective on gentrification, that treats it as a historic-cultural process associated primarily with inner-city London in the 1960s (for example, Maloutas 2012). Viewed this way, the process of gentrification is effectively fossilized, and disavowed of any applicability outside of a particular time and place/space: it is thus rendered lower than a 'mid-range concept'.

Some sceptics further argue that gentrification is a micro-economic process involving formal property rights and playing out in formal real estate markets only (for example, Ghertner 2015). Such a viewpoint reflects confusion in the midst of its attempt to intertwine reductionist theorization of urban change with the rich Marxist interpretations of gentrification, and displays a tendency (1) to regard cities in the Global South as qualitatively different and isolated from more general processes of capitalist accumulation; (2) to treat slums and informal settlements as distinct urban spaces where logics of capital accumulation cannot penetrate; (3) to disregard how deeply market and non-market processes are entangled in the same way, how formal and informal processes are fused together in the global economy; (4) to understate how much the operation of speculation and landlordism can be prevalent in informal settlements. From this perspective, any effort to apply the gentrification lens to other geographical contexts outside of the United Kingdom (and possibly North America) is seen as the imposition of Anglo-American hegemony. But adhering to such a perspective would also make it difficult to understand that the commodification of decommodified housing stocks has been a major thrust of gentrification in London too, as witnessed by the gentrification of council housing estates (Lees 2014). It also ignores the many other comparable precedents in North America, as well as in Latin America and Asia from the 1970s (for example, Janoschka et al. 2014). The variegated ways in which those occupying informal, non-market housing are dispossessed of their rights in many parts of the world are part and parcel of gentrification processes (see Lees et al. 2015).

Those who deny the application of 'gentrification' to non-Western cities should perhaps revisit the history of how the concept has evolved within the confines of the so-called Global North. By the 1970s, gentrification as a term and concept was appropriated by critics on the other side of the Atlantic, discussed in the context of mainly New York City but also other major cities in the eastern US, and indeed Canada. A number of young North American urban scholars saw gentrification as having resulted from two major forces inherent to capitalism: (1) the socio-cultural transformations in the aftermath of the 'baby boom' era; (2) the emerging importance of the real estate sector that took advantage of widening rent gaps. For more than two decades, gentrification debates battled back and forth over the 'post-industrial, new middle class' thesis and the 'rent gap exploitation' thesis over what had caused the rise of gentrification (see Lees, Slater and Wyly 2008). Importantly, both hypotheses never questioned the stretching of the gentrification concept beyond the domain of inner-city London in the 1960s; they were more concerned about the North American particularities that gave rise to a particular form of mutated gentrification (Ley 1980; Smith 1979; also see Slater 2006, for a full account of this historical debate). In a similar vein, readers should not be surprised by the scale and nature of contemporary gentrification in London, where expensive, new-build, often high-rise redevelopment came to dominate (Davidson and Lees 2010). This mutation has been supported by both New Labour and Tory policies of housing privatization and individual responsibility, and has led to soaring house prices, severe unaffordability issues, and unprecedented rates of displacement, not only of the most deprived segments of society but also of the relatively affluent middle classes.

The fossilization of gentrification also makes it difficult for critics to understand how urban processes coined as gentrification (especially with its focus on real estate capital, the recomposition of class, displacement of original land users and space commodification) have become increasingly pronounced in Asian and Latin American cities. For decades, a large number of non-Anglo-American cities have undergone substantial socio-spatial changes due to intensive state-led and/or private-led investment (often built upon growth coalitions between endogenous political and business elites), which have resulted in upward and unequal social re-stratification of neighbourhoods, *favelas*, *gecekondu* and *lilong* (Lees et al. 2015; López-Morales 2016a, forthcoming; Sánchez and Broudehoux 2013). There is a whole new global context which is seeing the predominance of capital over publicly oriented policy decisions regarding the use of urban space as an asset for the sake of capital accumulation: this is, however, nothing more than the corollary of decades of advancement of a relatively ample and adaptive array of state discourses and policies that range from extreme free-market ideology or neoliberalism (Harvey 2005) to market-oriented state developmentalism in the case of East Asia (Shin et al. 2016). Around the world, gentrification – as an explicit or implicit, or even as a hidden discourse – has become a major justification and goal for urban redevelopment in economies that depend heavily on the circulation of capital for commodification and exploitation of already urban or urbanizing space.

2.3   THE LINGUISTICS OF GENTRIFICATION

Attempts to investigate and conceptualize gentrification in non-Anglo-American cities face some familiar criticisms; such as, for example, that gentrification is difficult to translate into other languages as the term is too UK-specific. But, does it really matter whether or not gentrification as a term exists in a particular locality? Comparative urban studies on gentrification have produced significant achievements, calling for a more generic definition of gentrification to be adopted (Clark 2005) and asking researchers to pay attention to conjunctural factors that give rise to locally tuned processes of gentrification or actually existing gentrification.

Once we rescue gentrification from its confinement to the place specificities of 1960s London, and build upon the achievements of 20–30 years of comparative gentrification studies, we can broadly define gentrification as 'the commodification of space accompanying land use changes in such a way that it produces indirect/direct/symbolic displacement of existing users and owners by more affluent groups' (Shin et al. 2016: 458; see also the categories proposed by Janoschka et al. 2014). This is in line with Clark's (2005) call not to equate Ruth Glass's particularistic coining of the concept with its origin, calling instead for a more theoretically productive and intellectually inspiring 'generic gentrification' (Clark 2015) that can be applied as both an analytical tool and empowering political goal for the local grassroots to defeat, impede or regulate. The key to this perspective is the realization that generality and particularity are not mutually exclusive and can co-exist in theoretical and political realms. Similar awareness can be considered as one of the major tenets of comparative studies on gentrification; building on the work of the late Doreen Massey, who once argued that 'interdependence [of all places] and uniqueness [of individual places] can be understood as two sides of the same coin, in which two fundamental geographical concepts – uneven development and the identity of place – can be held in tension with each other and can each contribute to the explanation of the other' (1993: 64; cited in Lees et al. 2016: 6). It is perfectly possible to generalize gentrification as a process of land use change that results in the unequal appropriation of rents and causes the displacement of existing land users, while at the same time emphasizing the particular trajectories of how this process is shaped by the workings of the place-specific political, economic and social relations that co-exist in space.

At this point, it is useful to revisit the recent argument made by Ley and Teo (2014), who discuss how in Hong Kong the absence of linguistic expressions of gentrification does not preclude the ontological presence of gentrification as an actually existing urban process. Although the argument might seem a little obvious, we concur with them that it is possible to think of the ontological presence of gentrification in a given society, even though there is no such word as 'gentrification' being circulated in public or academic discourse. A comparative perspective on gentrification can suggest that gentrification as an urban process is often known by more localized forms of expressions such as *blanqueamiento* in Mexico (López-Morales 2016a) and 'urban redevelopment' in Seoul (Shin and Kim 2016). It may also be translated into an expression that is more useful for local populations, while retaining the core principle of gentrification in the translated version. For example, in South Korea, reflecting the growing popularity of gentrification in the media,[1] the National Institute of Korean Language, a government agency that works to translate foreign expressions into standard Korean, has suggested in May 2016 that in

---

[1]   According to Lee (2016), there were less than ten reports of 'gentrification' made by the media annually between 2004 and 2011, but the frequency of media reports referring to gentrification exploded, with 45 mentions in 2014, and 813 in 2015.

Korean, gentrification should be translated as *dungji naemolim*, literally meaning eviction/ displacement from one's nest/home.[2] While discussions about gentrification were largely confined to academic discourse, from 2015 it began to receive significant attention in the media and public discourse.

Latin American experiences inform us that theorizing gentrification should be 'sensitive enough to recognize that gentrification also means urban inequalities and segregation accentuated by the state responding to large-scale private interests' (López-Morales 2016a: 571). In Chile, for example, well before the term gentrification started to be used in the analysis of the unequal production of urban space in a highly neoliberalized housing market (López-Morales 2008), ample discussions took place to critically understand the effects of private-led residential redevelopment in the country's major cities (Sabatini et al. 2001). The importance of exploiting the potential to appropriate rents from land development has been historically so pronounced (as part of an institutional design by the state since the early 19th century aimed at increasing property tenure among the lowest strata of society) that there has been frequent conflict between the private exploitation of the commercial value of land and the 'right to stay put' of those living on that land (Wyly et al. 2010), or in simpler terms, between developers and petty landowners who are usually the ones facing unsurmountable barriers (for example, soaring housing prices and lack of financial loans) in finding replacement accommodation within redevelopment areas or nearby after selling their land (López-Morales 2016b). Following Clark (2005: 258), 'any process of change fitting this description is, to my [our] understanding, gentrification.'

2.4   THE STATE-DESIGNED NEXUS BETWEEN GENTRIFICATION AND DISPLACEMENT

One of the major characteristics of contemporary capitalism and gentrification is the scaling up of real estate projects. Increasingly it is an entire district or a neighbourhood that becomes subject to the intervention of real estate capital, resulting in wholesale clearance and reconstruction. Real estate capital has grown large in scale, hence the domination of big real estate corporations that have access to state institutions and finance, while smaller firms operate to pick up niche properties in the shadow of scaled-up projects. More importantly, however, the scaling up of real estate projects calls for a dedicated role for local and central states to clear barriers and obstacles, to facilitate the displacement of oppositional voices, creating *tabula rasa* conditions for real estate investment and the production of ideological discourses (Shin 2016; Slater 2014). To help facilitate private sector investment, governments assemble a range of preferential and subsidizing policies. Joined-up efforts by governments, government-affiliated agencies, developers and the media often produce stigmatization of neighbourhoods to be subject to 'revitalization', as if such areas and residents therein have lost their vitality and fallen into eternal disrepute or the so-called 'territorial stigma' (see Shin 2016; Lees 2014; Wacquant, Slater and Pereira 2014). Reinvestment and hence gentrification emerges as an alternative to real or

---

[2]   The announcement can be accessed here: http://news.korean.go.kr/index.jsp?control=page&part=view& idx=10332 (last accessed on 13 June 2017).

perceived persistent decay and dilapidation, a mythical presumption that forces people to believe that there is no other alternative. In similar vein to Defilippis (2004) and Lees (2014), Slater (2014) calls this a 'false choice urbanism', and says there is an urgent need to 'blast open this tenacious and constrictive dualism of "prosperity" (gentrification) or "blight" (disinvestment)' and reveal the intrinsic relationship between the two in a more fundamental process of uneven capitalist urbanization.

The scaling up of real estate projects leads to the rise of mega-gentrification and mega-displacement, which is enabled by the dispossession of people's rights through the workings of a growth alliance between the (central and/or local) state and (real estate) capital. Obviously, the nature of this alliance will differ across geographies. Very often, in the Global South, governments and developers are fused together through ownership shares or the close ties between developers and ruling families or political figures as in Abu Dhabi and Lebanon. The close nexus between large businesses and political elites in South Korea is another example of this politico-economic fusion (Shin and Kim 2016), and so is the 'state capitalism' that has emerged in mainland China. In Latin America, a more recent example includes the scandal of Adebrecht, the Brazilian construction group that is currently under investigation in several Latin American countries for possible cases of bribery in campaigns and the private accounts of top politicians including national presidents (*The Guardian* 2017).[3] Where there is a strong alliance between the state and real estate capital, it becomes increasingly difficult to challenge real estate development and resulting displacement.

As for mega-displacement and gentrification in post-colonial states, ethnic-religious tensions often become the sources of retribution against the marginalized, resulting in mega-displacement to set redevelopment and gentrification in motion. In Mumbai, for instance, the 1995 Maharashtra state elections led to the formulation of the state government's Slum Rehabilitation Scheme (SRS) that was to carry out large-scale slum clearance in order to clear ways for real estate and infrastructure construction in globalizing Mumbai (Doshi 2013). Eligibility for the resettlement of slum dwellers was based on paper-based evidences of residence in Mumbai prior to the cut-off date of the scheme. The SRS was to enable the involvement of real estate developers in redeveloping slums by introducing 'transferable development rights', which allowed developers to produce higher density market rate housing on cleared slums or elsewhere in the suburbs, on condition that developers also provided compensation units for eligible slum dwellers, although off-site resettlement was more popular among those affected. The Vision Mumbai redevelopment programme to transform Mumbai into the 'next Shanghai' resulted in 'Mumbai's "tsunami"' of mass clearance and eviction, demolishing about 45,000–90,000 informal structures and rendering 300,000–350,000 people homeless (see Doshi 2013; Ramesh 2005). Affected were those 'illegal' settlements which emerged after 1995. Xenophobic campaigns by the local political party aggravated the conditions of evictees further, as 'most Vision Mumbai evictees were ethnically North Indian or Muslim' (Doshi 2013: 858).

In promoting mega-gentrification, project financing becomes important, as an

---

3   Odebrecht is one of the key operators in the Porto Maravilha mega redevelopment in the (until a few years ago) derelict Zona Portuária (Sánchez and Broudehoux 2013).

individual developer (or even a consortium of developers) will often find it difficult to finance the entire project on its own. In this regard, the origin of capital becomes key to understanding the nature of the state-capital relationship, as well as the state-society relationship. National savings schemes such as the Central Provident Fund in Singapore or the National Housing Fund in South Korea have had a strong role to play in facilitating real estate construction in these countries, while foreign direct investment tends to be highlighted in recent years with regard to the rise of mega urban projects (Shatkin 2008). Surplus from a country or region often gets channelled into other regions in a geographical switching of capital (see Percival and Waley 2012 on Korean investment in Cambodian new town construction, and Kutz and Lenhardt 2016 on inward investment in Morocco). Sovereign wealth funds, as well as savings of middle- or upper-class families in Asia (for example, Singapore and China) have emerged as major investors in cities of the Global North, suggesting that the circulation of real estate capital has become quite complex and involves multiple directions between the Global North and the Global South and within each region.

While financialization plays a key role in the rise of (speculative) real estate projects (see Moreno 2014), how local governments make use of their planning powers to increase the financial viability of real estate projects is pivotal for urban development in the Global South in particular, where endogenous investors and major political elites work together with transnational investors. An exemplary case can be found in Mexico, which involves a public-private corporation called PROCDMX that cooperates with global financial players for the purpose of transforming entire districts in central Mexico City into transport corridors and hubs for luxury real estate investment. In this scheme, the Mexican state has privatized urban lands in core locations as public contributions to the public-private partnership, but at the same time guarantees the private sector's real estate operation by issuing 40-year-long contracts so that the private sector can extract rents from zoned urban space. Researchers and neighbourhood activists together wonder nowadays whether this carefully designed, sanitized new space of exception would be able to host/enlist any type of dissent, social deviation, grassroots cultural expressions or undesired actors (Gaytán 2016).

In many ways, the example of Mexico's PROCDMX chimes with the case of Buenos Aires's Puerto Madero mega-project, initiated in the late 1980s and since then having deeply transformed the city's old and derelict port area, Puerto Madero. It all started in 1989 when the city government transferred public land to the ad hoc, newly created Corporación Antiguo Puerto Madero (hereafter CAPM). The redevelopment of Puerto Madero was carried out under a prevailing neoliberal planning philosophy that widely failed to keep its initial promises of social mixing and public infrastructure provision: the result was a concentration of high-rise luxury condominiums and elite-oriented commercial land use that prevented social mixing. For instance, the highly segregated and enclosed Rodrigo Bueno shanty town located nearby lost access to the newly created 'ecological park' that was supposed to be open for public use according to the law that allowed the Puerto Madero operation (see Cuenya and Corral 2011; Garay et al. 2013). There, experts from Barcelona provided ideas and good-practice strategies for the CAPM operation (see Lees et al. 2016). Critics complain that although Puerto Madero has produced a new landscape pertinent to the world-city status of Buenos Aires, the area is separate from the rest of the city socially and economically, that the masses have been excluded from the project, and that the privatization of public resources such as public lands resulted in private investors' appropriation of enormous returns on their investment with comparatively minuscule collection of tax revenues (Garay et al. 2013).

2.5   THE STATE QUESTION

The above discussions about the state-designed nexus between gentrification and dispossession compels us to examine the state question. In Western Europe, there is a legacy of social democratic welfare statism, which has been an outcome of the post-war reconstruction and consensus between labour and capital. In this context, gentrification has a limited role to play if we assume the interventionist role of the state to provide collective consumption including housing welfare. The social democratic orientation of the state, and its legacy in the contemporary neoliberal world, would also create certain barriers to the full exploitation of real estate commodities. The disintegration of the post-war consensus and welfare statism, has therefore, served to accelerate gentrification processes in Anglo-American cities. The demise of Western Keynesian welfare statism has been accompanied by a state rhetoric that argues that gentrification is an inevitable outcome or the only means to revitalize post-industrial urban spaces constrained by a lack of public funding. Lang (1982: 1) goes as far as to claim that 'gentrification comprises one of the few urban success stories that is not dependent on a massive infusion of government moneys.'

The rhetoric of an incompetent state is frequently put forward in the Global South, where corrupt, ineffective or rent-seeking state officials are thought to have failed to provide basic urban services and functions. This is an incompetence that can be very functional for capitalist goals. In the context of a neglectful state that displays impotence in terms of bringing change and maintaining the urban core, private capital initiatives are often regarded as a viable alternative. For instance, Elshahed (2015) is sympathetic to the involvement of real estate capital, especially in a developer's (Al-Ismailia for Real Estate Investments) attempt to reuse and therefore salvage Egypt's modernist heritage building – Cinema Radio – without gentrification impacting on other current users in the vicinity (Elshahed 2015: 137). However, the ability of the private sector, formal or informal, to deliver key urban services needs to be viewed with care, especially with regards to their intervention in land and housing markets.

Contrary to incompetent state rhetoric, East Asian developmental statism is on the other end of the spectrum of understanding in terms of how the state has led the way to provide business-friendly environments as part of nation-building and maintaining state legitimacy (Castells 1992; Haila 2016; Woo-Cumings 1999). And, it is in this context that the rise of gentrification in East Asia is to be thought of. The lack of a mature civil society in East Asia is often pointed out as a reason for the brutal oppression of protesters against eviction by the state. This had been the case in South Korea, for example, in the early 1980s when there was an all-out attack on tenant protesters against a new redevelopment programme that resulted in large-scale new-build gentrification of dilapidated sub-standard neighbourhoods in Seoul (see Ha 2001; Kim 1999). China's urban redevelopment histories are also full of the violent use of state power to prevent local residents from hindering redevelopment progress (Shao 2013). It is also necessary to remember that in the historical context of urbanization, under the developmental state, the notion of private urbanism may simply be a myth that disguises the underlying and historic intervention of the developmental state in urban development. For example, Shin (2017) examines the case of smart city construction in Songdo, South Korea, and reveals that despite a more recent surge of smart city and private urbanism rhetoric associated with the Songdo City project, the characteristics of developmental state-led urbanization turned out to be persistent. These include the long-term commitment of the (local) state to realize the construction of a brand-new town, the developmental vision repackaged as green growth, and smart city promotion to adjust to the changes of the reigning urbanism. Moreover, profiteering from real estate projects, a key characteristic of speculative Korean urbanization, turned out to be the fundamental motive of both domestic and transnational developers, despite the dominant discourses of smart urban growth (see also Sonn, Shin and Park, 2017).

On the other hand, a longer trajectory of neoliberalization in Latin America provides a picture that can be contrasted with East Asian states. However, this is not a story of top-down neoliberal imposition but a story of endogenous political and economic interests engaging with global players, on their own terms and conditions. Redeveloping slums (read *slum gentrification*) has involved the workings of the state that often spearhead the changes. The story of Puerto Madero in Buenos Aires, aforementioned, is also one which saw the involvement of the state to eradicate shanty towns and displace local residents. So far, for at least two decades, the southern part of Buenos Aires (La Boca, the Barracas and Parque Patricios neighbourhoods, among others), which previously the state paid no attention to leaving slum dwellers in what became their neighbourhoods (see Rodriguez and Di Virgilio 2016), has increasingly witnessed the expansion of rent-seeking, culturally hip gentrification waves that are transforming the whole central city (Herzer et al. 2015). It is also illuminating to note that such attacks on shanty towns have historic precedents in the city. An unexplored case of state-led gentrification already occurred in 1977 during the eradication of a shanty town in the Bajo Belgrano district: an important reason for this state action was that the main stadium for the 1978 Football World Cup was located next to this *villa miseria*. Subsequently, in the 1990s and 2000s, the land was gradually redeveloped to accommodate luxury condominiums. In this case, mega-event driven displacement and state-led, neoliberal new-build gentrification, seem historically connected. The recent experiences of mega-scale redevelopment in Rio de Janeiro, for example, the ongoing redevelopment of Zona Portuária or Porto Maravilha also demonstrate the rise of state-led gentrification through the sanitization and commodification of urban space, combined with transforming public space into exclusive consumption space for urban elites (Queiroz Ribeiro and dos Santos Junior 2007; Sánchez and Broudehoux 2013).

2.6   CONCLUSION

As the real estate economy has become an increasingly dominant arena of capital accumulation, and as city-making has become an increasing part of the political ambition of governing elites, dilapidated and/or undesirable urban spaces have become subject to eradication and further commodification. Gentrification in this regard is a reflection of the state's political, ideological and economic project (Shin, forthcoming). This is the story of many countries in the Global South, which are increasingly integrated into the global circuits of capital and people, and as such experiencing the rise of new gentrifications or localized embryonic forms. In this chapter, we have argued that gentrification narrowly understood in a fossilized way (that is, gentrification equated with its classic form in 1960s London) is not a useful barometer through which to evaluate the experiences of other urban processes, either inside or outside of the usual suspects in gentrification studies. What comparative gentrification studies in recent years have taught us is the importance of de-centering the production of knowledge, incorporating emergent contextual discussions from elsewhere (and as it seems, literally from everywhere), and adhering to relational perspectives in order to understand how gentrification interacts with other locally available processes and discourses (see also Bernt 2016; Lees et al. 2016; López-Morales 2016a; Shin et al. 2016; Shin forthcoming). The de-centering of gentrification studies requires researchers to pay more careful attention to the historicity of urbanization and urban contestation. It also requires researchers to accept that gentrification may look completely different in places and societies we researchers do not yet know about or do not understand enough about as of now.

We conclude this chapter with a brief reflection on the construction of political alternatives in the fight against planetary gentrification. While this chapter has largely emphasized the workings of the state and capital in the Global South, it is also premature to simply assume that governments, developers and other state apparatuses are the only agents of mega-gentrification. With the growing affluence and expansion of middle classes in a number of global Southern countries that have seen the generation of wealth by their own industrialization and urban-based accumulation or the transfer of surplus capital from elsewhere (for example, King 2008; Koo 1991; Lett 1998; Tomba 2004), it is equally important to understand how the actions of the state-capital nexus have gained hegemony in their respective territories, and secured consent among a strata of residents, especially the property-owning middle classes who are attracted to securing gains from real estate investment. Such attention to state-society relations is particularly important, as the urban questions in the Global South are hard to detach from broader questions that emerge out of political mobilizations, which occasionally erupt to question state legitimacy. Where the support of the middle classes leans towards is significant in terms of how the state sustains its power vis-à-vis wider social movements. The resulting complexities provide both challenges and opportunities for anti-gentrification struggles in the Global South, which in turn can never be dissociated from those struggles that play out in the Global North.

The experience of Latin American urban struggles can be illuminating in this regard. Historically, Latin America is full of revolutionary moments in its history, starting with the independence wars in the early 19th century, followed by the Mexican and Cuban revolutions in the 20th century. Not only national political movements but also urban-based social uprising and revolutionary insurrection have also been prevalent (see Castells 1985). Latin America is currently seeing complex multi-scalar repertoires of social action, which are unfolding in extremely diverse urban contexts, ranging from Santiago to Buenos Aires to Mexico City, from disputes in micro-neighbourhoods to metropolitan-level conflicts. At a general level, urban social movements in Latin America show certain regularities such as class 'recomposition' on the one hand, exhibiting a growing cross-class consciousness of inequality which has emerged through spatial/local struggles against what Harvey (2010:181) calls speculative 'landed developer interests' in cities. On the other hand, such urban social movements display a seemingly contradictory, but much more variegated and in many ways 'creative', repertoire of protest performances, where claims are made for space, centrality and housing as social rights, yet somewhat detached from the language and histories of class struggle. These include the successful struggle in Mexico City to fend off the operation of private-public urban renewal agency as a neoliberal government apparatus, which has sought to carry out aggressive urban redevelopment and social cleansing (López-Morales, forthcoming), and the creative appropriation of neoliberal urban renewal policies in Buenos Aires to secure housing loans for supporting cooperative-style housing management and producing hundreds of low-cost, good quality social housing units all over the southern part of the city (Rodríguez and Di Virgilio 2016; see also Cociña and López-Morales, 2018; López-Morales 2016c). Anti-gentrification agendas increasingly occupy a central position, contributing to the formation of political alternatives and serving as a nexus between everyday struggles over lived space and larger social movement agendas. While we endeavour to locate gentrification in the Global South by not privileging the experience of Anglo-American cities, thinking of anti-gentrification strategies calls for the need to localize anti-gentrification fights while bearing in mind the possibility of the generalizability of such fights for cross-regional alliances. Thus, we envisage planetary use of the concept of gentrification as becoming more than normative.

ACKNOWLEDGEMENTS

Hyun Bang Shin acknowledges the support from the National Research Foundation of Korea Grant funded by the Korean Government (NRF-2017S1A3A2066514). Ernesto López-Morales acknowledges the support from the National Research Fund of Chile (Fondecyt Grant #1151287) and the Centre for Social Conflict and Cohesion Studies (COES, Fondap Grant #15130009).

REFERENCES

Bernt, M. (2016) 'Very particular, or rather universal? Gentrification though the lenses of Ghertner and López-Morales', *City*, 20(4): 637–644.

Castells, M. (1985) *The City and the Grassroots: A Cross-Cultural Theory of Urban Social Movements*, California: University of California Press.

Castells, M. (1992) 'Four Asian tigers with a dragon head: A comparative analysis of the state, economy, and society in the Asian Pacific Rim', in Appelbaum, R. and Henderson, J. (eds), *States and Development in the Asian Pacific Rim*, Newbury Park, CA: SAGE, pp. 33–70.

Chakrabarty, D. (2000) *Provincializing Europe: Postcolonial Thought and Historical Difference,* Princeton: Princeton University Press.

Clark, E. (2005) 'The order and simplicity of gentrification: A political challenge', in Atkinson, R. and Bridge, G. (eds), *Gentrification in a Global Context: The New Urban Colonialism*, London: Routledge, pp. 256–264.

Clark, E. (2015) 'Afterword: The adventure of generic gentrification', in: Lees, L., Shin, H. and López-Morales, E. (eds), *Global Gentrifications: Uneven Development and Displacement*, Bristol: Policy Press, pp. 453–456.

Cociña, C. and López-Morales, E. (2018) 'Unpacking narratives of social conflict and inclusion: Anti-gentrification neighbourhood organisation in Santiago, Chile', in: Rokem, J. and Boano, C. (eds), *Urban Geopolitics – Rethinking Planning in Contested Cities*, London: Routledge, pp. 171–188.

Cuenya, B. and Corral, M. (2011) 'Empresarialismo, economía del suelo y grandes proyectos urbanos: El modelo de Puerto Madero en Buenos Aires', *EURE*, 37(111), 25–45.

Davidson, M. and Lees, L. (2010) 'New-build gentrification: Its histories, trajectories, and critical geographies', *Population, Space and Place*, 16(5), 395–411.

Defilippis, J. (2004) *Unmasking Goliath: Community Control in the Face of Global Capital*, New York: Routledge.

Doshi, S. (2013) 'The politics of the evicted: Redevelopment, subjectivity, and difference in Mumbai's slum frontier', *Antipode*, 45(4), 844–865.

Elshahed, M. (2015) 'The prospects of gentrification in downtown Cairo: Artists, private investment and the neglectful state', in Lees, L., Shin, H.B. and López-Morales, E. (eds), *Global Gentrifications: Uneven Development and Displacement*, Bristol: Policy Press, pp. 121–142.

Garay, A., Wainer, L., Henderson, H. and Rotbart, D. (2013) 'Puerto Madero: Análisis de un Proyecto', *Land Lines*, July. [Online]. Available at: https://www.lincolninst.edu/pubs/2289_Puerto-Madero--An%C3%A1lisis-de-un-proyecto (last accessed 2 April 2017).

Gaytán, P. (2016) 'Espacio público: Entre el yosmart y la invención urbanita', *Metapolítica*, 20(95), 49–55.

Ghertner, A. (2015) 'Why gentrification theory fails in "much of the world"', *City*, 19(4), 546–556.

Ha, S-k. (2001) 'Substandard settlements and joint redevelopment projects in Seoul', *Habitat International*, 25, 385–397.

Haila, A. (2016) *Urban Land Rents: Singapore as a Property State*, Wiley-Blackwell.

Harvey, D. (2005) *A Brief History of Neoliberalism*, New York: Oxford University Press.

Harvey, D. (2010) *The Enigma of Capital and the Crises of Capitalism*, London: Profile Books.

Herzer, H., Di Virgilio, M.M. and Rodríguez, M.C. (2015) 'Gentrification in Buenos Aires: Global trends and local features', in Lees, L., Shin, H.B. and López-Morales, E. (eds), *Global Gentrifications: Uneven Development and Displacement*, Bristol: Policy Press, pp. 199–222.

Janoschka, M., Sequera, J. and Salinas, L. (2014) 'Gentrification in Spain and Latin America – a critical dialogue', *International Journal of Urban and Regional Research*, 38(4), 1234–1265.

Kim, S-h. (1999) 'The history of evictees' movement in Seoul', *Urbanity and Poverty*, 36, 51–77 [in Korean].

King, V.T. (2008) 'The middle class in Southeast Asia: Diversities, identities, comparisons and the Vietnamese case', *IJAPS*, 4(2), 73–109.

Koo, H. (1991) 'Middle classes, democratization, and class formation: the case of South Korea', *Theory and Society*, 20(4), 485–509.

Kutz, W. and Lenhardt, J. (2016) '"Where to put the spare cash?" Subprime urbanisation and the geographies of the financial crisis in the global South', *Urban Geography*, 37(6), 926–948.

Lang, M.H. (1982) *Gentrification Amid Urban Decline: Strategies for America's Older Cities*, Cambridge, MA: Ballinger Pub. Co.

Lee, S.Y. (2016) 'Neil Smith, gentrification, and South Korea', *Space and Society*, 26(2), 209–234 [in Korean].

Lees, L. (2012) 'The geography of gentrification: thinking through comparative urbanism', *Progress in Human Geography*, 36(2), 155–171.

Lees, L. (2014) 'The urban injustices of New Labour's "new urban renewal": The case of the Aylesbury Estate in London', *Antipode*, 46(4), 921–947.

Lees, L., Shin, H.B. and López-Morales, E. (eds) (2015) *Global Gentrifications: Uneven Development and Disparity*, Bristol: Policy Press.

Lees, L., Shin, H.B. and López-Morales, E. (2016) *Planetary Gentrification*, Cambridge: Polity Press.

Lett, D.P. (1998) *In Pursuit of Status: The Making of South Korea's 'New' Urban Middle Class*, Cambridge, MA: Harvard University Asia Center.

Ley, D. (1980) 'Liberal ideology and the postindustrial city', *Annals of the Association of American Geographers*, 70(2), 238–258.

Ley, D. and Teo, S.Y. (2014) 'Gentrification in Hong Kong? Epistemology vs. ontology', *International Journal of Urban and Regional Research*, 38(4), 1286–1303.

López-Morales, E. (2008) 'Destrucción creativa y explotación de brecha de renta: discutiendo la renovación urbana del peri-centro sur poniente de Santiago de Chile entre 1990 y 2005', *Scripta Nova*, 12(270). [Online]. Available at: http://www.ub.edu/geocrit/sn/sn-270/sn-270-100.htm (last accessed on 8 April 2017).

López-Morales, E. (2016a) 'Gentrification in the global South', *City*, 19(4), 564–573.

López-Morales, E. (2016b) 'Assessing exclusionary displacement through rent gap analysis in the urban redevelopment of inner Santiago, Chile', *Housing Studies*, 31(5), 540–559.

López-Morales, E. (2016c) 'Social internalization of risk in the housing market of Santiago, Chile, research on political economy', in Soederberg, S. (ed), *Critiquing Risk Management in Neoliberal Capitalism, Research on Political Economy*, 31, 79–105.

López-Morales, E. (forthcoming) 'Privatization of public and transport space in Mexico City: the birth of a political alternative', in Ahlert, M. and Von Borries, F. (eds), *Mexibility: Estamos en la ciudad, no podemos salir de ella*, Berlin.

Maloutas, T. (2012) 'Contextual diversity in gentrification research', *Critical Sociology*, 38(1), 33–48.

Massey, D. (1993) 'Power-geometry and a progressive sense of place', in Bird, J., Curtis, B., Putnam, T., Robertson, G. and Tickner, L. (eds), *Mapping the Futures: Local Cultures, Global Change*, London: Routledge, pp. 60–70.

Moreno, L. (2014) 'The urban process under financialised capitalism', *City: Analysis of Urban Trends, Culture, Theory, Policy, Action*, 18(3), 244–268.

Percival, T. and Waley, P. (2012) 'Articulating intra-Asian urbanism: The production of satellite cities in Phnom Penh', *Urban Studies*, 49(13), 2873–2888.

Queiroz Ribeiro, L. and dos Santos Junior, O. (2007) *As metrópoles e a questao social brasileira*, Rio de Janeiro: Revan.

Ramesh, R. (2005) 'Poor squeezed out by Mumbai's dream plan: India's biggest city is razing its shanty towns', *The Guardian*, 1 March. [Online]. Available at: http://www.theguardian.com/world/2005/mar/01/india.ran deepramesh (last accessed on 8 April 2017).

Rodríguez, M. and Di Virgilio, M. (2016) 'A city for all? Public policy and resistance to gentrification in the southern neighborhoods of Buenos Aires', *Urban Geography*, 37(8), 1215–1234.

Sabatini, F., Cáceres, G., and Cerda, J. (2001) 'Segregación residencial en las principales ciudades chilenas: Tendencias de las tres últimas décadas y posibles cursos de acción', *EURE*, 27(82), 21–42.

Sánchez, F. and Broudehoux, A-M. (2013) 'Mega-events and urban regeneration in Rio de Janeiro: Planning in a state of emergency', *International Journal of Urban Sustainable Development*, 5(2), 132–153.

Shao, Q. (2013) *Shanghai Gone: Domicide and Defiance in a Chinese Megacity*, Lanham, MD: Rowman and Littlefield.

Shatkin, G. (2008) 'The city and the bottom line: urban megaprojects and the privatization of planning in Southeast Asia', *Environment and Planning A*, 40, 383–401.

Shin, H.B. (2016) 'Economic transition and speculative urbanisation in China: gentrification versus dispossession', *Urban Studies*, 53(3), 471–489.

Shin, H.B. (2017) 'Envisioned by the state: Entrepreneurial urbanism and the making of Songdo City, South Korea', in Datta, A. and Shaban, A. (eds), *Mega-urbanization in the Global South: Fast Cities and New Urban Utopias of the Postcolonial State*, Routledge, pp. 83–100.

Shin, H.B. (forthcoming) 'Studying global gentrifications', in: Harrison, J. and Hoyler, M. (eds), *Doing Global Urban Research*, SAGE.

Shin, H.B. and Kim, S-h. (2016) 'The developmental state, speculative urbanisation and the politics of displacement in gentrifying Seoul', *Urban Studies*, 53(3), 540–559.

Shin, H.B., Lees, L. and López-Morales, E. (2016) 'Introduction: Locating gentrification in the global East', *Urban Studies*, 53(3), 455–470.

Slater, T. (2006) 'The eviction of critical perspectives from gentrification research', *International Journal of Urban and Regional Research*, 30(4), 737–757.

Slater, T. (2014) 'Unravelling false choice urbanism', *City: Analysis of Urban Trends, Culture, Theory, Policy, Action*, 18(4–5), 517–524.

Smith, N. (1979) 'Toward a theory of gentrification: A back to the city movement by capital not people', *Journal of the American Planning Association*, 45, 538–548.

Smith, N. (2002) 'New globalism, new urbanism: Gentrification as global urban strategy', *Antipode*, 34(3), 427–450.

Sonn, J.W., Shin, H. and Park, S.H. (2017) 'A mega urban project and two competing accumulation strategies: Negotiating discourses of the Songdo International Business District development', *International Development Planning Review*, 39(3), 299–317.

The Guardian (2017) 'Brazil's corruption scandal spreads across South America', 11 February. [Online]. Available at: https://www.theguardian.com/world/2017/feb/11/brazils-corruption-scandal-spreads-across-south-america (last accessed on 8 April 2017).

Tomba, L. (2004) 'Creating an urban middle class: social engineering in Beijing', *The China Journal*, 51, 1–26.

Wacquant, L., Slater, T. and Pereira, V.B. (2014) 'Territorial stigmatization in action', *Environment and Planning A*, 46, 1270–1280.

Woo-Cumings, M. (ed) (1999) *The Developmental State*, New York: Cornell University Press.

Wyly, E., Newman, K., Schafran, A. and Lee, E. (2010) 'Displacing New York', *Environment and Planning A*, 42, 2602–2623.

3. Beyond the elephant of gentrification: relational approaches to a chaotic problem

Freek de Haan

3.1 INTRODUCTION

As it appears today, gentrification has gone transcendental, homogenizing our minds (Schulman, 2012), our planet (Lees et al., 2016) and everything in between. Seemingly ubiquitous, its most prominent critics describe it as the socio-spatial expression *par excellence* of a still alarmingly globalizing capitalism, neoliberal urbanism, and middle class consumerism (for example, Smith, 2002, Lees et al., 2016). At the same time, however, many of those same observers feel a pressing need to gain knowledge of local specificities and how the arrival of such planetary forces is negotiated in different places, as it is suspected that the key to countering the process might be found there (for example, Lees et al., 2015). In between, on the one hand, the politically motivated urge to generalize and univocally define gentrification in its 'order and simplicity' (Clark, 2005) and, on the other, the nagging academic reflections of epistemic parochialism, researchers look to relational and postcolonial theories of multiplicity, process and non-linear translation for inspiration. A recent comprehensive review of the literature by Lees states this ambition as follows:

> A postcolonial perspective might help collapse (or prove?) the myth of the linear development of gentrification as travelling from the Global North to the Global South, replacing it with an ontology of relational multiplicity and an epistemology of multiple forms of knowledge in continual construction (Lees 2012: 166).

There are several important ontological and epistemological claims addressed in this statement that will occupy this chapter. Ontologically, there is the problem of gentrification 'itself' travelling our planet. From the current literature, a picture emerges of its diffusion as the spatially contextual expression of a globalizing neoliberal capitalism (Smith, 2002, Atkinson and Bridge, 2005). As a kind of spatial symptom, gentrification pops up wherever its political economic causes go, with local contingencies and resistances more or less able to mitigate the results. Informing this ontology is an epistemology with both 'legislative' and 'interpretivist' tendencies (Phillips, 2002). On the one hand then, there certainly is interpretive room for paradigmatically different descriptions of local particularities and aspects. Yet on the other, when it comes to explaining their existence, oftentimes a more or less implicit consensus sets in or is implied about gentrification's general definition and etiology (for example, 'few would disagree . . .' (Lees et al., 2015: 449)). Not surprisingly, these general/global to particular/local analytics of a rather legislative kind tie in with an all too familiar Anglo-Saxon dominated epistemic geography, which has raised many concerns about interpretive overgeneralization and the one-way 'travelling' of the arguably parochial concept of gentrification (Maloutas, 2012, Ley and Teo, 2014, Ghertner, 2015). Taken together, these ontological and epistemological geographies, reporting on the diffusion of both the process itself and its theorization, challenge the ambition stated by Lees to genuinely deal with gentrification as a 'relational multiplicity' and to study it through 'multiple forms of knowledge in continual construction' in order to be able to discriminate non-linear from 'linear development'. Much of the reason for sticking with these geographies anyway, apart from academic motivations (Maloutas, 2012), is a deep and sincere sense of political urgency. Any kind of letting go of the familiar unifying yet legislative concepts and narratives is felt to be a step toward relativism and to undermine the cause of battling those obvious injustices that accompany many gentrification processes. Yet it could be argued that on an affective-practice level, much of the urgency (and despair) is actually produced by those same grand narratives (cf. Gibson-Graham, 2006b, Latour, 2014), also in places where there might be less cause for such alarm. Apart from those places then, where an episteme of gentrification might be very welcome 'ontologically' (Ley and Teo, 2014), there could also be events that would warrant a more responsible introduction (that is, 'response-able', Barad, 2007). If gentrification is indispensable as a concept in current urban geography, it is also inescapably inadequate (cf. Chakrabarty, 2000) and we need to diversify ways of dealing with this. We need intellectual tools that allow us to slow down conclusions on gentrification's actual presence or absence in order to extract new possibilities from situations of empirical and ethical ambiguity. In contrast to the rather despairing visions of planetary emergency, I want to argue in this chapter for a more earthly gentrification. In the process I will present an outline of how relational approaches such as assemblage, actor-network and intra-action theory might open up new epistemic and methodological avenues for research on the issue, hoping to make some strides into the direction of that aspired relational ontology and constructivist epistemology. Different from traditional approaches to geography and gentrification, these radically relational theories are not predicated on the 'internal relations' (for example, Harvey, 1996) of parts, wholes, scales and their contradictory dialectics (in capitalism), but on 'relations of exteriority' (DeLanda, 2009), which have a life of their own, reducible to neither parts nor wholes. The chapter will run as follows. In the next section I will first try to find an opening into the 'relational multiplicity' of gentrification by revisiting the so-called 'Copenhagen interpretation of gentrification', which still describes fairly well the prevalent way of tackling the issue of its definition and explanation. In the third section I will propose in general terms an alternative way of describing the 'actualization' of gentrified spaces in terms of actor-network, assemblage and postcolonial approaches. In the section following this ontological exposition, I will suggest an epistemological strategy of 'counter-actualization' and apply it to some very familiar themes of gentrification. The last section will conclude with some thoughts on how to conduct our research (and ourselves) in future gentrification studies.

3.2   A NEW COPENHAGEN INTERPRETATION OF GENTRIFICATION

During the long first decade of gentrification debates, contributions and interventions were of a rather 'legislative' kind (Phillips, 2002), advancing either one best explanatory paradigm (for example, neoclassical, political economic, cultural, institutional) or attempting to integrate many into one. It was in response to the resulting impasse that Clark (1994) introduced the idea of a 'Copenhagen interpretation of gentrification', modelled after the prominent interpretation of quantum physics devised by Bohr and Heisenberg in the 1920s. Like its original, which dealt with the incommensurability of classical and quantum phenomena, Clark figured that the incompatibility of explanations of gentrification on a paradigmatic level should not exclude more than one of them having some truth value. Thus, many interpretations of gentrification, even though based on mutually exclusive abstractions (for example, capital, culture), could and should still be considered complementary (see also Lees, 1994). As such, and calling on another familiar (and very neo-Kantian) metaphor, the gentrification debate has also been characterized as a group of blind men groping around an elephant (Hamnett, 1991, Clark, 1992). As each one of them only accounts for one part of the gentrification elephant, they remain in disagreement about what it actually is. Consequently, the challenge becomes making the blind men communicate without them introducing their own legislative centrepieces and without too much 'reflexive categorization' of each other's accounts (on the contentious level of incommensurable paradigms that is). Today, this more low-level communication despite incomplete integration seems to have been achieved, it being argued that 'most gentrification researchers now accept that production and consumption, supply and demand, economic and cultural, and structure and agency explanations are all a part of "the elephant of gentrification"' (Lees et al., 2008: xxii). Acceptance of such a claim enables a refocusing of studies, away from discussion of definitions and causes, and towards an examination of local consequences of gentrification (Lees et al., 2008: 190).

Complementarity thus becomes a kind of interpretive compromise: the Copenhagen interpretation of gentrification. However, although surely having brought some relief in a rather tedious causal discussion, this seemingly less legislative and more interpretive solution (Phillips, 2002) has left us with a rather loose and (in the epistemic sense) idealistic dialectic of abstract generalities (that is, concepts hard to distinguish empirically or relate to concrete affairs with rigour and precision). Lees (1994), for instance, suggests a synthesis of Marxist economic and postmodern cultural paradigms by 'informing one set of ideas with another'. Arguing something similar, Phillips (2004) has more recently called for a 'trialectics' (Soja, 1996; Lefebvre, 1991) of material economic 'firstspace', symbolic cultural 'secondspace' and practically lived 'thirdspace' in order to engage with erstwhile neglected geographies of gentrification (in his case, the rural). As inspiring as these attempts at integrating the incommensurable may be, they both suffer from a dialectical (post)structuralism whose concepts are unavoidably like 'baggy clothes', with one abstraction's imprecision being compensated with another's (cf. Deleuze, 1988: 44).[1] Instead, a non-dialectical conception of complementarity, based on relations of exteriority, could prove instrumental in learning to appreciate with more precision gentrification's ontological multiplicity; that is, beyond a baggy, elephantine bundle of 'firstspace'

---

[1]   The thus deliberately blurry (Merrifield, 2006: 109) Lefebvrean triadic invites a lot of categorical confusion, also in distinguishing spaces of gentrification. See for example Phillips (2004) and Davidson (2009) on 'representations of space': are they 'lived' or 'conceived'? (Or see also, in a more general context, Merrifield (2006: 109–110) and Crang (2001: 201) on 'spatial practices': 'perceived' or 'lived'?) Cf. also DeFilippis (2004: 26) on Lefebvre's inspiring yet practically too abstract and imprecise analytical triad.

capitalist spatial practices, 'secondspace' neoliberal planning and 'thirdspace' postmodern consumer experience.

In the rest of this section I want to revisit the original Copenhagen interpretation through the work of physicist and feminist Karen Barad. This, I argue, will also throw a new light on Clark's Copenhagen interpretation, making of gentrification not a singular elephant subjected to many epistemologically incompatible viewpoints, but a true 'ontological multiplicity' in need of a different treatment. In the process, moreover, avenues will open up to 'bring down to Earth' the abstractions of old with the use of relational theories such as actor-network theory (cf. Phillips, 2010).

The Copenhagen interpretation of quantum physics, construed to cope with the so-called wave-particle paradox, often suggests more agreement than its creators actually shared. Bohr's notion of complementarity and Heisenberg's 'uncertainty principle' as initially proposed and as such widely adopted, were actually quite incompatible (Barad, 2007: 115). Whereas Heisenberg's is only an epistemic principle, Bohr's idea of complementarity, or what Barad calls his 'indeterminacy principle', concerns an ontic-semantic matter. The former, which addresses only the impossibility of knowing complementary subatomic events (such as the position and momentum of an electron), leaves intact the classical metaphysics that presupposes the pre-existence of individuated objects of measurement. Despite Heisenberg having conceded to Bohr's position at a later moment, it has been this ontologically restricted interpretation that has become hegemonic, as it fitted much better with a physics at that time still thoroughly classical in its outlook (Barad, 2007: 115–116).

However, with relations of complementarity becoming less of an epistemological matter of incommensurable abstractions, the specific physical reality of such relations becomes crucial. That is, in order to observe their occurrence, experimental circumstances have to be such that matter, classically thought to be made up of particles, starts exhibiting interference patterns. It is the famous 'double slit' setup that beautifully demonstrates this by having light or matter pass through a diffraction grating before landing on a screen behind it (see Figure 3.1). Even though starting out as a mere thought experiment, this double slit setup, and its many new variations involving so-called 'which-path detectors' or 'quantum erasers' (for further details, see Barad, 2007: ch.7), have recently become amenable to actual empirical testing, with some highly surprising results the relevance of which extends far beyond the subatomic world.[2]

Three of these results are important here, as they give solid clues on how to affirmatively conceptualize the (still negatively formulated) 'non-representational' realm of practices and relations of exteriority without recourse to phenomenological or (post-)structural dialectics and their internal relations. The first, already mentioned result is that the detection of particles physically terminates their wavelike behaviour (rather than just disturbing the measurement of their pre-existing wavelike properties). Second, rather than strictly distinctive, complementarity is continuous in the sense that it is possible to determine to a degree both wave and particle behaviour simultaneously but not both sharply at once.

---

[2]   It should be noted here that interference and diffraction phenomena are not bound to absolute scale and the interaction with the subatomic, but rather inherent (intra-active) to any kind of interaction (Barad, 2007). It is only that in the subatomic realm these phenomena become undeniably a feature of reality (that is, ontic) rather than an expression of our epistemic shortcomings (as classical science would have it).

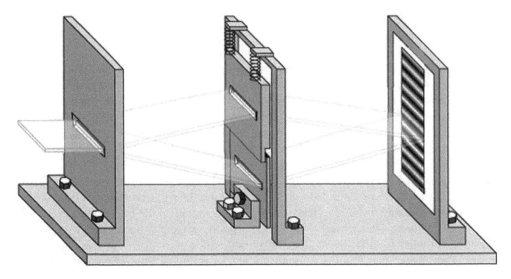

Source: Barad, 2007: 82.

Figure 3.1   The famous 'double-slit' setup

Furthermore, this continuous trade-off should be considered to be of a virtual nature, meaning that the mere capacity for particles to be distinguished in the setup (that is, distinguishability) already annuls the capacity for wavelike behaviour. As such, the setup first embodies an 'intra-active' entanglement or 'superposition' of more or less determinate capacities, rather than an interaction of separated components (such as 'particles').[3] Lastly, the experiments do not just subvert our classical notion of spatial separability (of individuals), but of time as well. Rather than merely serving as an unaffected external parameter, both bounded time and space are thus found to emerge from the experimental event itself. To summarize, what these experiments with diffraction reveal is a world of (scientific) practice that is constituted by a real ('physical') yet virtual continuum of intra-active gradients of distinguishability.[4] In this regard, complementarity becomes another name for the physical or synthetic incapacity for sharply enacting both wave and particle simultaneously and no longer a matter of incompatible analytic abstractions (such as 'wave' and 'particle'). Furthermore, observational distinctions and abstractions become nothing more than practically performed and contingent 'cuts' (for example, of cause/effect, subject/object) representing the practice (to itself) as an interaction of individual, pre-existing components.

Beyond the subatomic, the quantum experiments described by Barad can be seen as a kind of empirical corroboration of what (post-)actor-network theorists call 'ontological multiplicity' (Mol, 2002, Law, 2008). For example, like the subatomic events being enacted

---

[3]   In 'interaction' the pre-existence and individuality of relata is presupposed. 'Intra-action', by contrast, designates the genetic relation (vector) that precedes the relata. Like what assemblage theorists call a 'relation of exteriority' (DeLanda, 2009), it neither pre-exists in some part nor is interior to some whole.

[4]   On the difference between 'virtual reality' and 'real virtuality', see DeLanda, 2002: 30.

as either wave or particle, Mol observes how atherosclerosis is similarly multiple, enacted differently by the many diagnostic and treatment practices around a Dutch hospital. From this, she paradoxically concludes that 'the' vascular disease is more than one, as in positivism or transcendental realism, yet less than many, as in perspectival or cultural relativism. As Esbjörn-Hargens (2010) shows, this fractal, more-than-one-yet-less-than-many mode of existence can also be ascribed to the issue of climate change, which is perhaps already more like gentrification than particles or diseases in terms of its accorded scale. Rather than one thing-in-itself being partially observed by many blinded men, the 'elephant' of climate change thus becomes a monstrous 'multiple object' enacted differently according to methods ('cuts') practised (2010: 155). From here it is only a small step toward the problem of gentrification. Instead of assuming that we are dealing with an ultimately singular elephant of gentrification and that it is only our more or less correctable and integratable 'chaotic abstractions' barring us from seeing it right or whole, we need to find the conceptual instruments to deal with its inherently chaotic nature in a responsible way.

3.3   THE GENESIS OF GENTRIFIED SPACE: PROBLEMS, PRACTICES, INTERPRETATIONS, METRICS

To carefully extrapolate the insights of Barad and actor-network theorists to the problem of gentrification some intermediate theoretical steps are required. In this section I will therefore elaborate how an ontologically multiple or 'chaotic' problem of gentrification is resolved in practice with the deployment of interpretive and metric mediators. As will be explained, the latter mediators enact various, more or less dominant ontological and epistemological geographies of gentrification, including more or less parochial academic interpretations. The section will end with a few notes on how all this reflects back on our epistemology and ideas about causality.

Before gentrification is distinctly conceived or precisely measured it constitutes a chaotic multiplicity; that is, an ontologically 'objective' problem to be solved. Callon (2009), speaking of global warming rather than gentrification, compares the problem or 'issue' in such an objective yet undetermined (or 'totipotent') state to a biological stem cell that has not yet differentiated into a specialized one. Thus global warming constitutes a 'stem issue' first, before it is economized, politicized and scientized in specific ways, actualized for example in a carbon market. In a very similar way as Callon, Deleuze and Guattari (1987) have likened the state of a problem to that of an egg: a problem of which the mature animal born from it is but one possible 'solution' or actualization. What both Callon and Deleuze and Guattari aim at with these analogies is to conceive of problems as real and immanent to material processes and practices rather than mere projections of ideal or social transcendental subjects or structures (for example, Spector and Kitsuse, 1977). Their 'transcendental empiricism' attempts to trace the world in its problematic, embryonic genesis, rather than deduce a general representation from its supposedly mature form, which then retroactively passes for its ideal condition of possibility (for example, 'human subject' from white middle aged men or 'society' from modern national institutions). The world thus inquired becomes inherently problematic, even constituted by material-semiotic problems, with the apparently distinct entities populating our actual reality (for example, 'mature' animals, subjects, societies, markets) serving only as their temporary and incomplete 'solutions'. This implies that problems may be changed but never subsumed by their solutions and thus could be said to always outlive the latter. In our case we could say, even though the tendencies of social, economic and political displacement that constitute the problem of gentrification find their combined resolution in any actual state of a neighbourhood, those tendencies are never cancelled out by this actualization and keep haunting it; that is, the problem remains.

With genetic conditions related to their actualizations as problems to solutions, any actual space of gentrification could be considered conditioned by a real-life problem or 'stem issue' of gentrification. Inquiring into such conditions, rather like obtaining stem cells from highly specialized ones (Callon, 2009), would demand the extraction of some kind of diagram of the 'stem' problem of gentrification from actually enacted, narrated and measured spaces. Inevitably, our habitual use of language tends to fall short in this operation. However, in elaborating what has later been dubbed 'assemblage theory' (DeLanda, 2009), Deleuze and Guattari (1987) give us a recipe for attempting it nonetheless. As far as natural language goes then, a problem or multiplicity might best be described by an 'indefinite article + proper name + infinitive verb'.[5] Producing rather nonsensical expressions 'freed from all formal significances and personal subjectifica-tions' (Deleuze and Guattari, 1987: 263), this formula explores the limits of a language otherwise primed for generalization and the cancellation of multiplicity (cf. Deleuze, 1990). What if we perform this operation on problems of gentrification? Something in the way of 'a Notting Hill / Tarlabaşı / Hoogvliet to gentrify' could then capture those events of gentrification in their most desubjectified + singular + affective state.[6] In an intuited state, that is, still as far away removed (as language allows) from generalities of political ideology, culture and capital. In a way defaulting our preconceptions of 'gentrification generalized', it may thus translate into a first itinerary toward the development of less reductive accounts of gentrification: forget overarching cultures, political scales and economic systems (desubjectify), follow a neighbourhood by its proper name (singularize) and immerse yourself into its immense bundle of social, economic and political practices (be affected, response-able).

As it will turn out later, the formula specifically directs our attention to the practices of politicization, socialization and economization involved in the process of resolving or 'actualizing' the material-semiotic or 'virtual' problem of gentrification (cf. Callon, 2009). However, in order to further specify these practices we first need a more general idea of the type of earthly components through which they circulate and actualize themselves. Following (post-)actor-network theory (Law and Mol, 2001) we can describe the actualization of different spaces in terms of the mutability and mobility of the human and non-human mediators or 'actants' by which the issue is said to 'travel' geographically, from North to South or down the urban hierarchy, but also epistemically, from academic

---

[5]   First, the infinite verb (for example, to cycle, to renovate, to displace, to gentrify) designates an event comprising multiple dimensions of becoming or degrees of freedom (that is, practices). Second, the proper name, operating at the limit of classification, presents the singularity undergoing such becomings (for example, *this* neighbourhood, *that* city). Thirdly, the indefinite article introduces the assemblage as such, without preconceived center or subject (*the* capitalist system, *the* new middle class, *the* state).

[6]   Here, 'affective' should be understood as not only pertaining to (human) feelings or emotions, but in a transhuman (that is, between humans and/or non-humans), Spinozian sense, as designating any relational capacity to affect and to be affected (Deleuze and Guattari, 1987: 256–257).

to non-academic practices.[7] Most well-known are the so-called 'immutable mobiles', which bring about a Modern, intellectually domesticated Euclidean-type space (Latour, 1987). Without the construction of a metrically precise and materially mobile system of coordinates by such technoscientific actants, there would, for example, have been no Portuguese imperialism (or GPS for that matter). Likewise, yet more controversially, Newton's laws have been made universally valid (that is, beyond England) only through the mobilization of ships, letters and calibrated laboratory equipment. Developing Latour's concept further, employing notions of diffraction similar to Barad's, Law and Mol (2001) introduce mutable mobiles and mutable immobiles generating not Cartesian but 'fluid' and 'fire' spaces respectively.[8] Mutable mobiles, such as a Zimbabwe bush pump or a diagnosis of anemia, travel continuously through ecologies of practices, mutating fluidly and incrementally, transforming both themselves and their environment simultaneously. By contrast, mutable immobiles, such as signifiers of 'alcoholism' in addiction and liver treatment (Law and Singleton, 2004), or, of more importance here, building types, use values or property rights in a process of rezoning or gentrification (Guggenheim, 2010), mutate must faster and in much more discontinuous ways (that is, instantaneously, by decree). Rapidly producing one interpretive form after the other, like a flickering 'fire', they generate a phenomenological and communicative space; albeit with the price of always creating new 'immobile', positions and centres (variously signified reality, subject, structure, system, etc.).

When broadly applied to the issue of gentrification, we can translate these three ontologically differentiated forms of actants into metrics, interpretations and practices of gentrification. So first, immutable mobiles or metrics are the outcomes of all kinds of political, social and economic measurements such as polls, demographics and prices (of property, products or labour). Second, mutable immobile interpretations we find presented in newspapers, advertising, land registers, policy documents and in our field interviews in the form of statements and distinctions of right or left, class and ethnicity, attractive or ugly and, of course, of 'gentrification' itself. Third, practices include travelling and mutating capacities of, for example, charismatic leadership, writing policy documents, ads or business cases, accounting, aesthetic sensibility, everyday diplomacy or designing fashionable products.

Useful as this ontological distinction of spaces and their actants might already be, it remains rather static in the hands of actor-network theory.[9] To describe gentrification better as a process of actualization, we therefore need to relate these spaces genetically, which we do find in the proto-actor-network theory of Deleuze and Guattari (1987).[10]

---

[7]   In actor-network theory, the mediators in a network, be they human or non-human, are never entirely trivial intermediaries that simply transport some same force or cause. To explicitly acknowledge this, the term 'actant' has been devised to cover both human and non-human actors.

[8]   A possible fourth category of 'immutable immobiles', designating 'network space', I leave aside here, but suffice to say that within the ontology presented here it designates the problem itself (perhaps, one could say, as a topological 'attractor').

[9]   Much of the metaphysical stasis of the world of actor-network theory has to do with the theory's Whiteheadian 'actualism' (Harman, 2009). That is, when all the actors of a network are fully defined by their *actual* relations it becomes somewhat of a mystery how change happens.

[10]   Note that in 'recalling' actor-network theory, Latour (1999: 19) concedes with implicit reference to Deleuze and Guattari that 'actant-rhizome ontology' might have been a better (although less popularly attractive) name for the approach.

In their theory of assemblages, differential ('fluid'), projective ('fire') and metric spaces can be related in terms of their symmetry (under geometrical transformations) and it is the progressive 'breaking' of that symmetry that describes a trajectory of actualization, progressing from a still flexible and unformatted topological space to its metrically determined resolution (DeLanda, 2002, 2009).[11] Taking this as a general description of modern human ontogenetic processes, implies that metrics and interpretations of gentrification emerge from practices. This makes intuitive sense: in order to quantify (measure, evaluate or value) anything, qualitative choices are first to be made (present-absent, left-right, useful-redundant, etc.). Yet making such distinctions in turn requires actualizable capacities and skills to do so. Space is thus conceived here as thoroughly performative, as different actants actualize (enact, project, calculate) different spaces with no pre-existing Cartesian container (a technoscientific invention itself) through which they effortlessly travel from one global position to another. Maintaining metric space has to be part of the effort. Moreover, as Barad's experiments also demonstrated, it is not just space that is essentially performative but time as well. The actants, in their translation and co-evolutionary concatenation, can thus be said to constitute different material-semiotic spacetimes, histories or 'stories-so-far' (cf. Massey, 2005: 12). Whereas metrics as 'real abstractions' in practical use (cf. Sohn-Rethel, 1978) embody a promise of truthful representation (of value, popular will or observation) and thus write a universal or 'global' history of capital, democratic emancipation and scientific Enlightenment, interpretations allow for a 'planetary' multiverse of provincial and subaltern histories (cf. Chakrabarty, 2000, Spivak, 2003). Both of these histories, however, as with the spatial actualizations described above, arise from more rhizomatic becomings of earthly practices and problems.

Gentrification studies have not only been dominated by accurately perceivable and measurable 'firstspace' (Phillips, 2004) but by histories of equivalence as well (what postcolonial theorist Chakrabarty calls 'History 1'). As a prime example, the dialectic theory of uneven development underlying much of today's gentrification research (Smith, 2008), retains many developmentalist elements (Chakrabarty, 2000), as signalled by the often rather easy exclamations of global takeover of neoliberal capitalism and gentrification (for example, Smith, 2002; Atkinson and Bridge, 2005). Now the challenge (of relational theories) is not to propose a dialectical solution to this universalizing bias, compensating one grand narrative of planetary capitalism with a similarly rough category of 'context', 'contingencies' or 'Other' geographies (or 'history 2s'), but to conceive of both as concrete metric and interpretive constructions immanent to very specific sets of practices (of which some are academic). As such, both the formal abstractions of capitalism and its disenfranchised others are 'brought down to Earth' (cf. Phillips, 2010), restricted to and diffracted into the flat, chaotic concatenation of practices they are. This move immediately has an impact on the manifold ways that we in our academic or 'etic' work connect to other 'emic' practices.[12] Usually operating somewhere between the world of legislative

---

[11]   Geometrically, spaces can be arranged in terms of the symmetry they preserve under particular transformations, like rotating or stretching. In this regard, shapes that are wildly different in metric space, like a coffee mug and a donut, would by entirely equivalent in mouldable topological space (see DeLanda, 2002). The idea of 'symmetry-breaking' is borrowed from the physical science of critical transitions and could be said to describe the progressive emergence of 'order out of chaos' (Prigogine and Stengers, 1984).

[12]   The reflexive ethnographic distinction between etic and emic captures the difference between accounts of the world expressed in conceptual schemes regarded as meaningful by the scientific community and those of

metrics and more relativist interpretations, we either see ourselves as the bringers of truth, awakening the slumbering and liberating the oppressed, or at other times, as more modest hermeneutics, respectful of a diverse range of meanings. From the relational point of view, however, our explanatory and interpretive 'cuts' become an immediate, performative part of the problem and its actualization. In such an intra-active entanglement of etic and emic practices (cf. Barad, 2007), we need to be careful and responsible about our abstractions (Stengers, 2008: 50, Stengers, 2011). As an actant in the world, the concept of gentrification has in a way become both indispensable and inadequate (cf. Chakrabarty, 2000). This we have to deal with, not just by critically examining its application in different times and spaces all over the world (Lees et al., 2015), possibly refracting it into many different types (classic, state-led, slum, etc.), but also, in line with the previous section, employing it as a tool of diffraction capable of generating new ways of imagining and practising space (ways that might not amount to either a straightforward negation or further specification of the concept's meaning). The perhaps 'post-critical' (Felski, 2012) strategy of 'counter-actualization', to be explained in the next section, will provide a further rationale for this.

However, before moving on to this, a few words about causality are in order. Like etic/emic relations, notions of cause and effect change as well in the above discussed 'actualization theory'. Whereas empiricist science sees causation as a preferably quantitative logical description of constant conjunctions, critical (realist) accounts interpret these superstructural interactions as symptoms of deeper (infra)structural causal factors. For the 'flat ontology' proposed by relational approaches, in contrast, both kinds of implicit and explicit ontological stratifications are unwarranted, as such causal 'cuts' of reality have to be enacted by an epistemic assemblage. Actualization, the extension or 'cutting out' of a present space through an ontogenetic chain of actants, would then embody what we usually call *causation*, while 'counter-actualization' would be the concomitant *effectuation* of a time infinitely divided into potential (alternative, emergent) pasts and futures; that is, a restructuring of the virtual tendencies and capacities immanent to and conditioning that present (cf. DeLanda, 2002). Thus causation constructs and stabilizes, while effectuation, inevitably, and whether deliberately pursued or not, deconstructs and repotentializes, inducing alternative interpretations and emergent capacities. When we mostly emphasize the former process in our theoretical practices, we tend to take our own present reality as inevitable and retrospectively design possible explanations (structural determinants, functions of systemic survival) in the image of that actuality, thus giving rise to a rather static, deterministic and often fatalistic view of the world. However, when we (as 'transcendental empiricists') follow a path of counter-actualization, we trace down an embryonic or stem problem not at all resembling its mature actualization. This 'nonresemblance between the virtual and the actual', as Gibson-Graham (2006b: 202 n34) notes in her critique of 'capitalocentrism', makes for a more 'rigorous anti-essentialism to the understanding of causation, working against the nearly ubiquitous impulse to reduce complex [path-dependent and non-linear] processes of eventuation to the operation of one or several determinants [so that] it does not collapse what it aggregates into fewer

---

the natives being studied (Lett, 1990: 130–131). Although originating from a rather universalist structuralism (phon*etic*/phon*emic*), the distinction has, under the influence of postcolonial thought, come to designate a much more symmetrical hermeneutics.

categories, but spreads everything out to the limits of our tolerance for dimensionality and detail' (ibid.: xxx–xxxi). The latter operation is what I will describe in what follows as an epistemic strategy of counter-actualization.

3.4   COUNTER-ACTUALIZING GENTRIFIED SOCIETIES, MARKETS AND DEMOCRACIES

If a problem like gentrification, through its actualization, finds its resolution in metrics such as rising prices and changing demographics, it is only natural to start the task of problematization from there, as they provide a first empirical foothold and a provisional analytical demarcation amid a (desubjectified + singular + affective) multiplicity of travelling and mutating actants. What follows in this section is a further outline of this problematizing[13] strategy of counter-actualization (cf. Deleuze, 1990, DeLanda, 2002), and an illustration of what it might entail in the case of three important and familiar gentrification themes: social mix, capitalist property markets and neoliberal governance.

Let us start our journey of problematization from 'matters of fact'; that is, with actualized axioms and metrics of truth, money and power. To prevent 'category mistakes', we as Moderns subjects are in a way 'prepositioned' (Latour, 2013) by certain incommensurable 'symbolically generalized media' (Luhmann, 1997): by axiom money cannot buy you truth or power and vice versa.[14] As abstract, qualitatively indivisible and empty signifiers (cf. Laclau, 1996), these media of equivalence can only make the difference they make, as either unattainable regulatory ideals (cf. 'democracy' in poststructuralist theories or 'free market' in neoclassical economics) or, more practically and more commonly, by being divided quantitatively. In the Modern, axiomatic firstspace of metrics, scientific models and statistics quantify observations of nature and society, economic prices paid and investments made are a measure of some general utility, and political polls and other quantitative evaluations reflect how much decisions and plans represent the general will of the people. In these to-be-problematized terms, gentrification at any (axiomatic) scale appears simply as a changing demography, market and electorate (cf. Ley, 1980).

However, although they may, as 'real abstractions', be quite averse to much interpretation (at the cash register, just pay up, do not question the meaning of money, cf. Žižek, 2008), these metric realities, however axiomatized, always rely on prior qualitative, discursive choices (on some rare occasions, we do discuss the meaning of money). In and around a gentrifying neighbourhood, every social statistic is based on some classification (for example, livability or class) or theory (for example, attractiveness, social mix, class hegemony). Likewise, every price is a translation of some interpretation of use value (for example, historic character, exotic food) and every evaluation of power is rooted in ideological and strategic deliberations (for example, liberal versus social-democratic housing policy). A first step in counter-actualization then, is the familiar critical move of showing how 'matters of fact' are always the product of interpretation and discourse, and that

---

[13]   It needs to be remarked that 'problematization' here means quite the opposite of what Callon understands by the term, i.e. the translation of a (stem) issue into well-defined policy problems.

[14]   There may be other media of exchange added here, like lawfulness, beauty (as in art) or love (cf. Luhmann, 1997), although these are evidently less obviously quantified and axiomatized (but see Badiou, 2005).

Table 3.1   General scheme of the (counter-)actualization of intra-active practices

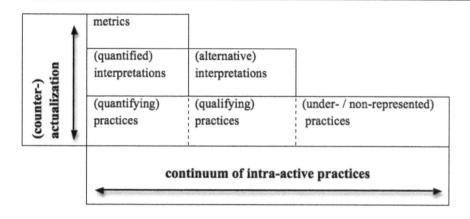

there are many alternative interpretations which are not (clearly) translated into official facts, payments or votes (for example, folk classifications, alternative use values, radical politics). Crucial however, is bringing down to Earth all these interpretations in a second step, by grounding them in the practices that generate them (for example, practices of statistics, accounting, organizing, writing, designing, gossiping), a move that also immediately brings our attention to those practices that lack or resist (clear) representation. Together then, these two moves of counter-actualization entail a progressive broadening of the range of intra-active actants (Table 3.1). In what follows I will apply this heuristic strategy to some familiar gentrification themes and debates.

3.4.1   Practices of Socialization

Without academic or folk practices of socialization, there is no society nor 'social facts' (cf. Latour, 2005a: 257).[15] Things are not social (or natural) in and of themselves but have to be constructed as such through all sorts of skills, techniques and objects. In terms of the foregoing types of actants enrolled we can distinguish (by the columns of Table 3.2) between metric, only interpretive and non-representational socialization practices. Metrics originate mostly from our academic and statistical institutions (for example, measuring demographic composition, social mobility, gentrification). Only very specific, (quasi-) theoretically motivated social categories enter and leave these practices (for example, class, ethnicity). However, many more very relevant distinctions will never be scientized. These include all kinds of identities of place and history, expressed in daily interactions and narratives ('the natives', 'those new people', 'there goes the neighbourhood', cf. for example, Butler and Robson, 2003). Thus a distinctive configuration of practices of socialization emerges, differentiated continuously according to their capacities for producing clear and

---

[15]   Of course, the idea of socialization suggested here is something very different from its classical sociological meaning of the internalization of the norms of society by an individual through upbringing and education. Quite the opposite, it is the performance of the social through representations such as 'individual' and 'society'.

Table 3.2   (Counter-)actualization of practices of socialization

(counter-)actualization ↕	counting and statistics	identification and representation	singularities
	social-demographic figures, tables and graphs		
	social indicators, classifications and theories	(non-quantified) social representations and community associations	
	methods, research skills within statistic and academic institutions	habitus, solidarity, recognition, distinction, resentment and indifference	(cultivation of) sad and joyful encounters, lines of flight (from identity)
continuum of intra-active practices of socialization: **counting and statistics – identification and representation – singularities**			

distinct social identities and their measurement. Of course, one recognizes here the metrics that legitimize policies of 'social mix' as well as the interpretive 'social tectonics' that critical academics take as indicative of its failure (Lees, 2008; Bridge et al., 2011, 2014).

However, there are also, in the outer right-hand cell, those very singular practices and events of socialization that somehow escape our usual institutional and everyday representations, but nevertheless turn up especially important to neighbourhood life. And it is here that a relational point of view could really make a difference, as other approaches tend to ignore this category as inconsequential. Reducing the 'geology of morals' (Deleuze and Guattari, 1987) of a neighbourhood to daily tectonics of sediment identities precludes the possibility of what we might call 'volcanic' ruptures or lines of flight breaking away from habitus. Some public events, places and spaces within a neighbourhood tend to exceed by virtue of their singularity the interpretive level of class dialectics and habitual interaction, not because they magically harmonize what is divided, but by intra-actively quilting people together through their indeterminate differences. In this regard, interviewing residents about their everyday grievances and their opinions on neighbourhood interaction and integration can be treacherous, as people then often feel compelled to speak in 'powerful negative generalizations' (Valentine, 2008: 332). More positive experiences are easily dismissed (especially by research) as they tend to be singularizing (rather than producing a cosmopolitan 'generalized respect for difference', Valentine, 2008: 332–333). However, observing and asking questions in that direction often reveals the best stories around events and places bearing proper names that signify a shared affective significance beyond class, political, ethnic or other fault lines (such as 'Schwendermarkt', 'Firuzağa Kahvesi', 'Ballroom Theater'). Empirical detection of these singular events requires response-able ethnographic work, a willingness to 'follow the actors' and suspend one's pre-established categories of the social and habitus (cf. Latour, 2005a). They might be embodied by a market square, a playground, a festival, a theatre event or a café, yet as events of intense 'co-becoming' they invariably transcend the generic 'third place' with its comfortable but separate co-existence (Blokland and Nast, 2014). They might be dormant and unintentionally activated when under threat, as when a public space is announced to be demolished and residents in multiple ways (re)connect with it, or they can be deliberately incited (although there are no guarantees here), as when a community art event manages to enrol a mixed cast and audience. When they work, they swarm with joyful as well as sad affects and write shared histories, connective dramas that can constitute the most affirmative (albeit non-revolutionary and non-assimilating) moments of 'social mixing'. They are those singularities of 'vertical tension' (Sloterdijk, 2012) that incite people to become the best of their selves, breaking out of their habitus, if only 'temporarily'.[16] Besides the undoubtedly necessary comfort of 'public familiarity' (Blokland and Nast, 2014), they are the condensations of improbable connections we must learn to cultivate below the radar of daily phenomenology and institutional oversight. That is, if we are prepared to appreciate diversity beyond the overly ambitious ideals of integration of both policy and its current critics.

3.4.2 Practices of (Real Estate) Economization

Gentrification is almost invariably explained as a function of capitalism, be it as the latest frontier of its uneven development (the product of a rent gap, Smith, 1982, Slater, 2014) or as a consequence of its post-industrialization and professionalization (Ley, 1980, Hamnett, 1991). However, this type of explanation, especially the former 'production' oriented theories, has a tendency to, on the one hand, overestimate capitalism's reach and, on the other, trivialize the heterogeneity of practices of computation, appraisal and construction by which rent gaps or (use) values are sociotechnically performed (thereby possibly obscuring many capacities for change, Gibson-Graham, 2006a, 2006b). To instead resist the strong 'epistemic pull of capital' (Gidwani, 2004: 537), insights of neo-institutional economists and *longue durée* historians like Braudel (1984) and DeLanda (1997) can be very helpful. As they rigorously restrict capitalism to 'hierarchies' and 'antimarkets', they effectively bar it from, on the one hand, covering all of social life, while on the other making it more akin to state bureaucracy than to small entrepreneurship and investments. Nonetheless, to faithfully describe 'economics in the wild', these insights need reinterpretation in terms of concrete practices of valuation and calculation, since neo-institutional 'transaction costs' still remain too abstract and rationalistic. Like society in the previous subsection, the economy and its markets have to be performed through practices of economization and marketization in order to exist (cf. Callon and Çalışkan, 2009, 2010, Latour and Lépinay, 2009).

More specifically, urban land and housing are not inherently economic but have to be performed that way 'in the wild' through specific calculative devices and scripts. And as in the case of a housing bubble (Smith et al., 2006), one can expect different economic practices of real estate economization at play in gentrifying neighbourhoods, varying from the very formal and financialized (Christophers, 2014) to the cultural and affective (Munro and Smith, 2008, Smith, 2011) (Table 3.3). At least three interesting complications

---

[16] As Sloterdijk (2012) keenly observes, in the classical understandings of Aristotle and Thomas Aquinas (which Bourdieu consciously disregards) the *habitus* or *hexis* is irreducible to the 'class within us' (i.e. to a culturally arbitrary expression of a deeper social structure). Unlike Bourdieu, they do not conflate social dominance (*pouvoir*) with practical achievement (*puissance*). We could demand the same of Bourdieuvian studies of social mixing and tectonics (e.g. Butler and Robson 2003, Davidson 2010, Jackson and Butler, 2015). When the neighborhood is no longer a zero-sum field, how do we summon the 'virtuous within us'?

Table 3.3   (Counter-)actualization of practices of real estate economization

(counter-)actualization			
	(prosthetic) prices, formulas, metric properties, point systems		
	'objectified' values, investment strategies, property and housing laws, faith in currency	non-quantified (alternative) use values and ideologies of housing, space and good living	
	valuing, price and calculative practices	passionate interests, media of discourse on housing within social and professional networks	(common) desires and capacities of dwelling and construction
	continuum of intra-active practices of real estate economics (cf. Smith, 2011): **hedonic/comparative pricing – behavioral-cultural rationality – affective**		

could result from this conceptualization in relation to the gentrification literature. First, calculations become intermeshed with discursive positions on use values and intense 'passionate interests' (Latour and Lépinay, 2009) and also with 'non-economized' marketized affects and capacities of common dwelling and construction. As with the heterogeneity of 'consumptive' motivations (Lees et al., 2008: 94–121), many more 'productive' interests and capacities may be included besides those of profit maximization (taken as primary in production accounts, Lees et al., 2008: 45–51). The latter can range from the highly regulated and financialized, comprising also social housing associations (Aalbers et al., forthcoming), to the more alternative arrangements, such as community land trusts and co-ops (cf. DeFilippis, 2004), to the non-economic and subaltern, including religious commons (Khalfan and Ogura, 2012) and squatting (Pruit, 2013). Second, this also implies that there is no natural distinction between 'market' and 'state' among calculative practices (cf. Lazzarato, 2015). Instead, following the more general lead of 'post-social' housing studies (Smith et al., 2006, Gabriel and Jacobs, 2008), we will encounter a whole jungle of economic skills, equipment and scripts (for example, valuation know-how, spreadsheet computations, rules of thumb, point systems, rent caps), with institutional representations (of 'social', 'state', 'market') possibly feeding into such assemblages by way of laws, plans and mission statements. Depending on such actants then, there are buyers and investors big and small, self-interested and socially committed, specialized and standardized, resident and absentee, operating close by and from a distance. Third, if we 'wish the neoclassical theories of urban land markets to become not true' (Lees et al., 2008: 48–49), or less true (by regulation or sociotechnical innovation, for instance), we would surely benefit from a deeper understanding of how they become true (Lees, 2014, for example, shows how they are constructed). Rent gaps are not 'out there' but have to be performed as such by framing operations of, for instance, estimating costs and benefits, securing attachment of buyers and setting prices (cf. Çalıskan and Callon, 2010).

Although space restricts me to further treat it here, it should be noted that practices of economization would also cover another important theme besides real estate (be it residential or commercial), which is the transformation of retail (for example, Bridge

Table 3.4   (Counter-)actualization of practices of politicization

	electoral, financial and scientific evaluations of power		
(counter-)actualization	political parties, offices, programs, rationalities, plans, regulations, laws, territories	political ideologies and movements (demonstrations, organizations etc.)	
	technologies of 'governing at a distance'	practices of power play, skills of networking and charisma	emerging, buzzing yet underrepresented concerns

continuum of intra-active political practices (cf. Latour, 2007):
governmentality – deliberative – Machiavellian – public problems – matters of concern

and Dowling, 2001, Zukin et al., 2009). The diagram of Table 3.4 would not change dramatically for this thematic, but since there is a lot less money involved in the transaction between producer and consumer, the emphasis would surely shift away from the calculative practices and move a bit more toward those of establishing qualitative use values ('cheap', 'authentic', 'local') and the non-representational, affective capacities of making and desiring (for example, craftsmanship). Like in the case of real estate economics, a more refined differentiation in terms of practices could thus be explored. For instance, and beyond rather facile frames of cultural arbitrariness (Bourdieu, 1984, Zukin et al., 2015), a contrast could be investigated between, amongst other features, those often small-scale entrepreneurial practices whose claims to authentic, healthy and more social living actually may have some purchase and those (often corporate chains) that merely fake and fetishize it (cf. Mallard, 2007, 2016). In sum, rather than having to envision some unimaginable post-capitalist world, we may thus engage more subtly with the rather concrete heterogeneity of practices of (housing) economization subsisting in our neighbourhoods (cf. Gibson-Graham, 2006b: xxxiv).

3.4.3   Practices of Politicization

In the (neo-)Marxist dominated gentrification literature, politics can be found just about anywhere, down to the most mundane interactions of neighbours (for example, Davidson, 2010, Paton, 2009). However, when located somewhat more precisely, we typically find the political at the 'frontier' (Smith, 1986: 34) in between the forces of capital (or 'economic profitability', Robinson, 1995) and their working class resistance (or 'neighborhood maintenance', Betancur, 2002). Recently, in the continental European literature in particular, this opposition has been slightly displaced by Rancièrean-inspired narratives of 'de-politicization' (Swyngedouw, 2009) in which urban space and gentrification are supposedly de-politicized by neoliberal governmentalities and their participation schemes, or 'police', troubled only by sparse eruptions of 'the political' proper (Uitermark and Nicholls, 2014). However, these dialectic and post-structuralist definitions of (de) politicization, police and the political proper, make it very hard to genuinely engage with those concerns and planning practices that complicate these distinctions, say when resistance comes from middle class liberals or, conversely, when working class people consciously cooperate with gentrification policies. Just about any academic work that blurs the aforesaid frontiers is condemned as an act of de-politicization itself and thus is complicit with gentrification and oppression (Slater, 2009, 2011: 580).

Other, relational approaches can offer a different take on the matter. As neither located in one specific place, such as a parliament, type of state, or particular class, nor 'everywhere', the political sphere can also be redescribed along a continuum of contrasting practices of politicization (cf. Latour, 2007: 818) (Table 3.3). Political concerns (or 'things', Latour, 2005b) provoked by the event of gentrification can then be observed to more or less successfully travel and mutate along that continuum, in 'search of their public' (cf. Dewey, 1954). Instead of having to fit a ready-made (for example, left-right) mould, a political thing (*res*) can thus actualize its republic (*res publica*) through a multiplicity of practices, from 'cosmopolitical' matters of concern to a Machiavellian power play to a fully established Foucauldian state apparatus 'governing from a distance' (cf. Latour, 2007: 818). This way, different events of gentrification will demand and allow for different practices of politicization, none of which are necessarily 'neoliberal' or 'de-politicized', from the circulation of concerns (of affordability, crime and so on), in the right-hand column, to their possible uptake by community leaders and organizations, in the middle, to participatory budgeting, city-wide referenda or policy evaluations in the left-hand column.

Freed from its one-fold frontier (with its standard resistance strategies), manifold practices come to channel the political issue(s) of gentrification. We can think of the buzz of concerns that somehow do not manage to find representation because of a static party politics at the lowest levels of democracy, or because of a complacent socialist government ('we do not have any gentrification here', cf. Franz, 2013: 263), or simply because of a lack of fit between the 'paper world' of bureaucracy and the verbalized concerns of the neighbourhood. Or think of the diplomatic and quasi-clientelistic ('Machiavellian') networks of community leaders, civil servants and politicians that cut across official alliances (and are often most effective in deflecting large-scale gentrification efforts) (cf. Erman and Coşkun-Yıldar, 2007, Yetiskul et al., 2016). Or, as a last example, how instead of instilling compliance 'from a distance', district level participatory planning boards are able to exploit an impotent, electorally fragmented city council and get things done for a neighbourhood. In every case, the devil will be in the details of practices (and their nonlinear intra-action), but that should not demotivate us from trying to delineate them more precisely without trying to remould them into grand oppositions.

3.5   ONTOLOGICAL MULTIPLICATION: POLITICIZATION × SOCIALIZATION × ECONOMIZATION

To complicate matters more, political, social and economic practices can be said to 'intra-act' as problems, imposing specific risks and opportunities on each other and generating an unceasing proliferation of new publics, groups and scarcities (cf. Callon, 2007). Most obviously for the subject at hand, many practices of housing economization immediately produce concerns of eviction, affordability or accessibility (for example, Marcuse, 1985).

It then remains to be seen whether and which paths of politicization (demonstrations, legal action, networking, party politics, deliberation) are practically feasible and desirable in relation to the market assemblage under study. Likewise, political regulation through rezoning, point systems or subsidizing can change in unexpected ways the economic calculations of investors and businesses (cf. Bernt, 2012). And in terms of socialization practices, we can think of how statistical categories of cultural difference (depicting 'integration', 'social mix' and 'balance') can seep into daily discourse, leading political concerns into racist directions rather than those of class struggle (cf. Uitermark and Duyvendak, 2008). Or how measurements and rankings of places in terms of crime or livability feed into real estate values (Gabriel and Jacobs, 2008: 534).

Of course there are many more possible overflowings that excessively spill beyond the frame of this chapter, but there is one important kind that involves we scholars in particular. Counter-actualization can also be thought of as a strategy enabling the diffractive super(im)position of our own (etic) practices and habits with those in the (emic) field. Risky and inconvenient questions can arise that may give us thought on whether and how to bring our 'gentrification' to the table. Questions such as, for example, can we imagine social mix as a practice of everyday diplomacy or civic craftsmanship, perhaps of cultivating singularity, rather than a 'gentrification by stealth'? Could the original working class residents take on the role of 'hosts' to the new 'guests' (maybe literally, in a community theatre), granting the former much more symbolic power than in their usual role as rather passive victims (possibly endowed with a sort of false consciousness)? Or can we think of 'middle class' religious practices as more than an anachronistic pastoral power or a mere pretext for a retreating state? Could they possibly reach the neighbourhood's most needy, there were social-democratic bureaucracies fail to do so? Or could they harbour practices of 'the common' beyond the standard public-private division? Could we find in deliberative democratic planning practices a genuine political outreach rather than a mere neoliberal technology to manufacture consent? Or can we, especially in the absence of other economically viable options, affirm those commercial practices promoting 'slow living'? Are we capable of seeing them as anything other than a simple displacement of the lifestyles of the poor? In short, are we currently capable of taking emic practices seriously in an affirmative way, not by uncritically surrendering to them, but such that we risk our own habitual (integrationist, victimizing, secular, demystifying, activist) conceptions of gentrification? Or, as the recent literature reviews of Slater (2006, 2009) seem to suggest, are these really just inappropriate, de-politicizing distractions? It probably depends on the singular problem at hand ('a Notting Hill / Tarlabaşı / Hoogvliet to gentrify'). In any case, we have to be careful that our abstractions do not obscure or even prematurely terminate the interstitial development of rare lines of flight (new singularities, affects and concerns) that might not readily identify as either positive and emancipatory or negative and revanchist practices (Lees et al., 2008: 195–234, cf. Caulfield, 1994).

While critical geographers rightfully deconstruct the bland positivism and functionalism of neoclassical and naturalist perspectives on urban life by positing a more fundamental spatial dialectic between capital and (abstract) labour, the 'political ecology' presented here grounds and diffracts these generalities into a heterogeneous multiplicity of practices, entertaining relations of exteriority (to which academic practices connect in modest yet possibly crucial ways). In the words of Latour (2004), our political ecology thus confronts us all with a perpetual challenge to 'progressively compose a common world'. In different (impersonal) capacities, or 'skills for the collective', we all have our responsibilities toward that purpose. Let (the) economists (in us) economize and construct civilized markets (Callon, 2009) and let politicians politicize and erect new, more inclusive republics (Latour, 2005b). As scientists, perpetually on the lookout for new relations and alliances, we are to stay perplexed and responsible (response-able), which in the case of gentrification studies means withstanding the epistemic pull of capital (and its 'firstspace' and 'History 1'), in our search for sources of resistance, but also by relaxing oppositions when possible to allow for diplomacy and the invention of new propositions and questions.

Our rhetorical and analytical skills are very much needed to co-write anti-gentrification handbooks such as those of LTF et al. (2014) in London or Phillips et al. (2014) in San Francisco. Yet as Lees et al. (2016) concur with reference to the Swedish context, specific strategies have to be developed for other places. For example, in my own non-academic writing for a bimonthly gazette of a Dutch neighbourhood, I take a more diplomatic and problematizing approach, saving my battle cries for those moments when they are obviously in place (also knowing well that a critical approach incites only counterproductive hostility there, from *all* parties, which I refuse to take as mere evidence of my right). Just as we have the critical moral duty to address exclusionary relations, and helping others to do so, we should also feel ethically obliged to actively look for unexpected vectors of connection and evolution (and to never assume a situation is not amenable to any such lines of flight, even, or especially in 'the South' where much of the commons have been less subject to state or market enclosure, citizens are often less deskilled in construction work and informalities can provide unexpected political leeway).

3.6   CONCLUSION

The framework presented here definitely complicates the world, making it more resistant to jumpy conclusions and quick fixes, yet it also opens a way into those interstitial zones of indeterminacy where new ways of living might await development. Moreover, it provides an opportunity to systematically lay more emphasis on *either* political *or* social *or* economic practices (even though they, their capacities, always interfere with each other). Perhaps this gives deeper, (urban) comparative analyses more of a chance, as the need lessens to immediately implicate the entire problem of gentrification in all aspects in every geographical case description (for which of course an 'ordered and simple' concept of gentrification is indispensable – yet inevitably inadequate). As such, a detour through these different ecologies of practices subtly slows down our analysis, forcing us to 'practice patience against the tyranny of emergency' (Gibson-Graham, 2006a: xxv) and defer our conclusions on the presence or absence of gentrification at a particular site. Again, this may be politically inappropriate in many cases, but the message here is to stay response-able and open as much as possible to that assessment.

The old Copenhagen interpretation of gentrification (Clark, 1994) gave us more interpretive leeway for engaging with all the particularities of its impact around the world, yet as the discourse developed henceforth, it also resulted in a rather taken for granted dialectic of grand determinants for a causal explanation. We should be wary however, of the all too opportunistic oscillations this situation allows for, between sweeping statements of a global, all-homogenizing gentrification with a clear and simple structural core and seemingly sophisticated displays of subalternism and planetarity. A return to the causal question in terms of more earthly, practical variables could indeed ward off this threat to our ambitions for a true ontological and epistemological multiplicity, and thus further refine and renew our understanding of its conditions. For this purpose we might, following Clark (2015), welcome a more 'generic' or, in terms of the new Copenhagen interpretation, 'diffractive' and question-generating notion of gentrification. A concept,

> [that] does not authorize any definition [but] suggests a way of addressing a situation whose eventual success will be the relevance of the questions to which it gives rise. [. . .] [a notion] that requires the highest power of invention: not to privilege any particular [political economic?] mode of knowledge (Stengers in Clark, 2015: 454).

We should not be scared of too much relativism just for fear of losing our 'political punch' against the conservative forces of this world. On the contrary, our relativism, or better, 'relationism' has never been radical enough. We need to develop a variety of intellectual tools, concepts sufficiently mutable and mobile to also foster capacitations beyond reactive resistance (cf. Hynes, 2013). Moreover, by our writing in whatever media and through participation in neighbourhood conventions and events, we could also strive to equip others – residents, entrepreneurs, social workers and civil servants who have a much more intimate knowledge of their cities' and neighbourhoods' singularities and practices – not just with facts and alternative ideas, but with the methods to counter-actualize their own practices. This primarily means having 'gentrification' propose the right questions, some of which are of a directly critical nature, while others can be more diplomatic and inquisitive.

REFERENCES

Aalbers, M., Van Loon, J. and Fernandez, R. (forthcoming) 'The financialization of a social housing provider', *International Journal of Urban and Regional Research*.
Atkinson, R. and Bridge, G. (eds) (2005) *Gentrification in a Global Context*, London: Routledge.
Badiou, A. (2005) *Being and Event*, London: Continuum.
Barad, K. (2007) *Meeting the Universe Halfway: Quantum Physics and the Entanglement of Matter and Meaning*, Durham, NC: Duke University.
Bernt, M. (2012) 'The "double movements" of neighbourhood change: Gentrification and public policy in Harlem and Prenzlauer Berg', *Urban Studies*, 49(14), 3045–3062.
Betancur, J. (2002) 'The politics of gentrification: the case of West Town in Chicago', *Urban Affairs Review*, 37(6), 780–814.
Blokland, T. and Nast, J. (2014) 'From public familiarity to comfort zone: the relevance of absent ties for belonging in Berlin's mixed neighbourhoods', *International Journal of Urban and Regional Research*, 38(4), 1142–1159.
Bourdieu, P. (1984) *Distinction: A Social Critique of the Judgement of Taste*, Cambridge, MA: Harvard University Press.
Braudel, F. (1984) *The Perspective of the World*, London: Collins.
Bridge, G. and Dowling, R. (2001) 'Microgeographies of retailing and gentrification', *Australian Geographer*, 32(1), 93–107.
Bridge, G., Butler, T. and Lees, L. (eds) (2011) *Mixed Communities: Gentrification by Stealth?*, Bristol: Policy Press.
Bridge, G., Butler, T. and Le Galès, P. (2014) 'Power relations and social mix in metropolitan neighborhoods in North America and Europe: moving beyond gentrification?', *International Journal of Urban and Regional Research*, 38(4), 1133–1141.

Butler, T. and Robson, G. (2003) *London Calling: The Middle Class and the Re-making of Inner London*, Oxford: Berg.

Çalışkan, K. and Callon, M. (2009) 'Economization, part 1: shifting attention from the economy towards processes of economization', *Economy and Society*, 38(3): 369–398.

Çalışkan, K. and Callon, M. (2010) 'Economization, part 2: a research program for the study of markets', *Economy and Society*, 39(1), 1–32.

Callon, M. (2007) 'An essay on the growing contribution of economic markets to the proliferation of the social', *Theory, Culture and Society*, 24(7–8), 139–163.

Callon, M. (2009) 'Civilizing markets: carbon trading between in vitro and in vivo experiments', *Accounting, Organizations and Society*, 34(3–4), 535–548.

Caulfield, J. (1994) *City Form and Everyday Life: Toronto's Gentrification and Critical Social Practice*, London: University of Toronto Press.

Chakrabarty, D. (2000) *Provincializing Europe: Postcolonial Thought and Historical Difference*, Princeton NJ: Princeton University Press.

Christophers, B. (2014) 'Wild dragons in the city: urban political economy, affordable housing development and the performative world-making of economic models', *International Journal of Urban and Regional Research*, 38(1), 79–97.

Clark, E. (1992) 'On blindness, centrepieces and complementarity in gentrification theory', *Transactions of the Institute of British Geographers*, 17(3), 358–362.

Clark, E. (1994) 'Towards a Copenhagen interpretation of gentrification', *Urban Studies*, 31(7), 1033–1042.

Clark, E. (2005) 'The order and simplicity of gentrification', in Atkinson, R. and Bridge, G. (eds) *Gentrification in a Global Context: The New Urban Colonialism*, London: Routledge, pp. 261–269.

Clark, E. (2015) 'Afterword: the adventure of generic gentrification', in Lees, L., Bang Shin, H. and López-Morales, E. (eds) *Global Gentrifications: Uneven Development and Displacement*, Bristol: Policy Press, pp. 453–456.

Crang, M. (2001) 'Temporalised space and motion', in May, J. and Thrift, N. (eds) *Timespace: Geographies of Temporality*, London: Routledge, pp. 187–207.

Davidson, M. (2009) 'Displacement, space and dwelling: placing gentrification debate', *Ethics, Place and Environment*, 12(2), 219–234.

Davidson, M. (2010) 'Love thy neighbour? Social mixing in London's gentrification frontiers', *Environment and Planning A*, 42(3), 524–544.

DeFilippis, J. (2004) *Unmaking Goliath: Community Control in the Face of Global Capital*, London: Routledge.

DeLanda, M. (1997) *A Thousand Years of Non-Linear History*, New York: Zone Books.

DeLanda, M. (2002) *Intensive Science and Virtual Philosophy*, London: Continuum.

DeLanda, M. (2009) *Deleuze: History and Science*, New York, NY: Atropos.

Deleuze, G. (1988) *Bergsonism*, New York: Zone Books.

Deleuze, G. (1990) *Logic of Sense*, London: Athlone Press.

Deleuze, G. (1994) *Difference and Repetition*, London: Athlone Press.

Deleuze, G. and Guattari, F. (1987) *A Thousand Plateaus: Capitalism and Schizophrenia*, London: Athlone Press.

Dewey, J. (1954) *The Public and its Problems*, Athens, Ohio: Swallow Press.

Erman, T. and Coşkun-Yıldar, M. (2007) 'Emergent local initiative and the city: the case of neighbourhood associations of the better-off classes in post-1990 urban Turkey', *Urban Studies*, 44(13), 2547–2566.

Esbjörn-Hargens, S. (2010) 'An ontology of climate change: Integral pluralism and the enactment of multiple objects', *Journal of Integral Theory and Practice*, 5(1), 143–174.

Felski, R. (2012) 'Critique and the hermeneutics of suspicion', *M/C Journal*, 15(1).

Franz, Y. (2013) *Between Urban Decay and Rejuvenation. Deliberate Employment of Gentrification in Neighbourhood Development: Case Studies from New York City, Berlin and Vienna*, Dissertation Universität Wien.

Gabriel, M. and Jacobs, K. (2008) 'The post-social turn: challenges for housing research', *Housing Studies*, 23(4), 527–540.

Ghertner, D. (2015) 'Why gentrification theory fails in "much of the world"', *City*, 19(4), 552–563.

GibsonGraham, J. (1996) *The End Of Capitalism (As We Knew It): A Feminist Critique Of Political Economy*, Oxford: Blackwell.

GibsonGraham, J. (2006) *A Postcapitalist Politics*, Minneapolis: University of Minnesota Press.

Gidwani, V. (2004) 'The limits to capital: questions of provenance and politics', *Antipode*, 36(3), 527–542.

Guggenheim, M. (2010) 'Mutable immobiles: change of use of buildings as a problem of quasi-technologies', in Farías, I. and Bender, T. (eds) *Urban Assemblages: How Actor-network Theory Changes Urban Studies*, London: Routledge, pp. 161–178.

Hamnett, C. (1991) 'The blind men and the elephant: the explanation of gentrification', *Transactions of the Institute of British Geographers*, 16(2), 173–189.

Harman, G. (2009) *The Prince of Networks: Bruno Latour and Metaphysics*, Melbourne: re.press.

Harvey, D. (1996) *Justice, Nature and the Geography of Difference*, Oxford: Blackwell.

Hynes, M. (2013) 'Reconceptualizing resistance: sociology and the affective dimension of resistance', *The British Journal of Sociology*, 64(4): 559–577.

Jackson, E. and Butler, T. (2015) 'Revisiting "social tectonics": the middle classes and social mix in gentrifying neighbourhoods', *Urban Studies*, 52(13), 2349–2365.

Khalfan, A. and Ogura, N. (2012) 'Sustainable architectural conservation according to traditions of Islamic waqf: the world heritage-listed stone town of Zanzibar', *International Journal of Heritage Studies*, 18(6), 588–604.

Laclau, E. (1996) *Emancipation(s)*, London: Verso.

Latour, B. (1987) *Science in Action: How to Follow Scientists and Engineers Through Society*, Milton Keynes: Open University Press.

Latour, B. (1999) 'On recalling actor-network theory', *The Sociological Review*, 47(S1), 15–25.

Latour, B. (2004) *Politics of Nature: How to Bring the Sciences into Democracy*, Cambridge, MA: Harvard University Press.

Latour, B. (2005a) *Reassembling the Social: An Introduction to Actor-Network-Theory*, New York: Oxford University Press.

Latour, B. (2005b) 'From realpolitik to dingpolitik: an introduction to making things public', in Latour, B. and Weibel, P. (eds) *Making Things Public: Atmospheres of Democracy*, Cambridge, MA: The MIT Press, pp. 4–31.

Latour, B. (2007) 'Turning around politics: a note on Gerard de Vries' paper', *Social Studies of Science*, 37(5), 811–820.

Latour, B. (2013) *An Inquiry into Modes of Existence: An Anthropology of the Moderns*, London: Harvard University Press.

Latour, B. (2014) *On Some of the Affects of Capitalism*, paper presented at Royal Academy, Copenhagen, 26 February.

Latour, B. and Lépinay, V. (2009) *The Science of Passionate Interests: An Introduction to Gabriel Tarde's Economic Anthropology*, Chicago: Prickly Paradigm Press.

Law, J. (2008) 'On sociology and STS', *The Sociological Review*, 56(4), 623–649.

Law, J. and Mol, A. (2001) 'Situating technoscience: an inquiry into spatialities', *Environment and Planning D: Society and Space*, 19, 609–621.

Law, J. and Singleton, V. (2004) 'Object lessons', *Organization*, 12(3), 331–355.

Lazzarato, M. (2015) *Governing by Debt*, South Pasadena, CA: Semiotext(e).

Lees, L. (1994) 'Rethinking gentrification: beyond the positions of economics or culture', *Progress in Human Geography*, 18(2), 137–150.

Lees, L. (2008) 'Gentrification and social mixing: towards an urban renaissance?', *Urban Studies*, 45(12), 2449–2470.

Lees, L. (2012) 'The geography of gentrification: thinking through comparative urbanism', *Progress in Human Geography*, 36(2), 155–171.

Lees, L. (2014) 'The urban injustices of New Labour's "new urban renewal": The case of the Aylesbury Estate in London', *Antipode*, 46(4), 921–947.

Lees, L., Shin, H. and López-Morales, E. (eds) (2015) *Global Gentrifications: Uneven Development and Displacement*, Bristol: Policy Press.

Lees, L., Shin, H. and López-Morales, E. (2016) *Planetary Gentrification*, Cambridge: Polity Press.

Lees, L., Slater, T. and Wyly, E. (eds) (2008) *Gentrification*, London: Routledge.

Lees, L., Slater, T. and Wyly, E. (eds) (2010) *The Gentrification Reader*, London: Routledge.

Lett, J. (1990) 'Emics and etics: notes on the epistemology of anthropology', in Headland, T., Pike, K. and Harris, M. (eds) *Emics and Etics: The Insider/Outsider Debate*, Newbury Park, CA: SAGE, pp. 127–142.

Ley, D. (1980) 'Liberal ideology and the postindustrial city', *Annals of the Association of American Geographers*, 70(2), 238–258.

Ley, D. and Teo, S. (2014) 'Gentrification in Hong Kong? Epistemology vs. ontology', *International Journal of Urban and Regional Research*, 38(4), 1286–1303.

London Tenants Federation, Lees, L., Just Space and Southwark Notes Archive Group (2014) *Staying Put: An Anti-Gentrification Handbook for Council Estates in London*, London: Calverts Co-operative.

Luhmann, N. (1997) *Die Gesellschaft der Gesellschaft*, Frankfurt am Main: Suhrkamp.

Mallard, A. (2007) 'Performance testing: dissection of a consumerist experiment', *The Sociological Review*, 55(s2), 152–172.

Mallard, A. (2016) 'Exploring urban controversies on retail diversity', in Blok, A. and Farías, I. (eds) *Urban Cosmopolitics: Agencements, Assemblies, Atmospheres*, London: Routledge, pp. 85–104.

Maloutas, T. (2012) 'Contextual diversity in gentrification research', *Critical Sociology*, 38(1), 33–48.

Massey, D. (2005) *For Space*, London: SAGE.

Merrifield, A. (2006) *Henri Lefebvre: A Critical Introduction*, London: Routledge.

Mol, A. (2002) *The Body Multiple: Ontology in Medical Practice*, Durham, NC: Duke University Press.

Munro, M. and Smith, S. (2008) 'Calculated affection? Charting the complex economy of home purchase', *Housing Studies*, 23(2), 349–367.

Paton, K. (2009) 'Probing the symptomatic silences of middle-class settlement: a case study of gentrification processes in Glasgow', *City*, 13(4), 432–450.

Phillips, M. (2002) 'The production, symbolization and socialization of gentrification: impressions from two Berkshire villages', *Transactions of the Institute of British Geographers*, 27(3), 282–308.

Phillips, M. (2004) 'Other geographies of gentrification', *Progress in Human Geography*, 28(1), 5–30.

Phillips, M. (2010) 'Counterurbanisation and rural gentrification: an exploration of the terms', *Population, Space and Place*, 16, 539–558.

Phillips, D., Flores, Jr. L. and Henderson, J. (2014) 'Development without displacement: resisting gentrification in the Bay Area', San Francisco and Oakland: Causa Justa – Just Cause.

Prigogine, I. and Stengers, I. (1984) *Order Out of Chaos: Man's New Dialogue with Nature*, Toronto: Bantam Books.

Pruijt, H. (2013) 'Squatting in Europe', in Squatting Europe Kollective (ed) *Squatting in Europe: Radical Spaces, Urban Struggles*, Brooklyn, NY: Autonomedia, pp. 17–60.

Robinson, T. (1995) 'Gentrification and grassroots resistance in San Francisco's tenderloin', *Urban Affairs Review*, 30(4), 483–513.

Schulman, S. (2012) *The Gentrification of the Mind: Witness to a Lost Imagination*, Berkeley: University of California Press.

Slater, T. (2006) 'The eviction of critical perspectives from gentrification research', *International Journal of Urban and Regional Research*, 30(4), 737–757.

Slater, T. (2009) 'Missing Marcuse: on gentrification and displacement', *City*, 13(2–3), 292–311.

Slater, T. (2011) 'Gentrification of the city', in Bridge, G. and Watson, S. (eds) *The New Blackwell Companion to the City*, Oxford: Blackwell Publishing, pp. 571–585.

Sloterdijk, P. (2012) *You Must Change Your Life: On Anthropotechnics*, Cambridge: Polity Press.

Smith, N. (1986) 'Gentrification, the frontier, and the restructuring of urban space', in Smith, N. and Williams, P. (eds) *Gentrification of the City*, Boston: Allen and Unwin, pp. 15–34.

Smith, N. (2002) 'New globalism, new urbanism: gentrification as global urban strategy', *Antipode*, 34(3), 427–450.

Smith, S. (2011) 'Home price dynamics: a behavioural economy?', *Housing, Theory and Society*, 28(3), 236–261.

Smith, S., Munro, M. and Christie, H. (2006) 'Performing (housing) markets', *Urban Studies*, 43(1), 81–98.

Spector, M. and Kitsuse, J. (1977) *Constructing Social Problems*, Menlo Park, CA: Cummings.

Spivak, G. (2003) *Death of a Discipline*, New York: Columbia University Press.

Stengers, I. (2008) 'Experimenting with refrains: subjectivity and the challenge of escaping modern dualism', *Subjectivity*, 22(1), 38–59.

Stengers, I. (2011) *Cosmopolitics II*, London: University of Minnesota Press.

Swyngedouw, E. (2009) 'The antinomies of the postpolitical city: in search of a democratic politics of environmental production', *International Journal of Urban and Regional Research*, 33(3), 601–620.

Uitermark, J. and Duyvendak, J. (2008) 'Civilising the city: populism and revanchist urbanism in Rotterdam', *Urban Studies*, 45(7), 1485–1503.

Uitermark, J. and Nicholls, W. (2014) 'From politicization to policing: the rise and decline of new social movements in Amsterdam and Paris', *Antipode*, 46(4), 970–991.

Valentine, G. (2008) 'Living with difference: reflections on geographies of encounter', *Progress in Human Geography*, 32(3), 323–337.

Yetiskul, E., Kayasü, S. and Ozdemir, S. (2016) 'Local responses to urban redevelopment projects: the case of Beyoğlu, Istanbul', *Habitat International*, 51, 159–167.

Žižek, S. (2008) *The Sublime Object of Ideology*, London: Verso.

Zukin, S., Lindeman, S. and Hurson, L. (2015) 'The omnivore's neighborhood? Online restaurant reviews, race, and gentrification', *Journal of Consumer Culture*, online first: 1–21 (journals.sagepub.com/doi/abs/10.1177/1469540515611203).

Zukin, S., Trujillo, V., Frase, P., Jackson, D., Recuber, T. and Walker, A. (2009) 'New retail capital and neighborhood change: boutiques and gentrification in New York City', *City and Community*, 8(1), 47–64.

4. Comparative urbanism in gentrification studies: fashion or progress?
Loretta Lees

4.1 INTRODUCTION

It has become fashionable of late to take on board the ideas of comparative urbanism in scholarship on gentrification (see Harris 2008; Lees 2012, 2014; Ley and Teo 2014; Lees, Shin and López-Morales 2015, 2016). This 'cosmopolitan turn' in gentrification studies, for want of a better description, marks a reorientation towards an emerging, broader field of comparative urbanism that aims to move towards a truly global urban studies. The question remains, however, how much progress can realistically be made in this endeavour given that methodological discussions of how to do comparative urbanism 'scientifically' have been few and far between. Such a question is made even more important in the face of numerous academics now climbing onto the bandwagon of 'comparative urbanism'[1] without recognizing its complexities and really doing no more than old-style comparison. It is also important given an emerging backlash against comparative urbanism (see for example, Smith 2013a, 2013b; Taylor 2013). Critics take issue with the assertions of new comparative urbanists that cities from the so-called Global South have been neglected in urban studies and that contemporary urban studies is ethnocentric. They argue that these new comparative urbanists' critiques oversimplify and misrepresent previous urban theory and studies. There are charges that a focus on ordinary cities is a provincial particularism, that ordinary cities proponents exclude certain cities while arguing for a 'more inclusive' global urban studies, that they confuse neo-Marxism with developmentalism and neoliberalism, and much more. This backlash is a little unpleasant (even masculinist,[2] indeed urban geography remains a quite male-dominated sub-discipline) and I think critique can be done in a different way, even if there are useful points to be taken from it.

In sum, comparative urbanism is in fashion. Ironically, it is a topic and indeed a label of great interest to journal editors (especially the *International Journal of Urban and Regional Research*[3]) and book publishers (especially Routledge) because it connects well to their key marketing ideas around internationalization and globalization. Indeed, globalization debates have fuelled the surge of interest in comparative urbanism (Nijman 2007). The field is also inter/trans/cross/multi-disciplinary, opening up different and wider markets

---

[1]   Many geography departments in the UK now market themselves as doing comparative urbanism or hosting comparative urbanists. Also, see Academia.edu for a long list of academics who list themselves as doing comparative urbanism.

[2]   Richard Smith's critique of Jenny Robinson is reminiscent of David Stoddart's (1991) attack on Mona Domosh (1991).

[3]   See http://www.ijurr.org/details/article/6080981/Introduction_to_a_Virtual_Issue_on_Comparative_Urbanism.html

of readership. The number of courses marketed around comparative urbanism is also on the rise, attracting international and cosmopolitan (middle class) students.

But is this progress? And how useful is it for gentrification studies? Surely any critical questioning of the value of comparative urbanism for gentrification studies (and indeed, other social sciences and humanities scholarship on the urban) must be located in relation to the *new* possibilities it offers for the social scientific evaluation of cities and urbanism. Key to this is recognizing that comparative urbanism is not simply comparing cities beyond 'the usual suspects'. It is not simply about comparing Global North cities with Global South cities or vice versa. It is not simply comparison; for me, like for other comparative urbanists such as Ananya Roy, Jenny Robinson, Sue Parnell, Colin McFarlane, and so on, it is about looking beyond the usual suspects in order to destabilise the 'truths' of Northern theory (and indeed, Southern theory), it is about destabilizing dominant procedures around comparability. It is not easy or straightforward, but rather messy and intellectually demanding.

4.2   COMPARATIVE URBANISM[4]

The arguments that comparative urbanists are now making are not new, for urban studies has long argued the need to rethink the way in which urban theory has developed. Lees, Shin and López-Morales (2016) point to urban sociologist and coiner of the term 'gentrification', Ruth Glass's (1964a) lesser known writings on 'Gaps in Knowledge', and other Marxists, like Henri Lefebvre's (2003; first pub 1970) concerns about the hegemony of the Euro-American industrialized city in urban theory. The comparative urbanist argument is that urban studies is colonial, hegemonic, and based on a selective number of presumed to be important cities, such as London, New York, and Tokyo, a selectivity fuelled not least by the global cities and world cities debates that have highlighted only a few large cities of the Global North and select others. As Robinson (2006: 13) argues in *Ordinary Cities*, contemporary urban theory has 'come to support a hierarchical analysis of cities in which some get to be creative, and others deficient, still tainted by the non-modern, placed on the side of the primitive.' McFarlane (2010) argues similarly that claims about 'the city' as a general category are too often made with the Global North implicitly in mind. Robinson (2010) argues further that urban studies makes assumptions about the incommensurability of wealthier and poorer places (cities or even neighbourhoods), assumptions which are reproduced throughout quite separate literatures. Accounts of wealthier cities are, more often, claimed to be universal, so that we witness an implicit comparativism. Robinson (2006: 41), like Roy (2009), makes a plea for a postcolonial urban theory that acknowledges the potential of learning from the experiences and accounts of urban life in different cities, where 'difference can be gathered as diversity, rather than as a hierarchical ordering or incommensurability.' The study of ordinary cities does not privilege the experiences of only certain cities in analyses and assumes them to be all part of the same field of

---

⁴   Some of the discussion and critique here developed out of a 2011 DAAD funded workshop in London and Berlin on comparative urbanism co-organized by Tim Butler, Loretta Lees, Talja Blokland, and Isle Helbrecht. Thanks to all who attended for their input, which is summarized in part here.

analyses. Robinson's overall aim is to bring into focus two aspects of cities by treating them as 'ordinary'.

First, she understands ordinary cities as 'unique assemblages of wider processes – they are all distinctive, in a category of one' (Robinson, 2006: 109). Second, she places ordinary cities within a world of interactions and flows: 'A vast array of networks and circulations of various spatial reach' (Robinson, 2006: 109). This implies that the urban is not determined by a specific type of city – whether 1920s Chicago or 1990s global cities such as London or New York. Instead, Robinson's understanding of the urban is akin to AbdouMaliq Simone's (2010: 3) understanding of 'cityness', which 'refers to the city as a thing in the making' that we take for granted and know implicitly. 'Cityness', he argues, has been 'largely peripheral to city life' (ibid, p. 5): the very dimension that characterizes the city – its capacity to continuously reshape the ways in which people, places, materials, ideas, and affect are intersected – is often the very thing that is left out of the larger analytical picture. For Simone and Robinson alike, comparative urban studies faces a new challenge, albeit one that we should have been aware of much earlier; that is, the hegemonic focus on cities in the Global North as if they should be a model for the development of cities everywhere. Of course, many of us left urban work in the Global South to Development Studies, and to be fair, it is hard to be a global urbanist – to know, to be an expert on – cities all over the world. Robinson asserts that, if we are to take all cities as ordinary cities and move away from comparing the usual suspects with the Global North and instead seek to compare processes between cities in unlikely comparisons, we would need to ask ourselves what sets of questions, what lines of theorizing, and what sort of methodologies would be suitable for this task. But here, Robinson (2010) leaves the challenge to others, when she argues for a 'comparative gesture', not a real 'comparative field'.

Ward (2010) discusses how the 1970s and 1980s did produce a comparative urban studies, mainly inspired by a Marxist perspective of seeking regularities and patterns through a grand and overarching theoretical lens that provided a cross-national comparative perspective. These studies, however, Ward argues (a little unfairly, I think), were hampered by an understanding of cities as bounded and discrete unities, and of geographical scales as fixed and pre-given. Indeed, in the 1970s and 1980s as part of the postmodern turn, there was a move away from comparative urbanism because it was seen to be part of the modernist project and prone to the fallacies of scientism/positivism and developmentalism. Ward argues that urban researchers need to move beyond these conceptions, the shortcomings of which not just postmodernists, but also postcolonial and poststructuralist theorists have made more than clear. But he is more cautious than Robinson and Simone, and asks the question as to whether a comparative urban studies can still be undertaken. For Ward, the answer is a 'Yes', as long as we keep being informed by past work and theorize back from empirical accounts of various cities. How that should be done, however, still seems a rather open question, given that comparative urbanism can be said to encompass, as a field of inquiry, the aim to develop 'knowledge, understanding, and generalization at a level between what is true for all cities and what is true for one city at a given point in time' (Nijman 2007: 1).

4.3   GENTRIFICATION STUDIES AND COMPARATIVE URBANISM

In 2012, I published a paper in *Progress in Human Geography* that asked gentrification studies to extend and rethink its earlier and longstanding work on the geography of gentrification in conversation with the new work on comparative urbanism. My concern was that there had been little to no discussion about appropriate theory to analyse gentrifications supposedly emerging in the Global South nor of how they might play out differently in the predominantly non-white cities of the Global South. I was also concerned about the rhetoric around the globalization of gentrification and 'gentrification generalized', as if (a) the process had moved North to South, West to East, and (b) that it was somehow the same everywhere. I wanted gentrification scholars to move away from an 'imitative urbanism' (from the idea that gentrification in the Global North has travelled to and been copied in the Global South) towards a 'cosmopolitan urbanism' (where gentrification in the Global South has a more expanded imagination). I felt that such a mind shift required a comparative imagination that could respond to this postcolonial challenge, and that this would have implications for how gentrification was being conceived (questioning the usefulness and applicability of the term 'gentrification' in the Global South) and how research was to be conducted (pushing us to learn new kinds of urbanism and involving multiple translations throughout the world) (Lees 2012). As Bourdieu and Wacquant (1999: 41) asserted earlier, 'the neutralization of the historical context . . . produces an apparent universalization further abetted by the work of "theorization"'. I was concerned about this in Marxist theorizations of the city in gentrification studies. Similarly, Harris (2008: 2423) argued that, rather than exporting Euro-centric understandings of gentrification to the Global South, we need to learn from the 'new sharp-edged forms' of gentrification emerging in the previously peripheral cities of the Global South. 'In this way, some of the more parochial assumptions, practices, and language of gentrification research can be "provincialized" and re-examined' (Chakrabarthy 2000).

Working in geography departments in colonized places, in New Zealand and Canada in the mid-1990s, opened my eyes to postcolonial theory and impacted some of my work back then (Lees and Berg 1995; Lees 2001). My longstanding interest in urban comparison can be found in my early work on an 'Atlantic Gap' between gentrification in London and New York City (see Lees 1994), where I illustrated that differences between the English and US land and housing markets and urban conservation practices had important effects on the gentrification process; and further comparisons with Paris (Carpenter and Lees 1995) whose central city, unlike in London and New York City, had remained middle class. The key theories of gentrification, I would come to argue, were 'made in place'. For example, the 'emancipatory city thesis' came out of more liberal Canadian cities such as Toronto and Vancouver and the 'revanchist city thesis' out of the much less liberal New York City (see Lees 2000).[5] I had long been concerned with how ideas about, and theories on, gentrification travelled problematically. In the 2000s, like Clark (2005) and

---

Harris (2008), I too wanted to see some dispute over the conventional truths, wisdoms, and time-space delineations of gentrification.

At the time, many were proclaiming that gentrification had gone global (for example, Smith 2002; Atkinson and Bridge 2005), but the 'extent of occurrence of the phenomenon from a global historical "perspective" remained largely uncharted' (Clark 2005: 260). Like Harris (2008), I wanted to see a more inclusive perspective on the geography and history of gentrification (see Lees 2000), but one informed by the new debates on comparative urbanism (see Lees 2012). I was persuaded by Ward's (2010) idea of a relational comparative approach, for 'stressing interconnected trajectories – how different cities are implicated in each other's past, present and future – moves us away from searching for similarities and differences between two mutually exclusive contexts and instead towards relational comparisons that use different cities to pose questions of one another.'

Any decentering of gentrification studies from theory originating in the Global North needs to be sensitive to and explore the different neoliberalisms associated with gentrifications around the world. There are superficial differences and similarities between gentrifications in the Global North and the Global South:

> . . . the long economic expansion and globalized credit boom across urban systems of the Global North drove gentrification outward from the urban core. The leveraged real-estate frenzy set the stage for an unprecedented crash and a wave of foreclosure driven displacements across many kinds of city neighborhoods . . . At the same time, transnational economic realignments and state-led redevelopment schemes transformed vast sections of the urban built environment of China, India, Brazil and elsewhere in the Global South . . . Contemporary urban renewal in the Global South dwarfs the bulldozed landscapes that enraged Anderson (1964) and, even in the US, the phrase is losing its stigma: Robert Moses . . . was the subject of a sympathetic, three-museum retrospective in New York in the Spring of 2007. All of these changes suggest that gentrification, displacement, and renewal have been respatialized and intensified in transnational urbanism (Wyly et al. 2010: 2604).

But there is a loose use and over-use of the term 'neoliberalism'. Neoliberalism at its simplest can be defined as the unleashing of the private market and the cutting back on government (public) intervention in the market (see Harvey 2005). It is *neo*-liberal because we have supposedly moved beyond and indeed all but destroyed the Western, post-war, Keynesian social contract made up of liberal politics and philosophies that sought to control the market in different ways. But when thinking about global gentrification, it does not make much sense to talk of neoliberalism in nations and cities that had never experienced liberalism, in this sense, in the first place. Moreover, neoliberalism had actually begun earlier in Latin American (Global South) countries such as Chile, than in the West, so the spread of global gentrification North to South via neoliberalism made little sense in this context. For me, the term 'neoliberalizations' (Larner 2003) is a better term, one attuned to the messiness of politics, lived experiences, and actual geographies, to the different contexts. This is why we titled a recent edited collection, 'Global Gentrifications' (see Lees, Shin and López-Morales 2015).

Despite being sceptical of big picture neoliberalism, sensitivity to different and similar

---

back the central city from poor and minority groups (see Lees 2000; and Lees, Slater and Wyly 2008 for more detail).

neoliberalisms and neoliberalizations is important for gentrification studies in particular, given the significant movement of capital worldwide into the secondary circuit of capital – investment in property. As Harris (2008: 2409) observed, mapping the 'global spread of policies and practices of gentrification', called for paying close attention to the connections between the market, the state, and civil society, and also the property and media elites who seem/ed to be pushing strategies of gentrification onto and up policy agendas. A turn to comparative urbanism was, I argued in the *Progress in Human Geography* paper, vital in the fight against gentrification too.

The timing of renewed interest in comparative urbanism – as the 2008 economic crisis hit and austerity agendas emerged – was an important one. It signalled a need to be much better attuned to the timings and intricacies of gentrifications worldwide. In the Global North, it was getting worse in some places, due to the financialization of housing and to developers pushing it in situations of austerity as the only choice out there. At the same time, stories about gentrification in the Global South were beginning to be published in the English- speaking world. In resistance to and fighting against gentrification, context and timing are paramount – you need to know the ground and time your fight well.

At the same time as I published the *Progress in Human Geography* paper, a Greek sociologist, Thomas Maloutas (2012), was asking whether the use of the Anglo-American term 'gentrification' facilitates or impedes understanding of processes of urban restructuring in different contexts. Like myself, he was voicing concern over the epistemological limits of current theorizations of gentrification. When gentrification is seen outside of Anglo-American cases, there is a danger, he argued, that we might equate apparently similar outcomes without paying enough attention to what could be quite different and contextually specific causes. This argument echoed the earlier heated debates in the 1990s about the contextual nature of gentrification, when a number of authors (especially Latin Americans) used diverse terminology for the same process; for example, *embourgeoisement*, *aburguesamiento*, *elitización*, urban reconquest, and so on. Like me (see Lees 1994; 2000), Maloutas argues for more attention to context in gentrification studies, but at the same time, that 'looking for gentrification in increasingly varied contexts displaces emphasis from causal mechanisms and processes to similarities in outcomes across contexts, and leads to a loss of analytical rigour' (p. 34).

He also asserts that there are three key reference points that are necessary conditions for gentrification: gentrification aesthetics, the presence of a middle-class (as a particularly well defined social segment), and post-industrialization. But this contradicts his overall thesis, as it ties 'gentrification' to the emergence of the post-industrial city in Northern and Western contexts. In addition, gentrification aesthetics are just an effect of gentrification, and the North American or West European middle-class is a historical socio-cultural particularity not necessarily evident in the Global South or East. There are plenty of cities in the Global South that have experienced gentrification but have not experienced deindustrialization and the move to post-industrialization (see, for example, He 2007, 2010 on gentrification in China; and Lees 2014). As such, Maloutas' (2012) argument about the contextual-attachment of gentrification falls back on the Western provincialism he seeks to unpick (for a more detailed critique, see Lees, Shin and López-Morales 2015).

More recently, Ley and Teo (2014) have explored the epistemological argument raised by Maloutas (2012). Like me, they were concerned that the use of the term/concept 'gentrification' outside of Euro-America represented a 'false rupture (a severing from its source region) and false universalisation (uncritically universalizing it)'. Given that the name 'gentrification' did not seem to exist in Hong Kong, they were concerned about the 'conceptual overreach' of 'gentrification' from the Anglo-American heartland to Asian-Pacific cities and specifically Hong Kong. But they concluded that just because the word 'gentrification' is missing from public and academic discourse in Hong Kong does not mean that it is not happening: 'It is only the critical view of gentrification in Euro-America compared with the neutral or even affirmative view of urban redevelopment (gentrification without the name) in Hong Kong that confounds the global symmetry.'

Ley and Teo (2014) is an example of valuable studies in the pipeline (some of which I outline in the next section) that question gentrification. Different takes on gentrification globally help us understand them properly so we can fight against this unjust process. Comparative urbanism allows us both to circumscribe the definition of gentrification in very different contexts, to distinguish its political valences – critical versus affirmative/neutral – and to conclude that its vectors of injustice may be different across time and space.

4.4 'DOING' COMPARATIVE URBANISM IN GENTRIFICATION RESEARCH

Scholars need to start asking 'ordinary questions' of comparative urbanism. While discussions of comparative urbanism are exciting and stimulating, how comparative urbanism may be achieved is not so obvious, leading to dismissals of the ordinary cities agenda as merely 'gestural' (Scott and Storper, 2015). Some of us in gentrification studies have taken up the gauntlet. The move from mere discussion of comparative urbanism towards actually 'doing' it is not easy, though. Concrete ideas as to how we might take forward a tangible research framework that takes seriously Ward's point about remaining informed by previous work is not straightforward, especially when it comes to methodologies and research methods in comparative urbanism.

The aim to decentre urban studies from the Global North often implies that certain research methods, especially those usually associated with positivism in even their lightest form, are to be thrown out and replaced by what can, at best, be termed 'academic impressionism'. The latter approach is certainly not by any stretch of the imagination what might be understood as 'scientific method'. I am of course not a positivist, but 'academic impressionism' is not robust enough a method for me either, certainly not for researching gentrification and importantly, using that research to fight this socially unjust process.

There are several methodological challenges to overcome in doing comparative urbanism. The first issue we are confronted with when looking at gentrification globally is to find Nijman's (2007) 'level between what is true for all cities and what is true for one city at a given point in time.' On the one hand, we are not to classify cities, because comparing differences in performance between cities globally would always imply a hierarchy. But if we are to stick to the idea that they are all a category of one, then what can we actually do? In some ways, comparative urbanism is trapped in the relativism that postmodern theory was charged with in the 1980s. And it is not surprising then that scholars who have argued for a new approach to comparative urban studies concern themselves with city government, governance, and the travelling of policies (see for example, Clark 2012).

After all, the themes and research questions that can be formulated around these do not need much reflection on the ideas that cities are not bounded, self-enclosed objects and that scales are not self-evident. Indeed, the plea for relational understandings is easy to live up to because such topics are primarily about how cities are actors that communicate and connect to other places. It is, however, a little more complicated, when, for example, one engages with core questions in urban geography and sociology; for example, processes and mechanisms that produce durable urban inequalities and their spatial expressions, such as gentrification. Avoiding urban classifications seems an impossible (and not always desirable) task, what might better be avoided is cultural dualisms. For example, the inner city versus suburb dualism central to urban studies makes little sense in countries that are gentrifying and suburbanizing at the same time, like China (see Lees, Shin and López-Morales 2016).

Further, I am not convinced that comparative urbanists are correct in their criticism that urban studies (in this case, gentrification studies) is lacking the methodological tools for comparing 'different' cities. In the view of comparative urbanists, it is either the theory that steers the construction of cases that is at fault or the methodology. And most comparative urbanists would argue, theory, more than anything else, should guide the construction of cases. While I share Jenny Robinson and AbouMaliq Simone's excitement over diversity, which is of course typical of the urban, I am concerned that this celebration of diversity could become nothing more than endless empirical accounts of the diversity of the urban, all of which may be fascinating in their own right, but which fail to do what Ward suggests we should do, theorize back from empirical cases. Indeed, theorizing back from empirical cases was a task that Atkinson and Bridge (2005) did not really do in their collection on gentrification in a global context, but other gentrification scholars have begun that process (see López-Morales 2010, 2011, on Chile; and Shin 2009, on South Korea). López-Morales, for example, reconceptualizes rent gap theory as 'gentrification by ground rent dispossession' in Santiago, contextually inflecting and indeed reinvigorating interest in rent gap theory globally.

So, if comparative urbanism is not to deteriorate into arbitrary urbanism, the task must be to think and theorize across cases. Harris (2008) began this when he looked at gentrification and public policy in London and Mumbai, and he ended up supporting Neil Smith's (2002) thesis about the increasing convergence between urban experiences in first and third world cities. Harris found that policy had a direct role in property speculation in both cities, that Mumbai was neoliberalizing in a similar way to London with state-sponsored gentrification and the rolling back of the state. Harris is clear, though, that gentrification did not simply project from heartland cities in the Global North to Mumbai in the Global South. There were, of course, transnational actors and imaginaries, but convergence was also a product of the desires of a powerful set of politicians and developers exploiting limited planning and land use policies in Mumbai. Harris also talks about the boomerang effect on institutions, apparatuses, and techniques of power in the West, even if he does not really elaborate much. Lees, Shin and López-Morales (2016) consider gentrification in a wider array of cities and argue that in a world that is increasingly urban, and where inner cities, suburbs and the rural are increasingly blurred distinctions, we are experiencing 'planetary gentrification'. Urban experiences in first and third world cities are converging, but that convergence is not always from core to periphery.

Harris does not discuss methodological tools, but Hyun Shin, Ernesto López-Morales and I thought hard about how we might compare the different cities in our work around the world. After much debate, we chose a grounded theory approach, an approach which operates almost in a reverse fashion from traditional social science research. Our first step was to collate as many stories (and therein, data) about gentrification or not from as wide a remit of cities, beyond the usual suspects, worldwide, as we could manage. The three of us had wide, international expertise that we pooled. Then we pulled out the main causes and grouped them together into a series of causal concepts. We then related them both to Northern theory on gentrification and to Southern theories that were out there on gentrification but little known. We began to think about new theory creation or whether previous theories remained valid. Our conclusion was that to flatten the globe and its multiple urban hierarchies with an appreciation of difference hides social injustices and neglects power relations, which are very apparent in the process of gentrification (see Lees, Shin and López-Morales 2015, 2016).

The second issue in using ideas from comparative urbanism to (re)investigate the supposed spread of gentrification globally and to unpack the idea of 'gentrification generalized' is quite simply the problematic classification or label of 'gentrification'. How can we study gentrification globally when (a) it is a Western concept framed by Western cities, and (b) without already implying that it exists globally? How can we find gentrification in places where it does not have that name? After all, we do not want to impose the category of gentrification on 'other' urban processes, or do we? Lemanski (2014) seems comfortable doing just that, reframing 'downward raiding'[6] in South African slums as 'hybrid gentrification'. Researchers who find bits and pieces of processes like gentrification, rather than overarching trends that can be comfortably categorized under existing or familiar definitions and theoretical frames, can still make contributions. The discovery and interrogation of these processes, even without the label 'gentrification', will broaden and enrich gentrification studies and even urban theory, and give rise to new understandings of the urban. They may even set new limits for the concept of gentrification.

A related issue is how do we select ordinary places for research without imposing gentrification on them and without running the risk of developing a new kind of parochialism? It could be argued that searching for gentrification across all comparative cases and contexts may actually play a role in the process itself, as the researcher-author brings the word into tangible reality, by applying it theoretically to a certain case. If s/he wishes to compare gentrification in two cities, then surely, one might assume, it must exist in both cases (whether it actually does or not). Fundamental questions such as these for comparative research need much more discussion and are to be welcomed.

Our selection of ordinary places mattered to us in light of the difficult politics of comparative urbanism and its comparative gestures. But case selection is always difficult for urban comparisons. Cases are always constructed. Selection requires an understanding of place and its particularities. One strategy might have been to seek out places with similar functions and use functional similarity in a context of diversity to study the urban comparatively. This means a more precise understanding of places and their peculiarities. Another way would have been to look at the urban transnationally, through mobilities,

---

[6]   Downward raiding is the process whereby middle-class families, themselves poorly housed, acquire the housing intended for low income groups because there are no alternatives.

drawing on Massey's (2007) argument that cities are part of widening networks and flows, which many urbanists now do. Overlapping connections might then be the 'location' of the research, rather than simply the selection of under-researched sites. Our strategy (see Lees, Shin and López-Morales 2015, 2016) was to seek out places beyond the usual suspects and to read across these places to identify similarities and differences amongst them, but also in comparison to longstanding, hegemonic examples from the Global North. We flattened the importance of all the places into one – no city or country was any more important than another – so they all became a category of one. Their differences were gathered as diversity, but we did not ignore their sameness when it was evident either. This relational comparative approach meant that the different cases from different cities around the world posed questions of each other, whether of middle class reproduction or revanchism or the use of military lands. Significantly, we were able to perform the methodological flattening of all our cities as a category of one because we used the idea of 'gentrification' as a comparator (evident or not) and our different linguistic skills enabled this as we were able to draw on various non-English literatures on urbanization.

The result we intended was that none of our cities appear exotic or parochial. We did not define the urban (or for that matter, gentrification) by a specific type of city. In fact, doing comparative urbanism in this way highlighted new processes such as the gentrification of military lands in cities as wide apart as Lagos, Karachi and Taipei. We found real evidence of exploitative processes of value extraction from the built environment in the Global South and East, processes which to date urban researchers working on/in the Global South and East have mostly overlooked. We also found that globally, the faster pace of financial capital mobility invested in real estate circuits of capital around the world has accelerated the uneven process of value extraction. This mobility, however, has not simply followed the trajectory of gentrification 'arriving' in the Global South and East from the North/West, and as such that 'neoliberal' trajectory really needs to be rethought. Importantly, we collated evidence globally of 'slum-gentrification' challenging assertions of old-time Global South experts such as Alan Gilbert that there is no such thing.[7] Our conclusion was that there are multiple gentrifications in a pluralistic sense, rather than Gentrification with a capital G. But what this means for gentrification studies we are only beginning to contemplate.

4.5   CONCLUSION

Comparative urbanism is in fashion, but to date progress has been slow. The scholarly promise of comparative urbanism remains unfulfilled, and urban studies has yet to meet the challenges comparative urbanists have posed for it. It will take time and it really is too soon to evaluate its progress (cr. Jayne 2013). Gentrification scholars have been at the forefront of trying to think through and *do* comparative urbanism, injecting much needed new ideas into gentrification studies. This is refreshing for this work has coincided with the 50th anniversary of Ruth Glass' (1964b) coining of the term 'gentrification'. Although doing comparative urbanism is much harder than discussing comparative

---

[7]   In an interview panel at the London School of Economics 2013.

urbanism, nevertheless, as a body of ideas, it deserves deeper attention from those in urban studies and beyond. In a world in which old economic and political hierarchies are breaking down, comparative urbanism could help re-imagine cities and urban practices in new ways, perhaps pushing urban theory into new subjects or perspectives so far unrecognized, devalued or neglected. Comparative urbanism, if a little too trendy right now in certain academic circles (although this seems to be dampening now), remains an exciting academic invitation, for comparison helps recover history. It shows that apparent similarity has different geographical origins. Moreover, similarities are not necessarily caused by global/transnational networks and mobilities. Gentrification is not generalized, but has generalizations – it is a pluralistic process.

Like Jenny Robinson (2010), I too want to build more globally attuned understandings of the urban and as discussed in this chapter, I have begun the hard work of having 'conversations' about gentrification and its multiple histories across cities worldwide. But on the flattening of the globe, gentrification scholars such as myself, Hyun Shin, and Ernesto López-Morales are interested in somewhat different (if interrelated) sorts of injustice. For Robinson it is the injustice of neglect and misrecognition of certain (southern/third world) cities while for us, it is the injustice of accumulation by dispossession and class exploitation. These two injustices cannot be separated. We need now to find a theoretical/ conceptual and methodological way forward that has political punch. We do not simply want to transcend the oppression of neglect based on location, but of human beings being cleared out of cities worldwide, socially cleansed simply because they do not have the money, the power, or the face that fits the new urban world.

REFERENCES

Atkinson, R. and Bridge, G. (eds) (2005) *Gentrification in a Global Context: The New Urban Colonialism*, London: Routledge.

Bourdieu, P. and Wacquant, L. (1999) 'On the cunning of imperialist reason', *Theory, Culture & Society*, 16(1), 41–58.

Carpenter, J. and Lees, L. (1995) 'Gentrification in New York, London and Paris: An international comparison', *International Journal of Urban and Regional Research*, 19(2), 286–303.

Chakrabarty, D. (2000) *Provincialising Europe*, London: Routledge.

Clark, E. (2005) 'The order and simplicity of gentrification – a political challenge', in Atkinson, R. and Bridge, G. (eds), *Gentrification in a Global Context: The New Urban Colonialism*, London: Routledge, pp. 256–264.

Clarke, N. (2012) 'Actually existing comparative urbanism: imitation and cosmopolitanism in North-South interurban partnerships', *Urban Geography*, 33(6), 796–815.

Domosh, M. (1991) 'Toward a feminist historiography of geography', *Transactions of the Institute of British Geographers*, 16(1), 95–104.

Glass, R. (1964a) *Urban-Rural Differences in Southern Asia: Some Aspects and Methods of Analysis*, Unesco Research Centre on Social and Economic Development in Southern Asia.

Glass, R. (1964b) *London: Aspects of Change*, London: MacKibbon and Kee.

Harris, A. (2008) 'From London to Mumbai and back again: gentrification and public policy in comparative perspective', *Urban Studies*, 45(12), 2407–2428.

Harvey, D. (2005) *A Brief History of Neoliberalism*, Oxford: Oxford University Press.

He, S. (2007) 'State-sponsored gentrification under market transition: the case of Shanghai', *Urban Affairs Review*, 43(2), 171–198.

He, S. (2010) 'New-build gentrification in Central Shanghai: demographic changes and socioeconomic implications', *Population, Space and Place*, 16(5), 345–361.

Jayne, M. (2013) 'Ordinary urbanism – neither trap nor tableaux: a response to Richard G Smith', *Environment and Planning A*, 45(10), 2305–2313.

Larner, W. (2003) 'Neoliberalism?', *Environment and Planning D: Society and Space*, 21, 509–512.

Lees, L. (1994) 'Gentrification in London and New York: An Atlantic Gap?' *Housing Studies*, 9(2), 199–217.

Lees, L. (2000) 'A Re-appraisal of Gentrification: towards a "geography of gentrification"', *Progress in Human Geography*, 24(3), 389–408.

Lees, L. (2001) 'Towards a critical geography of architecture: the case of an ersatz Colosseum', *Ecumene: A Journal of Cultural Geographies*, 8(1), 51–86.

Lees, L. (2012) 'The geography of gentrification: thinking through comparative urbanism', *Progress in Human Geography*, 36(2), 155–171.

Lees, L. (2014) 'Gentrification in the Global South?', in Parnell, S. and Oldfield, S. (eds), *The Routledge Handbook on Cities of the Global South*, Abingdon and New York: Routledge, pp. 506–521.

Lees, L. and Berg, L. (1995) 'Ponga, glass and concrete: a vision for urban socio-cultural geography in Aotearoa/ New Zealand', *New Zealand Geographer*, 51(2), 32–41.

Lees, L., Shin, H. and López-Morales, E. (eds) (2015) *Global Gentrifications: Uneven Development and Displacement*, Bristol: Policy Press/Chicago: University of Chicago Press

Lees, L., Shin, H. and López-Morales, E. (2016) *Planetary Gentrification*, Cambridge: Polity Press.

Lees, L., Slater, T. and Wyly, E. (2008) *Gentrification*, New York: Routledge.

Lemanski, C. (2014) 'Hybrid gentrification in South Africa: theorising across southern and northern cities', *Urban Studies*, 51(14), 2943–2960.

Lefebvre, H. (2003; first pub 1970) *The Urban Revolution*, Minneapolis: University of Minnesota Press.

Ley, D. and Teo, S.Y. (2014) 'Gentrification in Hong Kong? Epistemology vs. ontology', *International Journal of Urban and Regional Research*, 38(4), 1286–1303.

López-Morales, E. (2010) 'Real estate market, state-entrepreneurialism and urban policy in the "gentrification by ground rent dispossession" of Santiago de Chile', *Journal of Latin American Geography*, 9(1), 145–173.

López-Morales, E. (2011) 'Gentrification by ground rent dispossession: the shadows cast by large scale urban renewal in Santiago de Chile', *International Journal of Urban and Regional Research*, 35(2), 330–357.

Maloutas, T. (2012) 'Contextual diversity in gentrification research', *Critical Sociology*, 38(1), 33–48.

Massey, D. (2007) *World City*, Bristol: Policy Press.

McFarlane, C. (2010) 'The comparative city: knowledge, learning, urbanism', *International Journal of Urban and Regional Research*, 34(4), 725–742.

Nijman, J. (2007) 'Introduction – comparative urbanism', *Urban Geography*, 28(1), 1–6.

Robinson, J. (2006) *Ordinary Cities: Between Modernity and Development*, London and New York: Routledge.

Robinson, J. (2010) 'Cities in a world of cities: the comparative gesture', *International Journal of Urban and Regional Research*, 35(1), 1–23.

Roy, A. (2009) 'The 21st-century metropolis: new geographies of theory', *Regional Studies*, 43, 819–830.

Scott, A. and Storper, M. (2015) 'The nature of cities: the scope and limits of urban theory', *International Journal of Urban and Regional Research*, 39(1), 1–15.

Shin, H. (2009) 'Property-based redevelopment and gentrification: the case of Seoul, South Korea', *Geoforum*, 40(5), 906–917.

Simone, A. (2010) *City Life from Jakarta to Dakar: Movements at the Crossroads*, London and New York: Routledge.

Smith, N. (1996) *The New Urban Frontier: Gentrification and the Revanchist City*, London and New York: Routledge.

Smith, N. (2002) 'New globalism, new urbanism: gentrification as global urban strategy', *Antipode*, 34(3), 427–450.

Smith, R. (2013a) 'The ordinary city trap', *Environment and Planning A*, 45(10), 2290–2304.

Smith, R. (2013b) 'The ordinary city trap snaps back', *Environment and Planning A*, 45(10), 2318–2322.

Stoddart, D. (1991) 'Do we need a feminist historiography of geography and if we do, what should it be?', *Transactions of the Institute of British Geographers*, 16(4), 484–487.

Taylor, P. (2013) *Extraordinary Cities*, Cheltenham: Edward Elgar.

Ward, K. (2010) 'Towards a relational comparative approach to the study of cities', *Progress in Human Geography*, 34(4), 471–487.

Wyly, E., Newman, K., Schafran, A. and Lee, E. (2010) 'Displacing New York', *Environment and Planning A*, 42, 2602–2623.

PART 2

KEY/CORE CONCEPTS IN GENTRIFICATION STUDIES

5. From class to gentrification and back again
Michaela Benson and Emma Jackson

5.1 INTRODUCTION: CLASS, CLASS THEORY AND (SPACES OF) GENTRIFICATION

In this chapter, we argue for the need to carefully scrutinize the models of class that underlie understandings of gentrification and how they are mobilized, while also introducing more recent considerations from the sociology of class that focus on values and classificatory struggles (Skeggs 1997, 2004; Tyler 2015) into the study of gentrification. Our contention is that when rethinking gentrification to account both for the specificity of different contexts around the world and to speak to a planetary gentrification that can account for very different social, economic and political histories, different registers and languages of gentrification (Lees et al. 2016), it is timely to revisit and revitalize the understandings of class that have underpinned this body of research. In many ways, what we present here is a logical extension of concerns that, as Lees at al. (2016) remind us, have long been at the heart of urban theory that warn against the ethnocentric imposition of theories developed in Western European industrialized economies onto the reality of urbanization in other economic and social systems. Simply put, we question the extent to which conceptualizations of class variously developed to explain 19th-century labour relations and the class struggles emerging from industrialization (in Western European economies), and the manifestation of such relations of power through taste and consumption practices (cf. Bourdieu 1984), are fit to the purpose of critically analysing contemporary processes of gentrification the world over.

Following Imogen Tyler's (2015) provocation of class analysis more generally, we seek to develop the question: 'what is the problem that class describes' to consider (again) what is the problem that we try to describe when we present gentrification as a classed process? We argue that class is relational, situational and in progress, and that located, 'on the ground' studies based on qualitative work are important in complicating ideas of gentrification and its relationship to class. Gentrification through this lens emerges at once as a classed and classifying process that (re)produces inequalities and injustice. To explore these questions more fully, we examine in detail two recent monographs on class and gentrification, in two very different national and urban settings. These have been selected precisely to illustrate the complexity of relationships between the state and local articulations of class, how class formations interplay with and unfold in very different cultural and political contexts, including sites where class has not, at least officially, been acknowledged as part of the social structure.

The first of these is Kirsteen Paton's (2014) study of working-class people's perspectives on gentrification in Glasgow. Paton reiterates that gentrification in this context is a process that is motivated by not only the remaking of space but also the remaking of the working class through the manufacture of aspiration. However, as we discuss, she also explores how these interventions give rise to multiple and, importantly, ambivalent working-class experiences and identities in ways that are not captured so readily in much of the gentrification literature. The second example – Li Zhang's (2010) *In Search of Paradise* – explores the shift from state-provided housing to the emergence of private home ownership in Kunming, a regional city in China. In this way, she identifies a shift in how place-making plays out in Chinese cities. Zhang's ethnography perceptively argues that this is best understood as an, '*emergent* moment of class-making in a formerly socialist society that had passionately denied the existence of social class in its recent history' (p. 3). As housing emerges as a commodity, residence becomes a site of spatial distinction not previously attainable, place-making the grounds for the production of new class formations.

Before moving on to the discussion of these empirical cases, we start by revisiting the key conceptual and theoretical apparatus of gentrification research and social science approaches to understanding the relationship between class and space.

5.2   GENTRIFICATION, CLASS AND DISPLACEMENT

The original understanding of gentrification put forward by Ruth Glass (1964) to explain processes of residential transformation in London – the influx of the middle classes in to neighbourhoods and the corresponding displacement of the working class – describes how middle-class migration and investment in an area corresponds to shifts in demographics, changing the classed constitution of an area. More recent research on planetary gentrification (Lees et al. 2016) argues that understandings of this relationship between class and urban transformation carries the residues of the British example that it initially described, leading to a focus on the role of 'global gentrifiers (the global north and south's new middle classes)' (p. 110) rather than paying attention to the increasingly important role of '(trans)national developers, financial capital and transnational institutions'. However, Glass's (1964) perspective continues to influence research in this area because the urban transformations that gentrification intends to describe remain sites through which new class formations, relations and struggle may be produced. Within these considerations space figures prominently as something to be appropriated, fought and struggled over.

While gentrification has been predominantly a social phenomenon associated with urban contexts, as early sociological accounts (see for example Pahl 1965) and more recent calls for the recognition of planetary gentrification make clear, similar processes of capital accumulation act on place beyond the urban, extending to rural settings (Phillips 1998a, 1998b, 2004; Lees et al. 2016). Indeed, gentrification research, at least when understood as residential choice and emplacement of the middle classes has historically sought to challenge the dichotomy of the urban-rural divide. Indeed, Ray Pahl's (1965) work, *Urbs in Rure*, the vanguard of this body of work, bore witness to the counter-urban movement of the new middle classes and the transformation of rural areas around London through the development of the commuter belt. Documenting suburbanization, these works highlighted the relationship between the class formations brought about through widespread social and economic transformation in post-war Britain – notably the expansion and rise of the new middle class (see for example Abercrombie and Urry 1983; Goldthorpe et al. 1969) – and the transformation of space. As this earlier work demonstrated, these suburban environments were understood as fertile grounds for the reproduction of the new middle classes.

The relationship between wider social and economic transformations and gentrification is also well-captured in the accounts of 'pioneer' gentrification, new middle-class
formations articulated through the revaluation of urban living. As Ley (1996) describes
in his comprehensive study of Canadian cities, the new pro-urbanism of gentrifiers was
an outcome of the counter cultural politics of 1968, the experience of urban living of
the university educated middle class and a reaction to mass-produced environments
and the perceived conformity of the suburban lives of their parents. Per Ley (1996),
this 'new middle class' placed value on bespoke production and historic value, manifest
in the housing aesthetics and neighbourhood preservation elements of gentrification.
Such practices demonstrated the ways in which housing and neighbourhood aesthetics interplayed with the production of middle-class identities. Jager (1986) shows this
through his careful analysis of Victoriana, residential choice and class reproduction
through gentrification in Melbourne; Mendez (2008) also examines this in her account
of the middle classes in Santiago, Chile, and their pursuit of authenticity through
neighbourhood selection.

These studies explored how the consumption practices of the middle classes translate
into the construction of social boundaries that crystallize into spatial boundaries. In this
rendering, middle-class tastes and aesthetics are privileged, reflecting a wider shift from
the 1980s within class analysis towards the consideration of lifestyle and consumption
and their roles within (middle) class formation, inspired by Bourdieu's (1984) *Distinction*
(see for example Savage et al. 1992; Savage and Butler 1995). Within this theoretical
framework, claims to cultural practices become the grounds for judgement and status
discrimination, symbolic dominance exercised by the new middle classes in the pursuit of
social reproduction. This conceptualization of class formation has become hegemonic in
understanding the identities of middle-class incomers and their residential practices. This
is particularly well-illustrated by Butler and Robson's (2003) presentation of gentrifiers
in London who exhibit a 'metropolitan habitus', the capacity to live with difference as a
significant marker of their class formation. In this work, class formations have local inflec-
tions, the capitals, resources and assets of groups at the neighbourhood level structured
by and structuring place-specific mini-habituses. Writ large within this Western European
metropolitan habitus is a persistent tension between the middle-class ideal of social mixity
and the familiarity of others 'just like us' (see for example Butler and Robson 2003;
Bacqué et al. 2015). Within these studies of the middle classes and gentrification, place
takes a pivotal role within middle-class formation, bringing into sharp focus preferences
and dispositions, and the resources, assets and capitals that make this possible (Savage et
al. 2005; Benson 2013), while class struggle seems to take a backseat.

Importantly, many of these studies share the same methodological flaw: an *a priori*
categorization of incomers to a neighbourhood as 'middle class' and thus the subsequent
bounding of the research around this population. Such studies use gentrification as a
shorthand to talk about how places are appropriated by the middle classes to support their
own identity claims, how they experience the urban transformations of which they are a
part, and as such their insights into class relations are more limited. Our contention here is
that, for the large part, this research operationalizes gentrification as a way of describing
the population rather than identifying a process replete with class struggle. Further, it
reduces perspectives on gentrification to those who are the most likely beneficiaries of
this process (Slater, Curran and Lees, 2004; Slater 2006), the voices of those populations

most impacted by these urban transformations are silenced through the process (Lees 2014; Paton 2014).

Older critical sociologists and geographers took Glass's term in a different direction, linking it with wider processes of spatial and economic restructuring (e.g. Sassen 1991; Smith 1996). While a consensus emerged about the outcome of the process that gentrification describes, in terms of 'the re-creation of space for progressively more affluent users' (Hackworth, 2002: 815), there was a movement away from seeing middle-class people's preferences as the driver of the gentrification process in this body of literature. The middle classes were conceptualized not as the source, but as agents that are implicated in the urban changes that gentrification creates. An understanding of a different driver of gentrification underlies this approach, which is neatly encapsulated in Smith's (1996) argument that the physical deterioration of inner-city areas is 'a strictly logical, "rational" outcome of the operation of the land and housing markets' (p. 62). This insistence that we examine the structural processes that foster gentrification is why critical geographers have expressed frustration at broadsheet newspaper accounts of gentrification being driven by (pioneer) middle-class consumption choices. However, despite the insistence on the structural forces at play, this literature is still based on a model that reduces class to broad categories – the middle-class incomers and a displaced working class – and gentrification as a process where one replaces/displaces the other. In other words, class relations exist *a priori*, structuring the encounters taking place within these locations. This is a model that neglects the possibility that class relations are also shaped through encounter, through the changing dynamics of the housing market, localized forms of state intervention, and the specificities of localities. In other words, this work fails to grasp how the class struggle that gentrification is named after can generate new or ambivalent class positions.

The (Marxist) theoretical framing of class struggle between the middle class and the working class within this body of literature has become central to theoretical debates about the appropriation of space by the middle class and processes of displacement and stigmatization. In part, these understandings rest upon conceptualizations of the middle classes that position them in relation to labour relations, whether this is a middle class in the service of the elites and upper classes (being enticed by the local state or developers to be agents of neighbourhood improvement, for example) or an intermediary class position, with their actions and behaviours aimed at preserving their social position. Notably absent within these analyses is the possibility that the struggles over space relating to housing and residence that gentrification primarily describes, might allow for emergent class alliances and formations.

The focus on structural transformation central to the Marxist accounts of gentrification is a timely reminder of the lens onto such changes that the study of gentrification might offer. At a time when the economic performance of the world's mature economies is heavily reliant on housing, household debt through mortgages supporting increasing state indebtedness, a period Lapavitsas (2013) aptly describes in his eponymously named book *Profit Without Producing*, what then of class relations? How might this understanding of macroeconomic forces and increasing financialization shift our understandings of gentrification?

Contra the recent advocation in urban studies of planetary urbanism (Brenner and Schmid 2011; Wyly 2015), our approach to understanding social transformation takes context seriously (see also Lees 1994, 2003; Brown-Saracino 2009; Lees et al. 2016), a point reflected in our methodological preference for ethnographic research (Jackson 2015; Benson 2011; see also Lees 2003). This allows us to move beyond top-down models that we see as prevalent within these universalizing understandings of urban transformation to think on a range of different scales to consider what gentrification might look like, how it might be variously structured and framed, how it might in turn structure locales and class formations, in different locations. While earlier debates in this body of research can broadly be characterized as either promoting economic conditions or cultural practices as explanations for gentrification (see for example Smith 1979; Ley 1986) – although as Slater (2006) argues, both approaches were more nuanced than this binary opposition suggests – these work with *a priori* definition of who counts as working or middle class.

Slater's (2006) passionate treatise on the eviction of critical perspectives from gentrification research warned of the dangers in projecting a positive, almost celebratory image of gentrification that sees the influx of the 'creative class' as a marker of economic success, arguing for the urgent reintroduction of critical perspectives. We argue that such a critical perspective needs to be paired with a careful consideration of the complex practices and processes through which class formation and classificatory struggles operate within contemporary urban locations, and their implications for both people and place. Indeed, as Modan (2006) demonstrates in her ethnography of Mount Pleasant, a neighbourhood in Washington DC, how people talk about the places they live in and what it means to belong to these places, not only constructs the symbolic boundaries of inclusion and exclusion, but may have 'material implications for how those places develop and change' (p. 7). Simply put, such practices and processes are sites and moments in which power is exercised and realized, and deserve critical evaluation.

As we have outlined above, despite the proliferation of research on the classed process of gentrification there has been little consideration over what work the categories of class that are mobilized within it do. Therefore, there is a real need to reconsider class (as a concept) within gentrification research, to question what starting with understandings of class that are derived from occupational and income categories – reifying the power relations that stratified Western European industrial economies – and then simply applying them in analysis does to our understandings. We argue that such an approach runs the risk of shutting down understandings of gentrification that would see it instead as a process through which class and space are co-constituted. This is not to suggest that spatial struggles are the only place where class is made. Rather, just as earlier class and gentrification scholarship indicated how changing structures of labour reconfigured class positions, contemporary struggles over housing and urban space are one loci through which class relations, positions and identities may be constituted.

The perspective we advance here sees class as relational, situational and context dependent; urban transformation – a product and symptom of ongoing macroeconomic transformation – is both structuring of, and structured by, class relations. In this conceptualization, gentrification (naming one such urban transformation) becomes a site through which classificatory struggles are recast (I. Tyler 2015). Lees' (1994, 2003) longstanding assertion that gentrification research needs to take local context seriously further supports our call here for a revitalized understanding of class within gentrification research that takes seriously how class relations are articulated in and through localities (see Brown-Saracino 2009) and countries (Lees et al. 2016) and under what conditions.

With this in mind, we look at recent reconceptualizations of class. We explore what a spatial turn in this new landscape of class analysis might look like, a project that requires bringing the concepts of class and space that underpin gentrification research back into the light. As we argue, a reconsideration of these concepts offers a productive way of engaging with calls for more context-specific understandings of gentrification.

5.3   RETHINKING CLASS AND GENTRIFICATION

The last few years have seen renewed interest in social class within geography and sociology, and debates and disputes abound about how it should be conceived and theorized. Indeed, rising social and economic inequality makes class analysis more relevant than ever (Dorling 2014); inequality and struggle may have changed form, but they remain a significant and persistent presence (Atkinson 2015). Within this context, class as a concept names and reveals structural inequality (Savage 2015a; I. Tyler 2015). And yet there is a tendency within this work to resort to measurable categories proposed by stratification scholarship, which fix class position around income and occupation (Skeggs 2004, 2015; I. Tyler 2015).

The approaches to understanding class that we favour conceptualize class as a classificatory struggle framed around the pursuit of value. They are contextually agile and are therefore appropriate to the longstanding call for gentrification research to be more attentive to local particularities (Lees 1994). We consider this contribution to be twofold, focussing both on the fields of class analysis (which is based in Sociology and has tended to overlook space) and gentrification studies (which has been historically based in Geography and works with rigid models of class). Here we examine what the reframing of class analysis around classificatory struggles can contribute towards understandings of gentrification. Further, beyond gentrification studies, we think about what might be gained for studies of class by introducing spatiality into understandings of class exploitation and inequality.

5.3.1   Revisiting Class

We want to advocate for a dynamic approach to understanding class and how class is made, told and performed in and through struggles over power and authority. Class is relational, a project of classification and (de)valuation (Skeggs 2004; I. Tyler 2015); tied to material and economic relations, it is a site of exploitation. Class then defines a struggle for dominance in the field of power, the shoring up of positions through appropriation, demonstrating the exercise of symbolic violence that lies at its core (Skeggs 2004). As Imogen Tyler (2015) persuasively argues, this is an understanding underscored by a shift from reified 'class' identities and formations, towards a consideration over the ways in which class exploitation and relations are remade. Importantly, and building on the relational and intersectional approaches proposed by feminist class scholars (see for example Bradley 1995, 2014; Skeggs 1997, 2004; Crompton 2008), this approach sees class as inseparable from other social positions, such as gender and ethnicity.

At present within British class analysis, the works of Pierre Bourdieu occupy a particularly prominent position. Where earlier conceptualizations of class considered class relations as constructed through labour and property relations, speaking of post-war

France, Bourdieu (1984) identified 'culture' as an additional site through which these relations and class might be structured. Reflecting on the formation and reproduction of the petty bourgeoisie, he argued that culture and the judgements made on the grounds of taste that accompany these act as a site for status discrimination. This argument built on a wider conceptual framework that identified several forms of capital – social, cultural and symbolic – in addition to the economic (Bourdieu 1986). Imported to Britain in the late 1980s, this understanding of class formation was put to work initially to understand the fragmentation of the British middle classes at that time (see for example Savage et al. 1992; Savage and Butler 1995) – how varying levels of capitals, assets and resources combined to produce different formations within the middle classes. In the 2000s, Bourdieu's concepts became commonplace in the study of class in Britain (see for example Atkinson 2015, 2016).

Recently, the methodology that underscored Bourdieu's *Distinction* (1984), multiple correspondence analysis, has been revisited to plot British cultural tastes through large-scale surveys (see for example Bennett et al. 2008; Savage et al. 2015). These grandly claim to chart transformations in British class structure, and include the highly publicized Great British Class Survey (GBCS) (Savage et al. 2015; Savage 2015b). As scholars including Bradley (2014), Skeggs (2015), and I. Tyler (2015) assert, this recent use of Bourdieu describes class groupings in ways akin to what has otherwise been referred to as social stratification. As these feminist scholars argue, in further entrenching fixed ideas of class divisions the new models of class structure generated by this methodology fall short of critically reflecting on the ways in which class relations are transformed under contemporary political and economic conditions, instead reifying class identities. This timely reminder of the significance of macroeconomic contexts in the production of class relations is pause for thought about how we might reconceive of class and its relationship to wider structural transformation, but also, through focussing on processes, what a model of class that is mutable and adaptable to local particularities – rather than an ethnocentric imposition – might look like.

Bourdieu's ideas about different types of capital and his efforts to demonstrate that class extends beyond the socioeconomic and into the symbolic and cultural are useful additions to our understandings of class. However, as Skeggs (2004) argues, distinction – judgements over culture – is best understood as a practice of valuation where some people and some actions have value and others do not; they enable some people to claim legitimacy for their actions while for others legitimacy is denied. As Skeggs' (1997) ethnographic work with working-class women demonstrates, practices of valuation and their obverse feed into the formation of class and gender, divisions produced, naturalized and reaffirmed through the minutiae of everyday life. Being a subject of value does not only relate to classed forms of personhood but also ideas of respectability tied to nation, race and gender (Anderson 2015; Dhaliwal and Forkert 2015).

Skeggs' (1997, 2004) intervention renders visible the ways in which Bourdieu's (1986) model works to favour those able to convert capitals into status and social position. In other words, understandings of class framed in these terms privileges an understanding of value founded on exchange and accrual. As Skeggs (2004; see also Skeggs and Loveday 2012) argues, Bourdieu (1984) provides a compelling analysis of how the middle classes accrue forms of capital to become or maintain themselves as proper subjects. However, the taken-for-granted understanding of value as made through exchange negates other forms of value (e.g. use value) through which valuation could take place. As Skeggs' (2004) work demonstrates, aligning oneself with the subjects of value or else merely being defined by a lack of value is not inevitable. Privileging certain practices of valuation – which are, in and of themselves, emblematic of class divisions – to the exclusion of other processes, results in the foregone conclusion that some people are lacking in value. As Bradley (2014) argues, this is a significant methodological flaw, perpetuating the class divisions it sets out to challenge, a critique levelled at Bourdieu (1984) and the recent studies that have emulated his methodology to the ends of understanding class structure in contemporary Britain.

A further elaboration of this critique lies in Imogen Tyler's (2015) argument for a dynamic approach to understanding class, that allows for the possibility of recognizing new class relations emerging through contemporary struggles, and the new alliances that these conditions might instigate. In response to the Great British Class Survey and its efforts to propose new class formations attuned to contemporary social and economic contexts, she warns that we need to carefully (re)consider the social problem class describes and make certain that this lies at the core of our conceptual and empirical projects. Class as the production of inequality through social relationships is therefore mutable not fixed; this revised understanding of class challenges both conceptualizations that might present it as a form of identity politics – class(ed) identities as intransigent – or as in some way measurable, as stratification scholars might have it.

The theoretical framings provided by Skeggs (2004, 2015) and Tyler (2015), although inspired by ongoing conversations about class and how it operates in Great Britain, offer a series of considerations that are transferable to other contexts. They recognize that class formation and relations are dynamic, responsive to context and circumstances; they present these as produced through systems of value that privilege the lives, practices and actions of some over and above those of others. Importantly, class struggle emerges as a process through which inequality is produced and perpetuated. Such a conceptualization bolsters contemporary analyses of the injustices of contemporary urban renewal and gentrification, but might also allow for exploration of the ways in which these are not passively accepted but resisted by residents, as Lees (2014) has so powerfully described in her work with residents of London's Aylesbury Estate. Further, they do not assume a context or the transferability of classed identities that abstract them from sites of production, recognizing instead that these are relationally produced. Taken together, these theories constitute a radical shift in how we conceptualize class, calling for new methodological and conceptual considerations. Here we take these considerations forward, to argue for the value of these perspectives in thinking through diverse moments and spaces of gentrification in ways that recognize the particularity of these contexts and how class relations and exploitation play out within these.

5.3.2   Class – Space – Class

Our starting point in shifting focus towards the consideration of how class and space interplay lies in thinking again about the problem that gentrification seeks to describe. Our assertion here is simple: gentrification names a struggle over space, through which practices of valuation and ownership are writ large. We return here to our opening comments on ethnocentrism and the need for a conceptualization of class that allows for the possibility that class is not only wrought in and through employment relations. Indeed, to understand planetary gentrification (Lees et al. 2016) a conceptualization of class that can account for the ways that power relations and classificatory struggles play out through housing and land economies is urgently required.

We argue that gentrification is one site through which it might be possible to consider the spatial dimensions of classificatory struggles and practices of valuation that have, until now, been somewhat overlooked in these re-visionings of class. Against this background, we pose the following questions: (1) How do classificatory struggles manifest in and through place? (2) How do these struggles make class relations and place? (3) In what ways is class (with race and gender) lived, mobilized and conceptualized in these struggles over space? These questions lie at the core of our argument that these re-visionings of class offer important insights valuable in making sense of contemporary gentrification processes. Just as I. Tyler (2015) calls for a shift in understandings of class to privilege the dynamic ways in which class relations and social inequality are produced through classificatory struggles, there is a need to think about how place is conceived within our understandings of gentrification.

As we have argued elsewhere, place is not a blank canvas within which these processes unfold; it is remade through processes of gentrification and everyday practice (Benson and Jackson 2013). In short, place is dynamic, and as well as being a site of existing class relations, it is also a site that structures class relations and is reshaped through them. This framing approaches gentrification as a project of (re)valuing locations, in terms of both economic capital and the attribution of moral and symbolic significance to places. These processes of reclassification also rely on social and spatial boundary-making, other people and other places excluded or expelled from the image of the place that is being pursued by those who are seeking to transform it (Watt 2009; Holgersson 2014; Jackson and Benson 2015), place remade in their image in ways that are fundamentally classed and racialized (see for example K. Tyler 2003, 2012; Modan 2006; Benson and Jackson 2013). These, then, are also processes of class formation, in which space plays a *dynamic* role (de Certeau 1984; Lefebvre 1991; Massey 1994).

This active remaking of place simultaneously involves the devaluation of some people and locales, alongside revaluation, processes in which the middle classes may act as agents, but which might also be brought on by the state. This is particularly evident in Paton's (2014; see also Paton, McCall and Mooney, 2016) work on Glasgow, discussed in greater detail below, which demonstrates how state-led gentrification in that context is as much a project of restructuring citizens as it was about restructuring place: 'Devaluation of people and places not only contributes to the creation of a viable rent gap it also legitimises the use of gentrification as regeneration as being redemptive for these people and places' (Paton 2014: 187).

Focussing on the experiences and perspectives of prior residents, either those displaced by these processes or hanging on, managing to stay put, animates and complicates the (often binary) discussion of gentrification. Indeed we see this in Lees' (2014) close examination of New Labour's urban regeneration of London's Aylesbury Estate, where she documents the genealogy of urban injustice, the discursive construction of the 'sink estate', the practices that exclude residents from the regeneration, exposing 'a variety of unjust practices that have been, and are being, enacted on the Aylesbury Estate', while also looking 'at what the residents think about the whole process . . . and how they have resisted, and are resisting, dominant interests and practices' (p. 922). By documenting working-class experiences of and perspectives on gentrification, Paton (2014) finds ambivalence among her working-class interviewees towards this process. Glucksberg (2014) also registers this more unequivocal response from her interlocutors in south London, who had seen their council estate demolished, vividly encapsulated in the phrase 'we were regenerated out' (p. 97). These examples identify the coupling of the devaluation of place and devaluation of people as central to the logic of regeneration/gentrification (see Lees 2014). And yet, the differences in these analyses also connect to the specificities of the locales under examination – in Glucksberg's London case, displacement was more immediate and brutal, whereas in Paton's Glasgow case it was a slower burning process. This highlights how the local context of programmes of redevelopment and situational dynamics of classificatory struggles are significant in making sense of the production of inequalities (I. Tyler 2015); it is precisely in unpicking these differences that we can learn how regeneration both seeks to restructure classed environments and how this is lived, incorporated and resisted on the ground. As *Staying Put: An Anti-Gentrification Handbook for Council Estates in London* (Just Space, Lees, LTF and SNAG 2014) shows, there is a significant appetite for resistance to such urban processes and the economic and political structures that promote them.

Understood as a classificatory struggle along the lines that I. Tyler (2015) advocates, and her provocation to move beyond fixed and essentialist class identities, gentrification has the potential to remake both class and space. It renders gentrification a process in which class relations and place are best understood as mutually constitutive and a site *par excellence* to see this in action. It might produce unlikely alliances, and complex encounters with sites that bring together residents from different social backgrounds in shared struggles, as Brown-Saracino (2009) identifies in her ethnographic accounts of preservation practices in three neighbourhoods in the United States. This complicates understandings of gentrification, highlighting the value of understanding the nuances of how gentrification as a struggle over space – a process not only structured by, but also structuring of, class relations and inequalities – unfolds in different locations. In many ways, this is precisely the antidote to the well-rehearsed and popularized accounts of gentrification that either pit middle-class incomers against the original working-class residents or policy solutions that propose the introduction of middle-class residents as a panacea for structural problems such as under-investment and poverty (see Bridge, Butler and Lees 2011). Such analyses and accounts rest exactly on the reification of classed identities that I. Tyler (2015) warns against, leaving the wider structural forces that produce inequality unremarked on.

While we have focussed elsewhere on the way in which place-making interplays with classed identities, arguing that constituent identities are (continually) moulded through the creation and mundane maintenance of places (Benson and Jackson 2013), here we want to take an additional step in arguing that these practices of place-making are sites for the production of classed relations and classificatory struggles. This might seem a reiteration of longstanding arguments that present gentrification as a site of class struggle, but our innovation here is to think outside of a priori categorizations of class and to think instead about the ways in which particular processes and sites of gentrification play a role in the constitution of class relations; to see gentrification as struggles over value, power and authority; and to identify these as possible sites where new coalitions and allegiances emerge. We argue that this is an approach that is much more attentive to the nuances of contemporary classificatory struggles brought about by processes of social and economic transformation.

5.4 ETHNOGRAPHIC APPROACHES TO CLASS, SPACE, AND GENTRIFICATION

Making this shift in the conceptual framing of class and gentrification requires a similar reconsideration of methodology. It is perhaps unsurprising that the studies that we find the most useful in analysing the complexities of class formation and the development of inequalities through processes of gentrification are often ethnographic or highly inductive qualitative research that seeks to understand the lives and experiences of people living in particular locations. Lees (2003) argues for the usefulness of ethnography in investigating 'the ongoing social practices through which space is continually shaped and inhabited' (p. 111). Here we are extending this to argue that an ethnographic approach can produce a dynamic understanding of the production of class relations. Such methodological reflections further influence our discussion in the remainder of this chapter and the choices of two studies that we discuss in detail. These two examples illustrate the complex interplay of class and space and the transformation of these at their intersections, through gentrification.

5.4.1 Case Study One: 'Maybe the penthouse though!'

'Gentrification: A Working-Class Perspective' Kirsteen Paton (2014)

Given the argument advanced above, it may seem jarring that our first example has a title that promises 'a working-class perspective' but this title is a little misleading. From the outset Paton (2014) critiques not only the absence of working-class voices in studies of gentrification but also the denial of the complexity that is granted to the middle classes in gentrification studies (who are variously cast as 'the flâneur, the gentrifier, the cosmopolitan' (p. 1)). In her study, grounded in Partick, Glasgow – a predominantly working-class neighbourhood on Clydeside that borders the more affluent West End – Paton argues that gentrification is not only about the class restructuring of space but also about the attempted gentrification of working-class subjects.

The context of Glasgow is important here. In the wake of the decline of the shipbuilding industry, place-marketing campaigns since the 1980s have tried to shift the city's association with poverty and deindustrialization (including campaigns with the slogans 'Glasgow's Miles Better' (1984), 'Glasgow's alive' (1997) and more recently, 'People make Glasgow' (2014)). Such campaigns have been quite successful in attracting outside investment; however, as Paton argues, those who were not in-line with this 'Miles Better' city were those who 'have suffered most from the effects of restructuring [who] are deemed a problem and a deterrent to investment and who are subsequently targeted by neoliberal policy' (p. 60). This stigmatization, in tandem with the reification of the middle classes, impacted on housing policies which combined 'trickle-down economics with the promotion of self-help, bolstered by the manufacturing of aspiration via promoting home ownership' (p. 61). Paton's book is a chronicle of gentrification as a process that seeks to co-opt working-class residents into participating in, and buying into, gentrification as a hegemonic project through the 'manufacturing of aspiration' (p. 126).

The first ethnographic encounter in the book perfectly conjures the ambivalent working-class positions that arise from this. Paton meets Sylvie, at Sylvie's behest, not in a traditional Partick establishment but in one of the new bars. Talking over wine in the sunshine, Sylvie expresses mixed feelings over the new housing development but when the author mentions that she has been inside the development, Sylvie wants all the details. When the conversation turns to rent, Sylvie starts to work out what would be possible for her – she'd like to live there, 'Not all the way up, maybe halfway, with a wee balcony. Maybe the penthouse though!' Paton comments:

> her aspiration is as lofty as the high-rise itself, yet is slightly tentative, grading herself as being worthy of a place only halfway up. The key point is that she refuses to be excluded from the gentrification process taking place despite her lack of means, and that the proliferation of this type of development is the very housing trend that sees curtailed growth in social housing (2014: 4).

Sylvie cautiously includes herself into this gentrified future, which as Paton argues offers both (limited) new rewards and new injuries (2014: 125). As well as this soft cultivation of aspiration, Paton also explores how working-class people are formally invited to participate in the process – through, for example, consultation exercises – but then if they are seen to be making the wrong choices this is used to further malign them. Paton uses the example of the redevelopment of Mansfield Park, where the working-class residents' lack of interest in the park's redevelopment (that was to include a bandstand, an eco-play area and a 'meditation labyrinth') is met with frustration by the director of the local housing association:

> It's almost an aspirational thing [. . .] I was staggered by the comments I read from these people. What reasons are people in this [neighbourhood] not aspiring to something dynamic and vibrant and wonderful here and they have the opportunity to do so?

Helen goes on to suggest this lack of interest in participation is to do with a lack of self-worth, thus the process reinforces the idea of a working class that need to be fixed. However, this is not the only working-class experience of gentrification: Paton also describes how some working-class people find opportunities within these processes of change, for example Loretta who had become a developer and landlady, or Brian who had bought property in Partick in the 1970s and was encouraging his children to do the same (2014: 152). Paton argues gentrification is not a zero-sum game for working-class people but that their participation in it and the terms of engagement are unequal.

The project of gentrification in this case is one of intervening in the making of working-class subjects though the promotion of aspiration and commercial participation. But the results of this process are not those that are envisioned by the policy makers. In this case, a top-down project was not merely rolled out over the heads of a population but required their participation through aspiration and consumption. Rather, working-class people negotiate, resist and participate in gentrification in complex ways (cr. Modan 2006). Paton also finds little evidence of the middle classes mixing in and providing a social fix in the new residential developments, rather they see Partick as a step on the property ladder and are, in the main, perceived by their working-class neighbours as disinterested and aloof.

The impact of gentrification in this context is to reinforce the stigmatization of those who do not or cannot participate, while drawing in more to participate through home ownership or consumption that they cannot always afford. This, Paton argues, is the paradox of gentrification: 'gentrification simultaneously excludes and includes working class residents . . . [S]tate-led gentrification invites people to participate but this involves private consumption and it does not provide the means to achieve this' (2014: 155). Despite the different positions occupied by Paton's working-class participants in relation to gentrification, the overwhelming sense is one of gentrification as, if not 'cruel optimism' (Berlant 2011), then certainly cruel aspiration which plays a role in the restructuring of class identities: Paton argues, 'These restructured identities were classed, but not in the traditional sense. Instead they displayed neoliberal characteristics through narratives of choice' (2014: 185).

This study contributes to our argument in three broad ways: (1) It highlights how state-led projects of gentrification can be implemented to not only reshape place but also groups of people, their values, behaviour and aspirations; (2) it highlights that these projects are not merely rolled out onto people but are incorporated, resisted and lived with in a variety of ways; and (3) it complicates the stark opposition of incoming middle class and pre-existing working class in terms of their perspectives on gentrification. While working-class and middle-class groups make distinctions between each other and between others who occupy these broad categories, for Paton, the greatest differences between the middle classes and the working classes were their material positions and degree of choice about where they lived, rather than different cultural aspirations for the area.

5.4.2 Case Study Two: Housing in the Production of Class Differentiation

'In Search of Paradise: Middle-class Living in a Chinese Metropolis' Li Zhang (2010)
This second example provides further support for our argument for the need to reconsider the understandings of class and place that underpin gentrification research, particularly as this is extended to understanding urban processes ongoing around the world. The social and economic transformation of post-socialist China that Zhang (2010) describes renders highly visible the spatialization of class, the production of class relations and classificatory struggles. Throughout her discussion she presents class-making as a process of happening (ibid: 7), socially and economically produced through human relationships. Her ethnography astutely identifies the ways in which the privatization of homeownership in China goes together with the formation of a new, urban middle class; it reconfigures urban landscapes and brings into being middle-class lifestyles and subjectivities in ways that disturb understandings of the relationship between spatial configurations and class dynamics.

Zhang's (2010) focus is on Kunming, a regional city in southwest China, the capital of Yunnan Province. She describes the underdevelopment of the city under socialism, the shifts to the local economy brought in post-Mao, and the roles of tobacco and copper-mining industries within this; and, more recently, the expansion of tourism, trade and the service sector in the recent growth of the region's economy. Today, Kunming is a booming provincial economy, the site of considerable social and spatial polarization. The wider context of postsocialist transformation in China – which Zhang (2010) describes as a hybrid of socialist authoritarian rule and new neoliberal governing practices – and its local articulation in Kunming raise important questions about the relationship between class and space. As Zhang argues, 'I maintain that the politics of class, through the lens of homeownership and spatial reordering, lies at the heart of postsocialist transformations because it brings many critical cultural, political, and social issues together . . . postsocialist changes are not simply about the privatization of the economy or market liberalization but also about the making of new kinds of persons and class subjects' (Zhang ibid: 13; cr. Lees, Shin and López-Morales 2016).

Housing is a pivotal feature of this equation that presents the shift from socialism to postsocialism as a moment of class-making. The movement from publicly assigned and supplied housing under socialism to the privatization and commodification of housing made possible by the conditions of postsocialism, introduces spatial differentiation; importantly, this is housing development led by the state, and through which a (new) middle class is produced. Through the state-supported production of private housing, a new, more lifestyle-oriented class formation emerges; a significant factor in the formation of what Zhang (ibid) identifies as a 'new middle propertied strata' (*xinzhongchan jiecing*) of Kunming. Such a presentation of class-making through the terms of *jiecing* – a way of distinguishing on the grounds of socioeconomic difference – deliberately intends to dissociate contemporary change from the politically charged and violent moments of class struggle under socialism.

As Zhang (ibid) presents it, the changes to housing bring into being the prospects for class formation in postsocialist China. The private development of housing takes the form of the construction of residential communities, including gated complexes, rather than the construction of individual homes here and there. This spatial concentration of homes is significant to the development of the kinds of cultural differentiation and lifestyle practices that are associated with class formation. In the Chinese case, emergent class formation is further shaped through the work property developers and other intermediaries do; simply put, there is no *pro forma* for what it might mean to be middle class, what middle-class living might look like under conditions of postsocialism. Housing differentiation is the locus for the constitution of class difference and relations. This is a simultaneous process of making the new middle propertied *jiecing* and the cultural milieu of this class formation. As Zhang (2010) emphasizes, '[T]his is a process involving not only the political economy of housing and community production but also the cultivation of new lifestyles, mentalities, dispositions and aspirations among those who come to inhabit these places' (2010: 14). Property developers and intermediaries might then be understood to have *tabula rasa*, telling people what they want from their (private) homes, selling lifestyles and framing what different properties and residential environments mean and symbolize, producing and emplacing a new *jiecing* in the process.

So, where then and how do classificatory struggles manifest in and through place? These housing developments and their consumption first make visible the differences within the society. Indeed, consumption becomes a particularly acute marker of social stratification in the context of postsocialist China, marked precisely against the secrecy surrounding income and economic wealth. Further, set within a wider context in which state and public assets are dispossessed, the property developments that bring into being the new *jiecing* are intimately intertwined with the displacement, devaluation and relocation of other populations. Class-making therefore also entails the development of new class relations; labour activism, protests and legal action against real estate developers are some of the ways in which classificatory struggles emerge through this process and in these projects. Class relations also play out in the employment of migrant workers – in this case those from rural areas moving to the cities – to provide services in the employment of the new middle-class residents of these housing developments.

The ethnographic focus of Zhang's (2010) work makes clear the value of moving beyond top-down models for understanding gentrification, identifying the intricate ways in which class and space co-constitute. What Zhang (2010) describes in detail is precisely the interplay of property development, class-making and place-making. The context of postsocialist China and the emergence of distinct social classes within these urban settings provides an opportunity to make visible the way in which class and class relations are made in and through space. Further, it brings to bear a sense of how context – political, historical, local – matters to our understandings. Rather than an established and essentialized middle-class population moving in and displacing the working classes, the wider structural transformations within China and specifically in Kunming illustrate the dynamics of class formation and the development of new class relations in place.

5.5   CONCLUSION

In this chapter, we have proposed revisiting the understandings of class that underpin studies of gentrification with a view to making the latter a more malleable and adaptable concept. We have argued that the critical perspective on gentrification advocated by Slater, Curran and Lees (2004; see also Slater 2006), requires an attendant consideration of a critical perspective on class. This is a perspective that takes seriously the sites and moments at which class – as the struggle over value and worth – is produced, and the contextual and situational constitution of class formation.

Our tools of investigation and analysis need to be sharpened to shift the conversation from the blunt and binary lens within which gentrification research seems to become repeatedly entrenched – the structural and economic determinism of Marxist approaches versus the cultural lens oriented towards human agency; the gentrifier versus the non-gentrifier; the new middle class versus the working class. These binaries serve little more than to reify identities and stagnate debate, while gentrification – as the two cases we have discussed in this chapter identify – continues as a classed and classifying process full of contradiction and ambiguity.

However, we might also want to turn the lens back on to the concept of gentrification and ask how well-equipped a concept developed to describe the middle-class displacement of working-class populations in 1960s London is to describe processes of urban transformation ongoing in places such as China, which do not have the same frames of reference for understanding class. And yet, in reframing the discussion around an understanding of class that takes this as a struggle over value (Skeggs 2004, 2015; I. Tyler 2015), the making of the Chinese middle class through the development of exclusive housing complexes and the demands for a service class that this brings, that Zhang (2010) describes, may be brought into conversation with Paton's (2014) account of how working-class people in Glasgow navigate processes of urban transformation through which they and the place they live are repeatedly devalued.

Finally, these studies (Zhang 2010; Paton 2014) and others (see for example Modan

2006; Brown-Saracino 2009) are timely reminders of the methodological intervention required to test the limits of this reconceptualization of the relationship between class and gentrification. Such close-up analyses – qualitative and ethnographic – are to be celebrated for taking seriously wider structural transformation and economic forces and their local effects. These works – notably authored by female/feminist scholars – have a keen eye to wider structural transformation and economic forces, alongside contextual and situational specificity. The critical study of gentrification requires keeping a close eye on how people and places become devalued and marked out for intervention; how these processes are negotiated, participated in or resisted; and how such struggles can be genera-tive of (changing or coalescing) classed positions. Indeed, it is within such ethnographic and in-depth qualitative empirical research that we can uncover the critical perspective (on class) that Slater (2006; see also Slater, Curran and Lees 2004) laments as being absent from gentrification research.

We have argued that to understand planetary gentrification there is a need not only to critically evaluate the conditions through which knowledge of the urban has developed, but also to apply the same logic to the understandings of class that we mobilize within these. Drawing our inspiration from contemporary feminist scholars of class who have put forward a dynamic approach to understanding class as producing inequality and injustice through the struggle over value (Skeggs 2004, 2015; I. Tyler 2015), we have worked through how this reconceptualization of class might reanimate scholarly engage-ments with gentrification and urban redevelopment theoretically, conceptually and methodologically.

REFERENCES

Abercrombie, N. and Urry, J. (1983) *Capital, Labour and the Middle Classes,* London: George Allen and Unwin.
Anderson, B. (2013) *Us and Them?: The Dangerous Politics of Immigration Control,* Oxford: Oxford University Press.
Atkinson, W. (2015) *Class*, Cambridge: Polity Press.
Atkinson, W. (2016) *Beyond Bourdieu*, Cambridge: Polity Press.
Bacqué, M-H., Bridge, G., Butler, T., Benson, M., Charmes, E., Fijalkow, Y., Jackson, E., Launay, L. and Vermeesch, S. (2015) *The Middle Classes and the City: A Study of Paris and London,* London: Palgrave Macmillan.
Bennett, T., Savage, M., Silva, E., Warde, A., Gayo-Cal, M. and Wright, D. (2009) *Class, Culture, Distinction*, London: Routledge.
Benson, M. (2011) *The British in Rural France: Lifestyle Migration and the Ongoing Quest for a Better Way of Life*, Manchester: Manchester University Press.
Benson, M. (2013) 'Trajectories of middle-class belonging: the dynamics of place attachment and classed identities', *Urban Studies*, 51(14), 3097–3112.
Benson, M. and Jackson, E. (2013) 'Place-making and place maintenance: performativity, place and belonging among the middle classes', *Sociology*, 47(4), 793–809.
Berlant, L. (2011) *Cruel Optimism*, Durham: Duke University Press.
Bourdieu, P. (1984) *Distinction: A Social Critique of the Judgement of Taste*, Cambridge: Polity Press.
Bourdieu, P. (1986) 'The forms of capital', in Richardson, J. (ed), *Handbook of Theory and Research for the Sociology of Education*, New York: Greenwood, pp. 241–258.
Bradley, H. (1995) *Fractured Identities: Changing Patterns of Inequality*, Cambridge: Polity Press.
Bradley, H. (2014) 'Class descriptors or class relations? Thoughts towards a critique of Savage et al', *Sociology*, 48(3), 429–436.
Brenner, N. and Schmid, C. (2012) 'Planetary urbanization', in Gandy, M. (ed), *Urban Constellations*, Berlin: Jovis, pp. 10–13.
Bridge, G., Butler, T. and Lees, L. (2011) *Mixed Communities: Gentrification by Stealth*, Bristol: Policy Press.

Brown-Saracino, J. (2009) *A Neighborhood that Never Changes: Gentrification, Social Preservation, and the Search for Authenticity*, Chicago: University of Chicago Press.

Butler, T. and Robson, G. (2003) *London Calling: The Middle Classes and the Remaking of Inner London*, Oxford: Berg.

de Certeau, M. (1984) *The Practice of Everyday Life*, Berkeley: University of California Press.

Crompton, R. (2008) *Class and Stratification*, Cambridge: Polity Press.

Dhaliwal, S and Forkert, K. (2016) 'Deserving and undeserving migrants', *Soundings: A Journal of Politics and Culture*, 61, 49–61.

Dorling, D. (2014) *Inequality and the 1%*, London: Verso Books.

Glass, R. (1964) *London: Aspects of Change*, London: MacGibbon & Kee.

Glucksberg, L. (2014) 'We was regenerated out: regeneration, recycling and devaluing communities', *Valuation Studies*, 2(2), 97–118.

Goldthorpe, J., Lockwood, D., Bechhofer, F. and Platt, J. (1969) *The Affluent Worker in the Class Structure*, Cambridge, Cambridge University Press.

Hackworth, J. (2002) 'Postrecession gentrification in New York City', *Urban Affairs Review*, 37(6), 815–843.

Holgersson, H. (2014) 'Post-political narratives and emotions: dealing with discursive displacement in everyday life', in Jackson, E. and Jones, H. (eds), *Emotion and Location: Stories of Cosmopolitan Belonging*, London, New York: Earthscan Routledge.

Jackson, E. (2015) *Young Homeless People and Urban Space: Fixed in Mobility*, London: Routledge.

Jackson, E. and Benson, M. (2014) 'Neither deepest, darkest Peckham nor run-of-the-mill East Dulwich: the middle classes and their others in an inner-London neighbourhood', *International Journal of Urban and Regional Research*, 38(4), 1195–1210.

Jager, M. (1986) 'Class definition and the aesthetics of gentrification: Victoriana in Melbourne', in Smith, N. and Williams, P. (eds), *Gentrification of the City*, London: Unwin Hyman.

Just Space, Lees, L., LTF and SNAG (2014) *Staying Put: An Anti-Gentrification Handbook for Council Estates in London*.

Lapavitsas, C. (2013) *Profiting Without Producing: How Finance Exploits Us All*, London: Verso.

Lees, L. (1994) 'Gentrification in London and New York: an Atlantic gap?', *Housing Studies*, 9(2), 199–217.

Lees, L. (2003) 'Urban geography: new urban geography and the ethnographic void', *Progress in Human Geography*, 27(1), 107–113.

Lees, L. (2014) 'The urban injustices of new Labour's "New Urban Renewal": the case of the Aylesbury Estate in London', *Antipode*, 46(4), 921–947.

Lees, L., Bang Shin, H. and López Morales, E. (2016) *Planetary Gentrification*, Cambridge: Polity Press.

Lefebvre, H. (1991) *The Production of Space*, Oxford: Blackwell.

Ley, D. (1996) *The New Middle Class and the Remaking of the Central City*, Oxford: Oxford University Press.

Massey, D. (1994) *Space, Place and Gender*, Oxford: John Wiley & Sons.

Méndez, M. (2008) 'Middle class identities in a neoliberal age: Tensions between contested authenticities', *The Sociological Review*, 56(2), 220–237.

Modan, G. (2006) *Turf Wars: Discourse, Diversity, and the Politics of Place*, Oxford: Wiley-Blackwell.

Pahl, R. (1965) *Urbs in Rure: The Metropolitan Fringe in Hertfordshire*, London: Weidenfeld & Nicholson.

Paton, K. (2014) *Gentrification: A Working-Class Perspective*, Farnham: Ashgate.

Paton, K., McCall, K. and Mooney, G. (2016) 'Place revisited: class, stigma and urban restructuring in the case of Glasgow's Commonwealth Games', *The Sociological Review*.

Phillips, M. (1998a) 'Investigations of the British rural middle classes part 1: from legislation to interpretation', *Journal of Rural Studies*, 14(4), 411–425.

Phillips, M. (1998b) 'Investigations of the British rural middle classes part 2: fragmentation, identity, morality and contestation', *Journal of Rural Studies*, 14(4), 427–443.

Phillips, M. (2004) 'Other geographies of gentrification', *Progress in Human Geography*, 28(1), 5–30.

Sassen, S. (1991) *The Global City: New York, London, Tokyo*, Princeton: Princeton University Press.

Savage, M. (2015a) 'Introduction to elites: From the "problematic of the proletariat" to a class analysis of "wealth elites"', *The Sociological Review*, 63(2), 223–239.

Savage, M. (2015b) *Social Class in the 21st Century*, London: Penguin.

Savage, M. and Butler, T. (1995) 'Assets and the middle classes in contemporary Britain', in Savage, M. and Butler, T. (eds), *Social Change and the Middle Classes*, London: Routledge, pp. 345–358.

Savage, M., Bagnall, G. and Longhurst, B. (2005) *Globalization and Belonging*, London: SAGE.

Savage, M., Barlow, J. and Dickens, P. (1992) *Property, Bureaucracy and Culture: Middle Class Formation in Contemporary Britain*, London: Routledge.

Savage, M., Devine, F., Cunningham, N., Friedman, S., Laurison, D., Miles, A., Snee, H. and Taylor, M. (2015) 'On social class, anno 2014', *Sociology*, 49(6), 1011–1030.

Skeggs, B. (1997) *Formations of Class and Gender*, London: SAGE.

Skeggs, B. (2004) *Class, Self, Culture*, London: Routledge.

Skeggs, B. (2015) 'Introduction: Stratification or exploitation, domination, dispossession and devaluation?', *The Sociological Review*, 63(2), 205–222.

Skeggs, B. and Loveday, V. (2012) 'Struggles for value: value practices, injustice, judgment, affect and the idea of class', *The British Journal of Sociology*, 63(3), 472–490.

Slater, T. (2006) 'The eviction of critical perspectives from gentrification research', *International Journal of Urban and Regional Research*, 30(4), 737–757.

Slater, T., Curran, W. and Lees, L. (2004) 'Gentrification research: new directions and critical scholarship', *Environment and Planning A*, 36(7), 1141–1150.

Smith, N. (1996) *The New Urban Frontier: Gentrification and the Revanchist City*, London: Routledge.

Tyler, I. (2015) 'Classificatory struggles: class, culture and inequality in neoliberal times', *The Sociological Review*, 63(2), 493–511.

Tyler, K. (2003) 'The racialised and classed constitution of English village life', *Ethnos*, 68(3), 391–412.

Tyler, K. (2012) *Whiteness, Class and the Legacies of Empire: On Home Ground*, Basingstoke: Palgrave Macmillan.

Watt, P. (2009) 'Living in an oasis: Middle-class disaffiliation and selective belonging in an English suburb', *Environment and Planning A*, 41(12), 2874–2886.

Wyly, E. (2015) 'Gentrification on the planetary urban frontier: the evolution of Turner's noösphere', *Urban Studies*, 52(14), 2515–2550.

Zhang, L. (2010) *In Search of Paradise: Middle-class Living in a Chinese Metropolis*, Ithaca: Cornell University Press.

6. Gentrification and landscape change
Martin Phillips

6.1 INTRODUCTION

Landscape change has been a central, if rather neglected, aspect of gentrification. Davidson and Lees (2005, p.1170), for example, identify it as a defining feature of 'contemporary gentrification', along with 'the reinvestment of capital, . . . social upgrading of locale by incoming high-income groups; . . . and . . . direct or indirect displacement of low-income groups'. They develop this argument in the context of a study of large-scale, new-build developments along the Thames in London, interpreting these landscape changes through the concept of 'third wave or post-recession gentrification', which often involves state- and developer-led new-build gentrification of extensive areas. They draw on the work of Smith (2002b, p.433) who argued that in its third-wave, gentrification 'evolved into a vehicle for transforming whole areas into new landscape complexes', involving not only transformations in housing but also integration with developments in recreation, consumption and production. Gentrification, he argued, had changed in scale and form, such that 'the narrow residential rehabilitation projects that were so paradigmatic of the process in the 1960s and 1970s now seem quaint' (ibid., p.426), in comparison with many new-build developments.

Such arguments about the increasing scale and scope of new-build gentrification developments have been reinforced through a series of subsequent studies, including work on urban expansion and renewal, re-urbanization, post-suburbanization, social mixing, state-led gentrification and environmental gentrification. This work has repeatedly emphasized features such as capital investment, social recomposition and displacement, but landscape change also figures prominently in some accounts. He (2010), for example, documents how two state-led, new-build gentrification projects in Shanghai, China, effected a 'class remaking of the urban landscapes', whilst Shin (2015), Shin and Kim (2015), Hudalah (2015) and Ye (2015) highlight how gentrification, and an associated 'erasure and rebuilding' (ibid., p.495) of landscapes has occurred across areas of urban expansion into rural areas, as well as through the renewal or redevelopment of devalorized inner city spaces.

Whilst these studies all focused on Asian countries, the gentrification of spaces beyond the inner city has also been the focus of research in Europe and North America. Studies drawing on, and in some cases critiquing, notions of re-urbanization and post-suburbanization (e.g. Butler 2007; Charmes and Keil 2015; Davidson and Lees 2005; Rankin and Mclean 2014), have highlighted how suburban spaces in these areas have becomes sites of gentrification and experienced social and landscape transformations that challenge many long-established understandings of suburban space, such as it being a place of low density housing and high levels of physical, social and cultural homogeneity. These sites have hence often figured strongly in discussions of environmental/green/ecological gentrification, which have variously stressed how new-build gentrification can transform degraded landscapes, how environmental improvements can trigger gentrification, and how polluted landscapes can block gentrification (e.g. Checker 2011; Curran and Hamilton 2012; Dooling 2008; Hamilton and Curran 2013; Pearsall 2010).

A similar constellation of paradoxical arguments can be found in relation to discussions of social-mixing, which have included observations that gentrification is being 'incorporated into public policy . . . in the hopes of restructuring urban landscapes' (Wyly and Hammel 2005, p. 38), so that there would be more social mixing and integration, that gentrification is acting to produce 'an urban landscape increasingly segregated by class and race', and that the presence of 'certain groupings of populations and land uses' in an area can deter processes of gentrification (Ley and Dobson 2008, p. 2493).

Whilst such discussions of gentrification make frequent reference to the term 'landscape', it should be noted that none of the ones cited above actually include any substantive discussion of what the term landscape might mean, or even how it is being interpreted within a specific study. This is despite the term landscape being a long-standing subject of debate within human geography and many associated disciplines (e.g. see Sauer 1925; Winchester et al. 2013; Wylie 2007). A key aim of this chapter is to explicate some of the ways that gentrification researchers have employed conceptions of landscape, and point to some hitherto, as yet, rather underdeveloped strategies. The chapter will also explore how different conceptions of landscape connect to studies of gentrification other than those commensurable with notions of third-wave, large-scale, new-build gentrification as outlined above. Davidson and Lees (2005, p. 1165), for example, argue that the notion of landscape was 'evident in British sociologist Glass's (1964, p. xviii) coinage of the term "gentrification" and it has long offered some form of unity in the field'. Glass (1964, p. xiii), for instance, emphasized how the 'townscape' or visible 'face of the city' of London in the early 1960s was a juxtaposition of new and old, an account that subsequently has been viewed as indicative of the onset of an initial phase of 'sporadic gentrification' whereby gentrification was occurring in localized patches through the mediated agency of property owners (see Hackworth and Smith 2001; Smith 2002b). A mix of old and new can also be identified in much later instances of gentrification, with gentrification in the 1980s being viewed as a key dynamic in the formation of postmodern urban landscapes (see Ley 1987; Mills 1988). This chapter will explore how landscapes may have been transformed through various forms of gentrification and also seeks to deepen engagements with discussions around different conceptions of landscape. Specifically, the chapter will illustrate how gentrification studies can be viewed as enacting at least four distinct ways of conceptualizing landscapes.

6.2   GENTRIFICATION AND MATERIAL LANDSCAPES

The term 'landscape' has often been employed as a descriptor of, as Wylie (2007, p. 12) terms it, a 'world of physical features "out there" and that can be empirically accessed and described', often in visual registers as indicated by Duncan and Duncan's (2004, p. 37) description of landscapes as 'the visible surface of places', a phrase that has clear echoes of Glass's description of the landscape of London. More broadly, it is possible to identify four applications of such a concept of landscape within gentrification studies. The first is where the term landscape is used to describe a physical world on which gentrification comes to operate. Freeman (2006, p. 93), for example, describes the landscape of Harlem and Clinton Hill, in New York, as 'dotted with abandoned buildings', suggesting that this was the 'context' in which gentrification came to operate in these areas, although also noting that this context was not shared by all areas experiencing gentrification and highlighting how the landscapes of these two neighbourhoods had themselves been transformed prior to gentrification. He argues, for instance, that the landscape of Harlem in late 19th/early 20th centuries had been 'some of the most picturesque in Manhattan' (ibid., p. 49). In such cases, the term landscape is viewed largely as a passive entity: it refers effectively to the space or ground upon which gentrification operates.

This landscape perspective is often conjoined with use of the term landscape to describe a physical/material world that has been, at least in part, produced through the practices and processes of gentrification. Freeman (2006, p. 28), for example, argues that with gentrification, 'the vacant building and lots that dotted the landscape [of Harlem] began to disappear, replaced by renovated housing and gleaming new rowhouses and apartment buildings'. More generally, Smith (1996, p. 75) had described gentrification as a 'fabricant of the urban landscape', and argued that capital investment marked 'the return of capital to landscapes'. Smith's work repeatedly emphasized how capital investments involved physical transformations, which whilst often described in terms of changes to housing, housing stock and the 'built-environment', were also at times phrased as changes in landscapes. In relation to a study of the gentrification of Society Hill in Philadelphia, Smith wrote that capital investment and disinvestment 'represent overlapping stages in the evolution of a gentrified landscape' (Smith 1996, p. 1025). Earlier he had written that investments in housing constituted 'a permanent improvement in the landscape' (Smith 1979, p. 164), and also wrote about transformations of the 'built landscape' in an elaboration of his conceptions of rent gaps as a key determinant of gentrification (Smith et al. 1989). This latter study noted that whilst investment often involved the refurbishment of housing it could involve wider investments, a theme that was amplified in his later work on third-wave gentrification, which referred to the transformation of landscape complexes that were seen to consist not only of housing and facilities for business, retailing, leisure and recreation, but also 'open space' (Smith 2002b, p. 443). A key argument of this work was that the field of operation of gentrification had expanded to encompass a wider range of material objects, including the space between these objects.

Smith was not alone in making such observations. Zukin (1990), for instance, argued that gentrification was emerging as a 'socio-spatial complex of consumption', whereby capital investment focused initially on the refurbishment of housing becomes supplemented by investment in retail and cultural facilities, which whilst initially operating through 'specialized circuits', work together to transform an area into a 'scene' that itself comes to attract further, larger-scale, forms of capital investment. The result is, she argues, that areas of gentrification become transformed from 'an enclave – or an even smaller node – of upper-middle-class domestic consumption' through progressive linkage into wider circuits of capital, emerging first as 'new concentrations of "creative" services (advertising, architecture, publishing) that look for interesting locales at relatively cheap rents' and eventually 'a residential and commercial accessory to the major driver of capital investment, i.e. the financial district' (Zukin 1990, p. 50). She cites as an example of this final stage, the construction of Battery Park City and the Javits Convention Centre in the Hell's Kitchen area of New York, but her arguments could be applied across much of what Halle and Tiso (2014) describe as the 'Far West' of Manhattan.

This area includes the 'Meat Packing' (or MePa) District of New York City, which from the late 19th century through to the 1980s was an area of abattoirs, butchers and meat processing, although by the later period many of these businesses were struggling economically and there was abandonment and falling property values, features which can be viewed as indicators of an emerging rent gap in the area. Abandoned buildings and the growth of 'shadow economies' involving drugs and transsexual prostitution (Sholette 2011, p. 71), as well as the continuation of the meatpacking industry, led to the area becoming known, as Ferdman (2015, p. 25) puts it, as a 'sketchy destination, dark and desolate, notorious for its semi-abandoned warehouses and its stench'. However, this economy, as well as the area's low rents, began to encourage some movements into the area, including by businesses such as a supermarket focused 'on selling low-cost groceries in neighborhoods where . . . other chains were reluctant to locate . . ., a French restaurateur, [who] opened a diner . . . [and] in the late 1980s, a cluster of commercial art galleries' (Halle and Tiso 2014, p. 180). However, by 2008, the diner had closed, with the French restauranteur being unwilling to pay the escalating rental prices emerging as the area became the focus of increasingly large-scale investments, including the construction of large office, hotel and retail developments (Figure 6.1), and, in 2015, the Whitney Museum of American Art.

The contemporary landscape of the Meat Packing District contains the material products of the various phases and forms of gentrification that have occurred in the area, and indeed elements of prior activities: in Figure 6.1, a sign from a meat wholesaler has been retained as part of an entrance to an office block that has been built over an electrical goods retail establishment constructed behind a refurbished façade of buildings used by other meat-packing businesses.

Such a landscape is not unique to the Meat Packing District, Osman (2011, p. 11), for instance, described gentrified Brooklyn as being 'a layered landscape that retained the imprints of previous eras of economic restructuring'. Furthermore, Goldstein highlights how even in a landscape being restructured by large-scale international capital investment, remnants of formerly dominant activities may retain a presence in the landscape, albeit one marginalized in space as well as time:

> between the hours of two a.m. and ten a.m., echoes from an unfashionable industrial past resurface. Tractor trailers idle on Washington Street, whole carcasses are loaded into large refrigerated workrooms, and men who commute from Jersey and outlying boroughs still labor under cold fluorescents over bloodied power saws. In the early morning, the Meatpacking District continues, for the moment, to earn its name (Goldstein 2011, p. 23).

The persistence of past activities into the present highlights how the landscapes of gentrification are not simply the product of gentrification, nor indeed, as discussed earlier, simply a terrain over which gentrification comes to operate. Rather, as Patch (2004, p. 181) has observed, gentrification has to be 'embedded' in a landscape, and whilst gentrification processes might work to transform this landscape this does not mean that this 'will happen . . . or at least happen easily'. The concept of embedded gentrification highlights how material landscapes can act as an object against which, or around which, gentrification processes have to work, and which in some cases can act to block, or at least impede (Ley and Dobson 2008), gentrification. Such arguments, which might be viewed as a third perspective on material landscapes, are clearly evidenced in work on green/environmental/

*Figure 6.1   Retail and office development in the Meat Packing District, New York City
(Copyright: Author)*

ecological gentrification. Much of this work has focused on the redevelopment of urban
brownfield sites, many of which, as Pearsall (2013, p. 2297) notes, have come to be viewed
as environmentally contaminated areas 'regardless of whether ... formally tested',
thereby depressing property values and acting as 'a barrier to profitable redevelopment'
(Niedt 2006, p. 102). Studies such as Patch (2004), Ley and Dobson (2008) and Kern
(2015) have all highlighted how environmentally degraded landscapes – which might
merely involve areas which fail to exhibit 'interesting or socially approved architectural
signatures that provide landscapes of distinction' (Ley and Dobson 2008, p. 2473) – have
appeared to deter the onset of expected gentrification, although in many instances this has
at best only been a temporary stay, and in many cases, can be viewed as simply 'making
space' (Phillips 2000) ready for a subsequent phase of gentrification. Ley and Dobson
(2008, p. 2493), for example, argue that gentrification in the Grandview-Woodland district
of Vancouver has been impeded, in part, by the area's industrial activity that brought

in traffic and noxious smells, although also noted that rising house prices elsewhere in Vancouver had drawn in middle class migration from the early 2000s. They also record how earlier attempts to limit gentrification in neighbouring areas of Vancouver had 'perversely facilitated gentrification' (ibid., p. 2476), through checking new-build gentrification which both limited residential densities and preserved buildings which later became valued sites for refurbishment gentrification. More generally, research employing concepts such as environmental gentrification has highlighted that whilst contaminated brownfield sites may remain undeveloped for many years, such locations have become the focus of remediation activities which themselves may stimulate gentrification and/or be resisted as part of attempts to counter gentrification.

Some studies of environmental gentrification and other aspects of gentrification discussed in this section can be seen to enact a fourth perspective, which could be viewed as employing a 'landscape dialectic' (Mitchell 2002), whereby landscape form is seen to be both a creation of social processes and an actant that shapes and reshapes these processes. Dialectics as a term is widely associated with Marxism, and Marxist analysis of landscape dynamics – such as Harvey's (1975, p. 13) claim that capitalism involves 'a perpetual struggle in which capitalism builds a physical landscape appropriate to its own condition at a particular moment in time, only to have to destroy it, usually in the course of a crisis, at a subsequent point in time' – may be viewed as particularly appropriate to understanding the varying relationships between gentrification and landscape. As discussed in this section, the physical landscape of cities into which gentrification has come to be embedded has been produced in accordance with earlier capitalist demands, such as industrial production, before losing their value for such uses and their elements replaced or transformed through gentrification. However, destruction by, or incorporation into, the material landscapes of gentrification not only takes labour and resources to achieve, but the material character of landscapes can both encourage and deter gentrification. Landscapes, hence, become an active agent in the formation of landscapes of gentrification and non-gentrification.

The studies discussed hitherto have all been urban in focus, but all the perspectives on landscape and gentrification considered in this spatial setting can be identified in other spaces, including areas of wilderness and countryside. Research in North America, for instance, has identified residential development in the 'rural-urban fringe' as the cause of significant material and ecological landscape change, as 'forestland is removed to make way for homes; habitat for wildlife is destroyed; impervious surfaces are increased; and chemicals used to maintain vast lawns' (Kaplan and Austin 2004, p. 236). The last feature has been picked up in other work, with Hart (1998, p. 4), for instance, remarking that 'perhaps no culture group has had greater impact on the American landscape than the middle-class suburbanites who practice lawn worship', whilst Robbins (2007, p. xiii) has argued that 'the lawn is one of the largest and fastest growing landscapes in the United States'. Clearly not all of this growth can be laid at the door of gentrification, but as observed in Phillips et al. (2008, p. 55), with the onset of gentrification, areas such as gardens can become an 'object of investment and restructuring activity by gentrifiers', as well as new-build and even refurbishment acting to obliterate green spaces and habitats, when buildings and construction works occur in previously unbuilt on areas.

Reference to investment and restructuring by gentrifiers highlights how material landscapes can be actively produced through gentrification, with studies such as Abrams and Bliss (2013), Abram et al. (2013), Darling (2005), Hines (2010a; 2010b; 2012), Phillips (2005c; 2010b), Phillips et al. (2008) and Travis (2007) all highlighting transformations in landscapes associated with the arrival of gentrifiers into rural areas. As Nelson and Nelson (2010) note with respect to studies in the USA, developments such as ranchettes, gated-communities and private property enclosures have all been facets of gentrification-led landscape transformations. Particular attention has been paid in North America to transformations in Rocky Mountain West, which has been widely characterized as having experienced transitions from landscapes moulded by productive activities, such as mining, forestry, ranching and arable agriculture, to ones produced through a range of residential, recreational and other 'post-industrial' activities. Hines (2010b), for example, argues that areas of the Rocky Mountain West have become a 'post-industrial landscape of experience', focussed around attractive residences, recreational activity and an aesthetically pleasing and healthy environment. He adds that these landscapes have emerged at the expense of earlier industrial landscapes, although emphasizes that the latter landscapes still predominate across much of the regions, suggesting that the post-industrial landscapes of gentrification have emerged as islands of change 'in the midst of a relatively static, conservative, agricultural/industrial sea' (ibid., p. 509). Parallels here can be drawn with Patch's notion of embedded gentrification, with existing materialities of landscape acting as objects against which, or around which, processes of gentrification have to work. In Rocky Mountain West these existing material landscapes have included those of timber extraction and cattle ranching, activities that have been seen to block gentrification in some areas (see Beyers and Nelson 2000; Bryson and Wyckoff 2010), but are also undergoing transformations which release land for gentrification in other places (see Abrams et al. 2013; Bliss et al. 2010). Work in the UK has similarly both highlighted the significance for gentrification of the release of land from agriculture (see Phillips 2002; 2005a), and revealed situations where land is not being released from agricultural use, either because it is still economically valued for this use or a landowner is retaining land for other reasons. It has been shown how this may block gentrification but also how gentrification might be deterred by large-scale land-release for mass housing, if this results in large-scale population and housing growth that is viewed as creating a suburbanized landscape that fails to exhibit the 'rural' landscape desired by middle-class gentrifiers. Indeed, one might even apply the arguments of Zukin (1991, p. 142) that these areas have experienced de-gentrification in that 'developers acquire property from earlier residents who are wealthier and . . . more socially prominent', breaking the land into smaller plots on which to construct smaller, more standardized, forms of housing.

6.3 GENTRIFICATION AND LANDSCAPES AS SOCIAL SPACE

The emphasis on material landscape change was, at least in theory if not always in practice, conjoined within gentrification studies with consideration of the social drivers and consequences of such change, or as it might also be described, the social agents and victims of gentrification processes. The concept of landscape was itself also drawn into some expressions of such dynamics. Smith (1996, p. 39), for example, described gentrification as a 'class remake of the central urban landscape' and as 'a redifferentiation of the cultural, social and economic landscape' (ibid., p. 114). Such work adopts what

Henderson (2003, p. 182) describes as the 'social space' conception of landscape, in which landscape is taken to be constituted as humanly constructed 'space of any kind'. He adds that this conception is applicable to all manner of 'built environments', having 'no stake in any particular relationship between human beings, nor between humans and non-human nature' (ibid., p. 187). He argues this is both its great strength and ultimately a limitation, creating a notion of landscape that is too 'neutral' (ibid.), too abstract to convey much meaning and even perhaps too immaterial.

However, as Lees (2002, p. 102) remarks, the terms material and immaterial can be interpreted in a range of ways, often working as 'shorthand' for a variety of differences and tensions. She highlights, for instance, a distinction between the materialism of Philo (2000) and Jackson (2000), suggesting that in the former the material is 'associated with matter' whilst in the latter the material concerns the relationships between 'people and things'. In a sense the former materialization reflects the sense of landscape as discussed in the preceding section, whilst the latter can be connected to the 'social space' conception of landscape identified by Henderson (2003) and employed in some of the descriptions of gentrified landscapes by Smith (1996) in which observable features of a built environment are related to a landscape of social relations. Such a conception of landscape is clearly expressed in the work of Zukin, an early contributor to gentrification studies (Zukin 1982b), who later developed a wider interest in landscapes and argued that this term is frequently used as 'a sociological image' (Zukin 1991, p. 17), whereby visible features of a place evoke not only images of the social life that goes on in an area but also social relations of power.

A clear illustration of this line of argument, drawing directly on the work of Zukin, is Rofe's (2004) analysis of the changing urban landscapes of Newcastle in Australia. Interpreting landscape as the 'social meanings and narratives that are inscribed on a physical place' (ibid., p. 195), he argued that a city, widely viewed since its foundation in 1801 as a place of industry and a militant working class, and from the 1980s as a location of business closure, rising unemployment and 'social problems', was by the late 1990s being imagined, and indeed imaged, as a '"fab" landscape' of middle-class cosmopolitanism and de-industrial activity, in part as a consequence of gentrification (see also Winchester et al. 2013). He adds that whilst in this new landscape, 'affluence and power become emblematic', and displace the earlier social imaginary, it is both very clearly spatially concentrated – much of the city has not been gentrified – and also contested as many residents feel that they do not belong in this emergent landscape. This latter theme is very much emphasized in studies of resistance to gentrification, with Lees (2014), for example, highlighting both how gentrification projects are often accompanied by comments and images that establish social and moral contrasts between a normalized middle class and an in some way 'othered', and seemingly 'abnormal', working or under class, and how members of these stigmatized groups actively resent and resist this stereotyping and pathologizing, and the processes of gentrification that accompany them.

The work of Rofe (2004) and Lees (2014) focus on the way that people and organizations construct images of social identities and relations in association with physical localities or landscapes. Other work employing the 'social space' conception of landscape can be seen to be focused more upon employing their own, or others', academic social conceptions or imaginaries. Gentrification has indeed long been viewed as a 'key theoretical and ideological battleground' (Hamnett 1991, p. 174), with a range of quite divergent interpretations being advanced, debated and applied, often in a highly 'legislative' manner (Phillips 2002; 2010a). An illustration of this is provided by the debates between Hamnett (1991) and Smith (1992), with the former making use of Ley's (1980) analysis of the changing landscape of Vancouver to argue for an integrated, yet individual agency focussed interpretation of gentrification – or what Smith characterizes as 'philosophical individualism' – to be contrasted with his own, more collectivist interpretations of the social dynamics underpinning gentrification.

Postmodern and post-structuralist perspectives have arguably led to the adoption of more 'interpretive' approaches that work with a range of incommensurable theoretical positions, as well as potentially the 'bleeding' of the concept of gentrification 'into everyday parlance' (Savage 2016, p. 58). It can, however, still be argued that many studies use the term 'landscape' through a critical perspective, whereby landscapes are viewed as expressions of social relations of power, as illustrated by Zukin's (1991, pp. 16–17) claim that a landscape 'connotes a contentious, compromised product of society' because it is shaped through social processes of 'power, coercion and collective resistance'. Gentrified urban landscapes, she argues, reflect collective efforts of appropriation of space 'for elements of a new urban middle class', irrespective of their 'topography, building stock, and even existing populations' (ibid., p. 187).

Such critical perspectives can be seen to be widely enacted in gentrification studies, and indeed have not only been viewed as a key ingredient to the very concept (e.g. Slater 2006; 2008; Slater et al. 2004; Smith 1995; 1996) but also to have become of heightened significance, with Smith (2008, p. 197), for example, remarking that 'the class etching of the urban landscape that gave rise to the language of gentrification is, if anything, more intense today'. However, this perspective has faced a series of challenges. In gentrification studies, commentators such as Bernt (2016) have highlighted how recent years have seen not only claims concerning the heightened significance of a concept that highlights inequalities and injustices, but also growing epistemological and political unease about a concept that abstracts from context, or to draw on Savage's (2016, p. 209) discussion of methods in social science, 'lifts' social groups and processes of change out of 'physical landscapes', in order to construct them as a 'subterranean social landscape' which social scientists then seek to 'make visible'. More generally, the status and practice of critical research has been the focus of discussions in urban studies (e.g. Brenner 2009, 2011; Brenner and Schmid 2015), whilst as Wylie (2007, p. 97) notes, there has been continuing 'currents of unease' about the elision of the physical materiality of landscape in such accounts.

6.4 GENTRIFICATION AND SYMBOLIC LANDSCAPES

This unease over loss of materiality in landscape studies is, however, far from restricted to discussions of the critical approaches to landscape just outlined, but has also been prominent in discussions of what can be described as 'symbolic' or 'cultural' perspectives on landscape. One of the clearest illustrations of such a perspective is Daniels and Cosgrove's (1988, p. 1) description of landscape as 'a cultural image, a pictorial way of representing, structuring or symbolising surroundings'. They add that landscapes can be represented 'in a variety of materials and on many surfaces – in paint on canvas, in writing on paper, in earth, stones, water and vegetation on the ground'. Landscapes in this perspective are widely characterized as 'texts' as they are surfaces onto which meanings are written, and indeed read. Furthermore, attention is placed as much on how the landscapes are written or read as to what the texts of landscapes are about, a focus often expressed in terms of considering landscapes as 'a way of seeing' (Berger 1972; Cosgrove 1989), rather than as an object or surface being gazed at.

This understanding of landscape was an important constituent in the emergence of a so-called 'new cultural geography' in the late 1980s, although as Cosgrove (1990) observes, much of this new cultural geography was influenced by critical perspectives that viewed landscapes as expressions of power, with there being complex braidings between these perspectives. This is evident in gentrification studies, where Zukin (1991, p. 16) not only considered landscapes as embodiments of social relations of power but also viewed them as a 'symbolic representation', expressing cultural meanings and values. This viewpoint can be seen, to an extent, in her earlier study of gentrification in the SoHo District of Manhattan in the 1970s (Zukin 1982b), which suggested that this former industrial area had been gentrified through the combined actions of property owners, developers, affluent industrialists and aristocratic consumers, and a series of artists who came to construct open-plan studio and apartment spaces in multi-storey building blocks initially constructed for light manufacturing or warehousing. Zukin characterized this conjunction as the formation of an 'artistic mode of production' that bought about a 'seemingly modest redevelopment . . . based on arts and on historical preservation' (ibid., p. 188), although as later analysis has revealed, the trans-formations of SoHo went on to be extremely extensive and provide a model that was recreated in many, quite different, locations (see Cole 1987; Hamnett 2009; Podmore 1998; Shaw 2006; Smith 1996).

Amongst Zukin's arguments concerning the emergence of this mode of production is that it had a cultural dimension not only related to the creation of works of art but also in relation to the processes of inhabiting and reconstructing former industrial spaces. Noting that these spaces had been available for many years prior to the onset of their gentrification, she suggests that something must have changed to make people decide to occupy them and convert them to spaces of residence and artistic production. The change identified was an aesthetic, or *zeitgeist*, that involved people 'identifying in some existential way with an archaic past or an artistic style of life' (Zukin 1982b, p. 15). She says that this change occurred in the 1960s through an 'aesthetic conjuncture' of an emergent 'set of middle-class cultural values' (Zukin 1982a, p. 15), including 'a new cult of domesticity without an extended family structure', which acted to raise expectations of household focussed consumption 'to a luxury level', and an increased valuation of art and craft work stimulated by 'a professionalization and democratisation of arts and craft activities', which made artisanal and artistic products much more visible to urban audiences. The emergence of a gentrified landscape of loft living was, Zukin argued, a material expression of these cultural values as they were a construction that combined domestic residence with the production of art and crafts. Other cultural values identified as being also part of the conjuncture were a sense that the industrial age had ended and so there was a need to preserve some of its landscape elements, and a disenchantment with the modern, which not only reinforced a valuation of the past but also encouraged connections to expressions of counter-cultural values.

Zukin also argued that the media played an important role in promoting these values and the associated 'loft lifestyle', not least through illustrated magazine articles that portrayed both the spacious domestic space of loft apartments and the presence both of artistic workspaces and the products of art and design. The significance of the media in the formation of a gentrified 'loft landscape' was further highlighted by Podmore (1998), who suggested that representations of the SoHo loft circulated 'transregionally', including to Montréal, where films, magazines and novels, as well as property advertisements, made repeated references to the lofts of SoHo. She adds, however, that these representations also draw upon more localized imagery, as well as images of Paris, to create quite specific representations of the 'local loft landscape' (ibid., p. 299) of Montréal, a symbolic landscape that she argues, drawing on the work of Bourdieu (1984), is incorporated into the 'habitus', or everyday cultural judgements, of the inhabitants of the loft landscape. These residents not only sought to differentiate loft living, and loft residents, from other urban residents and residences, but also differentiate types of lofts and loft residents, including loft-style condominium apartments and 'authentic' lofts that were converted from former industrial spaces, 'loft artists' who lived and worked in their lofts, and 'loft dwellers' who used them solely as places of residence. Podmore (1998, p. 287) concludes by arguing that the loft landscape of Montréal is part of a symbolic system of 'classified and classifying practices' which, through the media, 'links the habitus of SoHo to other inner-city material landscapes, recursively creating a distinct lifestyle and taste pattern among North American inner-city middle classes'.

Podmore clearly adopts a symbolic conception of landscape and indeed quite explicitly distances herself from an approach to landscape that seeks to reveal the material social relations that underpin a landscape. She argues, for instance, that Zukin's analysis employs 'economic base/cultural superstructure arguments about urban change', and suggests that this acts 'to impede our understanding of the emergence of loft landscapes' (ibid., p. 283). Clearly not everyone accepts such arguments, with Zukin's analysis of SoHo being highly influential in subsequent accounts of gentrification in New York (e.g. Hackworth 2007; Hackworth and Smith 2001; Smith 1996), as well as viewed as a 'seminal text' in discussions of the role of artists in stage/phase models of gentrification (see Matthews 2010). However, Podmore's comments can be seen to point to the possibilities of adopting more symbolic conceptualizations of landscape.

Another set of works that can be seen to embrace such a perspective is that of Mills (1988; 1993) on the gentrification of Fairview Slopes in Vancouver. A key focus of this work was on the emergence of a 'postmodern landscape', where this is seen to involve 'a plethora of cultural signs and images which come together to form a messy social collage – or pastiche – of meanings' (Hubbard 2005, p. 295). In part this collage is constructed through the production of 'postmodern buildings', which have been designed to 'introduce variations in building surfaces, shape and size' (Phillips 2005b, p. 339), but can also emerge as a consequence of the co-presence in a landscape of different forms of gentrification (e.g. refurbishment, new-build) and earlier, as yet un-gentrified properties (see Figures 6.2 and 6.3). Fairview Slopes can be seen to encompass both of these aspects, having been transformed through a series of phases of development, including latterly ones which exhibit a pointedly 'postmodern . . . play of codes and symbols' (Mills 1988, p. 175). Mills explicitly draws inspiration from the conceptions of a 'new cultural geography' focussed on landscape as 'a way of seeing', arguing, for instance, that her focus was on considering

Figure 6.2   Postmodern buildings along the High Line, New York City (Copyright: Author)

what interpretations of social order 'gentrifiers write into, and read from, gentrified landscapes' (Mills 1993, p. 150). In a sense, this can be seen to echo conceptions of a social landscape as adopted by critical studies of gentrification, except that the writer and reader here was not the academic theorist of gentrification but the agents of gentrification themselves. She goes on to analyze the landscape of Fairview Slopes as a 'textual community'; that is, as a set of 'texts' that are written and read by particular sets of social actors. These include the images and words presented in property advertisements; the comments made by residents, architects and estate agents; and the symbolism 'made concrete in the landscape itself' (ibid., p. 154). These textual communities, she argues, create a series of symbolic codings or 'myths' of the landscape of gentrification.

Three symbolic constructions of Fairview Slopes' landscape are identified by Mills as warranting detailed discussion, namely as 'a distinctive area for a living investment', as 'city living at its best' and as a 'strategic location'. In the first case, Fairview Slopes is

Figure 6.3 Postmodern landscape along the High Line, New York City (Copyright: Author)

presented as a place where you can show, or even create, social status, an interpretation that Mills notes corresponds well with conceptions of gentrification as a form of 'positional consumption' or 'cultural capital accumulation', whereby people are investing in houses in part as a way of establishing a new social status. A second set of texts identified by Mills are those that present the area as 'city living at its best', which whilst also being interpretable as corresponding to academic conceptions that emphasize positionality and social status, are considered by Mills to be 'thoroughly geographical' in that these texts give value to the presence of 'urbanity'. The landscape was represented as 'best' because it was close to, but not in the city centre, and, even more significantly, it was not suburban. A third set of texts focussed on the practical advantages that the landscape could bring, both through its location and its material construction. These texts, for instance, stressed the centrality of the area within the city of Vancouver and how this enabled the minimization of journey times to work and leisure, as well as the physical design and construction of houses in the area, which were seen to minimize the inputs of labour associated with housework, gardening and the maintenance of properties.

As discussed in Phillips (2005b), a key feature of Mills' work is that whilst she notes parallels between the discourses of people in this area and a range of academic interpretations of gentrification, she does not use these to imply any sense of justifying or validating these academic interpretations. It is argued that she resists any attempt to 'look behind the image' (ibid., p. 345), focusing attention very much on the symbolisms being created and not seeing these as a surface expression of some social landscape, as implied within the critical approach of individuals such as Zukin. Whilst such a symbolic conception of landscape can be seen to be fully consonant with many post-structuralist strands of thought that have come to course through the contemporary social sciences, Mills' work can also be viewed as exhibiting many of the features that have led to a range of 'currents of unease' about the dematerialization of landscape, notably the seemingly exclusive emphasis on 'the constitution of intersubjective meaning systems . . . through the less-than-tangible, often-fleeting spaces of texts, signs, symbols . . . and imaginings' (Philo 2000, p. 33). For Lees (2001, p. 55), such a focus risks 'evacuating' the 'critical impulses' that characterized much of the initial impetus for the establishment of 'new cultural geography'.

Having said this, it is important to note that these concerns have been widely recognized, even amongst advocates of a symbolic conception of landscape. It has already been noted that Cosgrove (1990) identified complex braiding between symbolic and critical perspectives on landscape, and this can be identified across the work of many individuals identified with the 'new cultural geography'. Of particular relevance to the study of gentrification in this regard is Duncan and Duncan's (2004) study, *Landscapes of Privilege*, and associated works (e.g. Duncan 1973; Duncan and Duncan 2001, 2003). Although they do not use the term gentrification, their work on the township of Bedford, in New York State, can be seen to address many of the issues associated with the concept, including the in-migration of wealthy residents, the refurbishment and construction of new-build properties and the presence of exclusions and displacements. A key element of this work has also been on connecting these issues to the symbolizations of landscape, and how these are 'read both consciously and practically . . . by people who produce, value, and engage with them' (Duncan and Duncan 2004, p. 28). In a similar way to Mills, they explore a range of texts about the landscape of an area, including 'literature, painting, film, advertisements, and the landscape itself' (ibid., p. 32), identifying a series of discourses that 'define Bedford as a landscape', and also simultaneously, 'as a whole aestheticized way of life' (ibid., p. 32). These discourses encompass a range of landscape forms, including wilderness, countryside and village settlements, even though the authors characterize Bedford as 'a rural looking suburb, or exurb' (ibid., p. 24). As such, their work raises many interesting questions about the symbolic, as well as material, geographies of gentrification, in addition to highlighting the potential of developing symbolic analyses that are attentive to 'the social and political consequences that flow from . . .various readings . . . [of] landscapes' (ibid., p. 29).

The work of Duncan and Duncan clearly illustrates that symbolic approaches to gentrified landscapes are not only applicable to urban landscapes, and indeed there has long been a focus within landscape studies on rural spaces (e.g. see Kenzer (1985) on the significance of the rural in the work of Carl Sauer). The rise of 'new cultural geography' marked a significant shift in the focus not only towards symbolic conceptions of landscape but also to the study of urban spaces (Lees 2002), although rural studies were also heavily influenced by the 'cultural turn' towards the study of symbolic representations of rural space (see Cloke 1997; Holloway and Kneafsey 2004; Phillips 1998). Work such as Smith and Phillips (2001) and Phillips (2002; 2004) has sought to connect such work to the study of gentrification, with the former, for example, suggesting that in the Hebden Bridge area of West Yorkshire, two distinct cultural landscapes were of significance to gentrifiers, namely 'remote' and 'village'. In the former, desirable rural landscapes were seen to involve relative isolation from modern, capitalist society and placement in a historic and natural but challenging wild, 'Brontesque', landscape. In the latter, a more humanized/ socialized landscape was sought, with villages viewed as spaces of communal intimacy, support and safety. In studies of villages in West Berkshire, Norfolk and Leicestershire, I have highlighted a series of symbolic constructions of rurality that were of significance within processes of rural gentrification, including rurality as a 'space of nature' (Phillips 2005c; Phillips et al. 2008), a 'space of agriculture' (Phillips 2002) and as a 'non-suburban space' (Phillips 2002; 2004). The last of these very much echoes not only many of the observations made in Duncan and Duncan (2004) but also discussions of landscapes of desire and despair by Caulfield (1992; 1994) and Ley (1996). As outlined in Phillips (2004, p. 14), these studies can be read as implying that inner-city and rural areas are 'both seen as desirable alternatives to the "landscape of despair" of suburban space'.

Whilst the studies of Caulfield and Ley can be seen to enact elements of a symbolic conception of landscape, they clearly have other foci as well, including what is described in Phillips (2004), drawing on the work of Lefebvre (1991) and Soja (1996), as a 'thirdspace' geography of gentrification. This is concerned with 'space as directly lived' (ibid., p. 67), and the transformative potential of space (ibid., p. 69). These concerns can be seen to connect to a fourth perspective on landscape that has emerged over the last decade or so, which has been variously described as 'non-representational' (Waterton 2013), 'phe-nomenological' (Wylie 2007), 'post-phenomenological' (Wylie 2008), 'processual' (Wylie 2003), and 'vitalist' (Greenhough 2010), to list but a few titles. Whilst there are important differences between these stated approaches, they can, as Waterton (2013, p. 66) notes, all be seen to share a common feature, namely that they all consider landscape as being 'lived, embodied and tangled up' with how people '*do* things' (original emphasis) and also, with all manner of non- or more-than-human 'inhabitants' of landscapes.

6.5   GENTRIFICATION AND LIVED LANDSCAPES

Bound up with the focus on lived landscapes, it is possible to identify five further features that are common across most, if not all, of the named approaches and which can be seen to connect to the study of gentrification. First, there is a widespread concern to give more agency to landscapes: to not see them as a passive surface or material onto which material structures or meanings are simply inscribed or constructed. Reference has already been made to how the materiality of landscapes may act to both stimulate and block gentrification, and also to symbolic interpretations of landscape that appear to have influenced the in-migration of gentrification. Amongst such studies was the work of Smith and Phillips (2001) on the influence of 'remote' and 'village' landscapes, which are viewed as being encoded with meanings. As described, these landscapes could be viewed as mute surfaces onto which cultural meanings are encoded, both by contemporary gentrifiers and agents of gentrification such as estate agencies (see also Smith 2002a), but there are traces of material conditionings of these encodings. Smith and Phillips (2001, pp. 461–463), for instance, write about the 'roughness and darkness' of the 'millstone grit landscape' and how some gentrifiers 'revelled in the harshness of the moor top climate, which appeared to reinforce their affinity with the landscape'. Another study that could be seen to give agency to landscape is my research on 'baroque rurality' in a gentrified village in Leicestershire (Phillips 2014). The concept of baroque rurality highlights the diverse constituents of rural landscapes, and it is argued that a striking, but hitherto poorly recognized, feature of studies of rural in-migration is that they give agency to a large range of 'materialities of the rural', including vegetated surfaces, physical spatiality, chemical purity, sound, heat, light and the presence of water, as well as the 'visual appearance of landscapes'. However, whilst mentioned, the operation of these materialities rarely receives any sustained attention in studies of migration and rural gentrification, but rather is simply enrolled as a constituent of some highly abstract influence, such as environment, nature or, indeed, landscape.

The concept of baroque rurality connects to a second feature of these emergent approaches to landscape, which is a focus on the diverse constituents of landscape. For Ingold, for instance, even that most human focused of built environments, the home, is always a place of residence to much more than just people: 'the house has many and diverse animal inhabitants – more, perhaps than we are inclined to recognize. Sometimes special provision is made for them such as the kennel, stable or dovecote. Others find shelter and sustenance in its nooks and crannies' (Ingold 1995, p. 78). Landscapes are, as Ingold (2011, p. 116) remarks, '"cluttered" with every kind of thing, from hills and mountains to animals and plants, objects and artefacts', or as Wylie (in Merriman et al. 2008, p. 203) puts it, are 'intertwinings' of both human and the more-than-human. Over a decade ago I argued that gentrification research had yet to 'consider whether there are "extra social" or "natural" dimensions of gentrification' (Phillips 2005c, p. 1), an assessment that, as Bryson (2013) notes, might be seen to still broadly hold, despite the rise of research on environmental or ecological gentrification and the potential for quite directly connecting some of the conceptual lynchpins of gentrification studies to more-than-human inhabitants of landscapes.

A fourth feature of these new perspectives on landscape is their tendency to view landscapes as 'affectual', in that they impact people in a variety of ways beyond the cognitive and the visual, which has often been the principal ways that landscapes have been considered in previous approaches. It has, for instance, already been highlighted that advocates of symbolic perspectives on landscapes use phrases such as 'reading a landscape' and 'landscape as a way of seeing'. By contrast, recent landscape studies are often 'multi-sensual' and experiential in approach. As Waterton (2013, p. 69) puts it,

> in these approaches we find a landscape that involves a full range of sensory experiences: it is not only visual, but textured to the touch and resonating with smells, touch, sounds and tastes, often mundane in nature. It may be a moody landscape, dark, sharp and foreboding, or associated with memory, light, breezing and sweet, or, perhaps still, wildly atmospheric.

In my own work on rural gentrification I have explored the affective dimensions of a village landscape (Phillips 2014), examining people's emotional, semi-conscious and non-representational affective responses to plants, animals and material spaces, suggesting that whilst incoming gentrifier households often describe the countryside and rural natures through visual references, such as 'views from the house' or 'views from the car', other 'sensing of the countryside' tends to emerge once people have inhabited a village for some time.

Two other studies of gentrification that can be seen to connect to the affective study of landscapes are Patch's (2004) study of 'embedded gentrification' in Williamsburg,

New York City, and Kern's (2012) 'yoga informed' theoretical reflections on the potential significance of embodiment and emotion to the study of gentrification. Reference has already been made to Patch's work in discussions of material perspectives on landscape, and whilst this clearly is the principal focus of his examination of gentrification and landscape, his account provides a hint of how this could be connected to a more affective account of landscape when he writes that the artists moving in to Williamsburg: 'do not simply appropriate their industrial surroundings. In many cases they are enveloped in them, in the air they breathe, the sites they see and the spaces they sleep in. In Williamsburg, it means subjecting yourself and your family to low-quality living conditions' (Patch 2004, p. 182). Conducting a wider reflection on the scope for incorporating the study of emotion and embodied practices into gentrification studies, Kern highlights how certain embodied practices – such as 'seeking out local, artisanal and organic foods; dressing in particular fashions; or sitting in the coffee shop working on a laptop for hours' (Kern 2012, p. 32) – might act as 'markers of gentrification' that in a sense indicate 'as clearly as changes in the built environment or tenure structure' that one is entering a gentrified landscape. She further adds that gentrification often involves 'emotion-laden embodied practices' related to both contact and the avoidance of contact, such that gentrifiers might be seen to occupy an experiential 'bubble' that minimizes even 'verbal and visual contact' with bodies other than gentrifiers. This argument can be seen to have clear resonances with Butler and Robson's (2001, 2003) account of the 'tectonic' practices of gentrification, whereby social classes occupying the same landscape often live in distinct worlds, largely brushing past each other with little direct interaction between them. Kern also argues that there may be processes of emotional displacement occurring through gentrification, as embodied and emotional contacts and desires become regulated, both officially and through the self, and hence 'driven out or underground' (Kern 2012, p. 32). She also suggests that attention might be paid to the emotional dimensions of the counter-cultural and social justice facets of gentrification.

A final feature of these new studies of landscape that is closely related to the two previous points is that they reject a separation of landscape and analyst. Conceptions such as 'reading a landscape' imply some form of distancing between landscape and reader: the analyst in a sense steps out of a landscape in order to be able to view and decode its meanings. By contrast, notions such as dwelling and affect stress engagement, of being, as Wylie (2005, p. 239) puts it, 'in the thick' of a landscape. Connections to the study of gentrification might be made through the study of architecture and buildings, with Lees (2001) for example, promoting the idea that such studies need to be concerned 'with the inhabitation of architectural space as much as its significance', and hence 'engage practically and actively with the situated and everyday practices through which built environments are used' (see also Kraftl and Adey 2008). Such situated studies may actually not be alien to gentrification research given that many of the major studies of gentrification include some reference to periods of residence in landscapes of gentrification: Zukin (1982b, p. xiii), for instance, starts her study *Loft Living* with the words, 'I first became interested in living lofts as a loft dweller'.

6.6   CONCLUSION

This chapter has sought to foster greater reflection on the significance of landscape within the study of gentrification. It began by highlighting claims that landscape is a central, indeed perhaps, alongside others, a defining, feature of gentrification. It is, however, also a feature that has arguably been taken for granted: a persistent but often unremarked upon facet of gentrification. This can be viewed as surprising given that in other arenas, the concept of landscape has been the focus of considerable attention and debate. Four distinct understandings of landscape are identified as being, to a range of degrees and largely implicitly, present within gentrification studies, namely landscape as material/physical world; landscape as space of social life and social relations of power; landscape as a symbolic text or way of seeing; and landscape as lived space. It has also been stressed, particularly in relation to the second and third conceptions of landscape which are often viewed as connected to the 'new cultural geography' that emerged in the 1980s, that there is a complex braiding of approaches, a feature that is clearly evident in the work of Zukin whose writings have figured prominently in this chapter. Landscape, as much as gentrification, can be viewed as a 'congested and contested concept' (Phillips 2005, p. 477), and it is hence unsurprising that a range of tensions have surrounded the definition and employment of both. It has not been possible here to explore these tensions in great depth, but it is evident that in both gentrification and landscape studies, tensions have often been used productively to drive both theory and praxis into new terrains. This chapter has highlighted one new landscape of gentrification that is just beginning to be charted for exploration, namely its lived landscapes, but there are no doubt many more lying within, between and beyond those sketched out here.

REFERENCES

Abrams, J., Bliss, J. and Gosnell, H. (2013) 'Reflexive gentrification of working lands in the American west: contesting the "middle landscape"', *Journal of Rural and Community Development*, 8(3), 144–158.
Berger, J. (1972) *Ways of Seeing*, London: Penguin.
Bernt, M. (2016) 'Very particular, or rather universal? Gentrification through the lenses of Ghertner and López-Morales', *City*, 20(4), 637–644.
Beyers, W. and Nelson, P. (2000) 'Contemporary development forces in the nonmetropolitan west: new insights from rapidly growing communities', *Journal of Rural Studies*, 16(4), 459–474.
Bliss, J., Kelly, E., Abrams, J., Bailey, C. and Dyer, J. (2010) 'Disintegration of the U.S. industrial forest estate: dynamics, trajectories, and questions', *Small-Scale Forestry*, 9(1), 53–66.
Bourdieu, P. (1984) *Distinction*, London: Routledge.
Brenner, N. (2009) 'What is critical urban theory?', *City*, 13(2–3), 198–207.
Brenner, N. (2011) 'Assemblage urbanism and the challenges of critical urban theory', *City*, 15(2), 225–240.
Brenner, N. and Schmid, C. (2015) 'Towards a new epistemology of the urban?', *City*, 19(2–3), 151–182.
Bryson, J. (2013) 'The nature of gentrification', *Geography Compass*, 7(8), 578–587.
Bryson, J. and Wyckoff, W. (2010) 'Rural gentrification and nature in the Old and New Wests', *Journal of Cultural Geography*, 27(1), 53–75.
Butler, T. (2007) 'Re-urbanizing London Docklands: gentrification, suburbanization or new urbanism?', *International Journal of Urban and Regional Research*, 31(4), 759–781.
Butler, T. and Robson, G. (2001) 'Coming to terms with London: middle class communities in a global city', *International Journal of Urban and Regional Research*, 25(1), 70–86.
Caulfield, J. (1992) 'Gentrification and familism in Toronto: a critique of conventional wisdom', *City and Society*, 6(1), 76–89.
Caulfield, J. (1994) *City Form and Everyday Life*, Toronto: University of Toronto Press.

Charmes, E. and Keil, R. (2015) 'The politics of post-suburban densification in Canada and France', *International Journal of Urban and Regional Research*, 39(3), 581–602.

Checker, M. (2011) 'Wiped out by the "greenwave": environmental gentrification and the paradoxical politics of urban sustainability', *City and Society*, 23(2), 210–229.

Cloke, P. (1997) 'Country backwater to virtual village? Rural studies and "the cultural turn"', *Journal of Rural Studies*, 13(4), 367–375.

Cole, D. (1987) 'Artists and urban redevelopment', *Geographical Review*, 77(4), 391–407.

Cosgrove, D. (1989) 'Geography is everywhere: culture and symbolism in human landscapes', in Gregory, D. and Walford, R. (eds) *Horizons in Human Geography*, London: Macmillan, pp. 118–135.

Cosgrove, D. (1990) 'Landscape studies in geography and cognate fields of the humanities and social sciences', *Landscape Research*, 15(3), 1–6.

Curran, W. and Hamilton, T. (2012) 'Just green enough: contesting environmental gentrification in Greenpoint, Brooklyn', *Local Environment*, 19(9), 1027–1042.

Daniels, S. and Cosgrove, S. (1988) 'Introduction: iconography and landscape', in Cosgrove, D. and Daniels, S. (eds) *Iconography and Landscape*, Cambridge: Cambridge University Press, pp. 1–10.

Darling, E. (2005) 'The city in the country: wilderness gentrification and the rent gap', *Environment and Planning A*, 37(6), 1015–1032.

Davidson, M. and Lees L. (2005) 'New-build "gentrification" and London's riverside renaissance', *Environment and Planning A*, 37(7), 1165–1190.

Dooling, S. (2008) 'Ecological gentrification: re-negotiating justice in the city', *Critical Planning*, 15, 41–58.

Duncan, J. (1973) 'Landscape taste as a symbol of group identity: a Westchester County village', *Geographical Review*, 63(3), 334–355.

Duncan, J. and Duncan, N. (2001) 'The aesthetisation of the politics of landscape preservation', *Annals of the Association of American Geographers*, 91(2), 387–409.

Duncan, J. and Duncan, N. (2003) 'Can't live with them; can't landscape without them: racism and the pastoral aesthetic in suburban New York', *Landscape Journal*, 22(1–3), 88–98.

Duncan, J. and Duncan, N. (2004) *Landscapes of Privilege: The Politics of the Aesthetic in an American Suburb*, London: Routledge.

Ferdman, B. (2015) 'Off the grid: New York City landmark performance', *Performance Arts Journal*, 37(2), 13–29.

Freeman, L. (2006) *There Goes the 'Hood: Views of Gentrification from the Ground Up*, Philadelphia: Temple University Press.

Glass, R. (1964) *London: Aspects of Change*, London: MacGibbon and Kee.

Goldstein, B. (2011) 'Small hours in the Meatpacking District', *Gastronomica*, 11(4), 23–25.

Greenhough, B. (2010) 'Vitalist geographies: life and the more-than-human', in Anderson, B. and Harrison, P. (eds) *Taking Place: Non-Representational Theories and Geography*, Aldershot: Routledge, pp. 37–54.

Hackworth, J. (2007) *The Neoliberal City: Governance, Ideology, and Development in American Urbanism*, Ithaca: Cornell University Press.

Hackworth, J. and Smith, N. (2001) 'The changing state of gentrification', *Tijdschrift voor Economische en Sociale Geografie*, 92(4), 464–477.

Halle, D. and Tiso, E. (2014) *New York's New Edge: Contemporary Art, the High Line, and Urban Megaprojects on the Far West Side*, Chicago: University of Chicago Press.

Hamilton, T. and Curran, W. (2013) 'From "five angry women" to "kick-ass community": gentrification and environmental activism in Brooklyn and beyond', *Urban Studies*, 50(8), 1557–1574.

Hamnett, C. (1991) 'The blind men and the elephant: the explanation of gentrification', *Transactions of the Institute of British Geographers*, 16(2), 173–189.

Hamnett, C. (2009) 'City centre gentrification: loft conversions in London's city fringe', *Urban Policy and Research*, 27(3), 277–287.

Hart, J. (1998) *The Rural Landscape*, Baltimore: Johns Hopkins.

Harvey, D. (1975) 'The geography of capitalist accumulation: a reconstruction of Marxian theory', *Antipode*, 7(2), 9–21.

He, S. (2010) 'New-build gentrification in Central Shanghai: demographic changes and socio-economic implications', *Population, Space and Place*, 16(5), 345–361.

Henderson, G. (2003) 'What (else) we talk about when we talk about landscape: for a return to the social imagination', in Wilson, C. and Groth, P. (eds) *Everyday America: Cultural Landscape Studies after J.B. Jackson*, Berkeley, CA: University of California Press, pp. 178–198.

Hines, J. (2010a) 'In pursuit of experience: the postindustrial gentrification of the rural American West', *Ethnography*, 11(2), 285–308.

Hines, J. (2010b) 'Rural gentrification as permanent tourism: the creation of the "New" West Archipelago as postindustrial cultural space', *Environment and Planning D: Society and Space*, 28(3), 509–525.

Hines, J. (2012) 'The post-industrial regime of production/consumption and the rural gentrification of the New West archipelago', *Antipode*, 44(1), 74–97.

Holloway, L. and Kneafsey, M. (2004) *Geographies of Rural Cultures and Societies*, Aldershot: Ashgate.

Hubbard, P. (2005) 'Places on the margin: the spatiality of exclusion', in Phillips, M. (ed) *Contested Worlds: An Introduction to Human Geography*, Aldershot: Ashgate, pp. 290–316.

Hudalah, D., Winarso, H. and Woltjer, J. (2015) 'Gentrifying the peri-urban: land use conflicts and institutional dynamics at the frontier of an Indonesian metropolis', *Urban Studies*, 53(3), 593–608.

Ingold, T. (1995) 'Building, dwelling, living: how animals and people make themselves at home in the world', in Strathern, M. (ed) *Shifting Contexts: Transformations in Anthropological Knowledge*, London: Routledge, pp. 59–80.

Ingold, T. (2011) *Being Alive: Essays on Movement, Knowledge and Description*, London: Routledge.

Jackson, P. (2000) 'Rematerializing social and cultural geography', *Social and Cultural Geography*, 1, 9–14.

Kaplan, R. and Austin, M. (2004) 'Out in the country: sprawl and the quest for nature nearby', *Landscape and Urban Planning*, 69(2–3), 235–243.

Kenzer, M. (1985) 'Milieu and the "intellectual landscape": Carl O'Sauer's undergraduate heritage', *Annals of the Association of American Geographers*, 75(2), 258–270.

Kern, F. (2015) 'From toxic wreck to crunchy chic: environmental gentrification through the body', *Environment and Planning D: Society and Space*, 33(1), 67–83.

Kern, L. (2012) 'Connecting embodiment, emotion and gentrification: an exploration through the practice of yoga in Toronto', *Emotion, Space and Society*, 5(1), 27–35.

Kraftl, P. and Adey, P. (2008) 'Architecture/affect/inhabitation: geographies of being-in buildings', *Annals of the Association of American Geographers*, 98(1), 213–231.

Lees, L. (2001) 'Towards a critical geography of architecture: the case of an ersatz Colosseum', *Cultural Geographies*, 8(1), 51–58.

Lees, L. (2002) 'Rematerializing geography: the "new" urban geography', *Progress in Human Geography*, 26(1), 101–112.

Lees, L. (2014) 'The urban injustices of New Labour's "new urban renewal": the case of the Aylesbury Estate in London', *Antipode*, 46(4), 921–947.

Lefebvre, H. (1991) *The Production of Space*, Oxford: Blackwell.

Ley, D. (1980) 'Liberal ideology and the post-industrial city', *Annals of the Association of American Geographers*, 70(2), 238–258.

Ley, D. (1987) 'Styles of the times: liberal and neo-conservative landscapes in inner Vancouver, 1968–1986', *Journal of Historical Geography*, 13(1), 40–56.

Ley, D. (1996) *The New Middle Classes and the Remaking of the Central City*, Oxford: Oxford University Press.

Ley, D. and Dobson, C. (2008) 'Are there limits to gentrification? The contexts of impeded gentrification in Vancouver', *Urban Studies*, 45(12), 2471–2498.

Matthews, V. (2010) 'Aestheticizing space: art, gentrification and the city', *Geography Compass*, 4(6), 660–675.

Merriman, P., Revill, G., Cresswell, T., Lorimer, H., Matless, D., Rose, G. and Wylie, J. (2008) 'Landscape, mobility, practice', *Social and Cultural Geography*, 9(2), 191–212.

Mills, C. (1988) '"Life on the upslope": the postmodern landscape of gentrification', *Environment and Planning D: Society and Space*, 6(2), 169–189.

Mills, C. (1993) 'Myths and meanings of gentrification', in Duncan, J. and Ley, D. (eds) *Place/Culture/Representation*, London: Routledge, pp. 149–170.

Mitchell, D. (2002) 'Cultural landscapes: the dialectical landscape – recent landscape research in human geography', *Progress in Human Geography*, 26(3), 381–389.

Nelson, L. and Nelson, P. (2010) 'The global rural: gentrification and linked migration in the rural USA', *Progress in Human Geography*, 35(4), 441–459.

Niedt, C. (2006) 'Gentrification and the grassroots: population support in the revanchist suburb', *Journal of Urban Affairs*, 28(2), 99–120.

Osman, S. (2011) *The Invention of Brownstone Brooklyn*, Oxford: Oxford University Press.

Patch, J. (2004) 'The embedded landscape of gentrification', *Visual Studies*, 19(2), 169–187.

Pearsall, H. (2010) 'From brown to green? Assessing social vulnerability to environmental gentrification in New York City', *Environment and Planning C*, 28(5), 872–886.

Pearsall, H. (2013) 'Superfund me: a study of resistance to gentrification in New York City', *Urban Studies*, 50(1), 2293–2310.

Phillips, M. (1998) 'The restructuring of social imaginations in rural geography', *Journal of Rural Studies*, 18(2), 121–153.

Phillips, M. (2000) 'Making space for rural gentrification', in Hernando, F. (ed) *Proceedings of the 2nd Anglo-Spanish Symposium of Rural Geography*, Valladolid: University of Valladolid, section 1.2, pp. 1–21.

Phillips, M. (2002) 'The production, symbolisation and socialisation of gentrification: a case study of two Berkshire villages', *Transactions of the Institute of British Geographers*, 27(3), 282–308.

Phillips, M. (2004) 'Other geographies of gentrification', *Progress in Human Geography*, 28(1), 5–30.

Phillips, M. (2005a) 'Differential productions of rural gentrification: illustrations from North and South Norfolk', *Geoforum*, 36(4), 477–494.

Phillips, M. (2005b) 'People at the centre? The contested geographies of "gentrification"', in Phillips, M. (ed) *Contested Worlds: An Introduction to Human Geography*, Aldershot: Ashgate, pp. 317–352.

Phillips, M. (2005c) 'Rural gentrification and the production of nature: a case study from Middle England', in Ramirez, B. (ed) *Papers from the 4th International Conference of Critical Geography*. Mexico City. Accessed 23 July 2017 at www.academia.edu/ 877442/Rural_gentrification_and_the_production_of_nature_a_case_stu dy_from_Middle_England.

Phillips, M. (2010a) 'Counterurbanisation and rural gentrification: an exploration of the terms?', *Population, Space and Place*, 16, 539–558.

Phillips, M. (2010b) 'Rural gentrification and the built environment: exploring the connections', in Columbus, F. (ed) *Built Environment: Design, Management and Applications*, Hauppauge, New York: Nova Publishers, pp. 33–62.

Phillips, M. (2014) 'Baroque rurality in an English village', *Journal of Rural Studies*, 33, 56–70.

Phillips, M., Page, S., Saratsi, E., Tansey, K. and Moore, K. (2008) 'Diversity, scale and green landscapes in the gentrification process: traversing ecological and social science perspectives', *Applied Geography*, 28(1), 54–76.

Philo, C. (2000) 'More words, more worlds: reflections on the cultural turn and human geography', in Cook, I., Crouch, D., Naylor, S. and Ryan, J. (eds) *Cultural Turns/Geographical Turns: Perspectives on Cultural Geography*, Harlow: Prentice Hall, pp. 26–53.

Podmore, J. (1998) '(Re)Reading the "loft living" habitus in Montreal's inner city', *International Journal of Urban and Regional Research*, 22(2), 283–302.

Rankin, K. and McLean, H. (2014) 'Governing the commercial streets of the city: new terrains of disinvestment and gentrification in Toronto's inner suburbs', *Antipode*, 47(1), 216–239.

Robbins, P. (2007) *Lawn People: How Grasses, Weeds and Chemicals Make Us Who We Are*, Philadelphia: Temple University Press.

Rofe, M. (2004) 'From "problem city" to "promise city": gentrification and the revitalisation of Newcastle', *Australian Geographical Studies*, 42(2), 193–206.

Sauer, C. (1925) 'The morphology of landscape', *University of California Publications in Geography*, 2(2), 19–53.

Savage, M. (2016) 'The fall and rise of class analysis in British sociology, 1950–2016', *Tempo Social*, 28(2), 57–72.

Shaw, W. (2006) 'Sydney's SoHo syndrome? Loft living in the urbane city', *Cultural Geographies*, 13(2), 182–206.

Shin, H. (2015) 'Economic transition and speculative urbanisation in China: gentrification versus dispossession', *Urban Studies*, 53(3), 471–489.

Shin, H. and Kim, S.-H. (2015) 'The developmental state, speculative urbanisation and the politics of displacement in gentrifying Seoul', *Urban Studies*, 53(3), 540–559.

Sholette, G. (2011) *Dark Matter: Art and Politics in the Age of Enterprise Culture*, London: Pluto Press.

Slater, T. (2006) 'The eviction of critical perspectives from gentrification research', *International Journal of Urban and Regional Research*, 30(4), 737–757.

Slater, T. (2008) '"A literal necessity to be re-placed": a rejoinder to the gentrification debate', *International Journal of Urban and Regional Research*, 32(1), 212–223.

Slater, T., Curran, W. and Lees, L. (2004) 'Gentrification research: new directions and critical scholarship', *Environment and Planning A*, 36(7), 1141–1150.

Smith, D. (2002) 'Rural gatekeepers and "greentried" Pennine rurality: opening and closing the access gates?', *Journal of Social and Cultural Geography*, 3(4), 447–463.

Smith, D. and Phillips, D. (2001) 'Socio-cultural representations of greentrified Pennine rurality', *Journal of Rural Studies*, 17(4), 457–469.

Smith, N. (1979) 'Gentrification and capital: practice and ideology in Society Hill', *Antipode*, 11(3), 163–173.

Smith, N. (1992) 'Blind man's bluff or, Hamnett's philosophical individualism in search of gentrification', *Transactions of the Institute of British Geographers*, 17(1), 110–115.

Smith, N. (1995) 'Gentrifying theory', *Scottish Geographical Magazine*, 111(2), 124–126.

Smith, N. (1996) *The New Urban Frontier: Gentrification and the Revanchist City*, London: Routledge.

Smith, N. (2002) 'New globalism, new urbanism: gentrification as global urban strategy', *Antipode*, 34(3), 428–450.

Smith, N. (2008) 'On "The eviction of critical perspectives from gentrification research"', *International Journal of Urban and Regional Research*, 32(1), 195–197.

Smith, N., Duncan, B. and Reid, L. (1989) 'From disinvestment to reinvestment: tax arrears and turning points in the East Village', *Housing Studies*, 4(4), 238–252.

Soja, E. (1996) *Third Space: Journeys to Los Angeles and Other Real-and-Imagined Places*, Oxford: Blackwell.

Travis, W.R. (2007) *New Geographies of the American West*, Washington, D.C.: Island Press.

Waterton, E. (2013) 'Landscape and non-representational theories', in Howard, P., Thompson, I., Atha, W. E. and M. (eds) *The Routledge Companion to Landscape Studies*, London: Routledge, pp. 66–75.

Winchester, H., Kong, L. and Dunn, K. (2013) *Landscapes: Ways of Imagining the World*, London: Routledge.

Wylie, J. (2003) 'Landscape, performance and dwelling: a Glastonbury case study', in Cloke, P. (ed) *Country Visions*, Harlow: Prentice Hall, pp. 136–157.

Wylie, J. (2005) 'A single day's walking: narrating self and landscape on the South West Coast Path', *Transactions of the Institute of British Geographers*, 30(2), 234–247.

Wylie, J. (2007) *Landscape*, London: Routledge.

Wylie, J. (2008) 'Depths and folds: on landscape and the gazing subject', *Environment and Planning D: Society and Space*, 24(4), 519–535.

Wyly, E. and Hammel, D. (2005) 'Mapping neo-liberal American urbanism', in Atkinson, R. and Bridge, G. (eds) *Gentrification in a Global Context: The New Urban Colonialism*, London: Routledge, pp. 18–38.

Ye, M., Vojnovic, I. and Chen, G. (2015) 'The landscape of gentrification: exploring the diversity of "upgrading" processes in Hong Kong, 1986–2006', *Urban Geography*, 36(4), 471–503.

Zukin, S. (1982a) 'Loft living as "historic compromise" in the urban core: the New York experience', *International Journal of Urban and Regional Research*, 6(2), 256–267.

Zukin, S. (1982b) *Loft Living: Culture and Capital in Urban Change*, Baltimore: John Hopkins University Press.

Zukin, S. (1990) 'Socio-spatial prototypes of a new organization of consumption: the role of real cultural capital', *Sociology*, 24(1), 37–56.

Zukin, S. (1991) *Landscapes of Power: From Detroit to Disney World*, Berkeley: University of California Press.

7. Spatial capital and planetary gentrification: residential location, mobility and social inequalities

Patrick Rérat

7.1 INTRODUCTION

Gentrification in its various forms is about place and more precisely place competition or place appropriation between classes. In this chapter I argue that the choice of a place of residence is a strategic decision that enables individuals or households to gain locational advantages that are crucial in negotiating and mastering the spatial aspects of everyday life. The term 'spatial capital' (see Rérat and Lees 2011; Rérat 2016) has been used to conceptualize these locational advantages, revealing them to be an additional form of class-led appropriation of urban resources.

The conceptualization of spatial capital allows for the opportunity to re-read gentrification through the lens of mobility. Mobility is at the core of multiple transformations of contemporary societies and of 'an intense phase of time-space compression that (has) had a disorienting and disruptive impact upon political-economic practices, the balance of class power, as well as cultural and social life' (Harvey 1989: 284). This increase in mobility pertains to all aspects of society playing out as a spatial rupture of the places of everyday life, flexibility as a requirement on the job market, the multiplication of ways of moving and their increase in speed, etc. (see Urry 2007).

In this chapter I read the gentrification studies literature using spatial capital as a guiding thread. I develop the concept of spatial capital by broadening the lens of analysis to the planetary scale (Lees, Shin, and López Morales 2016) referring to studies in a wide range of spatial, social, economic and institutional contexts. After a discussion of the concept of spatial capital, I present more precisely how residential location and mobility are involved in gentrification processes. I address spatial capital (1) as an element of social differentiation, and (2) as a source of inequality.

7.2 SPATIAL CAPITAL AS A THEORETICAL TOOL

The notion of spatial capital as used here is mainly drawn from two authors: Jacques Lévy, a French geographer, who coined the term spatial capital in the 1990s, and Vincent Kaufmann, a Swiss sociologist, who developed the notion of motility.[1]

---

[1]   Other scholars propose terms such as network capital (Urry 2007) or mobility capital (Murphy-Lejeune 2002) to show how the use of space may be an asset.

7.2.1   Spatial Capital

Lévy defines spatial capital as the set of resources, accumulated by an actor, enabling her/him to engage with place and space, to profit, in accordance with her/his strategies, by the use of the spatial dimension of society (Lévy 2013: 147). The term capital refers to the work by Pierre Bourdieu. For him, individuals were not defined by social class but by the differing amounts of capital they possessed and their position in social space, which was made up of these different types of capital (Bourdieu 1984). He defined economic capital as financial assets and monetary income; cultural capital as an embodied disposition that reflects the habitus, it has two kinds – that incorporated through education and knowledge and the symbolic kind that demonstrates moral and aesthetic values; and social capital as that which is mobilized through social networks and relations. These different forms of capital are played out in the 'field', a kind of social arena in which Bourdieu recognizes the centrality of social relations to social analysis. Within a field the possession of capitals and the ability to deploy them allow an individual to gain social advantages.

Spatial capital is made up of the advantages brought by control over a series of geographic layouts in which scale is a determinant element (Lévy 2014: 48). It refers not only – or less – to the possibility of greater speed wrought by innovation in transport technologies (that enables travel across vast spaces) but more generally to the capacity to access quickly a certain type or a certain quantity of people or places (ibid.). Cities are spaces of multiple speeds and a high spatial capital means the utmost appropriation and articulation of the various scales and metrics (including the possibility to make use of pedestrian metrics).

Lévy (1994) distinguishes two components of spatial capital: position capital and situation capital. Position capital is related to a place and its spatial assets. It shows, notably, the importance of residential location in an urban region where space can be assimilated as a rare good and is an object of competition. Situation capital is related to an area, to a space appropriated by an individual through all kinds of mobility without abolishing distances but by mastering them. Mobility is one way to mitigate or compensate for a shortfall of position capital.

7.2.2   Motility

Kaufmann for his part stressed the necessity of addressing the phenomenon of mobility beyond the actual practices of individuals and of taking into account their potential mobility (Kaufmann 2002). He developed the notion of motility and defined it as the way an individual or a group takes possession and utilizes the field of possibilities with regards to movement relative to his/her personal aspirations and projects. It encompasses three interdependent elements: access, competence and appropriation (Kaufmann, Bergman, and Joye 2004; Flamm and Kaufmann 2006).

First, access is related to the 'range of possible mobilities according to place, time and other contextual constraints, and may be constrained by options and conditions. The options refer to the entire range of means of transportation and communication available and the entire range of services and equipment accessible at a given time. The conditions refer to the accessibility of the options in terms of location-specific cost, logistics and other constraints' (Kaufmann, Bergman, and Joye 2004: 750). This 'personal access rights portfolio' (Flamm and Kaufmann 2006) is closely linked to the place where an individual lives. The availability of means of transport and communication makes some places more desirable than others within an urban region and more likely to be appropriated by a dominant class. Second, competence refers to the skills and abilities of individuals that are necessary to make use of the supply of means of transport and communication. Skills are multifaceted and can be physical (e.g. the ability to cycle), acquired (e.g. a driving licence) or organizational (e.g. the ability to plan and synchronize activities). Finally, appropriation refers to the strategies, motivations, values and practices of individuals. It includes the way individuals interpret and act upon access and competences (be they perceived or real) and how they use their potential mobilities.

A second notion goes hand in hand with motility: the territory's hosting potential. For Kaufmann (2011), every territory has a specific ability to accommodate the projects of individuals. It is made up of factors such as the available networks (roads, trains, airports, etc.) and their levels of performance, as well as the spatial structure both in terms of morphology and functions (density, size, labour market, diversity of services, etc.). Every action assumes that the environment offers opportunities for realizing that project (Gibson 2014).[2] Consequently not all projects can be hosted anywhere: some areas are more able to cope with some projects, given their morphological characteristics, the laws that govern them, their accessibility, etc. (ibid.). The concept of (institutional) viscosity goes in the same direction; it was coined to balance the more agentive concept of motility with a theoretical account of structural conditions and to capture the variable degrees of resistance or facilitation offered by a structural context (Doherty 2015). It can 'analytically distinguish settings and systems that enable and support mobility (low viscosity) from those that make it difficult or impossible (high viscosity), and express relational degrees between them (being more or less viscous)' (ibid. 254).

7.2.3 Mobility as Capital

Several arguments for considering mobility as a capital have been put forward (for a more thorough discussion, notably with Bourdieu's work, see Lévy 1994, 2000; Kaufmann, Bergman, and Joye 2004; Kaufmann et al. 2015).

First, as for other forms of capital, an unequal level of spatial capital endowment characterizes different members of a society, reflecting the different degree of use, and mastery of, the spatial aspects of everyday life. In this sense, spatial capital is a factor in social differentiation. Individuals are not only endowed with varying degrees of mobility capital but also in different ways: 'unlike cultural, social or economic assets, which refer to hierarchical position, motility refers to both the vertical and horizontal dimensions of social position, thus highlighting not only new forms of social inequality but also making it possible for us to distinguish between different lifestyles based on an individual's relationship to time and space' (Kaufmann 2011: 40).[3]

Second, spatial capital can be accumulated and used for other social goods, it may

---

[2] Material artefacts are of utmost importance in a territory's potential. For example, the ability to live without a car, thanks to excellent public transport, helps to make such a way of life desirable and worth adopting (Kaufmann 2011).
[3] The same statement was made on spatial capital (Lévy 2000: 157).

be transformed into travel and it may be exchanged with other forms of capital. For example, a person could pay more money for their dwelling in order to benefit from what is perceived to be a more favourable location (locational advantage).

Third, spatial capital is not simply determined by the other forms of capital.[4] It depends on access, competence and appropriation that depend in turn on several variables such as residential location (availability of public transport, etc.), purchasing power (that enables the use of different means of transport, etc.), age (driving licence, etc.), awareness of environmental issues (in the choice to own a car, for example), mobility or migration experience, cognitive attitudes, and so on.

On the basis of the discussion of the theoretical framework of spatial capital the rest of the chapter analyzes how residential location and mobility are at play in gentrification.

7.3   SPATIAL CAPITAL AS AN ELEMENT OF SOCIAL DIFFERENTIATION

7.3.1   Spatial Capital and Gentrifiers' Residential Aspirations

A part of the gentrification literature has focused on gentrifiers' housing choices. It has explored the residential motivations to live in a central area expressed by some part of the middle to upper classes in a situation where suburbanization has been dominant in Euro-American contexts. Authors have asked what makes gentrifiers ('urban seeking middle class') different from suburbanites ('urban fleeing') (Butler 1997)?[5]

The literature that has investigated why the central city became attractive for the 'new' middle classes has identified two logics or sets of motivations. The first one, the valorization or distinction logic, is based on the urban way of life and on symbolic aspects such as conspicuous consumption, aesthetic values, and the rejection of suburbia as mass-produced, standardized, and socially undifferentiated (e.g. Caulfield 1994; Ley 1996). In terms of Bourdieu's conceptual frame, these aspects could be gathered under the concept of cultural capital. Less present in the literature are the second range of motivations, practical and utilitarian logics, stressing the convenience of urban life and questions of proximity and accessibility.

In three case studies of new-build gentrification in Switzerland (Rérat and Lees 2011; Rérat 2012, 2016) it was found that households moving to new central districts place location, proximity and mobility issues at the forefront of their motivations. The move allows them to acquire a specific spatial capital based on locational advantages and to capture advantages in both proximity and mobility. Living in a central area gives them an easy access to walking, cycling and urban public transport but also to the train system and its intercity connections.[6] The importance of these factors in the residential choices

---

[4]   Critiques have, however, been raised on whether Bourdieu's work lacks a sufficient spatial dimension and whether spatial capital is an independent capital (see for example Lévy 2014; Kaufmann et al. 2015; Mace 2015).

[5]   As discussed later, the distinction between suburbanization and gentrification is more and more blurred in many spatial contexts.

[6]   Although the car is far from being absent, its role is reduced notably in comparison with those who reside in the suburbs.

of these new-build gentrifiers indicates both the particular importance of spatial capital and their significant personal knowledge of the spatial capital of their chosen residential area. Their mobility patterns and practices show that they are both potentially hyper-mobile (they have accrued enough spatial capital to be very mobile, to use several means of transportation according to their needs) and hyper-fixed (they have strategically chosen particular fixed central city locations where they are locally rooted). They are 'mobile and rooted' and they move into dwellings, which they see as fixed points around which they organize their lifestyles.

Results on the importance of centrality, proximity and mobility have been found in several other contexts. The rediscovery of a place can generate a variety of spatial practices, such as in the Netherlands in reclaiming the streets as a living space by upper middle-class families (Karsten 2008). In London, Middleton (2008) found that walking played a key role in maintaining existing social relations and that walking made negotiating work, childcare and family life easier for gentrifiers. Hamnett and Whitelegg (2007) found that one-third of the gentrifiers they surveyed in Clerkenwell, London, said that their main residential motivation was the fact they could walk to their workplace. In Canadian cities, gentrifiers are characterized by a higher propensity to walk and to cycle to their workplace (Danyluk and Ley 2007; Barbonne 2008) and their everyday life rests upon proximity that is in opposition to life in the suburbs. Research in Norway underlines the attractiveness of central locations in reducing commuting distances and the need to use a car, as well as easier access to public services (Hjorthol and Bjornskau 2005).

Gentrification scholars have put forward several factors to interpret the importance of both mooring/fixity and mobility among the middle to upper classes. A first interpretation refers to the expression of left-liberal political values and of environmental beliefs (Danyluk and Ley 2007), and of the rejection of a suburban way of life (Caulfield 1994), and of the fact that gentrifiers valorize 'liberation from motor transportation' (Hjorthol and Bjornskau 2005: 353). These 'critical social practices'[7] (Caulfield 1994) or counter-cultural values go against the automobile-dependent suburbs and the hegemony of automobility (Urry 2004).[8] Such attitudes are even commodified by real estate developers as in the case of cycling in San Francisco (Stehlin 2015).

A more frequent interpretation – and non-exclusive – is that central locations help new middle-class households to combine work, social and family life. Such trends can be put in parallel with the increasing participation of women in the labour market (Bondi 1991) and the resulting growth in dual-career households or in relation to young urban parents (Karsten 2003). By contrast the suburbs are characterized as intrinsically patriarchal (Fishman 1987) with the time-space rhythms of separate spheres of work and daily life (Rose 1984) and automobile dependence (Newman and Kenworthy 1999). In the research on Swiss cities mentioned above, to live in a central area and to be able to reach other urban centres easily through rail connections is also a way to gain access and competence, and not always to be actually mobile but also as an insurance to be able to reach other labour markets (especially for young professionals at an early stage of their careers and in

---

[7]   Critical social practices are efforts made by people to resist institutionalized patterns of dominance and create new conditions for their social activities (Caulfield 1994: xiii).

[8]   They have, however, been predominantly observed in specific locations, such as the central areas of Western metropolises or in countries with a comparatively high modal share of alternatives to the car.

a context were work life is more fluid) (Rérat and Lees 2011). We find in these interpretations the idea of 'coping strategies' as identified by Butler and Robson (2003). By increasing their spatial capital these households reinforce their upper middle-class position and the interlinked patterns of mobility and fixity secure socio-spatial advantages.

The role and importance of proximity and mobility is however multifaceted. The mastery of spatial dimensions may imply strategies of selective social inclusion of the upper middle classes in the urban fabric. Andreotti et al. (2013) find, for example, that the upper middle classes in Milan, Madrid and Paris anchor themselves in their districts through the use of local infrastructures (leisure, consumption, etc.), and develop complex strategies of proximity and distancing with regard to other social groups. They therefore opt for 'partial exit' strategies, selecting the dimensions that they are willing to share with other social groups (especially in terms of their involvement in local community life). This ability to play with the double logic of participation/integration and disengagement/withdrawal (Hirschman 2004) constitutes another expression of spatial capital and shows the complex game of distance and proximity and its various meanings for gentrifiers.

This game is exemplified by the quality of schools which is of utmost importance for the middle to upper classes if their aspirations are to be realized or relative privileges maintained (Butler and Hamnett 2010). For Tonkiss (2013: 82):

> 'urban-seeking' gentrifiers who choose attractive locational positions in inner city neighbourhoods may prove to be 'urban-fleeing' when it comes to educational choices for their children. This means negotiating fixity and mobility in terms either of household relocations to the most desirable local catchments [. . .] or of daily out-migrations to more desirable schools [. . .].

Such households show a control over urban space where the ability to chose a neighbourhood as a place of residence (position capital) and/or the competence for mobility (situation capital) can be regarded as a resource in its own right (Barthon and Monfroy 2010).

These studies show that spatial capital is an element of social differentiation among the middle to upper classes. It helps to understand the diversity of residential choices among the middle to upper classes and the renewed attractiveness of central areas as a place of residence for parts of them. It highlights as well the importance of location and mobility in (enabling) certain lifestyles and the fact that central areas are not only places of urbanity, diversity, excitement, but also strategic locations. In that sense, these results runs counter to several ideas, such as the hypothesis that transport and communication are annihilating the benefits of concentration (as advanced by the literature on urban decline) or that gentrification is becoming somewhat irrelevant in a context of generalized suburbanization (Keil 2013).

7.3.2   Spatial Capital and Gentrification: Moving Beyond Critical Social Practices

There is a clear need to extend the scope of such studies beyond European and North-American contexts and to investigate further gentrifiers' spatial capital endowment as well as the uses and meanings of the duo mobility-fixity. This is even more relevant given two features of contemporary gentrification: the increasing diversity of gentrifiers and the increasing recognition of new geographies of gentrification both in terms of spaces and countries.

Gentrifiers' characteristics differ according to the form, the context, and the wave of gentrification. For Lees et al. (2016: 108), 'gentrifiers globally are [now] a much more diverse entity in terms of income (some are very rich, some lower-middle class), politics (some are liberal, some are conservative even authoritarian), and lifestyles (some are highly consumer-orientated, other much less so)'. Among them one group is of particular interest given the scope of this chapter: the highly mobile transnational class. Donzelot (2004) argues that gentrifiers are characterized by a certain degree of ubiquity. He asserts that they valorize proximity and its advantages, but as members of a global elite also want to be elsewhere on the globe quickly and easily through either real or virtual networks. This is the case of, for example, super-gentrifiers in London, for whom both local face-to-face communication and global presence were important (Butler and Lees 2006).

This echoes several empirical observations on transnational gentrification such as in Panama where redevelopment capital is local but the demand does not come from a single city-region but is transnational (Sigler and Wachsmuth 2016). Another compelling example of the tension between 'global wealth migration and local affordability' (Stiem 2016) is Vancouver. The globalization of the city's real estate market – due to the flood of foreign capital, mainly from China – has significantly driven the rise of housing prices. Housing prices have decoupled from the regional labour market, putting people employed locally at a major disadvantage.[9] 'Millionaire migrants' continue their professional activities and to build their fortune in China while their families settle in Vancouver (for various reasons such as the quality of life, children's education, geopolitical issues, etc.) (Ley 2010: 77). These 'astronaut families' display a specific and high spatial capital endowment that enables a way of life spread on two continents, that mitigates the effects of distance, and that is notably based on airline connections. Such a spatial capital greatly varies from the quest for proximity and the critical social practices discussed above.

Another point is the call made by several authors for a broader 'geography of gentrification' in order to take into account the contextuality of the phenomenon (Lees 2000). Two elements seem particularly relevant here: the spaces of gentrification in the global North and the specificities of cities/contexts in the global South. Regarding spaces of gentrification in the global North, the literature has extended the definition of 'gentrification' to encompass other spaces such as rural gentrification (Smith and Phillips 2001). At the same time, the distinction between gentrification and suburbanization has become less salient. For Lees et al. (2016: 211), 'planetary gentrification is not a reaction against suburbanization: indeed the two processes are increasingly blurred, as they are in the global North now too'. Case studies in New York and London, for example, have highlighted the suburban mindsets of super-gentrifiers (Lees 2003; Butler and Lees 2006). Less is known on the specific spatial capital of the households involved in forms and spaces other than in classic inner-city gentrification.

In the global South, greater attention is needed to gentrification processes where gentrifiers' spatial capital and housing choices are likely to differ from those observed in European and North-American case studies. A first difference is the definition of

---

[9]   Beyond the case of Vancouver, similar trends can also be observed in many contexts where tourism or second-homes act as drivers of gentrification. The same phenomenon happens for example in London where an inflated property market has been blamed on overseas investors such as Middle-Eastern oil wealth or Russian elites/oligarchs (Lees et al. 2016: 110).

the 'new' middle class,[10] its origin, its lifestyles, etc. In the global South, 'the term "new" middle class [. . .] refers to a newly emerging or expanding, modernizing middle class with new spending power and associated interest in consumerism' (Lees, Shin, and López Morales 2016: 83). These gentrifiers are not the same as the classic gentrifiers in the Euro-American context. When considering gentrification in the global South, 'the Western, consumption thesis and the idea of gentrification as a counter-cultural idea posited against the modern suburbs has no traction' (ibid. 96). By the same token 'with no experience of the post-war hegemony of suburban life, gentrifiers outside of Western cities will undoubtedly have different mindsets' (ibid.). Even though some authors show similarities with what has been observed in the North (see for example, Contreras Gatica 2011, on gentrification in Santiago de Chile), others underline the importance of economic capital and peoples' desire to accumulate wealth by investing in real estate properties as in the case of Hong Kong (Ley and Teo 2014) or Chinese cities (Ren 2008). In some cities, gentrification is also closely related to gated communities (Alvarez-Rivadulla 2007), which in the words of Hirschmann (2004) means a clear exit from parts of the city. This elite withdrawal can also be termed as 'separatism' or 'secession', it takes various built forms (from secured buildings to fortified enclaves), and is motivated by security concerns and by the 'discourse of urban fear' (Low 2001).

Spatial capital appears to be useful in analysing how privileged groups employ urban spaces, in combination with mobility, in ways which produce inequitable opportunities. More in-depth work on gentrifiers' motivations, spatial capital and lifestyles is crucially needed, all the more so in Southern cites which generally differ from their Northern counterparts in terms of urban form, population size, demographic dynamics, inequalities among classes, service and infrastructure provision, modal shares and state direction.

7.4   SPATIAL CAPITAL AS A SOURCE OF INEQUALITY

7.4.1   Spatial Capital and Evicted Populations

For gentrifiers the creation of spatial capital may be the result of strategies and residential choices. Gentrification may also lead to a contraction or destruction of spatial capital among the evicted populations, generating an additional source of inequality (Rérat and Lees 2011).

The eviction of lower income groups is a multifaceted process (Atkinson 2000; Davidson and Lees 2005; Davidson 2008). The most obvious form of eviction is direct displacement. Other forms include indirect economic displacement ('price shadowing'; inflation in land and property values in surrounding areas), community displacement (changes in neighbourhood governance and place identity), and neighbourhood resource displacement (transformation in the orientation of neighbourhood services and an increasing 'out-of-placeness'). Displacement goes beyond physical displacement and involves phenomenological displacement and loss of sense of place (Davidson 2008).

---

[10]   It has to be noted that important differences exist as well within the Global North. The term 'middle class' does not have the same meaning in English and in French for example (the English 'middle class' would be the middle to upper/high class in a French-speaking context).

In addition to the loss of their neighbourhood (and therefore of social capital) through gentrification, displacement can also result in a reduction of spatial capital. Few studies have directly addressed this issue despite its importance. Two studies in Shanghai for example showed that the dislocation of displacees from urban amenities and services is socially unjust and problematic. Evicted residents interviewed by Ren (2008: 39) summed up well the impact of displacement on spatial capital and on the access to services ('I don't want to live in the suburbs. There are no hospitals. It takes hours to get to the city and see a doctor by bus') and to job opportunities ('I can still make a living here in the city centre [. . .]. What can I do in the suburbs?'). Similarly, He (2010) shows that the residents evicted to the fringes of Shanghai were unable to commute from their new place of residence. With their displacement came the destruction of some important parts of their spatial capital. Their previous location was a guarantee to have access to many nearby amenities and work opportunities. The new peripheral location made them dependent on other forms of transportation that might be too expensive and not practical or quick enough.

These results raise the question of the importance of access and mobility. As said by Brand and Dávila (2011: 649), 'limited mobility constrains participation in urban life in general, and opportunities to expand work horizons, social and leisure activities, political and civic engagement. Lack of mobility turns geographical marginalisation into deeper social exclusion'. Peripheral locations may deepen the spatial mismatch between affordable neighbourhoods and available job opportunities. It limits people's ability to travel by foot and the high costs of public transport restrict people's movement to the strictly essential, as Ureta (2008) analyzed in Santiago, Chile.

More generally, as Lees et al. (2016: 76) argue, 'what the concept of spatial capital can inform us of is an understanding of what differentiates the gentrifiers from the gentrified is not only their economic power to purchase, assemble and/or speculate with land and properties, but also, crucially, their class differentiated material and immaterial accumulation of access to a wider range of spatial capital'. The displacement of low-income groups may involve a more difficult access to urban amenities and job opportunities. The new residential location may require a higher economic capital (e.g. the purchase of a car or of public transport tickets) or new skills (e.g. driving licence) and it may be characterized by a lower territory's hosting potential.[11] More studies are needed on displacement and on the ways displaced populations (have to) cope with the loss of spatial capital (strategies, tactics of resistance, adaptation, etc.).

7.4.2   Spatial Capital as an Uneven Impact of Transport Infrastructures

A further dimension of spatial capital in the gentrification literature is the uneven impacts of new transport infrastructures on spatial capital endowment among classes. As stated by Revington (2015: 1), 'relatively little work has considered how transportation systems may impact social equity through land use changes, particularly gentrification'. Public transit is widely thought of as a means of promoting social equity and it can make a real difference to isolated or deprived neighbourhoods. But 'if neighbourhoods receiving new

---

[11]   It could be said that such a move is for the middle-class suburbanites more a choice of lifestyle and residential aspirations. It also involves mobility practices that they need to master or be ready to adopt.

transit infrastructures gentrify, social equity will be undermined on two fronts: as existing residents endure housing affordability problems or are displaced, and as the mobility benefits of the new infrastructures fail to reach those it displaces' (ibid.).

The gentrification literature raises more generally the question of who benefits and who does not from transportation policies and infrastructures, or, to use the concept that frames this chapter, who is able to benefit from the generation of spatial capital. Indeed transport-oriented policies transform spatial opportunities in the city and they may (explicitly or not) be aimed at upper-income social groups (Blanco, Bosoer, and Apaolaza 2014). In other words, policy-led changes in transport access may allow one class to increase their chances of taking over a certain territory while the other class loses access to it (Lees, Shin, and López Morales 2016: 76).

The construction of transport infrastructures may be the catalyst for spatial restructuring and lead to the displacement of lower income groups (as discussed earlier in terms of general displacement whatever its cause, be it residential, commercial or infrastructural development). An obvious form of development-led displacement is direct displacement, which refers to the eviction of a population to build a transport infrastructure. In Brussels, for example, the extension of a station for high-speed trains, which was part of the Brussels International Development Plan, was a type of adaptation of urban spaces for globalization and led to the de-structuration of a popular neighbourhood (Van Criekingen 2008).

New infrastructures generate not only direct but also indirect displacement. Public transportation projects, the increased level of accessibility and planning policies may enlarge rent gaps, valorize the land surrounding the infrastructure, lead to skyrocketing property values, and increase displacement pressures. They may create locational advantages that attract gentrifiers and provide them with practical and convenient access to mobility options and eventually to urban amenities and services.

Such impacts echo a characteristic of gentrification in the global South: 'its widespread occurrence after the creation of new centralities in previously undervalued urban areas, but whose location has become strategic [. . .] for higher-status office or residential revitalization, or service provision' (Lees, Shin, and López Morales 2016: 75), which results in the 'neo-Haussmannization [. . .] that has peripheralized millions of people everywhere' (Lees, Shin, and López-Morales 2015: 443). In Santiago de Chile for example, the metro enlarged rent gaps and enabled new social classes to capture spatial capital (López-Morales 2010). Investments in transport infrastructures have also been reported to go along with the formalization of settlements or slums. In Mexico City, huge investments in transportation facilities were followed by the rezoning of vast areas that displaced low-income tenants and petty landowners from already formalized, yet highly underserviced, land, where they had lived for more than 30 years (Delgadillo 2016). In Manila, a metropolitan rail project led to the removal of informal settlements and the formalization of the land use, thereby opening the door to formal development (Choi 2016); while in Rio de Janeiro the whole redevelopment process in the city is underpinned by transport-oriented public investment penetrating the most emblematic favelas (Cummings 2015).

Another form of displacement (through housing price increase) may happen after the closing down of a transport infrastructure, the physical 'beautification' of areas and the creation of new urban amenities. In Seoul, the Cheonggye Stream had been buried to make room for an urban elevated highway in accordance with modernist planning principles. Its restoration in the 2000s induced an increase in land values in surrounding areas and 'accelerated land use change as land owners [sought] to maximize profits by attracting more affluent users who value[d] the newly created urban open space' (Lim et al. 2013: 199).[12] In Zurich, the Weststrasse ('West Street') was used as a transit route by a huge number of trucks between two highways and crossed a residential neighbourhood. The noise, pollution, filth and dangers caused by the motorized traffic meant very low rents that attracted a working-class population.[13] The construction of a new highway released the traffic from Weststrasse and investment was targeted at the improvement of public space. Houses were soon refurbished and rents increased triggering a quick turnaround of residents as documented by a eight-year photography report (Flühmann 2015). This raises a more global issue of whether liveability is a transformative use-value akin to the 'right to the city' (Lefebvre, Kofman and Lebas 1996) or an 'amenity that adds to exchange-value in space' (Stehlin 2015: 133).

In the examples discussed above, the mechanism of gentrification refers to the access dimension of spatial capital. There is a competition for space and for a location that enables the use of certain transportation means (but without suffering from the nuisances of transportation itself). In market economies this competition is expressed in land and housing prices and leads to the direct or indirect eviction of households with low economic capital to a location, in all likelihood, with a lower level of access (and with a lower hosting potential/higher viscosity).

Other mechanisms can be identified with respect to the uneven impact of transport infrastructures. In several US cities, protests have targeted corporate shuttles, such as in San Francisco with Google Buses. This figure of speech designs the luxury bus networks that are privately chartered and that transport 35,000 employees of the technological companies from San Francisco to Silicon Valley. Although being private these 'tech shuttles' use public bus stops to pick up tech employees 'using public money for private gains' and they even cause the deterioration of the public transit service (McCleave Maharawal 2014). This example shows – to use Doherty's metaphor (2015) – a differentiated impact on viscosity of urban space (higher for public transit users, lower for tech employees). It is also another dimension of the uneven endowment of spatial capital in the same territory due to the exclusion from (or denial of access to) a private service in a context of low public transit supply.

The uneven impact of transport infrastructure does not only rely on economic capital, location and access but also on the other dimensions of spatial capital. Brand and Dávil (2011) analyzed the *Metrocable* (aerial cable-car system) that was built in dense and hilly low-income informal settlements in Medellín, Colombia. The access factor is not really important (its cost was quite low even in comparison with alternatives such as buses) but appropriation was crucial. The *Metrocable* provides an infrastructural articulation of formal urban life and the main group of users is comprised of formal sector workers with long journey to work patterns. For social groups outside formal networks or whose

---

[12] A similar process was observed in New York where a decaying railroad viaduct was redeveloped into a celebrated public park: the High Line (Loughran 2014).

[13] While the construction of transport infrastructures or improvements may lead to gentrification, existing infrastructure may also produce nuisances, lower the quality of life and raise important issues in terms of environmental vulnerability and social justice.

everyday routines are circumscribed within the locality, the level of appropriation is much lower.

Another example is provided by the links between bicycle infrastructures and gentrification with a literature mainly based in the United States where the modal share of bikes in commuting trips (0.6%) is very low by international standards (Pucher and Buehler 2012; McKenzie 2014). In American cities such as San Francisco, cycling and bike schemes have become seen as forerunners of gentrification or synonymous with well-off white men. It is interesting to read this debate through the lens of spatial capital/motility. Access or skills do not seem to be the most important issue. US census data (McKenzie 2014) actually shows that bike use is negatively correlated with income (e.g. low-income commuters are the most likely to bike, which puts things into perspective on a national scale). The access to bike infrastructure is free to use and bikes are not expensive in comparison with other modes of transportation (except walking). The differences are mainly to be found in appropriation and the territory's hosting potential.

In terms of appropriation, cars and bikes convey different values, particularly among generations and social classes that may promote/hinder some mobility practices. The car has long been – and still is, at least partly – regarded as an important symbol of success and social status (Urry 2004), while bikes have long been the vehicle of the working classes for most of the 20th century.[14] Cycling nowadays has various meanings and images. A car-free identity may be countercultural and an embodied critique of decades of sprawl and car dependence (Horton 2006). It can also be seen as a practice of another race or class (either the elite who are able to chose to live more localized patterns of mobility; or the poorest who do not have a choice), as the calling into question of a social status symbol, as a threat to a way of life and as the start of neighbourhood change.

In terms of territorial hosting potential (cyclability or bikeability as it happens), bike infrastructures point to much deeper inequalities in American cities. For Stehlin (2015: 124), 'the real gains in bicycle space in select areas of core cities must be seen in the context of a vast, intensely car-dependent region in which the *possibility* of replacing the car trips by bicycle or mass transit is supremely uneven in distribution'. Urban structure and the degree of suburbanization of jobs, population and classes are indeed of utmost importance. Bike infrastructures are associated with unequal public resources, privilege and change (most of all when bike lanes appear when new people move in) but also with the symbolic appropriation of local space.

Spatial capital can be used to analyze the links between transport infrastructures and gentrification either through development-led displacement (direct or indirect), the way agencies plan infrastructures and their uneven impacts. This analytical framework highlights the various dimensions where inequalities may be at work. More research could be done to evaluate the impacts of transport infrastructures on housing prices and on the populations living in the adjacent areas (in terms of mobility practices, participation in the labour market, etc.). Moreover the research identified in this chapter deals mainly with transit, cycling and walking as sources of inequality. The dominant or hegemonic system of automobility and the many impacts of automobile dependence (in terms of social inequalities, externalities, environmental justice, household budget, etc.) (Newman and

---

[14]   When it was invented in the 19th century, the bicycle was first for the leisure of the *bourgeoisie*.

Kenworthy 1999; Urry 2004; Dennis and Urry 2009) have all but disappeared in Euro-America and should receive more attention.

7.5   CONCLUSION

Gentrification is a multi-faceted phenomenon. As it involves a form of class-led appropriation of urban resources, I argue that spatial capital can be a useful tool to analyze some of its mechanisms and impacts. Spatial capital refers to mastery or command over space, the ability to make profit from the spatial dimension of society, to make spatial choices in terms of both fixed location and mobilities, to organize one's life according to aspirations and constraints (Lévy 2014). This has also been expressed with the notion of motility which highlights three dimensions related to individuals: access (range of possible mobilities according to place and time), competence (physical, acquired, organizational) and appropriation (strategies, motivations, values) (Kaufmann, Bergman, and Joye 2004). The notion of a territory's hosting potential (Kaufmann 2011) or (institutional) viscosity (Doherty 2015) take into account more structural elements. Class inequalities may turn on access, competence, appropriation of (new) mobilities and urban space itself, which can be an object of political struggle.

In this chapter, this analytical grid has been applied to gentrification to highlight how spatial capital is an element of social differentiation. It contributes to explaining why central areas in the global North have become attractive for the 'new' middle class. Gentrifiers with a strategic move acquire a specific capital and are able to capture the advantages of both proximity/mooring and mobility (Rérat and Lees 2011). Their mastery of space, and their management of proximity and mobility, represent a complex strategy of participation/integration and disengagement/withdrawal with regard to other social groups (Andreotti, Le Galès, and Javier Moreno Fuentes 2013). However, gentrifiers have become a much more diverse entity and gentrification has taken place in other spatial contexts than just the inner cities of the global North (Lees, Shin, and López-Morales 2015). Further analysis of gentrification using the lens of spatial capital across a wider range of forms, spaces and countries is needed.

The chapter has also discussed spatial capital as a source of inequality. Gentrification may lead to a contraction of spatial capital among the evicted population, to loss of the resources enabling them to use the spatial dimension of society (e.g. access to job opportunities, services, urban amenities, etc.). An additional dimension is the uneven impacts of new transport infrastructures among classes (e.g. direct or indirect displacement, denied access to transport due to the price level, lack of skills or appropriation, etc.). Here again studies are needed on the ways displaced populations cope with the loss of their spatial capital, the strategies or tactics of resistance they adopt, and the mechanisms behind the uneven impacts of transport infrastructures.

The issues raised in this chapter are crucial in the debates on urban planning in a context characterized by the domination of the market, the withdrawal of the state and a higher than ever demand for well-positioned urban space. Gentrification raises the question of social justice in urban development, of the right to the city that implies equal access to housing, land, social rights and urban amenities, and commodities. Moreover, mobility practices are not only at the core of the functioning of societies but will be facing fundamental changes (Dennis and Urry 2009): global warming and oil depletion will require the transition to a low-carbon mobility and the diffusion of the autonomous car will have a disruptive and uneven impact on the way mobility is organized and practised in cities. The concept of spatial capital could be used as an analytical grid but also as a tool for planning practice (Mace 2015). By deconstructing the mechanisms behind the uneven use of the spatial dimensions of society, it could help to analyze how households are/are not able to exploit proximity and to use transportation supply. It could also help to evaluate the impact of transport infrastructures with respect to the needs of the various population groups in order to find ways to envision an urban development capable of integrating spatial justice.

REFERENCES

Alvarez-Rivadulla, M.J. (2007) 'Golden ghettos: gated communities and class residential segregation in Montevideo, Uruguay', *Environment and Planning A*, 39(1), 47–63.

Andreotti, A., Le Galès, P. and Javier Moreno Fuentes, F. (2013) 'Controlling the urban fabric: the complex game of distance and proximity in European upper-middle class residential strategies', *International Journal of Urban and Regional Research*, 37(2), 576–597.

Ascher, F. (1995) *Métapolis ou l'avenir des villes*, Paris: Odile Jacob.

Atkinson, R. (2000) 'Measuring gentrification and displacement in Greater London', *Urban Studies*, 37(1), 149–165.

Barbonne, R. (2008) 'Gentrification, nouvel urbanisme et évolution de la mobilité quotidienne: vers un développement plus durable ? Le cas du Plateau Mont-Royal (1998–2003)', *Recherches sociographiques*, 49(3), 423.

Barthon, C. and Monfroy, B. (2010) 'Sociospatial schooling practices: a spatial capital approach', *Educational Research and Evaluation*, 16(2), 177–196.

Blanco, J., Bosoer, L. and Apaolaza, R. (2014) 'Gentrificación, movilidad y transporte: aproximaciones conceptuales y ejes de indagación', *Revista de geografía Norte Grande*, 58, 41–53.

Bondi, L. (1991) 'Gender divisions and gentrification: a critique', *Transactions of the Institute of British Geographers*, 16(2), 190–198.

Bourdieu, P. (1984) *Distinction: A Social Critique of the Judgement of Taste*, Cambridge, MA: Harvard University Press.

Brand, P., and Dávila, J. (2011) 'Mobility innovation at the urban margins: Medellín's metrocables', *City*, 15(6), 647–661.

Butler, T. (1997) *Gentrification and the Middle Classes*, Aldershot: Ashgate.

Butler, T. and Hamnett, C. (2010) '"You take what you are given": the limits to parental choice in education in east London', *Environment and Planning A*, 42(10), 2431–2450.

Butler, T. and Lees, L. (2006) 'Super-gentrification in Barnsbury, London: globalisation and gentrifying global elites at the neighbourhood level', *Transactions of the Institute of British Geographers*, 31, 467–487.

Caulfield, J. (1994) *City Form and Everyday Life: Toronto's Gentrification and Critical Social Practice*, Toronto: University of Toronto Press.

Choi, N. (2016) 'Metro Manila through the gentrification lens: disparities in urban planning and displacement risks', *Urban Studies*, 53(3), 577–592.

Contreras Gatica, Y. (2011) 'La recuperación urbana y residencial del centro de Santiago: Nuevos habitantes, cambios socioespaciales significativos', *EURE (Santiago)*, 37(112), 89–113.

Cummings, J. (2015) 'Confronting favela chic: the gentrification of informal settlements in Rio de Janeiro, Brazil', in Lees, L., Shin, H. and López-Morales, E. (eds), *Global Gentrifications: Uneven Development and Displacement*, Bristol: Policy Press, pp. 81–100.

Danyluk, M. and Ley, D. (2007) 'Modalities of the new middle class: ideology and behavior in the journey to work from gentrified neighbourhoods in Canada', *Urban Studies*, 44(11), 2195–2210.

Davidson, M. (2008) 'Spoiled mixture – where does state-led "positive" gentrification end?', *Urban Studies*, 45(12), 2385–2405.

Davidson, M. and Lees, L. (2005) 'New-build "gentrification" and London's riverside renaissance', *Environment and Planning A*, 37, 1165–1190.

Delgadillo, V. (2016) 'Selective modernization of Mexico City and its historic center. Gentrification without displacement?', *Urban Geography*, 1–21.

Dennis, K. and Urry, J. (2009) *After the Car*, Cambridge; Malden, MA: Polity Press.

Doherty, C. (2015) 'Agentive motility meets structural viscosity: Australian families relocating in educational markets', *Mobilities*, 10(2), 249–266.

Donzelot, J. (2004) 'La ville à trois vitesses: relégation, périurbanisation, gentrification', *Esprit*, 303, 14–39.

Fishman, R. (1987) *Bourgeois Utopias: The Rise and Fall of Suburbia*, New York: Basic Books.

Flamm, M. and Kaufmann, V. (2006) 'Operationalising the concept of motility: a qualitative study', *Mobilities*, 1(2), 167–189.

Flühmann, C. (2015) *Weststrasse*, Zürich: Edition Frey.

Gibson, J.J. (2014) *The Ecological Approach to Visual Perception*, Hoboken: Taylor & Francis.

Hamnett, C. and Whitelegg, D. (2007) 'Loft conversion and gentrification in London: from industrial to postindustrial use', *Environment and Planning A*, 39, 106–124.

Harvey, D. (1989) *The Conditions of Postmodernity*, Oxford: Blackwell.

He, S. (2010) 'New-build gentrification in central Shanghai: demographic changes and socioeconomic implications', *Population, Space and Place*, 16(5), 345–361.

Hirschman, A.O. (2004) *Exit, Voice, and Loyalty: Responses to Decline in Firms, Organizations, and States*, Cambridge, MA: Harvard University Press.

Horton, D. (2006) 'Environmentalism and the bicycle', *Environmental Politics*, 15(1), 41–58.

Karsten, L. (2003) 'Family gentrifiers: challenging the city as a place simultaneously to build a career and raise children', *Urban Studies*, 40(12), 2573–2584.

Karsten, L. (2007) 'Housing as a way of life: towards an understanding of middle-class families' preference for an urban residential location', *Housing Studies*, 22(1), 83–98.

Karsten, L. (2008) 'The upgrading of the sidewalk: from traditional working-class colonisation to the squatting practices of urban middle-class families', *Urban Design International*, 13, 61–66.

Kaufmann, V. (2002) *Re-thinking Mobility: Contemporary Sociology*, Aldershot: Ashgate.

Kaufmann, V. (2011) *Rethinking the City: Urban Dynamics and Motility* 1st ed, Milton Park, Abingdon, Oxon; New York, NY; Lausanne, Switzerland: Routledge; EPFL Press.

Kaufmann, V., Bergman, M. and Joye, D. (2004) 'Motility: mobility as capital', *International Journal of Urban and Regional Research*, 28(4), 745–756.

Kaufmann, V., Ravalet, E., Dupuit, E. and S. Ecole polytechnique fédérale Lausanne (eds) (2015) *Motilité et mobilité: mode d'emploi*, Neuchâtel: Éditions Alphil-Presses universitaires suisses.

Keil, R. (ed) (2013) *Suburban Constellations: Governance, Land and Infrastructure in the 21st Century*, Berlin: Jovis Verlag.

Lees, L. (2000) 'A re-appraisal of gentrification: towards a geography of gentrification', *Progress in Human Geography*, 24, 398–408.

Lees, L. (2003) 'Super-gentrification: the case of Brooklyn Heights, New York City', *Urban Studies*, 40(12), 2487–2500.

Lees, L., Shin, H.B. and López-Morales, E. (eds) (2015) *Global Gentrifications: Uneven Development and Displacement*, Bristol, UK; Chicago, IL: Policy Press.

Lees, L., Shin, H.B. and López Morales, E. (2016) *Planetary Gentrification*, Cambridge, UK: Malden, MA: Polity Press.

Lefebvre, H., Kofman, E. and Lebas, E. (1996) *Writings on Cities*, Cambridge, MA: Blackwell Publishers.

Lévy, J. (1994) *L'espace légitime: sur la dimension géographique de la fonction politique*, Paris: Presses de la Fondation nationale des sciences politiques.

Lévy, J. (2000) 'Les nouveaux espaces de la mobilité', in Bonnet, M. and Desjeux, D. (eds) *Les territoires de la mobilité*, Paris: Presses universitaires de France, pp. 155–170.

Lévy, J. (2013) 'Capital spatial', in *Dictionnaire de la géographie et de l'espace des sociétés*, Paris: Belin, pp. 147–149.

Lévy, J. (2014) 'Inhabiting', in Lee, R. (ed), *The Sage Handbook of Human Geography*, Thousand Oaks, CA.: SAGE Publications Ltd, pp. 45–68.

Ley, D. (1996) *The New Middle Class and the Remaking of the Central City*, Oxford: Oxford University Press.

Ley, D. (2010) *Millionaire Migrants. Trans-Pacific Life Lines*, London: Wiley-Blackwell.

Ley, D. and Teo, S.Y. (2014) 'Gentrification in Hong Kong? Epistemology vs. Ontology', *International Journal of Urban and Regional Research*, 38(4), 1286–1303.

Lim, H., Kim, J., Potter, C. and Bae, W. (2013) 'Urban regeneration and gentrification: land use impacts of the Cheonggye Stream Restoration Project on the Seoul's central business district', *Habitat International*, 39, 192–200.

López-Morales, E. (2010) 'Real estate market, state-entrepreneurialism and urban policy in the "gentrification by ground rent dispossession" of Santiago de Chile', *Journal of Latin American Geography*, 9(1), 145–173.

Loughran, K. (2014) 'Parks for profit: the high line, growth machines, and the uneven development of urban public spaces', *City & Community*, 13(1), 49–68.

Low, S.M. (2001) 'The edge and the center: gated communities and the discourse of urban fear', *American Anthropologist*, 103(1), 45–58.

Mace, A. (2015) 'Spatial capital as a tool for planning practice', *Planning Theory*, 1–14.

McCleave Maharawal, M. (2014) 'Protest of gentrification and eviction technologies in San Francisco', *Progressive Planning*, 199, 20–24.

McKenzie, B. (2014) 'Modes less travelled – bicycling and walking to work in the United States: 2008–2012', *American Community Survey Reports*, 25, 1–18.

Middleton, J. (2008) 'London: the walkable city', in Imrie, R., Lees, L. and Raco, M. (eds), *Regenerating London: Governance, Sustainability and Community in a Global City*, London: Routledge, pp. 174–192.

Murphy-Lejeune, E. (2002) *Student Mobility and Narrative in Europe: The New Strangers*, London; New York: Routledge.

Newman, P. and Kenworthy, J. (1999) *Sustainability and Cities: Overcoming Automobile Dependence*, Washington: Island Press.

Pucher, J. R. and Buehler, R. (eds) (2012) *City Cycling*, Cambridge, MA: MIT Press.

Ren, X. (2008) 'Forward to the past: historical preservation in globalizing Shanghai', *City & Community*, 7(1), 23–43.

Rérat, P. (2012) 'Gentrifiers and their choice of housing: characteristics of the households living in new developments in Swiss cities', *Environment and Planning A*, 44(1), 221–236.

Rérat, P. (2016) 'Motivations résidentielles et pratiques de mobilité des classes moyennes supérieures dans les villes suisses', *Espaces et sociétés*, 164–165(1), 159–178.

Rérat, P. and Lees, L. (2011) 'Spatial capital, gentrification and mobility: evidence from Swiss core cities', *Transactions of the Institute of British Geographers*, 36(1), 126–142.

Revington, N. (2015) 'Gentrification, transit, and land use: Moving beyond neoclassical theory', *Geography Compass*, 9(3), 152–163.

Rose, D. (1984) 'Rethinking gentrification: beyond the uneven development of Marxist urban theory', *Environment and Planning D*, 1, 47–74.

Sigler, T. and Wachsmuth, D. (2016) 'Transnational gentrification: globalisation and neighbourhood change in Panama's Casco Antiguo', *Urban Studies*, 53(4), 705–722.

Smith, D.P. and Phillips, D.A. (2001) 'Socio-cultural representations of greentrified Pennine rurality', *Journal of Rural Studies*, 17(4), 457–469.

Stehlin, J. (2015) 'Cycles of investment: bicycle infrastructure, gentrification, and the restructuring of the San Francisco Bay Area', *Environment and Planning A*, 47(1), 121–137.

Stiem, T. (2016) 'Race and real estate: how hot Chinese money is making Vancouver unlivable', *The Guardian*. [Online] Available at: https://www.theguardian.com/cities/2016/jul/07/vancouver-chinese-city-racism-meets-real-estate-british-columbia?CMP=share_btn_tw.

Tonkiss, F. (2013) *Cities By Design: The Social Life of Urban Form*, Cambridge: Polity Press.

Ureta, S. (2008) 'To move or not to move? Social exclusion, accessibility and daily mobility among the low-income population in Santiago, Chile', *Mobilities*, 3(2), 269–289.

Urry, J. (2004) 'The "system" of automobility', *Theory, Culture & Society*, 21(4–5), 25–39.

Urry, J. (2007) *Mobilities*, Cambridge: Polity.

Van Criekingen, M. (2008) 'Urbanisme néolibéral et politiques de gentrification: main basse sur le quartier de la gare TGV à Bruxelles', *Géo-Regards*, 1, 113–125.

Visser, G. and Kotze, N. (2008) 'The state and new-build gentrification in central Cape Town, South Africa', *Urban Studies*, 45(12), 2565–2593.

8. Rent gaps
Tom Slater

8.1 'BOUNCEBACK-ABILITY'

In September 2016 Glasgow City Council launched its 'Resilience Strategy'. Supported by the Rockefeller Foundation's *100 Resilience Cities* competition, which awards generous grants to the 100 cities across the globe that it feels have demonstrated 'a dedicated commitment to building their own capacities to prepare for, withstand, and bounce back rapidly from shocks and stresses', it is a glossy document that sets out how Glasgow will 'maintain essential functions in the face of acute shocks and chronic stresses, but also grow and thrive through them' (p. 8). Apparently based on 'face-to-face conversations', workshops and on-line surveys with thousands of Glasgow residents, including children, the strategy identifies four 'pillars' around which resilience is to be built: 'empowering Glaswegians', 'unlocking placed-based solutions', 'fair economic growth', and 'fostering civic participation'. Announcing the launch of the document, Frank McAveety, Leader of Glasgow City Council, commented as follows:

> [T]he strategy document is a staging post in the conversation between Glasgow's citizens and its institutions about resilience. The strategy points to the route ahead and I've no doubt the journey will be accompanied by robust debate – Glasgow wouldn't have it any other way. This on-going dialogue will strengthen our resilience and allow us to face the future with confidence.[1]

In the spirit of 'robust debate', the first thing I would argue about this document is that it is presented in a manner that is truly excruciating. For example:

> During our conversations with Glaswegians on what makes Glasgow a resilient city we found that they like to talk of their 'bounceback-ability' factor – an ability to cope and even thrive through hard times (p. 18).

I am certain that if you were to visit a working-class part of Glasgow and utter the neologism 'bounceback-ability', you would be encouraged to leave. Similarly, I would venture that it is highly unlikely that schoolchildren anywhere in the city will embrace being 'young resilience ambassadors to develop leadership skills, share learning and champion creative new resilience ideas' (p. 75) and find an enthusiastic reaction from their classmates. This is partly because, as the document acknowledges, many areas of Glasgow are already extremely resilient places:

> The communities in the north of Glasgow are incredibly resilient in the face of a number of disproportionate stresses that are closely related to the post-industrial legacy of the area (p. 52).

---

[1] http://www.100resilientcities.org/blog/entry/glasgow-unveils-uks-first-city-resilience-strategy#/-_/.

This excerpt begs the question as to why a grand resilience strategy is necessary, and how people in Glasgow would feel about one being imposed. But it is in the discussion of the second pillar, 'unlocking place-based solutions', where we can see more of the political-economic intent behind this resilience strategy, and its relevance to questions of gentrification. The authors of the document are convinced that 'placemaking' is a wonderful design approach, as it 'contributes towards the creation of successful and resilient places, based upon balancing the relationship between the physical, social and economic characteristics of the area' (p. 50) – without taking a moment to reflect upon how people living where places are already made might feel about another vision of place being imposed on them. The placemaking approach is perhaps to be expected, however, as the Scottish Government has in recent years wholeheartedly bought into the ethos and methods of Andres Duany's 'New Urbanism' (see MacLeod 2013), which has 'placemaking' and post-political 'community engagement' at is core (and literally bought into it, as it paid Duany £250,000 for a week's consultancy work in 2010).

But a central goal issuing from the 'unlocking place-based solutions' pillar is 'to create an integrated resilience exemplar in the north of the city.' (p. 52). This is deemed necessary as 'patterns of investment, lack of active travel and public transport networks to neighbouring areas, and low availability of local employment opportunities' have resulted in 'stresses' of 'poverty and deprivation with high proportions of young people not in education or employment and significant issues surrounding addictions and mental health.' (ibid.) It is claimed that,

> The high concentration of vacant and derelict land in the north of Glasgow has also become a physical and social barrier to connectivity. It can often result in an environment that does not inspire pride in place and demotivates Glaswegians from taking advantage of active transport networks (pp. 52–53).

With problems pitched in such a way, the solution – written under the heading 'Resilience Value' – is predictable:

> The community, environmental and economic potential of derelict and vacant sites in Glasgow will be unlocked. By using 3D modelling to map vacant and derelict land we will be able to de-risk development by identifying new opportunities above and below ground. This will promote development opportunities associated with sites in order to attract developers and promote economic regeneration, compact city development and appropriate services (p. 53).

Disturbingly, the model for unlocking such 'potential' in urban land is the 2014 Commonwealth Games Athletes' Village, pitched in this document as 'one of the biggest success stories' where 'partnering agencies consulted intensively with local communities to build on community strengths and maximize social benefits' (p. 56). This is wildly at odds with what actually happened in the build up to that 2014 mega-event: the amplification of territorial stigma already affecting the East End of the city (Paton et al. 2017) which justified the forced eviction of residents whose homes were acquired through compulsory purchase before callous demolition to make way for the Athletes' Village (Porter 2009). The planner's eye view of working-class Glasgow can be read in the statement that 'the Games were an opportunity to bring vitality into areas of the city' (p. 55). As Ley (1996) has pointed out, the discourse of revitalization is 'objectionable, implying a sense of moral superiority in the process of residential succession, and imparting a mantle of less vitality to previous land uses and users.' (pp. 33–34).

This opening summary of Glasgow's resilience strategy points to the ongoing relevance of the rent gap theory in gentrification studies. As I aim to demonstrate, the theory helps explain how propitious political-economic conditions are created for the extraction of profit from urban land markets, and, far from being economistic or deterministic (as it is frequently critiqued or dismissed), it is a crucial theory to understand as part of a critical and/or resistant response to gentrification, and as a critique of the logic undergirding the process. In the Glasgow case above, the rent gap theory, understood and used as the scholar who devised it intended, is helpful in pinpointing and challenging a strategy which, dressed up in the positive rubric of building resilience, makes acceptable and palatable the claims to 'unlock economic potential' and 'de-risk development' to create 'opportunities associated with sites in order to attract developers'.

8.2 UNSETTLING CONSUMER SOVEREIGNTY

Wherever something new is being created, and thus in settlement and spatial planning also, the laws revealed through theory are the sole economic guide to what *should* take place (August Losch 1954: 359).

On the one hand, it seems unnecessary to provide a concise summary of Neil Smith's rent gap theory as this has been done many times before, and the original papers where the theory emerged are essential reading for anyone interested in gentrification, and also far more exciting to read than any summary! On the other, it seems very necessary to clarify the theory, as misunderstandings, errors of interpretation and sometimes downright lazy critiques still circulate widely and distort not only the debate over the theory, but the field of gentrification studies more generally.

The rent gap theory, stripped down to its bare essentials in its original formulation, is a Marxist critique of the highly influential neoclassical economic land use models of the Chicago School. Neoclassical economics continues to play a powerful ideological role in societies today, and in many instances is the undergirding logic driving urban policy, so it remains important to understand the battle for ideas in which Smith immersed himself throughout his career. That career started early; remarkably, the empirical study that led to the generation of the theory was an undergraduate dissertation in geography completed by Smith at the University of St. Andrews in 1977. Smith had spent a year as an exchange student in Philadelphia, where he had become captivated by the profound changes visited upon the neighbourhood of Society Hill. Having first noticed gentrification earlier in 1972, on Rose Street in Edinburgh, when a trendy new bar called *The Galloping Major* distinguished itself from neighbouring pubs by serving 'quite appetizing lunches adorned with salad' (Smith 1996: xviii), he felt that existing urban land use models and predictions regarding the miserable fate of central cities were inadequate in terms of explaining gentrification he had seen in Edinburgh and Philadelphia.

Smith was very sceptical of neoclassical models and predictions because of the *consumer sovereignty* paradigm undergirding them, which held that the rational choices of individual consumers of land and housing determined the morphology of cities.

Middle-class consumer demand for space, the neoclassical argument went, explained sub-urbanization – a process seen by many inside and outside academia to be the only future for all urban places. But the empirical reality of Society Hill – gentrification – seemed to call that paradigm into question. Smith could not accept that consumers were suddenly demanding en masse the opposite to what had been predicted, and 'choosing' to gentrify central city areas instead. In Society Hill he unearthed data showing that a majority of middle class people had never left for Philadelphia's suburbs because space was being produced for them via state-sponsored private sector development. This created hand-some profits for developers at the expense of working-class people who were displaced from central city space. His undergraduate dissertation was distilled and published in *Antipode* in 1979 (Smith 1979a), and that same year it was refined further in the *Journal of the American Planning Association* (Smith 1979b), where the pivotal theory of the rent gap was first articulated.

A starting point for Smith was that, in capitalist property markets, the decisive 'consumer preference' (with characteristic mischief he adopted the neoclassical language) is 'the preference for profit, or, more accurately, a sound financial investment' (1979: 540). As disinvestment in a particular district intensifies, as had happened in Society Hill, it creates lucrative profit opportunities for developers, investors, homebuyers and local government. If we wanted to understand the much-lauded American 'urban renaissance' of the 1970s, the argument and title of the rent gap essay went, it was much more important to track the movement of capital rather than the movement of people (the latter movement was the exclusive focus of the 'back to the city' rhetoric of the time, and the scholarship on it). Crucial to Smith's argument was the ever-fluctuating phenomenon of *ground rent*: simply the charge that landlords are able to demand (via private property rights) for the right to use land and its appurtenances (the buildings placed on it and the resources embedded within it), usually received as a stream of payments from tenants but also via any asset appreciation captured at resale. Landlords in poorer central city neighbourhoods are often holding investments in buildings that represented what economists and urban planners call the 'highest and best use' over a century ago; spending money to maintain these assets as low-cost rental units becomes ever more difficult to justify with each passing year, since the investments will be difficult to recover from low-income tenants. It becomes rational and logical for landlords to 'milk' the property, extracting rent from the tenants yet spending the absolute minimum to maintain the structure. With the passage of time, the deferred maintenance becomes apparent: people with the money to do so will leave a neighbourhood, and financial institutions 'redline' the neighbourhood as too risky to make loans. Physical decline accelerates, and moderate-income residents and businesses moving away are replaced by successively poorer tenants who move in – they simply cannot access housing anywhere else.

In late 1920s Chicago, Hoyt had identified a 'valley in the land-value curve between the Loop and outer residential areas. . . .[which] indicates the location of these sections where the buildings are mostly forty years old and where the residents rank lowest in rent-paying ability' (Hoyt 1933: 356–358). For Smith (1979b), this 'capital depreciation in the inner city' (p. 543), meant that there is likely to be an increasing divergence between *capitalized ground rent* (the actual quantity of ground rent that is appropriated by the landowner, given the present land use) and *potential ground rent* (the maximum that could be appropriated under the land's 'highest and best use'). So, Hoyt's land value valley, radically analyzed and reconceptualized, 'can now be understood in large part as the rent gap':

> Gentrification occurs when the gap is wide enough that developers can purchase shells cheaply, can pay the builders' costs and profit for rehabilitation, can pay interest on mortgage and construction loans, and can then sell the end product for a sale price that leaves a satisfactory return to the developer. The entire ground rent, or a large portion of it, is now capitalized: the neighbourhood has been 'recycled' and begins a new cycle of use (p. 545).

The elegance of the rent gap theory lies not just in what Ley (1996), one of Smith's more astute interlocutors, has referred to as its 'ingenious simplicity' (p. 42), but in its critical edge, its normative thrust. The flight of capital away from certain areas of the city – depreciation and disinvestment – has devastating implications for people living at the bottom of the urban class structure. The 'shells' referred to above do not simply 'appear' as part of some naturally occurring neighbourhood 'decay' – they are actively produced by clearing out existing residents via all manner of tactics and legal instruments, such as landlord harassment, massive rent increases, redlining, arson, the withdrawal of public services, and eminent domain/compulsory purchase orders. Closing the rent gap requires, crucially, separating people currently obtaining use values from the present land use providing those use values – in order to capitalize the land to the perceived 'highest and best' use. The rent gap thus highlights specific class interests, where the quest for profit takes precedence over the human need of shelter.

8.3   THREE CLARIFICATIONS

In an excellent discussion of the rent gap in the book *Gentrification*, Elvin Wyly noted the etymology of the word 'gap' – from the Old Norse for 'chasm', denoting a breach or wall or fence, a breach in defences, a break in continuity, or wide difference in ideas or views. He continued:

> The rent gap is part of an assault to breach the defensive wall of mainstream urban studies, by challenging the assumption that urban landscapes can be explained in large part as the result of consumer preferences, and the notion that neighbourhood change can be understood in terms of who moves in and who moves out. Scholars, therefore, take its implications very seriously (Lees et al. 2008: 55).

It is hardly surprising that the rent gap theory has been the subject of intense debate for nearly forty years. But those debates, often shot through with intractable ideological confrontations and petty bickering, became rather frustrating for many, leading to many cursory, dismissive summaries. It would be tedious to recite and summarize in any great detail the rent gap debates, and this task has been undertaken elsewhere (e.g. Lees et al. 2008: 39–86). Far more helpful at this juncture is to consider what can be learned from considering, as a body of scholarship, the most valuable lessons from studies that have grasped the importance of the political thrust of the rent gap from the outset, and understood its theoretical premises in order to conduct detailed empirical tests (e.g. Clark 1987; Kary 1988; Smith et al. 1989; Engels 1994; Yung and King 1998; Hammel 1999; O'Sullivan 2002; Darling 2005). Given the intense empirical grafting involved – there are no readily available variables to measure capitalized and potential ground rent, so scholars have to dig into planning archives and land records going back several decades in order to construct their own proxy indicators – few thorough empirical studies exist. Those that do, however, considered as a collective, are all valuable as part of a wider scholarly effort to understand the class transformation of space, wherever and under whatever conditions that transformation might be happening. From all those studies, and from Neil Smith's original writings, three things above all become clear about the rent gap theory.

1)   The rent gap theory is not narrowly economistic, but a theory of the state's role in creating the economic conditions for gentrification

Perhaps the most frequent charges levelled at the rent gap theory is that it is pure economic determinism (Hamnett 1991), that it 'overlooks regulatory contexts which may well discipline capital's freedom of expression' (Ley 1996: 42), that it has no place for a consideration of the role of 'extra-economic force', to use the language of recent arguments made by Ghertner (2014, 2015). I have never understood such criticisms. To be sure, rent gaps are produced by economic agents and actors (landlords, bankers, developers, realtors), and the theory was formulated as part of a broader critique of uneven development under capitalism, but the role of the state in the theory is far from laissez-faire or absent, but rather one of active facilitator, as Smith had found in Society Hill: 'The state had both a political role in realizing Society Hill, and an economic role in helping to produce this new urban space' (1979a: 28). It has been demonstrated multiple times in contexts where gentrification is occurring (particularly in recent years as gentri-fication – though never used in name by policy officials – has become a strategic urban development vision in many contexts) that the role of the state in producing rent gaps is direct and pivotal, to the point where rent gaps simply would not exist without the state (e.g. Uitermark et al. 2007; Glynn 2008; Hodkinson 2012; Kallin and Slater 2014; Paton 2010). As Kallin (2018) has pointed out in a study of a failed state-driven gentrification strategy in the Edinburgh district of Granton, 'if claims to difference are grounded in the notion that extra-economic force is alien to gentrification in "the West", then these are weak claims to difference' (p. 1). It is also worth noting that Neil Smith's undergraduate dissertation even carried the subtitle, "State Involvement in Society Hill, Philadelphia". Bernt (2016) complains about the 'essentially universalizing undercurrent which is at the core of the rent-gap theory' and argues that 'downplaying non-economic instances is deeply embedded within the reductionist conceptual architecture of the rent gap theory and integrating different institutional, social, cultural and political constellations has remained an enduring problem' (pp. 641–642). In my view, such charges are simply diver-sions in an epoch of vicious state-led accumulation strategies, and the ever-sophisticated mutation of neoliberal urbanism (Brenner et al. 2010; Harvey 2010). Perhaps the charges keep appearing because the original rent gap paper was rather muted on the role of the state, as its author's main mission was to critique the consumer sovereignty assumptions undergirding neoclassical land use models, even as the piece of empirical research that informed the theory had the state as core to the explanation of how gentrification was unfolding. But the point remains: conclusions should not be drawn about the rent gap theory unless one takes the trouble to read *all* the original studies closely.

2) *The rent gap theory helps us understand the circulation of interest-bearing capital in urban land markets, and speculative landed developer interests*

Writing in the immediate aftermath of the 2008 financial crisis, David Harvey (2010) remarked that speculative landed developer interests are 'a singular principle power that has yet to be accorded its proper place in our understanding of not only the historical geography of capitalism but also the general evolution of capitalist class power' (p. 180). He continued:

> Investments in rents on land, property, mines and raw materials thereby becomes an attractive proposition for all capitalists. Speculation in these values becomes rife. The production of capitalism's geography is propelled onwards by the need to realise speculative gains on these assets (p. 181).

In many capitalist economies, due to the decades-long shrinkage of the manufacturing sector, capital has switched from its primary circuit of industrial production to its second-ary circuit of accumulation, urban land and real estate markets, which runs parallel to the primary circuit. But the secondary has supplanted the primary in terms of its overall importance, often accounting for over 40% of all economic activity. One illustration: 76% of all bank loans in Britain go into property (and 64% of that into residential mortgages), and 87% of all household debt is tied up in mortgages. To address the crisis of continuous compound growth under long cycles of accumulation, capital has to devalue the existing capital fixed to the land, among other things, to reinvent investment opportunities for the absorption of a surplus (Harvey 2014). At times of crisis, speculation in land that is being devalued becomes rife. In Britain, the institutional arrangements behind the distribution of housing incentivize rampant land speculation: the urban housing market in the UK (London especially) has now become a place for very rich people – especially investors from overseas – to park their money at an annual rate of return of around 10%. Speculation means that more and more capital is being invested in search of rents and interest and future gains, rather than invested in productive activity – a trend towards a rentier form of capitalism: a parasitic economy characterized by the marked escalation of extracted unearned income. Rentiers make staggering fortunes simply from ownership of assets or resources that all of us need. They have everything to gain from the global circulation of interest-bearing capital in urban land markets, and from the municipal absorption of surplus capital via all kinds of debt-financed urbanization projects. Sayer (2015) has written a remarkable expose of the serious problem of extracted unearned income, and convincingly argues that one of the most dangerous myths of advanced capitalist societies is that the unearned income of the super rich is only fair given their 'hard work' (fictitious) and supposed talents as 'wealth creators' (yet they only create wealth for themselves).

The relevance of the rent gap theory to campaigns and struggles against speculative landed developer interests is that, as originally intended, it helps to

> redirect our theoretical focus toward the sphere of circulation. . ..[where] we can trace the power of finance capital over the urbanization process, and the patterning of urban space according to patterns of profitable investment (Smith 1979b: 24).

The function of rent under a capitalist mode of production is to underpin investment and reinvestment opportunity. A recent example of the speculative rentier class attempting to exploit the rent gap in London was the struggle over the New Era housing estate, built by a charitable trust in the 1930s to offer working-class Londoners affordable rental housing but for many years subject to disinvestment. Westbrook Partners is an investment firm based in New York City, which makes its billions by investing American pension savings in London land deals. Westbrook bought the New Era estate in March 2014 (initially a partnership deal with Benyon Estates, owned by the Conservative MP Richard Benyon, until he had to pull out due to public shaming), and immediately notified tenants that rents would rise to market values: from £600 a month for a two-bed flat to £2,400 a month (Chakrabortty 2014). Land value is not created from owning land – it is created from collective social investments in land, which landowners then extract as unearned income via private property rights. Exploiting the rent gap requires the expropriation of socially created use values: a form of structural violence visited upon working-class people in contexts that are usually described as 'regenerating' or 'revitalizing'. Instead of building shelter for people in need, the system encourages rentier capitalists to see who can best use their land-banking skills to anticipate the next housing bubble and survive the last one. In December 2014, however, there was a significant victory for residents of the New Era estate when Westbrook, under huge public pressure because of a campaign against its profiteering motives (led by young mothers on the estate), sold the land estate to the Dolphin Square Charitable Foundation, an affordable housing charity committed to delivering low cost rents to Londoners on low to middle incomes. The closure of rent gaps is not inevitable.

3)   Rent gaps are produced via the activation of territorial stigma

A signal contribution of the rent gap was to show that, first, the individual, personal, rational preferences in the housing market much cherished by neoclassical economists, and, second, the 'new middle class' dispositions towards a vibrant central-city (and associated rejections of bland, patriarchal suburbia) that intrigued liberal-humanist and feminist geographers, are all tightly bound up with larger, collective social relations and investments (core to the rent gap concept is that ground rent is produced by the labour power invested in land, and that consumer preferences are not 'exogenous' to the structures of land, property, credit, and housing). Contrary to the absurd recent intervention of a distinguished science writer drawing upon one dubious source (Ball 2014), consumer preferences and tastes visible in gentrifying neighbourhoods are not naturally occurring phenomena – they are deliberately made by agents seeking to extract profit from urban land, and usually in relation to a set of negative images about what places could become, or how they might remain, if they did not experience an upward economic trajectory. A tiresome charge against the rent gap theory is that it fails to predict which neighbourhoods will gentrify and which will not (missing completely the fact that it was never designed as a predictive model). But there is an unresolved analytic puzzle: why does it appear to be the case that gentrification rarely seems to occur first in the most severely disinvested parts of a city or a region – where the potential for substantial profit is at its greatest – but proceeds instead in devalorized, working-class tracts that are certainly disinvested but by no means the poorest or offering the maximum profit to developers? Hammel (1999) helpfully offered a clue:

Inner city areas have many sites with a potential for development that could return high levels of rent. That development never occurs, however, because the perception of an impoverished neighbourhood prevents large amounts of capital being applied to the land (p. 1290).

The challenge remains enticing – to consider the disparity between potential and capitalized ground rent in the context of how urban dwellers at the bottom of the class structure are discredited and devalued because of the places with which they are associated. The negative manner in which certain parts of cities are portrayed (by journalists, politicians and think tanks especially) has become critically important to policies geared towards their future. A mushrooming body of work points to a direct relationship between territorial stigmatization and the process of gentrification (Wacquant 2007; Gray and Mooney 2011; Slater and Anderson 2012; Kallin and Slater 2014; August 2014; Lees 2014; Thorn and Helgersson 2016), where neighbourhood 'taint' becomes a target and rationale for 'fixing' an area via its reincorporation into the secondary circuit of accumulation – yet sometimes the 'perception' Hammel outlines is so negative and entrenched that it acts as a symbolic barrier or diversion to the circulation of capital. In sum, as territorial stigmatization intensifies, there are major consequences for urban land markets, and therefore implications for rent gap theory. Such stigma serves economic ends, but also vice versa: examples abound under authoritarian urban regimes whereby the economics of inter-urban competition – with gentrification strategies at the core – are serving the brutal and punitive policies directed at working-class minorities, and particularly, at the places where they live (e.g. Kuymulu 2013; Sakizlioglu 2014).

8.4   PLANETARY RENT GAPS?

Up to the mid-2000s, there were hardly any studies of gentrification beyond the 'usual suspects' (cf. Lees et al. 2015, 2016). Almost everything scholars knew about the process, and the rich body of theory developed to understand it, came from (predominantly large) cities of the Global North. But the scale and pace of urban development in the Global South (and the extent of displacement), and the rise of postcolonial urban theory, has led to fascinating recent empirical and theoretical interventions, and changed the landscape of gentrification research in ways that are exciting and highly instructive for urbanists, regardless of where they are located. Three specific deployments of rent gap theory in the Global South are particularly striking, for they extend the theory in imaginative and creative ways. Whitehead and More (2007) examined the massive changes visited upon the central mills districts of Mumbai in the context of the 1980s informalization and decentralization (to the suburbs) of the textile industry in that city. Aided by an NGO organization actively supporting the 'relocation' of slum dwellers from those districts to the outskirts of Mumbai, mill owners and multinational developers seeking opportunities for commercial real estate realized that the (actively disinvested) land upon which the mills once worked was not at its 'highest and best use', and to gain maximum profit from the land they pushed successfully for changes to development regulations (which had stipulated that only one third of the mill lands could be used for real estate development). The result was an exclusive apartment and shopping mall development in a city where over 70% of residents officially live in 'slum' conditions. True to the original formulation of the rent gap thesis, the role of the state was far from laissez-faire:

> The state government has changed to become an organisation attracting off-shore and domestic investment to the island city, while service provision becomes secondary. It has been reshaped to enable, facilitate and promote international flows of financial, real estate and productive capital, and the logic of its policies can be read off almost directly through calculations of rent gaps emerging at various spots in the city (p. 2434).

The propitious role of the state in creating the disparity between capitalized and potential ground rent has also been illustrated by López-Morales (2010, 2011), in two striking papers on 'gentrification by ground rent dispossession' in Santiago, Chile. After the 1990 return to democracy in Chile (following 17 years of military dictatorship), various state policies were designed with a view to attracting professional middle classes into deeply disinvested parts of central Santiago, with varying degrees of success. From the 2000s onwards, however, a second phase of much larger scale state-sponsored entrepreneurial redevelopment has been taking place on formerly industrial sites, and on small owner-occupied plots in traditionally working-class peri-central areas known locally as *poblaciones*, all of which exhibit wide rent gaps in the context of a city that has positioned itself as one of the economic powerhouses of Latin America. López-Morales traced and mapped the policy-driven production and accumulation of potential ground rent in Santiago alongside the land devaluation produced by strict national building codes and the under-implementation of previous state upgrading programmes. Just as in the Mumbai case above, the state was critically important in the opening and closing of rent gaps, and also in creating the conditions for national and foreign speculation in urban land markets, for

> the way developers can acquire and accumulate large portions of inhabited land is by buying, at relatively low prices, from inner city owner-occupiers, and they often hold it vacant while passively waiting (or actively lobbying) to get building regulations loosened (López-Morales 2010: 147).

A third recent deployment of the rent gap thesis has been in a remarkable analysis by Wright (2014) of the gentrification of the centro historico of Ciudad Juarez on the Mexico-USA border in the wake of the carnage and devastation caused there by a transcontinental drugs war (2006–2012) instigated by both country's governments. Wright found rent gap theory to be highly applicable to explain a situation whereby

> in order to rescue the centro and augment its economic value, the city first needed to be economically and socially destroyed. The formerly vibrant downtown, in short, needed to be killed before it could be rescued (p. 2).

Wright weds feminist and Marxist approaches to accumulation by dispossession to explain a class struggle between, on the one hand, ruling elites intent on a strategy of denigrating the lives and spaces of working-class women and their children living in the centro in order to expand the rent gap and ultimately 'clean up' the area and 'reestablish' it as a place for upstanding families, and on the other, activists drawing public attention to the exploitation (in maquiladora factories and in sex work) of working poor women and especially to feminicidio (the killing of women with impunity):

activists used the language of feminicidio to launch a counter-offensive against the political and business elites who minimized the violence by declaring that the victims were not worth remembering. In so doing, they challenged the story that equated women's disappearance from public space, either through their deaths or through municipal social cleansing projects, with value. And, as such, they disabled a key technology for widening the rent gap between the places known for poor women and the places known for their disappearance (p. 9).

While gentrification plans were disrupted by activists for some time, this did not last, for those same policy and business elites then targeted young men caught up in the violence of the drugs war:

> Rather than refer to the male youth population that dominates the body count as the resident population of the city's poor working-class families, the mayor referred to them as 'venomous vermin' who had descended upon the city. . ... Such depictions. . .sought to whitewash the public memory of these young people who were being gunned down on the very streets that had raised them (p. 11).

This official 'politics of forgetting' is now working to close the rent gap and extract profits from massively devalorized spaces: 'the business leaders who are gobbling up the shuttered businesses and overseeing the massive physical reconstruction of the city that has its streets and buildings in rubble declare that everything is officially better as long as we forget about the past' (p. 11).

So, in these three contexts at least, the rent gap theory was helpful in explaining gentrification. This really seems to bother some urbanists working with postcolonial theory, not least Ghertner (2015) who published a piece entitled 'Why gentrification theory fails in much of the world'. He argues that the term 'gentrification' has been imposed by scholars on places where it does not fit, or where it makes little sense to struggles occurring at ground level; that it doesn't recognize the diversity of activities taking place where 'public land ownership, common property, mixed tenure, or informality' (p. 552) endure; that it is 'agnostic on the question of extra-economic force' (p. 553) (a highly questionable claim, see above); that 'Western' gentrification scholars 'see like capitalists' (ibid.) in their assumption that private land tenure/capitalist urbanization is everywhere; and that those scholars are not alert to forms of displacement which are driven by processes other than gentrification (such as the violent evictions taking place over privatization of non-private land tenures[2]). There is no space here for a full engagement with these interesting arguments – nor do I wish to get involved in what is becoming a tedious divide in urban studies between postcolonial/provincial and Marxist/political-economic urban theorists (counterproductive, given that, politically, these theorists usually share the same concerns about social injustices in cities). However, a brief observation vis-à-vis the logic of concept formation and theory building seems necessary. It almost goes without saying that it is very important to ask theoretical questions about the pertinence of certain concepts and whether they are helpful or not in dissecting urban processes beyond where they were formed. I know that a recent piece I wrote, 'Planetary Rent Gaps' (2017), has

---

[2]   An immediate reaction I had to this argument was that the privatization of non-private land tenures could be analysed as a gentrification strategy, when gentrification is defined appropriately as the class transformation of space, and not defined as Ghertner's 'nothing more than a rising rent environment and associated forms of market-induced displacement' (p. 552).

annoyed some postcolonial urbanists because I made the argument – drawing on available scholarship, such as that outlined above – that the fact the rent gap theory was developed in the US in the 1970s is not a valid reason to ignore it, nor indeed to 'unlearn' and then 'relearn' it, in very different contexts four decades later. The challenge is surely just to take it seriously, and if it turns out not to be useful in a certain context or struggle: then don't use it! Theories and concepts are perhaps best understood as our servants – we employ them, they are there to be useful to us if needed, to bring things to us that we did not have or see before, and to help explain phenomena that require careful scrutiny. It strikes me as anti-intellectual to write off a whole theory or concept for a whole region (or 'much of the world') simply because it isn't useful to one particular analyst working in one particular context. The postcolonial theorists would argue that, if there is anti-intellectualism, it is from those urban scholars who fire off essentialist generalizations without due regard for particular contexts and historical geographies. But Vivek Chibber (2016) offers a poignant reminder:

> Social theory is essentially about generalizing from one case to another. If you cannot generalize from one case to another, you don't have a theory. What you have is a very thick description of particular events. Unless you can say, what's happening in this event has a resemblance with and is driven by the same forces as events in other contexts, you don't have a social theory. So you cannot have a social theory whose central concept is difference because then it ceases to be a theory. It just ends up being endless descriptions of particular events.[3]

Furthermore, as Jamie Peck (2015) has recently highlighted, very few people are actually *doing* the systematic comparative work that the new comparative urbanists are calling for.

But at least from the research that is available, and still emerging, it seems to be the case that rent gap theory has a lot to teach us about gentrification in the Global South, and is far from 'less than adequate in much of the world' (Ghertner 2015: 554). In their excellent new book, *Planetary Gentrification*, Lees, Shin and López-Morales (2016) argue that the term 'gentrification' has not been stretched too far (contra Maloutas 2011) – it is unfolding at a planetary scale, even if changing conditions and local circumstances matter enormously. Even where the processes are not called 'gentrification' locally, or where there is no equivalent term, class-driven urban redevelopment is an embedded process in multiple Southern contexts. Finally, their synthesis of available research evidence points to the growing importance of secondary circuits of accumulation and the planetary shift to rentier extraction and what might be termed the robbery of value, rather than the production of value. Asset pursuit and asset stripping, via land grabbing and evictions, is a hallmark of contemporary urbanization and shows little sign of retreating on a planetary scale. It is not 'seeing like a capitalist' to consider rent gap theory in radically different contexts, nor is it an act of intellectual imperialism to do so, as long as one theory does not shut out the possibility of developing new theories which may teach us even more (Wyly 2015).

---

[3]   https://thecriticaltheoryworkshop.wordpress.com/2016/02/06/3/.

8.5   CLASS STRUGGLES NEED RENT GAP THEORY

It is fascinating to note the delightful rascality in where the rent gap paper appeared – in a mainstream planning journal as part of a special issue on neighbourhood 'revitalization', a term that made Neil Smith wince: 'it is often also true that very vital working-class communities are culturally devitalized through gentrification as the new middle class scorns the streets in favour of the dining room and bedroom' (1996: 32–33). The rent gap, taken seriously, forces analysts to confront class struggle, and the structural violence visited upon so many working-class people in contexts these days that are usually described as 'regenerating' or 'revitalizing'. Contrary to contemporary journalistic portraits of latte-drinking white 'hipsters' versus working-class people of colour, the class struggle in gentrification is between those at risk of displacement and the agents of capital (the financiers, the real estate brokers, policy elites, developers) who produce and exploit rent gaps. Housing itself is a class struggle over the rights to social reproduction – the right to make a life. This is a class struggle playing out within the realm of capital circulation largely between, on the one hand, those living in housing precarity, and on the other, finance capital and all its many tentacles.[4]

The Rockefeller *100 Resilient Cities* programme mentioned at the start of this chapter is effectively a neoliberal urbanist competition, where cash prizes are offered to the cities that get back to the desired status quo of capital accumulation and elite wealth capture as quickly as possible after 'shocks and stresses'. That there is a strong desire among urban managers to compete is evident in the fact that more than 1,000 cities registered to take part in the programme, and almost 400 formally applied for inclusion. 'Resilience', to the Glasgow planners and policy elites, means bracing yourself for economic and environmental catastrophes as everything will be fine in the end. It is not a strategy that leads us to question the structural and institutional conditions that are forcing people to be 'resilient' in the first place. Diprose (2015) has offered a particularly strong critique of the resilience logic and discourse:

> It is time to rid ourselves of resilience: to renounce responsibility for the economic crisis; to stop scapegoating people who are struggling; to refuse to submit to stress; to recognise healthy limits and do everything possible to sustain them. . ... Political reform and grassroots resistance can only work towards recovery if we work for the weak as well as the strong; if we promote a culture in which people do not just survive, but thrive. . . .Imagine if the time and effort invested in future-proofing ourselves was instead given to fully occupying the present, and to more determinedly realising the change we want to see (pp. 54–55).

Imagine, also, if those behind Glasgow's resilience strategy had asked participants, 'Would you rather "bounce back" from hard times, or resist and eliminate hard times?' The rent gap theory helps open up questions of resistance, and nudges the conversation in

---

[4]   A particularly fascinating recent deployment of rent gap theory has come from Wachsmuth (2017) who examined the explosion of Airbnb rentals in New York City and argued that potential ground rent is increased 'without any disinvestment having occurred, and without any need for big expensive renovations to capitalize on the opportunity.' This is because Airbnb gives landlords the choice to 'evict current tenants or decide not to find new ones when a lease ends . . . an enormous new opportunity for profit-making in urban housing markets where there is external tourist demand, and an enormous new risk of displacement and gentrification.'

the direction of what cities might look like without the structural and institutional forces producing gentrification.

REFERENCES

August, M. (2014) 'Challenging the rhetoric of stigmatization: the benefits of concentrated poverty in Toronto's Regent Park', *Environment and Planning A*, 46(6), 1317–1333.

Ball, P. (2014) 'Gentrification is a natural evolution', *The Guardian*, 19 November [Online]. Available at: http://www.theguardian.com/commentisfree/2014/nov/19/gentrification-evolution-cities-brixton-battersea.

Bernt, M. (2016) 'Very particular, or rather universal? Gentrification through the lenses of Ghertner and López-Morales', *City*, 20(4), 637–644.

Brenner, N., Peck, J. and Theodore, N. (2010) 'Variegated neoliberalization: geographies, modalities, pathways', *Global Networks*, 10(2), 1–41.

Chakrabortty, A. (2014) 'New Era estate scandal: families at the mercy of international speculators', *The Guardian*, 19 November [Online]. Available at: http://www.theguardian.com/society/2014/nov/19/new-era-estate-scandal-london-families-international-speculators.

Clark, E. (1987) *The Rent Gap and Urban Change: Case Studies in Malmö 1860–1985*, Lund: Lund University Press.

Darling, E. (2005) 'The city in the country: wilderness gentrification and the rent-gap', *Environment and Planning A*, 37(6), 1015–1032.

Diprose, K. (2015) 'Resilience is futile', *Soundings*, 58(5), 44–56.

Engels, B. (1994) 'Capital flows, redlining and gentrification: the pattern of mortgage lending and social change in Glebe, Sydney, 1960–1984', *International Journal of Urban and Regional Research*, 18(4), 628–657.

Ghertner, D. (2014) 'India's urban revolution: geographies of displacement beyond gentrification', *Environment and Planning A*, 46(7), 1554–1571.

Ghertner, D. (2015) 'Why gentrification theory fails in "much of the world"', *City*, 19(4), 552–563.

Glasgow City Council (2016) *Our Resilient Glasgow* [Online]. Available at: http://100resilientcities.org/strategies/city/glasgow#/-_/.

Glynn, S. (2008) 'Soft-selling gentrification?', *Urban Research & Practice*, 1, 164–180.

Gray, N. and Mooney, G. (2011) 'Glasgow's new urban frontier: "civilising" the population of "Glasgow East"', *City*, 15, 1–24.

Hammel, D. (1999) 'Re-establishing the rent gap: an alternative view of capitalised land rent', *Urban Studies*, 36, 1283–1293.

Hamnett, C. (1991) 'The blind men and the elephant: the explanation of gentrification', *Transactions of the Institute of British Geographers*, 17, 173–189.

Harvey, D. (2010) *The Enigma of Capital and the Crises of Capitalism*, London: Profile Books.

Harvey, D. (2014) *Seventeen Contradictions and the End of Capitalism*, London: Verso.

Hodkinson, S. (2012) 'The new urban enclosures', *City*, 16(5), 500–518.

Hoyt, H. (1933) *One Hundred Years of Land Values in Chicago*, Chicago: University of Chicago Press.

Kallin, H. (2018) 'The state of gentrification has always been extra-economic', in Benach, N. and Albet, A. (eds), *Gentrification as a Global Strategy: Neil Smith and Beyond*, London: Routledge.

Kallin, H. and Slater, T. (2014) 'Activating territorial stigma: gentrifying marginality on Edinburgh's periphery', *Environment and Planning A*, 46(6), 1351–1368.

Kary, K. (1988) 'The gentrification of Toronto and the rent gap theory', in Bunting, T. and Filion, P. (eds), *The Changing Canadian Inner City*, Dept of Geography, University of Waterloo.

Kuymulu, M. (2013) 'Reclaiming the right to the city: reflections on the urban uprisings in Turkey', *City*, 17(3), 274–278.

Lees, L. (2014) 'The urban injustices of New Labour's "New Urban Renewal": the case of the Aylesbury Estate in London', *Antipode*, 46(4), 921–947.

Lees, L., Shin, H. and López-Morales, E. (eds) (2015) *Global Gentrifications*, Bristol: Policy Press.

Lees, L., Shin, H. and López-Morales, E. (2016) *Planetary Gentrification*, Cambridge: Polity Press.

Lees, L., Slater, T. and Wyly, E. (2008) *Gentrification*, New York: Routledge.

Ley, D. (1996) *The New Middle Class and the Remaking of the Central City*, Oxford: Oxford University Press.

López-Morales, E. (2010) 'Real estate market, state entrepreneurialism and urban policy in the gentrification by ground rent dispossession of Santiago de Chile', *Journal of Latin American Geography*, 9(1), 145–173.

López-Morales, E. (2011) 'Gentrification by ground rent dispossession: the shadows cast by large scale urban renewal in Santiago de Chile', *International Journal of Urban and Regional Research*, 35(2), 330–357.

Losch, A. (1954) *The Economics of Location*, New Haven: Yale University Press.

MacLeod, G. (2013) 'New urbanism/smart growth in the Scottish Highlands: mobile Policies and post-politics in local development planning', *Urban Studies*, 50, 2196–2221.

Maloutas, T. (2011) 'Contextual diversity in gentrification research', *Critical Sociology*, 38, 33–48.

O'Sullivan, D. (2002) 'Toward micro-scale spatial modelling of gentrification', *Journal of Geographical Systems*, 4(3), 251–274.

Paton, K. (2010) 'Creating the neoliberal city and citizen: the use of gentrification as urban policy in Glasgow', in Davidson, N., McCafferty, P. and Miller, D. (eds), *Neoliberal Scotland: Class and Society in a Stateless Nation*, Newcastle: Cambridge Scholars Publishing, pp. 203–224.

Paton K., McCall, V. and Mooney, G. (2017) 'Place revisited: class, stigma and urban restructuring in the case of Glasgow's Commonwealth Games', *The Sociological Review*.

Peck, J. (2015) 'Cities beyond compare?', *Regional Studies*, 49(1), 160–182.

Porter, L. (2009) 'Planning displacement: the real legacy of major sporting events', *Planning Theory & Practice*, 10(3), 395–418.

Sakizliogliu, B. (2014) 'Inserting temporality into the analysis of displacement: living under the threat of displacement', *Tijdschrift voor Economische en Sociale Geografie*, 105(2), 206–220.

Sayer, A. (2015) *Why We Can't Afford the Rich*, Bristol: Policy Press.

Slater, T. (2017) 'Planetary rent gaps', *Antipode*, 49(s1), 114–137.

Slater, T. and Anderson, N. (2012) 'The reputational ghetto: territorial stigmatisation in St. Paul's, Bristol', *Transactions of the Institute of British Geographers*, 37(4), 530–546.

Smith, N. (1977) *The Return from the Suburbs and the Structuring of Urban Space: State Involvement on Society Hill, Philadelphia*. BSc Dissertation, Department of Geography, University of St. Andrews [Online]. Available at: http://www.geos.ed.ac.uk/homes/tslater/NeilSmithugraddiss.pdf.

Smith, N. (1979a) 'Gentrification and capital: practice and ideology in Society Hill', *Antipode*, 11, 24–35.

Smith, N. (1979b) 'Toward a theory of gentrification: a back to the city movement by capital, not people', *Journal of the American Planning Association*, 45(4), 538–548.

Smith, N. (1996) *The New Urban Frontier: Gentrification and the Revanchist City*, New York: Routledge.

Smith, N., Duncan, B. and Reid, L. (1989) 'From disinvestment to reinvestment: tax arrears and turning points in the East Village', *Housing Studies*, 4, 238–252.

Thörn, C. and Holgersson, H. (2016) 'Revisiting the urban frontier through the case of New Kvillebäcken, Gothenburg', *City*, 20(5), 663–684.

Uitermark, J., Duyvendak, J. and Kleinhans, R. (2007) 'Gentrification as a governmental strategy: social control and social cohesion in Hoogvliet, Rotterdam', *Environment and Planning A*, 39, 125–141.

Wachsmuth, D. (2017) 'Airbnb and gentrification in New York' [Online]. Available at: https://davidwachsmuth.com/2017/03/13/airbnb-and-gentrification-in-new-york/.

Wacquant, L. (2007) 'Territorial stigmatization in the age of advanced marginality', *Thesis Eleven*, 91(1), 66–77.

Whitehead, J. and More, N. (2007) 'Revanchism in Mumbai? Political economy of rent gaps and urban restructuring in a global city', *Economic and Political Weekly*, 23 June, 2428–2434.

Wright, M. (2014) 'Gentrification, assassination and forgetting in Mexico: a feminist Marxist tale', *Gender, Place & Culture*, 21(1), 1–16.

Wyly, E. (2015) 'Gentrification on the planetary urban frontier: the evolution of Turner's noosphere', *Urban Studies*, 52(14), 2515–2550.

Yung, C-F. and King, R. (1998) 'Some tests for the rent gap theory', *Environment and Planning A*, 30, 523–542.

9. Gentrification-induced displacement
Zhao Zhang and Shenjing He

9.1 INTRODUCTION

Displacement in gentrification studies is broadly defined as both the physical dislocation of people and the phenomenological eviction of people's sense of place (Davidson and Lees 2010). The concept, displacement, has also been used in relation to the construction of dams (Routledge 2003), metro stations (Choi 2016), and other types of development that have caused the destruction of local residents' everyday lives by forcing them to leave and resettle elsewhere. Since Peter Marcuse's (1985) seminal work on synthesising typologies of displacement based on the context of New York City between 1970 and the mid-1980s, displacement has been discussed widely in urban studies. In Marcuse's early typology, displacement was attributed to either direct last-resident displacement, direct chain displacement, exclusionary displacement or displacement pressure. In this chapter, we draw on and extend this work.

In the early days of gentrification studies, the focus very much rested on examining class-based population change (e.g. Hartman 1984; Atkinson 2000; Freeman and Braconi 2004). Gentrification-induced displacement in the Global North has had deep roots in industrial restructuring since the 1970s, when knowledge-based industries such as financial services and IT formed dense agglomerations in post-Fordist cities (Scott and Storper 2015). On the consumption side, a bourgeois lifestyle to some extent matched the industrial transformation from Fordist mass production to 'flexible accumulation' (Harvey 1987). In advanced industrial states, gentrification during that time reflected the transformation of industries, bringing in a population that fitted into higher value-added sectors (Scott 2011). In other words, gentrification in the 1970s marked the emergence of a new middle class (Ley 1994) or new professions in pursuit of a lifestyle different from that enjoyed by previous generations. Gentrifiers tended to be consumers with small families and preferred to be located close to their jobs, sources of entertainment and high-end catering services (Zukin 1987; Short 1989). Consequently, the working classes, who had previously occupied the inner city, were largely 'displaced' (or 'replaced' see Hamnett (2003); for a critique of the replacement thesis see Watt (2008), Davidson and Lees (2010), Lees (2014a)) by the middle classes. This process operated in concert with the dislocation of the existing working-class population and low-end businesses.

Apart from changes caused by globalised industrial and labour restructuring, national governments across the world, from the 1970s onwards, also gradually adopted upscale spatial strategies in the form of 'gentrification blueprints' to attract the middle classes. In particular, the so-called creative class were attracted to built-up socially-mixed neighbourhoods in central locations (Lees et al. 2016). On the production side, as characterised by Smith (1979: 538), rather than acknowledging gentrification as a 'back to the city movement' by the new middle class, what plays a much more decisive role in influencing the displacement process is 'how much productive capital returns to the area from the suburbs'. In the Global North, influenced by neoliberal policies in which social welfare has been offloaded and governance structures have been decentralised through state rescaling (Swyngedouw et al. 2002), local projects took more entrepreneurial steps to foster capital accumulation through the built environment (Harvey 1989). Furthermore, competition between different regions fostered changes in the form of massive infrastructure investment and upward urban redevelopment (Molotch 1976), to attract what was thought to be a more creative labour force (Florida 2004). Generally speaking, gentrification and gentrification-induced displacement in the Global North have long been dependent on laissez-faire policies as a prerequisite. Reduced public housing stock and aggressive spatial transformation, both driven by speculative capital, have been seen as key triggers for encroachment into pre-existing working-class neighbourhoods and the middle-class (re)taking of underinvested core urban areas, a notion defined by Smith (1996) as 'urban revanchism'.

Over time, with scholarly concerns zooming out from prominent global cities in the North Atlantic region, where the Industrial Revolution and historical immigration have played important roles in laying the foundations of class and race-based segregation, socio-spatial transformations in the Global South and East have begun to contribute nuanced empirical data and variables that enrich the theorisation and lens of gentrification across a much broader scope (Lees et al. 2015, 2016). For instance, upward spatial transformation in many newly industrialised states is not always associated with laissez-faire land and housing markets, but instead has been constantly manipulated by a strong state presence (e.g. He 2007). Gentrification-induced displacement in the 'developing' world has demonstrated other complex features, even coercive domicide against space-users' wills (e.g. Porteous and Smith 2001). Although residential displacement could be a vantage point from which to examine gentrification-induced displacement, the displacement engendered by gentrification goes far beyond its physical underpinnings – the cultural meanings behind erasing low-end businesses and killing off working-class communities and lifestyles should also be taken on board. Meanwhile, gentrification-induced displacement not only links to the very moment when an eviction takes place, but it also relates to the temporalities before, in the midst of, and after the eviction.

In the next section, we introduce the politico-economic basis of gentrification-induced displacement through the lens of 'accumulation by dispossession' and endogenous factors across different contexts. In the third section, typologies of gentrification-induced displacement are teased out, following that we discuss the socioeconomic impacts generated by gentrification-induced displacement in section four. In the fifth section, new trends and ideas related to the study of gentrification-induced displacement are outlined. The final section will suggest a more comprehensive stance from which to understand gentrification-induced displacement in the global context and possible solutions for reducing its adverse effects.

9.2   THE POLITICAL ECONOMY OF GENTRIFICATION-INDUCED DISPLACEMENT

9.2.1   Accumulation by Dispossession

Gentrification-induced displacement is associated closely not only with the physical dispossession of low-income or working-class populations and their cultures, but it can also be understood from a critical politico-economic viewpoint whereby it is part of a crisis-ridden capitalism revolutionising the old system by engendering new opportunities for accumulation. Based on Karl Marx's 'primitive accumulation' and Rosa Luxemburg's 'primitive and continuous accumulation', David Harvey (2003) has posited a framework for 'accumulation by dispossession', to explain how capitalism creates the conditions for constantly renewing and expanding reproduction rather than the one-off plundering of the peasantry which 'primitive accumulation' achieved. 'Accumulation by dispossession' has been found to be useful in explaining widespread neoliberal governance across the world since the 1970s, especially in urban-based socioeconomic transformations such as New Public Management in the UK and 'shock therapy' in post-communist states (Harvey 2005), where institutional design catered to the requirements of capital accumulation. According to Harvey (2003), privatisation, financialisation, the management and manipulation of crisis, and state redistributions are the top four features of accumulation by dispossession, and this contributes enormously to our understanding of the politico-economic basis for gentrification-induced displacement.

With regard to privatisation and financialisation, when the Fordist-Keynesian economic model dominated most parts of the world up until the 1970s, states used to engage actively in public housing provision as a 'means of labour', to sustain production and accumulation through the primary circuit of capital. Since the Oil Crisis and overproduction in the primary circuit of capital, the gradual adaptation of neoliberal policies in an array of liberal market economies has led to retreating government responsibilities in social welfare provision (Harvey 1978). Conversely, it has enhanced capital accumulation through the means of the urban built environment and the privatisation of public services, reflected in the shrinkage of public housing stock and an increase in mortgage consumption as a result of house purchases (Aalbers and Christophers 2014). In other words, private housing began to become sought after as a valuable financial asset and deviated from its basic structure and use value ever since (Harvey 1982). Given the residualisation of public housing provision and emerging speculative investment in the private housing market, poorly funded public housing neighbourhoods began to be overrepresented by the very poorest, while the private rent sector began to attract more affluent individuals/households so that they could stay in cities. To meet the demands of middle-class consumers (gentrifiers), whether in new-build developments (Davidson and Lees 2005) or urban regeneration schemes, these middle-class residents became potential competitors with public housing tenants for many of the same locations in the inner cities of the Global North. This dramatic change in housing provision from welfare to workfare widened socio-spatial inequality and brought about greater housing speculation, which then provoked gentrification-led displacement.

In terms of crisis manipulation and state redistribution, by implementing gentrification and displacement – from advanced Western European countries (Swyngedouw et al. 2002) to emerging Eurasian economies (Koch 2013) and Eastern Asian developmental states (Shin and Kim 2016) – state redistribution has been witnessed as an inevitable means of spatially sustaining capital accumulation. Taking Turkey as an example, the ruling Justice and Development Party (AKP) has carried out massive housing redevelopment and strategic gentrification projects in many major cities through the Turkish Housing Development Administration (TOKI) since the early 2000s in order to stimulate economic growth and create a populist rhetoric while consolidating the legitimacy of authoritarian governance (Çavuşoğlu and Strutz 2014). In China, from the Asian Financial Crisis in the late 1990s up until 2011, when large-scale public housing provision was reintroduced, accelerated housing privatisation and urban redevelopment, especially in the country's megacities, have marked the central state's intentional deployment of urban housing and redevelopment as a macroeconomic tool to help cope with regional and endogenous setbacks (He and Wu 2009). However, this spatial fix is not problem-free, since, for example, state-led neoliberal urban transformation has brutally destroyed the safety net for less affluent urban dwellers, which directly triggered the new public housing policies. The rights of Turkey's marginalised displacees, especially immigrants and ethnic minorities living in informal settlements (*gecekondu*), were taken (Lovering and Türkmen 2011). Gentrification and forced displacement in urban China induced a decade-long housing price inflation in tandem with property rights-based resistance on a nationwide scale (Hsing 2010; Wu 2015).

9.2.2 Endogenous Reasons for Gentrification-induced Displacement

As stressed by Smith (2002), gentrification has developed gradually into a 'global urban strategy', widely adopted by developing and newly industrialised states. We acknowledge that the aforementioned 'accumulation by dispossession' model and the intention to close the rent gap serve as fundamental economic drivers of gentrification and gentrification-induced displacement. From an ontological standpoint, it is easy to homogenise the rhetoric of 'worlding cities' or the practice of conducting upward urban redevelopment as policy mobility departs from the traditionally Global North-dominated paradigm (e.g. Roy and Ong 2011). For instance, the building of creative cities and industries mirrors the displacement of previous 'backwards' dwellers (e.g. Ren and Sun 2012), while the holding of mega-events has led residents to involuntarily leave neighbourhoods targeted for regeneration (Shin 2012).

From an epistemological perspective, however, scholars working in postcolonial contexts have increasingly been reminding us of the vernacular perspectives that provoke gentrification-induced displacement beyond well-documented experiences in the Global North (e.g. Ley and Teo 2014; Janoschka and Sequera 2016). Lees (2012) suggests that a more provincialised and comparative lens should be employed to gauge gentrification happening in different corners of the world, rather than oversimplifying it as a 'one-size-fits-all' theory. In particular, the nuances of land ownership, land development regimes and housing preferences/aesthetics at the local level could bring about pronounced impacts on detailed and context-sensitive policy implementation. For instance, in 'property states' (Haila 2000), where urban land is predominately state/publicly owned, such as Hong Kong, displacement imperatives are influenced enormously by the strong presence of local authorities, crony capitalists, and associated fiscal arrangements. Although gentrification terminology rarely appears in policy documents and media reports, the leases raised from this land, which are derived from 'crown leases' dating back to Hong Kong's colonial period, have contributed tremendously to local tax revenues. Public expenditure on urban infrastructure, such as metro networks, is sourced heavily from the adjacent property and premises leases. The transit-oriented development model has enhanced the proximity between upmarket commercial districts with high expected tax contributions and metro stations (Cervero and Murakami 2009), thus pricing out low-end businesses and working-class residents from the most convenient locations. Likewise, in Mainland China, where urban land is largely state-owned in tandem with a tradable land lease regime, the scarcity of local fiscal income incentivises subnational authorities to enter into large-scale gentrification projects by bulldozing rundown inner-city enclaves and relocating local residents to remote city outskirts (He and Wu 2009). This process not only helps reap lucrative tax revenues in addition to land conveyance fees, but it also simultaneously creates 'two housing markets' (Hsing 2010). As a typical East Asian developmental state, South Korea is deeply entrenched in large-scale displacement and housing redevelopment schemes, modernising its urban residential clusters from the 1980s onwards and producing 'vertical accumulation' through a unique high-rise housing culture, as a result of which the emerging middle class has embraced state-led gentrification (Park 2013). A recent study conducted in Latin American megacities, including Mexico City and Buenos Aires, by Janoschka and Sequera (2016), identifies 'symbolic violence' being widely adopted through claims of so-called 'architectural heritage' and 'cultural heritage' which are used to justify the rationality behind beautification and social cleansing in historic urban centres.

9.3   TYPOLOGIES OF GENTRIFICATION-INDUCED DISPLACEMENT

9.3.1   Direct Residential Displacement

In many ways, Marcuse's (1985) classification of residential displacement is still applicable to present-day gentrification studies. Firstly, he addressed both physical (e.g. harassment from landlords) and economic (e.g. rent increases) factors embedded within processes of displacement. Secondly, he suggested periodically counting the total number of displacees rather than only the last remaining resident in every housing unit. Thirdly, he proposed taking into account indirect and less measurable displacement by considering exclusionary displacement and displacement pressure which may not be traced immediately but might happen in the long term and in hidden forms (see Table 9.1). His vision has significantly influenced subsequent studies (e.g. Davidson and Lees 2005, 2010; Slater 2009) which claim that new-build gentrification has induced the displacement of the working-class population in both a direct and an indirect manner rather than through simple 'class replacement' (e.g. Butler 2007).

However, the definition of displacement by Marcuse (1985) is hinged largely upon the laissez-faire housing market and less interventionist urban policies dating back to the 1970s in New York City. Nowadays, direct residential displacement tends to be associated with more state-led and entrepreneurial actions (Lees et al. 2016). In different countries

Table 9. 1 Peter Marcuse's typologies of displacement and its adaptations

Direct last-resident displacement	Direct last-resident displacement is caused by both physical (e.g. harassment from landlords) and economic (e.g. rent increases) actions.
Direct chain displacement	This sort of displacement is counted beyond 'direct last-resident displacement' and includes previous households dislocated due to the deterioration of a building or rent increases.
Exclusionary displacement	This kind of displacement means households have previously had access to housing but are unable to access any at a later stage because it has been gentrified or abandoned.
Displacement pressure	Displacement pressure refers to the dispossession suffered by less affluent families during the transformation of the neighbourhoods where they live.

Source: Compiled from the definition of displacement given by Marcuse (1985) and its later adaptations by Davidson and Lees (2005, 2010) and Slater (2009).

across the world, lucrative redevelopment projects are frequently underlined with officially choreographed jargon and rhetoric, such as the ambiguously defined 'in the public interest' (Ren 2014), and 'obsolescence' (Kuyucu and Unsal 2010). Before sending in the bulldozers, schemes under the banner of 'slum renovation' or 'urban renewal' are at times appropriated to smooth the implementation of massive demolition, displacement and redevelopment projects.

Firstly, due to the long-term disinvestment and residualisation of public housing under neoliberal governance in the Global North, it is commonly downgraded and made a target for redevelopment. Despite nuanced policy orientations, 'social mixing' has been openly exploited in the Global North to deal with a series of social issues (Lees 2003, 2008; Bridge et al. 2011). For instance, in the US, 'social mixing' is a popular concept claimed as a progressive agenda through the 'dispersal of poverty' from distressed public housing projects (Crump 2002). The reality is that the HOPE VI programme of radical public housing transformation since the mid-1990s has not successfully accomplished its goal of poverty alleviation (Wyly and Hammel 1999). On the contrary, apparently racialised, class-based displacement and gentrification in former public housing estates have been documented and criticised (Lees 2014b; Goetz 2011; Bridge et al. 2011). In the Global South, obsolete neighbourhoods and informal settlements have also become easy targets for regeneration. For instance, 'the three olds' redevelopment[1] was employed in Guangzhou, the third largest city in China, and resulted not only in a wave of gentrification in the 2000s, but also in the demolition of many shelters for low-income groups, especially those living in dilapidated private, low-rise housing neighbourhoods and urban villages (*chengzhongcun*) (He 2012). In the case of Turkey, a large number of migrants, especially those from minority ethnic backgrounds living in informal settlements in large

---

[1] The three olds' redevelopment refers to the rejuvenation of old urban areas, old factories and old villages (see He 2012).

cities have been displaced and resettled to very remote locations, while their previous areas of residence have been strategically upgraded to cater to higher-end commercial and residential clients (Islam and Sakızlıoğlu 2015). Moreover, no matter whether in the Global South or the North, development-led displacement and mega displacement have been increasingly observed (Lees et al. 2016). For instance, holding mega-events not only serves the imaginative role of city branding and urban boosterism, but it also develops into a plausible justification for displacement and gentrification. In a long-term study of the aftermath of mega-events in Canadian cities, Olds's (1998) research testifies to the apparently forced eviction of communities caused by the Olympics and international expositions. More updated inquiries undertaken by Watt (2013) and Shin (2012) have further shown how the state's will can impose involuntary dislocation or displacement threats on working-class communities due to urban renewal, in these cases linked with mega-events in London and a series of major Chinese cities.

9.3.2   Indirect and Non-residential Displacement

9.3.2.1   Indirect displacement
Besides the aforementioned direct residential displacement, displacement induced by gentrification can be found in indirect or hidden forms, too. Although new-build gentrification does not normally dislocate pre-existing communities and can be built on brownfield sites (Shaw 2008), Davidson and Lees's (2005) research reminds us that indirect displacement should also be taken into account. Subsequent to 'price shadowing', which causes property price increases in areas adjacent to newly redeveloped sites, exclusionary displacement can occur, preventing many households from moving into previously affordable local areas (Davidson and Lees 2010; Lees et al. 2008). Recent studies have also found that a sought-after school's catchment area can create concentrations of families in upper income brackets, causing exclusionary displacement for less affluent households and their exclusion from high-quality educational resources (Wu et al. 2016; Butler et al. 2013).

At times, according to Marcuse (1985), although homes are not necessarily destroyed, arson and other forms of harassment perpetrated by landlords still exert significant displacement pressure on incumbent residents. Based on seminal work conducted by Newman and Wyly (2006), displacement pressure and deteriorating affordability not only price out some less affluent residents, but they also induce involuntary immobility, thus entrapping some tenants. Their 'staying put' and acceptance of high rents, substandard living conditions or overcrowding should be perceived as trade-offs. In some deprived neighbourhoods, although the bulldozers are not necessarily on the doorstep, the territorial stigmatisation of these neighbourhoods could exacerbate disinvestment and raise displacement pressures through the negative rhetoric used by the media and policymakers (August 2014; Kallin and Slater 2014).

9.3.2.2   Non-residential displacement
With regards to non-residential displacement, retail and tourism gentrification are sometimes major causes. Zukin (2008, 2009) talks about how the introduction of higher-end consumer culture and businesses sanitises the very 'authenticity' that gentrifiers in large American cities are looking for, pushing out pre-existing lower-end boutiques lacking in specific aesthetics and cultural taste. Retail gentrification not only denotes a

decline in traditional marketplaces and the unemployment of market traders (Gonzalez and Waley 2013), but it also indicates an uneven entrepreneurial landscape distanced from more mundane architectural appearances and largely replaced by modern-looking shopping malls (Hubbard 1996). Tourism gentrification has been witnessed in many parts of the world, with the aim of building tourist attraction sites and thus encouraging consumption-oriented activities (Gotham 2005). This can be seen in examples such as the 'Guggenheim Effect' in Bilbao, a city which strategically brought in more 'arts, culture and entertainment' to gentrify deprived inner-city areas (Vicario and Martinez Monje 2003: 2385). As a result, such museumisation fosters the dismantling of 'unmatched' businesses from core areas, which results in the eviction of low-end trade (Colini et al. 2009).

In many cities in the Global North, strategies to attract higher-income residents who could potentially contribute more to local tax revenues have played out unevenly in terms of social investment and have included revanchist behaviours such as restrictions over the use of public space (Atkinson and Easthope 2009) and the displacement of non-profit social services (De Verteuil 2011). In some Latin American cities with considerable informal employment, such as Mexico City, the livelihoods of street vendors have been jeopardised by the city's 'beautification' scheme, thereby accelerating the weakening of the street-trading culture (Crossa 2009). Furthermore, according to research carried out in Ecuador, already marginalised groups (e.g. indigenous beggars and street boys) have been dragged into worse conditions as a result of a revanchist urbanism, enforcing 'zero tolerance' and imposing the 'refinement' of non-white ethnic groups (Swanson 2007). Despite widespread social mixing policies across the globe, these policies are still very challenging to carry out in reality, as affluent social groups still tend to fence in and self-segregate themselves from low-income households (Lees 2008). This potentially contributes to intensified encroachment into public space and social services for the poor. De Verteuil (2011) reports that gentrification in London and Los Angeles has led to both the involuntary mobility (displacement) and involuntary immobility (entrapment) of non-profit services. For one thing, rent and overall cost increases in gentrified neighbourhoods have dragged down available social services to a very basic level. For another, the 'not-in-my-backyard' mentalities of gentrifiers constantly exert displacement pressure on client bases and push them away from high-end communities. The co-existing institutional and societal displacement of vulnerable groups has led to an increasing number of rough sleepers and homeless people (Blomley 2009; De Verteuil 2011).

From a more humanistic standpoint, Davidson (2009) suggests taking into account the displacement of everyday life and lived space, which is defined as 'phenomenological displacement' by Davidson and Lees (2010). The displacement of low-end commercial businesses, cultural settings and people's collective memories has a strong impact on pre-existing local communities and engenders a sense of losing one's place. Similarly, Atkinson (2015) puts forward an argument based on symbolic displacement, in which long-term residents suffer from an insecure and unfamiliar milieu, both before and after the actual dislocation.

9.4   IMPACTS OF GENTRIFICATION-INDUCED DISPLACEMENT

9.4.1   Impacts of Direct Residential Displacement

The impacts of direct residential displacement caused by gentrification vary somewhat, although from some policymakers' perspectives, massive residential displacement and relocation appear to yield socioeconomic benefits such as short-term rapid economic growth, poverty alleviation and social mixing. However, the consequences of these polices are not always as supposed.

In some developing countries, where urban renewal is taken as one of the key drivers of economic growth, property rights are always insufficiently protected. Forced displacement could induce protests and different forms of social contestation against the infringement of housing rights. In particular, when domicide, an extreme form of forced displacement achieved by violence and force, occurs, displacees, for instance in China (Shao 2013), have been reported to take legal and institutional action to challenge the 'barbaric displacement' carried out by local authorities, which eventually led to institutional and legislative adjustments. In the case of Turkey, domicide has not only provoked localised resistance against uneven processes alongside displacement and resettlement, but it also escalated into a nationwide anti-government social movement in 2013 (see Lovering and Türkmen 2011; Yörük and Yüksel 2014). When housing and human rights are subordinated to the myopic vested interests of political parties and politicians, gentrification-induced direct residential displacement can be politicised and induce large-scale bottom-up opposition.

With regard to poverty alleviation, for instance, housing voucher recipients and African-American recipients in particular, in the HOPE VI programme for distressed inner-city neighbourhoods in Chicago, set off a geographical shift in poverty in an outward direction to suburban areas. Consequently, it has been identified that a high re-concentration of race-based distressed neighbourhoods emerged on the city's outskirts, which were now home to those housing recipients previously displaced from the inner city (Sink and Ceh 2011). Likewise, displacement related to social mixing policies has been shown across a number of different contexts not to result in significant improvements in ethnic diversity or reductions in social inequality (Bridge et al. 2011). In fact, according to Walks and Maaranen (2008: 319) and other research conducted across the North Atlantic states over the past decade, 'the more that gentrification had progressed in a neighbourhood, the greater the reduction in levels of social mix'. In other words, worsened social polarisation and new social segregation were created.

Generally speaking, residential displacement has less desirable impacts on lower income groups, who are politically and economically subordinated to the hegemonic system due to elements such as race, origin and income. For instance, increasing homelessness has been witnessed as being directly linked with gentrification, whereby gentrifiers take the last piece of affordable space for the poor (Philip 1984). In Western Europe, such as in the Netherlands, the vulnerable legal status of ethnic minority groups and immigrants makes them easy targets for eviction and exposure to 'territorial, ethnic and class stigmatisation' (Sakızlıoğlu and Uitermark 2014: 1369). Similarly, Stabrowski's (2014: 813) findings in New York City articulate how gentrification produces spaces of 'prohibition, appropriation, and insecurity' by sweeping away highly concentrated Polish immigrants from certain neighbourhoods in Brooklyn. In less ethnically and culturally diversified countries, such as China, working class and migrant workers are often the victims of gentrification. Based on Shin's (2013) research in an urban village (Pazhou) in Guangzhou, in the absence of tenancy rights protection in China, migrant workers without local registration status are not entitled to compensation as private renters, regardless of any long-term tenancies or valuable contributions they have made to building the city.

9.4.2 Impacts of Temporalities and Displacement Pressure

Most previous studies into gentrification have focused on the outcomes of upward socio-spatial transformations. Only recently have temporalities and displacement pressures embedded in the process of gentrification-induced displacement begun to attract attention from scholars (e.g. Sakızlıoğlu 2014). Temporalities can be seen from two viewpoints: namely developers seeking to close rent gaps and encourage shorter-term turnover (Weber 2002). Firstly, local authorities and developers – at times intentionally – leave areas targeted for redevelopment in a dilapidated or unattended status, expecting the psychological stress engendered by anxiety and uncertainty to automatically disarm anti-displacement struggles within these deprived or stigmatised communities (Lees 2014b; Sakızlıoğlu 2014; Sakızlıoğlu and Uitermark 2014). Secondly, based on a study of inner-city gentrification in Nanjing, China (Zhang 2015), a large number of evictees could wait up to six years for resettlement housing. Although a rental allowance was offered during this transitional period, no official promise or agreement indicating the exact time of resettlement was provided. Protracted compensation plans for displacees offloaded financial pressure from local government and property developers in terms of paying back bank loans. Meanwhile, property developers acquired more substantial cash flow to reinvest in new projects. In China, the predicaments faced by displacees have been alleviated after a new ordinance governing residential relocation was enacted and large-scale affordable housing schemes were implemented since 2011. Besides passive waiting, resistance, especially in the midst of displacement pressures induced by retail/tourism gentrification, has also sometimes been organised proactively by traders and NGOs using place-making strategies to put a halt to or delay encroachment on a working-class trading environment (Crossa 2013; Buser et al. 2013).

9.4.3 Post-displacement Experiences Under Entrepreneurial Urbanism

Without prioritising human development, entrepreneurial urbanism and its associated large-scale direct displacement treats 'people as infrastructure' (Goldman 2011: 577), subordinated to greater economic development deployment. Residents living in social housing or overcrowded inner-city enclaves are often relatively marginalised people, including the elderly, as well as redundant and migrant workers. At times, due to small living spaces in dilapidated inner-city homes and limited compensation based on the structural value of these derelict dwellings, a large number of displacees are unable to receive in-situ resettlements. Under the entrepreneurial logic of urban governance, resettlement housing sites for displacees are often distributed across less accessible areas with low land rents (Hsing 2010). Lacking decent schools and well-matched working opportunities, these settlements have often turned into new poverty neighbourhoods (Sink and Ceh 2011).

Although housing space and housing quality might have been improved, underdeveloped public amenities (e.g. medical care, transportation facilities and schools) at these sites have created multiple deprivations for already vulnerable groups displaced from inner cities.

Aside from the obvious socioeconomic loss, psychological stress is an unavoidable post-displacement drawback. Displacees normally have to adapt to post-displacement living conditions and a new neighbourhood environment while dealing with losing a place of identity and re-establishing social networks. A quantitative study conducted by Desmond (2012) has pointed out the strong correlation between housing displacement and people's mental health, with severe post-displacement depression applying particularly to mothers. Gentrification and displacement under the entrepreneurial paradigm give credence only to capital accumulation and short-term economic gains via the built environment, such as strategising social mixing and household dispersal in distressed neighbourhoods in order to maximise profits (Davidson 2008). The socioeconomic requirements of displacees are always neglected, owing to the lack of visible economic returns. Without granting displacees sufficient training and employment chances at the very local level, vicious circles and pre-destined injustices are aggravated, e.g. the 'neighbourhood effect' which traps many poorly educated and badly paid households in these deprived areas (Slater 2013).

9.5   IDEAS FOR FURTHER RESEARCH

9.5.1   Financialisation-related Gentrification and Displacement

Extant gentrification studies have paid a good deal of attention to examining the incentives and logic of property developers and local states, but very few have been dedicated to analysing the extent to which financial capital has influenced processes of gentrification and displacement (for an exception see Webber and Burrows 2016 on the super rich in London). As argued by Lees et al. (2008: 179), the fourth wave of gentrification since the early 2000s in the US is strongly related to the 'intensified financiali[s]ation of housing combined with the consolidation of pro-gentrification politics and polari[s]ed urban policies'. Firstly, as part of the aforementioned accumulation by dispossession, financialisation means that land and housing are increasingly regarded as financial assets, with the exchange value being far more important than the use value (Harvey 1982). Meanwhile, the second aspect of financialisation demonstrates the integration between financial capital and the housing market. Overall high expectations regarding economic returns from mortgage lenders and investors have contributed to rapid increases in rent and housing prices (Lees et al. 2008).

In viewing urban housing as a financial asset that will appreciate in value, property developers and a small number of super-rich investors from Mainland China, including a considerable number of second- or multiple-home buyers, have created booming housing markets both at home and overseas (Wu 2015). Skyrocketing housing prices have not only brutally excluded migrant workers and less wealthy families from affordable housing and decent living environments in Mainland Chinese cities, but they have even contributed to making Vancouver one of the world's most expensive cities in which to buy a home (Ley 2015). A comparative study conducted by Fields and Uffer (2016) argues that the engagement of financial capital in public/social housing provision has weakened rental protection in a series of Global North cities. In several advanced liberal market economies, for instance, the catastrophic foreclosures and mortgage arrears rendered by the subprime mortgage crisis in the US (Aalbers 2012) and the bursting of the housing bubble in Ireland (Waldron and Redmond 2016), have also led to the eviction of many families who have defaulted on repaying their mortgage loans. Some of these were ex-gentrifiers who were once in pursuit of the 'middle-class dream' of owning decent homes but who dramatically became victims (displacees) of exploitative financial capital and, as such, 'losers' in gentrification. As such, we argue that the financialisation of the property market and people's treatment of housing as a financial asset, could lead to both direct and exclusionary displacement, a subject future research might investigate.

9.5.2   Some Other New Research Ideas

9.5.2.1   'Sandwich class'
Previous studies have focused on marginalised groups based on their race, ethnicity and deprived social backgrounds. Relatively marginalised groups have not received specific concern. Due to the limited buying power of early career employees and newly graduated students, skyrocketing housing prices have shut off their access to all but less desirable locations and housing conditions. Youth housing difficulties; in other words, the exclusionary displacement of urban youth, have developed into a worldwide phenomenon (Forrest and Yip 2013). For instance, owing to unaffordable housing prices and rents, a large number of newly graduated college students and migrant workers in China's megacities have been forced to squeeze into shabby shared rooms in urban villages, known as the 'ant tribes' (He 2015). In the Italian context, an unfriendly labour market and an absent welfare system have forced many youngsters in Milan to share apartments with others, sacrificing their privacy (Bricocoli and Sabatinelli 2016). Apparently, these urban dwellers do not necessarily suffer from absolute poverty, but their relatively deprived economic and social status have excluded them from gentrified areas of the city and negatively affected their pursuit of family and career development. Hence, zooming out from the traditional scholarly interest vis-à-vis very marginalised groups, the housing struggles of the 'sandwich class' also deserve our attention.

9.5.2.2   Displacement policies and implementation
More and more research has claimed that the state is increasingly playing a more decisive role in choreographing the pace of gentrification and displacement (e.g. He 2007; Lovering and Türkmen 2011; Paton and Cooper 2016). Therefore, it is very important to understand the way in which various legal settings bolster the occurrence of displacement. Some pioneering studies in the Turkish context have established that codifications have gradually legitimised the forced displacement of informal settlements in cities (Karaman 2013; Islam and Sakızlıoğlu 2015), while Shih's (2010a, 2010b) investigation in Shanghai reminds us that Chinese local governments have long been taking advantage of the legal system to promote urban growth via transforming the built environment. In the supposedly more democratic Netherlands, the deliberative participation and voting system of the city council, without transferring power to citizens, might even legitimise forced displacement rather than effectively enhancing social justice (Huisman 2014). Meanwhile, there are also certain non-institutional and informal practices within gentrification-induced

displacements. For instance, state officials of various ranks in Turkey may take advantage of pre-existing clientelistic networks to negotiate with displacees, in order to maximise profits and accelerate the dislocation process (Demirtaş-Milz 2013). More in-depth enquiries into the formal and informal practices of rules regarding displacement could potentially facilitate an enhanced understanding of the way in which state-led eviction is carried out on the ground.

9.6   CONCLUSION

In this chapter, we have employed an all-encompassing approach to provide an updated understanding of gentrification-induced displacement. After decades of theoretical exploration, gentrification-induced displacement is no longer treated purely as a side effect of gentrification in Euro-American cities (Marcuse 1985), for it has been observed widely across the world (Lees et al. 2015). Apart from the shared global political economy behind this controversial form of socio-spatial transformation, contextual factors, such as each country's institutional and economic features, also influence the scale, form, speed and resistance of gentrification-induced displacement. Over the past decade or so, empirical contributions from the Global South and East have largely enriched and diversified the epistemology of gentrification, as has been shown in the more inclusive reading of 'planetary gentrification' and its associated displacement (Lees et al. 2016). In this chapter, we too have tried to de-territorialise our narratives by incorporating examples from different continents, whilst embracing a comparative standpoint from which to address commonalities between these cases (Robinson 2011).

To curb the negative impact caused by gentrification-induced displacement, emphasis should be placed on institutionally constraining land and housing price speculation. As suggested by Combs (2015), to tame gentrification, Henry George's thoughts ought to be learnt, in that land should be viewed as a 'gift of nature', while all profit harvested from land should be recaptured through tax. Taxation on land/housing speculation through legislation helps to differentiate between ordinary urban users and speculators. A tax derived from land and housing speculation would help to reduce inequality and discrimination alongside urban redevelopment process. Alternatively, as inspired by relatively successful land use regulation practices in Singapore (Haila 2015), governments could be advised to consider intervening in speculation on state-owned land. Only when speculative behaviour in relation to land and property is controlled can the exploitation of private and financial capital in redevelopment projects be largely avoided.

The gentrification and displacement occurring in many newly-industrialised countries has been synchronised with the emergence of a 'new middle class' (Lees et al. 2016). Gentrification is not simply the transformation of housing stock – it is related even more closely to the resultant shift in housing classes. Besides concerns surrounding housing rights struggles, we suggest that scholarly attention should also be granted to pre-existing inequalities in social classes, especially in some former socialist and authoritarian states, by questioning why interest groups with ample political resources or proximity to crony capitalists tend to be speculators/gentrifiers, while the deprived social class are more likely to be marginalised further during upward urban redevelopment (e.g. Logan et al. 2009). Although urban resistance has attempted to draw attention to issues such as displacement, housing difficulties and social polarisation, the process of neoliberalisation has simultaneously intensified atomisation and led to people spending more time worrying about their group or individual interests (Mayer 2007). Despite assistance from conservationists and NGOs such as the 'Displacement Free Zone' organised by the Fifth Avenue Committee in the Lower Park Slope of New York City, which strives to protect local neighbourhoods and combat gentrification (Lees et al. 2008), anti-gentrification/displacement resistance still tends to be place-cum-class-based. The notion that people's atomised pursuit of potential windfall gains from redevelopment prevails, the politicised aim of creating an emancipatory space still has a long way to go. Bearing in mind that anti-gentrification resistance is a class struggle, only when people's personal ethics are mobilised in refuting spatial inequality (Marcuse 2015) and using residential mobility to counteract neoliberal hegemony in promoting homeownership (Maeckelbergh 2012) can more socio-spatial justice be achieved.

REFERENCES

Aalbers, M. (2012) *Subprime Cities and the Twin Crises*, Oxford: Wiley-Blackwell.
Aalbers, M. and Christophers, B. (2014) 'Centering housing in political economy', *Housing, Theory and Society*, 31(4), 373–394.
Atkinson, R. (2000) 'The hidden costs of gentrification: displacement in central London', *Journal of Housing and the Built Environment*, 15(4), 307–326.
Atkinson, R. (2015) 'Losing one's place: narratives of neighbourhood change, market injustice and symbolic displacement', *Housing, Theory and Society*, 32(4), 373–388.
Atkinson, R. and Easthope, H. (2009) 'The consequences of the creative class: the pursuit of creativity strategies in Australia's cities', *International Journal of Urban and Regional Research*, 33(1), 64–79.
August, M. (2014) 'Challenging the rhetoric of stigmatization: the benefits of concentrated poverty in Toronto's Regent Park', *Environment and Planning A*, 46(6), 1317–1333.
Blomley, N. (2009) 'Homelessness, rights, and the delusions of property', *Urban Geography*, 30(6), 577–590.
Bricocoli, M. and Sabatinelli, S. (2016) 'House sharing amongst young adults in the context of Mediterranean welfare: the case of Milan', *International Journal of Housing Policy*, 16(2), 184–200.
Bridge, G., Butler, T. and Lees, L. (2012) *Mixed Communities: Gentrification by Stealth?*, Bristol: Policy Press.
Buser, M., Bonura, C., Fannin, M. and Boyer, K. (2013) 'Cultural activism and the politics of place-making', *City*, 17(5), 606–627.
Butler, T. (2007) 'Re-urbanizing London Docklands: gentrification, suburbanization or new urbanism?', *International Journal of Urban and Regional Research*, 31(4), 759–781.
Butler, T., Hamnett, C. and Ramsden, M. (2013) 'Gentrification, education and exclusionary displacement in East London', *International Journal of Urban and Regional Research*, 37(2), 556–575.
Çavuşoğlu, E. and Strutz, J. (2014) 'Producing force and consent: urban transformation and corporatism in Turkey', *City*, 18(2), 134–148.
Cervero, R. and Murakami, J. (2009) 'Rail and property development in Hong Kong: experiences and extensions', *Urban Studies*, 46(10), 2019–2043.
Choi, N. (2016) 'Metro Manila through the gentrification lens: disparities in urban planning and displacement risks', *Urban Studies*, 53(3), 577–592.
Colini, L., Pecoriello, A.L., Tripodi, L. and Zetti, I. (2009) 'Museumization and transformation in Florence', in Porter, L. and Shaw, K. (eds), *Whose Urban Renaissance?: An International Comparison of Urban Regeneration Strategies*, New York: Routledge, 50–59.
Combs, J.L. (2015) 'Using Jane Jacobs and Henry George to tame gentrification', *American Journal of Economics and Sociology*, 74(3), 600–630.
Crossa, V. (2009) 'Resisting the entrepreneurial city: street vendors' struggle in Mexico City's historic center', *International Journal of Urban and Regional Research*, 33(1), 43–63.
Crossa, V. (2013) 'Play for protest, protest for play: artisan and vendors' resistance to displacement in Mexico City', *Antipode*, 45(4), 826–843.
Crump, J. (2002) 'Deconcentration by demolition: public housing, poverty, and urban policy', *Environment and Planning D: Society and Space*, 20(5), 581–596.

Davidson, M. (2008) 'Spoiled mixture: where does state-led "positive" gentrification end?', *Urban Studies*, 45(12), 2385–2405.

Davidson, M. (2009) 'Displacement, space and dwelling: placing gentrification debate', *Ethics, Place & Environment*, 12(2), 219–234.

Davidson, M. and Lees, L. (2005) 'New-build "gentrification" and London's riverside renaissance', *Environment and Planning A*, 37(7), 1165–1190.

Davidson, M. and Lees, L. (2010) 'New-build gentrification: its histories, trajectories, and critical geographies', *Population, Space and Place*, 16(5), 395–411.

De Verteuil, G. (2011) 'Evidence of gentrification-induced displacement among social services in London and Los Angeles', *Urban Studies*, 48(8), 1563–1580.

Demirtaş-Milz, N. (2013) 'The regime of informality in neoliberal times in Turkey: the case of the Kadifekale urban transformation project', *International Journal of Urban and Regional Research*, 37(2), 689–714.

Desmond, M. (2012) 'Eviction and the reproduction of urban poverty', *American Journal of Sociology*, 118(1), 88–133.

Fields, D. and Uffer, S. (2016) 'The financialisation of rental housing: a comparative analysis of New York City and Berlin', *Urban Studies*, 53(7), 1486–1502.

Florida, R. (2004) *Cities and the Creative Class*, New York: Routledge.

Forrest, R. and Yip, N-m. (2013) *Housing Young People*, New York: Routledge.

Freeman, L. and Braconi, F. (2004) 'Gentrification and displacement New York City in the 1990s', *Journal of the American Planning Association*, 70(1), 39–52.

Goetz, E. (2011) 'Gentrification in black and white: the racial impact of public housing demolition in American cities', *Urban Studies*, 48(8), 1581–1604.

Goldman, M. (2011) 'Speculative urbanism and the making of the next world city', *International Journal of Urban and Regional Research*, 35(3), 555–581.

Gonzalez, S. and Waley, P. (2013) 'Traditional retail markets: the new gentrification frontier?', *Antipode*, 45(4), 965–983.

Gotham, K.F. (2005) 'Tourism gentrification: the case of New Orleans' Vieux Carre (French Quarter)', *Urban Studies*, 42(7), 1099–1121.

Haila, A. (2000) 'Real estate in global cities: Singapore and Hong Kong as property states', *Urban Studies*, 37(12), 2241–2256.

Haila, A. (2015) *Urban Land Rent: Singapore as a Property State*, West Sussex: John Wiley & Sons.

Hamnett, C. (2003) 'Gentrification and the middle-class remaking of inner London, 1961–2001', *Urban Studies*, 40(12), 2401–2426.

Hartman, C. (1984) 'Right to stay put', in Geisler, C.C. and Popper, F.J. (eds), *Land Reform, American Style*, New York: CUPR Press.

Harvey, D. (1978) 'The urban process under capitalism: a framework for analysis', *International Journal of Urban and Regional Research*, 2(1–4), 101–131.

Harvey, D. (1982) *The Limits to Capital*, Chicago: University of Chicago Press.

Harvey, D. (1987) 'Flexible accumulation through urbanization: reflections on "post-modernism" in the American city', *Antipode*, 19(3), 260–286.

Harvey, D. (1989) 'From managerialism to entrepreneurialism: the transformation in urban governance in late capitalism', *Geografiska Annaler. Series B. Human Geography*, 71(1), 3–17.

Harvey, D. (2003) *The New Imperialism*, New York: Oxford University Press.

Harvey, D. (2005) *A Brief History of Neoliberalism*, Oxford: Oxford University Press.

He, S. (2007) 'State-sponsored gentrification under market transition: the case of Shanghai', *Urban Affairs Review*, 43(2), 171–198.

He, S. (2012) 'Two waves of gentrification and emerging rights issues in Guangzhou, China', *Environment and Planning A*, 44 (12), 2817–2833.

He, S. (2015) 'A review of "Housing inequality in Chinese cities", edited by Youqin Huang and Si-ming Li', *International Journal of Housing Policy*, 15(1), 97–100.

He, S. and Wu, F. (2009) 'China's emerging neoliberal urbanism: perspectives from urban redevelopment', *Antipode*, 41(2), 282–304.

Hsing, Y-t. (2010) *The Great Urban Transformation: Politics of Land and Property in China*, New York: Oxford University Press.

Hubbard, P. (1996) 'Urban design and city regeneration: social representations of entrepreneurial landscapes', *Urban Studies*, 33(8), 1441–1461.

Huisman, C. (2014) 'Displacement through participation', *Tijdschrift voor economische en sociale geografie*, 105(2), 161–174.

Islam, T. and Sakızlıoğlu, B. (2015) 'The making of, and resistance to, state-led gentrification in Istanbul, Turkey', in *Global Gentrifications: Uneven Development and Displacement*, Bristol: Policy Press, pp. 245–264.

Janoschka, M. and Sequera, J. (2016) 'Gentrification in Latin America: addressing the politics and geographies of displacement', *Urban Geography*, 37(8), 1175–1194.

Kallin, H. and Slater, T. (2014) 'Activating territorial stigma: gentrifying marginality on Edinburgh's periphery', *Environment and Planning A*, 46(6), 1351–1368.

Karaman, O. (2013) 'Urban neoliberalism with Islamic characteristics', *Urban Studies*, 50(16), 3412–3427.

Koch, N. (2013) 'Why not a world city? Astana, Ankara, and geopolitical scripts in urban networks', *Urban Geography*, 34(1), 109–130.

Kuyucu, T. and Unsal, O. (2010) '"Urban transformation" as state-led property transfer: an analysis of two cases of urban renewal in Istanbul', *Urban Studies*, 47(7), 1479–1499.

Lees, L. (2003) 'Visions of 'Urban Renaissance': the Urban Task Force Report and the Urban White Paper', in Imrie, R. and Raco, M. (eds), *Urban Renaissance? New Labour, Community and Urban Policy*, Bristol: Policy Press, pp. 61–82.

Lees, L. (2008) 'Gentrification and social mixing: towards an inclusive urban renaissance?', *Urban Studies*, 45(12), 2449–2470.

Lees, L. (2012) 'The geography of gentrification: Thinking through comparative urbanism', *Progress in Human Geography*, 36(2), 155–171.

Lees, L. (2014a) 'The death of sustainable communities in London?', in Imrie, R. and Lees, L. (eds), *Sustainable London? The Future of a Global City*, Bristol: Policy Press, pp. 149–172.

Lees, L. (2014b) 'The urban injustices of New Labour's "New Urban Renewal": the case of the Aylesbury Estate in London', *Antipode*, 46(4), 921–947.

Lees, L., Shin, H.B. and López-Morales, E. (2015) *Global Gentrifications: Uneven Development and Displacement*, Bristol: Policy Press.

Lees, L., Shin, H.B. and López-Morales, E. (2016) *Planetary Gentrification*, Cambridge: Polity Press.

Lees, L., Slater, T. and Wyly, E. (2008) *Gentrification*, New York: Routledge.

Ley, D. (1994) 'Gentrification and the politics of the new middle class', *Environment and Planning D*, 12(1), 53–74.

Ley, D. (2017) 'Global China and the making of Vancouver's residential property market', *International Journal of Housing Policy*, 17(1), 15–34.

Ley, D. and Teo, S.Y. (2014) 'Gentrification in Hong Kong? Epistemology vs. Ontology', *International Journal of Urban and Regional Research*, 38(4), 1286–1303.

Logan, J.R., Fang, Y. and Zhang, Z. (2009) 'The winners in China's urban housing reform', *Housing Studies*, 25(1), 101–117.

Lovering, J. and Türkmen, H. (2011) 'Bulldozer neo-liberalism in Istanbul: the state-led construction of property markets, and the displacement of the urban poor', *International Planning Studies*, 16(1), 73–96.

Maeckelbergh, M. (2012) 'Mobilizing to stay put: housing struggles in New York City', *International Journal of Urban and Regional Research*, 36(4), 655–673.

Marcuse, P. (1985) 'Gentrification, abandonment, and displacement: the linkages in New York City', *Journal of Urban and Contemporary Law*, 28(1), 195–240.

Marcuse, P. (2015) 'Gentrification, social justice and personal ethics', *International Journal of Urban and Regional Research*, 39(6), 1263–1269.

Mayer, M. (2007) 'Contesting the neoliberalization of urban governance', in Leitner, H., Peck, J. and Sheppard, E.S. (eds), *Contesting Neoliberalism: Urban Frontiers*, New York: The Guilford Press, pp. 90–115.

Molotch, H. (1976) 'The city as a growth machine: toward a political economy of place', *American Journal of Sociology*, 82(2), 309–332.

Newman, K. and Wyly, E. (2006) 'The right to stay put, revisited: gentrification and resistance to displacement in New York City', *Urban Studies*, 43(1), 23–57.

Olds, K. (1998) 'Urban mega-events, evictions and housing rights: the Canadian case', *Current Issues in Tourism*, 1(1), 2–46.

Park, J. (2013) *Institutional Explanations of Shaping a Particular Housing Culture in South Korea: A Case Study of the Gangnam District in Seoul*, unpublished thesis (PhD), The University of Sheffield.

Paton, K. and Cooper, V. (2016) 'It's the state, stupid: 21st gentrification and state-led evictions', *Sociological Research Online*, 21(3), DOI: 10.5153/sro.4064.

Philip, K. (1984) 'Gentrification and homelessness: the single room occupant and the inner city revival', *Urban and Social Change Review*, 17(1), 9–14.

Porteous, D. and Smith, S.E. (2001) *Domicide: The Global Destruction of Home*, Montreal and Kingston: McGill-Queen's University Press.

Ren, X. (2014) 'The political economy of urban ruins: redeveloping Shanghai', *International Journal of Urban and Regional Research*, 38(3), 1081–1091.

Ren, X. and Sun, M. (2012) 'Artistic urbanization: creative industries and creative control in Beijing', *International Journal of Urban and Regional Research*, 36(3), 504–521.

Robinson, J. (2011) 'Cities in a world of cities: the comparative gesture', *International Journal of Urban and Regional Research*, 35(1), 1–23.

Routledge, P. (2003) 'Voices of the dammed: discursive resistance amidst erasure in the Narmada Valley, India', *Political Geography*, 22(3), 243–270.

Roy, A. and Ong, A. (2011) *Worlding Cities: Asian Experiments and the Art of Being Global*, Oxford: John Wiley & Sons.

Sakızlıoğlu, B. (2014) 'Inserting temporality into the analysis of displacement: living under the threat of displacement', *Tijdschrift voor economische en sociale geografie*, 105(2), 206–220.

Sakızlıoğlu, B. and Uitermark, J. (2014) 'The symbolic politics of gentrification: the restructuring of stigmatized neighborhoods in Amsterdam and Istanbul', *Environment and Planning A*, 46(6), 1369–1385.

Scott, A.J. (2011) 'Emerging cities of the third wave', *City*, 15(3–4), 289–321.

Scott, A.J. and Storper, M. (2015) 'The nature of cities: the scope and limits of urban theory', *International Journal of Urban and Regional Research*, 39(1), 1–15.

Shao, Q. (2013) *Shanghai Gone: Domicide and Defiance in a Chinese Megacity*, Lanham: Rowman & Littlefield.

Shaw, K. (2008) 'Gentrification: what it is, why it is, and what can be done about it', *Geography Compass*, 2(5), 1697–1728.

Shih, M. (2010a) 'Legal geographies – governing through law: rights based conflicts and property development in Shanghai', *Urban Geography*, 31(7), 973–987.

Shih, M. (2010b) 'The evolving law of disputed relocation: constructing inner-city renewal practices in Shanghai, 1990–2005', *International Journal of Urban and Regional Research*, 34(2), 350–364.

Shin, H. (2012) 'Unequal cities of spectacle and mega-events in China', *City*, 16(6), 728–744.

Shin, H. (2013) 'The right to the city and critical reflections on China's property rights activism', *Antipode*, 45(5), 1167–1189.

Shin, H. and Kim, S-H. (2016) 'The developmental state, speculative urbanisation and the politics of displacement in gentrifying Seoul', *Urban Studies*, 53(3), 540–559.

Short, J. (1989) 'Yuppies, yuffies and the new urban order', *Transactions of the Institute of British Geographers*, 14(2), 173–188.

Sink, T. and Ceh, B. (2011) 'Relocation of urban poor in Chicago: HOPE VI policy outcomes', *Geoforum*, 42(1), 71–82.

Slater, T. (2009) 'Missing Marcuse: on gentrification and displacement', *City*, 13(2–3), 292–311.

Slater, T. (2013) 'Your life chances affect where you live: a critique of the "cottage industry" of neighbourhood effects research', *International Journal of Urban and Regional Research*, 37(2), 367–387.

Smith, N. (1979) 'Toward a theory of gentrification: A back to the city movement by capital, not people', *Journal of the American Planning Association*, 45(4), 538–548.

Smith, N. (1996) *The New Urban Frontier: Gentrification and the Revanchist City*, London: Routledge.

Smith, N. (2002) 'New globalism, new urbanism: gentrification as global urban strategy', *Antipode*, 34(3), 427–450.

Stabrowski, F. (2014) 'New-build gentrification and the everyday displacement of Polish immigrant tenants in Greenpoint, Brooklyn', *Antipode*, 46(3), 794–815.

Swanson, K. (2007) 'Revanchist urbanism heads South: the regulation of indigenous beggars and street vendors in Ecuador', *Antipode*, 39(4), 708–728.

Swyngedouw, E., Moulaert, F. and Rodriguez, A. (2002) 'Neoliberal urbanization in Europe: large-scale urban development projects and the new urban policy', *Antipode*, 34(3), 542–577.

Vicario, L. and Martinez Monje, P.M. (2003), 'Another "Guggenheim effect?" The generation of a potentially gentrifiable neighbourhood in Bilbao', *Urban Studies*, 40(12), 2383–2400.

Waldron, R. and Redmond, D. (2016) '(For)bearing the costs of reckless lending: examining the response to the Irish mortgage arrears crisis', *International Journal of Housing Policy*, 16(3), 267–292.

Walks, R.A. and Maaranen, R. (2008) 'Gentrification, social mix, and social polarization: testing the linkages in large Canadian cities', *Urban Geography*, 29(4), 293–326.

Watt, P. (2008) 'The only class in town? Gentrification and the middle-class colonization of the city and the urban imagination', *International Journal of Urban and Regional Research*, 32(1), 206–211.

Watt, P. (2013) 'It's not for us', *City*, 17(1), 99–118.

Webber, R. and Burrows, R. (2016) 'Life in an alpha territory: discontinuity and conflict in an elite London "village"', *Urban Studies*, 53(15), 3139–3154.

Weber, R. (2002) 'Extracting value from the city: neoliberalism and urban redevelopment', *Antipode*, 34(3), 519–540.

Wu, F. (2015) 'Commodification and housing market cycles in Chinese cities', *International Journal of Housing Policy*, 15(1), 6–26.

Wu, Q., Zhang, X. and Waley, P. (2016) 'Jiaoyufication: when gentrification goes to school in the Chinese inner city', *Urban Studies*, 53(16), 3510–3526.

Wyly, E. and Hammel, D. (1999) 'Islands of decay in seas of renewal: housing policy and the resurgence of gentrification', *Housing Policy Debate*, 10(4), 711–771.

Yörük, E. and Yüksel, M. (2014) 'Class and politics in Turkey's Gezi protests', *New Left Review,* 89, 103–123.

Zhang, Z. (2015) *Urban Redevelopment and Grassroots Resistance in the Chinese Context: A Case Study of the Historic Inner City of Nanjing*, unpublished thesis (PhD), University College Dublin.

Zukin, S. (1987) 'Gentrification: culture and capital in the urban core', *Annual Review of Sociology*, 13, 129–147.

Zukin, S. (2008) 'Consuming authenticity: from outposts of difference to means of exclusion', *Cultural Studies*, 22(5), 724–748.

Zukin, S. (2009) *Naked City: The Death and Life of Authentic Urban Places*, New York: Oxford University Press.

PART 3

SOCIAL CLEAVAGES IN
ADDITION TO CLASS

10. Non-normative sexualities and gentrification
Petra Doan

10.1 INTRODUCTION

Within the field of urban studies there is a rich literature on the topic of gentrification, but many of these sources fail to explore the role of non-normative sexualities in this process. Indeed, sexuality, as a topic for urban research, was largely ignored until the last two decades of the 20th century. There are a variety of possible reasons for this oversight, but one plausible explanation is that urban scholars and planning practitioners simply chose not to write about the presence of sexual and gender minorities because it was politically expedient to do so (Doan 2011a). However, by the late 1970s and into the 1980s a few seminal articles argued that gay men were clustering in urban areas and creating enclave-like environments in areas that had been deteriorating (Levine 1979; Castells and Murphy 1982; Castells 1983; Lauria and Knopp 1985; Knopp 1990). These findings opened the door to a different understanding of the relationship between non-normative sexualities and urban development that will be the focus of this chapter.

The vast majority of the literature on sexuality in cities has a focus on the Global North, especially Anglo-American cities in North America, Europe, and Australia. It is only recently that consideration of gentrification as a global social process has expanded properly with a useful emphasis on comparative urbanism (e.g. Lees et al, 2015, 2016; cr. Robinson 2006 on comparative urbanism). While there has been some debate about expanding the term gentrification to the Global South because its original concept of gentry seems narrow and colonial, Lees et al (2015) persuasively argue that Clark's (2005: 258) definition of gentrification – a process in which higher income land-users replace lower income land-users and increase capital investment in the neighborhood – remains useful at a global scale. The context in which this capital investment process occurs and the motivations of the investors may differ widely across the Global South and gentrification researchers should carefully reflect on the utility of their conceptual models in each situation (Lees et al. 2016). Evidence for the role of sexuality in this planetary process is, as yet, quite scarce. Lees et al. (2016) suggest that there is some evidence that gentrification in Buenos Aires may be linked in part to the development of gay tourism areas. Visser (2003, 2013) also notes the link between gay tourism and urban development in Cape Town, but cautions against applying the gayborhood concept across the Global South.

The critical issue with the use of gayborhood and associated Anglo-American terms to describe the development of LGBTQ neighborhoods is that the terms homosexual, gay, and lesbian are social constructions that emerged in the late 19th and early 20th centuries in the West partly in response to the strictness of Victorian era social norms. Foucault (1978) suggests that the idea of a separate homosexual identity was constructed as a means of stigmatizing unacceptable behavior by narrowly heterosexual and patriarchal institutions. The emergence of gay and lesbian identities in the 20th century was in turn a rejection of this stigmatization and an attempt to reclaim identity and in some cases to liberate specific urban spaces. While it is widely recognized that same-sex attractions and non-normative genders are found in every corner of the world and are a recurrent characteristic of human nature, the study of sexual identities and behaviors in urban areas requires a more nuanced understanding. Urban patterns of behavior that are clearly part of a gay identity in New York City or London may have little resonance in a different cultural context.

The first section of this chapter provides a brief review of the evidence that these non-normative identities have existed in nearly every era and location, although at times their visibility is constrained by social context. The next section will address the ways in which gays and lesbians in the West struggled to create safe urban residential locations. In particular, the chapter will address the ways that the peculiar formation known as gay and lesbian activism may have contributed to neighborhood formation that has been labelled gentrification. This section also explores the ways that other forms of non-normative sexuality, including sex work and porn shops, have worked against the forces of gentrification and urban development. Finally, although some commentators have proclaimed the end of the gayborhood, the chapter asks whether these formations will have new life in the Trumpist era in the US or whether new formations will need to be invented to ensure the preservation of LGBTQ community.

10.2   THE DIVERSITY OF SAME-SEX ATTRACTION ACROSS THE GLOBE

Occasional statements by political leaders such as Robert Mugabe and Mahmoud Ahmadinejad suggest that there are no gays in Africa or Iran because homosexuality was a Western invention transmitted to the rest of the word through colonialism and Western imperialism. These statements fly in the face of evidence that same-sex attraction is a widespread phenomenon that in many cases predates the colonial era. For example, in the African context there is considerable evidence of same-sex attraction and sexual activity that pre-dates and occurs simultaneously with the spread of colonial influence (Epprecht 2004; Tamale 2011; Leap 2002; Tucker 2009). Furthermore, there is evidence of same sex attraction in many parts of Latin America dating from the late 19th century (Salessi 1995; Montero 1995; Larvie 1991). Similarly, in South, Southeastern, and East Asia there is evidence of a continuing lesbian, gay and transgender presence (Thadani 1999; Rofel 1999; Silvio 1999; Jackson 1999; Gopinath 2005; Wei 2007). Finally, in the Middle East, same-sex attraction is not openly discussed, but is as much a part of the fabric of urban life as anywhere else (Ilkaracan 2002; Massad 2002; Whitaker 2006).

Throughout much of the Global South these same-sex subjectivities are troubled by the colonial and post-colonial imaginaries that undermine their autonomy by placing them within a homonationalist framework of gay and lesbian identity (Puar 2007) that perpetuates the hegemony of Western ideas (Cruz-Malave and Manalansan 2002). This chapter follows Visser's advice (2013) and will let others explore the ways that gentrification intersects with sexuality and urban developments across the Global South. Instead the chapter acknowledges the diversity of sexuality and gender across the globe, but will focus on the relationship between sexuality and urban development in North America, Europe, and Australia, allowing others from the Global South to explore the usefulness of these concepts in their environs.

10.3   EARLY PERSPECTIVES ON GENTRIFICATION ARE SILENT ABOUT SEXUALITY

Scholars who studied the first wave of gentrification for the most part had little to say about the relationship between sexuality and gentrification. The first wave of gentrification in the US context is generally linked to Federal urban renewal efforts in the late 1950s and early 1960s (Hackworth and Smith 2001). However, the spotty nature of this process produced isolated areas for reinvestment that some scholars labelled 'islands of renewal' in cities overwhelmed by the forces of sprawl (Berry 1985; Bourne 1993). Much of the early emphasis was on economic issues once Smith (1979) identified the 'rent gap' between what was charged for dilapidated structures and the rent those parcels could yield with improvements.

A subsequent 'second wave' of gentrification in the 1990s and 2000s was widespread, and differed from the earlier trend of isolated and incomplete renovation, with a more global pattern (Smith and Butler 2007). This round of gentrification can be linked to shifts in the housing finance system, to the privatization and demolition of public housing, and to changes in consumer preferences (Wyly and Hammel 1999). In addition, Lees (2000) found a further wave of super-gentrification was being stimulated by the consumption patterns of wealthy individuals who invested to regentrify certain neighborhoods in specific cities and reinvent them according to their needs.

Several scholars of gentrification did note in passing that gays appeared to be part of the urban scene from the 1970s onwards. Clay (1979) suggested that 'smart money will follow homosexuals in cities' (p. 31). Williams (1986) suggested that gentrifiers 'have typically been two-earner households (both heterosexual and homosexual), with partners pursuing careers in the professional and white-collar labor markets' (p. 69). Beauregard (1986) noted the complexity of gentrification processes, some of which were sparked by urban renewal, but others linked to the presence of gay men involved in neighborhood transformations such as that of the Castro in San Francisco (p. 40). Finally, LeGates and Hartman (1986) noted that one of the characteristics of 'in-movers' was that many are either single or in two-person households with no children, some of whom are gay men.

However, in many other studies there was very little discussion of sexuality, though it was likely a factor. For instance, Kerstein (1990) examined patterns of gentrification in the Hyde Park neighborhood in Tampa, Florida. This was a well-conceived and constructed analysis, but the author failed to mention the orientation of many of the early gentrifiers, since Hyde Park locally is considered the city's first gayborhood. Similarly, neither DeGiovanni (1983), who analyzed the Atlanta neighborhoods of Midtown and Inman Park, nor Chernoff (1980), who discussed 'social displacement' of older businesses by 'hippie' businesses linked to newer residents of adjoining neighborhoods in the Little Five Points area adjacent to Inman Park, mentioned the presence of gay men in Midtown or Inman Park or for that matter lesbians in Candler Park. This neglect flies in the face of the evidence that Atlanta's Midtown neighborhood by 1980 was already well known as a very gay place to be (Howard 1997), that the lesbian feminist bookstore Charis Books was one of the 'hippie' businesses in Little Five Points (Chesnut and Gable 1997; Sears 2001), and that some of the first and very influential gentrifiers in Inman Park were Bob Griggs and his partner, Robert Aiken (Anderson 2014).

10.4   SAME SEX SEXUALITY AND CITIES

It is impossible to understand the process of neighborhood formation and gentrification in gayborhoods without first exploring the complex social organizing that enabled such developments. Prior to the 1950s most gays and lesbians were scattered throughout the larger cities in North America. Twentieth century LGBT historians (Faderman 1991; Newton 1993; Kennedy and Davis 1993; Chauncey 1994; Stryker and van Buskirk 1996; Stein 2000) have documented the ways that gays and lesbians congregated in various bars and restaurants as well as in liminal public spaces such as bookstores, libraries, public parks, public toilets, piers, and other areas at the fringes of 'proper' society. Many of the businesses that welcomed gays and lesbians were located in marginalized areas such as the waterfront or industrial districts. 'Sometime during the fifties and sixties, in cities like New York and San Francisco, homosexuals began to reside in certain bohemian neighborhoods (Greenwich Village, North Beach) which offered higher degrees of tolerance as well as proximity to gay or lesbian gathering places' (Escoffier 1997: 130).

During this period, d'Emilio (1983) noted a considerable level of organization among LGBT individuals that was the precursor to organized resistance such as the 1966 riot at Compton's Cafeteria in San Francisco (Stryker 2008) and the 1969 rebellion at the Stonewall Inn in New York City. These events helped to catalyze the gay liberation movement and its later amendments (LG, LGB, LGBT, LGBTQ). For urban areas, these movements towards greater visibility also coincided with the emergence of clusters of residential areas around the LGBT-oriented businesses and institutions. Given the ongoing discrimination against LGBT people, these neighborhoods provided space for young gay men, lesbians, and some transgender people to explore their non-normative identities in relative safety.

By the end of the 1970s, Levine (1979) examined 27 possible concentrations of institutions catering to gay men and found that three identifiable gay ghettoes had emerged in New York, Los Angeles, and San Francisco. Other neighborhoods in those cities as well as in Chicago and Boston had concentrations of businesses, but did not appear to have significant gay residential density. Weightman (1981) also observed that gays contributed to neighborhood change through 'urban renovation and preservation programs, particularly in the restoration of decaying architecture' (p. 109).

Castells and Murphy (1982) presented more detailed analysis of gay men's residential patterns in the Castro District of San Francisco. Castells (1983) argued that an important component in the territorial clustering of gay men was their desire for political as well as social liberation. He noted that the Castro had become 'the world's gay capital, a new Mecca in the age of individual liberation' (p. 138). In particular, LGBTQ residents of the Castro District were crucial to the success of Harvey Milk in 1978, the first openly gay man elected to public office. Subsequent gay political influence can also be linked to residence since the creation of the city of West Hollywood in 1984 enabled the election of a gay majority on city council (Ward 2003). In addition, Davis (1995) argued that political redistricting would not have been possible without the strong support of gays and lesbians in Boston's South End.

San Francisco's leading role in gay history has been linked to several other important factors. Boyd (2003) suggested that same sex dances during the gold rush era might have been indicative of a wider tolerance for same sex activity in a location where the sex ratio was highly skewed by the presence of numerous young male prospectors who had come to California to find their fortune, and possibly to escape the traditional expectations of their parents in the 'city of bachelors'. In later years, areas such as the Barbary Coast near the waterfront and the Tenderloin district further inland became well known as places where establishments catered to those attracted to their own sex (Sides 2006). Frequent police crackdowns forced gay patrons away from these areas and towards North Beach (Stryker and Van Buskirk 1996).

A critical component of this liberation involved the creation of social organizations to protect the neighborhood's residents and businesses from police harassment. The owners and operators of many of the city's gay bars established the Tavern Guild to resist police harassment and protect bar owners and patrons from the all too frequent raids by the police. The success of this guild illustrated the importance of social organizations in the struggle for liberation. Boyd (2003) argued that tavern-based rights groups were complemented by other homophile organizations such as the Daughters of Bilitis and the Mattachine Society that by 1955 had formed local chapters and were actively organizing lesbians and gays to promote greater civil liberties. Both forms of organizing laid the groundwork for the development of the Castro as a liberated zone. However, not all queer-identified people have historically been included in strongly male-identified gayborhoods such as the Castro.

10.5   EXCLUSIONS FROM THE GAYBORHOOD

Bondi (1991) noted that while women have been portrayed as both the 'victims' and 'agents' of gentrification, much of the early literature had little to say about the ways that women were involved in gentrification. The same can be said about the role of lesbians in the gentrification of neighborhoods. There is less evidence on the evolution of lesbian spaces because women have lower incomes, more restricted access to capital, and must be concerned with the threat of male violence (Adler and Brenner 1992). Still, neighborhoods such as Park Slope in Brooklyn did develop strong lesbian identities (Rothenberg 1995; Lees, Slater and Wyly 2008; Senn 2013). However, Gieseking (2013) argued that gentrification eviscerated the ability of lesbians to hold physical territory, but barely diminished the area as an 'enacted neighborhood' (p. 196), which still functions as a kind of central node for many lesbians and queer women of varying classes and colors. In Manchester, lesbians found it difficult to create their own spaces within the gay village, which made them feel excluded (Pritchard et al. 2002). Podmore highlighted the ways that lesbian communities in Montreal were nearly invisible in the Boulevard St. Laurent area because of its large and diverse immigrant population (Podmore 2001, 2006). Similarly, in her study of lesbians in Ithaca, New York, Brown-Saracino (2011) found that for many queer women connections to the wider community were more important than living in a specifically queer neighborhood. She described her findings as follows: 'Many report that they once lived in "lesbian neighborhoods" in places such as Seattle and San Francisco in which queer women experienced physical and social isolation and that they moved because they wished to live outside the "ghetto".' (p. 371).

Florida and Mellender (2009) argue that gay populations act as urban pioneers and their location choices can have substantial positive effects on housing prices through an aesthetic-amenity premium. The resulting commodification of many gayborhoods created residential areas that are commodified habitation zones for white and wealthy gay men (Rushbrook 2002; Nast 2002; Nero 2005). Walcott (2007) suggested black gay men inhabited the margins of Toronto's queer spaces, although they had a powerful influence on the gay social scene and created 'imaginative conduits of queerness' (p. 243). Rosenberg (2017) argues that queer and trans youth of color have been systematically excluded from Chicago's Boystown. In Europe, as well, Bacchetta, El-Tayeb, and Hairtaworn (2015) argued against the conception that Europeans are homogeneously white and straight. Furthermore, they suggested that Queer People of Color (QPoC) in Europe were too often cast as 'deficient, inferior, and disentitled to life chances on account of their failed masculinities, femininities, and heterosexualities' (p. 769), and were often criminalized, displaced, or spatially confined. They remain violently excluded from the European landscape, where the intersection of race, gender, and sexuality produces a white Europe that continues to shape national and transnational structures.

Some scholars have argued that many young LGBTQ individuals are unable to find space in gayborhoods. For instance, Hanhardt (2008) described the way that LGBTQ young people of color in the West Village in New York City resisted the increasing gentrification of the area by organizing a group called FIERCE (Fabulous Independent Educated Radicals for Community Empowerment). According to Goh (2015) the most salient issue pursued by FIERCE was the redevelopment of Pier 40, which threatened to exclude young queer people from gathering there, one of the few remaining areas where young LGBTQ kids could gather and not be harassed. Elsewhere young LGBTQ people eschew traditional gay villages and seek their own spaces (Nash 2013a and Nash and Gorman-Murray 2014). Nash (2013b) used the term 'post-mo' to describe the identities of young queer people in Toronto who avoided the existing queer spaces of Toronto's gay village, and preferred to congregate in other parts of the city with a hip but not explicitly gay vibe. Ghaziani (2014) suggested that this post gay phenomenon was partly to blame for young gays who no longer choose to live in established places such as Boystown in Chicago. In Australia, young gays and lesbians appear to be less connected to the usual gay scene than earlier generations, but have not formally adopted the post gay identity yet (Lea et al. 2015). It is not clear whether these changes in the utilization of urban space are because these young people were more empowered and able to make their own spaces feel safe, or whether the assimilation of the gay village into the wider metro area has simply made them feel less comfortable in the existing gay village. Ghaziani (2015) argued that economic forces are an incomplete argument for why gayborhoods are in decline, because competing cultural and political developments – including the rate of assimilation of sexual minorities – expands the boundaries of where gays and lesbians feel comfortable living.

10.6   CRITICAL ELEMENTS IN GAYBORHOOD FORMATION

Residential patterns in many cities show periodic neighborhood clustering and then movement to new areas. Ghaziani (2014) suggested that gay bars often have served as anchor points in gayborhood formation, although Mattson (2015) demonstrated that in San Francisco gay districts had shifted from the Polk and SOMA neighborhoods to the homonormative Castro partly due to gentrification pressures in these other areas. Winkle (2015) traced the interconnected and shifting patterns of gay commercial districts as gay men's residential concentrations shifted northward away from Old Town into Boystown and eventually into Andersonville on the north side of downtown. Although Ghaziani (2014) suggested that this movement was partly linked to the post-gay trend, other factors such as increasing property values were also to blame. Gay areas in New York have seen similar shifts away from Greenwich Village (the location of the Stonewall Inn) northward into Chelsea, although as these areas gentrified spaces for queer youth of color were severely constrained (Goh 2015).

However, gay bars also serve other purposes unrelated to the immediately surrounding residential areas. Lewis (2015) studied gay men's residential and leisure activities in Washington DC and found that although the Dupont Circle area remained an important symbolic center for gay men, many gays no longer lived in that neighborhood. Others have suggested that bars remain venues for pilgrimages to reinforce LGBTQ identity (Howe 2001), as well as for 'lifestyle commuters' who explore urban establishments from a safe suburban location (Brekhus 2003). In a subsequent analysis, Lewis (2016) links the decline of gayborhoods to neoliberal development strategies that may be undermining the vitality of the 'very subjects they once valorized' (p. 15). 'The shift away from gay placemaking and toward the temporary performance of privatized gay identities in shared spaces means that the streetscapes of gay enclaves may no longer serve as sites of subcultural socialization' (Mattson 2015, p. 3157).

The ongoing theme of capital formation through investments in residential properties is made clear in a number of other cities. For instance, New Orleans experienced a clustering of LGBT people in neighborhoods adjacent to the French Quarter, most prominently the Marigny district. Lauria and Knopp (1985) suggested a close link between gay clustering and the gentrification of this neighborhood, since gay men were concerned with making secure capital investments in historic buildings. Knopp (1990) further detailed the careful organizing around historic properties and preservation that was a hallmark of this movement.

Similarly, the City of Toronto witnessed the evolution of a distinctive gay village surrounding the intersection of Church and Wellesley Streets (Nash 2005, 2006) that was experiencing considerable gentrification pressure (Bouthillette 1994). Although this neighborhood has remained relatively stable since its inception, the Gay Village has seen skyrocketing rents and has become unaffordable to many younger, less affluent LGBTQ individuals (Balkissoon 2009), as well as LGBTQ people of color (Catungal 2015).

Elsewhere, community activists have expressed concern that the arrival of new and more wealthy residents and the exodus of LGBTQ individuals has altered the essential nature of San Francisco's iconic Castro District. Buchanan (2007) described the worries of neighborhood activists who wondered if the Castro could survive as a queer place, while others questioned whether the whole concept of a gayborhood was passé? Although the rising property values of the early sweat equity owners in the Castro provided significant financial benefits to many gay men, the increasing numbers of condominium conversions exacerbated the housing situation for LGBTQ youth, retirees on fixed incomes, and all but the wealthiest newcomers. Others wondered if the dispersal of LGBTQ individuals would make it politically impossible to organize the community for future LGBTQ-related issues.

In Dallas, although increased property values were sought by gay real estate interests, these increases did not result in the assimilation of gay neighborhoods. Whittemore (2015) found LGBT individuals and their realtors contributed to the preservation and development of the Oak Lawn neighborhood. Further analysis of real estate advertisements in Dallas also confirmed the relative stability of the gay neighborhood (Whittemore and Smart 2015).

In Atlanta, the Midtown neighborhood has long been considered the heart of the LGBTQ community, but the redevelopment of the Peachtree Street corridor undermined the vitality of this queer neighborhood (Doan and Higgins 2011). City officials worked to administratively separate the corridor from the nearby gay area of Midtown in order to streamline redevelopment measures. In addition, they instituted rigorous code enforcement of existing gay bars and clubs (Doan 2014), resulting in the closure of many iconic gay bars on Peachtree and the construction of a series of high rise condominiums. Doan (2015) argues that the importance of capital formation was made clear in an interview with a gay city council member who stated that for him and some of his gay constituents the bottom line is their capital investment in land: 'Well, my mandate is to improve the quality of life of my constituents, it is to enhance the community in whatever way I can, and part of that effect is increased property values' (ibid p. 213).

In the 1990s, Miami Beach was a significant center of gay activism and nightlife (Kurtz 1999; Capo 2011) surrounded by declining housing stock inhabited by retirees from elsewhere. In recent years, significant capital investment and increasing property values have led some commentators to claim that gays were fleeing the city and moving to Broward County to the north (Lee 2005; O'Neill 2010), specifically the very gay city of Wilton Manors just outside Ft. Lauderdale (Ivy 2001). Kanai and Kenttama-Squires (2015) recognize these shifts as part of the commodification of gay spaces, but suggest these investments combined with significant pro-LGBTQ municipal policies are remaking the city into a gay-friendly area rather than a traditional gayborhood.

In the United Kingdom, several examples provide additional evidence about the mixed effects of redevelopment. Municipal officials in Manchester played a constructive role in neighborhood change. Quilley (1997) described the critical alliance between the Municipal Council and gay activists/business owners that promoted the gay district along Canal Street in Manchester. However, sometimes the presence of so many tourists drawn to enjoy its rather commodified queerness presented difficulties for gay men (Binnie and Skeggs 2004). Casey (2004) also reported on the impact of straight tourists on lesbian spaces in Newcastle upon Tyne. Similarly, in Spitalfields in East London, Brown (2006) argued that urban planners in conjunction with redevelopment interests sought to change the feel of the neighborhood by installing new street furnishings in order to 're-brand' the area as ethnic, but in doing so ignored the presence of gay men.

Some scholars have suggested that there is a regular progression in the evolution of queer spaces. Collins (2004) provided evidence from the London neighborhood of Soho to argue that gay village development follows a kind of evolutionary model. Collins' model suggests that neighborhoods must meet certain pre-conditions for gay businesses to consider moving there. Once these basic conditions are met, several gay-related stores, services, and bars begin to locate in the area. The success of these businesses stimulates an increasing concentration of businesses oriented to the LGBT community. As the neighborhood becomes more attractive, straight urban professionals are drawn to its chicness and begin seeking residences nearby, causing a further increase in rents. As a result, there is an assimilation of the formerly queer area into the mainstream. Binnie et al (2006) argued that some gentrification occurred as part of a shift towards 'cosmopolitan urbanism' in which ethnically distinct and architecturally significant neighborhoods began attracting more gay residents. Collins and Drinkwater (2015) have linked the decline of gay villages to several socio-technological innovations including sales of retail and entertainment venues in gay villages, purchases of existing residential properties, and the closure of gay pubs as more people use smartphones to connect.

Other authors described a less linear process. Ruting (2008) suggested that many gay neighborhoods in Sydney, such as Oxford Street, were frequently in a state of flux and have not been seamlessly assimilated back into heterosexual territory. Instead as areas lost their gay flavor, gays moved elsewhere. Gorman-Murray and Waitt (2009) have argued that some of these individuals move to 'gay-friendly' neighborhoods that are open and accepting of sexual differences, but these places cannot be considered gayborhoods.

Not all gay neighborhoods are in attractive upper income areas. For example, Matthews and Besemer (2015) found that in Scotland the LGBTQ population lives in the most deprived neighborhoods, challenging the assumption that such households enjoy a higher disposable income and greater locational choice when purchasing housing. The authors argued that neighborhoods with an overrepresentation of sexual minorities were mostly peripheral social housing, not gentrifying inner-city, neighborhoods.

Sometimes non-linear factors have also led to profound changes to gay neighborhoods. The direst of these impacts was linked to the devastating HIV/AIDS epidemic. One study found that one consequence of HIV/AIDS deaths in the gay community was diminishment of gayborhoods in the largest metropolitan areas in North America (Rosenfeld et al. 2012). Another study explored the same question using a sample of gay informants from 14 countries and found that the epidemic had led to communities that were undergoing structural decline and that gay men were assimilating into the suburbs (Rosser et al. 2008). Furthermore, the study found that declines in the numbers of gay clubs were linked to a shift to internet and social media-based dating apps as well as the aging of the gay population in many cities.

Despite these findings, there appears to be a clear preference among LGBT people for living in proximity to other LGBT people. Hayslett and Kane (2011) showed that in Columbus, Ohio, gays and lesbians tended to cluster in tracts with other gays and lesbians, suggesting that such residential choices may be linked to concerns with safety. Similarly, in Poland, Kusek (2015) reported that gays and lesbians also preferred to live in proximity to other LGBT people. In Paris, the Marais district was found to be similar to gay ghettos in North America, but developed its own unique gay sub-culture (Sibalis 2004).

10.7 TENSION BETWEEN OVERT SEXUALITY AND GENTRIFICATION

Hubbard et al (2009) noted that 'spaces of commercial sex – prostitution and pornography in particular – [are] often regarded as disturbing signs of a city's potential to harbour sexual [and social] disorder' (p. 186). Municipal officials often viewed these areas, often called 'red light districts' or 'sex zones', as blighted areas that had to be cleaned up. For instance, in New York City the local practice called social dancing long preceded the new residents who subsequently gentrified some neighborhoods and then called for strict enforcement of cabaret laws to shut down those pre-existing dance clubs (Hae 2011). Efforts by New York officials to prioritize gentrifying residents over existing dancing venues and their racial and sexual minority patrons are consistent with attempts to zone out other unwanted uses such as pornography in the Times Square area discussed by Papayannis (2000). These efforts in New York City are in sync with zero tolerance regulations in the United Kingdom that seek to ban any sex-related activities in specified areas to enable orderly social reproduction within the city (Hubbard 2004, 2012) that they are often in the process of gentrifying. Similarly, Sides (2006) argued that increases in downtown real estate values resulted in the decline of commercial sex districts in San Francisco through the use of restrictive zoning.

It is unfortunate that neighborhoods that are experiencing redevelopment and gentrification that have a distinct LGBTQ presence are frequently targets of 'heightened scrutiny' by municipal officials and strict interpretation of existing regulations. In Sydney, Australia, Prior (2008) has argued that land use and zoning regulations focused on gay bathhouses are 'guided by a range of discourses as to how they contaminate and pollute neighbourhoods, destroy their lifestyles and legitimate businesses, and, if placed too close to sensitive land uses such as schools or churches, can corrupt their vulnerable users' (p. 350).

Doan (2014) found that transgendered individuals in Midtown, Atlanta, were frequent targets of harassment by neighbourhood security patrols, even though such individuals may be so highly stigmatized that they may feel that 'sex work is their only employment option' (Doan 2011b, p. 105).

10.8   CONCLUSIONS

Queer spaces and especially gay male spaces have been under considerable pressure from gentrification and from claims that these spaces are not and perhaps have never been truly inclusive spaces. Despite the solidity of many of these claims, Brown (2013) suggested that these spaces still merit continued study and noted that 'while tales of its demise may ring true, and critiques of it abide, there also appear to be both cultural and material forces pushing for its endurance' (p. 463).

The complex ways in which capital and sexual orientation interact remain incompletely understood. Does the evolutionary model proposed by Collins (2004) continue to explain change in the 21th century? Should smart investors continue to 'follow the homosexuals' á la Clay? Or are the neighborhood change processes in Euro-American cities today somehow different than the evolutionary models that have been well studied in the latter half of the 20th century? Have social media apps completely displaced the gayborhood as a way to meet and greet potential partners or will there always be a need for proximity and community?

It remains to be seen whether the Trumpist era will reverse many of the gains of the past 20 years in the US, including same sex marriage, employment non-discrimination laws, and housing non-discrimination that are frequently inclusive of sexual orientation and gender identity. If some or all of these policies are reversed will the deflation of the 'post gay' balloon leave many wondering where have all the gayborhoods gone? It is too early to tell, but clearly analysis of the relationship between sexuality and urban redevelopment is likely to remain salient for many years to come.

REFERENCES

Adler, S and Brenner. J. (1992) 'Gender and space: lesbians and gay men in the city', *International Journal of Urban and Regional Research*, 16, 24–34.

Anderson, W. (2014) 'Spotlight on Incomparable Inman Park, Atlanta', *Georgia Globe Design News*, 14 February [Online]. Available at: https://wdanielanderson.wordpress.com/2014/02/14/spotlight-on-incomparable-inman-park-atlanta/ (accessed 14 November 2016).

Atkinson, R. and Bridge, G. (eds) (2005) *Gentrification in a Global Context: The New Urban Colonialism*, London: Routledge.

Bacchetta, P., El-Tayeb, F. and Haritaworn, J. (2015) 'Queer of colour formations and translocal spaces in Europe', *Environment and Planning D: Society and Space,* 33(5), 769–778.

Balkissoon, D. (2009) 'Exodus sees Church St. losing its gay village identity', *The Star,* 13 October [Online]. Available at: http://www.thestar.com/news/gta/2009/10/13/exodus_sees_church_st_losing_its_gay_village_iden tity.html (accessed 14 June 2016).

Beauregard, R.A. (1986) 'The chaos and complexity of gentrification', in Smith, N. and Williams, P. (eds), *Gentrification of the City*, Boston: Allen and Unwin, pp. 35–55.

Berry, B. (1985) 'Islands of renewal in seas of decay', in Peterson, Paul E. (ed), *The New Urban Reality*, Washington, DC: The Brookings Institution.

Binnie, J. (2004) 'Quartering sexualities: gay villages and sexual citizenship', in Bell, D. and Jayne, M. (eds), *City of Quarters: Urban Villages in the Contemporary City*, Aldershot: Ashgate, pp. 163–172.

Binnie, J. and Skeggs, B. (2004) 'Cosmopolitan knowledge and the production and consumption of sexualised space: Manchester's gay village', *The Sociological Review*, 52, 41–61.

Binnie, J., Holloway, J., Millington, S. and Young, C. (eds) (2006) *Cosmopolitan Urbanism*, London: Routledge.

Bondi, L. (1991) 'Gender divisions and gentrification: a critique', *Transactions of the Institute of British Geographers*, 16(2), 190–198.

Bourne, L.S. (1993) 'The myth and reality of gentrification: a commentary on emerging urban forms', *Urban Studies*, 30(1), 183–189.

Bouthillette, A.M. (1994) 'Gentrification by gay male communities', in Whittle, S. (ed), *The Margins of the City: Gay Men's Urban Lives*, Aldershot: Ashgate, pp. 65–83.

Boyd, N.A. (2003) *Wide Open Town: A History of Queer San Francisco until 1965*, Berkeley: University of California Press.

Brekhus, W. (2003) *Peacocks, Chameleons, Centaurs: Gay Suburbia and the Grammar of Social Identity*, Chicago: University of Chicago Press.

Brown, G. (2006) 'Cosmopolitan camouflage: (post) gay space in Spitalfields, East London', in Binnie, J., Holloway, J., Millington, J. and Young, C. (eds), *Cosmopolitan Urbanism*, London: Routledge, pp. 130–145.

Brown, M. (2013) 'Gender and sexuality II: there goes the gayborhood?', *Progress in Human Geography*, 38(3), 457–465.

Brown-Saracino, J. (2011) 'From the lesbian ghetto to ambient community: the perceived costs and benefits of integration for community', *Social Problems*, 58(3), 361–388.

Buchanan, W. (2007) 'S.F.'s Castro district faces an identity crisis: As straights move in, some fear loss of area's character', *San Francisco Chronicle,* 25 February [Online]. Available at: http://www.sfgate.com/cgi-bin/article. cgi?f=/c/a/2007/02/25/MNG2DOATDK1.DTL&type=gaylesbian (accessed 15 March 2017).

Capo, J. (2011) *It's not queer to be gay: Miami and the emergence of the gay rights movement, 1945–1995,* (unpublished doctoral dissertation, Florida International University, Miami, Florida).

Casey, M.E. (2004) 'De-dyking queer space(s): heterosexual female visibility in gay and lesbian spaces', *Sexualities,* 7(4), 446–461.

Castells, M. (1983) *The City and the Grassroots: A Cross-Cultural Theory of Urban Social Movements*, Berkeley: University of California Press.

Castells, M. and Murphy, K. (1982) 'Cultural identity and urban structure: the spatial organization of San Francisco's gay community', in Fainstein, N. and Fainstein, S. (eds), *Urban Policy: Urban Capitalism*, Volume 22 Sage Urban Affairs Annual Reviews, Beverly Hills: Sage Publications, pp. 237–259.

Catungal, J.P. (2015) 'The racial politics of precarity: understanding ethno-specific AIDS service organizations in neoliberal times', in Doan, P. (ed), *Planning and LGBTQ Communities: The Need for Inclusive Queer Spaces*, London: Routledge, pp. 235–248.

Chauncey, G. (1994) *Gay New York: Gender Urban Culture and the Making of the Gay Male World*, New York: Basic Books.
Chernoff, M. (1980) 'Social displacement in a renovating neighborhood's commercial district: Atlanta', in Laska, S.B. and Spain, D. (eds), *Back to the City: Issues in Neighborhood Renovation*, New York: Pergamon Press, pp. 204–218.
Chesnut, S. and Gable, A. (1997) 'Women ran it: Charis Books and more and Atlanta's lesbian-feminist community, 1971–1981', in Howard, J. (ed), *Carryin' On in the Lesbian and Gay South*, New York: New York University Press, pp. 241–284.
Clark, E. (2005) 'The order and simplicity of gentrification – a political challenge', in Atkinson, R. and Bridge, G. (eds), *Gentrification in a Global Context: The New Urban Colonialism*, London: Routledge, pp. 256–264.
Clay, P. (1979) *Neighborhood Renewal: Middle-class Resettlement and Incumbent Upgrading in American Neighborhoods*, Lexington, MA: Lexington Books.
Collins, A. (2004) 'Sexual dissidence, enterprise and assimilation: bedfellows in urban regeneration', *Urban Studies*, 41(9), 1789–1806.
Collins, A. and Drinkwater, S. (2015) 'Fifty shades of gay: social and technological change, urban deconcentration and niche enterprise', *Urban Studies*, 54(3), 765–785.
Cruz-Malave, A. and Manalanson, M. (eds) (2002) *Queer Globalizations: Citizenship and the Afterlife of Colonialism*, New York: New York University Press.
Davis, T. (1995) 'The diversity of queer politics and the redefinition of sexual identity and community in urban spaces', in Bell, D. and Valentine, G. (eds), *Mapping Desire: Geographies of Sexuality*, London: Routledge, pp. 285–303.
DeGiovanni, F. (1983) 'Patterns of change in housing market activity in revitalizing neighborhoods', *Journal of the American Planning Association*, 49(1), 22–39.
d'Emilio, J. (1983) *Sexual Politics, Sexual Communities: The Making of a Homosexual Minority in the United States, 1940–1970*, Chicago: University of Chicago Press.
Doan, P. (2011a) 'Why question planning assumptions and practices about queer spaces?', in Doan, P. (ed), *Queerying Planning: Challenging Heteronormative Assumptions and Reframing Planning Practice*, Farnham: Ashgate, pp. 1–18.
Doan, P. (2011b) 'Queerying identity: planning and the tyranny of gender', in Doan, P. (ed) *Queerying Planning: Challenging Heteronormative Assumptions and Reframing Planning Practice*, Farnham: Ashgate, pp. 89–106.
Doan, P. (2014) 'Regulating adult business to make spaces safe for heterosexual families in Atlanta', in Maginn, P. and Steinmetz, C. (eds), *(Sub)Urban Sexscapes: Geographies and Regulation of the Sex Industry*, London: Routledge.
Doan, P. (ed) (2015) *Planning and LGBTQ Communities: The Need for Inclusive Queer Spaces*, London: Routledge.
Doan, P. and Higgins, H. (2011) 'The demise of queer space? Resurgent gentrification and LGBT neighborhoods', *Journal of Planning Education and Research*, 31, 6–25.
Epprecht, M. (2004) *Hungochani: A History of Dissident Sexuality in Southern Africa*, Montreal: McGill-Queen's University Press.
Escher, A.J. and Petermann, S. (2000) 'Neo-colonialism or gentrification in the Medina of Marrakesh', *Space & Architecture*, 1(5), 34.
Escoffier, J. (1997) 'The political economy of the closet: notes toward an economic history of gay and lesbian life before Stonewall', in Gluckman, A. and Reed, B. (eds), *Homo-Economics: Capitalism, Community, and Gay and Lesbian Life*, London: Routledge, pp. 123–135.
Ettore, E.M. (1978) 'Women, urban social movements and the lesbian ghetto', *International Journal of Urban and Regional Research*, 2, 499–519.
Faderman, L. (1991) *Odd Girls and Twilight Lovers: A History of Lesbian Life in Twentieth-Century America*, New York: Penguin Books.
Florida, R. and Mellender, C. (2009) 'There goes the metro: how and why bohemians, artists and gays affect regional housing values', *Journal of Economic Geography*, 1–22.
Forsyth, A. (2011) 'Queerying planning practice: understanding the non-conformist populations', in Doan, P. (ed) *Queerying Planning: Challenging Heteronormative Assumptions and Reframing Planning Practice*, Farnham: Ashgate, pp. 21–51.
Foucault, M. (1978) *The History of Sexuality, Volume 1: An Introduction*, trans. R. Hurley, New York: Random House.
Ghaziani, A. (2014) *There Goes the Gayborhood?* Princeton: Princeton University Press.
Ghaziani, A. (2015) '"Gay enclaves face prospect of being passé": How assimilation affects the spatial expressions of sexuality in the United States', *International Journal of Urban and Regional Research*, 39(4), 756–771.
Gieseking, J. (2013) 'Queering the meaning of "neighbourhood": reinterpreting the lesbian-queer experience of Park Slope, Brooklyn, 1983–2008', in Taylor, Y. and Addison, M. (eds), *Queer Presences and Absences*, London: Palgrave Macmillan, pp. 178–200.

Goh, K. (2015) 'Place/out: planning for radical queer activism', in Doan, P. (ed), *Planning and LGBTQ Communities: The Need for Inclusive Queer Spaces*, London: Routledge, pp. 215–234.

Gopinath, G. (2005) *Impossible Desires: Queer Diasporas and South Asian Public Cultures*, Durham, NC: Duke University Press.

Gorman-Murray, A. and Waitt, G. (2009) 'Queer-friendly neighbourhoods: interrogating social cohesion across sexual difference in two Australian neighbourhoods', *Environment and Planning A*, 41, 2855–2873.

Hackworth, J. and Smith, N. (2001) 'The changing state of gentrification', *Tijdschrift voor Economische en Sociale Geografie*, 92(4), 464–477.

Hae, L. (2011) 'Legal geographies – the right to spaces for social dancing in New York City: a question of urban rights', *Urban Geography*, 32(1), 129–142.

Hanhardt, C.B. (2008) 'Butterflies, whistles, and fists: gay safe streets patrols and the new gay ghetto, 1976–1981', *Radical History Review*, 100, 61–85.

Hayslett, K. and Kane, M. (2011) '"Out" in Columbus: a geospatial analysis of the neighborhood-level distribution of gay and lesbian households', *City & Community*, 10(2), 131–156.

Howard, J. (1997) 'The library, the park, and the pervert: public space and the homosexual encounter in post-World War II Atlanta', in Howard, J. (ed), *Carryin' On in the Lesbian and Gay South*, New York: New York University Press, pp. 107–131.

Howe, A. (2001) 'Queer pilgrimage: the San Francisco homeland and identity tourism', *Cultural Anthropology*, 16(1), 35–61.

Hubbard, P. (2000) 'Desire/disgust: mapping the moral contours of heterosexuality', *Progress in Human Geography*, 24, 191–217.

Hubbard, P. (2004) 'Cleansing the metropolis: sex work and the policy of zero tolerance', *Urban Studies*, 41(9), 1687–1702.

Hubbard, P. (2012) *Cities and Sexualities*, Abingdon, Oxon: Routledge.

Hubbard, P., Matthews, R. and Scoular, J. (2009) 'Legal geographies – controlling sexually oriented businesses: law, licensing, and the geographies of a controversial land use', *Urban Geography*, 30(2), 185–205.

Ilkaracan, P. (2002) 'Women, sexuality, and social change in the Middle East and the Maghreb', *Social Research*, 69(3), 753–779.

Ivy, R. (2001) 'Geographical variation in alternative tourism and recreation establishments', *Tourism Geographies*, 3(3), 338–355.

Jackson, P. (1999) 'Same-sex sexual experience in Thailand', in Jackson, P.A. and Sullivan, G. (eds), *Lady Boys, Tom Boys, Rent Boys: Male and Female Homosexualities in Contemporary Thailand*, New York: Harrington Park Press, pp. 29–60.

Kanai, J. and Kenttamaa-Squires, K. (2015) 'Remaking South Beach: metropolitan gayborhood trajectories under homonormative entrepreneurialism', *Urban Geography*, 36(3), 385–402.

Kennedy, E. and Davis, M. (1993) *Boots of Leather, Slippers of Gold: The History of a Lesbian Community*, New York: Penguin Books.

Kerstein, R. (1990) 'Stage models of gentrification: an examination', *Urban Affairs Quarterly*, 25(4), 620–639.

Knopp, L. (1990) 'Some theoretical implications of gay involvement in an urban land market', *Political Geography Quarterly*, 9(4), 337–352.

Kurtz, S. (1999) 'Butterflies under cover: Cuban and Puerto Rican gay masculinities in Miami', *The Journal of Men's Studies*, 7(3), 371–390.

Kusek, W. (2015) 'Shifting the spotlight: suggesting a pragmatic approach to studying the Polish LGBT community', *Journal of Urbanism: International Research on Placemaking and Urban Sustainability*, 8(1), 82–96.

Larvie, S. (1999) 'Queerness and the specter of Brazilian national ruin', *GLQ: A Journal of Lesbian and Gay Studies*, 5(4), 527–557.

Lauria, M. and Knopp, L. (1985) 'Toward an analysis of the role of gay communities in the urban renaissance', *Urban Geography*, 6(2), 152–169.

Lea, T., de Wit, J. and Reynolds, R. (2015) '"Post-gay" yet? The relevance of the lesbian and gay scene to same-sex attracted young people in contemporary Australia', *Journal of Homosexuality*, 62(9), 1264–1285.

Leap, W. (2002) 'Strangers on a train: sexual citizenship and the politics of public transportation in apartheid South Africa', in Cruz-Malave, A. and Manalanson, M. (eds), *Queer Globalizations: Citizenship and the Afterlife of Colonialism*, New York: New York University Press, pp. 219–235.

Lee, G. (2005) 'Where the boys are, part 2: watch out, South Beach. Fort Lauderdale is making its moves as a top gay spot', *The Washington Post*, 15 May [Online]. Available at: http://www.washingtonpost.com/wp-dyn/content/article/2005/05/13/AR2005051300662.html.

Lees, L. (2000) 'A reappraisal of gentrification – towards a geography of gentrification', *Progress in Human Geography*, 24(3), 389–408.

Lees, L., Shin, H. and López-Morales, E. (2015) *Global Gentrifications: Uneven Development and Displacement*, Bristol: Policy Press.

Lees, L., Shin, H. and López-Morales, E. (2016) *Planetary Gentrification*, Cambridge: Polity Press.

Lees, L., Slater, T. and Wyly, E. (2008) *Gentrification*, New York: Routledge.

LeGates, R. and Hartman, C. (1986) 'The anatomy of displacement in the United States', in Smith, N. and Williams, P. (eds), *Gentrification of the City*, Boston: Allen and Unwin, pp. 178–200.

Levine, M. (1979), 'Gay ghetto', *Journal of Homosexuality*, 4(4), 363–377.

Lewis, N. (2015) 'Fractures and fissures in "Post-Mo" Washington, DC: the limits of gayborhood transition and diffusion', in Doan, P. (ed), *Planning and LGBT Communities: The Need for Inclusive Queer Spaces*, London: Routledge, pp. 56–76.

Lewis, N. (2016) 'Canaries in the mine? Gay community, consumption and aspiration in neoliberal Washington, DC', *Urban Studies*, 54(3), 695–712.

Massad, M. (2002) 'Re-orienting desire: the gay international and the Arab world', *Public Culture*, 14(2), 361–385.

Matthews, P. and Besemer, K. (2015) 'The "pink pound" in the "gaybourhood"? Neighborhood deprivation and sexual orientation in Scotland', *Housing, Theory and Society*, 32(1), 94–111.

Mattson, G. (2015) 'Style and the value of gay nightlife: homonormative placemaking in San Francisco', *Urban Studies*, 52(16), 3144–3159.

Montero, O. (1995) 'Julián del Casal and the queers of Havana', in Bergmann, E. and Smith, P. (eds), *¿Entiendes?: Queer Readings, Hispanic Writings*, Durham: Duke University Press, pp. 92–112.

Nash, C. (2005) 'Contesting identity: politics of gays and lesbians in Toronto in the 1970s', *Gender, Place & Culture: A Journal of Feminist Geography*, 12(1), 113–135.

Nash, C. (2006) 'Toronto's gay village (1969–1982): plotting the politics of gay identity', *The Canadian Geographer*, 50(1), 1–16.

Nash, C. (2013a) 'Queering neighbourhoods: politics and practice in Toronto', *ACME: An International E-Journal for Critical Geographies*, 12(2), 193–219.49: 243–252.

Nash, C. (2013b) 'The age of the "post-mo"? Toronto's gay village and a new generation', *GeoForum*, 57, 243–252.

Nash, C. and Gorman-Murray, A. (2014) 'LGBT neighbourhoods and "new mobilities": towards understanding transformations in sexual and gendered urban landscapes', *International Journal of Urban and Regional Research*, 38(3), 756–772.

Nast, H. (2002) 'Queer patriarchies, queer racisms, international', *Antipode*, 34(5), 874–909.

Nero, C. (2005) 'Why are gay ghettos white?', in Johnson, E. and Henderson, M. (eds), *Black Queer Studies: A Critical Anthology*, Durham: Duke University Press.

Newton, E. (1993) *Cherry Grove, Fire Island: Sixty Years in America's First Gay and Lesbian Town*, Boston: Beacon Press.

O'Neill, N. (2010) 'Gays leave unfriendly South Beach for Fort Lauderdale', *Miami New Times*, 14 January [Online]. Available at: http://www.miaminewtimes.com/2010-01-14/news/gays-areleaving-south-beach-for-fort-lauderdale/5/.

Papayanis, M. (2000) 'Sex and the revanchist city: zoning out pornography in New York', *Environment and Planning D: Society and Space*, 18, 341–353.

Podmore, J. (2001) 'Lesbians in the crowd: gender, sexuality and visibility along Montréal's Boulevard St. Laurent', *Gender, Place and Culture*, 8(4), 333–355.

Podmore, J. (2006) 'Gone "underground"? Lesbian visibility and the consolidation of queer space in Montréal', *Social and Cultural Geography*, 7(4), 595–625.

Prior, J. (2008) 'Planning for sex in the city: urban governance, planning and the placement of sex industry premises in inner Sydney', *Australian Geographer*, 39(3), 339–352.

Pritchard, A., Morgan, N. and Sedgley, D. (2002) 'In search of lesbian space? The experience of Manchester's gay village', *Leisure Studies*, 21(2), 105–123.

Puar, J.K. (2007) *Terrorist Assemblages: Homonationalism in Queer Times*, Durham, NC: Duke University Press.

Quilley, S. (1997) 'Manchester's 'new urban village': gay space in the entrepreneurial city', in Ingram, G., Bouthillette, A. and Retter, Y. (eds), *Queers in Space: Communities/Public Places/Sites of Resistance*, Seattle, WA: Bay Press, pp. 275–292.

Robinson, J. (2006) *Ordinary Cities: Between Modernity and Development*, London: Routledge.

Rofel, L. (1999) 'Qualities of desire: imagining gay identities in China', *GLQ: A Journal of Gay and Lesbian Studies*, 5(4), 451–474.

Rosenberg, R. (2017) 'The whiteness of gay urban belonging: criminalizing LGBTQ youth of color in queer spaces of care', *Urban Geography*, 38(1), 137–148.

Rosenfeld, D., Bartlam, B. and Smith, R. (2012) 'Out of the closet and into the trenches: gay male baby boomers, aging and HIV/AIDS', *The Gerontologist*, 52(2), 255–264.

Rosser, B., West, W. and Weinmeyer, R. (2008) 'Are gay communities dying or just in transition? Results from an international consultation examining possible structural change in gay communities', *AIDS Care: Psychological and Socio-medical Aspects of HIV/AIDS*, 20(5), 588–595.

Rothenburg, T. (1995) 'And she told two friends: lesbians creating urban social space', in Bell, D. and Valentine, G. (eds), *Mapping Desire: Geographies of Sexuality*, London: Routledge, pp. 165–181.

Rushbrook, D. (2002) 'Cities, queer space, and the cosmopolitan tourist', *GLQ: A Journal of Lesbian and Gay Studies,* 8(1&2), 183–206.

Ruting, B. (2008) 'Economic transformations of gay urban spaces: revisiting Collins' evolutionary gay district model', *Australian Geographer*, 39(3), 259–269.

Salessi, J. (1995) 'The Argentine dissemination of homosexuality 1890–1914', in Bergmann, E. and Smith, P. (eds), *¿Entiendes?: Queer Readings, Hispanic Writings*, Durham: Duke University Press, pp. 49–91.

Sears, J. (2001) *Rebels, Rubyfruits, and Rhinestones: Queering Space in the Post Stonewall South*, New Brunswick, NJ: Rutgers University Press.

Senn, C. (2013) 'Gentrification, social capital, and the emergence of a lesbian neighborhood: a case study of Park Slope, Brooklyn', *Urban Studies Masters Theses, Paper 7,* Fordham University, NY [Online]. Available at: http://fordham.bepress.com/urban_studies_masters.

Sibalis, M. (2004) 'Urban space and homosexuality: the example of the Marais, Paris' Gay Ghetto', *Urban Studies*, 41(9), 1739–1758.

Sides, M. (2006) 'Excavating the postwar sex district in San Francisco', *Journal of Urban History*, 32(3), 355–379.

Silvio, T. (1999) 'Reflexivity, bodily praxis, and identity in Taiwanese opera', *GLQ: A Journal of Lesbian and Gay Studies*, 5(4), 585–603.

Smith, D. and Butler, T. (2007) 'Guest editorial: conceptualising the socio-spatial diversity of gentrification: "to boldly go" into contemporary gentrified spaces, the "final frontier"?', *Environment and Planning A*, 39(1), 2–9.

Smith, N. (1987) 'Gentrification and the rent gap', *Annals of the Association of American Geographers*, 77(3), 462–465.

Stein, M. (2000) *City of Sisterly and Brotherly Love: Lesbian and Gay Philadelphia, 1945–1972*, Chicago: University of Chicago Press.

Stryker, S. (2008) *Transgender History*, Berkeley: Seal Press.

Stryker, S and van Buskirk, L. (1996) *Gay by the Bay: A History of Queer Culture in the San Francisco Bay Area*, San Francisco: Chronicle Books.

Tamale, S. (2011) *African Sexualities: A Reader,* Cape Town: Pambazuka Press.

Thadani, G. (1999) 'The politics of identities and languages: lesbian desire in ancient and modern India', in Blackwood, E. and Wieringa, S. (eds), *Same-sex Relations and Female Desires: Transgender Practices Across Cultures*, New York: Columbia University Press, pp. 67–90.

Tucker, A. (2009) *Queer Visibilities: Space, Identity, and Interaction in Cape Town*, London: Wiley-Blackwell.

Visser, G. (2003) 'Gay men, leisure space and South African cities: the case of Cape Town', *Geoforum*, 34(1), 123–137.

Visser, G. (2013) 'Challenging the gay ghetto in South Africa: time to move on?' *Geoforum*, 49, 268–274.

Walcott, R. (2007) 'Homopoetics: queer space and the black queer diaspora', in McKittrick, K. and Woods, C. (eds), *Black Geographies and the Politics of Place*, Boston: South End Press, pp. 233–245.

Ward, J. (2003) 'Producing "pride" in West Hollywood: a queer cultural capital for queers with cultural capital', *Sexualities,* 6, 65–94.

Wei, W. (2007) '"Wandering men" no longer wander around: the production and transformation of local homosexual identities in contemporary Chengdu, China', *Inter-Asia Cultural Studies*, 8(4), 572–588.

Weightman, B. (1981) 'Commentary: towards a geography of the gay community', *Journal of Cultural Geography*, 1, 106–112.

Whitaker, B. (2006) *Unspeakable Love: Gay and Lesbian Life in the Middle East*, London: Zaki Books.

Whittemore, A. (2015) 'The Dallas way: property, politics, and assimilation', in Doan, P. (ed), *Planning and LGBQ Communities: The Need for Inclusive Queer Spaces*, London: Routledge, pp. 39–55.

Whittemore, A. and Smart, M. (2015) 'Mapping gay and lesbian neighborhoods using home advertisements: change and continuity in the Dallas-Fort Worth metropolitan statistical area over three decades', *Environment and Planning A*, 48(1), 192–210.

Williams, P. (1986) 'Class constitution through spatial reconstruction? A reevaluation of gentrification in Australia, Britain and the United States', in Smith, N. and Williams, P. (eds), *Gentrification of the City*, Boston: Allen and Unwin, pp. 56–77.

Winkle, C. (2015) 'Gay commercial districts in Chicago and the role of planning', in Doan, P. (ed), *Planning and LGBQ Communities: The Need for Inclusive Queer Spaces*, London: Routledge, pp. 21–38.

Wyly, E. and Hammel, D. (1999) 'Islands of decay in seas of renewal: housing policy and the resurgence of gentrification', *Housing Policy Debate*, 10(4), 711–771.

11. Age, life course and generations in gentrification processes
Cody Hochstenbach and Willem Boterman

11.1 INTRODUCTION

Gentrification is generally defined as the class-based transformation of urban spaces (Lees et al. 2008). Although class is indeed central, gentrification is also the spatial manifestation of demographic processes embedded in a wider political economy. Gentrification is often understood as part of a specific life stage during young adulthood; a temporary phenomenon in the time-space trajectories of particular middle-class fractions (Bridge 2003). Although age is often implicitly discussed in gentrification studies, we argue that it should be treated as a key dimension to understand gentrification and the inequalities it brings about. Acknowledging the central role of demographic processes further opens up the debate about the global scope of gentrification and its specific geographical manifestations (Lees 2012), which are not just rooted in local configurations of class, but also in a wider national and local political economy around life course. It seems that the globalisation of gentrification as a primarily urban phenomenon and theoretical concept is mostly concerned with the ways in which global capital now sweeps across all corners of the planet. Gentrification is hence understood as a planetary strategy for capital accumulation and is mainly about class power (Lees et al. 2016). To some extent this is at odds with the complex ways in which gentrification is produced and practised in light of the specific historical trajectories of urbanization of Western cities. Gentrification in post-war America and Europe cannot be seen in isolation from suburbanisation and abandonment of inner cities; however, nor can it be seen separate from demographic transitions, the boom in single households and female emancipation.

In this contribution, we place age centre stage, and aim to unravel how it plays a role in different forms of gentrification. We do so by providing an overview of recent gentrification studies addressing age dimensions, drawing primarily on work from the 'Global North'. To investigate how age is implicated in gentrification processes, we focus on the concepts of life course and generation. In the residential domain, life-course transitions alter preferences and trigger residential moves, and are crucial moments that generate the conditions for (middle-class) households to move into or out of a gentrifying neighbourhood (Bridge 2003; Boterman and Bridge 2015). But they simultaneously confront low-income households with housing unaffordability, inaccessibility and displacement, foregrounding inequalities. Life-course transitions are not independent events: previous experiences, preferences and predilections accumulated during previous life stages and transitions, influence how households negotiate subsequent transitions. Moreover, life-course transitions bear some universality, but the specific ways in which life courses unfold and impact upon residential practices are highly contingent in space. Life-course transitions such as leaving the parental home are already differentiated between relatively similar Western welfare states (compare for instance the Netherlands and Sweden). The variation between and across countries of the Global North and Global South in terms of how the meaning of age and life courses are socially constructed is immense. Moreover, the very meaning of life-course transitions and the way it impacts residential practices is not stable over time.

In this regard, it is also imperative to consider the role of generations: baby boomers were crucial in driving gentrification as a counter process in many countries of the Global North in the 1960s and 1970s (Ley 1996). We argue that the ageing of this 'first generation' of gentrifiers contributes to new forms of gentrification, but also impacts subsequent generations. While it may seem very specific to this generation in Western countries, in many countries of the Global South, China being a prime example, the emergence of gentrification processes at unprecedented intensities is also linked to the rapid growth of the middle classes in general. Hence, a majority of the current gentrifiers in such contexts are also 'first generation'. This raises important questions about how we should understand the emergence of gentrification in ever more contexts in the light of intersections of life course, generation and class.

In this chapter, we highlight how multiple age groups are involved in different forms of gentrification. This is, we argue, necessary to understand the increasingly widespread scale at which gentrification and displacement operate. The remainder of this contribution will zoom in on the role of three different age groups in broader gentrification processes: (1) young people, (2) families, and (3) ageing groups. We specifically focus on the crucial role of life-course transitions, and the cumulative experiences and residential trajectories of particular generations. Finally, we consider the political economy of life course.

11.2   YOUNG PEOPLE AND GENTRIFICATION

Gentrification is most prominently associated with the life-course and residential trajectories of young people. These typically represent formative years in young people's transition towards full independence, and constitute a transitory period prior to settling down. During these years, many young people flock to inner-city environments where they can benefit from the close proximity of higher-education institutions, opportunity-rich labour markets, as well as amenities that cater to their specific tastes (Ley 1996, 2003; Smith and Holt 2007). In the 1960s, expanding university participation was important for specific fractions of the baby-boom generation to develop a more urban residential orientation. This was a counter process to more dominant suburbanization processes in Western societies though. To opt for an affordable inner-city environment was a way to distinguish oneself from other middle-class fractions and to reject the 'suburban' nuclear family (Wilson 1991; May 1996). Their choice for relatively cheap inner-city living arrangements had a clear financial rationale too, given the generally limited economic resources at disposal (Rose 1984; Caulfield 1994).

The typical life-course and residential trajectories of young people have changed over time. Higher education has continued to expand, making the city an ever more common destination for young people. Furthermore, young people increasingly extend a transitory life phase as they postpone settling down, marriage, and having children. Labour-market flexibilization and growing insecurities also push young people towards more flexible life arrangements. This creates a prolonged transitory life-course stage, often with a distinct urban orientation (Buzar et al. 2005; Van Criekingen and Decroly 2003). Consequently, gentrification no longer constitutes a rebellious counter process (Ley, 1996), but has become the default option in the residential and life-course trajectories of young middle-class households. It is part of the rite of passage of these young middle-class people towards adulthood.

At the same time, more and more inner-city neighbourhoods are growing unaffordable due to gentrification, forcing young people to make ever-sharper trade-offs regarding location: ongoing gentrification may have young people 'looking for the next best thing' and settling in those neighbourhoods that have so far remained largely untouched by gentrification, pushing the process' frontier (Kerstein 1990; Ley 2003).

11.2.1   Changing Housing-market Position

Given the crucial role ascribed to young people in gentrification, young people's housing position and opportunities will influence the form and intensity of gentrification processes. Since the global financial crisis and accompanying housing-market downturn, homeownership rates among younger age groups have fallen in virtually all European countries (Lennartz et al. 2016), as well as in a host of other contexts including North America, Australia and East Asia (Mykyta 2012; Stebbing and Spies-Butcher 2016; Forrest and Hirayama 2009). This trend should be considered part of long-term housing- and labour-market restructuring (Ronald 2008; Forrest and Hirayama 2015). Consequently, in many contexts, but most notably the United Kingdom (UK), the rise of a 'generation rent' has been identified: unable to buy a home, increasing numbers of young people have to rely on private-rental accommodation (McKee 2012; Clapham et al. 2014; Kemp 2015). More generally, young people find it increasingly difficult to acquire secure housing – either owned or rented – at all, resulting in the formation of capricious and chaotic housing pathways. Such pathways are marked by sequences of insecure, temporary and often semi-illegal living arrangements (Hochstenbach and Boterman 2015; Ford et al. 2002; Clapham et al. 2014). The overall destabilization of housing pathways must certainly not be considered solely the consequence of growing housing constraints and increasing labour-market insecurities. As remarked above, they are also part of a shift towards more flexible lifestyles and prolonged 'urban' living, prior to settling (Buzar et al. 2005; Mulder and Manting 1994; Van Criekingen and Decroly 2003).

So how does this influence gentrification processes? Despite growing housing insecurities, many young people retain a residential focus on increasingly expensive cities (Moos 2016). Unable to buy, these young adults have to rent. Investors and developers, eager to cater to these groups, consequently channel capital into the rental market. This contributes to a revival of private rent (Ronald and Kadi 2017), as well as the emergence of new forms of private-rental gentrification (Paccoud 2017). While rental gentrification is certainly not a new phenomenon – young, rather poor but upwardly-mobile 'marginal gentrifiers' are often associated with renting (Rose 1984; Van Criekingen and Decroly 2003) – in more recent times it has become increasingly integrated into speculative modes of urban development (Paccoud 2017; Fields and Uffer 2016). Effectively, rental gentrification is likely to contribute to exclusionary displacement (Marcuse 1986) with particular age and class dynamics (Van Criekingen 2010): young, mostly middle-class residents may be able and willing to negotiate housing constraints and overcome high rents by sharing an apartment, excluding lower-income family households from renting. Furthermore, high turnover rates allow landlords to frequently raise rents (ibid.). Finally, since security of tenure is often relatively low in private rent, low-income tenants may also be most likely to suffer direct displacement due to, for example, steep rental increases or landlord intimidation (Paccoud 2017). Yet, as young upwardly-mobile people may be inclined to accept precarious living arrangements themselves, they become more prone to displacement as well (cf. Hochstenbach and Boterman 2015).

11.2.2 Intergenerational Support

As constraints and insecurities on the housing market grow, young people are increasingly dependent on the parental home. Unable to find housing, growing numbers of young people prolong their stay in it (Lennartz et al. 2016), or use it as a safety net to deal with unexpected housing events (Sage et al. 2013). Moreover, parental support also shapes housing outcomes, for example through financial transfers to buy a home or pay rent (Helderman and Mulder 2007; Öst 2012). Such forms of intergenerational support have become more crucial in helping young people on their way as generational divides themselves are growing (McKee 2012; Forrest and Hirayama 2015). This exacerbates the intergenerational transmission of inequalities, deepening socio-economic dividing lines based on family background.

Intergenerational relations and parental support factor into processes of gentrification in both direct and indirect ways. In a study of Amsterdam, we have shown that parental wealth is a key predictor of young people's ability and propensity to move to up-market gentrification neighbourhoods (Hochstenbach and Boterman 2017). This directly contributes to gentrification processes as it allows young adults to tap into additional sources of wealth, driving up house prices in different tenures. Furthermore, new flows of capital are established. Parents, often living in suburban or rural locations, mobilize their wealth and invest it in urban neighbourhoods for their children. In a way this means that capital accumulated elsewhere 'urbanizes' (cf. Harvey 1985), flowing into gentrifying neighbourhoods. Such forms of parental support reflect intergenerational solidarity and social reproduction strategies, but are also often strategic investments to facilitate further wealth accumulation. Parents may particularly invest in gentrifying neighbourhoods because these are the sites where windfall gains may be expected. These investment strategies may have an interesting multigenerational dimension to them as parental financial capital is combined with their offspring's specific knowledge of the local housing market (i.e. where to invest).

Indirectly, parents do not only provide financial support, but also transfer social and cultural capital to get ahead on the housing market. Young people acquire preferences from their parents, which in turn inform residential location preferences and decisions (Hochstenbach and Boterman 2015). As the 'gentrifiers' of previous waves have aged and become parents, they are likely to pass on the preferences and tastes they acquired during these formative years in the life course, including a 'gentrification aesthetic'. They may expect their children to follow in their footsteps by moving to the city – notably to follow education (Rye 2011). Gentrification has therefore become a process that spans multiple generations. It figures ever more in the residential biographies of both the old and young, and it is reproduced across generations. This stands in stark contrast to early waves of gentrification, when the process was the outcome of young people rejecting parental household and residential arrangements (Ley 1996).

11.2.3 Apprentice Gentrifiers and Studentification

Education plays a key role in the expansion of gentrification. Due to the massive expansion of higher-education participation across contexts, growing numbers of young people gravitate towards urban areas to study (Smith and Sage 2014; also Fielding 1992). As a consequence, the early life-course trajectories of young people play out in urban settings increasingly often (Rérat 2012). During studenthood young people develop certain residential and social preferences, and internalize a specific way of life. Furthermore, studenthood often constitutes a gradual and 'sheltered' transition out of the parental home towards independence, as middle-class parents continue to lend support in various ways (Rugg et al. 2004). It can therefore be considered a crucial phase in the production and reproduction of a middle-class habitus (Chatterton 1999; Smith and Holt 2007: 150). Not only are these students on a trajectory to the middle classes, but the urban dimensions of student life are also likely to forge preferences for urban living. In addition, students tend to live among peers shaping future inclinations to live among likeminded people, an important dimension of gentrification processes in general (Smith and Holt 2007). Smith and Holt (2007) have therefore argued that students may be considered 'apprentice gentrifiers': their current and future residential preferences for specific urban areas are shaped by their spell as a student in the city.

Studenthood thus figures prominently in gentrification processes, because it represents a necessary precondition for the production of future gentrifiers (Smith 2005). Apart from this longer-term impact, students play a more direct role in gentrification processes in general (Ley 2003) as well as in the more specific process of studentification (Smith 2005; Hubbard 2008; He 2015). In its direct form studentification denotes the process where students concentrate in certain neighbourhoods, such as purpose-build student campuses but also existing neighbourhoods often located close to their university, the city centre, and amenities. Particularly in the latter case, studentification is likely to have notable repercussions. High residential turnover rates among students put pressure on local social cohesion. In addition, students' specific lifestyles, a neglect of public space, and student-specific businesses all impact how longer-term, non-student residents experience the neighbourhood. Therefore, in those neighbourhoods where studentification progresses, displacement pressures can take on rather extreme forms.

11.3 FAMILIES AND GENTRIFICATION

11.3.1 Gentrification as a Temporary Life Phase

The increase in higher-education participation is one of the main explanations for first wave gentrification as described above. The large numbers of young adults flocking to the city for study or work were to a large extent the result of fundamental demographic changes. The second demographic transition entailed the postponement of marriage and childbirth, thereby creating basically a new life-course stage in which young adults, especially women, had the opportunity to live independent lives after leaving the parental home and before settling down. These new generations of young adults fundamentally challenged traditional norms around many things, not least around parenthood, marriage and living alone or unmarried cohabitation. Many of them were first generation gentrifiers, members of a newly emerging middle class, who are argued to have developed an urban habitus, manifesting itself in a particular urban lifestyle revolving around consumption and new creative and service industries (Ley 1996; Butler and Robson 2003). This urban habitus of the new middle classes, however, is eventually challenged by events in the life course. Various scholars have shown that the urban lifestyle of new middle-class households is pressured by the birth of children (Bridge 2006). Entering the field of parenthood unsettles the relationship between habitus and field and raises the stakes in social reproduction (Boterman and Bridge 2015). The demographic literature has established that the birth of children triggers a reordering of priorities in terms of size, cost and location of housing (Rossi 1955). Most middle-class families have a preference for owning a larger home, with a garden in a child-friendly environment (Mulder 2006; Baldassare 1992). A large body of literature demonstrates that access to good schools is central for understanding the residential preferences of the middle classes as they enter into family formation (Butler and Hamnett 2007; Benson et al. 2015). In a range of different urban contexts, moving to the catchment area or school district of a high-quality primary or secondary school is argued to be an absolute priority (Wu et al. 2015; Butler and Van Zanten 2007; Lareau and Goyette 2014; Boterman 2013). As a result of the reordering of priorities, out of which housing and schooling emerge as key issues, many gentrifiers move out of the city when they have children. While oftentimes these residential trajectories lead to 'traditional' suburban locations (Bridge 2006; Boterman 2012b; Gamsu 2016), gentrifiers may also explicitly move to rural locations for reasons including good schools, a distinctive rural idyll, healthy environment, and sense of community (Phillips 1993, 2004; Smith and Higley 2012). For most middle-class households, an urban lifestyle only fits a specific stage of their life course and is hence a temporary phenomenon.

11.3.2   Family Gentrifiers

However, a number of studies have demonstrated that considerable numbers of middle-class households continue to be urban when they have children (Karsten 2007; Boterman 2012a; Goodsell 2013). This group, which has been referred to as family gentrifiers (Boterman et al. 2010; Karsten 2003; Lilius 2014) seems to be on the rise in various urban contexts, including New York City, London, Amsterdam and Berlin. Karsten (2003) argues that family gentrifiers stay in the city for three main reasons: they have invested heavily in localized social networks; the city provides them with a distinctive identity; and the city offers a time-space context that allows particularly mothers to manage their work-care balance. More generally, gentrification has been associated with increasing female participation in employment and consequently also the rise in dual earners, which gives these households a competitive edge on the housing market (Warde 1991; Rose 1989; Hamnett 2003). It is repeatedly argued that higher-educated women are the key agents of gentrification (Butler and Hamnett 1994). Family gentrification should therefore also be seen in the context of the intersection of class and gender (Bondi 1999; Van den Berg

2013; Boterman and Bridge 2015). Yet, although it has been convincingly explained why some middle-class families stay in the city and how they manage their every-day lives in respect to their consumption behaviour, their social networks, and their working careers (Brun and Fagnani 1994; Karsten 2003, 2007), few studies have investigated why and how urban family gentrifiers are different from gentrifiers that move out of the city. In other words: why does having children affect some middle-class households differently than others?

A longitudinal study with middle-class parents in Amsterdam demonstrates that specific fractions of the middle classes have specific residential trajectories when they have children. Depending on the sum and orientation of their economic social and cultural capital, some class fractions are more likely to stay in the inner city than others (Boterman 2012a). Specifically, relatively affluent households, with extensive social networks in the city, often working in the public sector, tertiary education, law, and creative industries, tend to stay in inner-city districts and continue to be gentrifiers after having children. They are able to combine the advantages of inner-city living while making only few compromises in terms of housing and – due to the proximity of good public schools – education. This group of high-paid dual earner families are both literally and figuratively the agents of more mature forms of gentrification. Households with similar cultural orientations who also rely on local social networks, but who command fewer financial resources, also tend to stay but have to make bigger compromises in terms of their housing situation. Lacking the economic capital to buy spacious housing in gentrified neighbourhoods they make sharper trade-offs between location and aspects of the home. They may buy or rent property in relatively cheap areas thereby indirectly or directly displacing other families from a non-native or lower-class background.

Finally, middle-class households that have the economic capital to buy property in gentrified parts of the city, but belong to other fractions of the middle classes, working for instance in business and finance, are more likely to suburbanize. These parents, often 'first generation middle class' (Reay et al. 2011), have other ideas about where to bring up children. They tend to stress the importance of homogeneity, space in and outside of the home, and also have more traditional divisions of labour between men and women (Boterman and Bridge 2015). Also, the issue of school choice seems to play a more central role (see also Reay et al. 2011). In this respect, they appear more similar in their residential trajectories to the traditional middle classes who massively suburbanized. It should be stressed that non-urban trajectories are highly differentiated and remain the most common form of residential mobility in the field of parenthood. Furthermore, these middle-class and high-earning families moving out of the city may drive gentrification processes in specific, distinct rural locations (Phillips 1993).

11.3.3   The Context of Family Gentrification

The way in which the residential trajectories of gentrifiers develop after the birth of children, however, appears to be highly influenced by local spatial and institutional context (Lees 2012). Bridge (2003, 2006) for instance argues that gentrification by families may not be 'sustainable' in the context of a provincial city (Bristol) because of the limited stock of 'gentrifiable' housing and good schools. In London, the wide range of residential environments and supply of historical homes, which are connected to the city via the extensive underground and train system, as well as the supply of good schools (education), enables the middle classes to maintain working careers and also their lifestyle via the consumption of urban amenities, such as restaurants, delis and theatres (Butler and Robson 2003). In London, the scale of the metropolitan area thus allows for a greater continuity of residential trajectories of gentrifiers.

In cities where gentrification is ubiquitous and where even the middle and upper classes are displaced from super-gentrified areas (Lees 2003; Atkinson 2016), such as London and New York City, housing for middle-class families is highly unaffordable. The huge boom in London's real estate market makes it almost impossible to stay in gentrified areas when a family needs to move for more space, although some are able to create more space via extensions or digging out the basement. In Northwest European cities where housing is also expensive but the real estate market is less affected by global capital, upper middle-class families are often among the most well-endowed households, particularly middle-class professionals with two substantial incomes. In those contexts, dual-income families may be among the most powerful displacers, particularly of non-native families and ageing working-class households.

This points to an interesting dynamic around age and class: family gentrification occurs often in areas where larger dwellings are inhabited by working-class households from which the children have usually moved out. Older working-class 'empty nesters' are replaced, and sometimes displaced, by a new generation of middle-class families. Although class is also central to this process, succession of one generation by the next is also a crucial dimension in its own right. As first-generation gentrifiers are now also becoming empty nesters and enter retirement, new questions around gentrification, generation, and life course emerge.

11.4   GENTRIFICATION AND OLDER GENERATIONS

11.4.1 Ageing

In a similar vein as leaving the parental home and entering the field of parenthood signify important transitions in the life course, in later life two transitions may be particularly associated with specific forms of gentrification: empty nesting and retirement. Empty nesting implies that the household becomes smaller, and generally entails a reduction of responsibilities for others, both emotionally and financially – although parental support to adult children is on the rise in many contexts (see McKee 2012; Forrest and Hirayama 2015; Albertini et al. 2007). This stage is in many Western contexts associated with a greater relative wealth, particularly when the household moves into smaller and cheaper housing (Painter and Lee 2009) or has paid off the mortgage debt. While empty nesting in principle decouples older households' attachment to family neighbourhoods and spacious homes, continuing employment generally means these households remain attached to the same location.

In a second stage of ageing, retirement may (but not necessarily so) reduce the disposable income of households. At the same time, retirement provides a greater time-budget allowing new leisure-oriented consumption, and travel. While there is a fairly extensive literature on retirement and the residential mobility of the relatively affluent elderly to the countryside, associated with rural manifestations of gentrification (Nelson et al. 2010; Philips 1993), there is much less explicit attention on older people in processes of urban gentrification.

In urban studies of gentrification older people are often described as victims or potential victims of displacement. Ageing is implicit, yet present, in analysis of class-based change in which older cohorts of working-class, blue-collar workers are gradually replaced by younger and higher-educated professionals (Hamnett 2003; Butler et al. 2008). Studies of class-based urban change often frame the elderly as 'weak' households that run the risk of being directly displaced (Atkinson 2000; Henig 1981), although an ageing working class enjoying security of tenure may also serve as a temporary brake to gentrification-induced population change (Hochstenbach and Van Gent 2015). Furthermore, it is often assumed that the elderly are most likely to be negatively affected in terms of belonging (Phillipson 2007), because gentrification is often said to be a disruption of the social and cultural life of the elderly. This type of research however, finds it difficult to separate issues of class and age as most of the neighbourhood's working-class communities affected by gentrification consist of older people and most urban elderly are lower educated than the new generation of gentrifiers.

Yet, there is increasing attention being paid to the intersection of age and class, as well as to variations in the way older people experience and react to neighbourhood change (Pinkster 2016). Studies from San Francisco and Montreal, for instance, point to a mixed experience of ageing in urban communities, which do entail economic displacement and experiencing a loss of place (Burns et al. 2011; Lehman-Frisch 2002). But, there is mixed evidence for how neighbourhood and urban change is experienced and how this is differentiated across class. Phillipson (2007: 336), for instance, differentiates between the quite nostalgic experiences of some elderly that are 'fixed' in space, which he calls 'the excluded', and the more elective forms of belonging of others who 'actively re-shape communities which are meaningful to them in old age'. Other research points to the intersection of age and ethnicity: in neighbourhoods where the ethnic composition of the population has changed over time, an ageing native working class may welcome gentrification as it brings in more native newcomers – in turn often related to nostalgic neighbourhood experiences (Ernst and Doucet 2014). Much of this differential experience of ageing is class related, but there is also a clear generational dimension. Much of the changes in the role of the elderly in spatial transformations could be ascribed to the ageing of the largest post-war generation in Western contexts: the baby boomers.

11.4.2 Gentrification and the Baby Boomers

The baby-boom generation played a crucial role in gentrification processes in North America and Europe. David Ley (1996) considers the rebellious and distinctive choices of this generation as quintessential for the revival of urban living, coming to fruition during the 1960s. Most baby boomers have now retired and are often parents to current generations of gentrifiers. Although of course this generation is diverse in various ways, generally speaking, baby boomers have been highly successful in building up housing and other wealth, retired relatively early, and are in better health than previous generations. Although older people are generally less residentially mobile than younger people, the current generation of 'young elderly' (60–75) may differ from previous generations also in this respect. Particularly higher-educated, affluent older people may mobilize their housing wealth to relocate in later life.

Most of the literature on gentrification and the residential mobility of older generations has focused on rural gentrification. This is argued to be growing due to the ageing of relatively affluent generations who seek out the countryside in search of the rural idyll (Nelson et al. 2010; Smith and Higley 2012). Rural gentrification is also fuelled through the acquisition of second homes (Paris 2009; Visser 2006). Not only do these homes serve as holiday addresses, they are often also vehicles for further wealth accumulation. The demand for second homes should, hence, be considered part of a turn towards a more speculative housing market as it forefronts housing as an investment. It is therefore likely to push up prices, contributing to gentrification and displacement, but also contribute to a loss in permanent population, eroding the customer base for everyday facilities (Smith and Higley 2012). This trend is also visible in cities where the affluent elderly may buy property for their children (see above) or as a pied-à-terre (Chevalier et al. 2012). There is also renewed interest by elderly households in urban apartments (Myers and Gearin 2001), they are willing to trade space for proximity to urban amenities. It had already been noted in some early studies of gentrification that loft-living and buying converted condominiums was popular among older households such as empty nesters (Ley 1986; Mills 1988). Although this has never been at the centre of gentrification research, recent case studies identify higher-educated and affluent, older age groups as agents of gentrification through the purchase of new-build apartments, condominiums, and lofts (Hamnett and Whitelegg 2007; Bounds and Morris 2006; Butler 2007). Furthermore, this group of high-educated and affluent retirees may prefer to 'age in place' and have the means to successfully do so. New-build developments in particular may cater to the demand by empty nesters and retirees for age-proof apartments in exclusive, enclosed, safe and relatively homogeneous environments (Rose and Villeneuve 2006). This contributes to forms of new-build gentrification, often on waterfronts or on brownfield sites (Davidson and Lees 2005; Butler 2007), but also relates to wealthy enclaves and gated communities in rural settings (Phillips 2000; Grant and Mittelsteadt 2004). Population ageing in most countries in the Global North (the US being an interesting exception) but also in countries such as Japan and China, may imply that older generations' investment and residential behaviour comes to play a greater role in gentrification processes. Patterns of ageing as well as the intersection of age and class differ between countries though. While in many countries in the Global North a relatively well-off generation is ageing, in many countries of the Global South the middle class tends to be smaller among older generations. It is hence likely that ageing has, and will continue to have, a variegated impact on the contemporary geography of gentrification.

11.4.3   Political Economy of Life Course

While the previous sections have focused on the life-course shaping gentrification processes, there is also what may be termed a political economy of life course. In the turn towards more speculative modes of gentrification, corporate and state actors have become more important agents. As more age groups become associated with gentrification, new niche markets open up creating opportunities for investors, states and speculative developers. Investors use specific identities and lifestyles as part of their investment and marketing strategies to facilitate the 'capital-led colonisation of urban space' (Davidson 2007: 493). And age plays an important part in this: the marketing strategies for many new urban development projects and the rebranding of neighbourhoods typically cater to a clientele that is high income, but also relatively young and childless (Young et al. 2006; Allen 2007). Likewise, luxury new-build projects may specifically be designed and branded to appeal to an ageing middle class. Although age may be mobilized in several ways, it frequently plays a role in efforts to 'sell' neighbourhoods or new developments, as it is part and parcel of promoted lifestyles where class and age intersect, and may thus be implicated in the commodification of (urban) space. Likewise, private parties recognize the importance of intergenerational support and hence market owner-occupied studios and other small apartments as an ideal investment opportunity for parents with university-attending children. And states may be eager to encourage such intergenerational support to boost demand for housing. For instance, in the wake of the housing-market downturn following the global financial crisis, the Dutch government made it temporarily possible for parents to transfer up to €100,000 tax free to their children to support with a house purchase.

By emphasizing how their developments meet the unfulfilled demands of specific age groups, investors push through, legitimize and normalize their projects. Ultimately, such projects may primarily serve private interests, and in fact do little to increase housing accessibility or affordability for any age group but instead propel elitist and exclusive forms of gentrification (Davidson 2007). This is not limited to high-end developments, but also extends into other domains such as student housing where developers promote exclusive forms of student living by renting out expensive rooms to students with few other options in tight housing markets (cf. Chatterton 2010).

State actors may use 'age' as a tool of de-politicization. States underscore how their housing policies will ultimately come to benefit certain age groups, which allows them to ignore, downplay, or conceal important class dimensions and middle-class politics. Although this issue has received little attention, a case study of Rotterdam shows that local urban policies to make the city more family friendly hold many implicit notions about class (Van den Berg 2013: 529): 'The neutral language of "families" and "amenities" disguises the way in which very specific families are targeted: the municipality will invest in amenities such as schools, sports clubs and childcare if it can attract the higher middle classes'. Lower-class families are in turn barely taken into consideration, and lower-class youths may even be targeted by punitive policies (ibid.). States may subsequently encourage developers to focus on particular groups, for instance by providing direct subsidies or by relaxing regulations when certain groups are the targeted clientele (Janoschka and Sequera 2016).

11.5   CONCLUSION

We have illustrated the importance of age, life course and generations in gentrification processes by focusing on key transitions among young people, families, and older households. While age certainly shapes residential preferences and is associated with particular constraints, life-course transitions are generally the key moments when households may opt into or out of gentrifying areas. Life-course transitions reshape people's preferences for, and expectations of, residential environments, and people are likely to adapt their residential arrangement accordingly (Clark and Dieleman 1996; Musterd et al. 2016). Life-course transitions trigger new trade-offs to be made. Moving into a gentrification area may be one particular strategy to negotiate altered preferences and constraints, and to realign habitus and field. Table 11.1 gives a schematic overview of various life-course transitions that are associated with young people, families and ageing people that may lead to gentrification. This is not to say that all people neatly follow the same life-course trajectories and transitions, nor that this scheme holds for each and every context. Nevertheless, as gentrification has become mainstream it becomes an ever more likely outcome of the negotiation of various life-course transitions. Developers recognize this and jump on those niche markets for profitable speculative housing development, and it provides states the opportunity to lure in those households they deem desirable.

This contribution has singled out the importance of tracking specific generations and age cohorts in gentrification processes: like young people and students, the baby-boom generation was crucial in kicking off incipient forms of gentrification across major cities in the Global North (Ley 1996). Having developed an urban middle-class habitus, some of them continue to gentrify in later life, with wealth previously accumulated through investing in gentrifying areas allowing them to do so. They are also the first generation to pass on a preference for gentrification to their offspring on a relatively large scale. The same goes for the intergenerational transmission of their accumulated wealth. The current generation of young people in Western cities is, however, confronted with a more difficult housing position requiring ever sharper trade-offs in relation to housing, including gentrification. Gentrification in the Global North has therefore become an increasingly multi-generational process, with different age groups involved. Indeed, in this context gentrification is an ageing process and pulling in older groups has been crucial to its expansion. The increasing diversity among gentrifiers allows the process to spread to more and different types of neighbourhoods, as well as to occur in different housing types and tenures (Table 11.1). Major cities in particular offer the setting where different forms of gentrification may get a foothold, while in smaller cities their occurrence depends to a greater extent on spatial and institutional context.

In the Global North gentrification has matured and is spreading laterally into new

Table 11.1   Different forms of gentrification with different age groups and life-course transitions

Age group	Life-course transition	Gentrification type	Property	Specific characteristic
Young people	Leaving parental home	Studentification	Student room, house sharing	Apprentice gentrifiers
	Graduation/labour market entry	Rental gentrification	Private rental, insecure	Flexible, insecure, temporary
Families	Settling down	Family gentrification	Owner-occupied family homes	Dual incomes; School choice
Older people	Having children			
Older people	Empty nesting		Lofts and condominiums;	Ageing in place; Investment strategy
	Retirement	Rural gentrification	Second homes	

niche markets, geographically variegating and sprawling. In rapidly urbanizing, emerging economies of the Global South gentrification and age may intersect in different ways. Here in many ways, urban gentrification remains mostly associated with younger people, most specifically with the emergence of a global new middle class (Lees et al. 2016: 84). Although parallels can be drawn in terms of capital investment and also in terms of consumption lifestyles, the way in which life courses, residential trajectories and transformation of urban space are intertwined differ quite fundamentally from American and European experiences. This is, we argue, important for understanding how we should understand gentrification's evolution from a significant yet relatively marginal counter current into a major force of urban change permeating into ever new corners of the globe (Hackworth and Smith 2001). Also in various countries of the Global South, notably China, gentrification is spreading through specific forms closely associated to age and life course – such as forms related to studenthood (He 2015) and family formation and school choice (Wu et al. 2015). It is important to draw in age, particularly life course, to better grasp the geography of gentrification as the manifestation of capital investment and class power in historically developed institutional and spatial contexts.

REFERENCES

Albertini, M., Kohli, M. and Vogel, C. (2007) 'Intergenerational transfers of time and money in European families: common patterns – different regimes?', *Journal of European Social Policy*, 17(4), 319–334.

Atkinson, R. (2000) 'Measuring gentrification and displacement in Greater London', *Urban Studies*, 37(1), 149–165.

Atkinson, R. (2016) 'Limited exposure: social concealment, mobility and engagement with public space by the super-rich in London', *Environment and Planning A*, 48(7), 1302–1317.

Baldassare, M. (1992) 'Suburban communities', *Annual Review of Sociology*, 18, 475–494.

Benson, M., Bridge, G. and Wilson, D. (2015) 'School choice in London and Paris – a comparison of middle-class strategies', *Social Policy and Administration*, 49(1), 24–43.

Bondi, L. (1999) 'Gender, class, and gentrification: enriching the debate', *Environment and Planning D: Society and Space*, 17(3), 261–282.

Boterman, W. (2012a) 'Residential mobility of urban middle classes in the field of parenthood', *Environment and Planning A*, 44(10), 2397–2412.

Boterman, W. (2012b) *Residential practices of middle classes in the field of parenthood*, PhD thesis University of Amsterdam.

Boterman, W. (2013) 'Dealing with diversity: middle-class family households and the issue of "black" and "white" schools in Amsterdam', *Urban Studies*, 50(6), 1130–1147.

Boterman, W. and Bridge, G. (2015) 'Gender, class and space in the field of parenthood: comparing middle class fractions in Amsterdam and London', *Transactions of the Institute of British Geographers*, 40(2), 249–261.

Boterman, W., Karsten, L. and Musterd, S. (2010) 'Gentrifiers settling down? Patterns and trends of residential location of middle-class families in Amsterdam', *Housing Studies*, 25(5), 693–714.

Bounds, M. and Morris, A. (2006) 'Second wave gentrification in inner-city Sydney', *Cities*, 23(2), 99–108.

Bridge, G. (2003) 'Time-space trajectories in provincial gentrification', *Urban Studies*, 40(12), 2545–2556.

Bridge, G. (2006) 'It's not just a question of taste: gentrification, the neighbourhood, and cultural capital', *Environment and Planning A*, 38(10), 1965–1978.

Brun, J. and Fagnani, J. (1994) 'Lifestyles and locational choices – trade-offs and compromises: a case-study of middle-class couples living in the Ile-de-France region', *Urban Studies*, 31(6), 921–934.

Burns, V., Lavoie, J. and Rose, D. (2011) 'Revisiting the role of neighbourhood change in social exclusion and inclusion of older people', *Journal of Aging Research*, 2012, 1–12.

Butler, T. (2007) 'Re-urbanizing London Docklands: gentrification, suburbanization or new urbanism?', *International Journal of Urban and Regional Research*, 31(4), 759–781.

Butler, T. and Hamnett, C. (1994) 'Gentrification, class, and gender: some comments on Warde's "Gentrification as Consumption"', *Environment and Planning D: Society and Space*, 12(4), 477–493.

Butler, T. and Hamnett, C. (2007) 'The geography of education: introduction', *Urban Studies*, 44(7), 1161–1174.

Butler, T. and Robson, G. (2003) *London Calling: The Middle Classes and the Re-making of Inner London*, Oxford: Berg Publishers.

Butler, T. and Van Zanten, A. (2007) 'School choice: a European perspective', *Journal of Education Policy*, 22(1), 1–5.

Butler, T., Hamnett, C. and Ramsden, M. (2008) 'Inward and upward: marking out social class change in London, 1981–2001', *Urban Studies*, 45(1), 67–88.

Buzar, S., Ogden, P. and Hall, R. (2005) 'Households matter: the quiet demography of urban transformation', *Progress in Human Geography*, 29(4), 413–436.

Caulfield, J. (1994) *City Form and Everyday Life: Toronto's Gentrification and Critical Social Practice*, Toronto: University of Toronto Press.

Chatterton, P. (1999) 'University students and city centres – the formation of exclusive geographies: the case of Bristol, UK', *Geoforum*, 30(2), 117–133.

Chatterton, P. (2010) 'The student city: an ongoing story of neoliberalism, gentrification, and commodification', *Environment and Planning A*, 42(3), 509–514.

Chevalier, S., Corbillé, S. and Lallement, E. (2012) 'Le Paris des résidences secondaires. Entre ville réelle et ville rêvée', *Ethnologie française*, 42(3), 441–449.

Clapham, D., Mackie, P., Orford, S., Thomas, I. and Buckley, K. (2014) 'The housing pathways of young people in the UK', *Environment and Planning A*, 46(8), 2016–2031.

Clark, W. and Dieleman, F. (1996) *Households and Housing: Choice and Outcomes in the Housing Market*, Transaction Publishers.

Davidson, M. (2007) 'Gentrification as global habitat: a process of class formation or corporate creation?', *Transactions of the Institute of British Geographers*, 32(4), 490–506.

Davidson, M. and Lees, L. (2005) 'New-build "gentrification" and London's riverside renaissance', *Environment and Planning A*, 37(7), 1165–1190.

Ernst, O. and Doucet, B. (2014) 'A window on the (changing) neighbourhood: the role of pubs in the contested spaces of gentrification', *Tijdschrift voor Economische en Sociale Geografie*, 105(2), 189–205.

Fielding, A. (1992) 'Migration and social mobility: South East England as an escalator region', *Regional Studies*, 26(1), 1–15.

Fields, D. and Uffer, S. (2016) 'The financialisation of rental housing: a comparative analysis of New York City and Berlin', *Urban Studies*, 53(7), 1482–1502.

Ford, J., Rugg, J. and Burrows, R. (2002) 'Conceptualising the contemporary role of housing in the transition to adult life in England', *Urban Studies*, 39(13), 2455–2467.

Forrest, R. and Hirayama, Y. (2009) 'The uneven impact of neoliberalism on housing opportunities', *International Journal of Urban and Regional Research*, 33(4), 998–1013.

Forrest, R. and Hirayama, Y. (2015) 'The financialisation of the social project: embedded liberalism, neoliberalism and home ownership', *Urban Studies*, 52(2), 233–244.

Gamsu, S. (2016) 'Moving up and moving out: the re-location of elite and middle-class schools from central London to the suburbs', *Urban Studies*, 53(14), 2921–2938.

Goodsell, T. (2013) 'Familification: family, neighborhood change, and housing policy', *Housing Studies*, 28(6), 845–868.

Grant, J. and Mittelsteadt, L. (2004) 'Types of gated communities', *Environment and Planning B: Planning and Design*, 31(6), 913–930.

Hackworth, J. and Smith, N. (2001) 'The changing state of gentrification', *Tijdschrift voor Economische en Sociale Geografie*, 92(4), 464–477.

Hamnett, C. (2003) 'Gentrification and the middle-class remaking of inner London, 1961–2001', *Urban Studies*, 40(12), 2401–2426.

Hamnett, C. and Whitelegg, D. (2007) 'Loft conversion and gentrification in London: from industrial to postindustrial land use', *Environment and Planning A*, 39(1), 106–124.

Harvey, D. (1985) *The Urbanization of Capital: Studies in the History and Theory of Capitalist Urbanization*, Oxford: Blackwell.

He, S. (2015) 'Consuming urban living in "villages in the city": studentification in Guangzhou, China', *Urban Studies*, 52(15), 2849–2873.

Helderman, A. and Mulder, C. (2007) 'Intergenerational transmission of homeownership: the roles of gifts and continuities in housing market characteristics', *Urban Studies*, 44(2), 231–247.

Henig, J. (1981) 'Gentrification and displacement of the elderly: an empirical analysis', *The Gerontologist*, 21(1), 67–75.

Hochstenbach, C. and Boterman, W. (2015) 'Navigating the field of housing: housing pathways of young people in Amsterdam', *Journal of Housing and the Built Environment*, 30(2), 257–274.

Hochstenbach, C. and Boterman, W. (2017) 'Intergenerational support shaping residential trajectories: young people leaving home in a gentrifying city', *Urban Studies*, 54(2), 399–420.

Hochstenbach, C. and Van Gent, W. (2015) 'An anatomy of gentrification processes: variegating causes of neighbourhood change', *Environment and Planning A*, 47(7), 1480–1501.

Hubbard, P. (2008) 'Regulating the social impacts of studentification: a Loughborough case study', *Environment and Planning A*, 40(2), 323–341.

Janoschka, M. and Sequera, J. (2016) 'Gentrification in Latin America: addressing the politics and geographies of displacement', *Urban Geography*, 37(8), 1175–1194.

Karsten, L. (2003) 'Family gentrifiers: challenging the city as a place simultaneously to build a career and to raise children', *Urban Studies*, 40(12), 2573–2584.

Karsten, L. (2007) 'Housing as a way of life: towards an understanding of middle-class families' preference for an urban residential location', *Housing Studies*, 22(1), 83–98.

Kemp, P. (2015) 'Private renting after the global financial crisis', *Housing Studies*, 30(4), 601–620.

Kerstein, R. (1990) 'Stage models of gentrification: an examination', *Urban Affairs Review*, 25(4), 620–639.

Lareau, A. and Goyette, K. (eds) (2014) *Choosing Homes, Choosing Schools*, Russell Sage Foundation.

Lees, L. (2003) 'Super-gentrification: the case of Brooklyn Heights, New York City', *Urban Studies*, 40(12), 2487–2509.

Lees, L. (2012) 'The geography of gentrification: thinking through comparative urbanism', *Progress in Human Geography*, 36, 155–171.

Lees, L., Shin, H. and López-Morales, E. (2016) *Planetary Gentrification*, Cambridge: Polity Press.

Lees, L., Slater, T. and Wyly, E. (2008) *Gentrification*, New York/London: Routledge.

Lehman-Frisch, S. (2002) '"Like a village": les habitants et leur rue commercante dans Noe Valley, un quartier gentrifie de San Francisco', *Espaces et Societes*, 108(1), 49–68.

Lennartz, C., Arundel, R. and Ronald, R. (2016) 'Younger adults and homeownership in Europe through the global financial crisis', *Population, Space and Place*, 22(8), 823–835.

Ley, D. (1986) 'Alternative explanations for inner-city gentrification: a Canadian assessment', *Annals of the Association of American Geographers*, 76(4), 521–535.

Ley, D. (1996) *The New Middle Class and the Remaking of the Central City*, Oxford: Oxford University Press.

Ley, D. (2003) 'Artists, aestheticisation and the field of gentrification', *Urban Studies*, 40(12), 2527–2544.

Lilius, J. (2014) 'Is there room for families in the inner city? Life-stage blenders challenging planning', *Housing Studies*, 29(6), 843–861.

Marcuse, P. (1986) 'Abandonment, gentrification and displacement: the linkages in New York City', in Smith, N. and Williams, P. (eds) *Gentrification of the City*, London: Unwin Hyman, pp. 153–177.

May, J. (1996) 'Globalization and the politics of place: place and identity in an inner London neighbourhood', *Transactions of the Institute of British Geographers*, 21(1), 194–215.

McKee, K. (2012) 'Young people, homeownership and future welfare', *Housing Studies*, 27(6), 853–862.

Mills, C. (1988) '"Life on the upslope": the postmodern landscape of gentrification', *Environment and Planning D: Society and Space*, 6(2), 169–190.

Moos, M. (2016) 'From gentrification to youthification? The increasing importance of young age in delineating high-density living', *Urban Studies*, 53(14), 2903–2920.

Mulder, C. (2006) 'Population and housing: a two-sided relationship', *Demographic Research*, 15, 401–412.

Mulder, C. and Manting, D. (1994) 'Strategies of nest-leavers: "settling down" versus flexibility', *European Sociological Review*, 10(2), 155–172.

Musterd, S., Van Gent, W., Das, M. and Latten, J. (2016) 'Adaptive behaviour in urban space: residential mobility in response to social distance', *Urban Studies*, 53(2), 227–246.

Myers, D. and Gearin, E. (2001) 'Current preferences and future demand for denser residential environments', *Housing Policy Debate*, 12(4), 633–659.

Mykyta, L. (2012) 'Economic downturns and the failure to launch: the living arrangements of young adults in the US 1995–2011', US Census Bureau Social, Economic, and Housing Statistics Division (SEHSD) Working Paper 24.

Nelson, P., Oberg, A. and Nelson, L. (2010) 'Rural gentrification and linked migration in the United States', *Journal of Rural Studies*, 26(4), 343–352.

Öst, C. (2012) 'Parental wealth and first-time homeownership: a cohort study of family background and young adults' housing situation in Sweden', *Urban Studies*, 49(10), 2137–2152.

Paccoud, A. (2017) 'Buy-to-let gentrification: Extending social change through tenure shifts', *Environment and Planning A*, 49(4), 839–856.

Painter, G. and Lee, K. (2009) 'Housing tenure transitions of older households: life cycle, demographic, and familial factors', *Regional Science and Urban Economics*, 39(6), 749–760.

Paris, C. (2009) 'Re-positioning second homes within housing studies: household investment, gentrification, multiple residence, mobility and hyper-consumption', *Housing, Theory and Society*, 26(4), 292–310.

Phillips, M. (1993) 'Rural gentrification and the processes of class colonisation', *Journal of Rural Studies*, 9(2), 123–140.

Phillips, M. (2000) 'Landscapes of defence, exclusivity and leisure: rural private communities in North Carolina', in Gold, J. and Revill, G. (eds) *Landscape of Defence*, Harlow: Prentice Hall, pp. 130–145.

Phillips, M. (2004) 'Other geographies of gentrification', *Progress in Human Geography*, 28(1), 5–30.

Phillipson, C. (2007) 'The "elected" and the "excluded": sociological perspectives on the experience of place and community in old age', *Ageing and Society*, 27(03), 321–342.

Pinkster, F. (2016) 'Narratives of neighbourhood change and loss of belonging in an urban garden village', *Social and Cultural Geography*, 17(7), 871–891.

Reay, D., Crozier, G. and James, D. (2011) *White Middle-Class Identities and Urban Schooling*, Basingstoke: Palgrave Macmillan.

Rérat, P. (2012) 'The new demographic growth of cities: the case of reurbanisation in Switzerland', *Urban Studies*, 49(5), 1107–1125.

Ronald, R. (2008) *The Ideology of Home Ownership: Homeowner Societies and the Role of Housing*, Basingstoke: Palgrave Macmillan.

Ronald, R. and Kadi, J. (2017) 'The revival of private landlords in Britain's post-homeownership society', *New Political Economy*, DOI:10.1080/13563467.2017.1401055.

Rose, D. (1984) 'Rethinking gentrification: beyond the uneven development of Marxist urban theory', *Environment and Planning D: Society and Space*, 2(1), 47–74.

Rose, D. (1989) 'A feminist perspective of employment restructuring and gentrification: the case of Montreal', in Dear, M. and Wolch, J. (eds) *The Power of Geography: How Territory Shapes Social Life*, London: Unwin Hyman, pp. 118–138.

Rose, D. and Villeneuve, P. (2006) 'Life stages, living arrangements, and lifestyles', in Bunting, T. and Filion, P. (eds) *Canadian Cities in Transition: Local Through Global Perspectives*, 3rd edition, Oxford: Oxford University Press, pp. 138–153.

Rossi, P. (1955) *Why Families Move: A Study in the Social Psychology of Urban Residential Mobility*, Glencoe: Free Press.

Rugg, J., Ford, J. and Burrows, R. (2004) 'Housing advantage? The role of student renting in the constitution of housing biographies in the United Kingdom', *Journal of Youth Studies*, 7(1), 19–34.

Rye, J. (2011) 'Youth migration, rurality and class: a Bourdieusian approach', *European Urban and Regional Studies*, 18(2), 170–183.

Sage, J., Evandrou, M. and Falkingham, J. (2013) 'Onwards or homewards? Complex graduate migration pathways, well-being, and the "parental safety net"', *Population, Space and Place*, 19(6), 738–755.

Smith, D. (2005) '"Studentification": the gentrification factory?', in Atkinson, R. and Bridge, G. (eds) *Gentrification in a Global Context: The New Urban Colonisation*, London: Routledge, pp. 72–89.

Smith, D. and Higley, R. (2012) 'Circuits of education, rural gentrification, and family migration from the global city', *Journal of Rural Studies*, 28(1), 49–55.

Smith, D. and Holt, L. (2007) 'Studentification and "apprentice" gentrifiers within Britain's provincial towns and cities: extending the meaning of gentrification', *Environment and Planning A*, 39(1), 142–161.

Smith, D. and Sage, J. (2014) 'The regional migration of young adults in England and Wales (2002–2008): a "conveyor-belt" of population redistribution?', *Children's Geographies*, 12(1), 102–117.

Stebbing, A. and Spies-Butcher, B. (2016) 'The decline of a homeowning society? Asset-based welfare, retirement and intergenerational equity in Australia', *Housing Studies*, 31(2), 190–207.

Van Criekingen, M. (2010) '"Gentrifying the re-urbanisation debate", not vice versa: the uneven socio-spatial implications of changing transitions to adulthood in Brussels', *Population, Space and Place*, 16(5), 381–394.

Van Criekingen, M. and Decroly, J. (2003) 'Revisiting the diversity of gentrification: neighbourhood renewal processes in Brussels and Montreal', *Urban Studies*, 40(12), 2451–2468.

Van den Berg, M. (2013) 'City children and genderfied neighbourhoods: the new generation as urban regeneration strategy', *International Journal of Urban and Regional Research*, 37(2), 523–536.

Visser, G. (2006) 'South Africa has second homes too! An exploration of the unexplored', *Current Issues in Tourism*, 9(4–5), 351–383.

Warde, A. (1991) 'Gentrification as consumption: issues of class and gender', *Environment and Planning D: Society and Space*, 9(2), 223–232.

Wilson, E. (1991) *The Sphinx in the City: Urban Life, the Control of Disorder, and Women*, Berkeley/Los Angeles/Oxford: University of California Press.

Wu, Q., Zhang, X. and Waley, P. (2015) 'Jiaoyufication: when gentrification goes to school in the Chinese inner city', *Urban Studies*, 53(16), 3510–3526.

12. Gentrification and ethnicity
Tone Huse

12.1 INTRODUCTION

How does ethnicity, or 'race' become a matter of gentrification? After all, gentrification is underpinned by economic inequality. It works through the unequal opportunities that people have in rising real estate markets – though often in pair with processes whose effects are more elusive, such as changing consumer preferences (Ley 1994, 1996), the commodification of symbolic economies (Zukin 1995), or urban policy that facilitates gentrification (Lees and Ley 2008). Unlike these processes, however, ethnic identities and relations are not necessarily of an economic nature. So why should they be relevant, or even interesting, to the gentrification researcher?

One answer to this question is that social geographies tend to overlap and cohere with ethnic geographies, and ethnic minorities are often overrepresented in lower income groups. Ethnic minority groups are thus less likely to be homeowners, and also more likely to live in poor areas of the city. They live in potential gentrification sites and are disproportionately vulnerable to displacement pressures. Which is perhaps why the precariousness of ethnic minorities is already widely recognised in the gentrification literature – scholars often mention that they are particularly vulnerable. Yet, in light of the enormous amount of research on gentrification[1] conspicuously little work has been done on how gentrification can reorder or amplify ethnic segregation (Lees 2000; Massey 2002; Powell and Spencer 2002; Rivilin 2002; Kirkland 2008; Moore 2009; Murdie and Teixeira 2011). Nor are there many studies that have sought to explain *how* ethnicity in itself can become a facet to the gentrification process. The ethnic dimension to gentrification is hence under-theorised. Indeed, it is 'perhaps most notable for its very absence from scholarly definitions of gentrification' (Kirkland 2008: 19).

In my own work, it is the respondents themselves that have brought up ethnicity as an issue relevant to gentrification (Huse 2014). Working in Tøyen Street, a multi-cultural street in Oslo, Norway, I conducted over 60 interviews with different stakeholders – shopkeepers, butchers, local politicians, activists, patrons of the local bars, present and former residents. I would begin all of the interviews with the same question: 'What do you think about the changes that are happening in this area?' When interviewing ethnic minority respondents, who were either immigrants or children of immigrants, I did not refer to their status as such. My interest was primarily in their role in the street, and in how they were experiencing growing gentrification pressures. Yet, without failure these respondents would themselves tie descriptions of the area's growing affluence to their own ethnic minority status. Actualised in stories of belonging, expressed as fears of displacement or

---

[1] Since Ruth Glass's (1964) coinage of the term 'gentrification', this field of study has produced more than a thousand research papers, journal articles, monographs, edited collections, books, book chapters, government evaluations and reports (Atkinson and Bridge 2005; Lees, Slater and Wyly 2008).

in ideas about their value to the area, ethnicity was made to matter in their descriptions of the gentrification process.[2] This pushed me to tackle the relationship between ethnicity and gentrification, and also the broader issue of how urban development affects on-going integration efforts. In doing so, I turned to the gentrification literature for clues as to how I could proceed.

I here learned that despite early warnings about gentrification and its displacement of poor, ethnic minority residents (Laska and Spain 1979; Logan 2013), as well as key gentrification writings having emphasised the ethnic dimension to gentrification (Smith 1996), there was very little research that interrogates the ethnicity–gentrification relationship. As for detailed statistical and comparative studies, only a few have been conducted, and their conclusions differ. Wyly and Hammel (2004: 1215), for instance, find in their analysis of 23 US cities that racial and ethnic discrimination in lending and insurance is intensified in the context of gentrification. Walks and Maaranen (2008; Walks 2009) study Canadian cities, and argue that gentrification reduces social and ethnic diversity. They further argue that gentrification leads to growing income polarisation and inequality in affected neighbourhoods. Freeman (2009: 2079, see also Freeman and Braconi 2004), on the other hand, finds that in the US gentrification may actually reduce income segregation. He also concludes that there is weaker, less robust evidence that gentrification increases racial segregation.

These inconsistencies can perhaps be ascribed to the difficulties of measuring gentrification (Atkinson 2004; Atkinson and Wulff 2009). Often there is a lack of proper and/or longitudinal data that describe the gentrifying area's residential composition, which then requires a methodology of working through indicators rather than more direct measures. It is also very difficult to measure the effects of displacement, as the displaced are often already dispersed and hard to track down. However, in light of recent debates over displacement, it is also likely that the diverging conclusions on how gentrification affects ethnic minority populations express two new fronts in gentrification research. Here, the stakes of the debate lie not in explaining the causes of gentrification, as was the case in the long-going debates over production- versus supply-side explanations (for an overview, see Lees, Slater and Wyly 2008), but in determining what injustices it produces (Slater 2006, 2009a).

This has in later years been widely discussed by gentrification scholars, and there is now growing recognition that mainstream urban research has neglected the changing conditions of the working classes (Slater, Curran and Lees 2004; Newman and Wyly 2006; Slater 2006; Wacquant 2008). Equally, studies on gentrification and ethnicity have largely focused on gentrifiers and their preferences (e.g. Prince 2005; Sullivan 2007; Boyd 2008; Moore 2009; Johnson 2015; Zaban 2015, 2016). There is, hence, a similarity between how this particular branch of gentrification research has evolved and gentrification research more generally, in that the consequences of gentrification for poor and working-class residents have not been adequately accounted for (Betancur 2011). That studies on

---

[2]   A similar type of linking between ethnic identities and gentrification is presented in Ramos-Zayas' analysis of race, class and space in Puerto Rican Chicago, where 'some residents have established parallels between gentrification in their current neighborhood, the Puerto Rican community's historical experiences being pushed out of other neighborhoods in Chicago marked for redevelopment, and the struggle over independence for Puerto Rico' (Tucker-Raymond and Rosario 2014: 4).

gentrification and ethnicity share this middle-class bias serves to underline the critique, as ethnic minorities are often much less privileged than are majority populations. The lack of gentrification research on ethnic minorities is also 'consistent with the general tendency for avoidance of racial discourse, the denial of the magnitude of racism, and the evasion of the topics of racial impacts, disparities and divisions' (Kirkland 2008: 29). However, as gentrification scholars are now becoming more attentive towards displacement and dispossession, there also seems to be a growing interest in the relationship between ethnicity and gentrification.

The majority of these more recent studies stem from a US context, a common thread being that gentrification is seen to perpetuate racial and ethnic inequality (Hwang 2015). This predominance of US scholarship is not surprising, in that the ethnic geographies of American cities have emerged from a particularly violent history (BondGraham 2007; Lees 2016); 'disinvestment, arson, redlining, public neglect, deindustrialisation, racism and urban renewal combined to make their settlement uniquely conflictive and unstable' (Betancur 2011: 389). Currently, the strong influence of neoliberal urban policy, combined with mass demolition of public housing (Goetz 2011) and aggressive crime control (Smith 2012), has made gentrification 'a crucial factor in the production of spatial inequality, displacement, homelessness and racial containment' (Lipman 2012: 97). Hence, gentrification is in the US often understood as the displacement of poor residents of colour by the white middle class (Massey 2002; Sullivan 2006; Kirkland 2008; Barrios 2010; Goetz 2011).

Notably, there are studies that emphasise so-called 'black gentrification', and which add nuance to the ways in which class and ethnic relations may play out in the context of gentrification (see e.g. Taylor 1992; Freeman 2006; Pattillio 2005, 2007; Boyd 2008; Moore 2009). However, as this chapter maintains a focus on non-gentrifier ethnic groups, the studies discussed here mainly concern the displacement of ethnic minority residents by the ethnic majority. Furthermore, the chapter concentrates on studies that deal explicitly with ethnicity and gentrification, and not merely with gentrification as set in an ethnically diverse context. A majority of these studies stem from the global north, which will then also be reflected in the chapter's discussions. However, as I return to in the conclusion, the emerging interest in how ethnic identities and relations are tied up with and affect gentrification processes is also reflected in works from outside the established sites of gentrification research. Several of these studies are presented alongside current concerns over global, or 'planetary' gentrification (Lees, Shin and López-Morales 2015, 2016) and thus represent not only a topical but also geographical expansion of gentrification studies.

12.2   DOUBLE EXPOSURE

An exemplary work that takes as its starting point the double exposure of low income, ethnic minority groups is Betancur's (2011) study of Latino communities in Chicago. Betancur here establishes that low-income groups' vulnerability towards gentrification is not purely economic. Displacement-associated loss will also be more severe for these groups, because they are highly dependent on place-based social fabrics. Adding to this, non-white ethnic minority groups appear to be challenged by racial discrimination. For contrary to European immigrants, who also developed place-based resources for self-help, and thereafter improved their social position significantly, the social mobility of the Latino communities has remained quite low. They have therefore become disproportionately vulnerable to aggressive urban restructuring schemes that now work through and promote gentrification. Powell and Spencer (2002), who also write in the context of the US, make a similar argument. Indeed, they maintain that the presence of ethnic minorities adds features to the gentrification process beyond those of a social and economic nature. Pointing to how the same US neighbourhoods that experienced white flight in the 1970s are now being re-occupied by white gentrifiers, they stress how notions of whiteness and white privilege are tied in with gentrification processes (Powell and Spencer 2002: 437).[3] Expressive of 'the myth of the white city', the association of 'whiteness with cleanliness and orderliness' and black people as 'a disruptive and threatening form of the urban "other"', gentrification reflects for Powell and Spencer (2002: 441) the 'desire to purify our environment and eliminate the blights associated with segregation and concentrated poverty.'

As I return to in the below discussion of territorial stigmatisation, this shows that where white privilege is involved there is often a close relationship between discursive power and a successful pro-gentrification agenda. Indeed, as is suggested by Zukin, Lindeman and Hurson's (2015) analysis of racial bias in social media restaurant reviews, one may also talk about 'discursive redlining' in the digital public realm, whereby readers are discouraged to venture into particular, majority-black areas. One should, however, be cautious of overestimating, or isolating the power of discourse in this context. For it is only when racism and ethnic stigma are coupled with a politics of distribution, be it by state-led gentrification or intense liberalisation, that discourses like that of 'the white city' begin to have material effects. Another Chicago study may shed light on this.

Rogers Park is a neighbourhood in Chicago that is frequently associated with ethnic and economic 'diversity'. Examining what this term actually represents, Berrey (2005) focuses on three groups: white real estate professionals and politicians; white progressive organisers; and black low-income housing advocates. What she finds is that diversity serves as a highly elastic term. There are different versions of it and these have rather different effects. The white pro-gentrification advocates, Berrey explains, tend to turn diversity into a proxy for mixed-income housing. White progressive organisers mobilise 'diversity' to raise concerns about structural inequality, but have simultaneously downplayed racial and class power disparities. This suggests that no matter how well-intended, 'a focus on neighbourhood diversity can overshadow the concerns of low-income, minority tenants, especially concerns about their rights' (Berrey 2005: 144). For whilst white stakeholders, be they pro-gentrification advocates or progressive organisers, frequently mobilise the diversity trope, 'the poor, African American subsidised housing activists rarely mention the word at all. Instead, they speak about discrimination and tenants rights' (Berrey 2005: 144).

Diversity, Berrey concludes, should not be embraced as an inherently good thing (e.g. Florida 2002), nor be dismissed as a symbol manipulated by urban elites (e.g. Mele 2000). Yes, diversity can be a proxy for gentrification, but it can also be mobilised – or denounced – within other social, political and economic contexts. As pointed out in Jones'

---

[3] In light of the post-2008 recession, it should also be added that there are signs that ethnic minority, inner-city neighbourhoods have been particularly vulnerable to both disinvestment and, thereafter, resurging gentrification (Tighe and Ganning 2015; Hyra and Rugh 2016).

(2015) discussion on gentrification and neoliberalism in Puebla, Mexico, cultural identities provide a field on which gentrification may both be imagined and resisted. Crucially, such contestations – be they an expression of 'white tolerance', 'black rights' or (post-)colonial identities – are intimately tied in with the political economy of gentrification. And at stake in these discursive struggles are the key qualities of urban life: the right to a safe and stable dwelling, to places of community and to the provision of basic needs, such as health care services and educational institutions.

Betancur and Berrey's two Chicago studies actualise the issue of ethnicity and gentrification in somewhat different ways. In Betancur's (2011) analysis, it is demonstrated how white privileging depends on the devaluation of ethnic minority communities. Gentrification appears as an aggressive strategy, where ethnic minority communities are targeted as dysfunctional and thus in need of improvement. In Berrey's (2005) work, the discourse of white privilege is added to and given nuance, yet similarly explored in light of quite aggressive pro-gentrification strategies. These analyses do not rule one another out, but expose the complexities embedded in the double exposure of low income, ethnic minority residents to gentrification pressures. Cast within the white image of the city they are framed as a problem to be dealt with, not a community member that under proper circumstances can improve their own livelihood. Importantly, this is a framing that mobilises ideas about ethnic minorities' influence on a particular place or neighbourhood – 'they' make the neighbourhood poor, the area 'bad' (Huse 2014). Which in turn helps to explain how gentrification can be presented as a legitimate strategy for dealing with what are basically social issues. For whilst improvement for a particular group of residents is often presented as the aim of urban renewal, the success of such renewal is very seldom measured in terms of their improved social mobility. Rather, it is the improved image of the neighbourhood that is held up as proof of success: 'poor' residents have been replaced by better ones.

12.3   TERRITORIAL STIGMATISATION

The association between gentrification, devaluation of ethnic minority communities and white privileging is far from unique to the US. Shaw (2011) describes it in her work on Aborigines in Sydney and Jones (2015) in his work on the Mexican city Puebla. Sakizlioglu and Uitermark (2014: 1369) even compare how it unfolded in the radically different settings of Amsterdam and Istanbul. In both cities, they argue, strategies of 'divide and rule' were executed 'by imprinting a stigma on the neighbourhood and classifying some of its residents as worthy of involvement while declassifying others' (Sakizlioglu and Uitermark 2014: 1383). These state-sanctioned strategies fed into territorial, ethnic and class stigmatisation and played a key role promoting gentrification.

A similar process occurred in Oslo in the mid-1990s, when parts of the inner-east city was framed by the then mayor as in danger of becoming an 'immigrant-ghetto' (Huse 2014). Significantly, and in contrast to the US, there are no large areas dominated by one ethnic minority in Norway. At the time, the majority population dominated all city districts, welfare programmes were strong and residential mobility to, from and within all city districts was high. To label any part of Oslo a ghetto was hence at best misguided (cf. Slater 2009b; Peach 1996). Nevertheless, the effect of Oslo politicians mobilising the ghetto-discourse was significant, much due to the policy that followed in the wake of these discursive acts. Publicly financed measures were implemented in order to make the inner-east 'more attractive for Norwegians' (Karlsen and Eriksen 1996), with increased attention being given to middle class preferences for 'attractive' urban living (Sæter and Ruud 2005). Gentrification was stated as a desirable outcome of the investments. The negative associations of the ghetto term were hence transmuted to signify the presence of non-whites, which in turn legitimised political measures that reinforced an already on-going gentrification process (Huse 2014). As Slater and Anderson (2011: 13) observe in the case of Bristol, ghetto labelling can be a powerful tool in efforts to justify pro-gentrification policy.

Bristol, Oslo, Amsterdam, Istanbul, Puebla and Sydney are very different cities, but they do share a history of gentrification being combined with forms of territorial stigmatisation – a process whereby the 'blemish of place' is 'superimposed on the already existing stigmata traditionally associated with poverty and ethnic origin or postcolonial immigrant status, to which it is closely linked but not reducible' (Wacquant, cited in Slater and Anderson 2011: 5). In Oslo, however, something quite different was simultaneously, and somewhat paradoxically, going on. Notions about diversity were being enrolled in strategies of branding the inner-east. As was stated by the very mayor who issued the 'immigrant-ghetto' warning: 'People on the west side should take a Saturday trip here. It is a fun part of town. Instead of using ten thousand kroner on a trip to the Far East, one can experience exoticism on Oslo's east side' (Karlsen and Eriksen 1996, my translation). The ethnic 'other', as Betancur (2011) remarks, became a selling point, the place branded as somewhere to experience difference.

12.4 ETHNIC PACKAGING

That urban authorities and enterprises engage in place branding and marketing is a rather common phenomenon and also a well-established subject of urban studies (e.g. Knox 1993; Zukin 1995; Mitchell 2003). Gentrification is often identified as an outcome of such commodification practices, much due to how they work in tandem with other measures that favour the presence of high-income groups. Multi-ethnic neighbourhoods are no exception to this commodification of neighbourhood character (Kaltmeier 2011). Rather, 'authenticity', 'diversity', 'multi-culturalism' and 'the exotic' are often mobilised as selling points (Zukin 2008; Huse 2014), with city districts or neighbourhoods being rebranded so as to 'represent sanitised "Otherness" made safe for mass-market consumption' (Lanegger 2016: 1302). Indeed, it has been suggested that urban policy makers should actively facilitate immigrant entrepreneurship in order to spur commercial gentrification. A form of 'ethnic gentrification' where newcomers 'reclaim' abandoned or neglected urban space (Airriess 2006; Arreola 2012; Hume 2015), is then thought to 'improve' and 'revive' neighbourhoods (Kloosterman and van der Leun 1999: 661).

An example of how ethnic culture is used in gentrification processes, and which speaks to how systematically this may be done, is the branding of four 'ethnic' Toronto districts – Corso Italia, Little Italy, India Bazaar and Greektown on the Danforth. Studying how these were selected as business improvement districts and consequently profiled as ethnic minority areas, Hackworth and Rekers (2005) point out how ethnic culture is produced to attract tourists and young urban professionals. The ethnic identity of the districts has also been embraced in the marketing of nearby residential areas, with gentrification as an outcome. Through these practices of 'ethnic packaging' immigrant cultures are thus incorporated in developers' strategic production of space. The intent is rarely, Hackworth and Rekers stress, to displace residents. Nonetheless, a multi-cultural urbanity is constructed that attracts more affluent users to these places.

Powell and Spencer (2002: 438) refer to a similar practice of producing attractive, multi-ethnic spaces in the US, albeit in a more critical light. Developers are not only selling place, they assert, they also use images of ethnic harmony to divert attention from racial conflicts: 'The terms "multiculturalism" and "diversity" are marketed by developers to avoid "ranking" oppressed groups in terms of the justness of their claims. This strategy sanitizes, ignores, and reifies the realities of racial discrimination and social injustice' (Powell and Spencer 2002: 438).

Comparable to how cultural identity (Jones 2015) and tropes such as 'diversity' (Berrey 2005) can be mobilised to suppress ethnic tension and undermine minority demands, ethnic packaging can represent a form of silencing. This point is supported by yet another US study, from the Southtown of San Antonio, Texas. De Olivier (2016) has here analysed the historical evolution of 'diversity' in successive waves of gentrification, and more generally, of how conceptions of ethnicity/race correspond to and evolve with modes of producing urban space. He finds that with the different gentrification phases the meaning of diversity changes, the result being that 'the amenity of diversity is increasingly attuned to capital interests and rendered less relevant as an ethic that benefits minority communities' (de Olivier 2016: 1301). De Oliver takes this to signify a transformation of 'cultural diversity', away from a social justice ethic and towards a lifestyle amenity, which then serves to legitimise cultural displacement.

Returning to the so-called 'exoticism' of Oslo's east side, and more specifically the Grønland neighbourhood, this has now become nationally known as an 'immigrant area'. Commercially the area is quite mixed, with shops and services aimed at immigrant groups from the larger Oslo region as well as at more affluent residents. In real estate adverts for dwellings, one can frequently find references to the area as 'colourful', 'multi-cultural', 'diverse' and also 'exotic'. During a period of intense new-build activity, a campaign for 'the new Grønland' was launched to present the area to newcomers. The campaign included a series of postcards with photos inscribed with the slogan 'my Grønland'. One of the postcards portrayed a close-up of halal meat; another, colourful Indian fabric. The Muslim butcher smiling behind the counter, or the woman in the traditional three-piece outfit, is however conspicuously missing, as pictures of non-whites in promotions of this 'colourful' neighbourhood generally tend to be. Instead of representing the diversity of Grønland, this instates a form of gentrification-tailored exoticism to be enjoyed and explored by the gentry. Here, the 'exotic' adds to the urban spectacle – to its 'well-composed' mix of service, accommodation, and culture – an ethnic twist. The non-white user, by the colour of his/her skin, is portrayed as part of the spectacle to be enjoyed, Grønland becomes a place of urban adventure for the affluent and white.

Importantly, this discourse is welcomed by many of the ethnic minority residents and shopkeepers I interviewed, in that it has a positive signal effect. One is seen as making a positive contribution. Contrary to what is often the case in Norwegian public debate today, ethnic packaging welcomes the presence of ethnic minorities. But when contrasted with the agency endowed in the middle class, with its supposedly superior ability to 'lift' so-called problem areas, the celebratory exoticism of ethnic packaging rings hollow. And as the emphasis on the 'exotic' reveals, the notion of an 'us' and 'them' is also present here. The wrapping is significantly different from that of ghetto labelling, but in advertising for potential residents and visitors it is the 'normal', majority-Norwegian one seeks to attract. Instead of being acknowledged as belonging to the urban environment in their own right, ethnic minorities – their bodies, their movements, their spatial representations – are reduced to sights, to an attraction. A form of 'social rendering' thus occurs, a process of community succession whereby the existing community is erased and an alternative one is reimagined (Lejano and González 2016: 1).

Why is it that ethnic packaging, or other 'salutes' to ethnic diversity so easily slip into some form or other of discrimination? One possible answer is that in the context of gentrification there will be an uneven distribution of resources – to buy, to sell, to stay put or be evicted, displaced. More often than not ethnic minorities are those with less resources. They therefore have less chance to gain from the opportunities created by what we may describe as their 'packaged presence'. Another answer, and one which also takes into account what Marcuse (1985) calls 'displacement pressure', is that there are cultural boundaries to participation in the 'new' and 'creative' areas of the city (Morgan and Idriss 2011). Transition is seen 'not as the enhancement and flourishing of the existing residential population but its replacement' (Lejano and González 2016: 10, see also Patch 2004). Existing communities are thus consistently devalued, which has also been recognised in gentrification research more generally. Smith (1982, 1996), for instance, identifies the stigmatisation of poor but vital neighbourhoods as one of the key facets to gentrification in New York. Betancur (2011: 399, see also Lipman 2012) shows how gentrification in Chicago undermines community building, 'splitting the community from within and from without'. The real tragedy of gentrification, he thus claims, is 'not market displacement *per se*, but community disintegration' (ibid) by which 'the elaborate and complex community fabric that is crucial for low income, immigrant, and minority communities' is harmed or destroyed (Betancur 2002: 807).

In light of this, gentrification can be seen as trying to fix something that is actually not broken, but that must be understood as such in order for the 'gentrification fix' to be deemed legitimate. Ethnic packaging then comes across as a form of social control, in that the presence of the ethnic 'other' is at once acknowledged and contained. A particularly acute example of this is given by Barrios (2010), who shows that in New Orleans, a city that has thrived on carnival and jazz tourism, the rituals and daily social practices of working class African Americans are being criminalised in the wake of gentrification. Lanegger (2016) provides another, perhaps subtler example. Examining commodification of Latino culture through skirmishes over street legitimacy in Denver, Colorado, he identifies how 'the rhythms of public space are changed to reinforce and reproduce gentrifier norms and practices, while the cultural practices of longtime residents become freighted with touristic eroticism' (Lanegger 2016: 1805).

Difference is simultaneously celebrated as a diverse pulse and flattened onto an even playing field, then honed into a powerful gentrification tool. Peering under the cloak, we find race and ethnic discrimination woven into the arbitrary subtexts of commonsense urbanity (Lanegger 2016: 1816).

On a more positive note, there are examples of how the representation of ethnic minority communities can be done so as to counteract, not produce ethnic stereotypes. Drew (2011), for instance, shows how tour guides in Chicago have developed quite sophisticated strategies for anti-racist representation. The guides engage tourists in the social issues that communities struggle with, such as gentrification and social inequality, as well as in the historical and structural causes of racial and social marginalisation. Key to this, Drew shows, is how it is the tourist and not the ethnic minority resident who is positioned as Other, thus avoiding the invocation of prevailing racialised constructions of their communities. Alternatively, local culture can be used to articulate demands over urban space, as was done through community-initiated planning in Vancouver's Downtown Eastside (Blomley 2004). Here, residents facing new-build displacement drew on the history and presence of indigenous peoples and working-class residents in order to develop an alternative vision for the Eastside and to formulate use-based claims to urban space.

12.5   SEGREGATION AND GENTRIFICATION

Unlike US studies, European scholarship rarely equates gentrification with white privilege. Nor is engagement with ethnicity as pronounced. In both urban research and politics there is, however, considerable interest in ethnic segregation and/or separation. Urban and national authorities are increasingly concerned over areas dominated by ethnic minorities, and express fears about the formation of so-called parallel societies, radicalisation of young Muslims and even terrorist cells. There are also long-standing concerns that living in minority-dominated areas prevents integration, as residents are assumed to be more vulnerable to social deprivation, isolation and reduced opportunities for work and education (Ireland 2008; Wessel 2009).

Studies on the segregation of ethnic minorities have much in common with studies on social mix policy, in that both fields ask whether residential segregation prevents upward social mobility (Musterd 2003, 2005; Atkinson 2008; Lees 2008; Musterd and van Kempen 2009; Semyonov and Glikman 2009; Bolt and van Kempen 2010; Bridge, Butler and Lees 2012; Ley 2012; Lipman 2012). Arguments for changing the residential composition – by attracting either members of the ethnic majority or more affluent residents – are fiercely debated within academic circles, but have gained considerable support among policy makers. With regard to ethnic mixing, or desegregation, an important assumption is that spatial proximity to the native majority encourages interaction and thus generates knowledge, tolerance and improved relations. Researchers have in this regard put much effort into measuring and monitoring segregation by means of quantitative methods, and into assessing how living in minority-dense areas influences social mobility and integration (Musterd and de Winter 1998; Musterd 2003; Ireland 2008; Bolt 2009; Musterd and van Kempen 2009; Wessel 2009; Bolt and van Kempen 2010; Phillips 2010). There are a few studies that mention the possibility that gentrification may impact desegregation efforts negatively (Musterd and de Winter 1998; Bolt and van Kempen 2013), but the relationship between integration and gentrification-induced change is yet to be explored.

However, studies on gentrification and school choice may indicate that ethnic desegregation by social mixing will not improve inter-ethnic relations. There is great variation between countries with regards to how education is organised and financed, which also means that there will be great variation in how educational institutions are entangled in gentrification processes. Studies from London (Butler and Robinson 2001, 2003; Ball and Vincent 2007; Reay 2007; Butler and Hamnett 2010; Hamnett and Butler 2011; Neal and Vincent 2013; Jackson and Butler 2015), Amsterdam (Boterman 2012, 2013) and Oslo (Huse 2014) do however indicate one strong resemblance: in areas that are undergoing gentrification, but that also exhibit a relatively high share of ethnic minority pupils in local schools, a large share of middle class parents will choose to either send their children to other schools or to move. Despite the role ascribed to schools as key integration arenas, their role in areas undergoing social and/or ethnic mixing can hence be limited. Indeed, as has been the case in Oslo, school choice can lead to a form of 'segmental white flight', where well-resourced parents of both ethnic minority and majority backgrounds are choosing to move away from minority dominated school districts (Huse 2014). As one Oslo journalist put it, 'Parents of all colours are fleeing' (Brandvold 2009). A rather peculiar situation then arises, where areas undergoing rapid gentrification and steep rises in real estate prices also exhibit a growing share of children living in poverty.

This situation is, however, not unique to Oslo. Studying two local schools in a Sydney suburb, Ho, Vincent and Butler (2015: 658) argue that gentrification has led to a rise in middle-class parents opting out of local schools in favour of private or more desirable public schools. In the US, white middle-class gentrifiers moving away from what they perceive as poor schools has led to the inclusion of schools in social mix schemes (Billingham and Kimelberg 2013; van den Berg 2013; Posey-Maddox 2014; Billingham 2015). In the case of Chicago, Lipman (2002, 2008, 2012; Lipman and Haines 2007) shows, comprehensive measures have been implemented in order to transform low-income communities and schools into mixed-income sites. The increased presence of middle-class students was hoped to alleviate the negative correlation between low-income groups and school performance. Instead, Lipman argues, these policies have led to racial containment and exclusion through gentrification. Rather than creating viable communities in which the urban poor have a right to place, new and exclusionary spaces are made available for middle class consumers, while low-income people of colour are displaced.

Whilst this is clearly a subject that needs to be studied further, there are, then, strong indications that policies that aim to mix poor, ethnic minority residents with more affluent incomers will not achieve the desired effects. Instead, the outcome may well be gentrification and the displacement of those whom the mixing was intended to benefit. Or, a form of 'intimate segregation' arises, where residents develop ways to avoid and structure inter-ethnic contact (Mumm 2008: 17, see also Butler and Robson 2001 and Jackson and Butler 2015 on 'social tectonics').

12.6   LOW-LEVEL URBAN GOVERNANCE

As it appears in gentrification studies, white privilege takes on highly variable forms. Different methods and objects of inquiry should therefore be pursued in approaching the subject. A particularly interesting group of studies, however, are those that link ethnic valuations and low-level forms of urban governance. Lanegger (2016) for instance, studies this through the social rhythms of public spaces. Asking 'Who belongs? When? Doing what?' (p. 1804) he finds that the governance of mundane practices quite effectively favours middle class modes of consumption. For instance, when parking regulations were changed, they were changed so that the temporal order of gentrifiers was habituated. At the same time, the original residents' use of public space was made more difficult. Describing the rolling out of bike lanes in Washington DC, Gibson (2015) further shows how such low-level regulations of urban space carry associations of cultural and ethnic identities, the bike lanes being considered as accommodating the desires of gentrifiers. DC is becoming 'younger, richer and whiter' (Gibson 2015: 239), he concludes, and the bike lanes have become an 'early warning' sign, 'a powerful visual implication that change was coming' (Gibson 2015: 242).

Studying Latino community gardens in New York City, Martinez (2010) shows how the re-zoning of these, from being restricted community spaces to public parks, worked to undermine Puerto Rican gardeners in particular. Here, likewise, low-level governance is exposed as a gentrification tool. What is perhaps most appealing in Martinez' account, however, is how she brings out a correspondence between cultural differences in uses of green spaces and contestations over how these should be regulated (Rosol 2012). The transformation of the gardens into park-like and publicly oriented spaces, Martinez argues, has worked in tandem with gentrification processes, thus facilitating a 'taming' of the neighbourhood in favour of white, middle class interests. The public park commons was not one in which the Latino gardeners would find the community and companionship so much appreciated in the gardens. That 'community' can be a problematic concept is also shown by Maskovsky (2006), who studied neighbourhood association conflicts in a traditionally African American neighbourhood in Philadelphia. African American residents here contested the neoliberal conception of residents as entrepreneurs, consumers, and neighbourhood citizen–volunteers. As is also observed by Powell and Spencer (2002) and Berrey (2005), a particularly problematic point was the disarticulation of questions concerning the politics of race from those concerning the politics of place. For whilst African American residents were indeed included in the different community organisa-tions, 'the insistence that they participate in a diverse, not a black, community' produced 'a new sense of racial inequality and new forms of class division in the new inner city' (Maskovsky 2006: 93).

By interrogating different forms of low-level governance, the works of Lanegger (2016), Gibson (2015), Martinez (2010) and Maskovsky (2006) provide a broad empirical take on the material and regulatory practices that position groups to benefit from gentrification processes. They show, in a manner of speaking, how class and ethnic privileging is made concrete. This could be a very interesting point to pursue in further research, as it would not only help develop our understanding of the double exposure of low income, ethnic minority groups to gentrification. It could also help local community groups identify key instances in which pro-gentrification agendas are achieved, and thus provide fruitful points of contestation. What these studies also tell us, is that the symbolic strategies of urban elites are often intimately linked to low-level forms of governance that re-inscribe how and by whom urban space may be used. Contrary to the classic example of the upmarket coffee shop, these are the material imprints of state-led or -assisted gentrifica-tion, which could open up avenues for political accountability and contestation that are perhaps more difficult to establish in the face of private market forces.

An example of such resistance is discussed by White (2015: 340), who analyses a conflict over drumming in a Harlem park. The conflict played out between a group of black drum-mers and two white police officers. The drummers were engaged in a 30-year-old tradition of drum playing in Marcus Garvey Park, the police were responding to a noise complaint from white residents in a nearby gentrified co-op. The drummers' protest against eviction was eventually successful, which White (2015: 345) ascribes to a 'racial belongingness' that draws on the public and racial imaginaries of Harlem as a black people's space. Established racial and cultural claims protect Harlem from the effects of non-black gentrification, White asserts. However, he continues, such claims are also problematic, in that they justify 'the construction and confinement of marginalized racial spaces' (White 2015: 348) – 'one might argue that racial belongingness is linked inextricably to practices of racial exclusion and subordination, inasmuch as racial claims to one space might only be seen as legitimate because of the racialised discrimination in other places' (White 2015: 348). Hence, White concludes, 'race both solidifies class resentment and promotes geographical structuring in a way that defies class categories' (p. 348). Kirkland (2008) also observes the two-sided nature of mobilising 'race' or ethnicity in community building. On the one hand, she maintains, race and ethnicity can underpin unification as well as claims to a neighbourhood or district. It could hence be a productive force against displacement (Kirkland 2008: 24). On the other hand, it can represent an added challenge, with racism and intolerance preventing inter-ethnic alliances between original residents seeking to resist gentrification. Studies of black gentrification – many of which are situated precisely in Harlem – further show that gentrification causes intra-ethnic conflict (Boyd 2008; Goetz 2011). In line with both Maskovsky (2006) and Martinez (2010), White's (2015) notion of racial belongingness thus brings out the need to scrutinise how ideas such as 'community' and 'urban public' actualise certain uses and constellations of users as well as specific modes of government.

A better understanding of how low-level governance works in conjunction with gentrification and ethnic privileging would, moreover, be especially useful for advancing understanding of indirect forms of displacement (Marcuse 1985). For although indirect displacement is most often expressed in affective terms – feelings of alienation and exclusion, a sense of loss of belonging, the want of past social networks – these are also outcomes of the material conditions of gentrification. A more sophisticated understanding of how these conditions are produced so as to facilitate privileged groups' needs and desires could then also provide a starting point for the formulation of other groups' rights and demands, and hence for a politics that can handle 'diversity' without prejudice.

12.7   CONCLUSION

The role of ethnicity and/or 'race' in gentrification processes is often ambiguous, and ethnic identifications may well be contradictory and multivalent (Sze 2010). Ethnic identities are 'produced in relation to larger structures, policy decisions and histories' (Sze 2010: 525), and there is a strong connection between the politics of place, the place of ethnic minorities in the city and the formation of ethnic identities (Huse 2014). To engage with the relationship between ethnicity and gentrification therefore requires sensitivity towards the geographical and historical context of ethnic minorities' position. The works presented in this chapter tackle this from different angles and by use of different methods. When read together, they show us that gentrification can be a powerful force in re-articulating the social and political conditions ethnic minorities live under. Often gentrification represents yet another phase in a long history of urban injustices, but it can also become the subject of contestation and community organisation. In resistance to gentrification, ethnic identities can provide a foundation for group formation, but ethnic relations can also be a hindrance to formulating broad community alliances, or even be used to justify gentrification (Berrey 2005; Martinez 2010; White 2015). There is as such no clear-cut story as to how gentrification will play out contra ethnic minorities that find themselves at odds with this process, and much work remains to be done in order to understand this well.

One important way forward is, as in gentrification research more generally, to develop better methods for measuring and monitoring displacement. Statistical data will of course be essential to this, but displacement studies should also examine the consequences of gentrification. What are the long-term effects on displaced residents? Do these vary between ethnic groups? How does gentrification affect social fabrics and for whom does change matter the most (Betancur 2002: 387)? Studies on displacement should hence be nuanced, so that we can begin to assess both how different groups are differently vulnerable, and how context plays into ethnic minority displacement. As shown in this chapter, there are several recent studies that recognise the double exposure of low income, ethnic minority groups, whilst also underlining the place-specific character that gentrification pressures entail. There is, however, little knowledge on how residential segregation differs between the regions of the world, as segregation research exhibits a certain contextual blindness (Maloutas and Fujita 2012; Yuan and Yat-sen 2014). Emerging scholarship on 'planetary gentrification' can contribute to filling this void. For as gentrification research is now beginning to include other sites and forms of gentrification than those traditionally examined, there are signs that studies on segregation and ethnic minority displacement will follow suit (Lees 2016; Lees, Shin and López-Morales 2016). For instance, Doshi (2013) has raised concerns over ethno-religious relations in Mumbai gentrification processes. Swanson (2007) interrogates the policing of indigenous street vendors and beggars in the Ecuadorian cities of Quito and Guayaquil, whilst Teppo and Millestein (2015) examine the intricate relationships between gentrification, morality, race and class in post-colonial Cape Town. Their studies are, literally, continents apart, but all give strong testimony to how the wider political situation of gentrification affects its outcome. In societies of highly unequal power relations and severe social inequality the unleashing of its 'revanchist' qualities will necessitate other responses than those produced in a Western context, making such scholarship not only very interesting but also urgent.

Much in line with how the expanding geography of gentrification studies is sensitising the field towards the wider political context of gentrification, the studies presented in this chapter show the need for an improved understanding of context. Not only is there great variation with regard to the history of ethnic minority settlements, or the type of gentrification they are undergoing, there are also significant differences between groups and individuals within these groups. For instance, in my study of Tøyen Street, I found that particular groups of non-Western women were more vulnerable to moving, as they depended on place-based social networks to counter isolation and handle domestic conflicts. As much as a 'geography of gentrification' (Lees 2000) is needed, the study of ethnicity and gentrification hence requires attention towards the specificities of the groups involved. Scholars who pursue the issue of gentrification and ethnicity could therefore benefit greatly from engaging with other fields of research, such as, for instance, critical race theory, post-colonialism or indigenous studies (Lees 2016).

Future research should also take into consideration the extended effects of gentrification. In Oslo, for instance, gentrification has been accompanied by very steep growth in real estate prices and inner-city districts are becoming economically unattainable for a growing number of people (Huse 2014). Accompanied by liberalisation of real estate markets and a growing shortage of public housing, successive waves of gentrification have gradually led to urban closure. Where newly arrived immigrants would previously seek out cheap housing in the centre of the city, there are now rising concentrations in Oslo suburbs as well as in smaller, adjacent cities. That gentrification is ordering urban space on a larger scale than the affected area, thus causing new ethnic geographies to emerge, is observed in other cities as well. In Toronto, for instance, the traditional transit zones for newly arrived immigrants are shifting, away from the gentrifying inner city and towards high-rise apartments in the suburbs that are being 'filtered down to visible minorities, recent immigrants, ethnic minorities, single parents, and unemployed and underemployed people' (Skaburskis and Nelson 2014: 898). Studying London and New York, Millington (2012; Hague 2013) argues that white middle-class gentrification and securitisation has led to the displacement of poverty, ethnic diversity, immigrants and asylum seekers to the urban periphery. Assessing housing markets in Southern European cities, Arbaci and Malheiros (2010) further identify how social mix policy and changes in tenure regimes have led to a sharp reduction of affordable rental dwellings, gentrification of central areas and the development of new middle class suburban areas. The lower income groups are hence excluded from the central municipal areas and pushed towards expanding urban peripheries. Processes of peripheralisation, Arbaci and Malheiros (2010: 251) observe, 'appear to go hand-in-hand with the increased housing hardship experienced by vulnerable groups, especially non-Western immigrants'.

When poverty is pushed out of the city and into the suburbs, Skaburskis and Nelson (2014: 898) warn, 'it becomes less visible, less seen, and less of a problem'. Emerging geographies of peripheral ethnic minority settlement thus tell us that gentrification has become a rather extensive force, with regional and political consequences beyond the places in which it unfolds. This 'spill-over gentrification' has particular effects on where ethnic minorities settle and should therefore be studied critically in regard to concerns over segregation and integration.

The research presented in this chapter demonstrates clearly that 'race' and ethnicity can play a crucial role in gentrification processes. On a final note, however, I would like to stress that it is important to not lose sight of how strategies such as ethnic packaging and ghetto labelling always work in tandem with wider struggles over the distribution of space. An exclusive focus on the negative effects of displacement, or on the cultural attitudes, personal motivations and consumer choices that guide the privileged, could easily mean that we lose sight of the underlying processes of real estate speculation and investment (Johnson 2015: 195). And whilst the demand for preserving and protecting communities from gentrification remains crucial, it should not overshadow the broader demand for urban housing markets that ensure affordability and access for all.

REFERENCES

Airriess, C. (2006) 'Scaling central place of an ethnic-Vietnamese commercial enclave in New Orleans, Louisiana', in: Kaplan, D. and Li, W. (eds), *Landscapes of the Ethnic Economy*, Lanham, MD: Rowman & Littlefield Publishers, pp. 17–33.

Arbaci, S. and Malheiros, J. (2010) 'De-segregation, peripheralisation and the social exclusion of immigrants: Southern European cities in the 1990s', *Journal of Ethnic and Migration Studies*, 36(2), 227–255.

Arreola, D. (2012) 'Placemaking and Latino urbanism in a Phoenix Mexican immigrant community', *Journal of Urbanism*, 5(1–2), 157–170.

Atkinson, R. (2004) 'The evidence on the impact of gentrification: new lessons for the urban renaissance?', *European Journal of Housing Policy*, 4(1), 107–131.

Atkinson, R. (2008) 'Commentary: gentrification, segregation and the vocabulary of affluent residential choice', *Urban Studies*, 45(12), 2626–2636.

Atkinson, R. and Bridge, G. (eds) (2005) *The New Urban Colonialism: Gentrification in a Global Context*, London: Routledge.

Atkinson, R. and Wulff, M. (2009) *Gentrification and displacement: a review of approaches and findings in the literature*, Report for the Australian Housing and Urban Research Institute [online]. Available at: http://www.ahuri.edu.au/publications/search.asp?ShowSearch=False&Search=Properties&Keywords=Rowland+Atkinson&Search-Author=True&Sort=Search-Title&Direction=DESC (accessed 10 June 2016).

Ball, S. and Vincent, C. (2007) 'Education, class fractions and the local rules of spatial relations', *Urban Studies*, 44(7), 1175–1189.

Barrios, R. (2010) 'You found us doing this, this is our way: criminalizing second lines, Super Sunday, and habitus in post-Katrina New Orleans', *Identities: Global Studies in Culture and Power*, 17(6), 586–612.

Berrey, E. (2005) 'Divided over diversity: political discourse in a Chicago neighbourhood', *City & Community*, 4(2), 143–170.

Betancur, J. (2002) 'The politics of gentrification: the case of West Town in Chicago', *Urban Affairs Review*, 37(6), 780–814.

Betancur, J. (2011) 'Gentrification and community fabric in Chicago', *Urban Studies*, 48(2), 383–406.

Billingham, C. (2015) 'Within-district racial segregation and the elusiveness of white student return to urban public schools', *Urban Education*, published online before print, DOI: 10.1177/0042085915618713, pp. 1–31.

Billingham, C. and Kimelberg, S. (2013) 'Middle-class parents, urban schooling, and the shift from consumption to production of urban space', *Sociological Forum*, 28(1), 85–108.

Blomley, N. (2004) *Unsettling the City: Urban Land and the Politics of Property*, New York: Routledge.

Bolt, G. (2009) 'Combating residential segregation of ethnic minorities in European Cities', *Journal of Housing and the Built Environment*, 24(4), 397–405.

Bolt, G. and van Kempen, R. (2010) 'Ethnic segregation and residential mobility: relocations of minority ethnic groups in the Netherlands', *Journal of Ethnic and Migration Studies*, 36(2), 333–354.

BondGraham, D. (2007) 'The New Orleans that race built: racism, disaster, and urban spatial relationships', *Souls*, 9(1), 4–18.

Boterman, W. (2012) 'Residential mobility of urban middle classes in the field of parenthood', *Environment and Planning A*, 44(10), 2397–2412.

Boterman, W. (2013) 'Dealing with diversity: middle-class family households and the issue of "black" and "white" schools in Amsterdam', *Urban Studies*, 50(6), 1130–1147.

Boyd, M. (2008) 'Defensive development: the role of racial conflict in gentrification', *Urban Affairs Review*, 43(6), 751–776.

Brandvold, Å. (2009) 'Flykter fra Vahl skole', *Klassekampen*, 27 August, p. 4.

Bridge, G., Butler, T. and Lees, L. (eds) (2012) *Mixed Communities: Gentrification by Stealth?*, Bristol: Policy Press.

Butler, T. (2003) 'Living in the bubble: gentrification and its "others" in North London', *Urban Studies*, 40(12), 2469–2486.

Butler, T. and Robson, G. (2001) 'Social capital, gentrification and neighbourhood change in London: a comparison of three south London neighbourhoods', *Urban Studies*, 38(12), 2145–2162.

Butler, T. and Robson, G. (2003) 'Plotting the middle classes: gentrification and circuits of education in London', *Housing Studies*, 18(1), 5–28.

Doshi, S. (2013) 'The politics of the evicted: redevelopment, subjectivity, and difference in Mumbai's slum frontier', *Antipode*, 45(4), 844–865.

Drew, E. (2011) 'Strategies for antiracist representation: ethnic tourism guides in Chicago', *Journal of Tourism and Cultural Change*, 9(2), 55–69.

Florida, R. (2002) *The Rise of the Creative Class: And How It's Transforming Work, Leisure, Community and Everyday Life*, New York: Basic Books.

Forbes-Boyte, E. (2009) 'Whiteout? Gentrification and colonialism in inner-city Sydney', *City*, 13(1), 153–156.

Freeman, L. (2006) *There Goes the Hood: Views of Gentrification From the Ground Up*, Philadelphia: Temple University Press.

Freeman, L. (2009) 'Neighbourhood diversity, metropolitan segregation and gentrification: what are the links in the US?', *Urban Studies*, 46(10), 2079–2101.

Freeman, L. and Braconi, F. (2004) 'Gentrification and displacement. New York City in the 1990s', *Journal of the American Planning Association,* 70(1), 39–52.

Fujita, K. and Maloutas, T. (eds) (2016) *Residential Segregation in Comparative Perspective: Making Sense of Contextual Diversity*, London: Routledge.

Gibson, T. (2015) 'The rise and fall of Adrian Fenty, Mayor-Triathlete: cycling, gentrification and class politics in Washington DC', *Leisure Studies*, 34(2), 230–249.

Glass, R. (1964) 'Introduction', in Glass, R. et al. (eds), *London: Aspects of Change,* London: McGibbon and Kee, pp. xiii–xlii.

Goetz, E. (2011) 'Gentrification in black and white: the racial impact of public housing demolition in American cities', *Urban Studies*, 48(8), 1581–1604.

Gonen, A. (2015) 'Widespread and diverse forms of gentrification in Israel', in Lees, L., Shin, H. and López-Morales, E. (eds), *Global Gentrifications: Uneven Development and Displacement*, Bristol: Policy Press, Ch. 8.

Hackworth, J. and Rekers, J. (2005) 'Ethnic packaging and gentrification: the case of four neighborhoods in Toronto', *Urban Affairs Review,* 41(2), 211–236.

Hague, E. (2013) '"Race", culture and the right to the city: centres, peripheries, margins', *Urban Studies,* 50(1), 232–234.

Ho, C., Vincent, E. and Butler, R. (2015) 'Everyday and cosmo-multiculturalisms: doing diversity in gentrifying school communities', *Journal of Intercultural Studies*, 36(6), 658–675.

Hume, S. (2015) 'Two decades of Bosnian place-making in St. Louis, Missouri', *Journal of Cultural Geography*, 32(1), 1–22.

Huse, T. (2014) *Everyday Life in the Gentrifying City: On Displacement, Ethnic Privileging and the Right to Stay Put*, Farnham: Ashgate.

Hwang, J. (2015) 'Gentrification in changing cities: immigration, new diversity, and racial inequality in neighborhood renewal', *The ANNALS of the American Academy of Political and Social Science*, 660(1), 319–340.

Hwang, J. and Sampson, R. (2014) 'Divergent pathways of gentrification: racial inequality and the social order of renewal in Chicago neighborhoods', *American Sociological Review*, 79(4), 726–751.

Hyra, D. and Rugh, J. (2016) 'The US great recession: exploring its association with black neighborhood rise, decline and recovery', *Urban Geography*, 37(5), 700–726.

Ireland, P. (2008) 'Comparing responses to ethnic segregation in urban Europe', *Urban Studies*, 45(7), 1333–1358.

Jackson, E. and Butler, T. (2015) 'Revisiting "social tectonics": the middle classes and social mix in gentrifying neighbourhoods', *Urban Studies*, 52(13), 2349–2365.

Johnson, C. (2015) 'Gentrifying New Orleans: thoughts on race and the movement of capital', *Souls*, 17(3–4), 175–200.

Jones, G. (2015) 'Gentrification, neoliberalism and loss in Puebla, Mexico', in Lees, L., Shin, H. and López-Morales, E. (eds), *Global Gentrifications: Uneven Development and Displacement*, Bristol: Policy Press, Ch. 14.

Kaltmeier, O. (ed) (2011) *Selling Ethnicity: Urban Cultural Politics in the Americas*, Farnham: Ashgate.

Karlsen, K. and Eriksen, T. (1996) 'Vil lokke nordmenn til Oslos østkant', *Dagbladet,* 26 September, p. 13.

Kirkland, E. (2008) 'What's race got to do with it? Looking for the racial dimensions of gentrification', *Western Journal of Black Studies*, 32(2), 18–30.

Kloosterman, R. and Van Der Leun, J. (1999) 'Just for starters: commercial gentrification by immigrant entrepreneurs in Amsterdam and Rotterdam neighbourhoods', *Housing Studies*, 14(5), 659–677.

Knox, P. (ed) (1993) *The Restless Urban Landscape*, New Jersey: Prentice Hall.

Lanegger, S. (2016) 'Right-of-way gentrification: conflict, commodification and cosmopolitanism', *Urban Studies*, 53(9), 1803–1821.

Laska, S. and Spain, D. (1979) 'Urban policy and planning in the wake of gentrification anticipating renovators' demands', *Journal of the American Planning Association*, 45(4), 523–531.

Lees, L. (2000) 'A reappraisal of gentrification: towards a "geography of gentrification"', *Progress in Human Geography*, 24(3), 389–408.

Lees, L. (2008) 'Gentrification and social mixing: towards an inclusive urban renaissance', *Urban Studies,* 45(12), 2449–2470.

Lees, L. (2016) 'Gentrification, race and ethnicity: towards a global research agenda?', *City and Community,* 15(3), 208–214.

Lees, L. and Ley, D. (2008) 'Introduction to special issue on gentrification and public policy', *Urban Studies*, 45(12), 2379–2384.

Lees, L., Shin, H. and López-Morales, E. (eds) (2015) *Global Gentrifications: Uneven Development and Displacement*, Bristol: Policy Press.

Lees, L., Shin, H. and López-Morales, E. (2016) *Planetary Gentrification*, Cambridge: Polity Press.

Lees, L., Slater, T. and Wyly, E. (2008) *Gentrification*, New York: Routledge.

Lejano, R. and González, E. (2016) 'Sorting through differences. The problem of planning as reimagination', *Journal of Planning Education and Research*, published online before print, DOI: 10.1177/0739456X16634167, pp. 1–13.

Ley, D. (1994) 'Gentrification and the new middle class', *Environment and Planning D*, 12(1), 53–74.

Ley, D. (1996) *The New Middle Class and the Remaking of the Central City*, Oxford: Oxford University Press.

Ley, D. (2012) 'Social mixing and the historical geography of gentrification', in Bridge, G., Butler, T. and Lees, L. (eds), *Mixed Communities. Gentrification by Stealth?*, London: Policy Press.

Lipman, P. (2002) 'Making the global city, making inequality: the political economy and cultural politics of Chicago school policy', *American Educational Research Journal*, 39(2), 379–419.

Lipman, P. (2008) 'Mixed-income schools and housing: advancing the neoliberal urban agenda', *Journal of Education Policy*, 23(2), 119–134.

Lipman, P. (2012) 'Mixed income schools and housing policy in Chicago: a critical examination of the gentrification/education/"racial" exclusion nexus', in Bridge, G., Butler, T. and Lees, L. (eds), *Mixed Communities: Gentrification by Stealth?*, London: Policy Press.

Lipman, P. and Haines, N. (2007) 'From accountability to privatization and African American exclusion – Chicago's "Renaissance 2010"', *Educational Policy*, 21(3), 471–502.

Logan, C. (2013) 'Mrs. McCain's parlor: house and garden tours and the inner-city restoration trend in Washington, DC', *Journal of Urban History*, 39(5), 956–974.

Marcuse, P. (1985) 'Gentrification, abandonment and displacement: connections, causes and policy responses in New York City', *Journal of Urban and Contemporary Law*, 28, 195–240.

Martinez, M. (2010) *Power at the Roots: Gentrification, Community Gardens, and the Puerto Ricans of the Lower East Side*, Lanham, MD: Lexington Books.

Maskovsky, J. (2006) 'Governing the "new hometowns": race, power, and neighborhood participation in the new inner city', *Identities: Global Studies in Culture and Power*, 13(1), 73–99.

Massey, D. (2002) 'Comment on "does gentrification hurt the poor?"', *Brookings-Wharton Papers on Urban Affairs*, Washington, DC: Brookings Institution.

Mele, C. (2000) *Selling the Lower East Side: Culture, Real Estate, and Resistance in New York City*, Minneapolis: University of Minnesota Press.

Millington, G. (2012) 'The outer-inner city: urbanization, migration and "race" in London and New York', *Urban Research & Practice*, 5(1), 6–25.

Mitchell, D. (2003) *The Right to the City. Social Justice and the Fight for Public Space*, New York: The Guilford Press.

Moore, K. (2009) 'Gentrification in black face? The return of the black middle class to urban neighborhoods', *Urban Geography*, 30(2), 118–142.

Morgan, G. and Idriss, S. (2011) 'The geography of the creative aspiration: class, ethnicity and mobility in a global city', paper presented at the *RC21 International Sociological Association Urban and Regional Development Conference*, 'The struggle to belong. Dealing with diversity in 21st century urban settings', 7–9 July 2011, Amsterdam.

Mumm, J. (2008) 'Report from the field: redoing Chicago: gentrification, race, and intimate segregation', *North American Dialogue*, 11(1), 16–19.

Murdie, R. and Teixeira, C. (2011) 'The impact of gentrification on ethnic neighbourhoods in Toronto: a case study of Little Portugal', *Urban Studies*, 48(1), 61–83.

Musterd, S. (2003) 'Segregation and integration: a contested relationship', *Journal of Ethnic and Migration Studies*, 29(4), 623–641.

Musterd, S. (2005) 'Social and ethnic segregation in Europe: levels, causes, and effects', *Journal of Urban Affairs*, 27(3), 331–348.

Musterd, S. and van Kempen, R. (2009) 'Segregation and housing of minority ethnic groups in Western European cities', *Tijdschrift voor economische en sociale Geografie*, 100(4), 559–566.

Musterd, S. and de Winter, M. (1998) 'Conditions for spatial segregation: some European perspectives', *International Journal of Urban and Regional Research*, 22(4), 665–673.

Neal, S. and Vincent, C. (2013) 'Multiculture, middle class competencies and friendship practices in super-diverse geographies', *Social & Cultural Geography*, 14(8), 909–929.

Nelson, L., Trautman, L. and Nelson, P. (2015) 'Latino immigrants and rural gentrification: race, "illegality", and precarious labor regimes in the United States', *Annals of the Association of American Geographers*, 105(4), 841–858.

Newman, K. and Wyly, E. (2006) 'The right to stay put, revisited: gentrification and resistance to displacement in New York City', *Urban Studies*, 43(1), 23–57.

de Olivier, M. (2016) 'Gentrification as the appropriation of therapeutic "diversity": a model and case study of the multicultural amenity of contemporary urban renewal', *Urban Studies*, 53(6), 1299–1316.

Patch, J. (2004) 'The embedded landscape of gentrification', *Visual Studies*, 19(2), 169–187.

Pattillo, M. (2005) 'Black middle-class neighborhoods', *Annual Review of Sociology*, 31, 305–329.

Pattillo, M. (2007) *Black on the Block: The Politics of Race and Class in the City*, Chicago: University of Chicago Press.

Peach, C. (1996) 'Does Britain have ghettos?', *Transactions of the Institute of British Geographers*, 21(1), 216–235.

Phillips, A. (2010) *Gender & Culture*, Cambridge: Polity Press.

Posey-Maddox, L. (2014) *When Middle-class Parents Choose Urban Schools: Class, Race, and the Challenge of Equity in Public Education*, Chicago: University of Chicago Press.

Powell, J. and Spencer, M. (2002) 'Giving them the old one-two: gentrification and the K.O. of impoverished urban dwellers of color', *Howard Law Journal*, 46(1), 433–490.

Prince, S. (2005) 'Race, class, and the packaging of Harlem', *Identities: Global Studies in Culture and Power*, 12(3), 385–404.

Prince, S. (2014) *African Americans and Gentrification in Washington, D.C.: Race, Class, and Social Justice in the Nation's Capital*, Burlington: Ashgate.

Ramos-Zayas, A. (2003) *National Performances: The Politics of Class, Race, and Space in Puerto Rican Chicago*, Chicago: University of Chicago Press.

Rivilin, A. (2002) 'Comment on "does gentrification hurt the poor?"', *Brookings-Wharton Papers on Urban Affairs*, Washington, DC: Brookings Institution.

Rosol, M. (2012) 'Book review: power at the roots: gentrification, community gardens, and the Puerto Ricans of the Lower East Side', *Urban Studies*, 49(5), 1155–1157.

Sæter, O. and Ruud, M. (2005) *Byen som symbolsk rom. Bypolitikk, stedsdiskurser og gentrifisering i Gamle Oslo*, Oslo: Universitetet i Oslo/Byggforsk forlag.

Sakizlioglu, N. and Uitermark, J. (2014) 'The symbolic politics of gentrification: the restructuring of stigmatized neighborhoods in Amsterdam and Istanbul', *Environment and Planning A*, 46(6), 1369–1385.

Semyonov, M. and Glikman, A. (2009) 'Ethnic residential segregation, social contacts, and anti-minority attitudes in European societies', *European Sociological Review*, 25(6), 693–708.

Shaw, W. (2011) *Cities of Whiteness*, Oxford: Blackwell Publishing.

Skaburskis, A. and Nelson, K. (2014) 'Filtering and gentrifying in Toronto: neighbourhood transitions in and out from the lowest income decile between 1981 and 2006', *Environment and Planning A*, 46(4), 885–900.

Slater, T. (2006) 'The eviction of critical perspectives from gentrification research', *International Journal of Urban and Regional Research*, 30(4), 737–757.

Slater, T. (2009a) 'Missing Marcuse: on gentrification and displacement', *City*, 13(2–3), 292–311.

Slater, T. (2009b) 'Ghettos', in Kitchin, R. and Thrift, N. (eds), *The International Encyclopedia of Human Geography*, London: Elsevier.

Slater, T. and Anderson, N. (2011) 'The reputational ghetto: territorial stigmatisation in St. Paul's, Bristol', *Transactions of the Institute of British Geographers*, 37(4), 530–546.

Slater, T., Curran, W. and Lees, L. (2004) 'Guest editorial', *Environment and Planning A*, 36(7), 1141–1150.

Smith, J. (2012) 'Maintaining racial inequality through crime control: mass incarceration and residential segregation', *Contemporary Justice Review*, 15(4), 469–484.

Smith, N. (1982) 'Gentrification and uneven development', *Economic Geography*, 58(2), 139–155.

Smith N. (1996) *The New Urban Frontier: Gentrification and the Revanchist City*, New York: Routledge.

Stillman, J. (2012) *Gentrification and Schools: The Process of Integration when Whites Reverse Flight*, New York: Palgrave Macmillan.

Sullivan, D. (2006) '"Assessing residents" opinions on changes in a gentrifying neighborhood: a case study of the Alberta neighborhood in Portland, Oregon', *Housing Policy Debate*, 17(3), 595–624.

Sullivan, D. (2007) 'Reassessing gentrification measuring residents' opinions using survey data', *Urban Affairs Review*, 42(4), 583–592.

Swanson, K. (2007) 'Revanchist urbanism heads south: the regulation of indigenous beggars and street vendors in Ecuador', *Antipode*, 39(4), 708–728.

Sze, L. (2010) 'Chinatown then and neoliberal now: gentrification consciousness and the ethnic-specific museum', *Identities*, 17(5), 510–529.

Taylor, M. (1992) 'Can you go home again? Black gentrification and the dilemma of difference', *Berkeley Journal of Sociology*, 37, 101–128.

Teppo, A. and Millestein, M. (2015) 'The place of gentrification in Cape Town', in Lees, L., Shin, H. and López-Morales, E. (eds), *Global Gentrifications: Uneven Development and Displacement*, Bristol: Policy Press, Ch. 21.

Tighe, J. and Ganning, J. (2015) 'The divergent city: unequal and uneven development in St. Louis', *Urban Geography*, 36(5), 654–673.

Timberlake, J. and Johns-Wolfe, E. (2016) 'Neighborhood ethnoracial composition and gentrification in Chicago and New York, 1980 to 2010', *Urban Affairs Review*, published online before print, DOI: 10.1177/107808 7416636483, pp. 1–37.

Tucker-Raymond, E. and Rosario, M. (2014) 'Imagining identities young people constructing discourses of race, ethnicity, and community in a contentious context of rapid urban development', *Urban Education*, published online before print, DOI: 0042085914550412, pp. 1–29.

van den Berg, M. (2013) 'City children and genderfied neighbourhoods: the new generation as urban regeneration strategy', *International Journal of Urban and Regional Research*, 37(2), 523–536.

Walks, R. (2009) 'Gentrification, social mix, and the immigrant-reception function of inner-city neighbourhoods: an updated analysis, 1971–2006', in *American Political Science Association 2009 Toronto Meeting Paper*. Available at: https://papers.ssrn.com/Sol3/papers.cfm?abstract_id=1451016##.

Walks, R. and Maaranen, R. (2008) 'Gentrification, social mix, and social polarization: testing the linkages in large Canadian cities', *Urban Geography*, 29(4), 293–326.

Wessel, T. (2009) 'Does diversity in urban space enhance intergroup contact and tolerance?' *Geografiska Annaler: Series B, Human Geography*, 91(1), 5–17.

White, K. (2015) 'Belongingness and the Harlem drummers', *Urban Geography*, 36(3), 340–358.

Wyly, E. and Hammel, D. (2004) 'Gentrification, segregation, and discrimination in the American urban system', *Environment and Planning A*, 36(7), 1215–1241.

Yuan, Y. and Yat-sen, S. (2014) 'Book review: residential segregation in comparative perspective: making sense of contextual diversity', *Urban Studies*, 51(8), 1764–1766.

Zaban, H. (2015) 'Living in a bubble: enclaves of transnational Jewish immigrants from Western countries in Jerusalem', *Journal of International Migration and Integration*, 16(4), 1003–1021.

Zaban, H. (2016) 'City of go(l)d: spatial and cultural effects of high-status Jewish immigration from Western countries on the Baka neighbourhood of Jerusalem', *Urban Studies*, published online before print, DOI: 0042098015625023, pp. 1–20.

Zukin, S. (1995) *The Cultures of Cities*, Cambridge, MA: Blackwell.

Zukin, S. (2008) 'Consuming authenticity: from outposts of difference to means of exclusion', *Cultural Studies*, 22(5), 724–748.

Zukin, S., Lindeman, S. and Hurson, L. (2015) 'The omnivore's neighborhood? Online restaurant reviews, race, and gentrification', *Journal of Consumer Culture*, published online before print, DOI: 10.1177/14695 40515611203, pp. 1–21.

13. Rethinking the gender–gentrification nexus
Bahar Sakızlıoğlu

13.1 INTRODUCTION

Gentrification alters the ways in which places are gendered and in doing so it reflects and affects the way gender is constructed and experienced. The ways places are gendered, as well as changes in gender constructions, may also affect the occurrence of gentrification. The concept of gentrification refers to a changing class composition – for example, Hackworth (2002) defines gentrification as 'the transformation of space for more affluent users' (p. 815). Yet, gentrification is also a product of, and invariably involves changes in, gender relations and the production of gender inequalities. Despite the expanding literature on gentrification, our knowledge on its relation to gender constitution remains limited.

The ways in which gender has been conceptualized and linked with gentrification have transformed from the early 1980s up until today. Thanks to some crucial feminist interventions in the literature (see Rose 1984; Bondi 1991, 1999; Bondi and Rose 2003), the research focus shifted from the role of women in gentrification processes to understanding gentrification as part of gender constitution, thus from categorical understanding of gender to conceptualizing gender as a set of social relations that are fundamentally structured by power relations in society. In this chapter,[1] I present a critical review of the existing literature pinpointing the gaps in our knowledge regarding the nexus of gender and gentrification. I call for a comparative and intersectional approach to investigate gendered geographies of gentrification. I conclude by underlining the need for feminist engagement with knowledge production about gentrification, as well as feminist praxis to contest gendered inequalities and dispossessions involved in gendered geographies of gentrification.

I begin by presenting the early work on gender and gentrification from the 1980s and 1990s, which focused on the role of women in gentrification and debated whether gender was a prime explanatory factor of gentrification. Secondly, I discuss geographer Liz Bondi's crucial interventions in the literature that reoriented our understanding of the link between gender and gentrification. I then focus on the recent work that has followed the path that Bondi blazed. Importantly, I then move on to discuss some future trajectories for research on gender and gentrification.

[1] This chapter has been written as a part of my post-doctoral research project entitled *Gendered Geographies of Gentrification*, and financed by the EU- H2020 Marie Curie IF programme with grant agreement No 658875. I want to thank Loretta Lees, Ebru Soytemel, Marguerite van den Berg and Justus Uitermark for their careful reading of and constructive comments on earlier versions of this chapter.

13.2 THE EARLY WORK ON GENDER AND GENTRIFICATION

The early research on gender and gentrification from the 1980s and 1990s evolved from studies with a focus on women's role in gentrification to studies debating the primacy of gender as an explanatory factor for/in gentrification.

13.2.1 Explaining the Role of Women in Gentrification

Women's role in gentrification has attracted scholars' attention since at least the 1980s. Researchers have discussed women both as actors in gentrification due to their demand for housing in gentrifying neighborhoods and bearers of gentrification as they are among the most vulnerable populations to displacement. Scholars have argued that with the increasing participation of women in the labour market, particularly the increasing number of career-oriented middle-class women with well-paid jobs (both as members of dual-earner households or as single households), the demand for gentrifying neighborhoods has increased (Ley 1986; Rose 1984, 1989; Smith 1987). Besides these factors related to the changing position of women in the labour market, the increasing number of women living alone (Rose and LeBourdais 1986) and postponing childbearing (Beauregard 1986) were also mentioned among the reasons for increased demand for housing in gentrifying areas. Scholars also discussed women as bearing the negative effects of gentrification – the increasing number of women with low paid jobs in the service sector, together with an increasing number of female-headed households, such as elderly women living alone and single mothers, issues that were among the factors that made women vulnerable to displacement (Bondi 1991).

13.2.2 Going Beyond the Dichotomy of Class versus Gender

While gentrification researchers had up until 1980 exclusively focused on capital flows and general consumer preferences, scholars such as Markusen (1981) argued that gentrification resulted from 'the breakdown of the patriarchal household' (ibid. p. 32). Rose (1984) underlined the need to study the link between gentrification and the changing gender division of labour. In her later work, Rose (1989) coined the concept of 'marginal gentrifiers' to refer to single women and LGBTQs with lower middle incomes. These groups were attracted to central city areas that offered both material benefits (such as a wide range of services, short commutes, etc.) and an emancipatory environment (see also Rose 1984; Smith 1987; Wekerle 1984).

Later the discussions on gender, class and gentrification revolved around the prioritization of gender (Warde 1991) or class (Butler and Hamnett 1994) in explaining gentrification. Sociologist Alan Warde (1991) argued that gender could better explain the production of gentrifiers compared to class. According to Warde, the ways career-oriented women responded to changes in the labour market and patriarchal pressures could explain different forms of gentrification. Opposing Warde's arguments, Butler and Hamnett (1994) discussed the importance of class in gentrification and how class affected the link between gender and gentrification. In a further attempt to move the debate beyond unproductive oppositions, Butler (1997) and Bondi (1999) insisted that rather than emphasizing either class or gender, scholars should focus on the complex and dynamic relationship between gender and class. But even though scholars acknowledged the interaction between class and gender in explaining gentrification, in many studies gender was subsumed under class or treated as a category rather than a social relation as was critiqued by Bondi (1999).

13.3 BONDI'S INTERVENTIONS: THE INADEQUACY OF EXISTING CONCEPTUAL FRAMEWORKS

Feminist geographer Liz Bondi played a significant role in (re)shaping the literature on gender and gentrification with two critical interventions. Firstly, in her seminal work on gender and gentrification, Bondi (1991) suggested a shift in research focus from the role of women in gentrification processes to understanding gentrification as gender constitution. She criticized the work that subsumed gender under class analysis, approaching gender as a category rather than a set of social relations. Bondi argued that such analyses ignored the gendered relations of oppression treating gender as an individual attribute. Rather she pointed to the importance of studying gentrification as gender constitution as well as class constitution. According to Bondi, class and gender were linked not only because gender inequality shapes class experience, but also as the formation of class embraces certain femininities and masculinities. Bondi argued that gentrification could be understood in a comprehensive manner only by paying attention to the dynamics of the mutual constitution of class, gender and space in gentrifying neighborhoods.

To widen the framework for studying gender and gentrification, Bondi (1991) made three suggestions: Firstly, instead of giving priority to one dimension of social differentiation – to class or gender – she suggested embracing a perspective that would investigate the dynamic relationship between class and gender and discuss the ways relations of oppression are negotiated and reconstructed through the process of gentrification. Secondly, Bondi argued that gender should be considered as a dynamic social relation and pointed to the importance of questioning how gentrification contributes to gender divisions in different contexts, rather than focusing on if gentrification involves a shift in power relations between men and women. Thirdly, Bondi also underlined the importance of approaching gender as a cultural construction, which meant that the research focus should be more on the meanings attached to femininities and masculinities rather than taking the gendered division of labour as the core of gender relations.

She argued that actors in gentrification negotiate their ideas about gender during the process of gentrification and exploring these ideas and the ways they are negotiated would give us more insight about the mutual construction of gender and space (Bondi 1991).

In her second intervention, Bondi (1999) emphasized the contextuality of gender constitution and gentrification. Gendered experiences of gentrification and the gendered production of space during gentrification varies in different contexts. She also underlined the importance of life course analysis to shed more light on the dynamics of the mutual constitution of gender, class and space.

Bondi's interventions have influenced the framing of the more recent literature on gender and gentrification in the 2000s.

13.4   MORE RECENT WORK ON GENDER AND GENTRIFICATION

Researchers responded well to Bondi's call for a more refined and comprehensive body of research on gender and gentrification. Recent research can be categorized into three general research areas in which scholars discuss the link between gender and gentrification: (1) Life course; (2) Neoliberal policy and the production of space; and (3) Class and gender in the everyday life of gentrifying neighborhoods.

13.4.1   Life Course: Family Gentrifiers

Bondi's call for conducting life course analysis to better understand gender in the context of gentrification was responded to by researchers who studied family gentrifiers in particular, and the relation of life course to gender in the context of gentrification at large.

Lia Karsten (2003, 2007) studied family gentrifiers whom she called young urban professional parents (YUPPs). YUPPs preferred to stay in the city centre as opposed to the general trend towards suburbanization for families in the Dutch context (and beyond). These mostly dual-earner families were made up of highly educated middle-class couples with children. Karsten (2003) showed how these family gentrifiers tried to combine childbearing and career-making by choosing to live in central neighborhoods where they could enjoy the convenience of living in proximity to work and facilities they needed and desired with respect to social reproduction too. The author discussed family gentrifiers' gendered practices as signaling a more equitable gendered division of labour, as men and women shared household duties and childcare equally.

Another study investigating the co-constitution of gender, space and class in relation to life course is that of Boterman and Bridge (2015) who focused on how middle-class couples changed their residential strategies after becoming parents in the cities of London and Amsterdam. Adding a comparative dimension to existing research on life course, class, gender and gentrification, Boterman and Bridge presented an invaluable analysis of the mutual constitution of gender, class and space based on Bourdieu's theory of habitus, field and capital. They showed how the use of neighborhood by gentrifier households becomes gendered after becoming parents and how particular contexts restrict or allow the ways gender roles and relations are negotiated during parenthood based on time-space constraints present in specific contexts. They argued that the institutional and spatial context of a particular city is very important in allowing and/or sustaining egalitarian gender practices and relations. More favorable childcare facilities, labour legislation, the scale of the city, duration and mode of commuting, etc. are the factors affecting how gender practices and relations are reconstituted during parenthood in different cities. They argue that an egalitarian gender division of labour is the case for a rather small fraction of the middle classes and that it is highly dependent on factors such as the proximity of work to house and labour market conditions etc. Another important finding that the authors discussed is that femininity was practised as a marker of class, i.e. cargo-bike mothers in Amsterdam (*bakfietsmoeders* in Dutch) and 'yummy mummy cafés' in London have become symbols of new middle-class culture. Boterman and Bridge also show the ways femininities and masculinities are practised during parenthood together with the meanings attached to them. Pointing to the contextually dependent ways that gender is constituted in relation to class and life course, they make a significant contribution to the study of gender, class, life course and gentrification.

13.4.2 Neoliberal Policy, Gender and Gentrification

Neoliberal city making at large, and gentrification specifically, both involve gender ideologies and representations that are mobilized by different actors involved in the production of space. The first set of research in the literature on this issue focused on how gendered revanchist neoliberal policies are. Papayannis (2000) argued that sex work is blamed for blight in disinvested city centres and that policy claims around saving these centres, displacing sex work, are associated with the revitalization of the city and thus capital accumulation. Likewise, Hubbard (2004) has shown that the neoliberal urban policy agenda and its promotion of gentrification are based on masculine ideas and practices. Hubbard argues that 'policies to remove the street-level sex work is no mere side-effect of the reassertion of capital but are fundamental in the re-centering of masculinity and the forging of new patriarchal arrangements in the Western post-industrial societies' (ibid. p. 678).

Along the same lines, Melissa Wright (2013) in her study of the livelihood strategies of sex workers in a gentrifying town, Cuidad Juarez, along the US-Mexico border, discussed how discursive processes helped to legitimize the violence against and displacement of sex workers and the working poor from the centre, as a means to increase the rent gap in the area. In a similar vein, in her study of gentrification in an ethnic minority neighborhood in Oslo, Tone Huse (2014) underlines that stigmatization based on gender medievalism was mobilized to legitimize gentrification in an ethnic minority neighborhood where many Muslims and ethnic minorities lived.

The second set of research has shown the ways city marketing strategies are gendered. For instance, Kern (2010, 2011) studied the gendered ideologies shaping the restructuring of the neoliberal city and showed how gender is used as a marketing strategy in the condominium market in Toronto. She discussed how condominium ownership, which boosted the image of urban women as 'emancipated' consumer citizens, did not actually emancipate women but reinforced patriarchal relations. Kern pointed to the importance of studying policy and decision making about gentrification from a gender perspective not only to map out gendered assumptions and ideas about work, family and home but also to critically discuss which women are tagged as 'desirable' and 'undesirable' in this process. Another important point she underlined is the importance of questioning the link between urban change and emancipation for women. New-build gentrification projects offer amenities such as proximity to the city centre, walkability, security etc., thereby re-appropriating and commodifying feminist visions. Kern discusses that women's freedom and autonomy are ripped of any redistributive or equity concerns. Commodifying these elements of urban life alters how gender is constituted!

Likewise, Van den Berg (2012, 2013) also shows the centrality of gender in the urban agenda as a tool in neoliberal city making. She discussed the use of femininity as a strategy to brand the city of Rotterdam from a masculine and industrial city to a feminine, creative, post-industrial city. According to the author, gendered urban strategies and ideologies of gender involved in urban restructuring, aspire to produce urban space for different gender relations, what she calls 'genderfication' (Van den Berg 2012, 2016). This policy targeting the attraction of middle-class families to the city, not only remakes gender relations but also brings about class upgrading and classed inequalities. Her analysis reveals the gendered nature of post-industrial city making as well as the importance of intersectional analysis in understanding gentrification.

To sum up, some scholars focused on the link between revanchist politics, gentrification and gender and others focused on the 'emancipated' femininity of the middle-class consumer citizen as a crucial aspect of the post-industrial city and policy making. These two sets of research show two sides of the same coin, as neoliberal policy and city making embrace certain femininities and masculinities while displacing or exterminating others.

13.4.3   Class and Gender in the Everyday Life of Gentrifying Neighborhoods

Researchers in this body of work have studied class, gender and gentrification in relation to two themes: 1) the social reproduction of communities; and 2) accumulation by dispossession.

13.4.3.1   Gender, class and the social reproduction of communities in gentrifying neighborhoods

Researchers here underline the important role of both lower income and middle-class women in the social reproduction of communities in gentrifying neighborhoods. To start with, Amy Mills (2007, 2010) made this argument in her in-depth ethnographic research on the constitution of gender and space in a gentrifying neighborhood in Istanbul. Mills presented a spatial analysis of the everyday constitution of gender and discussed multiple genderings of space in a neighborhood undergoing rapid change. She argued that the traditional neighborhood (*mahalle*) was constituted by the low-income women performing traditional gender roles in the *mahalle* and that these women made the neighborhood through the acts of knowing and their social networks of support. Mills showed how this *mahalle* network became socially exclusive to its members, especially when there was an influx of middle-class newcomers to the area with whom new lifestyles and non-traditional gender roles infiltrated and changed the neighborhood. The incoming women of higher socio-economic status had different understandings of privacy, preferring a rather stricter distinction between private and public space that did not comply with the fluid boundaries of home/street, private/public that existed in the *mahalle*. They also had non-traditional gender roles (they were working women, single and divorced women living alone) that could not easily be a part of the everyday gendered constitution of the *mahalle*. The middle-class women did try to be a part of the *mahalle* through the neighborhood association that the newcomers formed. This constituted a different and non-traditional way of relating to, and gendering of, space that came about in this gentrifying neighborhood in Istanbul. Mills asserted that women were still considered to be home and community makers even within the framework of modern urban life with non-traditional gender roles. In this process of gentrification, not only 'gendered belongings to community' but also 'what it means to be a woman' were being renegotiated. This detailed ethnographic analysis revealed gentrification to be both a classed and gendered process.

Secondly, Kirsteen Paton (2014) has produced a rich ethnographic study of gentrification that also discusses the gendered social reproduction of community in gentrifying neighborhoods. Her research illustrates how the construction of class is gendered, with a discussion not only of changing gender roles in work and community during neoliberal restructuring, but also of how femininities and masculinities are reconstructed in relation to class. Regarding the latter, the author shows that economic restructuring in the city of Glasgow deeply affected masculinities that were deemed redundant by the process of deindustrialization. Working-class men disassociating from their class position, embraced an 'adapt or die' strategy to be able to control their livelihoods. This idea of control in a time when working-class men in general were suffering a degrading experience due to economic and social change, the author argued, reconstructed and reinforced their masculinity in relation to class positions. As for femininity and class constitution, even though feminization of the service economy meant the breaking of traditional gender roles and class positions, Paton argued that working-class women aspired to increase their respectability through caring roles, taking an active part in the social reproduction of community in their gentrifying neighborhood; which became a heavier burden due to declining welfare services, ageing, drug addiction, and psychological problems, etc. Paton argues that 'the heavy burden of paid and unpaid labour brought about more exploitation of women and reinforced traditional gender roles' (ibid. p. 77).

Reminiscent of the argument Mills made about women's crucial roles in the social reproduction of communities and households in a gentrifying neighborhood, Paton points to the significant link between femininity and respectability that reinforced existing gender inequalities even though women's position in the labour market was changing, and they were more mobile both physically and financially.

In the same vein as these two studies, Jason Patch (2008) discussed the important role of new lower-middle-class and middle-class women entrepreneurs both in the production of gentrified space and in the social reproduction of gentrifiers' community in a gentrifying neighborhood. He argued for the importance of observing the gendered interactions these women made in the streets and stores – meeting, welcoming and acting as sources of information to the newcomers, so that they would get accustomed to and stay in the gentrifying neighborhood of Williamsburg, New York City. These women entrepreneurs avoided workplace discrimination in their stores and allowed flexibility for female employees. They also contested and negotiated masculinity in the streets as they constantly dealt with 'the guys on the street' (ibid. p. 113). According to the author, these women entrepreneurs, as 'the faces on the street' (ibid. p. 109), in contrast to what Jane Jacob's called 'eyes on the street' (ibid. p. 103), played a significant role in the production of this gentrified neighborhood and the construction of a gentrifier community.

Another important study was conducted by Leslie Kern (2013), who focused on the experiences of women working in gentrifying neighborhoods. Kern investigated work and gender in a gentrifying neighborhood and pointed to gendered vulnerabilities and precarity and how women worked to find a balance between capitalizing on gentrification and being under the threat of displacement. This ambivalent position involved using alternative informal and non-monetized practices to exchange support and engage with vulnerable people in the neighborhood. Creating these networks of support, women workers contributed not only to the social reproduction of the community but also to the production of gentrified urban spaces.

13.4.3.2   Accumulation by dispossession and gender: the experiences of the dispossessed
Perhaps the most important gap in the early literature was the exclusive focus on the role
and experiences of middle- and lower-middle-class women and LGBTQs in gentrification. Gender and sexuality were discussed in the early literature mainly in relation to the
emancipatory city thesis (Lees 2000), which argued that gentrification brought about
emancipation for groups suffering from patriarchy and homophobia, such as women
and LGBTQs. Scholars showed how gentrification helped these groups to contest and
alter oppressive gender relations. However, as Lees et al. (2008) noted, these studies
only focused on the experiences of middle-class women and LGBTQs, side-lining the
experiences of lower-class women and LGBTQs living and working in gentrifying areas.
Some recent work has addressed this gap in the literature focusing on the experiences and
contestation of women and LGBTQs living and working in gentrifying neighborhoods.

In her study of working-class women who were under threat of violent removal from
the city centre to make space for gentrification in Ciudad Juarez, along the Mexico-US
border, Melissa Wright (2013) argued that accumulation by dispossession was grounded
in the everyday struggles over social reproduction that the working poor engaged in to
defend the places in which they live and work. Examining the livelihood strategies of sex
workers in Ciudad Juárez, Wright discussed how these women rejected being removed and
contested the process of gentrification to safeguard their social reproduction.

Another study conducted by Zengin (2014) has discussed how transgender women
engaged in sex work in the gentrifying neighborhoods of Istanbul have experienced
chain displacement accompanied with increasing state violence against their livelihood.
Trans women were able to socially reproduce their community by building social support
networks in some central neighborhoods going through the early stages of gentrification,
where intellectuals, students, and artists had led marginal gentrification. But as gentrification proceeded, the police violently displaced these trans women with the support
of gentrifiers and the local community. Transgender women dispersed into adjacent
neighborhoods where they lacked the support and benefits of living as a community, and
down the line they were under threat of displacement in their new neighborhoods too due
to expanding gentrification.

Aslı Zengin is not the only scholar from Turkey who has investigated the dispossessions
women and LGBTQs bear together with the anti-displacement strategies they develop to
deal with these dispossessions. Soytemel (2013), in her paper on self-help neighborhood-
based networks of poor women in a gentrifying neighborhood in Istanbul, argued that
neighborhood-based social networks were very important in finding alternative accommodation once evicted, or in bypassing the officials who came to cut off the electricity
supply or to deliver eviction notices. Losing neighbourhood-based social networks was
fatal for these women who used collective strategies to survive economically and socially,
even under the threat of displacement.

In my own work (Sakızlıoğlu 2014), I found that some of the very low-income Kurdish
women in a gentrifying neighborhood in Istanbul were burdened with even heavier
consequences due to gentrification. These women could barely speak the official Turkish
language but enjoyed the presence of the Kurdish community in the neighborhood that
helped with their economic and socio-cultural survival. Gentrification not only meant
that these women would lose their homes but also their community and means of survival
too.

Tahire Erman (2016) has discussed how women in (slum housing) *gecekondu* areas, who were displaced and relocated to formal social housing estates on the peripheries of the Turkish capital, Ankara, suffered from displacement and dispossession from their neighborhoods but also from their means of social reproduction. Missing the practices of sitting in front of their houses, baking bread in their gardens, etc., which constructed the fluid boundaries of private and public in *gecekondu* areas, these women started appropriating public space in the formal social housing estates and carried *gecekondu* activities into these housing estates. This act of appropriation was a contestation to the imprisonment of former *gecekondu* women in their private houses in the new social housing estates.

In a study on experiences of displacement, Desmond (2012) underlined the vulnerability of women as evictees: he found that women are evicted at significantly higher rates than men in inner city black neighborhoods. In a later study, he documents the heavy burden of inequality on the shoulders of single mothers facing eviction (Desmond 2016). He also points to the importance of the gendered interactions between landlords and tenants that shape eviction processes. For instance, he found that a female tenant confronting her landlord was considered to be 'rude' and lesbians were considered to be 'tough' tenants. Showing how gendered the relations between tenants and landlords are, Desmond has opened up a new path of inquiry regarding the everyday gendered experiences of the dispossessed.

As for the question of how anti-displacement/dispossession strategies are gendered, Doshi (2013) has discussed how everyday practices of mitigating displacement in Mumbai slum areas were gendered, based on her in-depth study of two slum areas in the city. These gendered practices were found to be differentiated in these two different cases. Doshi, in her first case study of the Mankhurd slum area, argued that the SPARC Alliance – between an NGO and two grassroots groups – was based on the cooperation of evicted women residents and non-confrontational gendered participation asking for improvements in housing and sanitation. Underlining 'domesticated gendered subjectivities', SPARC made women collaborators in the negotiations, as the agents armed with the knowledge of home, sanitation, etc. In Doshi's second case study of the Mandala slum area, anti-eviction mobilization was more rights-based and the movement highlighted slum women's working-class backgrounds and experiences as opposed to SPARC's emphasis on women's social reproductive roles as housewives and mothers. Doshi highlighted the significance of understanding displacement politics based not only on class but also on gender and ethno-religious relations. Differentiated gender tactics against displacement have also been discussed in some studies on anti-displacement struggles in cities in Turkey. While in some neighborhoods women took the frontlines of the barricades (Ergin 2006), in other neighborhoods they were not at all or very little involved during the negotiations both due to patriarchal family structures and authority's embracing of the mostly male household head as the sole authority who would make decisions for his household during negotiations (Sakızlıoğlu 2014).

13.5 CRITICAL REFLECTIONS: TOWARDS A FUTURE RESEARCH AGENDA ON GENDER AND GENTRIFICATION

More recent research on gender and gentrification has responded well to Bondi's early criticisms. Most researchers now approach gentrification not by subsuming gender under class analysis but by looking at class and gender as co-constituted in the process. There is a growing body of work on the relationship of life course to gentrification and gender. There are, however, three issues that are not fully investigated in this literature. Firstly, we still know little about the link between gender and gentrification as cultural constructions (Bondi 1991). Bondi's earlier question of 'how changes in the sexual division of labor in the workplace, the community and the home . . . are negotiated through cultural constructions of femininity and masculinity' during the process of gentrification (ibid. p. 195) has not yet been fully addressed, even though some scholars have integrated this question into their research (Kern 2011; van den Berg 2013; Boterman and Bridge 2015). Secondly, the literature presents a partial picture, for most research has focused on how gentrification has positively affected the lives of women and LGBTQs with middle-class backgrounds. More recent work on gentrification has focused on the experiences of low income, dispossessed women and LGBTQs, yet we need to embrace an intersectional approach to grasp the experiences of women and LGBTQs from different class, race/ ethnicity, and age groups. As Lees et al. (2008) suggested, the question remains: 'Does the gentrifying inner-city act as an emancipatory space for all women' (p. 213) and for all LGBTQs? Thirdly, despite Bondi's emphasis on contextuality, the literature lacks comparative accounts that reveal the context dependent, as well as common elements, of how space and gender are mutually constructed.

To address these issues, I argue in this last section of the chapter that we need to integrate an intersectional and comparative perspective into our analysis of the mutual constitution of gender and space during gentrification processes. In the second part of this section, I want to discuss two neglected but important themes that are awaiting research interest.

13.5.1 An Intersectional and Comparative Lens on Gender and Gentrification

13.5.1.1 Inserting an intersectional perspective into gentrification and displacement research

Over a quarter of a century ago now, Knopp (1990) argued that the intersection of class, gender and sexuality should be taken into account in order to understand the different experiences of gentrification. It is now widely acknowledged in the literature that rather than giving priority to one dimension of social differentiation such as class, gender, race, age/life course, etc., researchers should take them all into account to examine how different axes of power are expressed, deconstructed, reconstructed and negotiated through the process of gentrification. Focusing on these aspects opens not only a theoretical possibility to better understand the contextual and complex functioning/s of power relations during the production of space for gentrification but also the question of how to construct a feminist politics across differences (based on class, age, sexuality, ethnicity/race or locality) to alter the regnant, oppressive organization and gender-ordered construction of space, be it patriarchal, sexist, racist, ageist, etc.

Even though there is an emerging literature integrating an intersectional perspective into gentrification and displacement research, there is still a lot of work that needs to be done. Integrating such a perspective into, for example, the literature on accumulation by dispossession, such as Doshi (2013) and Wright (2013) have done, will help us grasp how the mutual production of space and gender embodies, reflects, and alters, differentiated power relations in the contemporary neoliberal era.

Likewise, the tensions and interactions between constitutions of gender and class have recently entered the research lens of gentrification researchers, the key reference being Skeggs' work (1997) on the formation of gender and class. Skeggs has inspired some gentrification researchers such as Paton (2014), yet some important questions remain: How do ethnic minority and lesbian women both from a middle- and working-class background experience gentrification and displacement? How is gender articulated in contestations against accumulation by dispossession, gentrification and displacement in different contexts? What role does race play regarding the production of space and gender during gentrification processes? How similar or different are the experiences of religious middle-class women and non-religious middle-class women regarding gentrification processes in cities such as London, Berlin, Cairo, Istanbul, Marrakesh, among others? I think that engaging with and better incorporating the existing research on intersectionality as a critical inquiry and praxis (see Crenshaw 1991; Yuval-Davis 2006, among others) into gentrification research will enable better understanding of the complexities of the processes involved.

13.5.1.2 A comparative lens on gender and gentrification: gendered geographies of gentrification

To reveal the context dependent nature, as well as the common elements, of how space and gender are mutually constituted during gentrification processes, we need to employ a comparative perspective that would enable us to understand the connections among gender constructions and gentrifications in different settings. Some time ago, Lees (2000) highlighted the importance of the 'geography of gentrification' calling attention to how gentrification varies across different settings. To explore and theorize the diverse ways gender and space are mutually constituted in different contexts of gentrification, we need to carry this forward and focus on the 'gendered geographies of gentrification'. Doing so would mean also responding to recent calls for a comparative urbanism approach (Lees 2012; Robinson 2006); but also, drawing on post-colonial and feminist critiques of knowledge production, de-centering and nuancing hegemonic conceptualizations of gentrification and gender based on European and North American experiences. Aiming to link the mutual constitution of space and gender through different geographies of gentrification, a comparative approach would shed light on the connections among gentrifications as gender constitution, the gendered, racialized and classed constitution of space, and construction of femininities and masculinities during gentrification within, between, and beyond cities.

Researchers have pinpointed significant issues regarding different urbanization patterns, the role and culture of the middle classes, informality, and the role of the state, (among others see Lees et. al 2016) in questioning the usefulness of gentrification as a concept to explain similar processes in cities outside of the West. The point is then to approach the issues from a feminist perspective, and gender the discussion, which would mean underlining the significance of gender in understanding different geographies of gentrification.

We need to question our knowledge on the gender–gentrification nexus produced in/ for Western cities and investigate critically how the link between gender and gentrification plays out in different places. For instance, factors argued to have affected the occurrence of gentrification such as feminization of the labor force, changes in family structure etc., have different dynamics in different contexts that need to be discussed in detail to understand the contextual nature of gentrification. While questioning the relevance of what we know from the Western context for understanding new gendered geographies of gentrification is important, we also need to keep in mind the lessons learned from earlier feminist research, about thinking beyond dichotomies such as public/private, suburb/ inner city etc., in our understanding of gender and urban change. For example, we might want to unpack the relationship of gentrification to the emancipation of women, a body of work that focuses on the dichotomy of the suburb vs. the inner city in Europe and North America. Looking at gentrification in cities elsewhere, will, no doubt, mean engaging with and going beyond the dichotomies of urban and rural, traditional and modern, religious and non-religious, among others, to understand and contextualize gender roles, relations, inequalities, and the meanings attached to femininities and masculinities in relation to urban change.

Likewise, there is a need for contextualized studies of gender regimes in relation to gentrification, not only to map the institutional and spatial contexts to help better sustain and/or create egalitarian urban gender relations but also to understand the dynamics of gendered precarity and resistance to gentrification.

13.5.2   Neglected Themes in the Gender–Gentrification Nexus

13.5.2.1   Rural gentrification and gender

Gender has mostly been discussed in relation to urban gentrification, and the dichotomy of inner city vs. suburb living has been central to the construction of the argument that gentrification is emancipatory for women and LGBTQs. Martin Phillips is among the few researchers who have focused on the neglected link between rural gentrification and gender. Phillips (1993) started from the argument that gentrification resulted from the emergence of more class-symmetrical households. In his research, he found no evidence that there was increased class symmetry within the households who were rural gentrifiers. Indeed, he suggested that this argument could be reversed where rural gentrification was concerned. He found that class asymmetrical households moved to rural villages when they started families to provide a better, safer, greener place for their kids to grow up. In this sense, gentrification was in part 'the result of the perpetuation of patriarchal gender identities and associations' (ibid. p. 138). Phillips' research helps us ask more questions about: 1) the link between emancipation and gentrification; 2) the importance of life course in relation to rural and urban gentrification; 3) the impact of rural gentrification on gender relations and ideologies in rural areas together with the construction of rural femininities and masculinities; 4) the relationship between rural and urban gentrification; in other words, if rural gentrifiers were urban gentrifiers at a point in time, and vice versa; 5) questions regarding the gendered accessibility and affordability of centrality for rural and urban gentrifiers and non-gentrifiers.

These questions are important not only to understand the similarities and differences between rural and urban gentrification in relation to gender but also in relation to the ways we understand and conceptualize urban and rural.

Significantly, the geography of rural gentrification is expanding due to expansion of gentrification in many cities, which makes it unaffordable to many middle class households and marginal gentrifiers to stay put in the most gentrified cities. It has become especially important to investigate rural gentrification and gender in cities outside Europe and North America, where massive urbanization processes have brought about an increasing anti-urbanization sentiment amongst the middle classes. This has created a new demand for rural gentrification in rural and peripheral areas, as Qian and others (2013) have discussed in relation to China. New research needs to address different gendered geographies of rural gentrification in non-Western cities with a comparative perspective.

13.5.2.2   Dispossession and emancipation as the Siamese twins of gentrification

To unpack the relationship of urban change (gentrification in particular) to the emancipation of women and LGBTQs we need to approach the gendered processes of emancipation and dispossession as the Siamese twins of gentrification. In other words, gentrification brings about emancipatory gender relations and roles for some women and LGBTQs but at the cost of others' dispossession from their houses, neighborhoods, means of social reproduction, and access to city centres. Here we need to engage in: (1) an ethnography and political economy of emancipation; and (2) developing a feminist critique of, or gendering the theory of, accumulation by dispossession, to grasp the dynamics of emancipation and dispossession for women and LGBTQs during gentrification.

To start with the former, we need to question the unequal distribution of access to the centre and facilities among different class, ethnic, age, gender and sexuality groups. Mapping who is granted access to the centre and facilities in a convenient way, we can grasp the exclusions that urban policy brings about that act as forms of dispossession.

The appeal of the central city for those women who do not perform traditional gender roles and break the hegemony of the nuclear family has been well discussed in the literature, but we also need to ask more critical questions about:

(1)   how the notion of centrality changes in different cities and if the appeal of the centre is valid for different groups of women and LGBTQs in different cities that have different institutional, spatial structures and gender cultures (see Soytemel and Sen 2014). For example, how emancipatory are more homogenous gated communities located on urban peripheries, offering car-based convenience and facilities, in relation to gentrifying inner city neighborhoods?

(2)   the conflicts and collaborations regarding the ways women and LGBTQs question, contest and alter patriarchal and heterosexual norms in the everyday of the gentrifying inner city and beyond. How do visitors of a newly opened lesbian café interact with, meet, bypass, contest the visitors of a traditional coffee house in a gentrifying neighborhood in Istanbul, for instance? Or how do middle-class women in Cairo navigate, express themselves in, and make the gentrifying city?

My last point regarding the political economy and ethnography of emancipation, is about the experiences of domestic workers employed by gentrifier households and other workers in gentrifying neighborhoods, for it is important to understand the power relations involved in 'emancipation'. Likewise, the relations between different class, gender, sexuality, age, ethnicity groups in gentrifying neighborhoods can also tell us about the dynamics of power relations involved in gentrification and the emancipation that it brings to only some groups.

As for gendering accumulation by dispossession theory, Cindi Katz (2001, 2011) has made an invaluable contribution and suggested that discursive and material processes of capital accumulation aim at 'foreclosing the social reproduction of specified populations' as Wright (2013, p. 840) puts it. Katz (2011) analyzed accumulation by dispossession in everyday spaces criticizing the silence of Marxist work on social reproduction. She argued that capitalism discursively and materially disposes of some populations (such as sex workers, refugees, drug addicts, etc.) rendering their social reproduction impossible. She points to the importance of looking at the scale of everyday life in order to grasp the everyday struggles around continuing social reproduction as a contestation to accumulation by dispossession. In her own words: 'The scale of dispossession is witnessed not just in uneven geographical developments like colonialism, gentrification, suburbanization, or "urban renewal," but also at the intimate scales of everyday life. Foreclosure takes place – quite literally – at the very heart of people's existence' (Katz 2011, pp. 49–50).

Focusing on everyday gendered experiences of, and contestations over, gentrification and displacement as the manifestation of accumulation by dispossession would mean the gendering of the theory of accumulation by dispossession with a feminist perspective. Such a focus would not only help to connect the macro and micro framings of gendered dispossessions but also to understand the meanings attached to gendered dispossessions.

13.6   CONCLUSIONS

In this chapter, I have argued for deeper feminist engagement with the theory and process of gentrification, underlining the importance of approaching gentrification as a gender constitution process. Gentrification is no doubt a contested process as well as a contested concept. The gentrification literature has long reflected the big debates in the social sciences over the well-seated dichotomies of agency and structure, economy and culture, production and consumption, etc. Approaching gentrification as gender constitution, and doing so in relation to the formations of other social differentiations such as class, ethnicity, sexuality, has a critical and complex role to play in overcoming these binaries in our understanding of gentrification (Bondi 1999). It is notable that the gender–gentrification nexus has not been fully investigated in the ever-growing literature on gentrification. I believe that this has its roots in the gradual decrease of writings on gender in urban studies (Massey 1994; McDowell 1999) and space/place in gender studies (Alkan 2005; Mills 2010; Peake and Rieker 2013). Even though gentrification studies have kept pace with and incorporated newly emerging critical urban perspectives such as assemblage theory, planetary urbanization, etc., the question remains as to how and whether gender is incorporated into contemporary, critical gentrification research. As Peake (2016) argues, urban theory in the twenty-first century still lacks knowledge of, and inspirations from, feminist theory and praxis. Inserting a feminist understanding of gender and the urban (in relation to the rural), and putting it in relation to class, race/ethnicity, sexuality, age, etc., in our analyses of gentrification will not only enhance our understanding of gentrification, as gender serves as a critical tool to grasp and theorize the inequalities involved in the production of space. Such a perspective also helps eliminate the disciplinary boundaries between urban studies and feminist/gender studies.

In this chapter, I have argued for the need to incorporate an intersectional and comparative lens to study the gender–gentrification nexus. An intersectional approach would enable us to discuss the different and complex ways different axes of oppression cut across each other and are expressed and negotiated through the process of gentrification, while a comparative approach would make possible investigation of the gendered geographies of gentrification, focusing on how the gendered making of gentrification, both material and symbolic, and its gendered meanings and impacts on livelihoods, vary in different geographies.

Last but not least, I have discussed two neglected themes in gentrification research. Firstly, a feminist engagement with gendered geographies of gentrification requires moving away from the binary understanding of urban and rural and investigating gentrification in rural areas in relation to gentrification in city centres, shedding light on the rural element in urban gentrification and the urban in the rural gentrification. Such an engagement also goes beyond the regnant developmentalist/modernist approaches to understanding, on the one hand, the urban in the non-Western world (Peake 2016, p. 225), and on the other hand, the urban and rural. Secondly, I have discussed the need to approach gendered processes of emancipation and dispossession as the Siamese twins of gentrification. We need to question the political economy of emancipation while producing proper ethnographies of this process. Following Katz (2001, 2011) and Wright (2013), I believe it is time to critically engage with the theory of accumulation by dispossession from a feminist perspective to connect this macro theory to the micro, everyday experiences and meanings of gendered dispossessions and contestations to gentrification and displacement.

In a nutshell, I argue for a feminist engagement with gentrification theory building processes, employing gender as an analytical tool to investigate the inequalities and power relations involved in the production of space during gentrification. I also believe that such an engagement can help us to recognize the possibility of a space of intervention and of feminist praxis to correct the widespread gendered inequalities and dispossessions involved in processes of gentrification and to construct spaces that celebrate non-hierarchized differences.

REFERENCES

Alkan, A. (2005) *Yerel Yönetimler ve Cinsiyet: Kadınların Kentte Görünmez Varlığı* [Local Governments and Gender: The Invisible Presence of Women in Cities], Istanbul: Dipnot.

Beauregard, R. (1986) 'The chaos and complexity of gentrification', in Smith, N. and Williams, P. (eds), *Gentrification of the City*, Boston: Allen and Unwin.

Bondi, L. (1991) 'Gender divisions and gentrification: a critique', *Transactions of the Institute of British Geographers*, 16, 190–198.

Bondi, L. (1999) 'Gender, class and gentrification: enriching the debate', *Environment and Planning D: Society and Space*, 17, 261–282.

Bondi, L. and D. Rose (2003) 'Constructing gender, constructing the urban: a review of Anglo-American feminist urban geography', *Gender, Place & Culture*, 10(3), 229–245.

Boterman, W. and Bridge, G. (2015) 'Gender, class and space in the field of parenthood: comparing middle-class fractions in Amsterdam and London', *Transactions of the Institute of British Geographers*, 40(2), 249–261.

Butler, T. (1997) *Gentrification and the Middle Classes*, Aldershot: Ashgate.

Butler, T. and Hamnett, C. (1994) 'Gentrification, class and gender: some comments on Warde's "gentrification of consumption"', *Environment and Planning D: Society and Space*, 12, 477–493.

Crenshaw, K. (1991) 'Mapping the margins: intersectionality, identity politics, and violence against women of color', *Stanford Law Review*, 43(6), 1241–1299.

Desmond, M. (2012) 'Eviction and reproduction of urban poverty', *American Journal of Sociology*, 118(1), 88–133.

Desmond, M. (2016) *Evicted: Poverty and Profit in the American City*, New York: Crown Publishers.

Doshi, S. (2013) 'The politics of the evicted: redevelopment, subjectivity, and difference in Mumbai's slum frontier', *Antipode*, 45, 844–865.

Ergin, N. (2006) *Grassroots Resistance Against Urban Renewal, The Case of Güzeltepe, Istanbul.* Unpublished Master's Thesis, Department of Sociology, Middle East Technical University, Ankara.

Erman, T. (2016) *Mış gibi Site: Ankara'da Bir TOKİ-Gecekondu Dönüşüm Sitesi*. [Like a Housing Estate: A TOKI- Gecekondu Transformation Housing Estate in Ankara], Istanbul: İletişim Yayınları.

Hackworth, J. (2002) 'Post recession gentrification in New York City', *Urban Affairs Review*, 37(6), 815–843.

Hubbard, P. (2004) 'Revenge and injustice in the neoliberal city: uncovering masculinist agendas', *Antipode*, 36(4), 665–686.

Huse, T. (2014, *Everyday Life in the Gentrifying City. On Displacement, Ethnic Privileging and the Right to Stay Put*, London: Routledge.

Karsten, L. (2003) 'Family gentrifiers: challenging the city as a place simultaneously to build a career and to raise children', *Urban Studies*, 40, 2573–2584.

Karsten, L. (2007) 'Housing as a way of life', *Housing Studies*, 22, 83–98.

Katz, C. (2001) 'Vagabond capitalism and the necessity of social reproduction', *Antipode*, 33, 709–728.

Katz, C. (2011) 'Accumulation, excess, childhood: toward a countertopography of risk and waste', *Documents d'Anàlisi Geogràfica*, 57, 47–60.

Kern, L. (2010) 'Gendering reurbanisation: women and new-build gentrification in Toronto', *Population, Space and Place*, 16(5), 363–379.

Kern, L. (2011) *Sex and the Revitalized City: Gender, Condominium Development, and Urban Citizenship*, Vancouver: UBC Press.

Kern, L. (2013) 'All aboard? Women working the spaces of gentrification in Toronto's Junction', *Gender, Place & Culture*, 20(4), 510–527.

Knopp, L. (1990) 'Some theoretical implications of gay involvement in an urban land market', *Political Geography Quarterly*, 9, 337–352.

Lees, L. (2000) 'Reappraisal of gentrification: towards a "geography of gentrification"', *Progress in Human Geography*, 24(3), 389–408.

Lees, L. (2012) 'The geography of gentrification: thinking through comparative urbanism', *Progress in Human Geography*, 36(2), 155–171.

Lees, L., Shin, H. and López-Morales, E. (2016) *Planetary Gentrification*, Cambridge: Polity Press.

Lees, L., Slater, T. and Wyly, E. (2008) *Gentrification*, New York: Routledge.

Ley, D. (1986) 'Alternative explanations for inner city gentrification: a Canadian assessment', *Annals of the Association of American Geographers*, 76, 521–535.

Markusen, A. (1981) 'City spatial structure, women's household, and national urban policy', in Stimpson, C., Dixler, E., Nelson, M. and Yatrakis, K. (eds), *Women and the American City*, Chicago, IL: University of Chicago Press, pp. 20–41.

Massey, D. (1994) *Space, Place, and Gender*, Minneapolis, MN: University of Minnesota Press.

McDowell, L. (1999) *Gender, Identity and Place: Understanding Feminist Geographies*, Minneapolis: University of Minnesota Press.

Mills, A. (2007) 'Gender and *Mahalle* (Neighborhood) space in Istanbul', *Gender, Place & Culture*, 14(3), 335–354.

Mills, A. (2010) *Streets of Memory: Landscape, Tolerance, and National Identity in Istanbul*, Athens GA: University of Georgia Press.

Papayannis, M. (2000) 'Sex and the revanchist city: zoning out pornography in New York', *Environment and Planning D: Society and Space*, 18(3), 341–353.

Patch, J. (2008) '"Ladies and gentrification": new stores, residents, and relationships', in DeSena, R. and Hutchinson, R. (eds), *Gender in an Urban World*, Bingley: JAI Press.

Paton, K. (2014) *Gentrification: A Working-Class Perspective*, London: Routledge.

Peake, L. (2016) 'The twenty-first-century quest for feminism and the global urban', *International Journal of Regional and Urban Studies*, 40(1), 219–227.

Peake, L. and Rieker, M. (2013) 'Rethinking feminist interventions into the urban', in Peake, L. and Rieker, M. (eds), *Rethinking Feminist Interventions into the Urban*, Routledge: London and New York, pp. 1–22.

Phillips, M. (1993) 'Rural gentrification and the processes of class colonisation', *Journal of Rural Studies*, 9(2), 123–140.

Qian, J., He, S. and Liu, L. (2013) 'Aestheticisation, rent-seeking, and rural gentrification amidst China's rapid urbanisation: the case of Xiaozhou village, Guangzhou', *Journal of Rural Studies*, 32, 331–345.

Robinson, J. (2006) *Ordinary Cities: Between Modernity and Development*, London: Routledge.

Robinson, J. (2011) 'Cities in a world of cities: the comparative gesture', *International Journal of Urban and Regional Research*, 35(1), 1–23.

Rose, D. (1984) 'Rethinking gentrification: beyond the uneven development of Marxist urban theory', *Environment and Planning D: Society and Space*, 1, 47–74.

Rose, D. (1989) 'Toward post-Fordist families? Some implications of recent Canadian labour force restructuring for gender dynamics among inner-city and suburban households', *Zeitschrift fur Kanada-Studien*, 19, 147–162.

Rose, D. and Le Bourdais, C. (1986) 'The changing conditions of female single parenthood in Montreal's inner city and suburban neighborhoods', *Urban Resources*, 3, 45–52.

Sakızlıoğlu, B. (2014) *A Comparative Look at Residents' Displacement Experiences: The Cases of Amsterdam and Istanbul*. Unpublished PhD Thesis, Utrecht University, The Netherlands.

Skeggs, B. (1997) *Formations of Class and Gender: Becoming Respectable*, London: SAGE.

Smith, N. (1987) 'Of yuppies and housing: gentrification, social restructuring, and the urban dream', *Environment and Planning. D: Society and Space*, 5, 151–172.

Smith, N. (1996) *The New Urban Frontier: Gentrification and the Revanchist City*, London: Routledge.

Soytemel, E. (2013) 'The power of the powerless: neighborhood based self-help networks of the poor in Istanbul', *Women's Studies International Forum*, 41(1), 76–87.

Soytemel, E. and Sen, B. (2014) 'Networked gentrification: place making strategies and social networks of middle class gentrifiers in Istanbul', in Koçak, D. and Koçak, O. (eds), *Whose City is That? Culture, Design, Spectacle and Capital in Istanbul*, Cambridge Scholars Publications, pp. 68–94.

Van den Berg, M. (2012) 'Femininity as a city marketing strategy: gender bending in Rotterdam', *Urban Studies*, 49, 153–168.

Van den Berg, M. (2013) 'City children and genderfied neighborhoods. The new generation as urban regeneration strategy', *International Journal for Urban and Regional Research*, 37(2), 523–536.

Van den Berg, M. (2016) 'The discursive uses of Jane Jacobs for the genderfying city: understanding the productions of space for post-Fordist gender notions', *Urban Studies*, online research article, article first published online: 6 December 2016.

Warde, A. (1991) 'Gentrification as consumption: issues of class and gender', *Environment and Planning D: Society and Space*, 9(2), 223–232.

Wekerle, G. (1984) 'A woman's place is in the city', *Antipode*, 16, 11–19.

Wright, M. (2013) 'Feminicidio, narcoviolence, and gentrification in Ciudad Juárez: the feminist fight', *Environment and Planning D: Society and Space*, 31(5), 830–845.

Yuval-Davis, N. (2006) 'Intersectionality and feminist politics', *European Journal of Women Studies*, 13, 193–210.

Zengin, A. (2014) 'Trans-Beyoğlu: Kentsel Dönüşüm, Şehir Hakkı ve Trans Kadınlar' [Trans-Beyoglu: Urban Transformation, Right to the City and Trans Women], in Candan, A. B. and Ozbay, C. (eds), *Yeni Istanbul Çalışmaları: Sınırlar, Mücadeleler, Açılımlar* [New Istanbul Works: Limits, Contestations, Openings], Istanbul: Metis Yayınlar.

PART 4

TYPES OF GENTRIFICATION

14. Slum gentrification
Eduardo Ascensão

14.1 INTRODUCTION

In this chapter I define 'slum gentrification' (Lees 2014a) as the process of capital or material investment in poor and informal built environments, which can be associated with a new (or renewed) interest in the cultures of such places by mainstream urban cultures (in a particular city or globally), followed by changes in the built environment related to upgrade or renewal projects in those areas, and finally resulting in the partial or total substitution of incumbent populations from the sites of investment. Other gentrification scholars (e.g. Lees et al 2016; Lees 2014a,b) include formal built environments that have become stigmatized and disinvested as slums, like public housing estates in Euro-American cities.

As such, slum gentrification here encompasses both (1) the cultural and social re-appreciation of informal housing areas (which includes activities such as slum tours, other forms of cultural consumption known as favela chic or the more straightforward fact of a poor urban area becoming a de-stigmatized residential option), which, frequently in tandem with public urban upgrade programs, leads to a new appeal for slightly more affluent populations to move in, resulting in rises in rent prices and ultimately in the pushing out of the more vulnerable and lowest-income sections of the existing population, who may have lived on the site for decades; and (2) a different process, closer to classic slum clearance, where public- or private-led urban renewal projects lead to the displacement of incumbent slum populations to social housing in more peripheral and less valued locations, thus entailing a complete substitution of populations. Both processes are relationally porous, in the sense that elements usually associated with the first process can also appear on the second, and vice versa. Moreover, each sub-set takes slightly different forms across the world, with heterogeneous local variations placed within a continuum between one and the other. The one common element across different geographies and across the different segments of such continuum is that local variations of the gentrifying process tend to be mistaken for simple overflows coming from a general dynamics of urban improvement, with the problems associated with the gentrification of slum areas often depreciated as collateral damage by local governments, the real estate sector and other actors.

In abstract terms, the first process can be associated with consumption-related theories of gentrification (e.g. Ley 1996), only applied to informal, illegal or squatter settlements. This is because the typical subjects of this type of slum gentrification are middle-class individuals or households who visit or move to neighbourhoods considered 'authentic', 'dangerous' or 'popular' in order to 'consume' an urban experience that does not exist elsewhere in their city, with the resulting effects easily filed under a demand-driven urban economics. In reverse, the second process can be associated with production of space-related theories of gentrification (e.g. Smith 1979, 1996), in the sense that it often describes the unmistakable effects at a local scale of broader processes of national and transnational capital investment in cities as well as of the role that public policies and housing programs have in shaping the production of space of particular urban regimes. However, empirical evidence also suggests, as with other forms of gentrification, that the two explanations are not mutually exclusive (see Slater 2011) and sometimes co-exist in the same site, if not necessarily at the same time and usually in reference to different sections of the same settlement.

14.2   SLUM GENTRIFICATION I. TRICKLE OUT OF SITE: DYNAMICS OF GENTRIFICATION IN INFORMAL AREAS

The first process is relatively uncontested in the various literatures focusing on slums or on gentrification. It is easily identifiable by the existence of a social atmosphere where one or a series of informal settlements becomes culturally relevant to the larger metropolitan area they are a part of (to which they could originally be more or less disconnected) – via films, television programs, music, and so on – and subsequently the land and housing stocks which were outside the formal mechanisms of urban capitalism (but could already be regulated by local customs and resident associations) become commodified.

14.2.1   Tourism and State Intervention in the Celebrity Slum

Among those settlements are a number of 'celebrity slums' in different cities across the world. Names such as Rocinha, Vidigal or Santa Marta in Rio de Janeiro (Freire-Medeiros 2009; Cummings 2015; Ost and Fleury 2013); Dharavi in Mumbai (Mukhija 2003; McFarlane 2012), Kibera in Nairobi (Gulyani and Talukdar 2008) and Makoko or Ajegunle in Lagos, among others, have all undergone long processes of insertion into the touristic circuits of their respective cities (Freire-Medeiros 2009; Rolfes 2010; Frenzel 2014). They have also seen the set-up of more or less experimental interventions involving infrastructural upgrade and neighbourhood image re-branding in the area.[1] In addition, these settlements have seen their name and image used as metonyms for the 'slum' typology across the world, whether in globally distributed fiction films such as 'Slumdog Millionaire' (featuring both real and staged parts of Dharavi) or 'The Constant Gardener' (with scenes shot in Kibera); television documentaries such as the BBC's 'Welcome to Lagos' (with its episode 2 centered in Makoko); or popular academic books (Koolhaas et al 2001; Neuwirth 2006). All have helped to institute a common grammar on informal settlements in mega- or world-class cities, based on such paradigmatic slums.[2] These settlements are perfect illustrations of 'the slum as spectacle', a process whereby

---

[1]   The latter includes using specific parts of their urban morphology as visual motifs for the 're-branding' process, something which can be illustrated by the painting of Favela Santa Marta's main square (Praça Cantão) by the Dutch group Favela Painting in association with the Brazilian paint company Coral, owned by the AkzoNobel chemical corporation (Figure 14.1).

[2]   The celebrity slum is not exclusive to megacities in the Global South. Real Cañada Galiana in Madrid (Aguilera 2016); Le Samaritain in La Courneuve, Paris (idem); Cova da Moura in Lisbon (Beja-Horta 2006; Ascensão 2016); or the Ponte Mammolo refugee camp in Rome (Agostini 2011) are, albeit much smaller in population size, well-known cases of informal settlements in Europe.

'visualisations of [poverty and] stigma can become commodified' (Jones and Sanyal 2015: 432). In becoming subject to intangible commodification, they have also attracted (variable) capital investments into their local economies, resulting in more tangible forms of commodification. This is where slum gentrification begins.

One of the cities where the process is more advanced is Rio de Janeiro – also because favelas have been integral to the city since the early 20th century (Valladares 2006) – so to follow some examples located there illustrates the way the process can typically unfold. The first investments tend to be public programs aimed at the redevelopment of the areas. Initiatives such as the late 1990s Favela Bairro program (Riley et al. 2001), which rightly aim to upgrade settlements through the provision of sanitation infrastructure, collective services and housing upgrades, prepare the specific settlements where they are implemented for future capital investment. Alongside, public or private utility companies tend to use such initiatives as enablers to provide stable electric power, clean drinkable water or access to telecommunications to hitherto neglected populations; in other words, to open up new markets for their businesses (Ost and Fleury 2013). This is one of the main drivers of slum gentrification: relatively independent and informal economies suddenly become formalized, with untapped capital conducted to the formal economy. Living costs tend to go up, paving the way for gross inequalities in access to services, which previously were informally arranged and accessed. The question Ost and Fleury (2013) ask is if 'the market goes up the morro [the hill], does citizenship come down?' (idem: 635). The answer is often that, despite the different initiatives' benevolent intentions, it does not necessarily happen according to plan, with gentrification pressures appearing as a by-product of these investments.

Another type of state intervention in informal settlements that works as an indication of gentrification pressures, one complementary to that of infrastructural and housing amelioration, is bespoke or innovative community policing. It is a common feature around the world, from Pacifying Police Units in Rio (Yutzy 2012; Leite 2014; Menezes 2015) to panchayats in Indian slums (Roy et al. 2004). While they are frequently introduced by the conjoined desires of local governments and private companies to pacify and manage hitherto insurgent urban spaces, they often do respond to the real desires of inhabitants to defend themselves against the arbitrary violence of different actors in informal settlements – for instance in Rio's favelas, against the dual violence perpetrated against residents by the very corrupt military police, as well as by organized drug gangs (Machado da Silva 2008). Again, Ost and Fleury (2013: 660) have shown for the case of the Santa Marta favela in Rio de Janeiro how the installation of a police pacification unit (*UPP-Unidade de Polícia Pacificadora*) has meant a 200 percent increase in rents in the top areas of the neighbourhood and a 75 percent increase in the bottom ones.

At the end of this process of infrastructure upgrade and security normalization, it is common to witness the opening up of hotels and hostels inside or in the vicinities of the settlement (see Cummings 2015 for the case of Vidigal, in Rio). At this point, too, slum tours are typically instituted in the area.[3] Due to all these intersecting dynamics,

---

[3]   Slum tours range from activities set up by middle-class individuals from outside the settlements which may not produce a great deal of investment in the area, such as those at Rocinha in Rio (Freire-Medeiros 2011: 28); to tours and activities set up by residents themselves, who despite having to navigate the same media landscape and touristic system to canvass for clients are still able, for example, to provide decent salaries for tour

Source: Photo by author.

*Figure 14.1   Visual intervention at Favela Santa Marta's main square (Praça Cantão)
and tourists, 2015*

settlements undergo relatively abrupt increases in rent prices that change the rent structure
in the settlement (which becomes re-directed to tourism, the nearby-living lower middle
classes or cultural avant-gardes, the latter much like the pioneer gentrifiers of US and
UK cities in the 1950s–1960s [Moran 2007]), often displacing the most vulnerable of

guides from the neighbourhood and overall play a part in improving the settlement's social image for the rest of
the city (research observation, Favela Santa Marta, 2015, author).

the (already vulnerable) existing populations. Growing tourism is by no means the only indicator of slum gentrification, but it is its most visible.

14.2.2   Slum Landlordism and the Disjuncture in the Investment Cycle

Still in high-profile settlements, but where the tourism tail-end of the process does not exist (not in the same way, at least), a slightly more intricate and invisible type of gentrification is usually constituted by some sort of disjuncture in the investment-improvement-gentrification cycle, one that nonetheless ends up again pushing the most vulnerable slum residents out of site. This is especially the case where instead of self-built settlements with some form of owner-occupancy in place the prevalent type of access to housing is made through informal rental systems – slum real estate, as Gulyani and Talukdar (2008) designate it. In the example they provide, Nairobi, they note how the city's slums constitute low-quality but high-cost shelter for the urban poor in the city, and see very little of the earnings from this informal housing economy re-invested (by a politically connected slum landlord class, often government employees) to upgrade housing conditions, thus end up in a continuous 'sub-optimal equilibrium' (idem: 1917), one which provides housing for around 30 percent of the city's population. The disjuncture here is the absence of re-investment. In such situations, 'slum upgrade programs that create assets – such as housing with legal title – for slum residents that the better-off [also] lack are likely to be the subject of gentrification' (idem: 1921). It is poor eats very poor: once housing conditions or tenure are improved, home or deeds are quickly commodified and either grabbed by a slightly more affluent household or re-appropriated by the slum landlord class able to enforce evictions and passed on to those more affluent households.

14.2.3   Upgrade and Entrepreneurship in Ordinary Slums

Not dependent on the existence of slum landlordism but rather more exclusively related to the effects of slum upgrade projects, a comparable process exists in many, less renowned informal settlements around the world. For instance in Maputo, Mozambique, slum upgrade projects conducted under the aegis of UN Habitat in informal areas near the city centre, such as Mafalala, Polana Caniço A or Maxaquene, have meant that those on the lowest incomes and tenure status security have been pushed further out, to areas such as Zimpeto or Magoanine B and C (Jorge and Melo 2014). In Polana Caniço A (adjacent to the Sommerschield wealthy district), upgrade projects were immediately followed by the creation of a market to sell plots, which were informally transacted but sanctioned by municipal authorities. This means that those more vulnerable economically tend to sell and move away, substituted by lower middle-class individuals looking to build a detached, gated house. In addition, the PROMAPUTO plan in the area also meant the demolition of some of the settlement's sections to make way for new roads, so the atmosphere among residents was that 'the neighbourhood is not for us anymore' (idem: 65). Slowly, trickle out slum gentrification, not in the way of cultural appreciation or through slum landlordism but rather related to the settlements' proximity to the city centre, has seen the restructuring of these settlements' populations. Likewise, in Jakarta, Indonesia, Budiarto (2005) states that gentrification in upgraded *kampungs* can be explained in two layers.[4] The first is that land prices increase and 'dwellers quickly spot a financial profit which increases the chance of out-migration and the growth of *kampungs* in other areas' (idem: 5). This is 'trickle out slum gentrification' in its simplest form. The second is more complex and is that as the *kampung* morphological structure is messed about in upgrade projects, so are kinship and work relationships; leading to a type of social and mental displacement even whilst remaining immobile. In short, slum upgrade projects (modelled after the UN-Habitat intervention paradigm or not) tend to be followed by the rapid increase of land and house values in the upgraded settlements, often resulting in the peripherization of significant sections of the target populations.

Such prevailing universes of displacement can nonetheless, as McFarlane (2012) has shown, be recast within broader urban entrepreneurialism agendas and become internalized as such by residents and activists. In such a situation, much-needed capital, symbolic and associational investment into activities to improve the lives of slum dwellers (such as collective toilet blocks, micro-finance projects and individual or collective squatter tenure) become framed within a particular 'conception of poverty as socioeconomic potential and the poor as entrepreneurial subjects' (idem: 2796). Such projects' overriding ideology aims to 'transform spaces of poverty from an exploited proletariat to emerging markets that will be embraced by financially disciplined subjects' (idem: 2800); that is, slum dwellers themselves need to embrace these tenets in order to benefit from the projects. An instructive consequence is the way paid toilet blocks in informal settlements – for instance in Dharavi, Mumbai, which authors such as Appadurai (2001) at a certain point seemed to validate – commodify personal hygiene to such an extreme (Davis 2006: 141; McFarlane 2012: 2804) that people's bodily needs have to be relocated elsewhere; i.e. out in the open (Datta 2012: 130; Desai et al. 2015). The Finnish documentary film 'For Kibera!' (2015, directed by Kati Juurus) is a tongue-in-cheek illustration of the perversions of such situations. Following a radio DJ from the settlement, it shows a place where 200 NGOs work, yet are unable to significantly improve people's everyday lives; where EU-financed toilet blocks require the user to pay and are thus beyond the means of most residents, who then defecate in the open, contaminating water flows; where benign projects featuring automatic launderettes encroach on the livelihoods of people whose job is precisely to wash clothes for other residents; and finally where UN Habitat-sponsored medium-rise apartment blocks in construction 150 metres away will clearly not be for Kibera's poor residents but for lower middle-class (by Kenyan standards) new arrivals. The film shows that at the end of insistent cycles of philanthropic investment in the settlement – which as in other places is centered on the project-based temporalities that define the work of large humanitarian or development NGOs worldwide, leaping from site to site in search of the good project (Krause 2014) – gentrification looms.

These seemingly unrelated dimensions of life in informal settlements show that many such settlements have become spaces of social experimentation for forms of governing the precarious lives of the urban poor – much like colonial cities were in the early 20th century (Rabinow 1989). Desai and Loftus (2012) argue that at the core of the problem is

---

[4]   Jakarta experienced a mode of urban expansion locally designated as *desakota* (expressing a continuum between the village and urban lifestyles), which hinges on the different uses of the vernacular *kampung* urban form. In its poorest versions, the *kampung* (traditional village) is no longer associated with rural settings but with slums. Several such settlements in the city have been upgraded and gentrification ensued.

the way infrastructure investments in slum areas have become conduits through which a 'landlord class' switches capital from a primary to a secondary circuit. Thus they prescribe a specific research agenda for the near future:

> Without a clearer understanding of the circulation of capital through land in slum areas there is a serious risk that benevolent investments in infrastructure will merely strengthen powerful stakeholders operating within and across slum areas, while increasing the already precarious nature of slum dwellers' lives. (idem: 790)

14.3   SLUM GENTRIFICATION II. WHOLESALE GET OUT!: THE GENTRIFICATION OF ENTIRE INFORMAL AREAS

The need to understand the circulation of capital in slum areas directs us to the second sub-process of slum gentrification. It is one of a more direct and violent nature, and consists of wholesale clearance of slum areas as part of urban redevelopment plans that stretch beyond each given settlement. Such redevelopment plans tend to be driven in four different sub-modalities.

14.3.1   World-city Visioning and the 'Nuisance' of Slums

The first one involves city visioning projects aiming to attain world or global city status which earmark slum areas for reinvestment in processes of major spatial, economic and social restructuring of the city. The emblematic cases here are both Indian, Mumbai's Slum Rehabilitation Scheme, which introduced market incentives and developer participation in order to resettle slum dwellers and retrieve the entire, or parts of the cleared, space for middle-class developments (Mukhija 2003; Doshi 2013); and Delhi's urban middle classes' reclaiming of urban spaces from slums and slum dwellers with recourse to Public Interest Litigation, which sought to evict 'illegal settlements' on the grounds that they were/are environmental and societal nuisances (Ghertner 2010; Datta 2012: 67–83). They involve public-private partnerships in which the seduction of private developers to invest in slum areas is complemented with the guarantee that the state will enforce the rules towards off-site resettlement, i.e. displacement. However, this sub-modality is not an Indian particularity; it is replicated in other locations. In Lagos, Nigeria, Nwanna (2015) briefly mentions how, amidst a backdrop of massive demolition of houses in informal settlements in the rest of the city, some sections of the emblematic Makoko were razed with the justification of being 'environmental nuisances that undermined the mega-city status of Lagos' (idem: 313).

Forms of dispossession by the state which have parallels with cities' world-class aspirations but are compounded by other elements include those such as Luanda, Angola, where the re-privatization of land has often presupposed the clearance of long-standing informal settlements. The Luanda Sul/Talatona urban plan has overseen the forced and violent eviction of some of the oldest musseques (as informal settlements are called) in the city. Throughout the civil war, urban expansion in Luanda was fuelled by internal migration from conflict areas, with poor people settling in previously existing informal settlements (some of which were dated to colonial times) and expanding them. At the end of the war, all land was nationalized. Then, during the past decade renewal plans under the rubric of 'public good projects' justified that previously public land could be seized from squatter settlers living on it or from small farmers in the outer peripheries (on the latter, see Waldorff 2016). So for instance the plan that municipal company Edurb developed in collaboration with Brazilian private construction conglomerate Odebrecht (which has close ties to the Angolan regime), meant that settlements such as the Chicala neighbourhood and others were, or are to be, razed.[5] In this case, slum gentrification in bulk is the result of a previously Marxist, presently entrepreneurial contested political regime.

14.3.2   The Gated Highrise Template

The second sub-modality is constituted by slightly different national or transnational investments in urban space made in very particular prime locations, often catering to national and foreign wealthy populations; that is, condominiums and luxury highrises on the cleared land where informal settlements once existed. An illustration is Rio's Vila Autódromo (Silvestre and Oliveira 2012; Comité Popular da Copa 2015: 27; Villegas et al. 2016), a former fishing village with informal housing near the Olympic Park and the Bus Rapid Transit west line, which has been obstinately demolished and will make way for luxury highrise towers taking advantage of the lagoon environment, to be commercialized by the 'leasing company' involved in the construction of the Olympic Park. To an extent, it must be noted, these precisely located investments come on the back of previous citywide investments: for instance the Dharavi Redevelopment Plan in Mumbai (Weinstein 2014), pushed by millionaire Mukesh Mehta and other transnational real estate investors before the global recession of 2008 (it has since been abandoned), was clearly a culmination of the Slum Rehabilitation Scheme mentioned above. In Accra, Ghana, Gillespie (2016) identifies the Old Fadama informal squatter settlement near the city centre, an area reclaimed from swamp land by squatters which still provides an informal rental market to low-income populations, as being at risk of a similar process. Plans to redevelop it include passing the occupied public land to private investors to build high-rise mixed-use developments, and with it will come the eviction and displacement of the existing low-income squatters. One quote from a planning official involved in the redevelopment plan is illuminating regarding the plan's nature: '[It will be] a form of upgrading, but not the type of upgrading where we are going to legalise people staying here' (idem: 72). Evictions will obviously follow, is the message. The quote also illustrates a method that extends well beyond Accra or this sub-modality, one by which the terminologies coming from the diverse portfolio of possible state intervention in informal settlements (slum upgrade or rehabilitation programs, infrastructure provision, land titling schemes, and so on) are discursively re-worked by municipal authorities to mean much more blunt plans to simply demolish and remove low-income populations, all the while presenting them to potential investors or, unashamedly, to current residents, as benevolent 'upgrade' or 'redevelopment' plans. Finally, on the recurrence of the residential high-rise building type in these cases, it is historically ironic that the most common architectural template (the residential highrise) for this type of neoliberal urban restructuring is precisely the one

---

[5]   Social architect Paulo Moreira has established the Chicala Observatory (www.chicala.org), an online archive of the neighbourhood pending demolition, before people are displaced to mass housing 20 km away from Luanda's centre.

Source: Courtesy of Paulo Moreira.

Figure 14.2 Demolition 'for public good', Chicala, Luanda, 2015

233

which was pathologized for decades in Anglo-American urban studies (Newman 1972; Jencks 1977; Coleman 1985; cf. Jacobs 2006; Jacobs and Lees 2013). Over the past three decades, it has only needed to add the prefix 'luxury' or 'gated' to become the preferred housing type for affluent populations.

14.3.3 The Mega-event Urban Complex

Third, the zenith of slum gentrification in bulk occurs when it is connected to mega-events which require, or are the excuse for, substantive investment in public infrastructure, such as the Olympic Games, the football World Cup, the Commonwealth Games, International Fairs, and so on. For instance in Delhi, the 2010 Commonwealth Games led to as many as 200,000 people being forcibly evicted from their homes (HLRN Housing and Land Rights Network 2011); in South Africa, the 2010 football World Cup also involved dozens of thousands of evictions (Ngonyama 2010); and in Rio, sum totals are not yet finalized but preliminary official counts register 20,000 evicted families for the 2009–2013 period alone (Faulhaber and Azevedo 2015: 16). Significant shares of these people were slum/shack/favela dwellers, and to use HLRN's apt description, such processes tend to amount to 'planned displacement'. They take place during periods of strong economic growth that see the emergence of new middle classes, urban restructuring from industrial to service economies and when the mega-event 'fix' is too tempting to pass. In such circumstances, city administrations backed by national governments institute a state of exception regarding due procedure for evictions in areas where the urban poor reside, often cynically bending existing legislation and housing programs to the ulterior aims of beautification or of reserving prime urban space for future development for elites. For instance in Rio, the Minha Casa Minha Vida (MCMV) federal housing program was the preferential instrument to clear entire favelas or some of their sections near the Olympic venues while rehousing their inhabitants in MCMV estates 20 or 30 km away (idem: 67; see Figure 14.4). The mega-event syndrome (Müller 2015) has many different symptoms, among them being one of the more forceful drivers of slum gentrification (Davis 2011; Shin and Li 2013; Gaffney 2015). Finally, the amount of investment and political energy devoted by governing elites to the latter process is a clear indication that the displacement of poor populations from the sites of previous residence is not simply an unfortunate overflow of a broader movement for modernization for all (if it was so, in abstract it could be remedied, for example with in situ upgrading [see Huchzermeyer 2009]) but rather a conscious and inevitable outcome of freeing up space for more affluent populations.

14.3.4 Implementation Overflows of Urban Policies and Housing Provision

Fourth, up to a point slum gentrification can come from the unintended overflows of housing policies and programs which exacerbate rent gaps in informal areas in the process of being renewed and push the most vulnerable away. López-Morales (2011) tells of Santiago de Chile's inner city *poblaciones* (self-built working class areas, which are not exactly slums but rather the immediately better-off residential typology for the urban poor; see more below) where differential ground rents exist for incumbent populations or for large-scale developers in areas deemed for renewal. A state-subsidized market for renewal coupled with liberalizing regulatory tweaks mean that current owner-occupiers have access to a lower capital ground rent than market agents of renewal. López-Morales' focus is on a long disinvested municipality, where housing is of 'pure use value' (idem: 352) but which will undergo a rapid process of commodification leading to the displacement of incumbent populations in favour of large-scale developers. In Cape Town's Westlake district, Lemanski (2014) integrates the concept of downward raiding with that of gentrification to better explain the process of the sale of low-standard state-subsidized houses by low-income households to businesses and wealthy families from nearby areas (who use them as housing for their employees). She further explains how this raid into low-income public housing leaves the sellers destitute of any future public subsidy and potentially excluded from standard housing for life. Again this area is, albeit poor, not a slum (even if a significant share of the sellers will end up in informal settlements down the line). However, this kind of low-income variation of the 'right to buy' seems to be a worrying 'forerunner for the future rather than a unique outlier' (idem: 2953) and not just for South Africa: slum renewal projects coupled with individual tenure can be subject to a similar process, as mentioned above. In both these cases, applying the slum label is a slight overstretch given their housing types sit just above the slum category. However, it is also not completely false given their sub-standard housing conditions, their close relationship with slums – e.g. the residents of low-income public housing would otherwise be living in informal settlements and, indeed, may still end up in them – and the sense of being precursors to what may happen to informal settlements. Where the slum epithet is entirely appropriate is in analysis of the implementation wrongs of a slum eradication program in Lisbon (Ascensão 2015). The PER rehousing program (1993–present) involved the demolition of 30,000 shanty dwellings spread out in slum pockets across the metropolitan area and the rehousing of its residents in public housing estates. The program involved both in situ rehousing (with apartment blocks built on the sites of the previous informal settlements) – a just solution – and clearance and re-housing in more peripheral, segregated and underserviced housing estates across the metropolitan area. The Marianas, Fontaínhas or Pedreira dos Húngaros settlements were among the latter cases. In more complicated cases where the squatted land was privately owned and local governments failed to expropriate it in timely fashion, the original privileged locations were earmarked for residential development for the white middle classes and the mainly black immigrant poor populations were displaced to scattered destinations (discursively presented as a non-segregating option) or even left homeless if not deemed eligible for the program. The Quinta da Serra, Santa Filomena or Bairro 6 de Maio settlements were among the latter cases. In short, despite substantial public investment, only in the first of the three types of cases did this eradication program in Lisbon not involve some degree of slum gentrification.

All these four sub-modalities do not involve the fine-detail capitalist mechanisms of displacement at the house or street level which the 'trickle out' process described in the first section entails. Rather, they come as the result of citywide urban changes emerging from strategic national and transnational policies coupled with substantial public and private investments. Furthermore, there are circuitous relations between the four sub-modalities when one considers developments at particular locations, with specific projects involving elements of more than one sub-modality. Hence Vila Autódromo, clearly related to the mega-event set of circumstances, is also correctly listed above as an example of transnational investors 'redeveloping' informal urban areas into luxury highrises.

14.4   SLUM GENTRIFICATION, AN UMBRELLA DESIGNATION: HETERODOX COMPARISON AND POSTCOLONIAL URBAN THEORY

That all these different things have come under the broad conceptual umbrella of slum gentrification is a view that has been consolidating in the literature. Previously, gentrification in, and of, slum areas was a phenomenon identifiable in sparse information which mentioned the possibility that informal settlements could be, and indeed were being, gentrified (e.g. Mukhija 2002: 568; Davis 2006: 43). However, the process tended to be subsumed in those descriptions by the concurrent or alternative processes the authors addressed – upgrading policies, Haussmanization and so on. What recent work has brought about is the reconfiguration of slum gentrification as a process in itself. Such a bold conceptual move by Lees, Shin and López-Morales (2015, 2016) aims to get to grips with the fact that a variegated yet common process can be witnessed in many cities in the world:

Property-led (re)investment in spatially constrained slum areas, the visibly changing urban landscapes of the global South, the social 'upgrading' of locale by incoming higher-income groups, and the direct or indirect displacement (or threats of displacement) of the lowest income groups in society as a whole, are four factors usually occurring at the same time in many places in the 'informal' urban world (Lees et al 2016: 168).

Inspired by the cosmopolitanism of Robinson's (2006, 2015) work and calls for a more horizontal comparative urban research and a less West-centric urban theory, they wish to take insight from different places in the in/formal world, irrespective of where the cities they are located in stand in global or world hierarchies. Importantly, they shy away from diffusionist logics that gentrification is transposed from cities in the Global North to those in the Global South, as well as from evolutionist ones, where gentrification is only a thing of advanced economies.

Regarding slum gentrification in particular, they understand the polysemic nature of the word 'slum' and its associated problems; that slums differ between themselves, that some face the threat of state-led evictions or are constantly harassed by the police or mafia squads, while in others 'slum dwellers may have land titles and the forms of displacement are more subtle and less obvious' (Lees et al 2016: 145). They also acknowledge that 'there are cases where slum gentrification simply means slum removal, [whilst] in other cases, it means the gentrification of slums in situ by wealthier in-movers' (idem: 147). Yet they still seek to understand what is it that is going on in the informal world that seems to pertain to a single (but complex) movement. They do so under the umbrella of 'slum gentrification', and they are not alone.

Nevertheless, slum gentrification is not a fully stabilized concept yet, as it conflates existing or growing theorizations of what has happened to many informal settlements around the world over the past two decades – the exacerbation of mechanisms of displacement which were perhaps mitigated in the 1970s-to-1990s period[6] – but it is slowly being theorized. Such theorizations oscillate between robust re-appraisals of Marxist categories such as accumulation by dispossession (López-Morales 2011, 2016), the re-use of other

---

[6]   When research on squatter settlements that runs from Mangin (1967) to Turner (1976) to Santos (1977) to Gilbert (2000), to name only four, may have had some effect on policy.

concepts such as 'urban commons' and 'enclosures' (Gillespie 2016; Ghertner 2014) and more empirically inflected descriptions of what happens at specific locations, with the latter's terminology in close relation to the described events, such as 'marginal gentrification' (Doshi 2015), 'hybrid gentrification' (Lemanski 2014) or 'area gentrification' (Ascensão 2015). Although using different lexicons, these are important undertakings in the sense they enable to put in comparison cases which previously ran the risk of not being compared or put in parallel at all.

14.5 CRITIQUES AND THE SOCIAL USE OF THE CONCEPT

Slum gentrification as a separate concept and not merely a descriptive aside has been criticized, starting with its wording: that it reads uncomfortably regarding both its slum and gentrification parts. First, it reads uncomfortably regarding the slum part because – as the recent debate on the stand-alone use of the word has pointed out – it re-uses a derogatory term from the late 19th century to refer to city areas that have since been more objectively classified as informal, illegal or squatter settlements, as low-income areas or similar denominations, thus making an unwelcome comeback to broad sweeping denigrations of the urban poor (Gilbert 2007). This much is true, but given the return of the word was mostly driven by actors with global reach such as the UN through its Millennium Goals agenda and its agency UN Habitat (2003, 2007), it became dominant vocabulary. One of the positive aspects of this otherwise negative situation is that the 'slum' – whether construed as an epistemological shorthand for complex urban theories of poverty in contemporary megalopolis (Rao 2006) or as fine-detail explorations of its rhetoric uses by slum dwellers and policy-makers (Arabindoo 2011) – makes crystal clear that slums in late-19th-century European and American cities and slums in early-21st-century metropolises across the world have been produced by potentially comparable processes of uneven development and structural income inequality which have become a pressing global issue across different disciplines (e.g. Wilkinson and Pickett 2009; Piketty 2014). Urban studies is no different in this attention to inequality, therefore the power of the word slum to emphasize such historical lineages somewhat justifies its usage and should not be thrown away.

Second, it reads uncomfortably regarding the gentrification part because it refers to a process that is not located in areas usually associated with gentrification such as historical districts that undergo periods of strong disinvestment or other working- or middle-class areas in the city, but rather in very poor informal environments, hitherto considered to be outside the mechanisms of capital investment in the formal city (cf. Desai and Loftus 2013). It is also uncomfortable because using the gentrification term may seem to camouflage what in effect are processes of forceful urban renewal: the gentrification label suggests a more benevolent string of events than do forced evictions or displacement, therefore many authors feel uncomfortable in using it.

And still, the term has become increasingly used worldwide and one of the reasons it has is because the dynamics of slum gentrification are indeed similar to those of classic gentrification: a cycle of disinvestment (or under-investment, as explained below) in existing working or poor city areas; followed by pioneer movements into these areas (to visit, inhabit or research – yes, academics are among the forces that push gentrification through, albeit by any means its most negative one), related to cultural distinction or to opportunities for investment; these pioneer movements then become entangled in city-wide or area-based modernizing projects; the built environment is subject to significant change; the areas enter relatively more mainstream residential choices; and finally this results in higher rents and other economic disadvantages to incumbent populations such as increasingly unsecure tenure; ultimately pushing people away.

Among the most vocal critics of the use of the phrase to describe this particular string of events are development geographers who claim that there is no such thing as 'slum gentrification' (noted in Lees et al 2016: 214), that there already exist concepts such as slum clearance and forced evictions which cover the most important elements of the process. However, such criticisms fail to notice how key elements such as the 'replacement of populations' and the 'cycles of investment in the built environment' are subsumed within those concepts as secondary; whereas in the gentrification literature they are central, as their use by residents and activists in several different contexts attest to (see below). Within this first group of critics, there is a sense that their criticisms come from the wish to protect the field of development geography and some of its fetishistic solutions (the above-mentioned toilet blocks and micro-finance, but also pre-paid water and electricity meters; see Loftus 2013; Baptista 2015), which have often been pushed via consultancy, research projects and general policy advice. One more example of development 'fixes' are transportation infrastructure projects, which in several parts of the world have led to the indiscriminate expulsion of populations residing in settlements the projects were to cross. For instance in the implementation of Manila's North Rail-South Rail Linkage Project, 35,000 households were relocated from long-standing informal settlements near the tracks to eleven dispersed sites outside Metro Manila (Choi 2016: 585). In short, such critiques fail to fully acknowledge the complications of development models.

Another set of preoccupations comes from Ghertner's (2014) 'sympathetic critique' of the efforts to extend gentrification theory into the Global South and his preference to shift the discussion on contemporary forms of urban displacement from gentrification to the concept of accumulation by dispossession (curiously also used by some of the authors he later criticized in more severe terms, such as Ernesto López-Morales [Ghertner 2015]). First, he states that gentrification is the reinvestment of capital in disinvested space for he (quite correctly) argues that slums are not disinvested space but rather underinvested space, with an informal cycle of investment by poor residents over time (idem: 1558). In this sense, what he offers is simply a rigid formulation of the core mechanisms of gentrification (that it must entail investment in disinvested, not underinvested, space) in order to criticize its extension to contexts of slum demolition and displacement. It is a weak argument that falls short of the more productive approach of the planetary gentrification thesis (Lees et al. 2016), especially since it is quite easy to demonstrate that informal settlements indeed undergo a first cycle of investment from builders-residents, except it is done informally. That is indeed the essence of one of the more controversial researchers on land titling in informal settlements (yet very influential with global elites), Hernando de Soto (2000): to get this first cycle of investment (which comprises several instances of non-monetary exchanges and investment) into the formal economy.[7]

---

[7]   Furthermore, in a slight conceptual expansion to canonic gentrification theory, the argument can also be made that, from the start, the efforts of informal settlers in constituting their built environments is a form of sweat equity, although one which unlike that of pioneer gentrifiers in the Global North is not rewarded at a later

Ghertner's second argument is stronger and needs to be factored in, although it is a maximalist argument. Reflecting on empirical evidence from Delhi, he notes how 'slums are not a passive stage in land privatization, rather they function as a central vehicle for facilitating the alienation of public land to private developers' (Ghertner 2014: 1562). He then describes these forms of privatization along the lines of 'enclosures' that privatize common land into exclusively owned plots and do away with use rights to land. He argues that resistance needs to be against all forms of privatization of public land, and states that all that antigentrification struggles do is try to prevent the 'deepening commoditization' (idem: 1563) of something that was already commodified rather than a more fundamental move to resist the conversion of public land into the commodity form in the first place. Ghertner would do well to read the work by Lees and others on the conversion of public land (council estates/public housing) into a commodity in relation to new-build gentrification.

Of course, slum dwellers facing the demolition of their houses in many parts of the world do not protest against the privatization of public land, because by experience they know these arguments hold no sway for local governments and private investors steeped in a neoliberal state of mind. Instead, they shout 'Gentrification!' as one of the few rallying cries that still has some effect on public opinion and policy-makers worldwide (see Shin et al. 2016: 459–461). Evidence from the already-cited Santa Marta favela in Rio de Janeiro shows the typical set of circumstances where 'gentrification' is a socially relevant word. The residents of the peak of the favela, which encroaches on an environmentally protected natural park standing on public land, were notified to leave under a legal exception that waives standard administrative procedure for evictions in favelas in the case of the need to protect the environment or of landslide risk. However, the space resulting from the foreseeable removals will not be used to reinstate the natural park but very likely a hotel that will take advantage of the spectacular views (Ost and Fleury 2013: 658; Menezes 2015: 256–258). Furthermore, in this case the opportunity for the top of the favela to become a touristic attraction is facilitated, in terms of access for tourists, by the funicular (*plano inclinado*) which was put in place in 2008 following a Favela Bairro-type upgrade program implemented by the state government in the early 2000s (*Programa Estadual de Urbanização*). Again you see the role of public infrastructure projects to initiate processes of urban value increase. But the point is that in their activism against the threat of imminent evictions, the banners residents hung outside their houses, which were aimed at the tourists who take the funicular on different tours to the neighbourhood, read 'Gentrification' and 'World Cup for whom?' ('*Copa para Quem?*'); not 'Against the privatization of public land'. Residents know that the latter, however apt it could be to describe the case, is laughable in terms of media and policy impact. Gentrification, for the time being, is still not!

Because gentrification is the label that, no matter how derided or criticized, better gets under neoliberalism's skin, it is a particularly good one to contest and resist it. As Bernt (2016: 638) has also noted, it allows local activists, critical scholars and progressive planners to come together and enter into dialogue with policy-makers and even, to a limited

---

point (when re-selling their house after value appreciation) but is rather subject to dispossession (when evicted after the land is turned into a different use).

Figure 14.3   Contestation against gentrification at the peak of the Santa Marta favela in Rio de Janeiro, 2015

extent, top decision-makers. The latter still have to respond to the cries of gentrification in redevelopment plans, but no longer bother responding to those against the privatization of the public realm. In contexts of severe power imbalances, such as dialogues between slum dwellers and city officials, to have a concept which may seem too moldable yet is understood by everyone in its underpinning of different struggles across the world to fight evictions and displacement, is of great importance and should be appreciated.

14.6   HOW TO RESEARCH SLUM GENTRIFICATION?

Evidence for slum gentrification across the world is varied and undeniable. However, because it is a contested topic further research is much needed. Possible ways to study it include longitudinal studies, which involve large household surveys (e.g. Gulyani and Talukdar 2008), usually possible only with funding from large 'donor' organizations (such as the World Bank, UN Habitat or the EU), international 'cooperation' programs (such as Germany's GTZ, France's Coopération successor AFD, USAID, and so on) or large NGOs. Optimally, such large studies should be designed to include research assistants hired where the study is taking place – for instance slum dwellers embarking on undergraduate or graduate studies – so that the experience and data gathered during the research project can be used after it is over.

On a similar scale, research into long-term changes in population types (by income, ethnicity, etc.) in specific wards and municipalities, based on Census data, can be illuminating to pinpoint slum gentrification (Hammel and Wyly 1996). To an extent also dependent on access to official data (or more difficultly achieved through residents' own records), the production of displacement maps provides excellent visual illustrations of the gentrification process, whether the centrifugal displacement from one site only (e.g. London Tenants Federation et al 2014: 8–9 on the Heygate Estate in London) or a more networked circulation across an entire city (Faulhaber and Azevedo 2015: 67 on Rio de Janeiro). A great example of digital dissemination of efforts to map gentrification is the Anti-Eviction Mapping Project documenting the effects of gentrification on San Francisco Bay Area residents (see http://www.antievictionmap.com).

For more modest research endeavors, the simplest way of assessing whether a specific informal settlement is undergoing gentrification is to check for rent hikes (Yutzy 2012; Ost and Fleury 2013). It is easier said than done as rent prices in informal settlements are informally constituted and not publically published (not even on rental websites) but it is worth pursuing. Next on the list is to understand the assemblage of policy and capital formations for specific renewal projects. This involves looking at the global repertoire of policies and models of intervention to understand the localized use and adaptation of such global paradigms (titling, upgrade, etc.); as well as looking at which particular investments are being made at particular sites. The latter may involve financial prospectuses that circulate among investors and where foreseeable land rent may be explicit. The financialization of housing (Aalbers 2008; Rolnik 2013) is a worldwide phenomenon and financialized investment on homeownership for former slum dwellers is a small but integral part of it.

Interviewing and following displaced households into their new surroundings or new ones as they come in (slum gentrifiers) can provide insights into definitions of home and

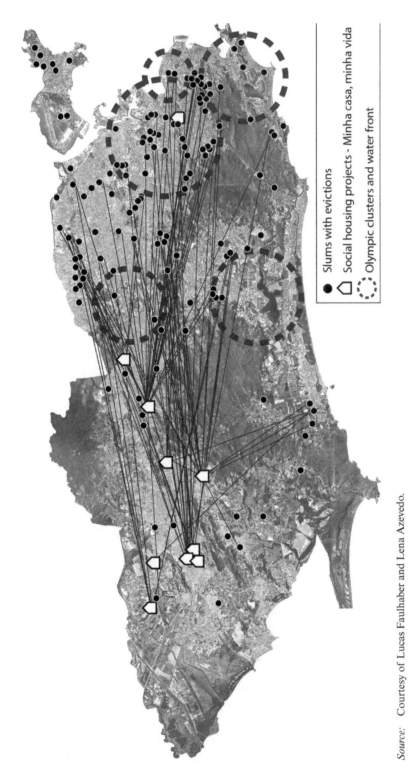

Source: Courtesy of Lucas Faulhaber and Lena Azevedo.

Figure 14.4 Displacement map of Rio de Janeiro

Legend:
- Slums with evictions
- Social housing projects - Minha casa, minha vida
- Olympic clusters and water front

dwelling in contexts of 'domicide' (Porteous and Smith 2001). Interviews and ethnographic research with local and outside housing activists, or with slum tour guides (Freire-Medeiros 2011; Durr 2012) will help us better understand the social and cultural background to gentrification in informal settlements. In addition, cultural geographers, anthropologists and sociologists may also want to investigate the discursive views on the slum in specific cities (such as the 'dangerous and insalubrious slum to be eradicated'; or the 'positive urban adaptation to be valued and capitalized'), present in media, policy documents or even in art and literature, as well as the cultures and lifestyles of early slum gentrifiers.

Other methods or combinations of methods to research slum gentrification can be added to the list, as this is a work in progress. One final item worth mentioning which can inspire researchers on slum gentrification in their future work goes back a few decades: Bunge's (1971) radical but hopeful method of 'setting up bivouac' in neighbourhoods at risk (in his case, Fitzgerald in Detroit in the late 1960s) was a partisan yet responsible and accountable method to 'see faithfully from another's point of view' (Merrifield 1995: 52). It included the use of extravagant indicators such as medical records of 'rat-bitten children', geo-referencing them in the city to point out the segregated spatiality of poverty and inequality (Bunge and Bordessa 1975: 326). Current researchers (in the present case, of settlements at risk of being razed) may take inspiration to be as bold and innovative to draw the attention of policy- and decision-makers to the injustices at work.

REFERENCES

Aalbers, M. (2008) 'The financialization of home and the mortgage market crisis', *Competition & Change*, 12(2), 148–166.

Agostini, G. (2011) *The forgotten housing demand: the urban slums in Rome, Italy*, Paper presented at the International RC21 conference 2011, [Online]. Available at: http://www.rc21.org/conferences/amsterdam2011/edocs/Session%2029/RT29-2-Agostini.pdf.

Aguilera, T. (2017) *Gouverner les Illegalismes Urbaines: Les Politique Publiques Face aux Squats et aux Bidonvilles dans les Regions de Paris et de Madrid (Governing urban illegalism: public policies against squats and slums in the Paris and Madrid regions)*, Paris: Dalloz.

Appadurai, A. (2001) 'Deep democracy: urban governmentality and the horizon of politics', *Environment and Urbanization*, 13(2), 23–43.

Arabindoo, P. (2011) 'Rhetoric of the "slum"', *City*, 15(6), 636–646.

Ascensão, E. (2015) 'Slum gentrification in Lisbon, Portugal: displacement and the imagined futures of an informal settlement', in Lees, L., Shin, H. and López-Morales, E. (eds), *Global Gentrifications: Uneven Development and Displacement*, Bristol, Policy Press, pp. 37–58.

Ascensão, E. (2016) 'Interfaces of informality: when experts meet informal settlers', *City*, 20(4), 563–580.

Baptista, I. (2015) '"We live on estimates": everyday practices of prepaid electricity and the urban condition in Maputo, Mozambique', *International Journal of Urban and Regional Research*, 39(5), 1004–1019.

Beja-Horta, A. (2006) 'Places of resistance: power, spatial discourses and migrant grassroots organizing in the periphery of Lisbon', *City*, 10(3), 269–285.

Bernt, M. (2016) 'Very particular, or rather universal? Gentrification through the lenses of Ghertner and López-Morales', *City*, DOI: 10.1080/13604813.2016.1143682.

Budiarto, L. (2005) 'Magersari: the spatial-culture of kampung settlements as an urban strategy in Indonesian cities and urban housing', *Proceedings of the XXXIII IAHS World Congress on Housing*, [Online]. Available at: http://www.repository.up.ac.za/dspace/bitstream/handle/2263/10394/Magersari%20the%20spatial-culture%20of%20kampung%20settlements%20as%20an%20u.pdf.

Bunge, W. (2011 [1971]) *Fitzgerald: Geography of a Revolution*, Athens, GA: University of Georgia Press.

Bunge, W. and Bordessa, R. (1975) *The Canadian Alternative: Survival, Expeditions and Urban Change*, Toronto: York University.

Cabannes, Y., Yafai, S. and Johnson, C. (2010) *How People Face Evictions*, London: Development and Planning Unit, University College London.

Choi, N. (2016) 'Metro Manila through the gentrification lens: disparities in urban planning and displacement risks', *Urban Studies*, 53(3), 577–592.

Coleman, A. (1985) *Utopia on Trial: Vision and Reality in Planned Housing*, London: Hillary Shipman Publishing.

Comité Popular da Copa (2015) *Rio 2016 Olympics: the exclusion games (Mega-Events and Human Rights Violations in Rio de Janeiro Dossier 4)*, Comité Popular da Copa [World Cup and Olympics Popular Committee of Rio de Janeiro, Rio de Janeiro].

Cummings, J. (2015) 'Confronting favela chic: the gentrification of informal settlements in Rio de Janeiro, Brazil', in Lees, L., Shin, H. and López-Morales, E. (eds), *Global Gentrifications: Uneven Development and Displacement*, Bristol: Policy Press, pp. 81–100.

Datta, A. (2012) *The Illegal City: Space, Law and Gender in a Delhi Squatter Settlement*, Farnham: Ashgate.

Davis, L. (2011) 'International events and mass evictions: a longer view', *International Journal of Urban and Regional Research*, 35(3), 582–599.

Davis, M. (2006) *Planet of Slums*, London: Verso.

De Soto, H. (2000) *The Mystery of Capital: Why Capitalism Triumphs in the West and Fails Everywhere Else*, London: Bantam Press.

Desai, V. and Loftus, A. (2013) 'Speculating on slums: infrastructural fixes in informal housing in the Global South', *Antipode*, 45(4), 789–808.

Desai, R., McFarlane, C. and Graham, S. (2015) 'The politics of open defecation: informality, body, and infrastructure in Mumbai', *Antipode*, 47(1), 98–120.

Doshi, S. (2013) 'The politics of the evicted: redevelopment, subjectivity, and difference in Mumbai's slum frontier', *Antipode*, 45(4), 844–865.

Doshi, S. (2015) 'Rethinking gentrification in India: displacement, dispossession and the spectre of development', in Lees, L., Shin, H. and López-Morales, E. (eds), *Global Gentrifications: Uneven Development and Displacement*, Bristol, Policy Press, pp. 101–119.

Dürr, E. (2012) 'Urban poverty, spatial representation and mobility: touring a slum in Mexico', *International Journal of Urban and Regional Research*, 36(4), 706–724.

Faulhaber, L. and Azevedo, L. (2015) *SMH 2016: Remoções no Rio de Janeiro Olímpico [SMH 2016: Removals in Olympic Rio de Janeiro]*, Rio de Janeiro: Mórula.

Freire-Medeiros, B. (2009) 'The favela and its touristic transits', *Geoforum*, 40, 580–588.

Freire-Medeiros, B. (2011) '"I went to the City of God": gringos, guns and the touristic favela', *Journal of Latin American Cultural Studies*, 20(1), 21–34.

Frenzel, F. (2014) 'Slum tourism and urban regeneration: touring inner Johannesburg', *Urban Forum*, 25, 431–447.

Gaffney, C. (2015) 'Gentrifications in pre-Olympic Rio de Janeiro', *Urban Geography*, DOI: 10.1080/02 723638.2015.1096115.

Ghertner, A. (2015) 'Why gentrification theory fails in "much of the world"', *City*, 19(4), 552–563.

Ghertner, A. (2014) 'India's urban revolution: geographies of displacement beyond gentrification', *Environment and Planning A*, 46, 1554–1571.

Ghertner, A. (2010) 'Calculating without numbers: aesthetic governmentality in Delhi's slums', *Economy and Society*, 39(2), 185–217.

Gilbert, A. (1999) 'A home is forever? Residential mobility and homeownership in self-help settlements', *Environment and Planning A*, 31, 1073–1091.

Gilbert, A. (2007) 'The return of the slum: does language matter?', *International Journal of Urban and Regional Research*, 31(4), 697–713.

Gillespie, T. (2016) 'Accumulation by urban dispossession: struggles over urban space in Accra, Ghana', *Transactions of the Institute of British Geographers*, 41, 66–77.

Gulyani, S. and Talukdar, D. (2008) 'Slum real estate: the low-quality high-price puzzle in Nairobi's slum rental market and its implications for theory and practice', *World Development*, 36(10), 1916–1937.

Hammel, D. and Wyly, E. (1996) 'A model for identifying gentrified areas with census data', *Urban Geography*, 17(3), 248–268.

HLRN Housing and Land Rights Network (2011) *Planned Dispossessment: Forced Evictions and the 2010 Commonwealth Games (Fact-finding Mission Report 14)*, New Delhi: HLRN.

Huchzermeyer, M. (2009) 'The struggle for in situ upgrading of informal settlements: a reflection on cases in Gauteng', *Development Southern Africa*, 26(1), 59–73.

Jacobs, J. (2006) 'A geography of big things', *Cultural Geographies*, 13, 1–27.

Jacobs, J. and Lees, L. (2013) 'Defensible space on the move: revisiting the urban geography of Alice Coleman', *International Journal of Urban and Regional Research*, 37(5), 1559–1583.

Jencks, C. (1978) *The Language of Post-Modern Architecture*, New York: Rizzoli.

Jones, G. and Sanyal, R. (2015) 'Spectacle and suffering: the Mumbai slum as a worlded space', *Geoforum*, 65, 431–439.

Jorge, S. and Melo, V. (2014) 'Processos e Dinâmicas de Intervenção no Espaço Peri-urbano: O caso de Maputo' [Intervention processes and dynamics in Peri-urban space: the case of Maputo], *Cadernos de Estudos Africanos*, 27, 55–77.

Koolhaas, R. and Harvard Project on the City, Boeri, S. and Multiplicity, Kwinter, S., Tazi, N. and Obrist, H. (2001) *Mutations*, Barcelona: Actar.

Krause, M. (2014) *The Good Project: Humanitarian Relief NGOs and the Fragmentation of Reason*, Chicago: University of Chicago Press.

Lees, L. (2014a) 'Gentrification in the Global South?', in Parnell, S. and Oldfield, S. (eds) *The Routledge Handbook on Cities of the Global South*, Routledge: New York, pp. 506–521.

Lees, L. (2014b) 'The urban injustices of New Labour's "new urban renewal": the case of the Aylesbury Estate in London', *Antipode*, 46(4), 921–947.

Lees, L., Shin, H. and López-Morales, E. (2016) *Planetary Gentrification: Uneven Development and Displacement*, Cambridge: Polity Press.

Leite, M. (2014) 'Entre a "guerra" e a "paz": Unidades de Polícia Pacificadora e gestão dos territórios de favela no Rio de Janeiro' [Between 'war' and 'peace': pacifying police units and governing favela spaces in Rio de Janeiro], *Dilemas: Revista de Estudos de Conflito e Controle Social*, 7(4), 625–642.

Lemanski, C. (2014) 'Hybrid gentrification in South Africa: theorising across southern and northern cities', *Urban Studies*, 51(14), 2943–2960.

Ley, D. (1996) *The New Middle Class and the Remaking of the Central City*, Oxford: Oxford University Press.

Loftus, A. (2006) 'Reification and the dictatorship of the water meter', *Antipode*, 38(5), 1023–1045.

London Tenants Federation, Lees, L., Just Space and Southwark Notes Archive Group (2014) *An Anti-gentrification Handbook for Council Estates in London*, London: Calverts Co-operative.

López-Morales, E. (2011) 'Gentrification by ground rent dispossession: the shadows cast by large-scale urban renewal in Santiago de Chile', *International Journal of Urban and Regional Research*, 35(2), 330–357.

Machado da Silva, L. (2008) *Vida sob Cerco: Violência e rotina nas favelas do Rio de Janeiro* [*Life Under Siege: Violence and Routine in Rio de Janeiro's Favelas*], Rio de Janeiro: Editora Nova Fronteira.

McFarlane, C. (2012) 'The entrepreneurial slum: civil society, mobility and the co-production of urban development', *Urban Studies*, 49(13), 2795–2816.

Menezes, P. (2015) *Entre o 'fogo cruzado' e o 'campo minado': uma etnografia do processo de 'pacificação' de favelas cariocas* [Between 'crossfire' and 'minefield': an ethnography of the 'pacifying' process in Rio's favelas], Unpublished PhD thesis, Instituto de Estudos Sociais e Políticos, Universidade do Estado do Rio de Janeiro.

Merrifield, A. (1995) 'Situated knowledge through exploration: reflections on Bunge's "Geographical Expeditions"', *Antipode*, 27(1), 49–70.

Moran, J. (2007) 'Early cultures of gentrification in London, 1955–1980', *Journal of Urban History*, 34(1), 101–121.

Mukhija, V. (2002) 'An analytical framework for urban upgrading: property rights, property values and physical attributes', *Habitat International*, 26, 553–570.

Mukhija, V. (2003) *Squatters as Developers?: Slum Redevelopment in Mumbai*, Aldershot: Ashgate.

Müller, M. (2015) 'The mega-event syndrome: why so much goes wrong in mega-event planning and what to do about it', *Journal of the American Planning Association*, 81(1), 6–17.

Neuwirth, Robert (2004) *Shadow Cities: A Billion Squatters, a New Urban World*, London: Routledge.

Newman, O. (1972) *Defensible Space: Crime Prevention Through Urban Design*, New York: Macmillan.

Ngonyama, P. (2010) 'The 2010 FIFA World Cup: critical voices from below', *Soccer & Society*, 11(1–2), 168–180.

Nwanna, C. (2015) 'Gentrification in Nigeria: the case of two housing estates in Lagos', in Lees, L., Shin, H. and López-Morales, E. (eds), *Global Gentrifications: Uneven Development and Displacement*, Bristol: Policy Press, pp. 311–327.

Ost, S. and Fleury, S. (2013) 'O Mercado Sobe o Morro. A Cidadania Desce? Efeitos socioeconômicos da Pacificação no Santa Marta' [The market goes up the Hill. Does citizenship come down? The socioeconomic effects of pacification at Santa Marta], *DADOS – Revista de Ciências Sociais*, 56(3), 635–671.

Piketty, T. (2014) *Capital in the 21st Century*, Cambridge: Harvard University Press.

Rabinow, P. (1989) *French Modern: Norms and Forms of the Social Environment*, Cambridge, MA: MIT Press.

Rao, V. (2006) 'Slum as theory: the South/Asian city and globalization', *International Journal of Urban and Regional Research*, 30(1), 225–232.

Riley, E., Fiori, J. and Ramirez, R. (2001) 'Favela Bairro and a new generation of housing programmes for the urban poor', *Geoforum*, 32, 521–531.

Robinson, J. (2006) *Ordinary Cities: Between Modernity and Development*, London: Routledge.

Robinson, J. (2015) 'Thinking cities through elsewhere: comparative tactics for a more global urban studies', *Progress in Human Geography*, 1–27.

Rolfes, M. (2010) 'Poverty tourism: theoretical reflections and empirical findings regarding an extraordinary form of tourism', *GeoJournal*, 75, 421–442.

Rolnik, R. (2013) 'Late neoliberalism: the financialization of homeownership and housing rights', *International Journal of Urban and Regional Research*, 37(3), 1058–1066.

Roy, A., Jockin, A. and Javed, A. (2004) 'Community police stations in Mumbai's slums', *Environment and Urbanization*, 16(2), 135–138.

Santos, B. (1977) 'The law of the oppressed: the construction and reproduction of legality in Pasargada', *Law & Society Review*, 12(1).

Shin, H. and Li, B. (2013) 'Whose games? The costs of being "olympic citizens" in Beijing', *Environment and Urbanization*, 25(2), 559–576.

Shin, H., Lees, L. and López-Morales, E. (2016) 'Introduction: locating gentrification in the Global East', *Urban Studies*, 53(3), 455–470.

Silvestre, G. and Oliveira, N. (2012) 'The revanchist logic of mega-events: community displacement in Rio de Janeiro's West End', *Visual Studies*, 27(2), 204–210.

Slater, T. (2011) 'Gentrification of the city', in Bridge, G. and Watson, S. (eds) *The New Blackwell Companion to the City,* Oxford: Wiley-Blackwell, pp. 571–585.

Smith, N. (1979) 'Toward a theory of gentrification: a back to the city movement by capital not people', *Journal of the American Planning Association*, 45, 538–548.

Smith, N. (1996) *The New Urban Frontier: Gentrification and the Revanchist City*, London: Routledge.

Turner, J. (1972) *Housing by People: Towards Autonomy in Building Environments*, London: Marion Boyars.

Valladares, L. (2006) *La Favela d'un Siècle à l'autre: Mythe d'origine, Discours Scientifiques et Representations Virtuelles*, Paris: Editions Maison des Sciences des Hommes.

Villegas, C., Esteban, K. and Nussbaumer, B. (2016) 'La ciudad esconde el proceso. La protesta popular en Vila Autódromo, Río de Janeiro' [The city hides the process. Popular protest in 'Vila Autodromo', Rio de Janeiro], *Íconos: Revista de Ciencias Sociales*, 56, 159–176.

Waldorff, P. (2016) '"The law is not for the poor": land, law and eviction in Luanda', *Singapore Journal of Tropical Geography*, 37, 363–377.

Weinstein, L. (2014) *The Durable Slum: Dharavi and the Right to Stay Put in Globalizing Mumbai*, Minneapolis: University of Minnesota Press.

Wilkinson, R. and Pickett, K. (2010) *The Spirit Level: Why Equality is Better for Everyone*, London: Penguin.

Yutzy, C. (2012) 'Increased state presence through the Unidade de Polícia Pacificadora in Santa Marta, Rio de Janeiro: the creation of the city's theme park and resulting social issues', *Revista de Estudos Urbanos*, 38(1), 127–146.

15. New-build gentrification
Mark Davidson

15.1 INTRODUCTION

In the 1990s and 2000s, the process of 'new-build gentrification' (Davidson and Lees 2005, 2010) took gentrification from modest mews (Glass 1964) to shimmering multi-million dollar residential towers. The scale and speed of neighbourhood transformation associated with this form of gentrification was striking. New-build gentrification became a central element of what was labelled 'third wave gentrification'. In 2001, Hackworth and Smith defined the latter process in the following way:

> Prophesies of degentrification appear to have been overstated as many neighbourhoods continue to gentrify while others, further from the city centre begin to experience the process for the first time. Post-recession gentrification seems to be more linked to large-scale capital than ever, as large developers rework entire neighbourhoods, often with state support (467).

Some 15 years on from this defining statement, three things jump out at the reader. First, the late 1990s concern with degentrification (also see Marcuse 1993) appears almost quaint from the vantage point of today's increasingly gentrified cities. Second, third wave gentrification contained two distinguishing features: the reliance on (i) corporate capital and (ii) governmental support. Simply put, transforming neighbourhoods – and, indeed, city regions – via new residential developments required large developers with lots of capital and the regulatory support of the state. Third, early conceptualizations of new-build gentrification overwhelmingly originated from North America and the United Kingdom. In doing so, this gentrification scholarship was closely connected to attempts to understand the state-forms associated with Third Way political ideology (see Giddens 1999). In early accounts of new-build gentrification (e.g. Davidson and Lees 2005), the 'state-led' prefix therefore often presumes a particular state-form; one closely connected to the centre-left effort to reform the harder edges of neoliberalism. These three distinctions remain critical, if often under-estimated, to current understandings of the history of gentrification(s).

Class-based, large-scale, capital-intensive transformations of modern urban space can arguably be dated to 29 June 1853; the day that Napoléon III instructed Georges Eugène Haussmann to '*aérer, unifier, et embellir*' Paris. In the works that continued until the 1920s, the transformation of Paris famously involved replacing working class quarters with an epoch defining bourgeois landscape. Harvey (2005) describes how this urban transformation was related to a very particular politico-economic situation: 'The surpluses of capital and labor power, so crushingly evident in 1848, were to be absorbed through a program of massive long-term investment in the built environment that focused on the amelioration of space relations. Within a year of the declaration of Empire, more than a thousand were at work on the construction site of the Tuileries . . .' (104).

This crisis of capitalist accumulation created two necessities. First, the state had to act in order to resolve a crisis of surplus capital. Second, in order to employ such large amounts of capital, the urban landscape would require a radical remaking. I note these two rather self-evident features of Harvey's synopsis in order to draw a necessary analogy between the nineteenth-century origins of new-build gentrification and its contemporary manifestations. New-build gentrification has predominantly, but not exclusively (see Smith 2011), been a process whereby large-scale capital and state power work in concert to transform the built form. This transformation is not principally a matter of residential preferences, policy choices or local land market fluctuation. Rather it fundamentally concerns the ways in which the urban process is continually shaped by capitalist processes.

Our starting point for understanding new-build gentrification should not therefore be the last 30 years of neoliberal urbanism, but rather our framing should be the much longer history of capitalism's relationship to urbanization. Within this history, we can find numerous examples of state-facilitated, large-scale capital investments serving to radically alter the class composition of neighbourhoods and, at a grander scale, recreate class relations more generally (see Harvey 2005). Such a reading means we must not only be sensitive to the inevitable geographical variations of the gentrification process, but also understand how successive waves of capitalist crisis accumulate to generate an accruing of the gentrification process.

This process of accrual is now reflected throughout the gentrification literature. Earlier debates surrounding new-build gentrification focused on the Anglo-sphere of the UK (Davidson and Lees 2005; Lambert and Boddy 2002), USA (Hackworth and Smith 2001; Smith 1996) and Australia (Shaw 2002). Now we see commentary on new-build gentrification from across the globe, with Asia (Moore 2015) and Latin America (López-Morales 2016) being particularly notable for the extent and intensity of new-build gentrification.

15.2   THE RISE OF NEW-BUILD-ISM: THIRD WAY GENTRIFICATION AND REGENERATION

Although it is possible to identify different forms of new-build gentrification across the history of urbanization, the term 'new-build gentrification' entered the urban lexicon during the 1990s and 2000s. In 1996, Neil Smith (39) made the following commentary on the gentrification processes he was observing at the time:

> How, in the large context of changing social geographies, are we to distinguish adequately between the rehabilitation of nineteenth-century housing, the construction of new condominium towers, the opening of festival markets to attract local and not so local tourists, the proliferation of wine bars and boutiques for everything and the construction of modern and postmodern office buildings employing thousands of professionals, all looking for a place to live? . . . Gentrification is no longer about a narrow and quixotic oddity in the housing market but has become the leading residential edge of a much larger endeavour: the class remake of the central urban landscape (cited in Davidson and Lees 2005: 1166).

What Smith was describing was later characterized as 'new-build gentrification' (Davidson and Lees 2005). The distinction Smith (1996) began to draw out is between a small-scale part of the urban process (i.e. the renovation of terraced townhouses by aspirant middle-class peoples) and a much more pervasive trend that itself is a defining part of the urban process. Whereas the processes that Ruth Glass described in 1964 were always somewhat marginal compared to parallel suburbanizations, the gentrification that Smith identified with 'the construction of new condominium towers' represented something quite different. The new condo boom that Smith observed was, and remains, the exemplary form of contemporary urbanization in places such as London (Davidson and Lees 2005, 2010) and Toronto (Kern 2010; Rosen and Walks 2015). Parallel processes have also rolled-out beyond the urban centres of the Global North, with cities such as Bangkok (Moore 2015) and Kuala Lumpur (Ortega 2016) experiencing new-build gentrifying development. In these cases, gentrification and state-led national economic development projects have often gone hand-in-hand. Indeed, in terms of intensity of neighbourhood transition and geographical extent, examples of new-build gentrification in the Global South now often appear to exceed those in cities such as London and Toronto (see Harris 2008; He 2010). On this point, the link between new-build gentrification and state power is critical.

This shift from a marginal, but significant, process to the exemplar for contemporary urban development necessitated the use of state power. This state power has come in various guises and forms. In some cases, state power has taken a particularly violent form, with governments using their powers of eminent domain (Carpenter and Ross 2009) and/or land ownership (Wu 2015) to instigate large-scale redevelopment schemes. In other times and places, policy recommendations and policy changes have incentivized some land uses and privileged some redevelopment actors over others (e.g. Hedin et al. 2012). In order to make gentrification the default program to produce economic growth and urban renewal, the state has again had to become a central actor within the urban process. And in order to take this role, the state – at least in democratic forms – has been required to provide justifications for its actions.

When Harvey (2005) describes the modernity at the centre of Haussmann's plans for Paris, he focuses on the need for the new regime to represent a historical break. Tomorrow's Paris would, at the request of Emperor Napoléon III, be created without reference to the past. The past was deemed irrelevant and the emerging city would adhere to a new and superior set of political values and ideas. Such an approach to urban renewal was to become symbolic of modern urbanization (Berman 1982). As processes of creative destruction have unfolded, so ideological explanations have been required to justify inevitable upheavals. The third wave of gentrification has often been intertwined with the advent of neoliberal politics and policy. In order to set about transforming the city along radically new lines (e.g. Urban Task Force 1999), a rejection of the past and/or an embrace of an alternate future has been necessitated. In the case of Haussmann's Paris, a rejection of the past became a political necessity. Today, such a rejection seems less important than modernist developmental promises and related claims about economic necessity that often serve to justify large-scale transformations of the urban form.

When London's riverside began to transform in the late 1990s and early 2000s (see Davidson and Lees 2005, 2010), the entire redevelopment process was at the same time being narrated by a new and ambitious centre-left policy agenda. Under Tony Blair's New Labour, urban policy was radically reformed. The government had commissioned the Richard Rogers-led *Urban Task Force* to come up with a new vision of Britain's cities. The policies and programs that emerged became shining examples of the Third Way (see Giddens 1999) political philosophy that underpinned the government's ideology. Third Way politics were meant to represent a distinct break from previous formulations of reformist socialism. What this meant for urban development was a notable shift in the language that explained urban development trajectories. Gentrification via wholesale neighbourhood redevelopment was cast as a project of social engineering and urban improvement. This project involved breaking down segregating urban geographies and installing new types of social mixing (Rose et al. 2013). Such a project required accompanying initiatives about social mixing and/or social integration (Davidson 2010).

Much of the 2000's British- and American-based literature on new-build gentrification is therefore situated within a common concern with social mixing policies (Lees 2008). An important question is implicit throughout this work: could the state-sanctioned expansion of gentrification be manipulated into a socially positive process? The promise of these politics was reduced segregation, economic benefits for low-income residents relating to gentrifiers deploying social capital in disinvested spaces, and the creation of more inclusive communities. Within the context of this seemingly new political program, a whole set of assumptions about gentrification and its social impacts were therefore being re-examined.

In Smith's 1979 description of the rent gap, he acknowledged that the state remained central to gentrification, even if private market actors seemed to be dominating in places such as Philadelphia:

> Once the rent gap is wide enough, gentrification may be initiated in a given neighborhood by several different actors in the land and housing market. . . . The state, for example, initiated most if not all of the early schemes, and though it plays a lesser role today, is still important. More commonly today, with private market gentrification, one or more financial institutions will reverse a long standing redlining policy and actively target a neighborhood as a potential market for construction loans and mortgages (545).

In contrast to Smith's early comments, third wave gentrification became manifest because the state opted to take a more active role in neighbourhood change. And with this, new-build gentrification became the principal vehicle by which the state's urban renewal objectives would be achieved. A confluence of surplus capital requiring large scale investment fixes (Christophers 2016) and the changing ideological basis of Anglo social democratic political parties therefore created the conditions for new-build gentrification to become a leading edge of contemporary urbanization.

15.3   A THEORY OF NEW-BUILD GENTRIFICATION?

Although the re-emergence of the state within gentrification processes enabled widespread new-build gentrification, its presence also created analytical and political complexities. Gentrification had traditionally been associated with the renovation of existing housing stock (cf. Glass 1964), whereas new-build construction was largely a concern of those studying new urban development (e.g. Gans 1982). The conjoining of new-build construction and neighbourhood reinvestment therefore presented conceptual challenges. These challenges were further complicated in places such as the UK and USA that were adopting Third Way (Giddens 1999) social policies aimed at using this conjoining to produce a 'positive' form of gentrification. Since a defining feature of gentrification is a distinctly inequitable outcome, displacement, the insertion of egalitarian policy objectives into the gentrification process potentially transforms gentrification into something else entirely: gentrification without displacement is not gentrification. Early debates on new-build gentrification were specifically concerned with this issue.

15.3.1 Residentialization or Gentrification?

In 2002, Lambert and Boddy published the results of a study into residential development in cities around the UK. Observing a growing number of new residential developments in places such as Bristol, they asked whether the concept of gentrification was an applicable descriptor:

> . . . core-area housing development in Bristol and other second tier UK cities has consisted mainly of corporate new build or conversion of former commercial or industrial buildings. This contrasts with the neighbourhood gentrification of early decades driven mainly by relatively better off households buying and renovating individual properties in generally lower income areas, for their own use. One implication is that there is no direct displacement of other social groups and lower income households as occurred with pre-recession gentrification. Gentrification in the sense of a process of social change based on 'invasion and succession' is, therefore a misnomer (21).

For Lambert and Boddy, the absence of direct displacement meant that the urban changes they were observing required a different explanation. The concept they developed was 'residentialization' and it was intended to describe a process of land use change distinct from gentrification. These land use changes involved the return and/or establishment of residential spaces within the cores of UK cities, particularly outside of London. While this process has parallels to gentrification in that it involves a reversal of centrifugal residential geographies in the industrial city, they felt it lacked the defining process of displacement and hence required a distinguishing concept.

This contention was picked up by Davidson and Lees (2005) when they developed the cases for and against the types of residential development described as examples of 'residentialization'. The case against focused on the pivotal issue of displacement, with Lambert and Boddy (2002: 18) arguing that the location of residential developments in brownfield sites meant the return of residents to core urban areas but did not involve displacement. This represents a powerful argument, since the UK state was, through a new set of urban policies, supposedly directing and conditioning capital reinvestment in the built form. By concentrating new-build onto brownfield sites and often requiring affordable housing allocations within new housing developments, policymakers promised to change neighbourhood class composition without displacing existing residents.

In response, Davidson and Lees (2005) presented a four-fold case against this interpretation. They claimed that gentrification has four defining elements: '(1) reinvestment of capital; (2) social upgrading of locale by incoming high-income groups; (3) landscape change; and (4) direct or indirect displacement of low-income groups' (1170). The first three elements, which are rather uncontentious, are shown to be present in cases similar to those examined by Lambert and Boddy (2002). Turning to displacement, Davidson and Lees (2005) presented evidence to suggest that displacement is taking place in neighbourhoods experiencing new-build gentrification/residentialization. They claimed: 'New-build developments will generate displacement by introducing a large population of gentrifiers into the community very quickly and will thereby act as beachheads from which the tentacles of gentrification can reach outward into the adjacent communities' (1184). By documenting the various ways in which new-build developments were enacting a class-based transition (see Davidson 2010) and pushing out working-class residents, Davidson and Lees (2005) demonstrated not only the applicability of the concept of gentrification, but also its political necessity.

By demonstrating that the defining elements of gentrification were present in cases of urban redevelopment along London's River Thames, Davidson and Lees (2005) provided a conceptual foundation to identify gentrification outside of its traditional locales (see Shaw 2002). However, another literature that emerged out of the Continental European context brought further challenges to those who wanted to mobilize the concept of new-build gentrification to describe emergent forms of urban change.

15.3.2   Reurbanization or Gentrification?

Reurbanization (Buzar et al. 2007; Haase et al. 2010) is a concept developed to describe the (re)growth of residential populations in a number of European cities. The concept is explicitly designed to capture a process that is similar, but ultimately different from gentrification (Haase et al. 2010). Reurbanization attempts to link demographic changes to transformations taking place within the structure of European and North American cities. The historical background to this is decades of suburban flight experienced in cities across the Global North. Reurbanization therefore seeks to describe the emergent counter-process in a similar way that gentrification has been described as a back to the city movement. Yet, according to Buzar et al. (2007) gentrification is not an accurate descriptor since, they claimed, it fails to capture the distinctive demographics, scales, housing preferences and social structures at play. Critically, this combination of distinctions means that the class dynamics of urban change processes in cities such as Ljubljana, Leipzig, Bologna and Lyon are said to be different when compared to gentrification in cities and regions not experiencing depopulation:

> Unlike gentrification, which affects only selected parts of the urban tissue and is associated with specific social groups and economic processes, reurbanisation is taking place throughout the inner city and is mobilising a much broader range of populations. Indeed, it would be difficult to describe as 'gentrification' the massive influx of international immigrants, young families and students into the lower end of the housing markets of all four cities (Buzar et al. 2007: 672).

The characterization of urban change within the reurbanization literature is therefore one that involves a largely vacant place becoming repopulated. Reurbanization is often described as a process of stabilization (Haase et al. 2010); after years of decline, city centres are characterized as moving towards a sustainable population and tax base.

Whereas gentrification involves a clear class transition, reurbanization is therefore more mixed. It is 'a process of repopulating the inner city with a variety of social groups and lifestyles' (Buzar et al. 2007: 671). This description of a process that simply repopulates an abandoned urban core has strong parallels with debates over social polarization (see Moulaert et al. [eds] 2003). Although proponents of the reurbanization thesis (Buzar et al. 2007; Haase et al. 2010) make a distinction between processes of social change occurring in cities placed differently within the urban hierarchy, some scholars working within large metropolitan centres made similar arguments (Hamnett 1994). Such characterizations of urban population transition have been questioned by scholars on the basis that existing social class measures often fail to understand the social composition and distinctions of the post-industrial city (Davidson and Wyly 2012; Watt 2008).

Debates on reurbanization therefore emphasize the impact of demographic shifts on urban processes, whereas concerns with residentialization (Lambert and Boddy 2002) focus more on the micro-scale social dynamics relating to changing land use. In each case, an argument is made against the concept of new-build gentrification principally on the basis of the absence of displacement. For those developing the concept of reurbanization, there is little or no working-class population to displace. For proponents of residentialization, the obvious absence of direct displacement from industrial or ex-industrial sites means the term gentrification is inapplicable. Although a case-by-case analysis of urban change would reveal varying degrees of transition, much of this disagreement stems from a fundamental misunderstanding about how gentrification generates multiple forms of displacement.

15.3.3 New-build Gentrification and Displacement

New-build gentrification can generate both direct and indirect displacement (Davidson 2010). Direct displacement is the most glaring injustice inflicted by gentrification processes. For new-build gentrification, this form of displacement tends to be associated with demolition (Lees 2014), where old structures are threatened or actually ripped down (Goetz 2011) and existing residents consequently moved out. Indirect displacement is a more slippery concept to deal with, since it involves a number of elements.

For Marcuse (1985) there are four displacement factors relating to gentrification: (i) direct last-resident displacement, (ii) direct chain displacement, (iii) exclusionary displacement, and (iv) displacement pressure. The last of these factors, displacement pressure, is critical for studies of new-build gentrification and, I would argue, gentrification in general. Marcuse describes displacement pressure in the following way:

> When a family sees the neighborhood around it changing dramatically, when their friends are leaving the neighborhood, when the stores they patronize are liquidating and new stores for other clientele are taking their places, and when changes in public facilities, in transportation patterns, and in support services all clearly are making the area less and less livable, then the pressure of displacement is already severe (Marcuse 1985: 207).

The different forms of displacement are important because the physical relocation of individuals from a home and neighbourhood means the loss of various things. This loss might be monetary, although displacement can also involve financial gains via the sale of property or statutory recompense. Even in such cases, however, there is still likely to be significant loss associated with displacement. What physical displacement almost inevitably means is a certain dislocation of one's lifeworld; a wrenching of one's being from its formative spatial existence: 'there is a need to ask why displacement matters at all: what does a loss of place constitute? How is a loss of space differentiated from a loss of place?' (Davidson 2009: 226). The answers to these questions involves recognizing the co-constitutive relationship between place and self (see Heidegger 1927[2008]; Lefebvre 1991).

When a neighbourhood becomes subject to gentrifying new-build development, this relationship between place and self can become radically altered. For an existing resident of a working-class neighbourhood, the rapid transition of retail and social services, along with a changing political community, can destroy a sense of belonging. A painful irony in many recent cases of new-build gentrification is that this is often the intent of policymakers. Ideas such as boosting social capital, generating integration and stimulating community participation often convert into a rejection of the existing community and an aspiration to replace it with something deemed more acceptable (Watt 2008). This linkage between processes of indirect displacement and state policy is one reason why new-build gentrification has become so powerful and pervasive. When dressed in the seemingly progressive rhetoric of centre-left social policy, new-build gentrification can appear a common sense solution for neighbourhood decline. The policies recast indirect displacement into a social good and, therefore, tend to legitimate displacement-causing gentrification processes. If we therefore limit our understanding of gentrification-induced displacement to the direct kind, as proponents of residentialization (Lambert and Boddy 2002) and reurbanization (Buzar et al. 2007) have tended to do, then we omit a full understanding of displacement and risk denying the crucial presence of state power with contemporary gentrification processes.

15.4   GLOBAL NEW-BUILD GENTRIFICATIONS

Debates concerning the concept of new-build gentrification emerged principally within the UK and USA contexts. As such, there are important questions to be examined with regards to how the concept might, or might not, be applied in different contexts (see Lees 2012; Maloutas 2011). This section reviews the variety of ways that the concept of new-build gentrification has been applied over the past decade. The principal objective is to demonstrate how a variety of new-build gentrifications have been identified. Far from there being the mono-dimensional process of new-build gentrification that many early Global North centred debates implicitly presumed, the new-build gentrification literature has now identified and examined a whole range of urban transformations.

In identifying how the concept of new-build gentrification has been utilized to understand urban change outside of its points of conceptual origin, I am rejecting some of the post-colonial critiques circulating in urban studies (e.g. Ghertner 2014; Robinson 2015). Although post-colonial urban research comes in various iterations, its core concern is that the exporting of theory from the 'Global North' to the 'Global South' tends to misinterpret and misrepresent sets of processes that are, ultimately, indigenously derived and contextually embedded (Robinson 2015). For some gentrification scholars, this means we must reject the application of concepts that are intricately bound up with attempts to understand the Global North metropolis (Maloutas 2011). Others find it necessary to supplement Global North theories with those developed from within different contexts, therefore developing hybrid approaches (Lemanski 2014). The approach taken here in order to trace out the geographies of new-build gentrification is derived from the definition of gentrification developed by Davidson and Lees (2005; see above). This definition seeks to outline the most basic elements of a class-based neighbourhood transition under capitalism.

A further reason why this definition is used in order to understand a diversity of cases is its analytical modesty. It does not assume, as Ghertner's (2014) recent work suggests, (a) an assertion of responsibility for displacement, (b) any particular processes of tenure priority or transformation, or (c) allocations or mobilizations of force. It does, however, assume that the process of gentrification involves land assuming a higher and better use as defined under capitalism. Furthermore, it does not imply that the process takes place in the same way, involves the same actors, or generates the same outcomes in all places. It simply outlines the most basic features of class-based neighbourhood transition under capitalism. Consequently, it is assumed that the concept can be used in places that satisfy the conditions of (a) operating under capitalism and (b) involving class-based competition over residential space. In the sections that follow, four key dimensions of the new-build gentrification literature are critically reviewed: (a) new-build gentrification and the state; (b) new-build gentrification and its consequent forms of displacement; (c) new-build gentrification and its implication in real estate development; and (d) new-build gentrification and gentrifiers.

15.4.1 New-build Gentrification and the State

The state has remained a central theme of the new-build gentrification literature, with the theme of state as policy maker, urban strategist and shaper of outcomes being particularly notable (Davidson and Lees 2005; Hackworth and Smith 2001; Smith 1996). Collectively these accounts have tended to involve an exploration of the strong connection between neoliberal states and new-build gentrification, although this relationship is not determinate and a growing literature exists on the connection between new-build gentrification and (post-)socialist states (see Bernt 2016; Ren 2015). The relation between new-build gentrification and the state is therefore varied with context and iteration being important to producing very particular types of new-build gentrification. New-build gentrification is commonly associated with the importation and localization of urban policy. As described by Smith (2002; also see Davidson and Lees 2005), gentrification became a blueprint for urban policy across the globe. New-build gentrification has been at the forefront of this process, with states adopting gentrifying urban renewal programs from elsewhere (see Harris 2008; Zhang et al. 2013) and applying them within their own locales (although we now know that there were in fact earlier, endogenous examples of new-build gentrification in, for example, South Korea, see Lees, Shin and López-Morales 2016). New-build gentrification has therefore become a manifestation of broader processes of policy mobility (McCann and Ward 2011), where urban policy models are developed and transmitted across a vast array of cities.

Although this transference of policy is widely acknowledged to involve the adoption of gentrifying strategies, as Harris (2008) explains in the context of British models being adopted in Mumbai, the outcome of this process is far from simply replication of neighbourhood change:

> The practical politics of gentrification need to be understood as contingently realised across different global contexts. Although Lower Parel's gentrification has been framed by transnational actors and urban imaginaries, it has also been the product of the whims and wherefores of a powerful nexus of politicians, builders and developers exploiting and profiting from Mumbai's poorly implemented and monitored land use policies and planning controls (2423).

Harris follows this cautionary note with an acknowledgment that the contextually dependent manifestations of new-build gentrification in Mumbai generated potential for learning to occur in ways that transmitted knowledge back to the perceived places of origin of gentrification processes.

In other locations, this process has played out differently. In China, the centrality of the Communist state has resulted in a highly particularized set of processes. In Shanghai, an enthusiastic embrace of new-build gentrification by state officials has resulted in state powers being used to instigate large-scale demolition processes and large-scale direct displacement processes. The nuances of the debate in the UK (see Boddy and Lambert 2002; Davidson and Lees 2005) have, on this issue, not been required. Outside of Shanghai, similar utilizations of state power are evident in China, with cities like Yuexiu adopting gentrifying strategies in a vibrant, historical urban centre (see Zhang et al. 2013). Here again, context is centrally important since new-build gentrification is not premised on brownfield conversion or substantial disinvestment.

Whether in China, the Philippines (Ortega 2016), New Zealand (Murphy 2008) or Sweden (Hedin et al. 2012), new-build gentrification has often required and/or utilized state powers to instigate large-scale neighbourhood transformation. In each case, we can find the defining features of new-build gentrification present (Davidson and Lees 2005) and yet the variation in process and outcome are most striking. In terms of state power, it is possible to identify degrees of policy replication, varying amounts of state violence and different versions of amelioration.

15.4.2 New-build Gentrification and its Consequent Forms of Displacement

Across the new-build gentrification literature, it is now clear that the process is not only responsible for significant indirect displacement (Davidson and Lees 2005, 2010) but also significant amounts of direct displacement (Bromley and Mackie 2009; He 2010). The variety of displacements associated with new-build gentrification again demonstrates how the defining features of the process cannot be used to forecast any specific outcomes.

In the most extreme cases, new-build gentrification has generated extensive and violent displacement processes. Ortega (2016) has recently described how the coalescence of global city strategy, international real estate capital, and gentrification has generated an aggressive and violent process of displacement in Manila:

> Creating 'world-class' spaces of wealth, production, and consumption in Manila rests upon the dispossession of the urban poor, particularly informal settlers. Beyond posh facades of condominium buildings or green gardens of mixed-use developments, the ugly face of gentrification lies in its war against informality. The spatialities of recent demolitions illustrate how profit-oriented lure of 'world-class' developments reconfigure the relationship of informal settlers and local officials, eventually trumping their political claims. This very same lure masks the brutality of eviction and legitimizes their expulsion to distant relocation sites (48).

Similar descriptions of large-scale direct displacement can be found in China (He 2010) and, to a lesser extent, in Taiwan (Hsu and Hsu 2013).

Elsewhere, less explicitly violent forms of displacement have been commonly found. In Europe, issues of displacement are often bound up with social policy initiatives, where a desire to produce social mix (Davidson 2008) has accompanied concerns about gentrification-induced displacement. In Amsterdam, efforts to produce neighbourhood social mixing have been attempted through the liberalization of housing markets and privatization of social housing stock (Boterman and van Gent 2014). Such policy programs, as elsewhere (see Van Criekingen 2010), have tended to open up some vulnerable populations to displacement pressures. In Sweden, a neoliberal turn has made privatization and tenure transformation a central part of contemporary urban process, with the inevitable creation of displacement pressures where none previously existed (Hedin et al. 2012).

Subtle forms of indirect displacement also continue to be associated with state-led efforts to increase urban densities. In Davidson and Lees' (2010) examinations of London, the policy-led effort to increase residential densities using brownfield land was linked to a host of displacement processes. These same types of displacement processes have been identified in cities such as Tokyo (Lutzeler 2008) and Bangkok (Moore 2015), where attempts to 'reurbanize' sections of the inner city have set in motion displacement processes that are forcing long-term residents from their neighbourhoods.

15.4.3   New-build Gentrification and its Implication in Real Estate Development

In recent years, a sub-set of the new-build gentrification literature has begun to trace out the varied ways in which this relationship between new-build gentrification and real estate capital has been structured. Gentrification scholars have often found this link to real estate capital is bound up with state-led renewal attempts (Davidson 2007). In these cases, state actors have acted to incentivize investments in areas of strategic concern. For example, in Atlanta, Georgia, Immergluck (2009) found that real estate speculation and consequent gentrification was highly correlated with planning initiatives. In other locations, such as Barcelona (see Arbaci and Tapada-Berteli 2012), it has been state demolition programs that have instigated new geographies of real estate investment. In the Chinese context, Liang and Bao (2015) found that real estate development and new-build gentrification were united by tourism policies in Shenzhen.

López-Morales (2016) has offered one of the first studies into how real estate capital activity engages in new-build gentrification. In his study of new-build gentrification in Santiago, Chile, he found that developers undertook a set of strategies in order to extract maximum profits from their exploitation of the rent gap and, simultaneously, reduce resistance from existing residents. Through the establishment of monopoly positions, López-Morales' study explains how real estate capital can work in concert with the state in order to produce processes of (i) monopolistic buying power, (ii) blockbusting, (iii) construction-led deterioration, (iv) redlining, and (v) abandonment and deliberate deterioration. This work powerfully demonstrates how real estate investors are not passive in their exploitation of rent gaps, but rather that they actively create the rent gaps necessary for gentrification and foster the conditions necessary for maximum profit exploitation.

Although there is much more work to be done on how real estate actors engage with and enact the processes of new-build gentrification, the existing literature demonstrates a variety of intersections between state and capital and the construction of strategies by real estate actors to enact particularly violent forms of gentrification.

15.4.4   New-build Gentrification and Gentrifiers

The relationship between new-build gentrification and gentrifiers remains one of the most under-examined parts of the process. Although classical gentrification studies often alluded to how particular subjects became engaged/made through the process (Bridge 2006), new-build gentrification has less obvious connections. New-build gentrification is, by definition, a much more commodified process that almost universally involves the gentrifier being the purchaser of a finished commodity. Such a relationship can lead to questions over whether those in gentrifying new-build developments are gentrifiers at all, since the processes of subject formation traditionally associated with gentrifiers appear largely absent.

Existing literature has demonstrated a strong connection between new-build gentrification and mobility. In his work on Swiss gentrification, Rerat (2012) has shown that new-build gentrifiers have a strong desire for 'the convenience of urban life' (221), meaning that proximity to urban centre amenities and mass transit corridors are crucial considerations for gentrifying residents. This mirrors the findings of Butler and Robson (2004) in their multi-neighbourhood study of gentrification in London. They similarly found that gentrification, where renovation- or new-build based, had become a coping strategy for those in the high intensity, long working-hours, post-industrial workforce. In the different context of Bangkok, Moore (2015) finds a similar correlation, with the installation of rapid mass transit being highly correlated with gentrifying urban development. New-build gentrification therefore shows, at least in relation to proximity and mobility, similarities to classical 'back to the city' gentrification processes. However it remains unclear if urbane attitudes are also associated with this desire for city centre proximity.

Kern's (2010) studies on the gender dimensions of new-build gentrification suggest that the relationship between new-build gentrifiers and urbane attitudes might be complex:

> Through the commodification of fear and safety, of women's freedom and women's sexuality, neoliberal processes of privatization, securitization and capital accumulation are able to circulate with increased speed through expanding markets. Moreover, women's everyday lives and urban identities are shaped by this tension, drawing middle-class and professional women into the project of the revanchist, entrepreneurial city (211).

Here, urban and anti-urban sentiments both serve to fuel processes of new-build gentrification in Toronto. In the context of the real estate development process, the secure 'safe' spaces of the closeted new-build condo complex stand in paradoxical complementarity with the perceived dangers of the city. Whether the same tensions exist with regards to other facets of subjectivity in the new-build gentrification process remains largely unknown, although Butler and Robson's (2004) late 1990s and early 2000s account of gentrifiers in London suggests that similar complexes exist in relation to education.

15.5   CONCLUSIONS

The process of new-build gentrification has proliferated over the globe during the past two decades. Although it takes radically different forms across place and time, through tracing out its defining features it is possible to examine how a particular modality of urban change produces a variety of neighbourhood class-based transformations. Yet, there are many aspects of this still-emerging process that we know too little about.

First, there are some analytical and conceptual developments that can improve existing understandings. Although Smith (1996, 2002) and Davidson and Lees (2005, 2010) have provided accounts of the process in its early forms, a detailed account of the forms and evolution of new-build gentrification within and across contexts is yet to be written. Second, existing work on comparative perspectives has failed to develop persuasive typologies of new-build gentrification. Too often the concept is used either in a wholesale fashion or critiqued and abandoned. Charting a course between these positions (e.g. Lemanski 2014) in order to understand the diversity of the process will remain an on-going challenge. Many empirical gaps also exist. Many cities and regions that have become incorporated into global real estate development processes, such as Beirut and Moscow, and the concomitant gentrification remain under-studied. Like gentrification studies more generally, we also continue to know too little about the varied forms and combinations of displacement associated with new-build gentrification.

Beyond the particular theoretical and empirical concerns of the gentrification literature, there is also a growing need to examine how new-build gentrification became a part of the broader urbanization process under neoliberal capitalism (Harvey 2012). Over the past decade, new-build gentrification in places such as London and New York has rapidly accelerated. The scale of residential developments has grown as the process has become incorporated into both middle-class and elite housing markets. Gentrification may have started out as a small-scale urban phenomenon, but current new-build gentrification processes highlight how central it has become to the recreation of urbanized capitalism itself. This has generated numerous new questions. In terms of geography, new-build gentrification has become a suburban phenomenon in places like East Asia (Hudalah et al. 2016), making the 'back-to-the-city' trope less useful. As new-build gentrification has also become driven by speculation in real estate markets, the relationship between gentrifying neighbourhood change and gentrifiers is also mutating. Unpicking how new-build gentrification has become constitutive of broader politico-economic processes, through state planning, capital circulation and debt-financing, is therefore becoming a more urgent task. It is also a task that will require gentrification research to expand beyond its traditional boundaries. For example, neighbourhood-based analysis may have to be supplemented with an analysis of real estate networks and financial assemblages. As gentrification has transcended the neighbourhood, so must its researchers.

REFERENCES

Arbaci, S. and Tapada-Berteli, T. (2012) 'Social inequality and urban regeneration in Barcelona city centre: reconsidering success', *European Urban and Regional Studies,* 19, 287–311.

Berman, M. (1988) *All That Is Solid Melts into Air: The Experience of Modernity,* reissue edition, New York: Penguin Books.

Bernt, M. (2016) 'How post-socialist is gentrification? Observations in East Berlin and Saint Petersburg', *Eurasian Geography and Economics,* online early, 1–23.

Boterman, W. and van Gent, W. (2014) 'Housing liberalisation and gentrification: the social effects of tenure conversions in Amsterdam', *Tijdschrift voor Economische en Sociale Geografie,* 105, 140–160.

Bridge, G. (2006) 'It's not just a question of taste: gentrification, the neighbourhood, and cultural capital', *Environment and Planning A,* 38, 1965–1978.

Bromley, R. and Mackie, P. (2009) 'Displacement and the new spaces for informal trade in the Latin American city centre', *Urban Studies*, 46, 1485–1506.

Butler, T. and Robson, G. (2004) *London Calling: The Middle Classes and the Remaking of Inner London*, 1st edn, Oxford; New York: Bloomsbury Academic.

Buzar, S., Hall, R. and Ogden, P. (2007) 'Beyond gentrification: the demographic reurbanisation of Bologna', *Environment and Planning A*, 39, 64–85.

Christophers, B. (2016) 'For real: land as capital and commodity', *Transactions of the Institute of British Geographers*, 41, 134–148.

Criekingen, M. (2009) 'Moving in/out of Brussels' historical core in the early 2000s: migration and the effects of gentrification', *Urban Studies*, 46, 825–848.

Davidson, M. (2009) 'Displacement, space and dwelling: placing gentrification debate', *Ethics, Place and Environment*, 12, 219–234.

Davidson, M. (2010) 'Love thy neighbour? Social mixing in London's gentrification frontiers', *Environment and Planning A*, 42, 524–544.

Davidson, M. and Lees, L. (2005) 'New-build "gentrification" and London's riverside renaissance', *Environment and Planning A*, 37, 1165–1190.

Davidson, M. and Lees, L. (2010) 'New-build gentrification: its histories, trajectories, and critical geographies', *Population, Space and Place*, 16, 395–411.

Davidson, M. and Wyly, E. (2012) 'Class-ifying London', *City*, 16, 395–421.

Doucet, B., R. van Kempen, and Weesep, J. van (2011) "We're a rich city with poor people': municipal strategies of new-build gentrification in Rotterdam and Glasgow', *Environment and Planning A*, 43, 1438–1454.

Gans, H. (1982) *The Levittowners: Ways of Life and Politics in a New Suburban Community*, New York: Columbia University Press.

Ghertner, D. (2014) 'India's urban revolution: geographies of displacement beyond gentrification', *Environment and Planning A*, 46, 1554–1571.

Giddens, A. (1999) *The Third Way: The Renewal of Social Democracy*, Cambridge: Polity Press.

Glass, R. (1964) *London: Aspects of Change*, London: MacGibbon & Kee.

Goetz, E. (2011) 'Gentrification in black and white: the racial impact of public housing demolition in American cities', *Urban Studies*, 48, 1581–1604.

Haase, A., Kabisch, S., Steinführer, A., Bouzarovski, S., Hall, R. and Ogden, P. (2010) 'Emergent spaces of reurbanisation: exploring the demographic dimension of inner-city residential change in a European setting', *Population, Space and Place*, 16, 443–463.

Hackworth, J. and Smith, N. (2001) 'The changing state of gentrification', *Tijdschrift voor Economische en Sociale Geografie*, 92, 464–477.

Hamnett, C. (1994) 'Social polarisation in global cities: theory and evidence', *Urban Studies*, 31, 401–424.

Harris, A. (2008) 'From London to Mumbai and back again: gentrification and public policy in comparative perspective', *Urban Studies*, 45, 2407–2428.

Harvey, D. (1978) 'The urban process under capitalism: a framework for analysis', *International Journal of Urban and Regional Research*, 2, 101–131.

Harvey, D. (2005) *Paris, Capital of Modernity*, 1st edn, London: Routledge.

Harvey, D. (2013) *Rebel Cities: From the Right to the City to the Urban Revolution*, 1st edn, London: Verso.

He, S. (2010) 'New-build gentrification in Central Shanghai: demographic changes and socioeconomic implications', *Population, Space and Place*, 16, 345–361.

Hedin, K., Clark, E., Lundholm, E. and Malmberg, G. (2012) 'Neoliberalization of housing in Sweden: gentrification, filtering, and social polarization', *Annals of the Association of American Geographers*, 102, 443–463.

Heidegger, M. (1927[2008]) *Being and Time*, Harper.

Hsu, J. and Hsu, Y. (2013) 'State transformation, policy learning, and exclusive displacement in the process of urban redevelopment in Taiwan', *Urban Geography*, 34, 677–698.

Hudalah, D., Winarso, H. and Woltjer, J. (2016) 'Gentrifying the peri-urban: land use conflicts and institutional dynamics at the frontier of an Indonesian metropolis', *Urban Studies*, 53(3), 593–608.

Immergluck, D. (2009) 'Large redevelopment initiatives, housing values and gentrification: the case of the Atlanta Beltline', *Urban Studies*, 46, 1723–1745.

Kern, L. (2010) 'Selling the "scary city": gendering freedom, fear and condominium development in the neoliberal city', *Social and Cultural Geography*, 11, 209–230.

Lambert, C. and Lambert, C. (2002) 'Transforming the city: post-recession gentrification and reurbanisation', paper presented at the XVI AESOP Congress, Volos, Greece, 10–15 July.

Lees, L. (2008) 'Gentrification and social mixing: towards an inclusive urban renaissance?', *Urban Studies*, 45, 2449–2470.

Lees, L. (2012) 'The geography of gentrification: thinking through comparative urbanism', *Progress in Human Geography*, 36, 155–171.

Lees, L. (2014) 'The urban injustices of New Labour's "New Urban Renewal": the case of the Aylesbury Estate in London', *Antipode*, 46, 921–947.

Lees, L., Shin, H. and López-Morales, E. (2016) *Planetary Gentrification*, Cambridge: Polity Press.

Lefebvre, H. (1992) *The Production of Space*, 1st edn, Oxford, UK; Cambridge, MA, USA: Wiley-Blackwell.

Lemanski, C. (2014) 'Hybrid gentrification in South Africa: theorising across southern and northern cities', *Urban Studies*, 51, 2943–2960.

Liang, Z.-X. and Bao, J.-G. (2015) 'Tourism gentrification in Shenzhen, China: causes and socio-spatial consequences', *Tourism Geographies*, 17, 461–481.

López-Morales, E. (2016) 'Gentrification in Santiago, Chile: a property-led process of dispossession and exclusion', *Urban Geography*, 37, 1109–1131.

Lützeler, R. (2008) 'Population increase and "new-build gentrification" in Central Tōkyō', *Erdkunde*, 62, 287–299.

Maloutas, T. (2012) 'Contextual diversity in gentrification research', *Critical Sociology*, 38, 33–48.

Marcuse, P. (1985) 'Gentrification, abandonment, and displacement: connections, causes, and policy responses in New York City', *Urban Law Annual: Journal of Urban and Contemporary Law*, 28, 195–240.

Marcuse, P. (1993) 'Degentrification and advanced homelessness: new patterns, old processes, Netherlands', *Journal of Housing and the Built Environment*, 8, 177–191.

McCann, E. and Ward, K. (2011) *Mobile Urbanism: Cities and Policymaking in the Global Age*, University of Minnesota Press.

Moore, R.D. (2015) 'Gentrification and displacement: the impacts of mass transit in Bangkok', *Urban Policy and Research*, 33, 472–489.

Moulaert, F., Rodriguez, A. and Swyngedouw, E. (2003) *The Globalized City: Economic Restructuring and Social Polarization in European Cities*, Oxford: Oxford University Press.

Murphy, L. (2008) 'Third-wave gentrification in New Zealand: the case of Auckland', *Urban Studies*, 45, 2521–2540.

Ortega, A. (2016) 'Manila's metropolitan landscape of gentrification: global urban development, accumulation by dispossession and neoliberal warfare against informality', *Geoforum*, 70, 35–50.

Ren, J. (2015), 'Gentrification in China?', in L. Lees, H.B Shin and E. López-Morales (eds), *Global Gentrifications: Uneven Development and Displacement*, Bristol: Policy Press, pp. 329–348.

Rérat, P. (2012) 'Gentrifiers and their choice of housing: characteristics of the households living in new developments in Swiss cities', *Environment and Planning A*, 44, 221–236.

Robinson, J. (2016) 'Thinking cities through elsewhere: comparative tactics for a more global urban studies', *Progress in Human Geography*, 40, 3–29.

Rose, D., Germain, A., Bacqué, M., Bridge, G., Fijalkow, Y. and Slater, T. (2013) '"Social mix" and neighbourhood revitalization in a transatlantic perspective: comparing local policy discourses and expectations in Paris (France), Bristol (UK) and Montréal (Canada)', *International Journal of Urban and Regional Research*, 37, 430–450.

Rosen, G. and Walks, A. (2015) 'Castles in Toronto's sky: condo-ism as urban transformation', *Journal of Urban Affairs*, 37, 289–310.

Shaw, K. (2002) 'Culture, economics and evolution in gentrification', *Just Policy: A Journal of Australian Social Policy*, 28, 42–50.

Smith, D. (2011) 'What is rural gentrification? Exclusionary migration, population change, and revalorised housing markets', *Planning Theory and Practice*, 12(4), 596–605.

Smith, N. (1979) 'Toward a theory of gentrification: a back to the city movement by capital, not people', *Journal of the American Planning Association*, 45, 538–548.

Smith, N. (1996) *The New Urban Frontier: Gentrification and the Revanchist City*, London; New York: Routledge.

Smith, N. (2002) 'New globalism, new urbanism: gentrification as global urban strategy', *Antipode*, 34, 427–450.

Urban Task Force (1999) *Towards an Urban Renaissance*, London: Routledge.

Van Criekingen, M. (2010) '"Gentrifying the re-urbanisation debate", not vice versa: the uneven socio-spatial implications of changing transitions to adulthood in Brussels', *Population, Space and Place*, 16, 381–394.

van Gent, W. (2013) 'Neoliberalization, housing institutions and variegated gentrification: how the "third wave" broke in Amsterdam', *International Journal of Urban and Regional Research*, 37, 503–522.

Visser, G. and Kotze, N. (2008) 'The state and new-build gentrification in Central Cape Town, South Africa', *Urban Studies*, 45, 2565–2593.

Watt, P. (2008) 'The only class in town? Gentrification and the middle-class colonization of the city and the urban imagination', *International Journal of Urban and Regional Research*, 32, 206–211.

Wu, F. (2015) 'State dominance in urban redevelopment beyond gentrification in urban China', *Urban Affairs Review*, 1078087415612930.

Zhang, X., Hu, J., Skitmore, M. and Leung, B. (2014) 'Inner-city urban redevelopment in China metropolises and the emergence of gentrification: case of Yuexiu, Guangzhou', *Journal of Urban Planning and Development*, 140(4).

16. The gentrification of social housing
Melissa Fernández Arrigoitia

16.1 INTRODUCTION

Gentrification is broadly understood as a multifaceted process of contemporary capital-ism that slowly strips away the working class characteristics of particular locations to turn them into areas where only (or mainly) those with greater financial and cultural capital (the middle class 'gentry') can afford to live, work or play. Whatever its global permutations, the unfolding of this process is consistently linked to a growing lack of affordable housing for those who need it the most, and in many countries it has been directly related to, if not dependent upon the reduction of social housing via displace-ment, expulsions and dispossession (Lees et al. 2008; Lees 2014a,b; Sassen 2015; Brickell et al. 2016; Janoschka and Sequera 2016). Indeed, the provision and maintenance of social housing, whether rented or owner-occupied, state-provided or as informal settlements, can counteract some of the effects of gentrification by guaranteeing affordable homes to those who are otherwise excluded from them.

But social housing does not emerge (or disappear) in a vacuum. It is inextricably tied to a plethora of other housing, urban and planning policies that are often deeply invested and entangled in the neoliberal politics and practices of gentrification. These tend to be sanitised through a discursive repertoire of legitimation that includes phrases or 'rewords' (Mendes 2011; Lees 2003) such as 'social mixing', 'poverty deconcentration' and 'urban renewal'. Government inputs (or lack thereof) into social housing are also interrelated to the broader market dynamics of land values and real-estate investments (Rolnik 2013; Madden and Marcuse 2016). As Lees, Shin and López-Morales (2015) argue, the multiple forms, mutability and complexity of property rights and tenure relations globally makes the gentrification analytic both as a concept and a process one that is 'constitutive of diverse urban forces at work' (p. 3) – essential. Its multi-pronged contingency means that social housing policies and practices are not innocent altruistic mechanisms of (re)distribu-tion. In the context of austerity, economic crises and the retrenchment of welfare states, they are also tools that work with the private market in ways that make the displacement of existing populations from central city areas not only possible but legitimate. This, in turn, enables the unequal socio-spatial development, polarisation and segregation of the urban poor (Lees et al. 2008). The loss of public housing is connected to increased levels of homelessness and vulnerability, and can be deeply gendered and racialised putting certain women, for instance, in more precarious circumstances (Dehavenon 2000; Desmond 2016).

It is against this background that this chapter explores social housing as both an object *of* gentrification (i.e., a domain impacted by gentrification) and a key instrument *for* it (i.e., a domain that facilitates gentrification). The first section below sets out what the differences and similarities are between these two orientations. The second section identifies three principal mechanisms– privatisation, social mixing, and new construction on city peripheries – through which these forms of gentrification take place. It discusses each of these in relation to national and regional examples – particularly those regions my own work has focused on. I juxtapose cases that exemplify the process of 'social housing gentrification' in order to contribute to a discussion within a now well-established call by urban studies scholars to decentre the Global North as *the* nexus of gentrification (Lees, Shin and López-Morales 2016). While there is an ongoing debate as to the applicability of the term in diverse contexts,[1] gentrification has been taking place in various guises inside and outside the West for some time. The goal here is not to be exhaustive but to produce knowledge that highlights the 'regularities' (Lees et al. 2015: 8) of gentrification processes across different contexts.

Social housing is also of course, more than an instrument of policy. At its core, it is a lived experience of home and community. Its gentrification must therefore also be understood through the eyes of residents resisting these moves and proposing alternative logics of urban (and suburban, rural or peripheral) life. The final section looks at some examples of local activism as embodied political resistance to gentrification, and heeds some lessons from them. It extends the gentrification analytic by building on feminist geopolitics to include a 'more than housing' approach to the topic at hand and identifies existing or proposed alternatives to the gentrification of social housing in both the Global North and South. The conclusions offer some tentative ideas about areas that could benefit from further scholarly inquiry.

16.2   SOCIAL HOUSING AS AN OBJECT *OF* AND TOOL *FOR* GENTRIFICATION

Before moving on, it is worth clarifying the analytic distinction I make between the gentrification *of* social housing and social housing as a tool *for* gentrification. It is an important one when identifying and decoupling the overt and subtle relations between gentrification and social housing.

In the first instance – as an object *of* gentrification – this pertains to cases where social housing is targeted for a reduction of units or residents through partial or full removal. Here, social housing residents are directly affected through actions such as evictions and displacement (Marcuse 1985; Slater 2010), and the physical structures themselves are either demolished or refurbished. It also includes cases where paying social housing rents or attending to living costs becomes untenable because of gentrification-related pressures (see Marcuse 1985, on indirect displacement and/or Harvey 2001, on 'accumulation by dispossession'). In certain Global South contexts, these analytic frameworks have been extended beyond the pricing out of long-term residents from central city areas via rent rises and higher costs of living to include the element of force in social housing removals as integral to the typologies of gentrification (Janoschka et al. 2014; Ghertner 2014). The *of* in the phrase underscores how the desire for more gentrified landscapes and environments can lead to the social and material 'unmaking' of public housing homes (Brickell and Baxter 2014; Lees 2014a,b).

---

[1]   For debate on gentrification as 'a choice between unreflective universalism and essentializing individualization', see Bernt 2016; Ghertner 2014; López-Morales 2015; and Slater 2015.

On the other hand, as a tool *for* gentrification – the production or alteration of social housing schemes can also be used by policy-makers and housing practitioners as a political, economic and material artefact of construction that facilitates the division and appropriation of space. This is the case when new peripheral projects that liberate prime central city land for new investments are created, or when policies are devised in ways that promote exclusion within existing or new-build social housing (by, for example, favouring certain 'deserving' tenants according to a financial logic that effectively prices out long-term residents). In its instrumentation *for* gentrification, the proactivity that appears to underlie the creation of some social housing disguises the more subtle (and perverse) ways in which gentrification is mobilised though selective provision and spatial distinction.

While the form and content of these two approaches can differ, they are not mutually exclusive and often coincide in practice. In a mixed-income social housing regeneration project, for example, total numbers of dwelling units can be reduced through partial demolition and resident displacement (i.e., gentrification *of* social housing), at the same time that new 'social' units can be built to target a more middle class demographic that 'diversifies' the socio-economic landscape (i.e., the 'mixed communities' tool *for* gentrification). In both instances, the underlying incentives and effects are often the same: the reduction of social housing units vis-à-vis private market ones, the replacement of previous low-income residents with new more affluent ones and the gentrification (sold as 'social mix') of the adjoining areas where the buildings stand or stood (see Bridge et al. 2011). This 'social cleansing', as many have come to label this process, tends to ignore or minimise the everyday emplacement that already exists in social housing communities where,

> . . .the deep roots working class people grow in the places where they reside – a use-value conception of space – are secondary to the totally dominant exchange-value (profit) ethos and mandate of those responsible for housing provision and urban planning (Slater 2013: 288).

Crucially, both are also likely to draw from a long-established history of discursive repertoires that pivot on the figure of the social housing resident (and their associated housing typology) as stigmatised and demonised 'other' (Fernández Arrigoitia 2014). Fuelled initially by an American school of socio-environmental determinism that linked public housing building typologies with racialised anti-social behaviour (Newman 1972; Rainwater 1970; Yancey 1971), this idea was successfully transferred to the United Kingdom (UK) by Alice Coleman's 'science of deign disadvantagement' and adopted during Thatcher's era of social housing privatisation (Coleman 1985; Jacobs and Lees 2013: 1565). The specific labelling of social housing 'others' varies between countries and regions of the world but is part of a continuum in global symbolic 'otherings' that maps onto local vernaculars of stigmatised difference (e.g., racialised, gendered and classed) and housing typologies (e.g., high-rises and slums/favelas/gecekondu).

The discourses that conflate residents' social status with buildings' architectural form circulate most emblematically in relation to modernist post-World War II high-rise social housing towers. In Western cities such as Chicago, Glasgow and St. Louis these 'big things' (Jacobs 2006; Jacobs et al. 2003) were initially perceived as objects of love and admiration that would reorder urban space and its working class inhabitants according to dominant visions of appropriate development and 'progress'. They were later condemned and rejected as failed objects of disgust and derision in need of interventions such as demolition (Jacobs and Lees 2013). These socio-material histories matter not just to the emotions and imaginations buildings inspired at particular moments in 'modern' time (Kaasa 2014) but to how that effect travels through time, informing future policies that determine the form social housing takes. The transnational *long-duree* of this material-aesthetic-emotional bind works to justify the displacement and dispossession of working-class and low-income groups which, in turn, makes gentrification possible or, at the very least, more publicly presentable.

Let us then now turn to explore some of the mechanisms through which the gentrification of social housing – in both of the forms described above – is most typically materialised across a number of settings.

16.3   THE MECHANICS OF SOCIAL HOUSING GENTRIFICATION

16.3.1   Privatisation and Tenure Conversion

One of the most recognisable patterns signalling the gentrification of social housing is a turn away from state responsibility for housing provision (where there had previously been one) toward its privatisation (Lees 2014a,b). Generally defined as the sale of state-owned assets to the private sector (i.e., individuals, housing associations or corporations), its intensity and manifestations are highly dependent on the socio-cultural heritage of individual national housing systems and welfare states (see Scanlon et al. 2014). The logic through which privatisation (which includes tenure conversions, from public to private rental, or ownership) spurs gentrification is simple:

> As the acquisition of owner occupied housing generally requires more financial capital or income than entering (social) rental housing, particularly in high-demand areas, tenure conversions typically entail that new residents will be of a higher social economic status (Boterman 2012: 140).

In other words, the sale of state rentals through market dynamics summons gentrification by allowing relatively higher-income residents seeking the valued amenities (spatial, natural or public) of the previously low-income public housing units to buy these out. The desire to privatise social housing, or construct private affordable units through public-private partnerships (more on the latter below), is typically connected to capitalist pushes for homeownership as a tenure that presumes housing wealth and security in later life and is ideologically entrenched (especially in North America and the UK) as a form of legitimate middle-class aspirational citizenship.[2] Despite the devastating aftermaths of the global financial crisis and its established links to private homeownership bubbles, as well as the disastrous effects of the construction of 'vivienda popular' (popular housing) in countries such as Chile and beyond from the 1970s onward (Caldeira 2016), the privatisation of social housing continues to be enthusiastically supported by neoliberal

---

[2]   See Madden and Marcuse (2016) for a recent discussion that debunks the myths of homeownership, revealing its ideological status and highlighting its role as a system of alienation, oppression and liberation.

austerity agendas that favour disinvestment from social housing and associated severe public spending cuts.

In the UK, and other European contexts, the main tool that facilitated the privatisation of a previously robust social housing sector was the Right to Buy policy (first instituted in 1980) characterised by the selling of discounted council homes to sitting tenants. Restrictions on building new social housing and large-scale voluntary transfers of council housing to other landlords have also led to a gradual but steep reduction of the social sector and its stock, as well as a shift in ownership structures towards owner-occupation (see Table 7.1 in Scanlon et al. 2014: 106; Murie 2016). Sell-offs for home-ownership are often justified by the continued existence of new-build construction; but the balance between these two is often not one-to-one, and sell-offs (or privatisation/tenure-conversion) can far-exceed new social housing construction (Hedin et al. 2012).

A stark and 'revanchist' (Smith 1996) incarnation of the UK's Right to Buy model has been taking shape since 2015 by providing discounts to tenants who want to purchase their previously protected Housing Association property. The recent Housing White Paper (DCLG 2017: 60) announced a funding extension for this pilot scheme. A new 'Right-to-Rent' regime has also been operating since 2016 requiring landlords, homeowners and letting agents to conduct immigration checks on future tenants. Finally, despite being ruled out, the conservative government proposed the idea of a 'pay to stay' policy where social housing tenants would be charged market rents (tapered) once they exceeded a particular earning threshold. These are pernicious and racially infused shifts in discourse, governance, policy and practice that are contributing to the gentrification of many urban neighbourhoods and rapidly dismantling the safety nets protecting the vulnerable.

Seen also in contexts as diverse as New Zealand, Estonia, Central and Eastern European countries (Hegedus et al. 2013; Kährik 2003; Thorsnes and Kidson 2015), the Right to Buy policy has facilitated the almost wholesale privatisation of social housing and a sharp decrease of the sector (via different national processes) through give-away financial schemes and the restitution principle which returned or compensated presocialist era owners and landlords. In Hungary, the privatisation of social housing stock has taken place alongside urban reconstruction and rehabilitation programmes, and new social housing allocation policies that favour the middle classes including an ad hoc allocation tendering procedure that allows for local municipalities to choose households considered to be 'better off' (i.e., can pay higher rents) and financial incentives (grants) to 'export' the poor, have led to the gentrification of urban centres (Hegedus 2014). This multi-layered phenomenon resonates in cities as diverse as London, Istanbul, Lisbon, Rome and Madrid, where a lack of affordable homes and historically low levels of public housing have been symptomatic of larger economic crises, gentrification trends and a rollback of the welfare state (see Mathivet 2012).

A large study that looked at the socio-spatial effects of tenure conversion in inner city Stockholm (from public housing rental units to privately owned cooperatives) found that individuals with higher disposable incomes and education levels were replacing less affluent ones, younger people were replacing older populations and a growth in a 'back to the city' movement among families with children was taking place at the same time (Andersson and Magnusson Turner 2014). These concomitant shifts nourish gentrification because they 'reduce the public sector, increase segregation, and generate less affordable housing in Stockholm for those who cannot access cooperative or home ownership tenure' (ibid., p. 26). Such trends in residential segregation support assertions that to understand the relations between policy, gentrification and urban social patterning, it is imperative to investigate the intersections of demography, ethnicity and social class because 'trends in the converted section of the housing market are not just mirroring income developments but also seem to reflect trends in ethnic segregation, as well as demographic trends such as a renewed interest among families to live in the inner city' (Boterman 2012). In other words, there is a financial, political, moral and cultural economy at play in the creation of a gentrified environment that tends to benefit the deserving – classed, gendered and racialised – few.

16.3.2 'Social Mixing'

Connected to but distinct from privatisation and tenure change, urban policy and planning directives that promote 'socially mixed' neighbourhoods also play a strong hand in the gentrification of social housing by enabling the reduction of low-income social tenants present in a particular area and the introduction of wealthier ones in the name of 'redevelopment' (Bridge et al. 2011). 'Social mixing', in this sense, is a form of exclusionary displacement related to both rent- and value-gap theories that often takes place and is made legitimate when local authorities seek to 'regenerate', 'upgrade', 'renew' or 'revitalise' neighbourhoods. Policies supporting these kinds of programmes are part of the 'elastic yet targeted' (Lees et al. 2016: 99) structure of gentrification that claims that bringing in higher income market residents to areas considered disadvantaged or in decline will lead to less segregation or poverty concentrations, while engendering greater diversity and inclusivity (Lees 2008; Lees et al. 2008; Lees and Ley 2008). The idea is that bringing the tastes, wealth, morals and culture of middle class populations closer to poorer populations will remedy the problems popularly associated with social housing 'residualisation' (read in certain countries as ethnic segregation and concentration) and its social 'types'. Running through the artificial production of mixity are highly gendered and raced ideologies about cities, bodies, safety and fear (Baxter and Lees 2009; Kern 2010).

Social mix strategies and techniques have been implemented in many countries through-out the world through a range of policies, programmes and practices that, while distinct and operating at varying scales and temporalities, also bear many similarities (Bridge et al. 2011). In Asian cities such as Beijing and Shanghai (Ha 2014; Kim et al. 2010), urban redevelopment programmes have for a very long time been characterised by the kinds of demolitions, large-scale clearances and new-build construction that are more typi-cally associated today with Western cities. Seoul's urban development and high-density reconstruction, Shin and Kim argue (2016), have always been property led; gentrification, therefore, can be understood as endogenous to such places (see also Ha 2015).

One of the largest programmes to date has been the United States' HOPE VI (Home Ownership and Opportunities for People Everywhere) programme – a large-scale public housing, mixed-income redevelopment programme adopted in the early 1990s by the Federal Department of Housing and Urban Development (HUD) as a way to transform 'severely distressed' public housing by altering their physical form through partial or total demolition (National Commission on Severely Distressed Public Housing 1992). Seen as a tool for deconcentrating poverty it was rolled out differently by individual states. In economically depressed and colonial contexts such as the Caribbean territory of Puerto

Rico, a joint commission set up in 1991 between HUD and the local housing authority (PRPHA) opted for the total demolition of all of its tall public housing buildings and their replacement with mixed-income ones (in scattered low-rises, commonly called 'walk-up' apartments). This programme and the concomitant growth in the use of Section 8 vouchers and Low-Income Housing Tax Credits (LIHTC) have contributed to the shrinking of an already weak public housing sector (Vale 2002). As Desmond (2016: 303) has so powerfully demonstrated in his ethnographic account of evictions in America,

> . . .two of every three poor renting families get no federal assistance. . .This drastic shortfall in government support, coupled with rising rent and utility costs alongside stagnant incomes, is the reason why most poor renting families today spend most of their incomes on housing.

Supported by the intensified surveillance and policing of spaces, this policy has also been linked to territorial stigmatization, systemic forms of discrimination and crucially, to increased displacement and gentrification (Dinzey Flores 2007, 2012, 2013; Oliver-Didier 2016; Lees 2004, 2008: 2454; Engle Merry 2001; Smith 2006: 278). As I have argued elsewhere,

> HOPE VI is specifically being used with the affluent and middle class aesthetics in mind as a device through which to transform urban space by refurbishing city centres, 'cleaning out' whatever remnants of pre-modern living may be left scattered around the corners and alleys of those centres [. . .]. By peripheralizing and dispersing the poor, the interests of private industries, particularly construction and development ones, are being protected and urban social justice and a fair distribution of resources are adversely affected [. . .] (Fernández Arrigoitia 2010: 23–24).

In the UK, an equivalent move towards large-scale 'urban regeneration' – or 'state-led gentrification' (Lees et al. 2008; Watt 2009) – has involved demolishing existing social housing estates to give way to new densely built 'mixed community' schemes, stripping established forms of diverse urban life and community of its socio-economic complexity. Such erosions have been facilitated by government-backed planning instruments such as viability assessments that allow for-profit developers to negotiate down their affordable housing obligations (or, Section 106) if they can demonstrate that including social housing would make their scheme financially 'unviable'. While exact figures vary, the net loss of London council homes due to partial or full regeneration is significant and unquestionable.

Instituting mixed-income programmes in the US and the UK often involves negotiating with original residents who will be displaced, offering distant substitute units or insufficient financial compensation (Lees 2014a). These negotiations are also true of large slum redevelopment schemes in cities such as Mumbai that offer only a few of the original dwellers the possibility of on-site resettlement. Brokered by community leaders, these deals form part of a 'speculative displacement' (Goldman 2011) that requires residents to wait indefinitely for compensation or resolution. Allocation of scarce affordable housing units is also mediated by discriminatory identity-markers and by loopholes in local policies that allow new upper-income invasion (Doshi 2015: 112). In some Indian cities, state-led mixed income programmes have existed since the 1970s (Lees et al. 2016: 129) but the possibility of creating or maintaining a real 'mix' has been diminished by neoliberal trends that favour slum clearances and luxury gated developments and lifestyles (Kumar and Fernández Arrigoitia 2015).

There is mounting evidence in places ranging from Santiago de Chile and Toronto to London, Puerto Rico and India that the assumptions behind mixed-income developments and policies – mainly that proximity between social groups will lead to poverty deconcentration, to upward mobility or to a reduction of class-oriented fear and exclusions – are unfounded (Lees 2008). Findings from studies of low-income household displacement in cities such as San Francisco (Dagen Bloom et al. 2015) directly contradict one of the key arguments used by proponents of these schemes – that by generating more market rate housing, accessibility and affordability will ensue. Without the right economic conditions, no amount of mixing and diversity will lead to better opportunities (Ruiz-Tangle and López 2014).

In places marked by deep and historical racial tensions and prejudices, as well as other class and gender divides, an influx of middle-class populations can actually lead to greater tensions, divisions and senses of surveillance, with spatial rules and social policies dominated by middle class cultures and aesthetics (Clark 2002; Joseph et al. 2011). New middle-class neighbours in Toronto's first public housing redevelopment project, for instance, framed the outdoor socialising of low-income neighbours as deviant, devaluing the input, ideas or physical presence of tenants, women and racialised youth (August 2014). In Johannesburg, where the municipality is embarking on massive mixed-income, mixed-tenure housing developments (Mbembe and Nuttall 2008; Mosselon 2017), these often lead to 'Nimbyism, rent increases, exclusionary displacement, socio-economic segregation, and political isolation' (Winkler 2013: 32). These social impacts are coupled with the argument that,

> Targeting investment and implementing large-scale projects on the few sites where market-driven redevelopment is viable will only reinforce inequality in the context of an uneven geography of land values (August 2014: 1177).

16.4   DISPLACEMENT TO NEW PERIPHERAL SOCIAL HOUSING

Market-driven redevelopment projects that seek to 'renew' (read, cleanse) central city areas perceived as declined through urbanisation and mixed-income housing projects of the kind described above can reinforce inequalities through an aesthetics, politics and logic of gentrification. In countries as different as Turkey, India and Brazil to the UK, Canada and China, this is not just about speculative investment in central city areas, but also about achieving 'global' or 'world-class' city status by replacing populations deemed undesirable or unproductive within those spaces with newer economic, 'creative' or 'cultural' capital (Lees et al. 2016). These longings for an embodied urban change are usually premised on raced, classed and gendered understandings of order, morality and progress (Fusté 2010).

Displacement can take place before or after gentrification. When displacement leads to new urban development projects of various kinds including mixed-income housing of the kind described before, moving people is the mechanism through which gentrification is facilitated. While the outcomes, experiences, violence and dispossession that results from such displacements can be equally strong in the Global North and South, development induced displacement appears to be more aggressive in the Global South, where bulldozers can sometimes raze houses outright and without warning (Lees et al. 2016; also Brickell et al. 2017). In Delhi, where there are long-standing struggles over the privatisation of land (enclosure) and the end of the public city (communing), displacement of the working classes and slum removals are pursued directly by the state with the use of extra-economic force (Ghertner 2014: 1562–1564). While Ghertner argues that in the Indian context this does not amount to gentrification, state-led (or legitimated) removals almost invariably have the effect of reducing the amount of official or unofficial social housing in the re-valued central areas and displacing low-income residents into small and distant low-cost housing complexes built by private investors in publicly subsidised urban fringe-land. Johannesburg's 'Better Building Programme', a regeneration policy that prioritises 'homeownership, privatization, and the break up of concentrated poverty' has, for instance, enabled the eviction of many of the most vulnerable inner city residents without suitable alternatives being provided (Winkler 2009: 364).

While these peripheral, new-build projects can provide some necessary social housing (rented or owner-occupied, depending on the country's policy), their creation in distant and disconnected peri-urban areas creates and reproduces the marginality of its residents (who are often already the subjects of multi-generational displacements). It does so by denying residents full participation in urban or community life – making their circulation for work and sociality difficult. In the absence of urban infrastructure, including transport, schools and health facilities, this landscape of additional needs reflects and reproduces the devaluation of particular urban subjects as an underserving underclass. It does so unevenly, and disproportionately impacts women who continue to carry child and other social reproduction and domestic labour responsibilities. By being out-of-sight, it also creates the ideal environment for discrimination, impunity and abuse against and within those communities.

The creation of social housing in peripheries does not just provide housing after gentrification is underway; it can also facilitate gentrification by providing homes to low-income residents previously inhabiting newly re-valued land ripe for urban speculation. Rio de Janeiro's implementation of the Brazilian social housing programme *Minha Casa, Minha Vida* (MCMV) is a case in point of how housing and urban development trends leading to gentrification can coincide and make the displacement of inner-city lower-income populations out to peripheries not only possible, but inevitable. Devised by the Ministry of Cities under the 2008 Growth Acceleration Programme (PAC) to generate economic activity and increase the workforce, MCMV is a federal housing construction programme (currently in its third phase of construction) that resembles the mass modernist post-war public housing projects of some European countries and the United States. Planned to accommodate means-tested families through owner-occupation, this programme has undoubtedly responded to a housing need. It has also been instrumental in sheltering the estimated hundreds of thousands of residents displaced from favelas who have had to be relocated because of the local government's vast urban redevelopment projects, including a series of new Bus Rapid Transit (BRT) lines; a range of World Cup and Olympics sport installations; and a number of tourism-related infrastructures, including the redevelopment of the entire Port (Porto Maravilla) area.

In these 'voluntary' resettlements, the element of 'free' choice becomes questionable. . .it is about how the legitimate uses and users of newly valued central city spaces are being re-defined and delimited in a context of competing (and highly unequal) interests. . . There is, at the moment, a conflict between 'the right to the city' and commercial purposes in the favour of the latter, as political will and financial pressures combine to the detriment of informal urban workers and dwellers. If delivering 'public good', in a phase of modernist upgrade, follows a voracious market-driven land policy, the city may run the risk of alleviating a social and economic segregation which will limit the much-needed access to decent and affordable housing (Fernández Arrigoitia 2013).

In this light, having a solid social housing construction project in place to offer as alternative accommodation makes development led displacement through evictions and resettlements more effortless and easily justifiable. It also facilitated the gentrification of central city favelas, which were formerly the only housing possibility for poor inhabitants of the city (Steele 2013).

The construction of mass social housing projects on the peripheries of Indian cities such as Chennai (Figures 16.1 and 16.2) are exhibiting another, more pre-emptive function for displacement and gentrification, as they are built en masse by new internal migrants to sit empty, awaiting future evicted inhabitants from nearby shantytowns, who are usually longer-term migrants (Kumar and Fernández Arrigoitia 2015). Here, new peripheral social housing construction is contributing to a cycle of urban entrapment that keeps the most vulnerable in positions of exclusion and precarity. Like in Istanbul, the relocation of inhabitants away from metropolitan centres into peripheral social housing complexes acts as a form (amongst others) of symbolic and material/physical

Source: Author, August 2015.

Figures 16.1 & 16.2   *Chennai is witnessing mega peri-urban public and private property developments like these social housing and luxury towers, along the same main road*

violence (Angell et al. 2014; Lovering and Türkmen 2011; Mooney 1999; Van Criekingen 2013).

16.5   SOCIAL HOUSING AS RESISTANCE TO GENTRIFICATION

In light of the hyper-commodified housing landscapes of cities around the world, the mere existence of truly affordable and accessible public housing rental units can be seen as a form of active resistance – a socio-material counterpoint to dominant city-making visions via gentrification. The survival of these spaces and their residents should be understood in part through the lived 'extra economic' forces that continually produce them. If we consider the affective, emotional, material and intimate geopolitical life (Brickell 2012a,b) of social housing's domestic and community spaces, then everyday acts of maintenance and quotidian interactions can emerge as resistant and political in scope (Lees 2014a; Lees and Ferreri 2016). Home-making, here, takes place with and despite rules, regulations or removal threats; and informal livelihood practices and sociality can defy the material, political and symbolic bordering of targeted raced/gendered/classed populations (Fusté 2010; Oliver-Didier 2016). By valuing the way individuals and groups make sense and meaning of the past, present and future of their homes, the relevance of subjectivity, culture, history and politics in opposing (or surrendering to) gentrifications is highlighted. This feminist multi-sensorial/temporal/scalar framework also moves us away from the 'either/or' debate that has dominated gentrification studies as primarily about commodification via rent-gap theory (Bernt 2016: 7).

Resistance is also always contingent and configured through historic and evolving links to a range of networks, places and political actors. Traditional forms of protest can vary in scope – from private tenancy rights and affordability in urban, peri-urban and more rural settings to environmental standards or overcrowding; and they can differ in form – from public demonstrations and petitions to documentary films and mural painting. They can be local while generating broader national or international alliances with similar causes. The recent upsurge of resistance to evictions and displacements linked to urban gentrification and loss of the commons across public housing contexts represents a form of global or 'planetary' challenge to common forms of urban dispossession (see Lees et al. 2018).

Brutal waves of neoliberal austerity programmes have attacked public welfare provision and already dwindling social subsidies, with deep impacts on housing. When the state intervenes in this way to foster policies and programmes that lead to the displacement of lower-income residents, its role in alleviating poverty becomes questionable and its hand in the gentrification (read, reduction) of public housing more explicit (Goetz 2013; Bridge et al. 2011). In inner London, where low-income social housing residents are being disproportionately affected by mega-gentrification and displacement, residents, activists, scholars, artists and local politicians have converged around the erosion and denial of the right to adequate and affordable shelter, and against the social cleansing agenda most famously associated with the demolition of the Heygate Estate in Elephant & Castle (Lees and Ferreri 2016). The interest and actions garnered by this case served as a teaching ground of sorts for the on-going battle on the nearby Aylesbury Estate, based on the human rights of resident leaseholders,[3] a public inquiry yielded a surprise rejection by the government of the local council's compulsory purchase orders (CPOs). Another group who managed to secure their social housing units through occupation and media tactics despite enormous pressures to move out was Focus E15. In both cases, as in so many other social housing communities, it was women who led the resistance.

In Latin American contexts (Casgraine and Janoschka 2013), gentrification processes have been noted as incomplete because wholesale neighbourhood take-over is almost always patchy. This makes its politics and material manifestations (logics) unique spaces for community organisation and resistance. In Puerto Rico, a post-colonial nation with strong links to both Latin American and US politics and culture, public housing residents

---

[3] Specifically, it was found to breach the European Convention on Human Rights (ECHR) 'in respect of Articles 1 (right to quiet enjoyment of property) and 8 (right to respect for private and family life).' Acknowledging that, 'as a consequence of the CPO they will be separated from their family and friends and they will be unable to afford to return to the estate' (Coffey 2016: 42).

Source: Alvin Cuoto, 2010.

Figure 16.3   Residents fighting the demolition of Las Gladiolas housing towers (San Juan, Puerto Rico) come together with other island-wide communities threatened by displacement

contesting HOPE VI demolitions in 2006 were not only composed of vocal individuals with ties to workers' unions and to other local social and legal aid groups defending vulnerable communities. Over time, they also developed relations with the Latin American 'Grito de los Excluidos' movement and to its global anti-displacement campaign, as well as to the local chapter of Amnesty International which supported anti-demolition activism on the grounds of race and gender discrimination, tied into long-standing public health issues as well. Ambivalence and subterfuge were important to the way individuals coped with the pressures to move out, while direct and legal actions were also necessary as pressure tactics. While these incarnations of community activism and resistance are not exactly new – residents and communities facing housing injustices have always organised or resisted –

Source: Author, August 2013.

*Figure 16.4   Residents of Villa Autódromo (Rio de Janeiro) unite with academics,
activists and human rights lawyers to discuss relocation threats due to
Olympic Stadium construction*

the most recent movements have successfully turned the question of 'the housing crisis'
into a topic of mass political protest (Edwards 2016; Watt and Minton 2016). Other
notable examples of recent resistance come from Spain and the US, where mortgage
market defaults, foreclosure and affordability crises, have galvanised new waves of far-
reaching condemnations, activisms and radical grassroots political movements such as
the PAH (Plataforma de los Afectados por las Hipoteca) (see Annunziata and Lees 2016).

Many if not all of the movements quoted above have produced alternative technical,
evidence, planning and design documents to contest official versions of public housing
redevelopment. In Rio de Janeiro, for example (see Figure 16.4), a popular planning
document was created between residents, urban scholars and planners, architects and
legal experts to present a community vision and alternative to the government's proposed
evictions and resettlements of their historic homes due to an Olympic construction
project (AMPAVA 2016). Designed to resist 'an unjust, unjustifiable, and illegal removal
attempt', their holistic urban, economic, social and cultural programme was awarded the
international 2013 Urban Age award in symbolic recognition and support of their cause.

While some gains were achieved and the mayor now uses the case as a 'model eviction' where some families have been given the opportunity to remain in reconfigured spaces and new-built homes, the majority were displaced (some very violently) and moved to MCMV resettlement sites. In another case, the 'Preserve Rosewood Courts' group in Texas drew up a 'People's Plan to Preserve Austin's Public Housing' (Preserve Rosewood 2016), linking the struggles of affordable housing and historic preservation in their eastern corner of the city ('one of the most gentrified zip codes in the nation') to rising rents and property values. They argued that gentrification should be tackled by valuing the cultural and material heritage as well as racial histories of what they uncovered and documented as America's oldest black public housing, which the Austin Housing Authority was looking to demolish and redevelop. In London, an anti-gentrification handbook was co-produced by scholar-activists, organisations and council tenants providing other social housing communities threatened by displacement guidance on resisting the demolition of their council estates (The London Tenants Federation, Lees, Just Space and SNAG, 2014); a similar version has now been produced in Sweden.

16.6　CONCLUSION

This chapter has addressed cases from across the world, reflecting the growing academic, media and popular interest in, and literature on, this topic, as well as the varied and precise causes, mechanisms and effects that can be attributed to social housing's gentrification in diverse global landscapes. While not claiming to be an exhaustive account, the transnational approach employed here echoes and responds to what are now well established calls for decentring the Global North as *the* nexus of gentrification knowledge.

In many parts of the world, the privatisation, demolition, reduction, replacement or transformation of social housing has become inseparable from processes of urban renewal and regeneration which commands the displacement or removal of lower-income groups from revalued city land in order to reach their 'middle-classification' goals. The production, changes to and contestations over social housing today are therefore impacted by, but also implicated in, processes of gentrification. This nexus makes the provision, maintenance or elimination of social housing a unique lens into the power and complexity of gentrification.

Slater (2013), like the scholar-activists researching and contesting the gentrification of public housing on the ground referred to in this chapter, has been absolute in his pronouncement of what needs to happen at this stage:

> The solution is simple, but way off a political radar locked on dismal austerity measures: the preservation and restoration of what public housing is left, together with the mass construction of new public housing, amidst an extended programme of basic income and living wage security, and substantial investment in education (p. 389).

This is being echoed by an increasing number of academics, activists and politicians. But there is also a recognition of the difficulties in implementing wholesale transformation and support for incremental reforms to housing policy. Government intervention on the housing market through rent stabilisation and robust public housing programmes are some of the protective factors that can limit the displacement effects of gentrification

(Lees 2014a). Heeding these lessons, the Parisian city government officially disabled displacement in central working-class neighbourhoods or zones in 2016 in order to prevent 'ghettoization' or social segregation. Its underlying anti-market logic recognises the problems with current mainstream social housing and affordability models and encourages social mix through mechanisms of permanence rather than 'renewal'.

In those places where 'mixed income' schemes and urban redevelopment has been the go-to mechanism of gentrification, direct investment in maintaining existing public housing and building new affordable homes should be prioritised over redeveloping to attract the middle classes. Investment in community development and other programmes can be key towards a 'more meaningful, effective and transformative change' (August 2014: 1178).

There is an evident need for more independent and critical social housing research, as well as for gathering historical, current and strategic data on displacement within and across cities to greater political effect. In the context of Latin America, Janoschka and Sequera (2016: 6) argue that in order to transform the naturalised order of displacement, there needs to be a stronger analytic focus on the discourses that have come to naturalise it. This is not just about top-down political discourses justifying gentrification processes, but also about the multiple, everyday, popular practices that constitute a 'naturalised' or 'idealised' urban order. As postcolonial and feminist readings of the home remind us, these are not apolitical spaces of private domesticity, but politically charged environments with great stakes in the future of urban territories.

REFERENCES

AMPAVA (2016) *Plano Popular da Vila Autódromo: Plano de Desenvolvimento Urbano, Economico, Social e Cultural* [Online]. Available at: https://comitepopulario.files.wordpress.com/2012/08/planopopularvilaauto-dromo.pdf.

Andersson, R. and Magnusson Turner, L. (2014) 'Segregation, gentrification, and residualisation: from public housing to market-driven housing allocation in inner city Stockholm', *International Journal of Housing Policy*, 14(1), 3–29.

Angell, E., Hammond, T. and Van Dobben Schoon, D. (2014) 'Assembling Istanbul: buildings and bodies in a world city', *City*, 18(6), 644–654.

Annunziata, S. and Lees, L. (2016) 'Resistance to displacement in Southern European cities during austerity gentrification', *Sociological Research Online* [Online]. Available at: http://www.socresonline.org.uk/21/3/5.html.

August, M. (2014) 'Negotiating social mix in Toronto's first public housing redevelopment', *International Journal of Urban and Regional Research*, 38(4), 1160–1180.

Baxter, R. and Lees, L. (2009) 'The rebirth of high-rise living in London: towards a sustainable, inclusive, and live-able urban form' in Imrie, R., Lees, L. and Raco, M. (eds), *Regenerating London: Governance, Sustainability and Community in a Global City*, London: Routledge, pp. 151–172.

Boterman, W. and Van Gent, W. (2014) 'Housing liberalization and gentrification. The social effects of tenure conversions in Amsterdam', *Tijdschrift voor Economische en Sociale Geografie*, 105(2), 140–160.

Brickell, K. (2012a) 'Geopolitics of home', *Geography Compass*, 6(10), 575–588.

Brickell, K. (2012b) '"Mapping" and "doing" critical geographies of home', *Progress in Human Geography*, 36(2), 225–244.

Brickell, K. and Baxter, R. (2014) 'For home unmaking', *Home Cultures*, 11(2), 133–143.

Brickell, K., Fernández Arrigoitia, M. and Vasudevan, A. (2017) *Geographies of Forced Evictions: Dispossession, Violence, Resistance*, Palgrave Macmillan.

Bridge, G., Butler, T., and Lees, L. (eds) (2011) *Mixed Communities: Gentrification by Stealth?*, Bristol: Policy Press. (Republished 2012 by University of Chicago Press).

Caldeira, T. (2016) 'Responses to the global city: the urban question in the twenty-first century, A dialogue with Teresa Caldeira', *ÍCONOS*, 56, 149–155.

Casgraine, A. and Janoschka, M. (2013) 'Gentrificación y resistencia en las ciudades latinoamericanas. El ejemplo de Santiago de Chile', *Andamios – Revista De Investigación Social*, 10(22), 19–44.

Clark, S. (2002) 'Where the poor live: how federal housing policy shapes residential communities', *Urban Anthropology*, 31(1), 69–92.

Coffey, L. (2016) *CPO Report to the Secretary of State for Communities and Local Government*. 29 January 2016 [Online]. Available at: https://southwarknotes.files.wordpress.com/2009/12/aylesbury-cpo-inspectors-report.pdf.

Coleman, A. (1985) *Utopia on Trial: Vision and Reality in Planned Housing*, London: Hilary Shipman Publishing.

Dagen Bloom, N., Umback, F. and Vale, L. (2015) *Public Housing Myths: Perception, Reality and Social Policy*, Ithaca: Cornell University Press.

Department for Communities and Local Government – DCLG (2017) *Fixing our broken housing market*, February 2017 [Online]. Available at: https://www.gov.uk/government/collections/housing-white-paper.

Desmond, M. (2016) *Evicted: Poverty and Profit in the American City*, New York: Crown.

Dinzey-Flores, Z. (2007) 'Temporary housing, permanent communities: public housing policy and design in Puerto Rico', *Journal of Urban History*, 33(3), 467–492.

Dinzey-Flores, Z. (2012, 'Where rights begin and end in Puerto Rico's gated communities', *Singapore Journal of Tropical Geography*, 33(3), 198–211.

Dinzey-Flores, Z. (2013) *Locked In, Locked Out: Gated Communities in a Puerto Rican City*, Philadelphia: University of Pennsylvania Press.

Doshi, S. (2015) 'Rethinking gentrification in India: displacement, dispossession and the spectre of development' in Lees, L., Shin, H.B. and López-Morales, E. (eds), *Global Gentrifications: Uneven Development and Displacement*, Bristol: Policy Press.

Edwards, M. (2016) 'The housing crisis in London', *City: Analysis of Urban Trends, Culture, Theory, Policy, Action*, 20(2), 222–237.

Engels, B. (1999) 'Property ownership, tenure and displacement: in search of the process of displacement', *Environment and Planning A*, 31, 1473–1495.

Engle Merry, S. (2001) 'Spatial governmentality and the new urban social order: Controlling gender violence through law', *American Anthropologist*, 103(1), 16–30.

Fernández Arrigoitia, M. (2010) *Constructing 'the other', practicing resistance: public housing and community politics in Puerto Rico*. PhD thesis, The London School of Economics and Political Science (LSE) [Online]. Available at: http://etheses.lse.ac.uk/335/.

Fernández Arrigoitia, M. (2013) 'Relocating homes and lives in Rio's Olympic city', *Urban Age Rio de Janeiro Conference Newspaper* [Online]. Available at: https://lsecities.net/media/objects/articles/relocating-homes-and-lives-in-rios-olympic-city/en-gb/.

Fernández Arrigoitia, M. (2014) 'Unmaking public housing towers: the role of lifts and stairs in the demolition of a Puerto Rican project', *Home Cultures*, 11(2), 167–196.

Fusté, J. (2010) 'Colonial laboratories, irreparable subjects: the experiment of (b)ordering San Juan's public housing residents', *Social Identities*, 16(1), 41–59.

Ghertner, A. (2014) 'India's urban revolution: geographies of displacement beyond gentrification', *Environment and Planning A*, 46, 1554–1571.

Goetz, E. (2013) *New Deal Ruins: Race, Economic Justice, and Public Housing Policy*, Ithaca, NY: Cornell University Press.

Goldman, M. (2011) 'Speculative urbanism and the making of the next world city', *International Journal of Urban and Regional Research*, 35, 555–581.

Ha, S. (2015) 'The endogenous dynamics of urban renewal and gentrification in Seoul', in Lees, L., Shin, H. and López-Morales, E. (eds), *Global Gentrifications: Uneven Development and Displacement*, Bristol: Policy Press.

Harvey, D. (2001) *Spaces of Capital*, Edinburgh: Edinburgh University Press.

Hedin, K., Clark, E., Lundholm, E. and Malmberg, G. (2012) 'Neoliberalization of housing in Sweden: gentrification, filtering and social polarization', *Annals of the Association of American Geographers*, 102(2), 443–463.

Hegedus, J. (2014) 'Social housing in Hungary' in Scanlon, K., Whitehead, C. and Fernández Arrigoitia, M. (eds), *Social Housing in Europe*, Chichester: Wiley Blackwell.

Hegedus, J., Lux, M. and Teller, N. (eds) (2013) *Social Housing in Transition Countries*, New York: Routledge.

Jacobs, J. (2006) 'A geography of big things', *Cultural Geographies*, 13, 1–27.

Jacobs, J. and Lees, L. (2013) 'Defensible space on the move: revisiting the urban geography of Alice Coleman', *International Journal of Urban and Regional Research*, 37(5), 1559–1583.

Janoschka, M. and Sequera, J. (2016) 'Gentrification in Latin America: addressing the politics and geographies of displacement', *Urban Geography*, 37(8), 1175–1194.

Janoschka, M., Sequera, J. and Salinas, L. (2014) 'Gentrification in Spain and Latin America – a critical dialogue', *International Journal of Urban and Regional Research*, 38, 1234–1265.

Joseph, M., Khare, A. and Bartz, N. (2011) 'On-the-ground realities of mixed-income development in Chicago:

operational challenges and social dynamics, Colloquy presentation', Urban Affairs Association Annual Meeting, 16–19 March, New Orleans, LA.

Kaasa, A. (2014) 'Revolutionary affect: feeling modern in Mexico City', in Jones, H. and Jackson, E. (eds), *Stories of Cosmopolitan Belonging: Emotion and Location*, Abingdon: Routledge.

Kährik, A. (2003) 'Socio-economic residential differentiation in post-socialist Tallinn', *Journal of Housing and the Built Environment*, 18(1), 49–73.

Kern, L. (2010) 'Selling the "scary city": gendering freedom, fear and condominium development in the neoliberal city', *Social & Cultural Geography*, 11(3), 209–230.

Kim B-W., Kwon N. and Gil J-H. (2010) 'Analysis of the commercial characteristics about the Samcheongdong-gil gentrification', *Journal of the Korean Regional Economics*, 5, 83–102 (in Korean).

Kumar, S. and Fernández Arrigoitia, M. (2016) *The urbanisation-construction-migration nexus (UCMnSA) in 5 cities in South Asia*. A report for DFID [Online]. Available at: http://eprints.lse.ac.uk/65861/.

Lees, L. (2003) 'Visions of "urban renaissance": the urban task force report and the urban white paper', in Imrie, R. and Raco, M. (eds), *Urban Renaissance? New Labour, Community and Urban Policy*, Bristol: Policy Press, pp. 61–82.

Lees, L. (2008) 'Gentrification and social mixing: towards an urban renaissance?', *Urban Studies*, 45(12), 2449–2470.

Lees, L. (2012) 'The geography of gentrification: thinking through comparative urbanism', *Progress in Human Geography*, 36(2), 155–171.

Lees, L. (2014a) 'The urban injustices of New Labour's "new urban renewal": the case of the Aylesbury Estate in London', *Antipode*, 46(4), 921–947.

Lees, L. (2014b) 'The death of sustainable communities in London?', in Imrie, R. and Lees, L. (eds), *Sustainable London? The Future of a Global City*, Bristol: Policy Press, pp. 149–172.

Lees, L. and Ferreri, M. (2016) 'Resisting gentrification in its final frontiers: learning from the Heygate Estate in London (1974–2013)', *Cities*, 57, 14–24.

Lees, L. and Ley, D. (2008) 'Introduction to special issue on gentrification and public policy', *Urban Studies*, 45(12), 2379–2384.

Lees, L., Annunziata, S. and Rivas-Alonso, C. (2018) 'Resisting Planetary Gentrification: the value of surviv-ability in the fight to stay put', *Annals of the Association of American Geographers*, 108(2), 346–355.

Lees, L., Shin, H. and López-Morales, E. (eds) (2015) *Global Gentrifications: Uneven Development and Displacement*, Bristol: Policy Press.

Lees, L., Shin, H. and López-Morales, E. (2016) *Planetary Gentrification*, Cambridge: Polity Press.

Lees, L., Slater, T. and Wyly, E. (2008) *Gentrification*, New York: Routledge.

López-Morales, E. (2015) 'Gentrification in the Global South', *City*, 19(4), 564–573.

Lovering, J. and Türkmen, H. (2011) 'Bulldozer neoliberalism in Istanbul: the state-led construction of property markets, and the displacement of the urban poor', *International Planning Studies*, 16(1), 73–96.

Madden, D. and Marcuse, P. (2016) *In Defense of Housing: The Politics of Crisis*, London: Verso.

Marcuse, P. (1985) 'Abandonment, gentrification, and displacement: the linkages in New York City', in Smith, N. and Williams, P. (eds), *Gentrification of the City*, Routledge, pp. 153–177.

Mathivet, C. (2012) 'Presentation of the Passerelle issue' in *Housing in Europe: Time to Evict the Crisis*, Issue 7: Passerelle and AITEC [Online]. Available at: http://aitec.reseau-ipam.org/IMG/pdf/Passerelle_7_ENG-light.pdf.

Mbembe, A. and Nuttall, S. (2008) 'Introduction: Afropolis', in Nuttall, S. and Mbembe, A. (eds), *Johannesburg: The Elusive Metropolis*, Durham, NC: Duke University Press, pp. 1–33.

Mendes, L. (2011) 'Cidade pós-moderna, gentrificação e a produção social do espaço fragmentado', *Cadernos Metropolis*, 13(26) (julho), 473–495.

Millard-Ball, A. (2000) 'Moving beyond the gentrification gaps: social change, tenure change and gap theories in Stockholm', *Urban Studies*, 37(9), 1673–1693.

Mooney, G. (1999) 'Urban "disorders"' in Brook, C., Mooney, G. and Pile, S. (eds), *Unruly Cities? Order/Disorder*, London: Routledge, pp. 52–56.

Mosselson, A. (2017) '"Joburg has its own momentum": Towards a vernacular theorisation of urban change', *Urban Studies*, 54(5), 1280–1296.

Murie, A. (2016) *The Right to Buy? Selling Off Public and Social Housing*, Bristol: Policy Press.

National Commission on Severely Distressed Public Housing (1992) *The Final Report of the National Commission on Severely Distressed Public Housing*, Washington, DC.

Newman, O. (1972) *Defensible Space: Crime Prevention Through Urban Design*, New York: Macmillan.

Oliver-Didier, O. (2016) 'The biopolitics of thirdspace: urban segregation and resistance in Puerto Rico's Luis Lloréns Torres Public Housing Project', *Housing, Theory and Society*, 33(1), 1–22.

Preserve Rosewood (2016) *A Jewel in the Violet Crown: A People's Plan to Preserve Austin's Public Housing* [Online]. Available at: www.preserverosewood.org.

Rainwater, L. (1970) *Behind Ghetto Walks: Black Family Life in a Federal Slum*, Chicago: Aldine.

Rolnik, R. (2013) 'Late neoliberalism: the financialization of homeownership and housing rights', *International Journal of Urban and Regional Research,* 37(3), 1058–1066.

Ruiz-Tangle, J. and López, E. (2014) 'Él studio de la segregación residencial en Santiago de Chile: revision crítica de algunos problemas metodológico y conceptuales', *EURE*, 40(119), 25–48.

Scanlon, K., Whitehead, C. and Fernández Arrigoitia, M. (eds) (2014) *Social Housing in Europe*, Chichester: Wiley Blackwell.

Shin, H. and Kim, S-H. (2016) 'The developmental state, speculative urbanisation and the politics of displacement in gentrifying Seoul', *Urban Studies,* 53(3), 540–559.

Slater, T. (2013) 'Expulsions from public housing: the hidden context of concentrated affluence', *Cities*, 35, 384–390.

Slater, T. (2015) 'Planetary rent gaps', *Antipode*, 49, 114–137.

Smith, J. (2006) 'Mixed-income communities: designing out poverty or pushing out the poor?' in Bennet, L., Smith, J. and Wright, P.A. (eds), *Where Are Poor People to Live? Transforming Public Housing Communities*, New York: M.E. Sharpe.

Smith, N. (1996) *The New Urban Frontier: Gentrification and the Revanchist City*, London: Routledge.

Steele, F. (2013) 'Brazil property: buyers target homes in Rio's "pacified" favelas', *Financial Times*, 13 September [Online]. Available at: https://www.ft.com/content/5a4c57ea-1612-11e3-a57d-00144feabdc0.

The London Tenants Federation, Lees, L., Just Space and Southwark Notes Archive Group (SNAG) (2013) 'Challenging "the new urban renewal": the social cleansing of council estates in London', in Campkin, B., Roberts, D. and Ross, R. (eds) *Urban Pamphleteer #2 'London: Regeneration Realities'*, London: Urban Lab, UCL, pp. 6–10.

The London Tenants Federation, Lees, L., Just Space and SNAG (2014) *Staying Put: An Anti-Gentrification Handbook for Council Estates in London* (hardcopy and electronically).

Thorsnes, P. Alexander, R. and Kidson, D. (2015) 'Low-income housing in high-amenity areas: long-run effects on residential development', *Urban Studies*, 52(2), 261–278.

Van Criekingen, M. (2013) *Forced Evictions in Istanbul,* Cities Unica Euromaster in Urban Studies. Urban Economic Geography, ULB Brussels, 2011/2013 [Online]. Available at: http://www.hlrn.org/img/violation/merve_Forced_Evictions_in_Istanbul.pdf.

Watt, P. (2009) 'Housing stock transfer, regeneration and state-led gentrification in London', *Urban Policy and Research,* 27(3), 229–242.

Watt, P. and Minton, A. (2016) 'London's housing crisis and its activisms: introduction', *City: Analysis of Urban Trends, Culture, Theory, Policy, Action*, 20(2), 204–221.

Winkler, T. (2009) 'Prolonging the global age of gentrification: Johannesburg's regeneration policies', *Planning Theory*, 8(4), 362–381.

Winkler, T. (2013) 'Believing in market forces in Johannesburg', in Porter, L. and Shaw, K. (eds), *Whose Urban Renaissance? An International Comparison of Urban Regeneration strategies*, Abingdon: Routledge, pp. 25–33.

Yancey, W. (1971) 'Architecture, interaction and social control: the case of a large-scale public housing project', *Environment and Behaviour,* 3, 3–21.

17. Tourism gentrification
Agustín Cocola-Gant

17.1 INTRODUCTION

Gentrification caused by tourism is increasingly affecting places around the world. Although some scholars have noted that tourism threatens the right to 'stay put' of existing populations (e.g. Colomb and Novy, 2016; García-Herrera et al., 2007; Gladstone and Préau, 2008; Gotham, 2005), a conceptualisation of how this phenomenon occurs has not been fully considered. This chapter brings into conversation the literature on tourism and gentrification and shows how both processes intersect in several ways. Special attention is given to the extent to which tourism can be interpreted as a gentrifying process that causes different forms of displacement. Although tourism gentrification has especially been noted in cities, the process also affects non-urban spaces, in particular the coastal and rural contexts. In this regard, tourism gentrification can be seen as an example of 'other geographies of gentrification' (Phillips, 2004).

The growth of tourism is a worldwide phenomenon and residents experience tourism-driven gentrification in both the North and the South. However, the way in which the process occurs is different in different places. The literature highlights two scenarios in which tourism gentrification takes place. First, in advanced capitalist economies research notes that tourism and gentrification tend to coexist and, moreover, that both processes feed into each other. Although research has traditionally regarded tourism as an isolated phenomenon implicitly assuming it takes place in tourist bubbles or precincts (Judd, 1999), in recent years the development of tourism has generally occurred in places that have not been planned as tourist spaces. Instead, tourism tends to overlap with gentrified areas, especially because gentrification provides consumption facilities and a middle-class sense of place that attracts further consumers. I explore this literature in the first section of the chapter. In this regard, I suggest that the attraction of visitors accelerates the pressure of gentrification as the intensification of land use pushes up the value of commercial and residential properties. New spaces of consumption have the ability to increase land values and this process explains why property owners are particularly interested in promoting local tourism growth (Logan and Molotch, 2007).

Second, research highlights that tourism gentrification is particularly important in peripheral economies that rely on tourism as a factor for development and growth. In other words, in places where the lack of highly paid professional jobs offers fewer possibilities for the occurrence of classical gentrification but, instead, where spaces are dominated by the purchasing power of visitors. In the Mediterranean, Caribbean or the Asia-Pacific region, the arrival of visitors opens up new investment opportunities in the built environment and leads to a process of tourist urbanisation that includes not only large-scale resorts and second homes but also housing rehabilitation in historic areas. From a postcolonial perspective, this geography highlights a tourism gentrification that has largely been neglected in a gentrification literature that has principally focused on cities from advanced capitalist economies in the North. In this regard, the chapter shows a geography of gentrification (Lees, 2012) that challenges the conventional ways of theorising the process of gentrification from the perspectives of the Anglo-American world.

Finally, in the last section I bring together different examples from the North and the South and suggest that tourism causes three forms of displacement: residential displacement, commercial displacement and place-based displacement. While residential and commercial displacement are related to the power of tourism to increase land values, place-based displacement refers to the loss of place experienced by residents as the consumption of space by visitors effectively displaces them from the places they belong to. In this regard, displacement is economic, but also cultural and linked to the introduction of new lifestyles that undermine the use value of neighbourhoods as residential spaces.

17.2   TOURISM AND GENTRIFICATION IN ADVANCED ECONOMIES

A starting point in conceptualising the process of urban tourism gentrification is to recognise that tourism does not exist in isolation from the rest of the city but instead overlaps and coexists with other processes of consumption and production of urban space. In this regard, some scholars have studied the emergence of urban tourism in relation to, and as a result of, other contemporary processes of urban restructuring, in which gentrification plays a crucial role. For example, in the explanation of urban tourism, research has often referred first, to interurban competition for mobile capitals and consumers to cope with the economic and fiscal problems brought on by suburbanisation and deindustrialisation (e.g. Judd, 1999; Meethan, 2001). Second, studies have pointed to the emergence of a new middle class increasingly concerned with the consumption of pleasure and entertainment (e.g. Fainstein and Gladstone, 1999; Judd, 1999; Mullins, 1991). Together these two strands of research suggest that the emergence of urban tourism is linked to the implementation of revitalisation strategies aimed at bringing capital and people – residents and visitors alike – back to cities. In other words, the explanation of urban tourism mirrors the logic of the 'back to the city movement' used to explain the advent of gentrification (Lees et al., 2008): the reinvestment of capital in disinvested working-class areas and the consumption power of the new middle class and their demand for urban living. As a result, the occurrence of both tourism and gentrification needs to be regarded as the consequence of the same process of economic and spatial restructuring in which changes in the political economy of cities have been matched by changes in patterns of consumption and employment.

In addition, research shows that tourism and gentrification tend to coexist in similar urban environments and indeed that they mutually reinforce each other. Some authors note that gentrification usually becomes a precursor for the promotion of place (Fainstein and Gladstone, 1999; Judd, 2003; Maitland and Newman, 2008; Novy and Huning, 2009). The proliferation of gentrified landscapes creates tourist-friendly spaces as they provide visitors with sanitised areas, consumption opportunities and a middle-class sense of place. For instance, Terhorst et al. (2003: 85) found that in Amsterdam the amenities and services that emerged with gentrification – restaurants, trendy bars, antique shops, or art galleries – played an important role in improving Amsterdam's image, causing these areas to become 'more attractive to day-trippers and tourists, particularly those who are themselves gentrifiers in their home country'. By way of contrast, other authors showed that extensive investment in the promotion of tourism eventually led to the creation of considerable housing demand and encouraged gentrification (Spirou, 2011; Torres and Momsen, 2005).

From a cultural political economy perspective, the simultaneity of tourism and gentrification results from the key role that culture and consumption activities play in urban economic development strategies (Amin and Thrift, 2007; Ribera-Fumaz, 2009; Zukin, 1995). The crisis of deindustrialisation expanded the consumption functions of urban centres and interurban competition seeking to attract mobile capital and 'the consumer dollar' (Harvey, 1989). In such a post-industrial context, the future of most cities would depend on them being desirable places for consumers to live in or visit and, accordingly, revitalising urban cores usually involves the rebranding of cities as spaces of leisure and pleasure. Phillips (2002) reminds us how culture-side explanations of gentrification have emphasised the importance of amenities and consumption activities in order to attract new middle-class residents, and how residential gentrification is actually associated with and stimulated by the development of commercial spaces and entertainment facilities such as gourmet restaurants, museums, marinas or art galleries. In a similar way, authors such as Florida (2002) and Lloyd and Clark (2001) suggest that economic innovation and growth occurs where highly skilled mobile workers wish to locate and, for this reason, urban policies should focus on quality of life concerns, cultural amenities, and opportunities for consumption and recreation. Although culture-side approaches to gentrification such as those of Ley (1996) or Mills (1988) did not link the development of amenities and recreation facilities to notions of tourism, such environments are precisely the spaces consumed by visitors. In this regard, Judd (2003: 31) notes that 'it is increasingly difficult to distinguish visitor from "local" spaces because leisure, entertainment, and cultural sectors are sustained as crucially by local residents as by out-of-town visitors'. Consequently, urban revitalisation strategies have produced new services and amenities catering to middle-class consumers and, in doing so, they have marketed the tourist and the gentrified city at the same time.

However, there are other ways to examine the intersection between tourism and gentrification that complicates the classed dynamics of visitors and gentrifiers as middle-class users. Research on gender, ethnicity or sexuality shows how people are always more than undifferentiated consumers. For instance, the literature on sexuality and the city reveals that consumption practices are also gendered and framed by heteronormative identities. Regarding gay-friendliness, studies have explored how it has come to be used as a form of cultural capital that makes cities more desirable for the 'creative class' and how it also plays a crucial role in the production of events and spectacles to attract tourism (Bell and Binnie, 2004; Hubbard and Wilkinson, 2015; Waitt et al., 2008). However, those studies also show that a heteronormative cultural economy tolerates gay identities only if they conform to acceptably commodified expressions. Some forms of sexual diversity, such as gay male subcultures, are considered intolerable and only a respectable notion of gay identity is promoted as a safe form of exotic difference. Other authors illustrate how forms of consumption of space are framed by the norms of masculinity and gender divisions. Chapuis (2016) shows how the gentrified Red-Light district of Amsterdam is consumed by male visitors as an opportunity to adopt an accentuated virile posture while, by contrast, female visitors generally describe their consumption experience as uncomfortable or dangerous.

The overlap of tourism and gentrification has also been noted in non-urban contexts, particularly in rural areas (Donaldson, 2009; Phillips, 2002) and in coastal villages (Freeman and Cheyne, 2008). On the one hand, both rural and coastal gentrification have been linked to the charm and natural environment that those locations provide for people who seek a place to retreat from the urban milieu or to retire to. Not surprisingly, for Hines (2010), rural gentrification is a form of 'permanent tourism'. On the other hand, rural and coastal areas have been restructured into having a primarily tourist economic base. Here both recreational facilities and the expansion of second homes play a crucial role. As Phillips (2002) highlights, in the context of a post-productivist countryside, many rural areas have become valorised for leisure facilities to serve both resident and visiting middle-class people.

I have shown that the literature explains the coexistence of tourism and gentrification as a consequence of, first, the tendency of the middle classes to consume similar environments and, secondly, the importance of culture and consumption facilities in strategies for economic development. In either case, it is important to note how this coexistence affects real estate markets and leads to the displacement of low-income communities. I argue that tourism accelerates the pressures of gentrification as the demands of visitors increase rent extraction possibilities. The coexistence of tourism and gentrification means that the arrival of new consumers to areas that were already affected by gentrification intensifies land uses and so pushes up both residential and commercial property values. For instance, in the case of Berlin, several authors show how the pressure of gentrification can be exacerbated by visitors (Füller and Michel, 2014; Häussermann and Colomb, 2003; Novy and Huning, 2009). Tourism has contributed to rising rents and evictions and has caused lower-income residents to blame visitors for a new wave of gentrification. The specific way in which tourism increases rent extraction possibilities and consequently exacerbates the pressure of gentrification-induced displacement will be explored below.

So far, I have shown that tourism and gentrification can be considered co-actors in the production of post-industrial landscapes. I have explored a literature that focuses predominantly on advanced capitalist economies. The next section will explore a different scenario, considering peripheral economies that have barely experienced classical gentrification. I will explore a literature that focuses on places in which the leisure industry has been the most feasible way of engaging in territorial competition and where the lack of a local middle-class is supplanted by the purchasing power of visitors.

17.3   TOURISM GENTRIFICATION IN PERIPHERAL ECONOMIES

Tourism gentrification is especially important in places where tourism represents a central factor for development and growth. An overview of case studies on tourism gentrification shows a geography that covers secondary cities in the North such as New Orleans or San Diego (Gladstone and Préau, 2008; Gotham, 2005; Spirou, 2011) but especially the global South, from Latin America (Hayes, 2015b; Hiernaux and González, 2014; Janoschka et al., 2014; Janoschka and Sequera, 2016; Nobre, 2002; Scarpaci, 2000) to the

Mediterranean, including Spain (Cocola-Gant, 2016; Franquesa, 2011; García-Herrera et al., 2007; Morell, 2009; Vives Miró, 2011), Portugal (Nofre, 2013; Pavel, 2015), and Croatia (Kesar et al., 2015), and from South Africa (Donaldson, 2009) and Mauritius (Wortman et al., 2016) to the Asia-Pacific region (Liang and Bao, 2015; Pleumarom, 2015). I argue that in these places, as the consumption power of the middle-classes is smaller than in advanced economies, tourism comes to supplant the lack of local demand that real estate capital needs for the realisation of surplus value. The purchasing power of visitors stimulates real estate markets and, in such a context, the classical gentrifier is supplanted by visitors as consumers of places. Although visitors have a crucial role to play, this is more as consumers rather that producers of the process. In this sense, it is worth noting that authors have stressed the agency of the state and capital for whom the creation of tourist destinations is a key element for the geographical expansion of capitalism (Britton, 1991; Gotham, 2005; Janoschka et al., 2014).

In understanding this geography of tourism gentrification, several points need to be stressed. First, a starting point should consider the different role that places play in the spatial division of labour. For peripheral economies, tourism represents the easiest way of attracting capital and consumers. For instance, the history of urban tourism in Spain shows that the phenomenon started at the end of the nineteenth century when cities promoted their historic centres as a way of compensating for their lack of industrialisation (Cocola-Gant, 2014; Cocola-Gant and Palou i Rubio, 2015). In recent decades, the spatial division of labour has intensified as a result of the territorial competition and economic restructuring that emerged after deindustrialisation. Harvey (1989) argues that cities can compete in regards to key command functions in finance or information as well as with the spatial division of consumption. He notes that whereas competition within the former is peculiarly tough, less advanced economies can still compete to attract mass consumption and tourism. For instance, in regards to Bilbao, Vicario and Martínez Monje (2005) illustrate how the 'Guggenheim effect' has failed to attract strategic services and professionals. Rather, it has increased the importance of urban leisure activities and the result has been a new landscape of entertainment that has multiplied the number of visitors.

Second, and as a consequence of this uneven development of capitalism, the progression of gentrification in places that focus on tourism as a tool of engaging in territorial competition is less related to the consumption demand of a local middle class and more to the effects of tourists as consumers of places. The gap between the purchasing power of visitors and local residents leads to a market pressure on both housing and services that makes places increasingly unaffordable for the indigenous population. In Latin America, for instance, where the middle-classes are far smaller than in the North (Díaz-Parra, 2015; Lees et al., 2016) and urban workers are incorporated into the labour market in degrees and forms that include high levels of self-help and informality (Betancur, 2014), research shows that gentrification 'is more the result of their "touristification" and the urban politics of local governments, than of processes based on the actions of middle class gentrifiers' (Hiernaux and González, 2014: 55). In Rio de Janeiro, for instance, in the context of preparation for the city's 'mega-events' in which favelas were targeted for redevelopment, the new consumers of place increasingly are young Americans and Europeans who are attracted to the favela experience (Cummings, 2015).

With regards to tourists as consumers of places, it is worth noting the relevance of transnational lifestyle migrants. Lifestyle migration has been conceptualised as a hybrid form of mobility between migration and permanent or residential tourism (Janoschka and Haas, 2014; Williams and Hall, 2000). Because lifestyle migrants possess higher economic capital than the indigenous inhabitants, they have been targeted as a way of boosting economies in several locations (Hayes, 2015b; Janoschka and Haas, 2014). Although research on the links between lifestyle migration and gentrification remains in its infancy, processes of gentrification in which lifestyle migrants acted as pioneer gentrifiers have been noted in a number of places, including urban, rural and seaside contexts (Blázquez-Salom, 2013; Hayes, 2015a; Sigler and Wachsmuth, 2016; Van Noorloos and Steel, 2015; Wortman et al., 2016). The important point is that the demand of these 'transnational gentrifiers' creates possibilities for profitable real estate reinvestment in markets where such opportunities would not have existed on the basis of local demand (Sigler and Wachsmuth, 2016). Research shows that in these places lifestyle migrants play a central role in the real estate market, both as purchasers of homes for personal consumption and as investors.

Finally, in peripheral economies the demand of visitors is crucial in opening up new real estate opportunities as it supplants the lack of local middle-classes. In the 1970s, Lefebvre (1991: 353) noted that in the Mediterranean 'tourism and leisure become major areas of investment and profitability, adding their weight to the construction sector, to property speculation, to generalized urbanization'. Processes of tourism urbanisation have been especially noted in seaside and rural areas via the construction of large-scale tourist infrastructures and second homes (Blázquez-Salom, 2013; Mullins, 1991; Wortman et al., 2016). However, it is also important to note how the link between tourism and the production of space also affects urban spaces that have traditionally been the focus of gentrification research; that is, housing rehabilitation and historic preservation. For instance, with the demise of the Soviet Union, Scarpaci (2000) shows that Cuba had to turn to tourism development in order to attract foreign direct investment. As a consequence, the historic city – *La Habana Vieja* – was rehabilitated in the 1990s via investment which came principally from hard-currency operations in tourism. The result was the relocation of residents outside the area, the construction of tourist infrastructures and the provision of consumption services for visitors. The rehabilitation of housing by tourism investors needs to also be related to the change from housing as shelter towards housing as an investment vehicle and the potential to convert housing into tourist accommodation. In recent years, such a conversion has been linked to the phenomenon of holiday rentals (Cocola-Gant, 2016; Pavel, 2015). In the case of Lisbon, for instance, where the growth of tourism was seen as a 'fast policy' solution towards overcoming the post-2008 crisis, and where the liberalisation of the housing market took place in 2012 as a condition of the European Union's bid to 'rescue' Portuguese banks and the state, the result has been a wave of housing rehabilitations in which local residents have been evicted in order to open new hotels and short-term leases. The way in which tourism-oriented rehabilitation threatens the residents' right to stay needs to be related to a wider conceptualisation of tourism-driven displacement, a point considered below.

17.4   TOURISM GENTRIFICATION AND DISPLACEMENT

Tourism gentrification is a process in which the growth of visitors threatens the existing population's right to 'stay put'. In this regard, a conceptualisation of tourism gentrification needs to explain how tourism-driven displacement takes place. This conceptualisation is crucial for gentrification research but especially for public policy as it challenges the assumption that the growth of visitors is inherently positive. In this section, I bring together several examples from both the global North and the South to better understand why the growth of tourism is displacing communities and local businesses.

I suggest that tourism gentrification causes three interrelated forms of displacement: residential displacement, commercial displacement, and place-based displacement. With regards to residential displacement, the growth of tourism affects the housing market in several ways. First, as Logan and Molotch (2007) highlight, the intensification of land use causes property prices to surge and, accordingly, new spaces of tourism consumption have the ability to increase land values. In this regard, tourism accelerates gentrification as the increase of house prices, on the one hand, makes it more difficult for low-income residents to remain, and, on the other hand, enables only affluent users to move into the area concerned. This process has been noted by research in several destinations in both the North and the South (Cocola-Gant, 2009; Fainstein and Gladstone, 1999; Franquesa, 2011; Gladstone and Préau, 2008; Gotham, 2005; Morell, 2009; Spirou, 2011; Vives Miró, 2011; Wortman et al., 2016). For instance, in New Orleans, Gotham (2005) and Gladstone and Préau (2008) show that, as a result of the growth of tourism, the city centre experienced an increased escalation of property values, with this escalation resulting in the conversion of affordable single-family residences into expensive condominiums, pushing out lower-income people.

Second, the growth of tourist accommodation accelerates processes of residential displacement, especially because it involves increasing conversion of housing into accommodation for visitors. Here both traditional tourist infrastructures such as hotels and the current expansion of holiday rentals must be considered. On the one hand, in places where historic preservation has been fuelled by tourism, and consequently where housing rehabilitation has been driven by tourism investors, the opening of hotels tends to involve the rehabilitation of previous residential buildings (Pavel, 2015; Vives Miró, 2011). On the other hand, the spread of holiday rentals is seen by a range of communities as a new threat that is accelerating the difficulties in accessing housing (Cocola-Gant, 2016; Colomb, 2012; Füller and Michel, 2014; Kesar et al., 2015; Opillard, 2016; Peters, 2016). The phenomenon of holiday rentals needs to be related to the role that housing plays as an asset in which money can be invested and stored. As tourism has the ability to increase property values, it allows investors to store their surplus capital in the residential market of tourist destinations and in the meantime to rent them to visitors. Indeed, research reveals that, far from 'sharing', behind Airbnb there is a new opportunity for capital accumulation in which the suppliers are, less single families that occasionally rent the homes in which they live, and more investors and landlords that are renting out residential properties permanently (Arias-Sans and Quaglieri-Domínguez, 2016). In this sense, housing in historic cities is again being rehabilitated by tourism investors, in a process in which tenants are supplanted by transient visitors as the former represent barriers to capital accumulation.

In this change from housing to tourist accommodation it is important to note how displacement takes place. On the one hand, both the opening of hotels and vacation rentals involves the direct displacement of residents (Cocola-Gant, 2016). On the other hand, the process takes housing units off the market and, in so doing, accelerates the escalation of house prices (Cocola-Gant, 2016; Opillard, 2016; Peters, 2016). In central areas of Barcelona, for instance, 16.8% of housing units are listed on Airbnb and in 2015 rent prices rose by 18% (Cocola-Gant, 2016). Although the occurrence of direct displacement could be more visible, crucially the process makes it increasingly difficult for residents to find affordable accommodation. This is an example of what Marcuse (1985) calls 'exclusionary displacement' (see also Slater, 2009). In this sense, the difficulties in finding affordable accommodation accelerates 'classical' gentrification as only middle- and upper-class individuals can afford to move to the area.

With regards to commercial displacement, during the 1980s and 1990s the literature observed that the main consequence of tourism in processes of neighbourhood change was commercial gentrification (Fainstein and Gladstone, 1999; Sandford, 1987; Zukin, 1995). As a consumption activity, the demands of visitors results, on the one hand, in the expansion of retail facilities, restaurants, nightlife pubs and other opportunities for entertainment and, on the other, to the displacement of the working class and local stores used by the indigenous residents. After the growth of tourism in 2000, the commercial gentrification caused by tourism has been observed worldwide (Bromley and Mackie, 2009; Cocola-Gant, 2015; Gotham, 2005; Häussermann and Colomb, 2003; Hoffman, 2003; Liang and Bao, 2015; Nofre, 2013; Spirou, 2011; Terhorst et al., 2003). The rising land value observed in tourist areas also affects commercial properties, and this increase is central to understanding the substitution of local stores by amenities for visitors. Research shows that local businesses are replaced by franchises as the former cannot afford the escalation of property values. As Gotham (2005: 1112) notes in regards to New Orleans, 'the last of the corner cafes and local coffee shops are today competing for space with some of the largest corporations in the world'.

Finally, I suggest that tourism gentrification needs to be regarded as a process of place-based displacement. The experience of living in spaces of tourism consumption is the cause of everyday tensions at the neighbourhood scale making residential life increasingly difficult. Although residents may not experience residential displacement, the domination of space by visitors can displace them from the places they belong to. In regards to this, the conceptualisation of displacement proposed by Davidson (2008, 2009) and Davidson and Lees (2010) is crucial. The authors argue that although displacement tends to be reduced to the specific moment in which a resident moves out, this understanding leaves important aspects of space silenced. In particular, they suggest that gentrification creates a new social and cultural context in which the indigenous residents feel a sense of dispossession from the places they inhabit, or 'loss of place': 'the places by which people once defined their neighbourhood become spaces with which they no longer associate' (Davidson, 2008: 2392). Although this theme needs further empirical studies, in the case of tourism gentrification, research has documented a number of issues.

First, tourism-driven commercial gentrification removes the services and local stores that residents use on a daily basis (Cocola-Gant, 2015; Terhorst et al., 2003). Second, regarding the privatisation of public spaces that tends to occur in tourist areas, several authors note that residents complain that there is an decreasing amount of space left for non-commercial activities (Degen, 2004; Häussermann and Colomb, 2003). Importantly, both local stores and public areas tend to be spaces of encounters for long-term residents. Their displacement means that meeting-places disappear and that residents lose gathering areas that are central for community life. Third, a central concern of residents in several tourist destinations is a perceived reduction in their quality of life. In particular, research has documented conflicts resulting from noise and night-time activities (Gravari-Barbas and Jacquot, 2016; Nofre, 2013); over-densification of public spaces, which especially affects the elderly (Cocola-Gant, 2015; Peters, 2016); or environmental pressures such as the production of waste or air pollution, which is particularly important in cruise destinations (Colomb and Novy, 2016; Vianello, 2016). Finally, in the context of residential tourism, it has been noted that transnational migrants are visibly distinct from the local population in term of status, behaviour, language or cultural values, and that this social and cultural differentiation leads to polarised and fragmented urban environments (Hayes, 2015b; Van Noorloos and Steel, 2015; Wortman et al., 2016).

As a consequence, tourism gentrification involves a deep mutation of the place in which long-term residents can lose the resources and references by which they define their everyday life. Although place-based displacement is still an unexplored topic, I suggest that the loss of place experienced by residents could be the cause of a progressive out-migration from tourist areas that affects both low- and middle-income people, including those who were gentrifiers in earlier rounds of the process. The cultural dimension of displacement poses new questions for research as traditionally the process has been analysed through the lens of the housing market and not through place-based dynamics.

17.5 CONCLUSIONS

This chapter has brought together the tourism and gentrification literatures with the intention of providing a conceptualisation of tourism gentrification. I have shown that in advanced economies the literature has generally adopted a cultural economy approach and has explored the relationship between visitors and gentrifiers as consumers of similar environments. In peripheral economies, however, research has taken a political economy perspective in which the creation of destinations by the state and private capital is central for economic development. In either case, tourism opens up possibilities for real estate investment, introduces differentiated lifestyles and poses several risks for indigenous residents. In other words, tourism plays a crucial role in the production and consumption of space and leads to different forms of displacement. It is for this reason that tourism needs to be seen as a form of gentrification.

As a first attempt to put into conversation different cases from both the North and the South that have noted the role that tourism plays in processes of gentrification, this chapter is not a final conceptualisation. Rather, it may be a starting point for future cases in different contexts. In fact, for a better understanding of tourism gentrification we need detailed empirical and comparative studies. I suggest that we need to pay attention to several issues that are particularly relevant. The first one is the relationship between housing and tourism. Housing supply and affordability are becoming central issues worldwide, but the role played by tourism has been overlooked. In this chapter, however, I have shown different examples in which tourism exacerbates the difficulties in accessing housing. In this regard, empirical studies about the impacts of holiday rentals are needed. But also, it is especially important to explore the extent to which investors store their surplus capital in the residential market of tourist destinations. A political economy of housing (Aalbers and Christophers, 2014) has neglected this fact. It seems that residents in tourist areas may be competing for housing not only with visitors but with the super-rich.

A second point of interest concerns the cultural effects of tourism and how the arrival of visitors to residential areas has the potential to disrupt the everyday lives of residents. The implication of such effects has increased in the 21st century as a consequence of the growth of low-cost and party tourism. Several cities in Europe, for instance, are now destinations for young visitors that seek sex, cheap alcohol and night clubs (Nofre, 2013). In my experience of doing fieldwork in Barcelona, residents are selling their properties to tourism investors but a critical reason for moving out is simply noise. The host and guest relationship poses relevant questions for research. However, and probably because tourism research has a strong tradition in the analysis of tourism management and planning, authors have traditionally focused on visitor satisfaction and consumer experience (Ashworth and Page, 2011). Only a few narratives have focused on the host's experience of the encounter (Robinson, 2001). Cultural geographers interested in ideas of encounter have also overlooked the interactions between visitors and host communities (Gibson, 2010). Critical research, however, should reverse this lack of consideration and focus more on the way in which the host community space and cultural practices are exposed to the arrival of visitors.

Finally, in recent years there has been an increased concern among communities and local authorities regarding evidence that shows a progressive population decline in tourist areas (Kesar et al., 2015; Pavel, 2015). This is clearly seen in places such as Venice, which has lost half its population in the last 30 years. Empirical studies are needed in order to build detailed stage models of tourism gentrification. I suggest, however, that although in an initial stage, tourism may be seen as a solution to bring capital and consumers back to cities, it has the potential to result in a final substitution of residential life by tourism. In understanding this process, we have to take into account that all forms of displacement analysed earlier take place at the same time and mutually reinforce each other. The pressure on the housing market, the lack of commercial services that residents need and the loss of place resulting from the encounter with visitors makes it increasingly difficult for residents to use neighbourhoods as spaces for social reproduction. In such a scenario, displacement is not just the out-migration from a place, but it also means the impossibility for, and lack of willingness of, residents to access tourist areas. The occurrence of displacement is not simply more intense than in classical processes of gentrification, but it may lead to a situation in which long-term residents would be replaced by transient consumers and tourism investors.

REFERENCES

Aalbers, M. and Christophers, B. (2014) 'Centring housing in political economy', *Housing, Theory and Society*, 31(4), 373–394.
Amin, A. and Thrift, N. (2007) 'Cultural-economy and cities', *Progress in Human Geography*, 31(2), 143–161.
Arias-Sans, A. and Quaglieri-Domínguez, A. (2016) 'Unravelling Airbnb. Urban perspectives from Barcelona', in Russo, P. and Richards, G. (eds), *Reinventing the Local in Tourism. Travel Communities and Peer-produced Place Experiences*, London: Channel View, pp. 209–228.

Ashworth, G. and Page, S. (2011) 'Urban tourism research: Recent progress and current paradoxes', *Tourism Management*, 32(1), 1–15.

Bell, D. and Binnie, J. (2004) 'Authenticating queer space: Citizenship, urbanism and governance', *Urban Studies*, 41(9), 1807–1820.

Betancur, J. (2014) 'Gentrification in Latin America: overview and critical analysis', *Urban Studies Research*, 4, 1–14.

Blázquez-Salom, M. (2013) 'More villas and more barriers: gentrification and the enclosure of rural land on Majorca', *Méditerranée. Revue géographique des pays méditerranéens*, 120, 25–36.

Britton, S. (1991) 'Tourism, capital, and place: towards a critical geography of tourism', *Environment and Planning D: Society and Space*, 9(4), 451–478.

Bromley, R. and Mackie, P. (2009) 'Displacement and the new spaces for informal trade in the Latin American city centre', *Urban Studies*, 46(7), 1485–1506.

Chapuis, A. (2016) 'Touring the immoral. Affective geographies of visitors to the Amsterdam red-light district', *Urban Studies* online.

Cocola-Gant, A. (2009) 'EL MACBA y su función en la marca Barcelona', *Ciudad y Territorio: Estudios Territoriales*, 159, 87–101.

Cocola-Gant, A. (2014) 'The invention of the Barcelona Gothic Quarter', *Journal of Heritage Tourism*, 9(1), 18–34.

Cocola-Gant, A. (2015) 'Tourism and commercial gentrification', in *The Ideal City. Between Myth and Reality. RC21 Conference*, Urbino: ISA, pp. 1–25.

Cocola-Gant, A. (2016) 'Holiday rentals: the new gentrification battlefront', *Sociological Research Online*, 21(3), 10. Available from: http://www.socresonline.org.uk/21/3/10.html.

Cocola-Gant, A. and Palou i Rubio, S. (2015) 'Tourist promotion and urban space in Barcelona. Historic perspective and critical review, 1900–1936', *Documents d'Anàlisi Geogràfica*, 61(3), 461–482.

Colomb, C. (2012) 'A city for whom? Urban tourism, neighbourhood conflicts and planning policy in Berlin and Barcelona', in *The Second ISA Forum of Sociology (August 1–4, 2012)*, CONF, Buenos Aires: ISA.

Colomb, C. and Novy, J. (2016) 'Urban tourism and its discontents: an introduction', in Colomb, C. and Novy, J. (eds) *Protest and Resistance in the Tourist City*, London: Routledge, pp. 1–30.

Cummings, J. (2015) 'Confronting favela chic: the gentrification of informal settlements in Rio de Janeiro, Brazil', in Lees, L., Shin, H. and López-Morales, E. (eds) *Global Gentrifications: Uneven Development and Displacement*, Bristol: Policy Press, pp. 81–99.

Davidson, M. (2008) 'Spoiled mixture: where does state-led "positive" gentrification end?', *Urban Studies*, 45(12), 2385–2405.

Davidson, M. (2009) 'Displacement, space and dwelling: placing gentrification debate', *Ethics, Place and Environment*, 12(2), 219–234.

Davidson, M. and Lees, L. (2010) 'New-build gentrification: its histories, trajectories, and critical geographies', *Population, Space and Place*, 16(5), 395–411.

Degen, M. (2004) 'Barcelona's Games: the Olympics, urban design, and global tourism', in Sheller, M. and Urry, J. (eds) *Tourism Mobilities: Places to Play, Places in Play*, London: Routledge, pp. 131–142.

Díaz-Parra, I. (2015) 'A back to the city movement by local government action: gentrification in Spain and Latin America', *International Journal of Urban Sciences*, JOUR, Routledge (ahead-of-print): 1–21.

Donaldson, R. (2009) 'The making of a tourism-gentrified town: Greyton, South Africa', *Geography*, 94(2), 88–99.

Fainstein, S. and Gladstone, D. (1999) 'Evaluating urban tourism', in Judd, D. and Fainstein, S. (eds) *The Tourist City*, New Haven and London: Yale University Press, pp. 21–34.

Florida, R. (2002) *The Rise of the Creative Class: And How It's Transforming Work, Leisure, Community and Everyday Life*, New York: Basic Books.

Franquesa, J. (2011) '"We've lost our bearings": Place, tourism, and the limits of the "mobility turn"', *Antipode*, 43(4), 1012–1033.

Freeman, C. and Cheyne, C. (2008) 'Coasts for sale: gentrification in New Zealand', *Planning Theory & Practice*, 9(1), 33–56.

Füller, H. and Michel, B. (2014) '"Stop being a tourist!" New dynamics of urban tourism in Berlin-Kreuzberg', *International Journal of Urban and Regional Research*, 38(4), 1304–1318.

García-Herrera, L., Smith, N. and Mejías Vera, M. (2007) 'Gentrification, displacement, and tourism in Santa Cruz de Tenerife', *Urban Geography*, 28(3), 276–298.

Gibson, C. (2010) 'Geographies of tourism: (un)ethical encounters', *Progress in Human Geography*, 34(4), 521–527.

Gladstone, D. and Préau, J. (2008) 'Gentrification in tourist cities: evidence from New Orleans before and after Hurricane Katrina', *Housing Policy Debate*, 19(1), 137–175.

Gotham, K. (2005) 'Tourism gentrification: The case of New Orleans' Vieux Carre (French Quarter)', *Urban Studies*, 42(7), 1099–1121.

Gravari-Barbas, M. and Jacquot, S. (2016) 'No conflict? Discourses and management of tourism-related tensions in Paris', in Colomb, C. and Novy, J. (eds) *Protest and Resistance in the Tourist City*, London: Routledge.

Harvey, D. (1989) 'From managerialism to entrepreneurialism: the transformation in urban governance in late capitalism', *Geografiska Annaler*, 71, 3–17.

Häussermann, H. and Colomb, C. (2003) 'The New Berlin: marketing the city of dreams', in Hoffman, L., Fainstein, S. and Judd, D. (eds) *Cities and Visitors: Regulating People, Markets, and City Space*, Oxford: Blackwell, pp. 200–218.

Hayes, M. (2015a) 'Into the universe of the Hacienda: lifestyle migration, individualism and social dislocation in Vilcabamba, Ecuador', *Journal of Latin American Geography*, 14(1), 79–100.

Hayes, M. (2015b) 'Introduction: the emerging lifestyle migration industry and geographies of transnationalism, mobility and displacement in Latin America', *Journal of Latin American Geography*, 14(1), 7–18.

Hiernaux, D. and González, I. (2014) 'Turismo y gentrificación: pistas teóricas sobre una articulación', *Revista de Geografía Norte Grande*, 58, 55–70.

Hines, J. (2010) 'Rural gentrification as permanent tourism: the creation of the "new" West Archipelago as postindustrial cultural space', *Environment and Planning D: Society and Space*, 28(3), 509–525.

Hoffman, L. (2003) 'Revalorizing the inner city: tourism and regulation in Harlem', in Hoffman, L., Fainstein, S. and Judd, D. (eds) *Cities and Visitors: Regulating People, Markets, and City Space*, Oxford: Blackwell, pp. 91–112.

Hubbard, P. and Wilkinson, E. (2015) 'Welcoming the world? Hospitality, homonationalism, and the London 2012 Olympics', *Antipode*, 47(3), 598–615.

Janoschka, M. and Haas, H. (2014) 'Contested spatialities of lifestyle migration. Approaches and research questions', in Janoschka, M. and Haas, H. (eds) *Contested Spatialities, Lifestyle Migration and Residential Tourism*, New York: Routledge, pp. 1–12.

Janoschka, M., Sequera, J. and Salinas, L. (2014) 'Gentrification in Spain and Latin America – a critical dialogue', *International Journal of Urban and Regional Research*, 38(4), 1234–1265.

Janoschka, M. and Sequera, J. (2016) 'Gentrification in Latin America: addressing the politics and geographies of displacement', *Urban Geography* online: 1–20.

Judd, D. (1999) 'Constructing the tourist bubble', in Judd, D. and Fainstein, S. (eds) *The Tourist City*, New Haven and London: Yale University Press, pp. 35–53.

Judd, D. (2003) 'Visitors and the spatial ecology of the city', in Hoffman, L., Fainstein, S. and Judd, D. (eds) *Cities and Visitors: Regulating People, Markets, and City Space*, Oxford: Blackwell, pp. 23–38.

Kesar, O., Dezeljin, R. and Bienenfeld, M. (2015) 'Tourism gentrification in the city of Zagreb: time for a debate?', *Interdisciplinary Management Research*, 11, 657–668.

Lees, L. (2012) 'The geography of gentrification: thinking through comparative urbanism', *Progress in Human Geography*, 36(2), 155–171.

Lees, L., Shin, H. and López-Morales, E. (2016) *Planetary Gentrification*, Cambridge: Polity Press.

Lees, L., Slater, T. and Wyly, E. (2008) *Gentrification*, London and New York: Routledge.

Lefebvre, H. (1991) *The Production of Space*, Oxford: Blackwell.

Ley, D. (1996) *The New Middle Class and the Remaking of the Central City*, Oxford: Oxford University Press.

Liang, Z-X. and Bao, J-G. (2015) 'Tourism gentrification in Shenzhen, China: causes and socio-spatial consequences', *Tourism Geographies*, 17(3), 461–481.

Lloyd, R. and Clark, T. (2001) 'The city as an entertainment machine', in Gotham, K. (ed) *Critical Perspectives on Urban Redevelopment*, New York: Elsevier, pp. 357–378.

Logan, J. and Molotch, H. (2007) *Urban Fortunes: The Political Economy of Place*, 2nd edn, Berkeley and Los Angeles: University of California Press.

Maitland, R. and Newman, P. (2008) 'Visitor-host relationships: conviviality between visitors and host communities', in Hayllar, B., Griffin, T. and Edwards, D. (eds) *City Spaces–Tourist Places: Urban Tourism Precincts*, New York and London: Elsevier, pp. 223–242.

Marcuse, P. (1985) 'Gentrification, abandonment, and displacement: connections, causes, and policy responses in New York City', *Journal of Urban and Contemporary Law*, 28, 195–240.

Meethan, K. (2001) *Tourism in Global Society. Place, Culture, Consumption*, New York: Palgrave.

Mills, C. (1988) '"Life on the upslope": The postmodern landscape of gentrification', *Environment and Planning D: Society and Space*, 6(2), 169–190.

Morell, M. (2009) 'Fent barri: heritage tourism policy and neighbourhood scaling in Ciutat de Mallorca', *Etnográfica*, 13(2), 343–372.

Mullins, P. (1991) 'Tourism urbanization', *International Journal of Urban and Regional Research*, 15(3), 326–342.

Nobre, E. (2002) 'Urban regeneration experiences in Brazil: historical preservation, tourism development and gentrification in Salvador da Bahia', *Urban Design International*, 7(2), 109–124.

Nofre, J. (2013) '"Vintage nightlife": Gentrifying Lisbon downtown', *Fennia-International Journal of Geography*, 191(2), 106–121.

Novy, J. and Huning, S. (2009) 'New tourism areas in the New Berlin', in Maitland, R. and Newman, P.

(eds) *World Tourism Cities: Developing Tourism off the Beaten Track*, London and New York: Routledge, pp. 87–108.

Opillard, F. (2016) 'From San Francisco's 'Tech Boom 2.0' to Valparaíso's UNESCO World Heritage Site: resistance to tourism gentrification in a comparative political perspective', in Colomb, C. and Novy, J. (eds) *Protest and Resistance in the Tourist City*, London: Routledge, pp. 129–151.

Pavel, F. (2015) *Transformação urbana de uma área histórica: o Bairro Alto. Reabilitação, Identidade, Gentrification*. PhD Dissertation. Lisbon: Universidade de Lisboa.

Peters, D. (2016) 'Density wars in Silicon Beach: the struggle to mix new spaces for toil, stay and play in Santa Monica, California', in Colomb, C. and Novy, J. (eds) *Protest and Resistance in the Tourist City*, London: Routledge.

Phillips, M. (2002) 'The production, symbolization and socialization of gentrification: impressions from two Berkshire villages', *Transactions of the Institute of British Geographers*, 27(3), 282–308.

Phillips, M. (2004) 'Other geographies of gentrification', *Progress in Human Geography*, 28(1), 5–30.

Pleumarom, A. (2015) 'Tourism: a driver of inequality and displacement', *Resurgence. Special Issue: Global Tourism Growth: Remedy or Ruin?*, 301(1), 5–10.

Ribera-Fumaz, R. (2009) 'From urban political economy to cultural political economy: rethinking culture and economy in and beyond the urban', *Progress in Human Geography*, 33(4), 447–465.

Robinson, M. (2001) 'Tourism encounters: inter-and intra-cultural conflicts and the world's largest industry', in AlSayyad, N. (ed) *Consuming Tradition, Manufacturing Heritage: Global Norms and Urban Forms in the Age of Tourism*, London and New York: Routledge, pp. 34–67.

Sandford, M. (1987) 'Tourism in Harlem: between negative sightseeing and gentrification', *Journal of American Culture*, 10(2), 99–105.

Scarpaci, J. (2000) 'Reshaping Habana Vieja: revitalization, historic preservation, and restructuring in the socialist city', *Urban Geography*, 21(8), 724–744.

Sigler, T. and Wachsmuth, D. (2016) 'Transnational gentrification: globalisation and neighbourhood change in Panama's Casco Antiguo', *Urban Studies*, 53(4), 705–722.

Slater, T. (2009) 'Missing Marcuse: on gentrification and displacement', *City*, 13(2–3), 292–311.

Spirou, C. (2011) *Urban Tourism and Urban Change: Cities in a Global Economy*, New York and London: Routledge.

Terhorst, P., Ven, J. van de and Deben, L. (2003) 'Amsterdam: it's all in the mix', in Hoffman, L., Fainstein, S. and Judd, D. (eds) *Cities and Visitors: Regulating People, Markets, and City Space*, Oxford: Blackwell, pp. 75–90.

Torres, R. and Momsen, J. (2005) 'Gringolandia: the construction of a new tourist space in Mexico', *Annals of the Association of American Geographers*, 95(2), 314–335.

Van Noorloos, F. and Steel, G. (2015) 'Lifestyle migration and socio-spatial segregation in the urban(izing) landscapes of Cuenca (Ecuador) and Guanacaste (Costa Rica)', *Habitat International*, 1–8.

Vianello, M. (2016) 'The "No Grandi Navi" campaign. Protests against cruise tourism in Venice', in Colomb, C. and Novy, J. (eds) *Protest and Resistance in the Tourist City*, London: Routledge.

Vicario, L. and Martinez Monje, P. (2005) 'Another "Guggenheim effect"? Central city projects and gentrification in Bilbao', in Atkinson, R. and Bridge, G. (eds) *Gentrification in a Global Context. The New Urban Colonialism*, Book Section, London and New York: Routledge, pp. 151–167.

Vives Miró, S. (2011) 'Producing a "successful city": neoliberal urbanism and gentrification in the tourist city – the case of Palma (Majorca)', *Urban Studies Research*, 1–13.

Waitt, G., Markwell, K. and Gorman-Murray, A. (2008) 'Challenging heteronormativity in tourism studies: locating progress', *Progress in Human Geography*, 32(6), 781–800.

Williams, A. and Hall, C. (2000) 'Tourism and migration: new relationships between production and consumption', *Tourism Geographies*, 2(1), 5–27.

Wortman, T., Donaldson, R. and Westen, G. (2016) '"They are stealing my island": Residents' opinions on foreign investment in the residential tourism industry in Tamarin, Mauritius', *Singapore Journal of Tropical Geography*, 37(2), 139–157.

Zukin, S. (1995) *The Cultures of Cities*, Oxford: Blackwell.

18. Retail gentrification
Phil Hubbard

18.1 INTRODUCTION

Brixton in London has had a changeable reputation in the eyes of the British media. In the 1960s and 1970s, obvious problems of deprivation and social disorder were blamed squarely on the area's recently arrived Caribbean immigrant population, while the rioting of the 1980s and 1990s was deemed symptomatic of the criminality of young black residents, and seldom seen as a valid reaction to police harassment, economic marginalisation or social stigma. But in recent years, different discourses have emerged, cataloguing the transformation of the borough from that of a 'lawless ghetto' to a hip and sought-after neighbourhood caught up in the regeneration maelstrom that has enveloped London in the wake of the 2012 Olympics (Campkin, 2013). Part of this story involves the blending of Brixton's ethnicised identity into a narrative concerning London's cosmopolitanism – and the construction of an urban brand that has encouraged gentrification through the consumption of multiculturalism (Butler, 2002; Lees, 2016). This gentrification has attracted some fairly negative headlines, with media accounts emerging which have highlighted existing residents' rather futile attempts to resist the rising tide of gentrification, with property prices rising on average by 75% over a ten-year period, outstripping rises in trendy Shoreditch, neighbouring Clapham and up-and-coming Peckham.

The story of Brixton's gentrification is one that is very familiar to those of us that have followed London's over-heated housing markets in the last decade, albeit in this instance the normal preoccupation with class conflict has been overlain with specific concerns about the displacement of the black Caribbean population that has long relied on forms of social and cultural capital embodied in Brixton's rich range of 'ethnic' stores and traditional street markets (see Figure 18.1). In media reporting, this is evidenced via a focus on the displacement of businesses that have long served the area's black population, many established by members of the initial 'Windrush' generation that arrived in the late 1950s. Eye-watering rent increases have caused many traders to up sticks, with Caribbean cafes, barbers, pubs and foodstores closing in the face of a gentrification that seems hard to resist. Sometimes the new alliances of class and capital causing this are formidable indeed: for example, Network Rail, a major landowner in the area, is evicting 21 traders with businesses under Brixton's infamous arches, seeking to reinvent this area as the Atlantic Village market, doubling rents with an eye to replacing the motley mix of hairdressers, nail bars, grocers, fabric shops and traders selling reggae CDs, with a more profitable range of businesses, prompting fierce opposition from local resident groups. Numerous media stories have then documented the disappearance of 'local' shops from Brixton, and their replacement by champagne and cheese stores, trendy pop-up barista coffee shops and niche cocktail bars. This then is not a story about local-run businesses being replaced by retail multiples or global corporations, but one where a set of independently

Figure 18.1   Electric Avenue, Brixton

run business is replaced by a new set of independent businesses, albeit ones owned by richer, whiter incomers.

This type of gentrification story, involving the transformation of 'local' shopping streets into spaces of middle class consumption, is one that occasionally captures media headlines, but remains little examined in urban studies. Indeed, retail transition – which is often slow and piecemeal (Kern, 2015a) – tends to excite less academic commentary than the type of 'scorched earth' gentrification associated with the redevelopment of council estate housing, or the spectacular urban transformations associated with the super-rich's colonisation of already-affluent neighbourhoods (the 'super-gentrification' that is producing new 'gilded ghettos' in many world cities (Atkinson, 2016). So, while retail change is something often noted in studies of gentrification, it is rare to find gentrification scholars saying anything particularly profound about the role of retail change in wider processes of gentrification. This is surprising given local shopping spaces constitute one of the most obvious battlegrounds of gentrification, with the social and economic transitions characteristic of gentrifying neighbourhoods often most palpable at street-level as established stores close and new ones open. This oversight is doubly perplexing given it is now widely accepted that gentrification represents much more than the simple rehabilitation of working class housing, being a concept that describes the generic production (and management) of urban space for middle-class consumption of all kinds (Rankin and MacLean, 2015).

This said, there is an emerging, but patchy, literature that is beginning to acknowledge the importance of retail transformation in effecting neighbourhood change (e.g. Bridge and Dowling, 2011; Deener, 2007; Gonzalez and Waley, 2014; Schlack and Turnbull, 2016; Hentschel and Blokland, 2016; Kasinitz and Zukin, 2016; Rankin et al, 2016; Yu et al, 2016). This literature suggests that, from London to New York, from Shanghai to Sydney and beyond, it is possible to find instances where changes to local shopping streets are not just indicative of local social transformations, but drive those very transformations by changing the social, cultural and economic character of a given locality, and instigating significant exclusionary pressures. Here, the emergence of new types of retail outlets is seen to precipitate the out-migration of populations who can no longer afford to shop in the neighbourhood where they live. As Peter Marcuse (1985: 207) asserts, when a family sees 'the stores they patronise are liquidating and new stores for other clientele are taking their places . . . then the pressure of displacement is severe'. This implies that retail gentrification needs to be taken seriously as something that can presage residential gentrification, and should not be dismissed as incidental to the 'real' business of property speculation, house-building and corporate gentrification.

This chapter accordingly argues for increased attention to be paid to retail gentrification, defined here as involving the up-scaling of shops and related businesses, and the concomitant displacement of the local stores and services on which working class residents rely. Drawing mainly on UK and US examples, and foregrounding questions of fashion, style and taste, this chapter stresses the role retail change has in changing the 'atmosphere' of a neighbourhood, instigating displacement pressures that weigh most heavily on the poorest and most vulnerable, ultimately encouraging the colonisation of inner city districts by middle class, consumer values.

This chapter begins by reviewing the extant literature on the role of retail change in gentrification. This review focuses on one of the key dimensions of retail gentrification – i.e. the displacement of existing businesses via processes of 'boutiquing' – showing that this has generally negative impacts on the poorest dwellers most reliant on 'local' or 'ethnic' stores in their everyday lives. While the majority of studies focus on such shops as spaces fulfilling residents' economic needs (i.e. providing affordable foodstuffs), in this chapter I also highlight the role that shops play in working class and ethnic communities as spaces of sociality and generosity. The disappearance of familiar and well used shops in inner city districts is something that I argue can be devastating for longer term residents, encouraging forms of displacement and (self-) exclusion that can encourage subsequent forms of residential gentrification.

18.2   RETAIL UP-SCALING AND THE BOUTIQUING OF LOCAL SHOPPING STREETS

Most shopping streets are characterised by change. Stores and formats transform over time, and the mix of independent stores and corporate-owned 'multiples' ebbs and flows. In times of economic downturn, recessionary pressures can result in a glut of vacant premises, as was the case in the 2009 'retail recession' in Britain. Despite this, most shopping streets are thought to exhibit considerable resilience in the face of economic boom and slump, adapting to changing circumstances by up-scaling or down-scaling, depending on the spending power of local consumers (Wrigley and Dolega, 2011). However, a major trend over recent decades has been the relative down-scaling of many local shopping streets, particularly in inner city neighbourhoods, with corporate retail capital moving out of town to more profitable locations. In Britain, the rise of out-of-town retailing from the 1980s onwards was identified as a major factor in the decline of some inner-city shopping streets, their devotion to forms of convenience, discount and 'ethnic' retail serving 'disadvantaged' consumers often contrasted with the spectacle of the out-of-town mall that caters overwhelmingly for the mobile middle classes (Williams et al, 2001). While these trends took sometimes exaggerated forms in those British cities abutting Regional Shopping Centres (e.g. Meadowhall in Sheffield or Merry Hill in Dudley), most towns and cities felt the impact of out-of-town (and later, online) retailing, echoing the trends observed much earlier in continental Europe and North America (Herrmann and Beik, 1968).

Given this spatial restructuring of retail capital, many inner-city districts became characterised by locally run stores catering to the needs of local working-class consumers, especially those belonging to ethnic communities whose tastes were poorly served elsewhere. Such streets are often characterised by 'ethnic' grocery stores, beauty shops and restaurants, but also discount stores and outlets associated with more residualised forms of consumption such as liquor stores, sex shops and betting shops, as well as pawnbrokers, charity shops and second-hand stores. But, conversely, it is this 'local' character and vernacular style that has subsequently been seized upon as retail capital seeks new, more profitable sites for its own realisation, exploiting the 'rent gap' between current and potential land values. While this can be associated with the return of corporate retail capital, such as that embodied in the form of metropolitan style brands such as *Starbucks*, *American Apparel* or *Gap* (M. Smith, 1996; Hankins, 2002; Mermet, 2016), more routinely it is independently run 'bohemian' or 'hipster' stores that first co-opt offbeat elements of street culture, and signal the beginnings of the incorporation of a deprived or 'ethnic' neighbourhood within the middle class cognitive map of the consumer city. This has been something observed in numerous gentrifying districts around the world once characterised as dangerous or sketchy but now discoursed as authentic, cool and edgy (see, e.g., Fuller and Michael (2014) on Kreuzberg, Berlin, or Murdie and Teixeira (2010) on Little Portugal, Toronto). Perhaps the best-known example here is Wicker Park, Chicago, famously described by Lloyd (2002) as 'neo-Bohemia' on the basis of the transformation of its main street (Milwaukee Avenue) from a partly derelict Latino neighbourhood street into one characterised by cafes, art galleries and funky shops frequented by Mac-wielding creatives and tattooed, cycling 'hipsters'. This, once little-known industrial district, has become known as one of the US's hippest neighbourhoods, the transformation of its retail offer reflecting its metamorphosis from an ethnic 'ghetto' to an arty, creative hub.

A key argument that can be pulled from the literature is that marginalised shopping streets are not instantly transformed into glossy spaces of spectacular super-rich consumption via a sudden influx of corporate retail capital, but undergo a slow transition from spaces of 'toxic' or insalubrious consumption into neighbourhoods offering a form of 'crunchy chic' to middle-class consumers (Kern, 2015b). This is a form of retail that is discoursed as more meaningful, greener and interesting than the retail offer elsewhere, and one seen to be embedded in particular local traditions. Shopping in these neighbourhoods hence bequeaths cultural capital on the 'knowing' consumer prepared to step outside the mainstream to experience something more local and 'authentic' than the out-of-town retail experience (Zukin, 2008).

Retail gentrification has nonetheless taken different forms over time, varying significantly from nation to nation. For example, in the 1980s and 1990s, the replacement of local pubs by 'yuppie' wine bars was a sure-fire sign of incipient gentrification. However, in more recent times, the first sign of retail gentrification has been the emergence of 'hipster urbanism' in the form of edgy art galleries, bijou vintage boutiques and shabby-chic coffee shops, 'pop-up' outlets that quickly become known as the haunt of the bearded, flannel-shirted trendsetters whose presence serves to discourse certain inner city districts as both authentic and cool (Cowen 2006). The emergence of such outlets also helps embed myths of creativity in specific neighbourhoods, with a proliferation of 'proper' barista coffee shops indicating that the area is becoming populated by homeworking creative and artistic types (the 'coffice' being a neologism that describes the café as the ideal working environment where background noise provides a 'buzz' but where there are no colleagues or family members to provide a distraction).

In the last decade or so, there have been several notable studies of gentrification that have explicitly looked at the significance of independently run wholefood shops, boutiques and hipster bars in marking out some spaces as ripe for gentrification (e.g. Pascual-Molinas and Ribera-Fumaz, 2009; Sullivan and Shaw, 2011; Anguelovski, 2016). In these studies, the replacement of corner cafes by 'real' coffee shops, convenience grocery stores by wholefood delis and pubs by bars serving cocktails in jam-jars is seen to be a vital first stage in a gentrification process that culminates in the upscaling of entire neighbourhoods. Perhaps the most influential account of such 'boutiquing' is that provided by the New York-based cultural commentator Sharon Zukin. Focusing on the case of Harlem (Manhattan) and Williamsburg (Brooklyn), Zukin has asserted that independently run boutiques 'mark out' particular neighbourhoods as safe for commercial investment, constructing a marketable image of inner city cosmopolitanism that can be seized upon by property developers and retail consortia alike. Noting the often modest beginnings of retail gentrification, she suggests that the economic and cultural entrepreneurs establishing new businesses in previously deprived districts do so to fabricate an 'aura of authenticity' based on the working class history of the area. In the process, they seek to establish a reputation among a youthful, artistic, alternative clientele, hoping to attract a broader middle class consumer base via good write-ups in the local media and word-of-mouth. In time, rents rise, with the synergistic combination of retail and residential gentrification ultimately producing neighbourhoods associated with conspicuous consumption and middle class rituals of belonging. The outcome is local shopping streets no longer characterised by traditional, immigrant or family-owned stores but dominated by the 'global ABCs of gentrification: art galleries, boutiques and cafes' (Zukin et al, 2016: 31).

Here, Zukin et al's attention to the interaction of cultural and economic values follows in the tradition of Jager (1986), Mills (1988), Ley (1994) and others who foregrounded the consumption values of the gentrifying middle class when explaining the remaking of the central city. The argument here is well-rehearsed. Pioneer gentrifiers, lacking the resources to copy upper-class consumer habits, rely on the revival and refurbishment of older, cheaper properties that are prized for their aesthetic potential, and they set about furnishing their house with similarly recycled and vintage goods. This can even manifest in 'poor chic' (Halnon, 2002), the process in which the middle classes seek to display distinction via the 'victorious' aesthetic consumption of lower-class symbolism. But poor chic does not involve the simple purchase, and display, of second-hand goods. It requires serious disposable income to clean and restore such goods, turning the merely shabby into 'shabby chic'. Working class authenticity is cherished, but in the process, it is symbolically consumed until little trace of its 'dirty' working class background remains. The same can be said of retail transformation, with sketchy neighbourhoods becoming 'crunchy' or 'hip' neighbourhoods via the emergence of boutiques before ultimately becoming fully fledged 'trendy' neighbourhoods known internationally for their designer stores and Michelin-starred restaurants (Kern, 2015b).

Emergent landscapes of 'authentic' (or at least independent) retailing can thus be seen as a first step in embedding middle class values in formerly working class areas. For example, Ley's (1994) influential study of gentrification in Vancouver suggested that inner city embourgeoisement was most obviously manifest in the opening of small-scale antique shops, boutiques, French restaurants and galleries in districts that had been previously identified as lower status. For Ley, this linked to the pivotal role of artists in gentrification, with the gentrification of many neighbourhoods starting via the emergence of such artistic and 'bohemian' stores, with these slowly linking to other forms of 'creative capital' such as those associated with advertising, architecture and publishing. Ultimately this created a local service economy almost entirely oriented to upper middle class populations. Similarly, when describing change in the inner West districts of Sydney (Glebe, Newtown, Balmain, and Rozelle), Dowling and Bridge (2001) noted a shift in retail and food outlets away from ethnic-run grocery stores towards delis offering 'exotic' gourmet food to cook or reheat at home (the latter being indicative of middle class 'time poor, cash rich' lifestyles). The conclusion here was that new retail outlets were precipitating a more thoroughgoing process of gentrification by offering the middle classes means of acquiring, and displaying, distinction through the consumption of goods in what were regarded as authentic, exotic or cosmopolitan spaces.

The fact that the first sign of retail gentrification in many neighbourhoods is the emergence of independently-run boutiques and cafes helps explain why the disappearance of traditional, local stores is not necessarily recognised as gentrification per se (Zukin et al, 2009). In contrast to situations where new-build gentrification is accompanied by wholesale retail redevelopment, and the emergence of corporate retailing, independent hipster stores seemingly embody a resistance to the globalisation of retail, with new proprietor-owned stores often represented as being preferable to the chains that dominate out-of-town and city-centre retailing. Indeed, these businesses often espouse forms of locally based production, and promote crafted goods rather than the mass produced. For example, hipster bars favour microbrews and real ale over mass produced, imported lagers; wholefood shops offer organic and 'green' produce, eschewing fast food cultures; and vintage clothing stores represent a welcome reaction to sweatshop, disposable fashions. There is also a resolute focus on durable goods rather than the transient or immaterial (e.g. the vinyl record over the mp3, the book over the kindle). As such, working class residents are not always resentful of their arrival, recognising that hipster businesses are diversifying the range of goods and services available on some local shopping streets, and that their owners are investing where others might not (Paton, 2010). Rather than viewing them as competition, existing independent traders and businesses can also be welcoming of these new stores, particularly in instances where they are more in keeping with the local business ethos than multiple chains such as *Starbucks* or *Subway*.

But, as Maly and Varis (2015) point out, hipster cultures are translocal, and the search for distinction via authenticity shares certain characteristics whether in the US, Germany, or UK (with the consumption of real coffee, vintage clothes, craft beer, and indie music appearing indexical). In the process, through interactions with hipster consumers from elsewhere, and increasing mediation, these neighbourhoods become gradually incorporated into global consumer cultures, even if a residuum of local culture survives (Zukin and Kosta, 2004). This is certainly what is happening in Brixton, where the reputation of the area for edgy nightlife, a diverse retail offer and music has encouraged the in-migration of white hipster and middle class investors, such as the French-Italian couple who established the second branch of their *Champagne and Fromage* deli in Brixton Village in 2013 (Figure 18.2), prompting protests from local anarchist groups. Alongside other

Source: Ewan Munro, licensed under creative commons, CC BY SA 2.0.

Figure 18.2   Boutiquing Brixton: fromage and champagne

new businesses such as *Barrio Brixton* (a Havana-themed cocktail bar which opened in 2016) and *Brixton Blues Kitchen* (opened 2015), this type of business continues Brixton's reputation as a melting pot of world cuisines, but is run by incomers who are white and evidentially wealthier than the owners of shops that have recently closed in the district, such as *Chicken Jerk*, the Eritrean *Dhalak* diner, and *A&C Convenience Store* on Atlantic Road, run by the same Greek Cypriot family for generations. To again quote Zukin et al (2009: 52), under current conditions of globalisation, the new outlets 'provide a material base for new kinds of cosmopolitanism that ignore old expressions of ethnic homogeneity and contrast with cultural forms, including consumption spaces, which embody low-status identities'.

So, while hipster stores exude authenticity and celebrate local distinctiveness, they are inevitably caught up in processes that valorise particular neighbourhoods through a selective appropriation of particular traditions or place-based values. Here, literatures on 'global gentrification' demonstrate that local character is a highly marketable commodity in place promotion, but one seldom associated with immigrant or 'ethnic' neighbour-hoods per se (Bridge, 2007). Rather, what sells is a form of consumption in which knowl-edgeable white entrepreneurs turn marginal neighbourhoods into ones characterised by a more navigable and 'safer' version of cosmopolitanism. Incoming hipster businesses are complicit in this process given they trade on the caché of being in an edgy multicultural neighbourhood, but offer forms of consumption easily intelligible to the white middle class readers of the Sunday supplements and style magazines. This suggests an almost-complete enrolment of hipster cultures within an infrastructure of gentrification that involves international lifestyle commentators, restaurant reviewers, and real estate agents discoursing particular neighbourhoods as cosmopolitan and cool. Counter-claims – that independent retailing is the saviour of the High Street – nonetheless remain widespread, informing retail regeneration policy at both national and local levels despite the lack of evidence that hipsterfication could ever benefit the local working class populations most reliant on local shopping streets (Hubbard, 2017).

18.3   RETAIL CHANGE, DISPLACEMENT AND RESENTMENT

While the literature on retail gentrification remains somewhat sparse, there is an emerging consensus that even small-scale retail changes can precipitate significant changes in the social and cultural character of a given locality, with the arrival of hipster businesses and boutiques especially important. As has been the case in theorisations of residential gen-trification (e.g. Hackworth and Smith, 2001), this can result in teleological models which provide a generalised description of how this proceeds. In effect, a process of change is hypothesised which goes through distinct phases. The first is the emergence of one or two key 'hipster' businesses that begin to change the appearance of local shopping streets that, before their arrival, had been characterised as possessing only maligned forms of ad hoc, 'ethnic' and discount retailing. Such new, stylish hipster stores and boutiques hence provide the basis of a powerful discourse of neighbourhood change. In a second phase, it becomes apparent that these new stores can provide the type of vintage, one-off and bespoke goods that middle class consumers from elsewhere seek as a means of emphasis-ing their taste and distinction. These goods can include the type of accoutrements and fittings that are valued by those pursuing gentrified living in period housing: second-hand furniture, antiques, and vintage fabrics, for example. As more middle class consumers descend on the neighbourhood, these types of boutiques become more numerous. In a third phase, these stores become sites not just where the middle class seek particular niche goods, but spaces for the social reproduction of a gentrifying habitus, becoming 'hang-outs for both bohemians and gentrifiers or places for social networking among stroller-pushing parents and underemployed artists and writers' (Zukin et al, 2009: 47). Fourthly, and finally, the shopping street is transformed from a local space serving long-term residents to one entirely devoted to middle class displays of taste and distinction:

> Designer shops, art galleries, bars and restaurants form the background to a landscape of people in semi-public space (tables on the footpath they must pay to occupy) watching the passing parade and sipping chardonnay from a boutique winery, beer from a microbrewery, coffee from organic beans grown in the developing country du jour (Shaw, 2008: 2).

Kate Shaw's description of a local shopping street thoroughly integrated in a spectacle of middle class consumption returns us to Neil Smith's (1996) argument that gentrification is primarily manifest in the reinvention of inner city districts as landscapes of leisure, being consumerist 'playscapes' catering only to the affluent (see also MacLeod and Ward, 2002).

Though this sequence of retail gentrification is persuasive, and widely noted, whether retail gentrification will always result in the displacement of poorer populations remains moot given retail mix might in some cases be beneficial for local working class populations (Freeman, 2011). Quite where displacement fits into these putative phases of retail change is then open to speculation. Indeed, studies suggest these displacement processes can take different forms, from the forced departure of established traders who can no longer afford rents in a given neighbourhood through to the 'pricing out' of shoppers who find that their local High Street no longer offers the goods they need at a price they can afford (Deener, 2007). Less frequently noted, but no less significant, is the difference retail change can make in terms of altering the 'atmosphere' evident in given locales, making some longer-term residents feel palpably 'out of place' in neighbourhoods they traditionally regard as home. A number of US studies have focused on this, suggesting that this tendency is particularly pronounced when white, hipster stores replace stores run by ethnic minorities, creating a different sense of place. For instance, in their study of Portland, Oregon, Sullivan and Shaw (2011) report that both incoming and established white residents looked positively on retail change, whereas the local black population had more mixed reactions and stated most new stores did not cater to their needs and incomes. Here it appeared their apprehension was largely due to feeling culturally excluded and uncomfortable in the stores they felt were aimed squarely at white populations. In their examination of New York City, Zukin et al (2016) similarly argue that low-income ethnic minority residents typically equate new, upscale consumption spaces with majority 'white' interests, and although they sometimes appreciate the better goods and services that new stores make available, often feel that retail change is working in the interests of incomers. Put simply, while many middle class white consumers appear reticent to visit retail businesses run by non-white proprietors in US inner city neighbourhoods, black consumers report feeling out of place in spaces where the dominant clientele is both affluent and white.

The suggestion here is that ethnicity may be as important as class for understanding retail-induced displacement, with a language of exclusion sometimes suggesting clear limits to who is perceived to belong on particular shopping streets. In the US context, the long-standing division of black and white populations seems massively important, albeit that some studies note a fracturing of the black population between those poorer black populations who oppose gentrification and those middle class blacks who might sometimes be implicated in retail gentrification processes themselves (Moore and Diez Roux, 2006). But questions of ethnicity do not only intersect with class, as Greenberger's (2003) study of Greenpoint in Brooklyn shows. Here, it was apparent that 'new entrepreneurial businesses' run by white incomers were experienced as exclusionary by many of the area's older residents, including an established white Polish community that felt the area's past was being lost.

Clearly, a nuanced understanding of retail gentrification requires the type of intersectional analysis that is now *de riguer* in many studies of neighbourhood change (Schroeder, 2014). North American studies clearly provide some pointers here by showing the complex ways retail capital can be caught up in complex struggles over space and place, implicated in processes of racial and ethnic exclusion. In the UK, the ethnic dimensions of retail change are less regularly invoked. Nonetheless, in their study of class dispositions in South London, Benson and Jackson (2013) highlight the ways that white, middle class affiliations with particular spaces can be mapped onto, and out of, local consumer spaces that are imagined as either 'white' or, conversely, 'multicultural'. Interviewing middle class gentrifiers, they found that local shopping streets were regularly cited as marking the boundary between desired spaces and those imagined as Other. For example, respondents regularly mentioned Rye Lane (Peckham) and East Dulwich High Street as marking out the boundary between different neighbourhoods: while the former was rarely frequented by these middle class respondents, who viewed it as a declining, shopping street characterised by 'Arab and North African' businesses, East Dulwich 'village' was conversely identified as a space of benign cosmopolitanism more readily incorporated into their middle class worldview. Coincidentally, Suzanne Hall's (2011: 2572) ethnography of 'ordinary' High Streets in South London identified Rye Lane – alongside other 'superdiverse' shopping streets – as an important space of social and cultural life for the less affluent. As she notes, shopping streets such as Rye Lane or Walworth Road are repeatedly devalued in policy circles, perhaps because of their association with super-diverse 'ethnicised' retail, whereas shopping streets in white-dominated gentrified neighbourhoods are frequently held up as models of what a diverse and sustainable shopping street should look like.

Taken together, these examples make it clear that middle class notions of 'cosmopolitan retail' extend to incorporate certain 'exotic' forms of retailing, but not others. This suggests that middle class identification intersects with ethnicity in distinctive ways that can devalue certain retail landscapes at the same time it renders others as 'exotic' and even 'authentic'. These examples also highlight that the languages used to describe retail landscapes are replete with notions that confirm distinctions of Self and Other. This idea is explicit in the work of Hagemans et al (2016), who argue that outsiders routinely describe Dutch inner city shopping streets dominated by migrant businesses as messy, dirty and dangerous. While this tendency is most obvious in white descriptions of the stores and business characterised as non-white, it is also something more generally evident in descriptions of 'working class' retail environments. For example, Gonzalez and Waley

(2012: 6) suggest that in Britain, street markets in working class areas are now dominantly seen as 'cheap, unruly, wild, dirty, backwards' with traders 'regarded as being loud, rude, whingeing'. In their view, calls for markets to attract a wider range of urban residents – including 'the young, sleek suited, pin-striped city dwellers and professionals' (Gonzalez and Waley, 2012: 7) – betray a thoroughly classed language which imposes a symbolic violence on the less affluent by describing a retail space they frequent as 'out of place' in the contemporary city. Their case study of the reinvention of Leeds' Kirkgate Market by a local authority keen to attract inward investment and tourism is echoed further north, with the closure of 'Paddy's Market' in Glasgow being seen to underpin what Paton (2010) characterises as the middle-class colonisation of this city. As she acerbically observes, 'the place is full of cafés for the café latte mob with their wee cakes' (Paton, 2010: 219). Indeed, throughout the UK there are examples where markets have been upgraded and renovated by local authorities, with Farmers' Markets seen as a better lure for consumers than street markets offering a mixture of food, clothes, DVDs, stationary and household cleaning products, often at 'knock-down' prices. The disappearance of 'traditional' street markets is important for more than economic reasons: such markets played a vital role in the reproduction of working class communities by providing a form of socially connective retailing, especially important in superdiverse neighbourhoods (Dines, 2009).

Here the role of retail policy in encouraging gentrification also needs to be highlighted, with city governors encouraging displacement through the replacement of an economy of necessity and thrift with one of distinction and display:

> In the gentrified market, the focus is on specialty produce, particularly food (organic, hyper-local, artisanal), vintage clothes and independent fashion designers. The idea of a market as a gastronomic destination is emphasized. Essential goods such as affordable fresh fruit, vegetables, meat and fish become secondary or disappear, or for example rather than sell fresh fruit, stalls sell prepared trays with cut fruit at much higher prices. Customers also change. The market becomes a destination for higher-income shoppers looking for a special produce or tourists who are prepared to pay much higher prices. There's a sense of 'distinction' of shopping at a market to differentiate oneself from the standardised supermarkets (Gonzalez and Dawson, 2015: 21).

Crucially, while street markets were important spaces of working class sociality, as well as economic reproduction (Watson and Wells, 2005; Dines, 2009), their transformation has been widely celebrated in policy circles, suggested to have restored the fortunes of so-called struggling shopping streets. Witness, for example, Mary Portas' (2011) government-commissioned review of the British High Street: though intended to address the obvious problems of vacant premises on many local shopping streets, the recipe for retail revival espoused in her report is one privileging up-market Farmer's Markets, craft production, and 'pop-up' galleries over the type of consumption that might thrive in less affluent communities (see Hubbard, 2017).

In Britain, policy documents addressing the 'decline' of high streets have rarely noted the specific needs of the disadvantaged or working-class consumer per se. Rather, they have articulated a wider concern with improving the vitality of shopping streets by transforming their offer to target those middle class and affluent consumers who predominantly shop online and out of town. But it is equally important to stress that many of state initiatives encouraging retail revival have been introduced with reference to improving both the social diversity and conviviality of local shopping streets. Inevitably, this generates a number of contradictions. For example, ordering devices such as CCTV and securitisation are justified in terms of making shopping spaces more comfortable with an eye to increasing the social mix, not eviscerating it. Indeed, one of the earliest and most important studies of British town centres in the wake of the move of retail 'out of town' – Ken Worpole's (1992) *Towns for People* – placed much emphasis on fear of crime and anxiety, and the detrimental impact this was having on local shopping streets. Following this, a number of authors made similarly impassioned pleas for reviving High Streets by making them safer, seeing this as vital in fighting the decentralisation tendencies that were encouraging many consumers and activities away from town centres. For example, Oc and Tiesdell (1997: 237) offered a programmatic vision that suggested that making High Streets safer for the 'most vulnerable' (referring explicitly to women and the elderly) would ultimately make it safe for 'everybody', seeing no necessary connection between securitisation and the exclusion of (for example) working class men or ethnic 'Others'.

But even if contemporary retail policy seldom expresses an antipathy towards particular types of shoppers, it often specifies particular types of outlet that are seen to have a malignant or toxic impact on the 'ecology' of the High Street because they attract populations regarded as inherently antisocial. In the UK, for example, the broad promotion of social diversity conflicts with the apparent intolerance expressed for businesses including bookmakers, lap dance clubs, fast food restaurants, discount alcohol outlets or money-lenders, all of which are regularly accused of coarsening the street and 'blighting' town centres (Townshend, 2016). Many local councils in the UK have introduced 'saturation' policies designed to prevent the opening of such stores (via licensing and planning controls), typically targeting the inner city shopping streets where these are most numerous. Here the policy language justifying such measures figures such premises as potentially criminogenic, and also accuses them of confronting consumers with unhealthy lifestyle options. For example, in 2015, the Royal Society for Public Health (RSPH) presented research that showed distinct concentrations of bookmakers, fast food takeaways, and payday lenders in places experiencing high levels of morbidity and premature mortality. By contrast, healthy shopping streets were identified as supporting social interaction and mental well-being thanks to their higher concentrations of pharmacies, health centres, museums, art galleries, leisure centres and libraries. The recommendation of the RSPH, like that of Portas, was that tighter regulation is needed to prevent local shopping streets being 'over-run' by unhealthy businesses.

Negative depictions of local shopping streets, identifying them as in need of regeneration, thus proliferate in the policy literature. It is this type of negativity that has encouraged the emergence of coalitions of councillors, shopkeepers and landlords seeking to improve the fortunes of these streets, with Business Improvement Districts and Town Centre Management schemes often explicit in their targeting of wealthier discerning consumers. This is something Heather McLean and colleagues have noted in the regeneration of Toronto's inner suburban shopping streets:

> Redevelopment proponents express a common desire to reinvent suburban commercial strips into 'higher' value, 'green' and 'creative' neighbourhoods that emulate gentrified downtown commercial areas. They hope that regeneration initiatives will attract artists and middle class consumers of culture by combining infrastructure development with neighbourhood-scale efforts to reinvent streets with high-end coffee shops, bicycle repair facilities and farmers' markets. However, such strategies territorialize dis-invested neighbourhoods, presenting them as

empty and blighted, marking stores frequented by low-income residents as lacking and in need of improvement. In turn, these planning trends displace concerns about structural inequalities (McLean et al, 2015: 1302–1303).

Intuitively, widening the class appeal of inner city shopping streets appears to make good sense, with the promotion of a diverse and inclusive high street promoting an ideal of city life strongly embedded in contemporary urban policy. Yet, viewed from a critical perspective, the notion that town centres cater primarily to disadvantaged consumers and need to be 'regenerated' according to the tastes of middle class consumers is an example of what Neil Smith (1996) famously termed 'revanchism': a class-based revenge that inevitably fuels displacement and gentrification.

So at a time when concepts of 'diversity' and 'mixed-use' shopping streets are 'rendered in rather reductive-instrumentalist terms as being socially desirable' (Griffiths et al, 2013: 1177), it is important to question whether these very notions are based on a definition of diversity and inclusion which privileges white, middle class behavioural and consumerist norms. These questions of course take different inflection beyond Britain, but there are, as Zukin et al (2015) note, repetitive tropes of authenticity which characterise 'up and coming' districts irrespective of whether one is looking at retail gentrification in Brooklyn, Amsterdam, Toronto or even Shanghai, albeit in the latter case it is streets run by internal migrants that appear most vulnerable to gentrification. In all cases, it is more upscale and globally legible forms of consumption that triumph, and more affordable, everyday consumption that suffers. As Stephen Miles (2012) contends, we hence need to be wary in terms of buying into myths of urban conviviality reproduced via positive images of cosmopolitan shopping streets given such images perpetuate a myth of common prosperity, rather than what is likely to be the more uncomfortable reality that lies beneath. In the context of the contemporary city, this reality is a city increasingly divided between established migrants and more recent arrivals, as well as between rich and poor.

18.4   CONCLUSION

To date, retail change has not figured particularly prominently in the literatures on urban gentrification. Nonetheless, Dowling and Bridge (2001: 99) assert that retail landscapes 'provide a particularly sensitive indicator of the balance of forces in gentrified neighbourhoods', a conclusion mirroring Smith and Williams' (1986: 3) summation that residential gentrification is intimately linked to the emergence of 'modern "trendy" retail and restaurant districts' which constitute 'a visible spatial component of wider social transformation'. From Brixton in London to Brooklyn in New York City, from Shimokitazawa in Tokyo to Sodermalm in Stockholm, there are innumerable examples of shopping streets once associated with working class and immigrant groups now catering to flannel-shirted hipsters with ironic haircuts, yummy mummies pushing Bugaboo strollers, and creative types clutching MacBooks. These neighbourhoods of vinyl record stores, curated coffee shops, and vintage furniture stores are then well on their way to becoming clichés, instances of retail transition which demonstrate the close connection between retail regeneration and the arrival of a wealthier, hipper gentrifying class. But in this chapter, it has been emphasised that such retail change is not merely indicative of gentrification: it deserves to be theorised and studied in its own right as a distinctive form of gentrification that can precede (and precipitate) other social, cultural and economic processes of gentrification, including residential gentrification. This argument is made on the basis that retail change alters more than the goods and services available in different communities: it also profoundly changes the way different neighbourhoods are represented, experienced and lived, often alienating and displacing longer-term residents in the process.

Reviewing the literature on retail gentrification, this chapter has suggested that the up-scaling of local shopping streets rarely benefits the poorer residents most reliant on local facilities, initially integrating their neighbourhoods within trans-local circuits of hipster notoriety and, over time, involving them in global processes of property investment and corporate speculation that are little interested in the needs of longer term residents. The speed – and precise outcome – of this gentrification process is of course variable, dependent on local contingencies including retail rental levels and vacancy rates, and much also depends on the nature of the existing retail offer and its pattern of ownership. This noted, it is clear much more needs to be said about the rhythm and pacing of retail gentrification in different contexts (Kern, 2015a). Likewise, the embodied and sensory aspects of this process remain poorly articulated, with the way that new, hipster businesses alienate or repel long-term shoppers, especially those from ethnic or minority groups, needing to be more fully documented. The work of Suzanne Hall (2012), provides some important signposts towards the type of detailed ethnographic investigation that is needed here, while comparative studies of the type summarised in the collection by Zukin et al (2016) show how we might place such accounts in a richer theoretical context via engagement with the concept of comparative urbanism. However, the connections between global gentrification and retail gentrification remain weakly theorised, perhaps not surprisingly given the seeming absence of studies on retail gentrification in the global South (but see Lees, Shin and López-Morales, 2016, for some examples, especially on street vendors cleared out of those public spaces to be gentrified). This given, it remains clear that post-millennial retail geography is yet to make a truly significant contribution to understandings of gentrification as a global phenomenon, implying the need for a renewed dialogue across disciplinary divides about how consumption spaces are implicated in urban change and conflicts in a variety of globalisation arenas.

REFERENCES

Anguelovski, I. (2016) 'Healthy food stores, greenlining and food gentrification: contesting new forms of privilege, displacement and locally unwanted land uses in racially mixed neighborhoods', *International Journal of Urban and Regional Research*, 39(6), 1209–1230.

Atkinson, R. (2003) 'Domestication by cappuccino or a revenge on urban space? Control and empowerment in the management of public spaces', *Urban Studies*, 40(9), 1829–1843.

Atkinson, R. (2016) 'Limited exposure: social concealment, mobility and engagement with public space by the super-rich in London', *Environment and Planning A*, 48(7), 1302–1317.

Benson, M. and Jackson, E. (2012) 'Place-making and place maintenance: practices of place and belonging among the middle classes', *Sociology*, 47(4), 793–809.

Bridge, G. (2007) 'A global gentrifier class?', *Environment and Planning A*, 39(1), 32–46.

Bridge, G. and Dowling, R. (2001) 'Microgeographies of retailing and gentrification', *Australian Geographer*, 32(1), 93–107.

Butler, T. (2002) 'Thinking global but acting local: the middle class in the city', *Socological Research Online*, 7(3), http://www.socreonline.org.uk/713/timbutler.htm.

Campkin, B. (2013) *Remaking London: Decline and Regeneration in Urban Culture*, London: IB Tauris.

Cowen, D. (2006) 'Hipster urbanism', *Relay: A Socialist Project Review*, 13, 22–23.

Deener, A. (2007) 'Commerce as the structure and symbol of neighborhood life: reshaping the meaning of community in Venice, California', *City and Community*, 6(4), 291–314.

Dines, N. (2009) 'The disputed place of ethnic diversity: an ethnography of the redevelopment of a street market in East London', in Imrie, R., Lees, L. and Raco, M. (eds) *Regenerating London: Governance, Sustainability and Community in a Global City*, London: Routledge.

Freeman, L. (2011) *There Goes the Hood: Views of Gentrification from the Ground Up*, Temple University Press.

Füller, H. and Michel, B. (2014) '"Stop being a tourist!" new dynamics of urban tourism in Berlin-Kreuzberg', *International Journal of Urban and Regional Research*, 38(4), 1304–1318.

Gonzalez, S. and Waley, P. (2012) 'Traditional retail markets: the new gentrification frontier?', *Antipode*, 45(4), 965–983.

Gonzalez, S. and Dawson, G. (2015) 'Traditional markets under threat: why it's happening and what traders and customers can do', http://tradmarketresearch.weebly.com/uploads/4/5/6/7/45677825/traditional_markets_under_threat-_full.pdf.

Greenberger, N. (2013) *Changing Retail Dynamics in Greenpoint, Brooklyn*, unpublished thesis, Columbia University.

Griffiths, S., Vaughan, L., Haklay, M. and Jones, E. (2008) 'The sustainable suburban High Street: a review of themes and approaches', *Geography Compass*, 2(4), 1155–1188.

Hackworth, J. and Smith, N. (2001) 'The changing state of gentrification', *Tijdschrift Voor Economische en Sociale Geografie*, 92(4), 464–477.

Hall, S. (2012) *City, Street and Citizen: The Measure of the Ordinary*, London: Routledge.

Halnon, K. (2002) 'Poor chic: the rational consumption of poverty', *Current Sociology*, 50(4), 501–516.

Hankins, K. (2002) 'The restructuring of retail capital and the street', *Tijdschrift voor Economische en Sociale Geografie*, 93(1), 34–46.

Hattori, K., Kim, S. and Machimura, T. (2016) 'Tokyo's living streets: the paradox of globalized authenticity', in Zukin, S., Kasinitz, P. and Chen, X. (eds) *Global Cities, Local Streets*, New York: Routledge.

Hentschel, C. and Blokland, T. (2016) 'Life and death of the great regeneration vision: diversity, decay, and upgrading in Berlin's ordinary shopping streets', in Zukin, S., Kasinitz, P. and Chen, X. (eds) *Global Cities, Local Streets*, New York: Routledge.

Herrmann, R. and Beik, L. (1968) 'Shoppers' movements outside their local retail area', *The Journal of Marketing*, 32(4), 45–51.

Hubbard, P. (2017) *The Battle for the High Street: Retail Gentrification, Class and Disgust*, Basingstoke: Palgrave.

Jackson, P. and Holbrook, B. (1995) 'Multiple meanings: shopping and the cultural politics of identity', *Environment and Planning A*, 27(12), 1913–1930.

Jager, M. (1986) 'Class definition and the aesthetics of gentrification: Victoriana in Melbourne', in Smith, N. and Williams, P. (eds) *Gentrification of the City*, New York: Routledge.

Kasinitz, P. and Zukin, S. (2016) 'From ghetto to global: two neighbourhood shopping streets in New York City', in Zukin, S., Kasinitz, P. and Chen, X. (eds) *Global Cities, Local Streets*, New York: Routledge.

Kern, L. (2015a) 'Rhythms of gentrification: eventfulness and slow violence in a happening neighbourhood', *Cultural Geographies*, doi: 10.1177/1474474015591489.

Kern, L. (2015b) 'From toxic wreck to crunchy chic: environmental gentrification through the body', *Environment and Planning D: Society and Space*, 33(1), 67–83.

Lees, L. (2016) 'Gentrification, race and ethnicity: towards a global research agenda', *City and Community*, 15(3), 208–214.

Lees, L., Shin, H. and López-Morales, E. (2016) *Planetary Gentrification*, Cambridge: Polity Press.

Ley, D. (1994) 'Gentrification and the politics of the new middle class', *Environment and Planning D: Society and Space*, 12(1), 53–74.

Lloyd, R. (2002) 'Neo–bohemia: art and neighborhood redevelopment in Chicago', *Journal of Urban Affairs*, 24(5), 517–532.

MacLeod, G. and Ward, K. (2002) 'Spaces of utopia and dystopia: landscaping the contemporary city', *Geografiska Annaler. Series B, Human Geography*, 84(3–4), 153–170.

Maly, I. and Varis, P. (2015) 'The 21st-century hipster: on micro-populations in times of superdiversity', *European Journal of Cultural Studies*, 1367549415597920.

Marcuse, P. (1985) 'Gentrification, abandonment and displacement: connections, causes and policy responses in New York City', *Journal of Urban and Contemporary Law*, 28(1), 195–240.

Mermet, A. C. (2016) 'Global retail capital and the city: towards an intensification of gentrification', *Urban Geography*, online early, http://dx.doi.org/10.1080/02723638.2016.1200328.

Miles, S. (2012) 'The neoliberal city and the pro-active complicity of the citizen consumer', *Journal of Consumer Culture*, 12(2), 216–230.

Mills, C. (1988) '"Life on the upslope": the postmodern landscape of gentrification', *Environment and Planning D: Society and Space*, 6(2), 169–190.

Moore, L. and Diez Roux, A. (2006) 'Associations of neighborhood characteristics with the location and type of food stores', *American Journal of Public Health*, 96(2), 325–331.

Murdie, R. and Teixeira, C. (2010) 'The impact of gentrification on ethnic neighbourhoods in Toronto: a case study of Little Portugal', *Urban Studies*, 48(1), 61–83.

Oc, T. and Tiesdell, S. (eds) (1997) *Safer City Centres: Reviving the Public Realm*, London: SAGE.

Papachristos, A., Smith, C., Scherer, M. and Fugiero, M. (2011) 'More coffee, less crime? The relationship between gentrification and neighborhood crime rates in Chicago, 1991 to 2005', *City and Community*, 10(3), 215–240.

Pascual-Molinas, N. and Ribera-Fumaz, R. (2009) 'Retail gentrification in Ciutat Vella, Barcelona', in Porter, L. and Shaw, K. (eds) *Whose Urban Renaissance?*, London: Routledge.

Paton, K. (2014) *Gentrification: A Working-Class Perspective*, Farnham: Ashgate.

Portas, M. (2011) *The Portas Review. An Independent Review into the Future of Our High Streets*, London: HMSO.

Rankin, K. and McLean, H. (2015) 'Governing the commercial streets of the city: new terrains of disinvestment and gentrification in Toronto's inner suburbs', *Antipode*, 47(1), 216–239.

Rankin, K., Kamizaki, K. and McLean, H. (2016) 'Toronto's changing neighbourhoods: gentrification of shopping streets', in Zukin, S., Kasinitz, P. and Chen, X. (eds) *Global Cities, Local Streets*, New York: Routledge.

Schlack, E. and Turnbull, N. (2015) 'Emerging retail gentrification in Santiago de Chile: the case of Italia-Caupolicán', in Lees, L., Shin, H. and López-Morales, E. (eds) *Global Gentrifications: Uneven Development and Displacement*, Bristol: Policy Press.

Schroeder, C. (2014) '(Un)holy Toledo: intersectionality, interdependence, and neighborhood (trans)formation in Toledo, Ohio', *Annals of the Association of American Geographers*, 104(1), 166–181.

Sibley, D. (1995) *Geographies of Exclusion: Society and Difference in the West*, New York: Psychology Press.

Smith, M. (1996) 'The empire filters back: consumption, production, and the politics of Starbucks coffee', *Urban Geography*, 17(6), 502–525.

Smith, N. (1996) *New Urban Frontier: Gentrification and the Revanchist City*, London: Routledge.

Sullivan, D. and Shaw, S. (2011) 'Retail gentrification and race: the case of Alberta Street in Portland, Oregon', *Urban Affairs Review*, 47(3), 413–432.

Townshend, T. (2016) 'Toxic high streets', *Journal of Urban Design*, 1–20.

Worpole, K. (1992) *Towns for People: Transforming Urban Life*, Milton Keynes: Open University Press.

Watson, S. and Wells, K. (2005) 'Spaces of nostalgia: the hollowing out of a London market', *Social and Cultural Geography*, 6(1), 17–30.

Williams, P., Hubbard, P., Clark, D. and Berkeley, N. (2001) 'Consumption, exclusion and emotion: the social geographies of shopping', *Social and Cultural Geography*, 2(2), 203–220.

Wrigley, N. and Dolega, L. (2011) 'Resilience, fragility and adaptation: new evidence on the performance of UK High Streets during global economic crisis and its policy implications', *Environment and Planning A*, 43(10), 2337–2363.

Yu, H., Chen, X. and Zhong, X. (2016) 'Commercial development from below: the resilience of local shops in Shanghai', in Zukin, S., Kasinitz, P. and Chen, X. (eds) *Global Cities, Local Streets*, New York: Routledge.

Zukin, S. (2002) 'What's space got to do with it?', *City and Community*, 1(4), 345–348.

Zukin, S. and Kosta, E. (2004) 'Bourdieu off-Broadway: managing distinction on a shopping block in the East Village', *City and Community*, 3(2), 101–114.

Zukin, S. Kasinitz, P. and Chen, X. (eds) (2016) *Global Cities, Local Streets*, New York: Routledge.

Zukin, S., Trujillo, V., Frase, P., Jackson, D., Recuber, T. and Walker, A. (2009) 'New retail capital and neighborhood change: boutiques and gentrification in New York City', *City and Community*, 8(1), 47–64.

19. Gentle gentrification in the exceptional city of LA?
Juliet Kahne

LA is simply one of the best currently available counterfactuals to conventional urban theory and practice, and as such, it is a valuable foundation for excavating the future of cities everywhere (Dear and Dahnman, 2008: p. 268).

19.1 GENTRIFICATION IN THE EXCEPTIONAL CITY?

This chapter adds to the literature on planetary gentrification (Lees, Shin and López-Morales, 2016) by going to another city where gentrification has only seemingly, relatively recently, emerged. Not a city in the global south, but a city in the global north, albeit one that straddles both first world and third world in its own right (Rieff, 1991). The city of Los Angeles was the only large North American city *not* to feature in gentrification scholarship in the 1980s and 1990s. In fact, Los Angeles had long been seen as an 'exceptional city' (Scott and Soja, 1996) following its own distinctive trajectory. Indeed, Los Angeles, described by the LA School as a young, sprawling, suburban, centreless, multinucleated city was not the sort of place one would expect to find gentrification. And seemingly the LA School did not mention its presence (e.g. Dear, 2000, 2002), after all it would contradict their postmodern, centrifugal model. The LA School argued that Los Angeles is a city made up not of concentric rings like in the Chicago School model (see Park, Burgess and McKenzie, 1925), but rather a hotchpotch of concentrated, smaller, sporadic urban communities spread throughout the landscape. For them (see Dear, 2000; Dear and Flusty, 1997) the inner-city's Central Business District (CBD) was not the focus of LA, the heart of the city, development and politics, that everything stems out from. Nevertheless some urban scholars (ironically including some from the LA School itself) began to highlight or mention gentrification in LA in the mid-1990s into the 2000s, even if in very little detail (see Davis 1990, 1992; Beauregard, 1991; Scott and Soja, 1996; Dear and Flusty, 1997; Keil, 1998; Boudreau and Keil, 2001; Monhan, 2002; Lin, 2008). A decade into the C21st, and simultaneously at the time I was completing my research in Los Angeles, other authors such as Reese, Deverteuil and Thach (2010) also started to highlight this gap in the literature, providing a little more detail in their discussion of Los Angeles as an example of 'weak-centre' gentrification, but still adhering to the dominance of the LA School model:

> Being a more polycentric city-region, Los Angeles is characterised by a 'weak centre' pattern of gentrification, in which the process of centripetal gentrification is muted, since there is far less need for higher classes to live near the centre, or there is no dominant centre at all [. . .] Studying Los Angeles should therefore provide an interesting counterpoint to gentrification and displacement within strongly centred urban regions (pp. 313–314).

This academic 'outing' of gentrification in LA echoed the editorial pieces on gentrification that began to proliferate in the *Los Angeles Times* and *LA Weekly*. Media reports focused

Note: In Downtown LA, historic buildings such as the old Metro building seen here, have been turned into lofts and apartments

Source: Author, 2010.

Figure 19.1   'Downtown is looking up'

on the 'visible' and thus controversial gentrifications in the eastern section of Los Angeles, near and within the Downtown area, for example, Silver Lake and the neighbouring Echo Park, and such accounts have only increased in number over time (e.g. Geffner, 2005; Welch, 2005; Zahniser, 2006; Papademetropoulos, 2008; DiMassa and Bloomekatz, 2009; Vincent, 2009; Hawthorne, 2010; Xia, Winton and Allen, 2012; Medina, 2016). Reports were initially concerned that not only was gentrification potentially displacing residents, but also threatening the identity and cohesiveness of many historic neighbourhoods throughout the city. The gentrification they discussed was developer- and city-led but also through sweat equity, it was both historic preservation and new-build, residential and retail, large scale and small scale, and also policy led, as seen with the Adaptive Reuse Ordinance (ARO) that kicked off loft-living style gentrification in Downtown LA (see Zukin, 1989). In other words, it did indeed *all come together* in LA (Soja, 1989), in this case, lots of different types of gentrification at the same time.

In 1999, things really changed. The City of Los Angeles adopted the ARO, which allowed developers to expedite the purchase of historic buildings in Downtown Los Angeles (this has since extended to other areas), and quickly turn them into new housing – most of it loft-like units and condos (see Figure 19.1). The ordinance '[. . .] provides for an expedited approval process and ensures that older and historic buildings are not subjected to the same zoning and code requirements that apply to new construction' (City of LA, 2011). Since then, over the past two decades the CBD, and LA's inner-city in general, has grown in scale and cultural significance, shifting what was once a Westside focus to an Eastside one. The entire downtown area of Los Angeles has since become a major hotbed of gentrification in the city, attracting large amounts of capital creating an entirely new landscape of consumption based on a physical and cultural foundation that was there since the beginning of Los Angeles's existence as a city – very much contradicting the LA School's 'centre-less' city idea.

The LA School's Mike Davis discussed the visceral nature of gentrification in downtown LA in the 2nd edition of *City of Quartz*, sharing his frustration with an important aspect of Los Angeles politics that stems from its neoliberal past. He lamented how Antonio Villaraigosa, Los Angeles's then mayor, had been seen as a beacon of hope in terms of shifting politics in Los Angeles away from the power of secret political cliques, boosterism and their exploiting motives – but Villaraigosa turned out not to be that beam of hope. As Davis (1990) wrote:

> The former rebel from east of the River is now the jaded booster of a 'Downtown renaissance' that promotes super-cathedrals, billionaire sports franchises, mega-museums, Yuppie lofts, and drunken Frank Gehry skyscrapers at the expense of social justice and affordable housing. He endorses an evil plan to expel the majority of the homeless from Downtown in order to satisfy the greed of its landowners and gentrifiers (p. x).

Davis (1990), however, despite having quite an accurate vision of the process downtown that was to continue to take place for the next decade, did not discuss the new urbanism and smart growth initiatives behind much of this redevelopment. For some Los Angeles communities had already experienced higher rents associated with smart growth strategies, as reports like this one highlighting a report on Koreatown by Apisakkul et al. in 2006 suggests:

> Los Angeles communities have already experienced higher rents associated with smart growth strategies. One report discusses gentrification and the risk of displacement in ethnic enclaves in Los Angeles – stating that existing city growth strategies have catered to the city's higher income working professionals. The report found that low-income renters and families with children and seniors with limited incomes were most vulnerable to displacement. Meanwhile, smart growth measures like the adaptive reuse ordinance in Los Angeles have produced mostly homes affordable to families making over $90,000 per year (Cowing, 2012: p. 3).

In an interview in the *Los Angeles Times*, Tom Slater (2006) criticized this thus:

> Gentrification is a serious issue when housing laws fail to protect tenants, when affordable housing is nonexistent and when no new public housing is being built because of widespread fears of re-creating the unacceptable conditions of L.A.'s existing housing projects, like Imperial Courts in Watts. Even if people are not made homeless, the conversion of dilapidated hotels into swanky apartments means that there are fewer housing options for poorer citizens, and if this happens on a large scale, it puts massive pressure on already stretched voluntary organizations, charities and social assistance providers. People living on the streets and in the single-room-occupancy hotels of Downtown L.A. have enough to cope with already without being hosed out of the way for iPod-wearing, latte-drinking professionals strolling to work in Bunker Hill (p. 2).

The gentrification that Davis described and that Slater highlights is not very 'weak centre', it is not different to gentrification processes found in other US. downtowns, it is not exceptional, and more importantly it was a prelude to what has emerged since – for large-scale development and 'regeneration' *is* taking place in Downtown Los Angeles and surrounding neighbourhoods, causing a significant amount of conflict. Moving forward to 2016 we can see how complications of the process have escalated, become more apparent, and spread onwards from areas such as Silver Lake into so many neighbourhoods, as the recent battle against gentrification in East LA's Boyle Heights demonstrates (see Delagadillo, 2017). As a recent displacement map created by the Urban Displacement Project – a research and action initiative led by UC Berkeley (Zuk and Lim, 2015) – shows, LA is gentrifying like other U.S. cities, just a little later in the day.

Indeed, the media has been excited to show the LA public the city's new gentrification frontiers. Back in 2007 a restaurateur and semi newcomer to the Silver Lake area, Dana Hollister, took an *LA Times* reporter (George, 2007) into decrepit parts of Downtown Los Angeles and talked about the LA River as being at the edge of the Wild, Wild West (cr. Smith, 1986), as an area with potential:

> Oh yeah, I'm callin' on this one. It's a killer view of the city and it's beautiful. You've got parking, safe parking. I wonder what they're asking for this? This is a magnificent building! And look at this how great are those bridges with all of that tagging all over? How beautiful would this be to live in? You feel like you're in Brooklyn. And look over there [. . .] look how beautiful. I see apartment buildings under the bridges! At the base. I mean, think of the view. How pretty is this? It would be like living under the Golden Gate Bridge. How cool would that be? (p. I.12)

Yet interestingly, she demonstrates a real awareness of her role in such a process, as she expresses what could be best described as 'gentrifier's guilt', which was not something reported on NYC's gentrification frontier back in the 1980s and 1990s (e.g. Smith, 1986, 1996):

> You have to be sensitive . . . because, really, your neighbors are your business partners. They are what allow you to exist. So if you're not aware of their needs and are not addressing what has come before you, then you're not going to fit in. And you are actually going to become extinct. So *gentle gentrification* is realizing where you're appropriate. It's not about just plunking something down because there is an opportunity. Is it an educated opportunity? Is it an enlightened kind of business? And sometimes it's not ready (p. I.12; emphasis added).

It could be hypothesized then that because gentrification came relatively late to LA, in comparison to other U.S. cities, it has emerged at a time when the public are much more aware of its negative impacts and want to limit some of these. However it should be noted that such concerns are not necessarily about limiting the negative impacts of gentrification on those who are most vulnerable, but more so that many do not want to lose what attracted them to a neighbourhood in the first place. For most gentrifiers, there is a balance to be struck. This notion of a gentler, softer, more self-aware, more limited form of gentrification has been expressed in the neighbourhood of Silver Lake – a historic enclave just northwest of gentrifying Downtown LA – which is discussed below as a case study based on research conducted between 2008–2010.

19.2   THE CASE OF SILVER LAKE: GENTLE, SOFT OR WEAK GENTRIFICATION?

At first glance, Silver Lake (see Figure 19.2) does not appear to be a typical case of a gentrified inner city neighbourhood. Within the grid like and segregated micro areas of Los Angeles, Silver Lake exists as its own little parcel. Located near Downtown Los Angeles, and just east of the tourist centre of Hollywood it is situated in a rather central urban location. However its location in relation to the rest of the city of Los Angeles allows it seclusion since it is on the eastern fringes of the city and much of it is situated in hills.

The hills of Silver Lake provided a cradle for what was soon to be seen as the 'jewel'

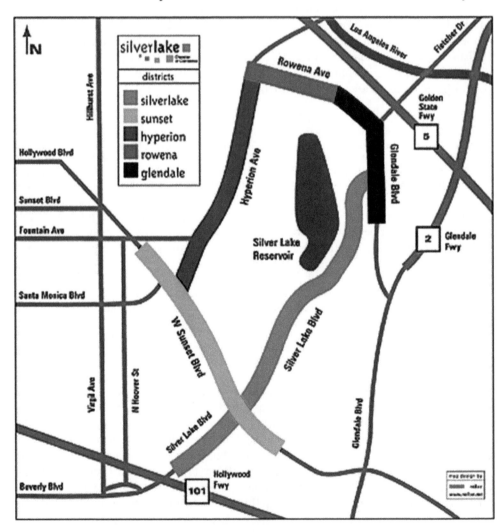

Source: Silver Lake Chamber of Commerce, 2010.

Figure 19.2   Map of Silver Lake

Note: View from a wealthier residential area in Silver Lake's hills just off Sunset Boulevard, looking east towards Downtown LA. Silver Lake's location gives it a rural feeling in the middle of the city.

Source: Author, 2010.

Figure 19.3 Silver Lake is strongly characterized by its hills and central urban location

of the neighbourhood, the Silver Lake Reservoir, which was built in 1906–1907 (*Los Angeles Times*, 1907). This is largely because the hills created a very non-urban space in a very urban location (see Figure 19.3), providing a feeling of nature in the city due to the mixture of the reservoir, the hills, and the various views of Los Angeles from the hilltops. The rolling hills and their views of the reservoir were the initial attraction for people to move to Silver Lake in the early 1900s and both remain major attractors of the neighbourhood today. Away from the ocean and near Downtown Los Angeles, Silver Lake is strongly characterized by these hills, the Silver Lake Reservoir, and the lack of exclusivity experienced in so many other hill-like areas of Los Angeles, giving it a physical sense of place like no other in Los Angeles.

After the Silver Lake Reservoir was developed in the early 1900s, the area quickly saw a wave of inhabitants. This was primarily because some of the very first film studios opened up in what was then called the Edendale vicinity (Los Feliz/Silver Lake/ Echo Park), and as a result the landscape quickly became a home to those involved in this industry (Shiel, 2012). Walt Disney for example spent a number of years going from practically declaring bankruptcy to becoming the creator of Mickey Mouse in the neighbourhoods of Los Feliz and Silver Lake (Mannheim, 2002; Susanin, 2011).

Eventually, like Disney, many film studios moved out of the area to locations such as nearby Burbank seeking more production space to house the large success that motion pictures were having (Bible, Wanamaker and Medved, 2010). However, even after so many studios left, the area continued to sustain a creative community because of those who chose to remain in their new enclave.

Silver Lake sits in one of the older parts of Los Angeles that was further developed in the 1920s after the film studios came and went. Because Silver Lake is an older neighbourhood, it also has a much more urban, walkable form and pattern of development than other parts of Los Angeles, in addition to having an abundance of historic housing stock. It is very well connected to Downtown Los Angeles, and given that the historic Red Car line used to run through Silver Lake making travelling to other areas throughout LA easy, the foundation is there for it to be an ideal central, urban location, particularly as Los Angeles's transport system continues to advance.

By way of comparison to many LA neighbourhoods Silver Lake provides an inviting, walkable space, as newcomer 'Jonah', expressed in interview:

> Silver Lake is very walkable, I mean I walked here to meet you! On the weekends I hardly ever use my car to get around. And there is so much local neighbourhood stuff, so I walked to breakfast, I walked to the Farmers Market, and even if I don't walk, I can drive places in like 2 minutes to other things. So it's great in that it's so close to local things, and local town centres, but also close enough to other centers like Downtown, but I have the benefit of having a big back yard, and a parking garage, and a big enough house, so its kind of like so its like a really big mix of suburban amenities and urban amenities I guess? And I feel it comes without the negatives of either. I mean sometimes you get some of the urban negatives, like crime or graffiti or something, and I have noticed that has improved in the past three years on my street – Interview, Jonah, 2010.

Jonah's comment demonstrates the benefits of Silver Lake's walkable urban form. To have this kind of walking environment is unusual, and a luxury in Los Angeles, and this in itself creates a very alternative space (a more integrated social alternative to a more exclusive and segregated way of being seen in other parts of LA). This correlates well with the literature on gentrification and spatial capital (e.g. Rérat and Lees, 2011). This is not only because of the ability to walk, but because of the environment one is actually walking through. 'Shannon' also discussed walkability comparing her experiences in New York City to Silver Lake and emphasizing the cultural impact of being able to do this in LA:

> I love that you can walk everywhere here. I love that there's all these little outdoor cafes and people are just you know, nice. People live in the 'city' in Silver Lake in a way that they don't in many other parts of LA, where you're kinda hermetically sealed in your house, and then your car. And to worsen it people are like 'ohhh I want the big back yard with a deck' and then they don't really live in the city. As opposed to in Silver Lake where people are out, they're at the coffee shops, they're at the bars, they're at the farmers market, they're walking around, people walk to things here, and so there's much more of a sense of community just because there are people out on the streets, it's not you know, a ghost town the way it is in many other neighborhoods in LA – Interview, Shannon, 2011.

It is perhaps no coincidence then that the neighbourhood has been associated with gentrification, given its walkable urban nature in an otherwise sprawling, suburban city. Indeed, its residents feel that any adjustments or additions to the neighbourhood ought to enable this pedestrian environment – one where people can get out of their cars, wander around near their homes, engage with other people in the community, and enjoy the cultural amenities that Silver Lake has to offer. With traffic being such an issue for residents across Los Angeles County, and with ever increasing petrol prices and a lack of public transport, Angelenos are clearly avidly searching for ways to make their commutes easier and more economical. Silver Lake, like a number of other nearby neighbourhoods, offers this to its residents, and people are catching on.

In the media report above, Dana Hollister referred to 'gentle gentrification' in LA. Wiest and Zischner (2006) investigated what they call 'soft' or 'controlled' gentrification in East German cities, where they claimed that displacement did not actually take place. In Silver Lake, residents have taken action to preserve the character and scale of the neighbourhood, and in so doing tried to block displacement of long-term residents and businesses alike. So, on the other hand, it could be said that Silver Lake is not experiencing gentrification at all, but what Brown-Saracino (2004, 2007, 2010) calls 'social preservation'. This is still different to what Ley and Dobson (2008) call 'gentrification limited', for Silver Lake residents seem to like a state of pre-mature or immature gentrification, or in other words, a gentrification that is 'just right'.

Social preservationists are people who actively work to maintain community authenticity and diversity both in the landscape and social networks. According to Brown-Saracino (2007) the difference between gentrifiers and social preservationists rests not necessarily in their actions, but in their intentions and interests. In other words, there are many similarities between gentrifiers and social preservationists, but their ideals stem from a different set of beliefs and needs rooted mainly in the reasons for living in a particular neighbourhood (appreciation of ethnic diversity in social preservation as opposed to a future in the housing market in gentrification).

Silver Lake is diverse and has long attracted creative types. Its creative community primarily developed from the motion picture studios that were built there in the 1910s and 1920s, but this extended to painters, writers, and other artists rather than just movie stars, animators and producers. Over the next few decades Silver Lake became known as a refuge for artists and their supporters (Hurewitz, 2007), as a result, a bohemian identity emerged. In the gentrification literature scholars often discuss the influx of a creative or bohemian community as a precursor to (or as a result of) gentrification (e.g. Caulfield, 1994), but in the case of Silver Lake, the creative community has always been there. Zukin (1989) talks about early stage gentrifiers being attracted to fringe or alternative locations in the city which have a sense of authenticity – this can often be found in the original architecture of an area, the cultural diversity amongst the existing residents, or even a range of independently owned shops (see Zukin, 2008). Often these locations offer a strong sense of place, and tend to be low income, immigrant populated, inner city areas, with a wealth of neglected historic architecture or disinvested urban spaces that support a lifestyle on the fringes of society, where big money is just not that evident, even if it exists. Such a place could easily be identified as Silver Lake.

A local architect and author, Barbara Bestor, who wrote *Bohemian Modern Living in Silver Lake* (2006) notes:

> In the 1930's and 1940's many progressives, communists, artists, and a Latino population migrated to Silver Lake while the rest of the city grew more conservative and economically and racially divided (p. 1).

This knowledge was also shared by resident 'Gloria' who had lived in the Silver Lake/Echo Park area for over 30 years:

> We had heard about this community as being sort of a lefty community and it was near downtown and it was very diverse . . . so we lived here, in an area which is called 'Red Hill'. There used to be a lot of people here who were in the communist party, and a lot of the old lefties have stayed around – Interview, Gloria, 2011.

Silver Lake for most of its history was a fairly white, middle class area, yet during the later mid-20th century as Downtown Los Angeles experienced its version of 'white flight', Silver Lake (and indeed Echo Park) experienced an economic downturn for a short period. The area developed a reputation for crime and gang activity, especially during the 1970s, 1980s and early 1990s. During that time Silver Lake and the surrounding areas (Echo Park even more so) became heavily populated immigrant neighbourhoods that were generally lower income. This is a pattern seen in many other U.S. cities that have experienced gentrification.

After the 1980s, Silver Lake began to divide into two distinct areas: the 'Hills' as locals called them, in a 'leafy amphitheater' setting around the Reservoir, and the 'Flats', a more 'bustling working class' part of the neighborhood mostly to the south of Sunset Boulevard, where Latino but also a mixture of other ethnicities existed (Ramos, 1984). The majority of people surveyed or interviewed in Silver Lake between 2008–2010 had lived in other parts of Los Angeles previously, and often in somewhat similar neighbourhoods before moving. In fact, many of the respondents were from New York, or lived in Hollywood just before Silver Lake. No one had ever lived in the Westside areas such as Beverly Hills, Santa Monica, Pacific Palisades, Culver City, or Westwood – considered the more wealthy, exclusive and generally more sterile areas of Los Angeles in terms of diversity. Resident 'Marion' described her situation:

> Diversity was the reason we moved here. We moved here because I need a mix of people, and a mix of houses, a mix of everything. I'm a New Yorker so it is the closest to that kind of mix that I probably could find in well, Southern California really. The diversity is probably the most important thing for me. When we were living in the valley I felt like everybody was the same, houses were the same, everything was dull. But I don't feel that way here. I feel like, everybody is different. Ethnically, financially, age, nationality – Interview, Marion, 2011.

To help explain why this might be, another resident, 'Sylvia', described her view of why Silver Lake feels like New York City, demonstrating that there is a major draw to the area based on diversity, lifestyle, belonging and familiarity:

> [. . .] having grown up in New York where it's a melting pot, you just see all types of people, you know, all colors and just very open about everything, and very accepting about everything I feel like Silver Lake has that same sort of vibe. It's not just all, you know, women in their Juicy Couture sweats, or with their Yoga mats, it's a different, more diverse vibe. And that to me, well that's what I grew up with so that's what I'm more comfortable with. I think also here if you meet people from New York, a lot of them live in Silver Lake, cause people are just drawn to what they grew up with, who you're used to whatever, and it's a similar vibe, you know? You've got that kind of like, little bit of East Village vibe in Silver Lake, but you get the benefit of living in a house with a garden, and being able to drive to work, and having a little bit more space but you still get that kind of New York vibe which I really appreciate – Interview, Sylvia, 2010.

Another newcomer from New York called 'Marie' also suggested that there is a specific 'type' of person who lives in Silver Lake, and that this person is different to someone you would find in other parts of Los Angeles:

> I think that there's a very specific type of person who is drawn to Silver Lake. The person who wants to live in Manhattan Beach is not Silver Lake demographic. Somebody who wants to live in Beverly Hills is not Silver Lake demographic. I think it's very artsy, people are more creative here, they're a little bit more liberal, but you know, maybe they care a little bit more about other people, and about the neighbourhood they live in. Altogether it's just a different kind of view of things and the way I describe it to some of my friends from other places is that, the only people you see with boob jobs in Silver Lake are the trannies . . . – Interview, Marie, 2010.

From residents' accounts, old and new, Silver Lake's cultural evolution was clearly slow-growing and highly organic – like a fine tomato. Old timers and newcomers alike expressed how they found solace in a place that seemed to retain its unique historic identity, diversity and character, which they felt was unusual in Los Angeles. This was a more 'gentle gentrification', making the distinction between 'what had gentrified' and 'what had not gentrified' rather difficult. But, gentrification pressures were everywhere. Indeed as Zukin (2008) says:

> Authenticity . . . becomes an effective means for new residents to cleanse and claim space; since it is they and the media for which many of them work who define the term, it reflects their own self-interest (p. 745).

Silver Lake's gentrifiers were not too different from the neighbourhood's old timers – alternative, diverse, and full of pride for their neighbourhood. The term 'gentrifier' seemed too negative a label for them as it was evident they believed in social preservation. Based on how residents identified themselves, most of them felt they had little other choice than to live in Silver Lake, and if anything, they were aware and concerned about gentrification and displacement of not only long-term residents, but of themselves. It is evident that more discussion needs to take place surrounding the rather general label of 'gentrifier', as in this case the gentrifiers demonstrated characteristics of social preservationists (like so many pioneer gentrifiers elsewhere – see Lees, Slater and Wyly, 2008), but in Silver Lake, ultimately and unsurprisingly, social preservation failed.

19.3 A CREATIVE HUB MOVES TOWARDS MATURE GENTRIFICATION

As well as being identified as diverse, Silver Lake is also known for its music scene. Through the 1990s, Silver Lake began to be known as one of the main hubs for American Indie Rock music. Many major musicians and bands have since been associated with Silver Lake, some of the most famous are Elliot Smith, Beck, Local Natives, and Silversun Pickups (named after a local corner store), but this does not include the large number of already famous musicians that lived in the area, such as Flea from the Red Hot Chili Peppers who helped open up a non profit music school in the neighbourhood, The Silver Lake Conservatory of Music. Such musicians and bands have furthered a 'Silver Lake' identity in the public eye, and are indirectly responsible for attracting new residents wishing to be part of it:

> When Beck (notable music artist) moved to Silver Lake in the late 80s, it wasn't trendy at all. It was backwater – but it did offer cheap housing, a significant draw for a high school dropout without a steady paycheck. You could measure how Beck and Silver Lake have gentrified (while holding onto a few scruff marks) at a concert he gave there in January (2005) in a club called Spaceland. [. . .] The crowd was made up of college kids and young professionals, those who could afford to live in what is now a high rent neighbourhood or would be able to someday. Still, the vibe in Spaceland had not changed much since the time that Simpson of the Dust Brothers first saw Beck perform there, just before the 'Loser' tour (Lubow, 2005).

Soon, Silver Lake became an even better known creative hub, and again, noticeably gentrifying, as seen in Szanto (2003):

> Silver Lake and Los Feliz are rapidly being settled by artists and young creative types who are fostering a do it yourself scene. Houses, parking lots, empty cinemas, and storefronts have become provisional art galleries; weekend long interdisciplinary minifestivals are publicized mainly by word of mouth. The atmosphere recalls the old La Cienega days, but the gentrification of these formerly working class neighbourhoods is unrelenting. Commercial galleries and hip boutiques are already moving in (p. 414).

Coming back to Dana Hollister (George, 2007), this Silver Lake 'newcomer', represents the people that came to Silver Lake and its surrounding neighbourhoods after it became just a little more mainstream, once it was a little *safer*, a little more *on trend*, and when the housing was still very reasonably priced in comparison to other 'desirable' neighbourhoods in Los Angeles. These newcomers demonstrated slightly different tastes and characteristics to those of Silver Lake old-timers – a little more money, more of a focus on upscale goods, more property investment hungry, and, despite her evidence of a conscience, both attitudes are seen quite clearly in Hollister's words. Such differences between pioneer gentrifiers and their followers are real but they often get squashed together under the umbrella term 'gentrification', especially when the description and definition of gentrification and its stages are blurred in sources such as the media. Saying gentrification exists is easy. Defining the actors involved in the process, and their role, is not. It is in Silver Lake where we see this crisis of culprits.

Indeed, other accounts in the *Los Angeles Times* such as in McNamara (2002) told a different story, where change seemed to be taking place more quickly, was more evident, and posed more of a threat to Silver Lake's long standing identity:

> Walking along Sunset Boulevard, between the clean white chic of Rain Heron and the recently artsified Alvarado Arts Building, it is impossible not to notice how fabulous this stretch of the street is. Splattered by the gentrification that has been spilling out from Los Feliz/Silver Lake into Echo Park during the last five or six years, these 20 or so blocks are perhaps the perfect mix of the real and terminally hip. Coffeehouses elbow Laundromats, gallery space stands alongside taco stands, boutiques bloom next to mattress stores and tchotchke emporiums (McNamara, 2002).

Although the description is one of a mixed, interesting, eclectic place, it is also describing a place that is changing from one set of tastes to another – and this was back in 2002. Today, Silver Lake has specialty shops, restaurants and other services that serve a much more upscale clientele, that is more familiar with what we know as 'gentrified' areas – not the bohemian, multi-cultural enclave it once embodied. What is interesting is that the types of small businesses coming in existed before in Silver Lake, it is just that there are now more of them and they seem to cater to a slightly different market, a more upscale market. It is as if previous businesses have not just been displaced, but replaced.

The general take in gentrification studies is that pioneer gentrifiers regardless of their liberal intentions, trigger or instigate gentrification and displacement (see Lees, Slater and Wyly, 2008). Therefore pioneer gentrifiers are relatively low impact, but controversial. They move into a neighbourhood at a point when housing and rent prices are quite low, and often part of the attraction. Yet they are pioneers because unlike other middle class urban dwellers they are willing to deal with the risks and tensions of living in marginal inner city areas. However, the very fact of their inhabitation clears the way for future, less 'risk oblivious' (see Clay, 1979) gentrifiers in the process's second wave. This seems to best describe what is taking place in Silver Lake, counteracting any social preservation thesis.

The relationship between gentrified neighbourhoods and minority populations has long been discussed (e.g. Castells, 1983; Knopp, 1990). The gay population of Silver Lake had, and still has, a major presence in the area, and has influenced much of the entire area's known cultural identity, particularly in the minds of Angelenos. However, based on what was witnessed and heard from residents in the neighbourhood, this is one of many demographics in Silver Lake that is diminishing – something that cannot simply be determined by census tracts analysis.

Silver Lake's gay population is not only present in Silver Lake, but it was, and is, very politically active, as seen in Kenney (2001):

> Silverlake would not be the neighborhood it is without the decades of public activism both in the neighborhood and across the city. The Mattachine Society was founded here, early gay activists 'liberated the bars' and kicked out the police, and some of the first nonbar gay businesses opened up on Sunset Boulevard in the heart of the neighborhood (p. 197).

The gay (and political) community continues to be vibrant in Silver Lake, and has even been coined as 'the true gay mecca' (Trykowski, 2013). Yet as the area becomes more appealing to the mainstream, gay culture is under threat of being displaced, and there was already evidence of this in 2012.

An iconic gay haunt, the Black Cat Tavern, was a bar in Silver Lake that was famous for being a site of the gay rights movement. The bar was raided by the LAPD on New Year's Eve in 1967 where people were beaten and arrested. A few weeks later, further demonstrations took place collaborating with other 'counter culture' groups as a response to being targeted by the police. This coincided with many similar gay rights protests that were taking place throughout the U.S. around this time, such as in San Francisco and New York City, and pre-dates the famous Stonewall Riots that took place in New York City's Greenwich Village. The demonstration at the Black Cat was seen to be one of the first gay rights protests in the U.S. (Kenney, 2001).

The Black Cat Tavern eventually closed and was later reopened as LeBarcito (see Figure 19.4), a Latino gay bar that stood for many years serving the gay community in Silver Lake, in addition to its counterpart Le Bar, which was only a short distance away (it closed down in the early 2000s). Activist and resident Wes Joe was responsible for getting the location historic status as a Historic Cultural Monument in 2008, meaning the space is worthy of preservation. This seemed like a clear example of social preservationism, and

Note: Many other restaurants and bars in the area also closed down around 2012.

Source: Author, 2013.

Figure 19.4   Site of historic Le Barcito/Black Cat Bar before it became a gastropub in 2012

an excellent example of how resident involvement and community activism in Silver Lake was being enacted, keeping the cultural landscape intact and preserved, and it appeared to be an example of the community fighting displacement. But in 2012, LeBarcito was purchased by a hip restaurateur, and turned into a gastropub, with pricy food and a complete renovation of the interior's historic elements. In respect for the bar's historic status, the owner kept the name of the bar, part of the original sign, and placed historic photos of the political events that took place there along the walls of the bar. The owner actually lives in Silver Lake, and as a result is an example of the kind of newcomer that lives in this area – one who embraces the community history and culture, yet simultaneously contributes to its change. The new gastropub opened at the end of 2012, and elicited mixed feelings from residents. The activist himself, Wes Joe, responded to this change in a 2012 article in *The Eastsider* magazine simply stating, 'things change'. Others spoke out in frustration on the comments section in the same announcement, referring to the displacement of a minority culture that had long found a safe space in Silver Lake:

> This was a great bar and a venue that I went to for years. While there seems to be lots of gastro-pubs serving all the latest trends in food, popping up all over this hood it's not quite as easy to go

back and create a dive-y bar and the strong community following Le Barcito represented in the community. This bar's absence is being felt by many – it was a unique place to stop by and grab a drink. With the recent closing of The Otherside and the closing of Le Bar several years back, and the many other gay bars that have closed in the area – the local gay community continues to take a hit as far as community spaces to gather in the area. I guess all the 'gay friendly' artists in the area aren't really savvy to the unique needs that come from gay men having a public space to gather and socialize. Guess we don't need that since I have 'Grinder' right? Our community continues to get shoved aside to our new online ghetto. That bar wasn't just about hooking up – it provided a real sense of gay space for many people. The new spot . . . guess we'll see, might be good food and a fun place, but it won't be Le Barcito and the Sunset Junction is less for it (Comments, *The Eastsider*, 2012).

It can be seen here that even in a neighbourhood with strong community activism and support, this long-standing gay bar gentrified anyway, reflecting the wider changes in the neighbourhood.

However, the gay community is far from being the only community being affected by gentrification in Silver Lake. In fact, the Latino community in Silver Lake, it is safe to say, has taken the biggest hit as seen in census tract analysis alone. But it is also apparent visually, simply on the disintegration of an abundance of shops and delis that catered to this community for decades. For example, La Parrilla was a restaurant that had been in Silver Lake for at least 20 years. The restaurant had seen better days and did not exactly have the best Mexican fare compared to its beloved nearby counterparts such as El Conquistador (which was not only owned by long-term Latino/gay residents, but has also since closed down), but La Parilla was still in service to the community. The location was on the fringes of Silver Lake, near Echo Park, one of the pockets that is still more highly Latino and currently in a stage of transition. By 2012, this part of Silver Lake had already started to see change, particularly with the opening of trendy bars such as Mohawk Bend nearby in Echo Park. What is interesting is not so much that La Parrilla closed down, but that this Mexican restaurant was replaced by another Mexican restaurant – just one that is more upscale, and one that serves a new clientele (see Figure 19.5). Instead of traditional *platos*, we see a large selection of expensive beer, and specialty tacos. The décor went from a more traditional and colorful Mexican style to a grey-toned, modern and minimal facade – much more a representation of the gentrification aesthetic (Bridge, 2006). Again, businesses swapped from one set of 'tastes' to another (e.g. Bridge, 2006), and this demonstrates an obvious change in Silver Lake. There is clearly a new market in the neighbourhood, and Diablo Taco, however better the food, highlights this change. El Diablo however is not the only signifier of change – this is one of many bars and restaurants that have opened up in Silver Lake catering to this new customer base, while older places such as La Parilla keep disappearing. This sort of 'upscaling' comes as no surprise, and as we see in Silver Lake, many actually welcome it. But what is important to note is that despite community efforts to protect or save a place of particular cultural meaning, as we see with the Black Cat, its destiny was still the same as La Parilla. So it raises the question – what sort of change truly lies in the hands of the community? It seems here that despite all efforts, the market clearly dictates what stays, and what goes.

Note: Amenities are not just displaced but 'replaced'. La Parrilla in 2009, became Diablo Taco in 2013, serving the new tastes of the neighborhood.

Sources: Left: The Eastsider 2011; right: Author, 2013.

Figure 19.5   Gentrification maturing in Silver Lake

19.4 CONCLUSION

LA seems to be an example of planetary gentrification par excellence – it is a place where there is little difference between city and country (Zukin, 2010), and the urban and the rural blur into each other on LA's beaches, mountains, valleys and deserts. Silver Lake exemplifies this well with its urban walkability yet hillside location that actually makes it feel rural – a best of both worlds situation. Traditional distinctions between urban and rural, city and suburb, urban and regional are not clear-cut in LA, calling for the removal of centre-periphery binary thinking (cr. Merrifield, 2014; Lees, Shin and López-Morales, 2016). LA is also a place where the developed and underdeveloped worlds collide, as Shiel (2001) has said:

> [. . .] this notional positioning of Los Angeles as some kind of global core to which the rest of the world can be viewed as periphery must be balanced by the recognition that if Los Angeles is a paradigm, it is so not merely because it can be proposed as one of the world's most 'advanced' urban societies but also because it can be proposed as one of the world's most 'backward' urban societies – a tense and often violent combination of First and Third World realties in one (albeit highly segregated) space. Thus Los Angeles contains uneven development internally while accentuating it on the world stage (p. 7).

This does not make LA 'exceptional' however as Shiel seems to argue, for the city demonstrates the same characteristics as planetary urbanization everywhere, and that also lends itself to gentrification.

Similar to how gentrification taking place in Los Angeles is making it more similar than different to other cities of its size and scale, Silver Lake also is not exceptional, for its gentrification may have been 'gentle' for a time but its impacts are far from unique. In fact, it is now far beyond a tipping point as it transitions into maturity. The intentions of any in-mover might have been benign in Silver Lake (as with pioneer gentrifiers in London and NYC in the 1960s), but the outcome is just the same. Silver Lake, a progressive arts district since the early twentieth century, for so long remained a contrast to Los Angeles' Westside-centric developer-chic landscapes, and maintained a bohemian enclave and relatively consistent commercial and residential landscape despite waves of city- and developer-led gentrification surrounding it on all sides. But gentrification has strengthened and moved forward in Silver Lake as well as in its surrounding sister neighbourhoods, where the process is also not so gentle.

In their discussion of planetary gentrification and operationalizing the 'new' comparative urbanism, Lees, Shin and López-Morales (2016) state that it is not enough to just look at the global south but to look at third world urbanisms in first world cities (as well as vice versa); in a city like LA where it has long been argued that first world and third world come together (cr. Rieff, 1991), this makes a lot of sense. In fact, journalists often compare Silver Lake to so many of its lookalikes in other western cities (and certainly an aesthetic that can be seen in non-western cities) – Williamsburg and Bushwick in Brooklyn, Shoreditch and Bethnal Green in London, Prenzlauer Berg or even more so Neukölln in Berlin, and it is likely that Silver Lake's characteristics can be found in neighbourhoods everywhere – the gentrification aesthetic is also planetary. Silver Lake, although still a 'jewel' of Los Angeles, is not unique but joins, if not exemplifies, similar urban neighbourhoods around the world where despite providing a sense of place, gentrification is by no means gentle (see Figure 19.6).

Link at: https://www.flickr.com/photos/keithhamm/9412052498.

Source: Photo by Keith Hamm, Flickr Creative Commons.

Figure 19.6   Evidence of a less gentle gentrification in Silver Lake, 2013

As this chapter has shown, LA fits with the gentrification literature and indeed, the actual process on the ground is escalating. It seems then that Los Angeles is developing more like other cities around the world, and in fact is *not*, as the introductory quote to this chapter says, 'counterfactual'.

REFERENCES

Apisakkul, M. et al. (2006) 'Gentrification and Equitable Development in Los Angeles Asian Pacific American Ethnic Enclaves', *Little Tokyo Service Center* and A3PCON, 20, 38.

Beauregard, R. (1991) 'Capital restructuring and the new built environment of global cities: New York and Los Angeles', *International Journal of Urban and Regional Research*, 15(1), 90–105.

Bestor, B. (2006) *Bohemian Modern: Living in Silver Lake*, New York: Harper Collins.

Bible, K., Wanamaker, M. and Medved, H. (2010) *Location Filming in Los Angeles*, Charleston, SC: Arcadia Publishing.

Boudreau, J.-A. and Keil, R. (2001) 'Seceding from responsibility? Secession movements in Los Angeles', *Urban Studies*, 38(10), 1701–1731.

Bridge, G. (2006) 'It's not just a question of taste: gentrification, the neighbourhood, and cultural capital', *Environment and Planning A*, 38, 1965–1978.

Brown-Saracino, J. (2004) 'Social preservationists and the quest for authentic community', *City and Community*, 3(2), 135–156.

Brown-Saracino, J. (2007) 'Virtuous marginality: social preservationists and the selection of the old-timer', *Theory and Society*, 36(5), 437–468.

Brown-Saracino, J. (2010) *A Neighborhood That Never Changes*, Chicago: The University of Chicago Press.

Castells, M. (1983) *The City and the Grassroots: A Cross Cultural Theory of Urban Social Movements*, Berkeley: University of California Press.

Caulfield, J. (1994) *City Form and Everyday Life: Toronto's Gentrification and Critical Social Practice*, Toronto: University of Toronto Press.

City of Los Angeles (2011) *Adaptive Reuse Ordinance*, available from http://preservation.lacity.org/incentives/adaptive-reuse-ordinance.

Clay, P. (1979) *Neighborhood Renewal: Middle-Class Resettlement and Incumbent Upgrading in American Neighborhoods*, Lexington, MA: D.C. Health.

Cowing, A. et al. (2012) 'Getting there together: tools to advocate for inclusive development near transit', *Public Counsel*, 1–23, http://www.mitod.org/pdf/20120208_TOD_Advocates_Guide.pdf.

Davis, M. (1990) *City of Quartz: Excavating the Future in Los Angeles*, 2nd edn, New York: Verso.

Davis, M. (1992) 'Fortress Los Angeles: the Militarization of Urban Space', in Sorkin, M. (ed) *Variations on a Theme Park: The New American City and the End of Public Space*, New York: Hill and Wang, pp. 154–180.

Dear, M. (2000) *The Postmodern Urban Condition*, Oxford: Blackwell.

Dear, M. (2002) 'Los Angeles and the Chicago School: Invitation to a debate', *City and Community*, 1(1), 5–32.

Dear, M. and Dahmann, N. (2008) 'Urban politics and the Los Angeles School of Urbanism', *Urban Affairs Review*, 44(2), 266–279.

Dear, M. and Flusty, S. (1997) 'The iron lotus: Los Angeles and postmodern urbanism', *Annals of the American Academy of Political and Social Science*, 551, 151–163.

Delgadillo, N. (2017) 'The neighborhood that went to war against gentrifiers', *City Lab*, 1 March, https://www.citylab.com/equity/2017/03/the-neighborhood-that-went-to-war-against-gentrifiers/518181/.

DiMassa, C. and Bloomekatz, A. (2009) 'L.A. to announce Broadway makeover', *Los Angeles Times*, 28 January, http://www.latimes.com/local/la-me-broadway28jan28-story.html.

Geffner, D. (2005) 'Inevitably, renewal leads to gentrification (who owns downtown?)', *Los Angeles Business Journal*, 28 March, 81.

George, L. (2007) 'Dana Hollister: she's the girl with the x-ray eyes', *Los Angeles Times*, 29 April, http://articles.latimes.com/2007/apr/29/magazine/tm-hollister17.

Hawthorne, C. (2010) 'City walk: time to return to LA's core', *Los Angeles Times*, 8 August, http://articles.latimes.com/2010/aug/08/image/la-ig-downtown-20100808.

Hurewitz, D. (2007) *Bohemian Los Angeles: and the Making of Modern Politics*, Berkeley: University of California Press.

Keil, R. (1998) *Los Angeles: Globalization, Urbanization and Social Struggles*, New York: J. Wiley & Sons.

Kenney, M. (2001) *Mapping Gay L.A.: The Intersection of Place and Politics*, Philadelphia: Temple University Press.

Knopp, L. (1990) 'Some theoretical implications of gay involvement in an urban land market', *Political Geography Quarterly*, 9(4) October, 337–352.

Lees, L., Shin, H. and López-Morales, E. (2016) *Planetary Gentrification*, Cambridge: Polity Press.

Lees, L., Slater, T. and Wyly, E. (2008) *Gentrification*, New York: Routledge.

Ley, D. and Dobson, C. (2008) 'Are there limits to gentrification? The contexts of impeded gentrification in Vancouver', *Urban Studies*, 45(12), 2471–2498.

Lin, J. (2008) 'Los Angeles Chinatown: tourism, gentrification, and the rise of an ethnic growth machine', *Amerasia Journal*, 34(3), 110–125.

Lubow, A. (2005) 'Beck at a certain age', *The New York Times*, 6 March, http://www.nytimes.com/2005/03/06/magazine/beck-at-a-certain-age.html?mcubz=2.

Mannheim, S. (2002) *Walt Disney and the Quest for Community*, Aldershot: Ashgate.

McNamara, M. (2002) 'L.A. at large: a tour of Bohemia's back alleys', *Los Angeles Times*, 25 September, http://articles.latimes.com/2002/sep/25/news/lv-artcrawl25.

Medina, J. (2016) 'Gentrification protesters in Los Angeles target art galleries', *Los Angeles Times*, 5 November, https://www.nytimes.com/2016/11/05/us/los-angeles-gentrification-art-galleries.html?mcubz=2.

Merrifield, A. (2014) *The New Urban Question*, London: Pluto Press.

Monhan, T. (2002) 'Los Angeles studies: the emergence of a specialty field', *City and Society*, 14(2), 155–184.

Papademetropoulos, L. (2008) 'The real gentrification story', *Los Angeles Times*, 3 July, http://www.latimes.com/opinion/la-oew-papademetropoulos3-2008jul03-story.html.

Park, R., Burgess, E. and McKenzie, R. (1925) *The City*, Chicago: University of Chicago Press.

Ramos, G. (1984) 'Silver Lake: residents of all stripes are drawn to an evolving community', *Los Angeles Times*, 18 November, C1.

Reese, E., DeVerteuil, G. and Thatch, L. (2010) '"Weak-center" gentrification and the contradictions of containment: deconcentrating poverty in Downtown Los Angeles', *International Journal of Urban and Regional Research*, 34(2), 310–327.

Rérat, P. and Lees, L. (2011) 'Spatial capital, gentrification and mobility: evidence from Swiss core cities', *Transactions of the Institute of British Geographers*, 36(1), 126–142.

Rieff, D. (1991) *Los Angeles: Capital of the Third World*, New York: Touchstone.

Scott, A. and Soja, E. (eds) (1996) *The City: Los Angeles and Urban Theory at the End of the Twentieth Century*, Berkeley: University of California Press.

Shiel, M. (2001) 'Cinema and the city in history and theory', in Shiel, M. and Fitzmaurice, T. (eds) *Cinema and the City: Film and Urban Societies in a Global Context*, Oxford: Blackwell, pp. 1–18.

Shiel, M. (2012) *Hollywood Cinema and the Real Los Angeles*, London: Reaktion Books.

Silver Lake Nearly Ready (1907) *Los Angeles Times*, 25 November, p. II2.

Slater, T. (2006) 'The downside of upscale', *Los Angeles Times*, 30 July, 1–2, http://articles.latimes.com/2006/jul/30/opinion/op-slater30.

Smith, N. (1986) 'Gentrification, the frontier, and the restructuring of urban space', in Smith, N. and Williams, P. (eds) *Gentrification of the City*, London: Allen & Unwin, pp. 15–34.

Smith, N. (1996) *The New Urban Frontier: Gentrification and the Revanchist City*, New York: Routledge.

Soja, E. (1989) *Postmodern Geographies: The Reassertion of Space in Critical Social Theory*, London: Verso.

Susanin, T. (2011) *Walt Before Mickey: Disney's Early Years, 1919–1928*, Jackson: University Press of Mississippi.

Szanto, A. (2003) 'Hot and cool: some contrasts between the visual art worlds of New York and Los Angeles', in Halle, D. (ed) *New York and Los Angeles: Politics, Society, and Culture – A Comparative View*, Chicago: University of Chicago Press, pp. 393–422.

The Eastsider (2012) 'A new (fancy) life for Silver Lake's Black Cat Tavern', 10 October, http://www.theeastsiderla.com/2012/10/storefrontreportanewfancylifeforsilverlakesblackcattavern/.

Trykowski, T. (2013) 'Move over, West Hollywood Silver Lake is the true gay mecca', *LA Weekly*, 19 April, http://www.laweekly.com/news/move-over-west-hollywood-silver-lake-is-the-true-gay-mecca-4173444.

Vincent, D. (2009) 'Escape from LA-la land', *The Guardian*, 17 April, https://www.theguardian.com/travel/2009/apr/18/los-angeles-silver-lake-guide.

Welch, M. (2005) 'Hipsters send Times into tizzies', *Los Angeles Times*, 3 April, http://www.latimes.com/news/la-op-tent3apr03-story.html.

Wiest, K. and Zischner, R. (2006) 'Upgrading old housing areas in East German inner cities – processes and development paths in Leipzig', *Deutsche Zeitschrift für Kommunalwissenschaften*.

Xia R., Winton, R. and Allen, S. (2012) 'Chalk protests at downtown L.A.'s ArtWalk draw a defiant new line', *Los Angeles Times*, 13 July, http://articles.latimes.com/2012/jul/13/local/la-me-0714-artwalk-20120714.

Zahniser, D. (2006) 'Welcome to gentrification city', *LA Weekly*, 23 August, http://www.laweekly.com/news/welcome-to-gentrification-city-2144884.

Zuk, M. and Chapple, K. (2015) *Urban Displacement Project*, UC Berkeley, http://www.urbandisplacement.org/map/socal.

Zukin, S. (1989) *Loft Living: Culture and Capital in Urban Change*, Brunswick, NJ: Rutgers University Press.

Zukin, S. (2008) 'Consuming authenticity', *Cultural Studies*, 22(5), 724–748.

Zukin, S. (2010) *Naked City: The Death and Life of Authentic Urban Spaces*, New York: Oxford University Press.

20. New directions in urban environmental/green gentrification research
Hamil Pearsall

20.1 INTRODUCTION

In cities around the world, residents, activists, and government officials call for urban environmental improvements, such as brownfield redevelopment, additional green space, and expanded bike infrastructure, as part of the transition to a more sustainable, livable city. A mainstream perception is that such changes provide benefits to all residents across the city, and further, that they will address environmental justice concerns by benefitting those who have suffered the greatest environmental burdens. However, residents, activists, and scholars have started to question the motivations, processes, and impacts of such 'improvements' that tend to raise property values and attract wealthier and whiter residents. Low-income residents, homeless residents, tenants in informal housing, and people of color, have found themselves excluded from the benefits of these new environmental amenities and vulnerable to unintended, yet negative, consequences, such as residential, commercial, or industrial displacement.

This chapter reviews gentrification processes that accompany the types of urban environmental changes that are often featured as key parts of urban sustainability plans and discusses how communities and residents are addressing this dilemma in urban greening and sustainability. Although gentrification processes are not confined to cities, environmental gentrification scholarship has focused on urban contexts, possibly as a reflection of the current emphasis on making cities more sustainable. Additionally, the majority of research is based in North American and European cities, with some research situated in the 'Global East'.

20.2 CONCEPTUALIZING ENVIRONMENTAL GENTRIFICATION

Greening and economic development have become increasingly coupled as more and more cities have embraced sustainability and sustainable development as a key component of economic growth plans (Pearsall and Pierce, 2010; Pearsall et al., 2012). In some contexts, greening efforts may serve as one of, or one component of, many structural drivers of gentrification, such as municipal subsidies to large real estate developers, subsidies for housing renovations, or aggressive mortgage financiers, that contribute to the uneven development of cities (Hamnett, 1973; O'Loughlin and Munski, 1979; Smith, 1979a; Wyly and Hammel, 1999). In other contexts, greening efforts may appear at the behest of a new gentrifying class that wants to live in an urban setting that has access to an array of green amenities. These new residents may use their wealth, political connections, or other means to demand environmental improvements and realize their ideal green aesthetic.

The emergence of the term 'environmental gentrification' is often linked to a study by Sieg et al. (2004) finding increases in prices in neighborhoods with notable improvements in air quality based on their study in Southern California from 1990–1995. Their findings were reinforced by economists Banzhaf and Walsh's (2008) study of how changes in pollution levels impact population and demographic composition and Banzhaf and McCormick's (2006) study of gentrification processes associated with the remediation and redevelopment of locally unwanted land uses (LULUs). Concurrently, the National Environmental Justice Advisory Council (NEJAC) published a report detailing the 'unintended' impacts of urban environmental policies, particularly the remediation and reuse of brownfields redevelopment, in five communities in the United States (NEJAC, 2006). They highlighted gentrification concerns and included a series of recommendations to reduce negative impacts for vulnerable populations, such as displacement or exclusion from the cleanup planning process.

Perspectives on the relationship between urban greening and gentrification have expanded since these initial empirical studies of pollution remediation in the 2000s. New terms such as 'ecological gentrification' or 'eco-gentrification' and 'green gentrification' have emerged, offered by scholars from fields such as geography, planning and sociology, to convey different aspects of the gentrification processes that precede, accompany, or follow sustainability planning or urban greening efforts. There has been little discussion of the differences in these terms, and to some extent it appears that they have emerged from different scholars, in different fields, to describe similar processes. A brief comparison of terms and usage follows and is summarized in Table 20.1.

Many quantitative studies of American cities adopt Banzhaf and Walsh's (2008, pp. 24–5) definition of environmental gentrification as 'in a world where households sort in response to changes in environmental quality, the bulk of the benefits of a policy that successfully cleans up dirtier neighborhoods where the poor live may actually be captured by rich households'. This definition emphasizes the distributional and outcome-oriented aspects of greening, suggests a market-led process, and focuses on the class-based dimensions of gentrification impacts. This definition implies a rather unpoliticized process that unintentionally accrues benefits to the rich while displacing the poor. Subsequent studies drawing on qualitative approaches or other disciplinary perspectives have highlighted additional aspects of gentrification processes, including: (1) acknowledgement that environmental gentrification is racialized, (2) recognition of multiple negative impacts, in addition to residential displacement, and (3) description of the political processes that enable or create environmental gentrification (Table 20.1). For instance, Gould and Lewis (2012), who described the process as 'green gentrification', also included in their definition that such environmental improvements exacerbate racial inequalities, in addition to economic ones, based on a study of a public park renovation in Brooklyn, New York. In a similar vein, Anguelovski's (2015) study of food gentrification in Jamaica Plain, Boston (MA) noted the white privilege of the alternative food movement that supported a healthy food store (Whole Foods) over a Latino market. Secondly, Dooling (2009), through her study of how the creation of new green spaces in Seattle impacted homeless populations, recognized that physical displacement, though a critical negative impact of gentrification, is not the only one and was also accompanied by exclusion from the green spaces and the

Table 20.1 Key terms and definitions commonly used in environmental gentrification research

Name of process	Source of definition	Definition	Key Aspects
Environmental Gentrification	Sieg et al. 2004	'significant price increases in communities with large improvements in air quality and price decreases in communities with small air quality improvements. Distributional effects of environmental policies seem to be pronounced with opportunities for the lowest income households to lose because the induced increases in their housing prices are not fully offset by the air quality improvements they can afford to enjoy' (1074–1075)	• Distributional impacts • Class • Market-led perspective
	Banzhaf and Walsh 2006	'in a world where households sort in response to changes in environmental quality, the bulk of the benefits of a policy that successfully cleans up dirtier neighborhoods where the poor live may actually be captured by rich households' (24–25)	• Distributional impacts • Class • Market-led perspective
	Checker 2011	'environmental gentrification builds on the material and discursive successes of the urban environmental justice movement and appropriates them to serve high-end redevelopment that displaces low income residents' (210)	• Distributional and procedural impacts • Class • Market-led and gentrifier-led perspectives
Ecological Gentrification	Dooling 2009	'the implementation of an environmental planning agenda related to public green spaces that leads to the displacement or exclusion of the most economically vulnerable human population while espousing an environmental ethic' (621)	• Distributional and procedural impacts • Class • Primarily market-led perspective
Green Gentrification	Gould and Lewis 2012	'without clearly focused public policy intervention, in situ environmental improvements will tend to increase racial and class inequality, and decrease environmental justice, a process we refer to as "green gentrification"' (114)	• Distributional and procedural impacts • Class and race • Market-led perspective

planning process. Finally, Checker (2011) observed that city officials and developers used the language and aims of environmental justice advocates to promote improving green space access in an underserved neighborhood in Harlem, New York City. Yet, ultimately, this green space served wealthy and white populations. By examining how city officials and the neighborhood redevelopment corporation appropriated language of equity and justice, Checker illuminated the political processes that linked greening and gentrification in this park restoration effort.

20.3   EXPLAINING ENVIRONMENTAL GENTRIFICATION

The majority of studies conceptualize environmental gentrification as supply-side/ market-led gentrification, drawing on Smith's (1979b) explanation of a rent gap, or the difference between the actual ground rent and potential ground rent under different types of redevelopment scenarios. In the case of an 'environmental' rent gap, pollution – in air, soil, or water – makes places less attractive to residents and subsequently depresses property values – up to 45% according to Bryson (2013). When the pollution source is removed or site remediated, property values rebound (Hurd, 2002; Dale et al., 1999; Kohlhase, 1991; De Sousa et al., 2009; Roddewig, 1996). A study of site cleanups across the US also supported this remediation-rebound pattern (Gamper-Rabindran et al., 2011). This study further found that property values were not the only thing to change following the remediation of hazardous waste sites; an increase in mean household income and percentages of college-educated residents – two often-employed indicators of gentrification – also accompanied the site cleanups.

Nationwide and citywide quantitative studies of environmental gentrification have suggested that the relationship between cleanups and gentrification is place-specific and complex. For instance, brownfield redevelopment facilitated gentrification only in certain vulnerable neighborhoods in New York City (Pearsall, 2010), primarily those with other gentrifying factors, such as proximity to Manhattan, while brownfield redevelopment in Portland, Oregon, did not create gentrification patterns (Eckerd, 2011). Checker (2014) noted that certain brownfields in Staten Island were more attractive for redevelopment because of their waterfront locations, versus brownfields located inland near other toxic facilities. Finally, Abel and White (2011) attributed gentrification patterns in Seattle (WA) to broader trends in deindustrialization, rather than as a direct result of improvements in air quality and gentrification. Additional studies find that supply-side/market-led perspectives may not provide an adequate explanation of gentrification, particularly when gentrification may precede greening activities.

Demand-side/gentrifier-led environmental gentrification, after Ley (1994) and other consumption theorists, occurs when gentrifiers identify environmental quality or other green amenities as a priority for their post-industrial and professionalized city and use their wealth and political leverage to advance this agenda. Mir and Sanchez (2009) provided an excellent example of this process in Chicago, Illinois, where there were significantly more complaints and inspections of car repair shops in gentrified neighborhoods, even though enforcement remained consistent across all (i.e. gentrified and ungentrified) neighborhoods. Other studies have uncovered how wealthy residents use environmental quality or sustainability goals to justify gentrification. Baviskar (2003) coined the term 'bourgeois environmentalism' to describe the ways in which the rise of environmentalism embraced by the growing middle class in India has been used to justify the removal of slums or other activities (e.g. defecation in parks) portrayed as dirty or unnatural (see Lees, Shin and López-Morales, 2016, on bourgeois environmentalism as gentrification). She notes that 'upper-class concerns around aesthetics, leisure, safety, and health have come significantly to shape the disposition of urban spaces' (ibid., p. 90). While these studies show either consumption-side or production-side perspectives, Curran and Hamilton (2013) also reiterate that a thorough explanation of environmental gentrification may draw on both production-side and consumption-side theories, as supported by other gentrification research (e.g. Lees et al., 2008; Hamnett, 1991; Clark, 2005).

Other scholars have employed explanatory frameworks that draw on theories of urban development and sustainability from various fields (e.g. critical sustainability studies, planning). Perhaps most notably, several scholars (e.g. Rosol, 2013; Goodling et al., 2015; Long, 2016; Tretter, 2013a) have applied While et al.'s (2004) concept of an 'urban sustainability fix', inspired by Harvey's concept of a 'spatial fix', to explain how capitalism interacts with sustainable development goals in post-industrial North American cities such as Austin, Texas; Vancouver, British Columbia; and Portland, Oregon. Other studies (e.g. Abel and White, 2011; Dale and Newman, 2009), have embraced a planning frame by drawing on Campbell's (1996) 'sustainability triangle' that describes conflicts among three dimensions of sustainability (ecology, economy, and equity) by focusing on tensions that emerge as cities try to achieve economic development and social justice (titled 'the development conflict') and environmental protection and social justice (titled 'the property conflict'). Finally, Schuetze and Chelleri (2015) propose the concept of the 'sustainability fallacy' to describe the challenges faced by the extensive and ambitious plan to redevelop downtown Seoul, Korea, into a green smart city, though they use this term in a descriptive rather than explanatory way.

20.4   WHAT SPARKS ENVIRONMENTAL GENTRIFICATION?

While brownfield redevelopment, the addition of new parks, or new transit-oriented developments do not necessarily create gentrification, they can catalyze gentrification or be used by certain actors to justify or accelerate processes that displace and marginalize certain residents. Subsequently, in some cases, such as the park renovation project in Harlem, New York City (Checker, 2011) or the remediation of the industrial Gowanus Canal in Brooklyn, New York City (Miller, 2016), residents vulnerable to gentrification opposed efforts to improve environmental quality and access to environmental amenities. Paradoxically, these vulnerable populations tend to be subjected to the most extreme environmental justice concerns. At first glance, opposition to urban environmental projects may seem confusing or contradictory, thus environmental gentrification research has helpfully uncovered the unintended and negative consequences of greening and how they unfold in different cities (Table 20.2). This research serves as a critical step towards finding a solution to Wolch et al.'s (2014) 'urban greening paradox', where the addition of green space in underserved neighborhoods leads to increases in the cost of living that can ultimately displace or exclude the longtime residents it was intended to serve. As Table 20.2 highlights, research has identified an array of catalysts to environmental

Table 20.2　Gentrification catalysts

EG catalyst	Actors	City	References
Bike infrastructure	Bike advocacy groups	Chicago, Los Angeles, Portland, Milwaukee, San Francisco, Chicago, Seattle	Lubitow, Zinschlag and Rochester 2015; Lugo 2015; Stehlin 2015; Hoffman 2016
Brownfield redevelopment	Developers, city government	New York City, Portland	Checker 2014; Curran and Hamilton 2012; Hamilton and Curran 2013; Pearsall 2010, 2012, 2013
Park creation/ restoration	City government, park advocacy groups	New York City, Malmö (Sweden)	Checker 2011; Gould and Lewis 2012; Litke, Locke and Hass 2015; Millington 2015; Sandberg 2014
Waterfront redevelopment	City government, private developers, residents	Ahmedabad, Delhi, Chennai, New York City, North Carolina, Seoul, Toronto	Bunce 2009; Checker 2014; Follman 2015; Lim et al. 2013; Sharan 2015; Youth et al. 2015
Smart growth/ ecodensity	City government, developers, environmental interest groups	Austin, Vancouver, Seoul	Quastel 2009; Rosol 2013; Schuetze and Chelleri 2015; Tretter 2013
Community-oriented greening	City government, urban farmers, residents, non-profits	Baltimore, New York City	Battaglia 2014; Reynolds 2015

gentrification, ranging from private to public, top-down to bottom-up, and site-specific to city-wide, as well as the specific aspects that create unjust processes and unintended and adverse impacts.

Brownfield redevelopment in North American cities has come under particular scrutiny from environmental gentrification scholars, who have highlighted associated demographic changes, power-laden political processes, and vulnerable populations. As reviewed above, early research on environmental gentrification focused on improvements to air quality or the remediation of contaminated land, such as brownfields or hazardous waste sites, primarily in North American cities. Several national and regional studies suggest that gentrification, characterized by the displacement of low-income and minority residents, follows brownfield redevelopment and hazardous site cleanups (Gamper-Rabindran et al., 2011; Gamper-Rabindran and Timmins, 2011; Essoka, 2010). City-specific projects have uncovered some additional aspects of remediation practices and their connections to gentrification. Dale and Newman (2009), for example, found that brownfield redevelopment projects in Victoria and Toronto reduced diversity and equity. Research in New York City highlighted the characteristics of populations vulnerable to displacement, such as low-income and elderly populations, as well as those living in rent stabilized housing (Pearsall, 2010), and active industries and blue collar workers (Curran and Hamilton, 2012). Kern's (2015) study in Toronto, Ontario, reminds us of important racial components of environmental gentrification, observing that remediation of toxic sites was accompanied by displacement of black bodies in one former industrial neighborhood. Finally, in Spokane, Washington, Bryson (2012) traced the political processes surrounding the remediation and redevelopment of a brownfield site, documenting how civic leaders who heavily promoted and facilitated this private redevelopment failed to acknowledge or consider negative impacts for residents vulnerable to displacement from increases in property values. While this research on environmental remediation has analyzed impacts in the neighborhoods where remediation occurs, it has not considered what remediation in one neighborhood means for environmental conditions and demographic impacts in other neighborhoods. Better engagement with environmental justice scholarship could improve the multi-scalar perspective on environmental remediation.

Activists and scholars have also critically examined the impacts of densification or smart growth planning in an era of neoliberalism (Rérat and Lees, 2011; Quastel et al., 2012). Compact urban form provides locational advantages that gentrifiers value, including reduced travel time and associated costs, and improved mobility. Rérat and Lees (2011) suggest that gentrifiers benefit from 'spatial capital' gained from inhabiting inner city residences in dense, 'sustainable' neighborhoods. Quastel (2009), Quastel et al. (2012) and Rosol (2013) note that Vancouver's municipal EcoDensity plan capitalized on this notion of density as gentrification. They suggest that this plan represented little more than state-sponsored support of developers aiming to market environmental amenities and the concept of 'livability' to wealthy residents interested in living in downtown Vancouver. Quastel (2009) also highlighted the role that green consumerism played in developers' appropriation of environmental discourses without addressing the need for affordable housing. Vancouver is not the only city to fail to deliver on affordable housing promises; Addison et al.'s (2013) review of smart growth planning revealed that affordable housing is often challenging to include in sufficient supply, particularly because smart growth principles reduce the amount of land available for housing (Downs, 2005).

Residents, activists and scholars have also examined the impact of green building policies on neighborhood housing values and characteristics, uncovering multiple ways in which green design can simultaneously create and reflect gentrification. Chegut et al.'s (2013) study of green buildings in London made a clear connection between green buildings and gentrification, finding that these buildings raise nearby property values, although also noting that each addition to the green housing stock decreased the rents and property values of such buildings. Beyond this property value impact, Mehdizadeh and Fischer suggest that national green building policies create symbols of gentrification:

> As being green becomes in vogue, and the next way to compete with the 'Joneses', communities will market themselves to the wealthy as 'green'. Conceivably, 'green' may become a code word for safe, rich, professional, and privileged (Mehdizadeh and Fischer, 2013, p. 6).

Boeing et al.'s (2014) study of the neighborhood-scale green building certification (LEED-ND) in a gentrifying neighborhood in Oakland, California, provided further perspectives on this issue, finding that neighborhoods that failed to meet environmental certification criteria often contained longtime residents who viewed their neighborhood as livable and employed valuation criteria different to those promoted in LEED-ND. Their study indicated that efforts to comply with environmental certification may ignore the needs of current residents and instead redesign neighborhoods to attract a new (and likely wealthier) crowd.

Waterfront redevelopment has also been tied to greening or cleaning efforts. Unsurprisingly, many studies find that these state-sponsored projects lead to displacement of residents. Cities with slums or informal settlements have witnessed extensive displacement patterns associated with a newfound interest in waterfront property. In Delhi, India, the Yamuna River was cleared of slums to make way for two large mega-projects, in hopes of creating a 'world class' riverfront (Follmann, 2015; Sharan, 2015). A similar process unfolded along the Sabarmati River in Ahmedabad under the pretense of 'inclusive' redevelopment (Desai, 2012), and in Chennai, where an estimated 18,000 families were displaced from the Cooum River as a result of development and environmental restoration efforts (Coelho and Raman, 2010).

Research in post-industrial cities in the United States and Seoul, South Korea, has also highlighted how redevelopment that leverages the waterfront as amenity, displaces industries and working waterfronts. Curran (2004, 2007) observed industrial displacement along the waterfront in the rapidly gentrifying Williamsburg in Brooklyn, New York City, in the early 2000s. Subsequent research also linked the installation of park space or other green waterfront amenities to the loss of industrial space. In Seoul, South Korea, Lim et al. (2013) found that the Cheonggye Restoration Project led to the displacement of industrial uses in the historic business district and that land use changes associated with the river restoration project were aimed at wealthier users. This pattern also emerges in smaller cities in North America. Coastal fishing communities across the USA have become gentrification hot spots, threatening long-time marine-based economies and their workers: Colburn and Jepson's (2012) study of close to 3,000 fishing communities argued that both resource-dependent residents and their culture, developed over decades of a fishing economy, were displaced by in-migration of higher-income populations who were often retired and seeking the amenities afforded by waterfront access. In Toronto, Ontario, Bunce (2009) found that even public waterfronts are subject to gentrification in the neoliberal city, where city officials provide developers with access to pursue private projects for large-scale urban revitalization.

In other cities, too, public space has become a sort of gentrification battleground. In response to environmental justice concerns about the inequitable distribution of parks across cities, many sustainability plans call for improving green space access in underserved neighborhoods by creating new parks or renovating existing ones. Despite the appearance of good intentions, activists and residents have critiqued the outcomes, such as 'richening' and 'whitening' observed by Gould and Lewis (2012), as well as planning processes that exclude longtime residents (Checker, 2011). In Seattle, Washington, Dooling (2009) noted that the addition of city-maintained public green spaces ultimately served to displace homeless people who lived in them, and excluded these populations from discussions concerning creating new parks in the future.

The creation of the High Line in New York City, an elevated linear park constructed on a defunct railway, points towards the heightened gentrification impacts associated with private-public partnerships. Though the High Line is part of the municipal park system in New York City, its development and maintenance is led by a 'friends' group that act as non-profit caretakers of the park and raise 98% of the annual budget (Friends of the High Line, 2016). Several studies reveal large-scale displacement of residential and commercial occupants following the creation of this internationally renowned park space that serves as a global attraction in New York City's post-industrial Meatpacking District (Littke et al., 2015; Patrick, 2014; Millington, 2015). As Littke et al. (2015, p. 367) observed, 'great landscaping does not make great places', pointing to the damaging effects of such dramatic gentrification (which has been celebrated by the city's administration as economic development). From a different perspective, Patrick (2014) also noted how plants, labeled as invasive, have been displaced by the creation of the park. His 'more than human' relational analysis shows the irony of one plant surviving the challenging industrial and post-industrial growing conditions being designated as undesirable, and systematically removed: 'it hardly seems ethical that *A. altissima* should bear the weight of being demonized as invasive when the very conditions for its survival are intertwined with the forms and structures of urbanization in late capitalism' (ibid., p. 936). Patrick's study reminds us that the impacts of gentrification go beyond human populations and that we should continually question so-called environmental improvements and whose interests they serve.

Another type of green public amenity that is linked to gentrification is bike infrastructure, often presented as a sustainable transit option, alongside public transportation, to reduce car congestion and CO_2 emissions. Rather than focusing on the impact of bike lanes on property values, as with many of the studies of brownfield redevelopment or green space creation or renovation, research conducted primarily in US cities, has revealed how bike planning has become both racialized and failed to accommodate the needs of communities that intersect the bike lanes. Hoffman's (2016) book *Bike Lanes are White Lanes* describes how bike advocates have, perhaps unintentionally, created a white community of advocacy in Portland (Oregon), Milwaukee (Wisconsin) and Minneapolis (Minnesota). Lugo's (2015, p. 308) research in Seattle reinforces this sentiment, in that she found that some communities viewed bike lanes as a way to help people to pass through their neighborhoods: 'In Seattle the entrenchment of sustainable development as city policy made bicycle infrastructure seem like yet another benefit that would accrue to white environmentalists'. Not all research concluded that bike infrastructure is part of (or a symbol of) gentrification, and this will be addressed below in a section on responses to environmental gentrification.

Activists have also observed how small-scale, community-oriented greening activities conducted by residents themselves can reflect the green interests of gentrifiers, as well as acting as a symbol or catalyst for accelerating gentrification. It is, perhaps, in this area of research that the embedded processes of market-led and gentrifier-led gentrification are best illuminated, as it is difficult to disentangle these two aspects of environmental gentrification at this fine scale. Certainly, Baviskar's (2002) discussion of bourgeois environmentalism in Delhi, and its impact on environmental regulations and urban space, showed how the aesthetic interests of the middle class can guide development of city-wide environmental regulations that displace vulnerable populations. As an indication of how residents have become sensitive to symbols of gentrification, residents in Baltimore opposed street tree planting in certain neighborhoods (Battaglia et al., 2014). In New York City, Reynolds (2015) observed that urban agriculture, despite its association with socially just practices, did little to challenge structural racism in the neighborhood. However, in a counter example in Liverpool, England, Thompson (2015) notes that grassroots greening, in the form of guerilla gardening led by residents who remained in the increasingly abandoned Granby neighborhood, set the stage for an effective Community Land Trust that rehabilitates houses, as opposed to demolishing them and serving to further devalue the neighborhood.

20.5 INCLUDING SOCIAL JUSTICE AND EQUITY AS PART OF URBAN ENVIRONMENTAL CHANGES

Efforts such as the Community Land Trust described above, hold promise for preventing displacement, although McKendry and Janos (2015) suggest that even deliberate efforts to elevate the social equity and justice components of greening projects face considerable challenges in overcoming the logic of neoliberal urbanism and technocratic sustainable development approaches. Despite this, residents, community groups, and activists have drawn on a variety of strategies to oppose environmental gentrification processes. Some strategies employed are similar to those used by environmental justice activists, such as collective neighborhood action, community organizing, and direct tactics, while others are different approaches afforded by specific urban environmental conditions, such as environmental policies and regulations. Pearsall and Anguelovski (2016) provide a review and analysis of responses to environmental gentrification processes, and this section complements their analysis by discussing the ways in which efforts at resistance gain traction in different contexts.

20.5.1 Is it Up to the Individual?

Arguably, the scale at which responses or resistance strategies occur has become increasingly scrutinized and relevant in neoliberal cities that silence community protests, sponsor urban renewal and gentrification, and roll back social services providing safeguards for those living in gentrifying neighborhoods. Pearsall's (2012) study of resistance to gentrification in New York City points out how strategies implemented at the individual scale, such as owning a home, became the most effective way of safeguarding vulnerable residents from displacement, as other community or city-wide support systems, such as rent stabilization, were eroded. This shift – placing burden on the individual to be resilient to neighborhood change – marginalizes already vulnerable residents (e.g. renters). Further, research in Chicago (Hoffman, 2016; Lubitow et al., 2015), Delhi (Baviskar, 2011), New York (Checker, 2011, 2014), and Seoul (Schuetze and Chelleri, 2015) suggests that the voices of these vulnerable individuals are not always heard. For instance, residents who participated in planning meetings to discuss the restoration of Morningside and Marcus Garvey Parks in New York City, expressed frustration at the restoration effort being co-opted by a new gentrifying population: 'Residents were encouraged to accommodate a technocratic compromise that shunned politics as unseemly and counter-productive, and that sought instead only to engage "community" at the level of governance' (Checker, 2011, p. 225). While the formal planning process seemingly promised 'meaningful involvement' from all residents, ultimately contributions from specific residents – those who were whiter and wealthier – were adopted by the planners. Lubitow et al. (2015) make similar observations regarding bike lane infrastructure in Chicago, Illinois. Although certain residents raised concerns about adding new bike lanes to their neighborhoods, these concerns went unheeded in the 'community' planning process that bike advocates oversaw. Bike advocates – similar to the park restoration advocates in New York – made problematic assumptions about what was best for neighborhoods, leading community members and scholars to urge advocates to rethink the role of biking: 'Bicycles have great potential to revolutionise how people use and interact with public space, but a truly just and socially sustainable bike infrastructure must incorporate community concerns and avoid strictly technological, universalised assumptions about the use and value of bicycles' (ibid., p. 2650). Thus, given the power dynamic embedded in a 'community' planning process that is led by those with more power, it seems likely that the residents most vulnerable to the changes proposed by the process will be only superficially involved.

Lugo's (2015) comparison of bike advocacy in Seattle and Los Angeles reminds us that cultural sensitivity and inclusion can improve the social justice dimension of bike infrastructure expansion efforts in cities. In Seattle, she found that residents questioned the imposition of bike infrastructure in their neighborhoods, noting that such infrastructure was not intended to serve the neighborhoods that it crossed. Lugo contrasted this example with the bicycling communities in Los Angeles, where biking was found to be part of a network of social movements, thus placing social justice and equity as part of the bike discussion. She observed:

> Too often, urban planners, designers, and developers fail to engage ethnographically with the spaces they wish to improve, ignoring the cultural distinctions that imbue public spaces with meaning. . . When bike advocates focus on changing infrastructure rather than building networks among existing residents, urban neighborhoods become design products rather than lived places (ibid., p. 307).

Lugo found that the presence and inclusion of people in discussions and planning helped prevent gentrification. This act of including opinions and concerns from residents as a meaningful part of planning processes has gained traction in other contexts too. In East Baltimore, Maryland, where residents indicated that they did not want street trees because of perceptions of gentrification, city officials recognized that community involvement was important for realizing their urban tree canopy cover (UTC) goal (Battaglia et al., 2014). Having this feedback from residents from East Baltimore helped tree planting advocates reframe their approach to defining 'Possible' UTC and to incorporate residents' attitudes towards trees.

20.5.2   Far-reaching Impacts of Community Activism

Hackworth and Smith (2001) suggested that large-scale protests, such as the Tompkins Square Park protests in the early 1990s (Smith, 1996), became less common in the neoliberal context, yet scholars have documented important community-led activism/protests against environmental gentrification processes. These studies reveal mixed results, though in some cases the efforts have succeeded in stopping or slowing particular developments or initiatives. For instance, threats to demolish urban gardens in New York City's Lower East Side, to make way for affordable and market rate housing, was met with highly visible protests by the gardeners, and ultimately the involvement of the state, as well as celebrity Bette Midler's non-profit, the New York Restoration Project (Schmelzkopf, 2002). In

Austin, Texas, environmental justice activists from 'People Organized in Defense of Earth and Her Resources' (PODER) challenged a municipal smart growth plan for its inattention to racial inequalities and gentrification potential across the city. Tretter (2013b) observed that PODER had to reframe this perceived social problem (of racial inequity) into environmental terms in order to get the attention of the city's environmentalists and advocates of the SMART growth plan. Ultimately, the plan was not approved, though largely due to economic reasons. Additionally, even though some smart growth principles were subsequently adopted into other city policies, affordability was incorporated into these plans.

Other studies have also observed how community activism has influenced perceptions of environmental plans and changes, even if they have not stopped them. For instance, Quastel (2009) and Rosol (2013) examined how social justice advocates critiqued the superficial efforts to incorporate affordability and livability in Vancouver's sustainability plan. Rosol (2013, p. 2251) argues that even though an ecodensity bill was approved by city council, it 'failed as a hegemonic project', as critics questioned the project for its lack of affordable and livable plans. In Jamaica Plain, Boston (MA), a coalition of Latino residents, college students, and older residents came together to oppose 'food gentrification' via the opening of Whole Foods (Anguelovski, 2015). One particular concern was that 'Whole Foods', an expensive 'healthy' food store, would replace the local 'Hi-Lo' supermarket that served the local community and was known as one of the best Latino markets in the state. The 'Whose Food/Whose Community?' coalition leveraged a highly visible campaign through protests, comments in newspaper and online forums to protest the opening of Whole Foods, which they saw as a sign of gentrification to come and the loss of the neighborhood's Latino identity. While such activism is important, Checker's (2014) study of state-sponsored gentrification in Staten Island's North Shore found that such participation in formal planning processes, even if meaningful, requires considerable attention, time, and resources from activists.

20.5.3 'Just Green Enough' as a New Approach to Resisting Environmental Gentrification

The examples above describe activist efforts to oppose a particular development, plan or initiative, and Miller (2016, p. 293) suggests that some residents have used pollution 'as a protective barrier against the ill effects of green gentrification'. However, Curran and Hamilton (2012) discovered that activists and residents have avoided gentrification without compromising environmental quality or environmental improvements. Based on work in Brooklyn, Hamilton and Curran (2013) observed what they call 'gentrifier-enhanced environmental activism', highlighting how longtime residents worked with gentrifiers to redevelop brownfields along Newtown Creek, a contaminated industrial waterway. They positioned this term as different and complementary to local environmental justice efforts, where 'successes were won by countering gentrifiers' voices rather than cultivating cross-class alliances' (ibid., p. 1561, citing Keil and Boudreau (2006) and Checker (2011)), with it enacting a focus on strategic alliances that can keep the interests of longtime residents at the center of discussions. They found that this arrangement facilitated the redevelopment of contaminated and underutilized properties in Greenpoint in a way that was consistent with the needs of longtime residents and maintained the industrial fabric of the neighborhood. In Curran and Hamilton (2012), they coin the term 'just green enough' to describe a process where redevelopment initiatives remediate and redevelop land without catalyzing gentrification processes or displacing residents. Their case study in Greenpoint provided an exciting solution to Wolch et al's (2014) green space paradox, and it suggests an approach for centering social justice and equity in greening processes.

Curran and Hamilton developed the concept of the 'just green enough' approach based on their case study in Greenpoint, Brooklyn, and it is worth asking to what extent or how it could be a viable solution in other locations. Arguably, a particular set of institutional structures helped waterfront redevelopment in Greenpoint become equitable and community-sensitive. Notably, in 2010, Newtown Creek was designated a Superfund site, one of the most contaminated sites in the USA, which provided funding and regulatory oversight, including mechanisms for community involvement, as part of the remediation process. Additionally, Greenpoint had a well-organized and committed group of organizers. Pearsall (2013) observed a similar outcome in the nearby Gowanus Canal in Brooklyn, where many residents advocated for a Superfund designation, willingly accepting the stigma of living near a Superfund site so that they could have more input in the redevelopment process. However, as Miller (2016) observed, private investment had occurred before the full remediation of the Gowanus Canal, complicating the goals of affordability and stability that many longtime residents wanted.

Institutional structures, specifically state or national legislation, have been used in other contexts to improve the social equity outcomes of environmental improvements. Addison et al. (2013) emphasized the importance of legislation to synchronize definitions and expectations of affordability in different cities, particularly given the challenges that smart growth proponents face in incorporating adequate affordable housing. In Malmö, Sweden, Sandberg (2014) discussed the successes of city ecologists in designating a former quarry, used previously as a scenic amenity for nearby condominium owners, as a nature preserve. This designation was enabled by environmental regulations and required the quarry to provide access to the public (rather than exclusively maintaining it as scenery for wealthy condominium owners). Of course, all environmental laws may not be so benevolent to vulnerable communities; Ghertner (2010) describes how environmental regulations were used to justify the removal of slums in Delhi in the 1990s.

Finally, additional research points to the importance of context and design for providing a space that is 'just green enough'. While the formalization of space into parks may catalyze gentrification, vacant land or other informal spaces, such as river banks, may provide a unique green space that is sheltered from gentrification (Rupprecht et al., 2015). Foster's (2014, p. 124) research on the 'Petite Ceinture', an abandoned railway in Paris, France, supported this idea, revealing that 'vacant' land provided an important space for ecological and socio-cultural interactions that 'disrupt the dominant logic of urban development'. On the other hand, Baviskar (2011) and Follmann (2015) show how informal waterfront spaces can become attractive to developers, as observed by developments on the Yamuna River in Delhi, resulting in the displacement of extensive slum settlements. From a design perspective, Ngom et al. (2016) noted that the configuration of greenspace can influence gentrification potential. In Quebec City, Canada, they found that linear parks designed for walking or cycling improve social equity outcomes, particularly when compared to parks in Montreal (Canada), which tend to be placed in the densest (and wealthiest) parts of the city. They emphasized the need for attention to accessibility and quality, as opposed to a narrow focus on increasing per capita greenspace.

20.6 CONCLUSION

While the growth of environmental gentrification research over the last decade has built a strong and interdisciplinary foundation for understanding the socio-spatial dimensions of urban sustainability planning and associated environmental improvements, there is much ground for future research to cover. To begin, environmental gentrification research would benefit from connecting theories and methods from currently disconnected literatures in urban geography (e.g. gentrification), human-environment geography (e.g. political ecology), and even ecology (for example Patrick, 2014) to more fully accommodate the human and ecological dimensions of environmental gentrification. Secondly, and related, 'environmental gentrification' research would benefit from moving beyond urban conceptualizations of gentrification to consider rural gentrification, which would also provide new theoretical and methodological insights (e.g. Phillips et al., 2008). Third, as mentioned previously, attention to flows of pollution or environmental burdens across spaces and places would improve the scalar lens of this work; little environmental gentrification research has investigated the consequences of displacing polluting facilities or the pollution itself to other neighborhoods or regions. Fourth, although there is some research from the 'Global East' and other cities around the world, the majority of research is based in North American and European cities. Further examining environmental gentrification in additional locations and in non-Western settings would improve our understanding of greening and gentrification processes and how they unfold in different social, economic, cultural, political, and environmental contexts. Finally, the majority of environmental gentrification resistance research draws on large-scale or major moments of resistance (e.g. protests, opposition to formal projects). Further, a more nuanced approach to understanding how everyday acts of resistance influence the processes and patterns of environmental gentrification in rapidly changing neighborhoods would provide an important perspective on the broader impacts of small-scale actions and how they contribute to the creation of just and equitable green cities.

REFERENCES

Abel, T. and White, J. (2011) 'Skewed riskscapes and gentrified inequities: environmental exposure disparities in Seattle, Washington', *American Journal of Public Health*, 101, S246-S254.

Addison, C., Zhang, S. and Coomes, B. (2013) 'Smart growth and housing affordability: a review of regulatory mechanisms and planning practices', *Journal of Planning Literature*, 28, 215–257.

Anguelovski, I. (2015) 'Alternative food provision conflicts in cities: contesting food privilege, injustice, and whiteness in Jamaica Plain, Boston', *Geoforum*, 58, 184–194.

Banzhaf, H. and McCormick, E. (2006) 'Moving beyond cleanup: identifying the crucibles of environmental gentrification', *Andrew Young School of Policy Studies Research Paper Series*.

Banzhaf, S. and Walsh, R. (2008) 'Do people vote with their feet? An empirical test of Tiebout's mechanism', *The American Economic Review*, 98, 843–863.

Battaglia, M., Buckley, G., Galvin, M. et al. (2014) 'It's not easy going green: obstacles to tree-planting programs in East Baltimore', *Cities and the Environment (CATE)*, 7, article 6.

Baviskar, A. (2003) 'Between violence and desire: space, power, and identity in the making of metropolitan Delhi', *International Social Science Journal*, 55, 89–98.

Baviskar, A. (2011) 'What the eye does not see: the Yamuna in the imagination of Delhi', *Economic and Political Weekly*, 46, 45–53.

Boeing, G., Church, D. and Hubbard, H. et al. (2014) 'LEED-ND and livability revisited', *Berkeley Planning Journal*, 27, 31–55.

Bryson, J. (2012) 'Brownfields gentrification: redevelopment planning and environmental justice in Spokane, Washington', *Environmental Justice*, 5, 26–31.

Bunce, S. (2009) 'Developing sustainability: sustainability policy and gentrification on Toronto's waterfront', *Local Environment*, 14, 651–667.

Campbell, S. (1996) 'Green cities, growing cities, just cities?: Urban planning and the contradictions of sustainable development', *Journal of the American Planning Association*, 62, 296–312.

Checker, M. (2011) 'Wiped out by the "greenwave": environmental gentrification and the paradoxical politics of urban sustainability', *City & Society*, 23, 210–229.

Checker, M. (2014) 'Green is the new brown: "old school toxics" and environmental gentrification on a New York City Waterfront', in Isenhour, C., McDonogh, G. and Checker, M. (eds) *Sustainabiltiy in the Global City: Myth and Practice*, New York: Cambridge University Press, pp. 157–179.

Chegut, A., Eichholtz, P. and Kok, N. (2013) 'Supply, demand and the value of green buildings', *Urban Studies*, 51, 22–43.

Clark, E. (2005) 'The order and simplicity of gentrification: a political challenge', in Atkinson, R. and Bridge, G. (eds) *Gentrification in a Global Context: The New Urban Colonialism*, London: Routledge, pp. 261–269.

Coelho, K. and Raman, N. (2010) 'Salvaging and scapegoating: slum evictions on Chennai's waterways', *Economic and Political Weekly*, 45, 19–23.

Curran, W. (2004) 'Gentrification and the nature of work: exploring the links in Williamsburg, Brooklyn', *Environment and Planning A*, 36, 1243–1258.

Curran, W. (2007) '"From the frying pan to the oven": Gentrification and the experience of industrial displacement in Williamsburg, Brooklyn', *Urban Studies*, 44, 1427–1440.

Curran, W. and Hamilton, T. (2012) 'Just green enough: contesting environmental gentrification in Greenpoint, Brooklyn', *Local Environment*, 17, 1027–1042.

Dale, A. and Newman, L. (2009) 'Sustainable development for some: green urban development and affordability', *Local Environment*, 14, 669–681.

Dale, L., Murdoch, J. and Thayer, M. et al. (1999) 'Do property values rebound from environmental stigmas? Evidence from Dallas', *Land Economics*, 75, 311–326.

De Sousa, C., Wu, C. and Westphal, L. (2009) 'Assessing the effect of publicly assisted brownfield redevelopment on surrounding property values', *Economic Development Quarterly*, 3, 95–110.

Desai, R. (2012) 'Governing the urban poor: riverfront development, slum resettlement and the politics of inclusion in Ahmedabad', *Economic and Political Weekly*, 47, 49–56.

Dooling, S. (2009) 'Ecological gentrification: a research agenda exploring justice in the city', *International Journal of Urban and Regional Research*, 33, 621–639.

Downs, A. (2005) 'Smart growth: why we discuss it more than we do it', *Journal of the American Planning Association*, 71, 367–378.

Eckerd, A. (2011) 'Cleaning up without clearing out? A spatial assessment of environmental gentrification', *Urban Affairs Review*, 47, 31–59.

Essoka, J. (2010) 'The gentrifying effects of brownfields redevelopment', *Western Journal of Black Studies*, 34, 299.

Follmann, A. (2015) 'Urban mega-projects for a "world-class" riverfront – the interplay of informality, flexibility and exceptionality along the Yamuna in Delhi, India', *Habitat International*, 45, 213–222.

Foster, J. (2014) 'Hiding in plain view: vacancy and prospect in Paris' Petite Ceinture', *Cities*, 40, 124–132.

Friends of the High Line (2016) *About the High Line*, available at: http://www.thehighline.org/about.

Gamper-Rabindran, S., Mastromonaco, R. and Timmins, C. (2011) 'Valuing the benefits of superfund site remediation: three approaches to measuring localized externalities', Working Paper No. 16655 ed. Cambridge, Massachusetts: National Bureau of Economic Research.

Gamper-Rabindran, S. and Timmins, C. (2011) 'Hazardous waste cleanup, neighborhood gentrification, and environmental justice: evidence from restricted access census block data', *The American Economic Review*, 101, 620–624.

Ghertner, D. (2010) 'The nuisance of slums: environmental law and the production of slum illegality in India', in Anjaria, J. and McFarlane, C. (eds) *Urban Navigations: Politics, Space and the City in South Asia*, Routledge India, 23–49.

Goodling, E., Green, J. and McClintock, N. (2015) 'Uneven development of the sustainable city: shifting capital in Portland, Oregon', *Urban Geography*, 36, 504–527.

Gould, K. and Lewis, T. (2012) 'The environmental injustice of green gentrification', in DeSena, J. and Shortell, T. (eds) *The World in Brooklyn: Gentrification, Immigration, and Ethnic Politics in a Global City*, Plymouth, Maryland: Lexington Books, pp. 113–146.

Hackworth, J. and Smith, N. (2001) 'The changing state of gentrification', *Tijdschrift voor economische en sociale geografie*, 92, 464–477.

Hamilton, T. and Curran, W. (2013) 'From "five angry women" to "kick-ass community": gentrification and environmental activism in Brooklyn and beyond', *Urban Studies*, 50, 1557–1574.

Hamnett, C. (1973) 'Improvement grants as an indicator of gentrification in inner London', *Area*, 5, 252–261.

Hamnett, C. (1991) 'The blind men and the elephant: the explanation of gentrification', *Transactions of the Institute of British Geographers*, 16, 173–189.

Hoffman, M. (2016) *Bike Lanes are White Lanes: Bicycle Advocacy and Urban Planning*, Lincoln: University of Nebraska Press.

Hurd, B. (2002) 'Valuing superfund site cleanup: evidence of recovering stigmatized property values', *Appraisal Journal*, 70, 426–437.

Keil, R. and Boudreau, J-A. (2006) 'Metropolitics and metabolics: rolling out environmentalism in Toronto', in Heynen, N. and Kaika, M. (eds) *In the Nature of Cities: Urban Political Ecology and the Politics of Urban Metabolism*, New York: Routledge, pp. 40–61.

Kern, L. (2015) 'From toxic wreck to crunchy chic: environmental gentrification through the body', *Environment and Planning D: Society and Space*, 33, 67–83.

Kohlhase, J. (1991) 'The impact of toxic waste sites on housing values', *Journal of Urban Economics*, 30, 1–26.

Lees, L., Shin, H. and López-Morales, E. (2016) *Planetary Gentrification*, Polity Press: Cambridge.

Lees, L., Slater, T. and Wyly, E. (2008) *Gentrification*, New York: Routledge.

Ley, D. (1994) 'Gentrification and the politics of the new middle class', *Environment and Planning D: Society and Space*, 12, 53–74.

Lim, H., Kim, J. and Potter, C. et al. (2013) 'Urban regeneration and gentrification: land use impacts of the Cheonggye Stream Restoration Project on the Seoul's central business district', *Habitat International*, 39, 192–200.

Littke, H., Locke, R. and Haas, T. (2015) 'Taking the high line: elevated parks, transforming neighbourhoods, and the ever-changing relationship between the urban and nature', *Journal of Urbanism: International Research on Placemaking and Urban Sustainability*, 9, 1–19.

Long, J. (2016) 'Constructing the narrative of the sustainability fix: sustainability, social justice and representation in Austin, TX', *Urban Studies*, 53, 149–172.

Lubitow, A., Zinschlag, B. and Rochester, N. (2015) 'Plans for pavement or for people? The politics of bike lanes on the "Paseo Boricua" in Chicago, Illinois', *Urban Studies*, 53, 2637–2653.

Lugo, A. (2015) 'Can human infrastructure combat green gentrification? Ethnographic research on bicycling in Los Angeles and Seattle', in Senhour, C., McDonogh, G. and Checker, M. (eds) *Sustainability in the Global City*, New York: Cambridge University Press, pp. 306–328.

McKendry, C. and Janos, N. (2015) 'Greening the industrial city: equity, environment, and economic growth in Seattle and Chicago', *International Environmental Agreements: Politics, Law and Economics*, 15, 45–60.

Mehdizadeh, R. and Fischer, M. (2013) 'The unintended consequences of greening America: an examination of how implementing green building policy may impact the dynamic between local, state, and federal regulatory systems and the possible exacerbation of class segregation', *Energy, Sustainability and Society*, 3, 1.

Miller, J. (2016) 'Is urban greening for everyone? Social inclusion and exclusion along the Gowanus Canal', *Urban Forestry & Urban Greening*, 19, 285–294.

Millington, N. (2015) 'From urban scar to "park in the sky": terrain vague, urban design, and the remaking of New York City's High Line Park', *Environment and Planning A*, 47, 2324–2338.

Mir, D. and Sanchez, A. (2009) 'Impact of gentrification on environmental pressure in service micro-enterprises', *Business Strategy and the Environment*, 18, 417–431.

NEJAC (2006) 'Unintended Impacts of Redevelopment and Revitalization Efforts in Five Environmental Justice Communities', Washington D.C.: US Environmental Protection Agency.

Ngom, R., Gosselin, P. and Blais, C. (2016) 'Reduction of disparities in access to green spaces: their geographic insertion and recreational functions matter', *Applied Geography*, 66, 35–51.

O'Loughlin, J. and Munski, D. (1979) 'Housing rehabilitation in the inner city: a comparison of two neighborhoods in New Orleans', *Economic Geography*, 55, 52–70.

Patrick, D. (2014) 'The matter of displacement: a queer urban ecology of New York City's High Line', *Social & Cultural Geography*, 15, 920–941.

Pearsall, H. (2010) 'From brown to green? Assessing social vulnerability to environmental gentrification in New York City', *Environment and Planning. C, Government & Policy*, 28, 872–886.

Pearsall, H. (2012) 'Moving out or moving in? Resilience to environmental gentrification in New York City', *Local Environment*, 17, 1013–1026.

Pearsall, H. (2013) 'Superfund me: a study of resistance to gentrification in New York City', *Urban Studies*, 50, 2293–2310.

Pearsall, H. and Anguelovski, I. (2016) 'Contesting and resisting environmental gentrification: responses to new paradoxes and challenges for urban environmental justice', *Sociological Research Online*, 21.

Pearsall, H. and Pierce, J. (2010) 'Urban sustainability and environmental justice: evaluating the linkages in public planning/policy discourse', *Local Environment*, 15, 569–580.

Pearsall, H., Pierce, J. and Krueger, R. (2012) 'Whither Rio+ 20?: Demanding a politics and practice of socially just sustainability', *Local Environment*, 17, 935–941.

Phillips, M., Page, S. and Saratsi, E. et al. (2008) 'Diversity, scale and green landscapes in the gentrification process: traversing ecological and social science perspectives', *Applied Geography*, 28, 54–76.

Quastel, N. (2009) 'Political ecologies of gentrification', *Urban Geography*, 30, 694–725.

Quastel, N., Moos, M. and Lynch, N. (2012) 'Sustainability-as-density and the return of the social: the case of Vancouver, British Columbia', *Urban Geography*, 33, 1055–1084.

Rérat, P. and Lees, L. (2011) 'Spatial capital, gentrification and mobility: evidence from Swiss core cities', *Transactions of the Institute of British Geographers*, 36, 126–142.

Reynolds, K. (2015) 'Disparity despite diversity: social injustice in New York City's urban agriculture system', *Antipode*, 47, 240–259.

Roddewig, R. (1996) 'Stigma, environmental risk and property value: 10 critical inquiries', *The Appraisal Journal*, October, 205–218.

Rosol, M. (2013) 'Vancouver's "EcoDensity" planning initiative: A struggle over hegemony?', *Urban Studies*, 50, 2238–2255.

Rupprecht, C., Byrne, J., Ueda, H. et al. (2015) '"It's real, not fake like a park": Residents' perception and use of informal urban green-space in Brisbane, Australia and Sapporo, Japan', *Landscape and Urban Planning*, 143, 205–218.

Sandberg, L. (2014) 'Environmental gentrification in a post-industrial landscape: the case of the Limhamn quarry, Malmö, Sweden', *Local Environment*, 19, 1068–1085.

Schmelzkopf, K. (2002) 'Incommensurability, land use, and the right to space: community gardens in New York City', *Urban Geography*, 23, 323–343.

Schuetze, T. and Chelleri, L. (2015) 'Urban sustainability versus green-washing – fallacy and reality of urban regeneration in downtown Seoul', *Sustainability*, 8, article 33.

Sharan, A. (2015) 'A river and the riverfront: Delhi's Yamuna as an in-between space', *City, Culture and Society*, 7, 267–273.

Sieg, H., Smith, V., Banzhaf, H. et al. (2004) 'Estimating the general equilibrium benefits of large changes in spatially delineated public goods', *International Economic Review*, 45, 1047–1077.

Smith, N. (1979a) 'Gentrification and capital: practice and ideology in Society Hill', *Antipode*, 11, 24–35.

Smith, N. (1979b) 'Toward a theory of gentrification a back to the city movement by capital, not people', *Journal of the American Planning Association*, 45, 538–548.

Smith, N. (1996) *The New Urban Frontier: Gentrification and the Revanchist City*, London: Routledge.

Thompson, M. (2015) 'Between boundaries: from commoning and guerrilla gardening to community land trust development in Liverpool', *Antipode*, 47, 1021–1042.

Tretter, E. (2013a) 'Sustainability and neoliberal urban development: the environment, crime and the remaking of Austin's downtown', *Urban Studies*, 50, 2222–2237.

Tretter, E. (2013b) 'Contesting sustainability: "SMART growth" and the redevelopment of Austin's Eastside', *International Journal of Urban and Regional Research*, 37, 297–310.

While, A., Jonas, A. and Gibbs, D. (2004) 'The environment and the entrepreneurial city: searching for the urban "sustainability fix" in Manchester and Leeds', *International Journal of Urban and Regional Research*, 28, 549–569.

Wolch, J., Byrne, J. and Newell, J. (2014) 'Urban green space, public health, and environmental justice: the challenge of making cities "just green enough"', *Landscape and Urban Planning*, 125, 234–244.

Wyly, E. and Hammel, D. (1999) 'Islands of decay in seas of renewal: housing policy and the resurgence of gentrification', *Housing Policy Debate*, 10, 711–771.

21. Gentrification, artists and the cultural economy
Andy Pratt

21.1 INTRODUCTION

This chapter examines the changing nature of the relationship between gentrification and the cultural economy in theory and practice; it also highlights a gap in debates about gentrification. Whilst the role of culture in the gentrification process has received much attention, the cultural economy has not. The gap stems from tendencies to instrumentalise culture, to reduce it to consumption, and to ignore its value(s) and the means of its production. This chapter focuses on a complex and sometimes misunderstood field, that of cultural production. The paradox that we encounter is that cultural workers and artists are often portrayed as both the causes and the victims of gentrification. An important step in my argument is to broaden and contextualise debates about gentrification to make sense of this paradox. I will argue that gentrification – if we take Ruth Glass's (1964) classical definition of the process as displacement of former residential tenants – should also be further explored in relation to movements and displacements between manufacturing, office, retail and cultural sites. Such changes, outside of residential-residential moves, have not been subject to nuanced analyses of social and political agency in respect to cultural workers and artists. On one hand, artists have been portrayed as dupes and uni-dimensional; on the other hand, the economic contribution of cultural (production) activities has been under-valued (see Park 2016; d'Ovidio and Rodríguez Morató 2017).

Formerly industrialised inner cities of North America and Europe have been through a particularly intense pattern of social and economic change over the last 50 years. This process has involved rebuilding and transforming spaces, often into quite different uses. This transformation primarily has not involved residential property (although there have been transformations of residential spaces in tandem: it is the latter that has been the focus of much of the gentrification literature). The picture has been of old manufacturing infrastructure (factories and warehouses, storage and related transport, especially port-related activities) either being razed to the ground and replaced by new buildings, or refurbished; in both cases the site is converted into other uses: sometimes offices, other times residential, and exceptionally cultural.

The causes of this transformation lie in the process of de-industrialisation (of mainly North American and Western European cities), and the concomitant industrialisation of East Asia. The outcomes in each city are different as local responses have been mobilised; however, they are commonly bundled under the label of the emergence of the 'post-industrial' city. Gentrifying cities in North America and Western Europe experienced, first depopulation and then re-population of the inner city; in many cases, at the same time, the balance of employment shifted to the service sector, in notable cases financial services. It is important to underline that this involved a double movement in labour markets: of former industrial workers out, and new service workers in: very few workers made the transition in person. This had important implications for housing stock, and housing demand (see Lees, Slater and Wyly, 2008).

A less-reported trend is that concerning the cultural economy; as a productive sector in cities it has also grown in relative and absolute importance. Indeed, many would argue that the growth of creative employment, and the demand for creative employees, is a characteristic of the post-industrial, or knowledge, economy (Pratt 2007; Hutton 2015). In addition, there have been substantial shifts in the governance regimes of North American and West European cities and nation states which in general terms have been characterised by a shrinking of the state (that is, reducing the responsibilities of the state for collective guidance and provision of goods and services), and a focus on importing economic growth activities through competition. This latter competitive practice ranges from the attraction of companies and sectors of the economy that are perceived to be growing, to the attraction of tourist and visitor spending. To attract investment and to compete with other cities, urban governments have developed many tools starting with subsidies, and extending to lifestyle and branding. Culture has become an important instrument in the city booster toolkit (Palmer-Rae Associates 2004; Florida 2008; Anholt 2010; Kong 2012).

The processes outlined above are complex and manifold, and it is not the intention to explore them in detail here. My point is to underline the fact that the Euro-American inner city has become a major opportunity for developers to exploit the 'rent gap' opened up in the redevelopment process. Arguably, economic restructuring, especially globalisation, provides the most fertile ground for gambling on revaluation of land uses and property: a foundation of the gentrification process. Following from this my concerns in this chapter are first, to widen the focus from housing to the economy more generally; and secondly, to argue that culture (as heritage, or experience; or, as practice) is a common theme which is generally in the background. The aim here is to foreground the ways in which culture plays a part in urban transformations. Finally, to highlight the neglect, or/and the instrumentalisation of culture in the global cities paradigm (Pratt 2011a), and analyses framed by the concept of the 'creative class' (Pratt 2011b); and instead to encourage more attention to situated analyses in the spirit of comparative, or planetary, urbanism.

The gentrification literature has already begun substantive debate over the relationship between gentrification and globalisation (Lees 2003; Atkinson and Bridge 2005; Butler and Lees 2006; Lees, Shin and López-Morales 2016); in addition, there has also been a long-running debate about the relationship between culture and gentrification. To embrace the transformations wrought by the emergent cultural economy I want to argue that these debates need to be extended further. I will re-inforce a relatively neglected aspect of this new trend to include not just residential to residential 'upgrading' (classic gentrification), but also including transitions such as manufacturing to residential, manufacturing work to cultural work, and cultural work to residential uses (see Zukin, Trujillo et al. 2009; Curran 2010; Yoon and Currid-Halkett 2014; Hubbard 2016; Kim 2016). Displacement of less powerful actors by more powerful actors characterises these transitions, moreover it presages a cultural change, not simply one of consumption and identity (as already discussed in the gentrification literature), but also one of cultural production and cultural value(s) (Jung, Lee et al. 2015; Grodach, Foster et al. 2016).

I want to make the case that the displacement of artistic and cultural workers is not the 'victimless crime' that it appears to be as presented in much urban regeneration literature;

it has significant negative impacts on the livelihoods and economic output of one of the few growing sectors of contemporary economies. Moreover, this continual displacement of artists and cultural workers undermines the delicate cultural ecosystems that sustain such economic and cultural output in our cities.

The chapter is divided into three parts. Part I, opens up the debate about the artist and the city. The second part reviews the urban regeneration regimes that have implicated culture and produced distinct cultural gentrification effects. The third part, pulls the focus away from cultural consumption and instrumentalism and explores how a concern for cultural production re-configures the fate of the cultural worker in the city.

21.2   PART I: ARTISTS AND THE CITY

In this part I want to introduce the subject 'caught in the middle': the cultural worker. I will show that we need to understand the related, but often dislocated, flows of production and consumption in the city. I will represent these through the contrast of the figures of the artist and the hipster. Second, I revisit a classic of gentrification, Zukin's (1982) work on 'loft living' in New York City, and suggest that some further contemporary lessons can be learned.

21.2.1   Artists and Hipsters

It is difficult to avoid debates about gentrification today, but they have a different character to those of former years. In addition to the working-class family being forced out of their property and replaced by a middle-class family, other common characters include the cultural worker (artist) and cultural consumer (Hipster). An emblematic case is that of the 'Cereal Killer' shop in Brick Lane, London (Khomami and Halliday 2015; see Figure 21.1). This is a store selling boutique breakfast cereal at vastly inflated prices, which has clearly attracted a market who are willing to pay. However, Brick Lane is on the 'fault line' between the City of London and Tower Hamlets, a predominantly poor and ethnically diverse community dominated by social housing; it is one of the poorest boroughs in the United Kingdom. The 'hipster' shop, of which Cereal Killer is emblematic, and the lifestyle and cultural milieu that surrounds it, has become a notable feature of many North American and European cities in recent years (see http://www.cbc.ca/news/thenational/hipster-haters-crash-cereal-cafe-1.3255706).

A common trope of inner urban cultural redevelopment these days is the Hipster. It is a term widely and loosely used, but refers to a style and affectation of an artistic producer; in its current stylistic manifestation with a throwback to a Victorian fashion sensibility; it is a subculture that has powerful consumption effects. The Hipster is a dedicated cultural consumer who puts 'taste' at the top of the agenda. Associated with this trend is the extreme consumption choices offered for products such as coffee or beer: the craft beer scene being one example. It is clearly a complicated phenomenon, but what unites it is that it requires considerable disposable income to maintain the lifestyle which is, like most sub-cultures, manifest by conspicuous consumption. Despite its affectation of 'craft' and 'making' it is a form and practice of consumption. As will be noted later, what Richard Florida (2002) refers to as the Creative Class, or David Brooks (2000) refers to

Figure 21.1   Cereal Killer Café, Brick Lane, London, target of anti-gentrification activists

as Bourgeois Bohemians, overlaps with the Hipster; the common feature being a focus on (a variety) of cultural consumptions, and the purchasing power to attract suppliers.

It is not surprising that 'Cereal Killer' became a flash-point in demonstrations about rising property prices (not just residential prices), and the displacement of people and activities from traditional neighbourhoods. A similar manifestation of 'hipster' consumer outlets can be found in many property 'hot spots' in London, and across the world. Indeed, they are perceived by property professionals, or even praised, as an index of an area 'coming up' (being gentrified). The transformation offered by developers is derelict industrial sites made over into luxury condominiums. The shock is not simply of cultural and economic transformation, but also the physical scale. As an example, the development of Bishopsgate Goods Yard, which is part of the back story of the 'Cereal Killer' demonstrations, is planned to be one of the tallest in London. So, the point is that residential and commercial property transformation is closely linked with cultural consumption (see the recent work on touristification discussed in Lees, Shin and López-Morales 2016; and retail gentrification and hipsters in Zukin, Trujillo et al. 2009, and Hubbard 2016).

But, there is another side to the story. Brick Lane has been an emblematic epicentre of the growth of cultural and artistic workers in East London; it is not a consumption sub-culture but a 'scene' (Straw 2001), a community of artistic practice (Mar and Anderson 2010). For 25 years, artists have moved to the cheaper property of the East End (deserting West and Central London) (Green 1999). Initially they used short let housing as live-work spaces, these have been supplemented by 'art factories', larger industrial spaces converted into artist studios. The Truman Brewery Site, on Brick Lane, is an exemplar (Oakley and Pratt 2010). As the name suggests this was a redundant brewery that was converted into cultural studio spaces. Other models of space provision are also found, from the not-for-profit, artist-owned, studio providers such as (in London) Acme and Space, to the short-life housing owned by local authorities. What unites these property forms is that they are vehicles to insulate tenants (artists) from property price inflation, a form of social rent control. More successful artists – those with a global audience – also have studios near Brick Lane, but they have been able to own them in their own right (for example Tracey Emin, and Gilbert and George). What has been referred to as the greatest concentration of artists in Europe, has been facilitated by forms of studio provision that have been devised in opposition to upgrading/gentrification. However, it is not a form that is secure, nor guaranteed. We will revisit this in Part III.

The phenomenon is not confined to London, a notable example is the article that David Byrne (2013) (curator and formerly in the band Talking Heads) wrote about New York City, bemoaning the fact that artists could no longer afford to have studio space, let alone live, in the inner city. This is especially poignant as New York, especially the area around SoHo, was in effect given a new life when artists moved in in the 1970s. The very notion of the 'loft' as an artistic space was coined here.

We can add yet another layer of significance here, that cities such as London and New York now promote themselves as desirable locations for tourism and living, as well as for work, on the basis of the presence of this cultural buzz (Mayor of London 2012). For the most part artists are instrumentalised as creators of a playground for Hipsters, BoBo's and the Creative Class: what city mayors now consider as a necessary bauble to attract the latest hi-tech producer to the city. At the same time, this creates the conditions to precisely undermine the possibility of creative producers remaining in the city. This has been an ongoing, and naturalised, aspect of urban regeneration. The economic (as opposed to the cultural and social) dimensions of the cultural and creative industries have become more important in cities in the last decade. For example, by 2010 in London, they counted as the fourth largest employment sector (Freeman 2010).

Thus, it is very clear that the artist and cultural worker is being displaced from the inner city. The dominant policy and political discourse is that artists can simply move on and regenerate another neighbourhood; in fact, it is often presented as 'wonderful and necessary' that they should (see Park 2016). This process can be characterised as a vicious cycle of artistic gentrification. One would expect that artists would be cherished given their seemingly 'Midas touch' to property markets; but far from it, they would perhaps be better characterised as 'cannon fodder'. The economic role of the cultural and creative industries has until recently been overlooked at both national and urban scales (Buitrago Restrepo and Duque Márquez 2013; NESTA 2013). The well-known artist Grayson Perry (2014) has a 4-part cartoon illustrating this process in his book *Playing to the Gallery: Helping Contemporary Art in its Struggle to Be Understood*. Image 1 shows a decaying factory building, possibly squatted by artists; image 2 has the building now renamed 'old industry studios', it is clearly managed studio space; in image 3 the building has another makeover, this time it is labelled a 'creativity hub' fronted by a trendy café, and is obviously a fancy co-working space for new media workers. The coup de grâce is image 4, the building has been torn down and rebuilt in a modern style and is called 'Bohemia apartments'. This process, and its ever-decreasing time-scale, presents major challenges for the creative, and urban, economy.

Before beginning to reconnect the opposing aspects of production and consumption, culture and economy, we need to understand how we have framed the debate thus, this requires us to revisit debates about the global city and culture. In the following part of the chapter, I will review the policy and practices that flow from normative misconceptions. In Part III they are reconnected.

21.2.2   The Global City

Debates rooted in the Global City paradigm as exemplified by Sassen (2001) characterise a massive transformation of world urbanism and the emergence of a 'super-league' of 'command and control centres' of the global economy – the Global City – rooted in the power of the financial services. Sassen and Castells (1989) have pointed to the emergence of the dual, or polarised, city as a result: between rich and poor, between those linked to a local economic system, or a global one.

In a series of papers, Loretta Lees (Lees 2003; Butler and Lees 2006) and colleagues have developed an argument for the emergence of super-gentrification in some cities associated with the huge sums paid to workers in the financial services sector. This is an argument that has a correspondence with the social polarisation thesis of those writing about the Global City. The elite gentrification of older and established housing stock is beyond the reach of even the locally 'very well off'; other manifestations of this emergence of a super elite have been plotted across many global cities, especially associated with either elite gated communities and buildings, or the construction of massive basements to existing large properties. Some displacement is going on here, but between the rich and the super-rich.

A key weakness of the Global Cities paradigm literature has been its understanding of culture. King (1995) has stressed the importance of colonialism, and cultural diasporas; but this has tended to be swept up as a part of a debate about labour markets and migration. A similar economic reductivism applies to the cultural economy which is generally characterised as a dependent 'service' of the core economy, having little if any autonomous significance, and none in respect to the economic realm (Pratt 2011b). In part this deficit is a function of history, the cultural economy was not significant in cities 25 years ago, although it is now. Today, rightly, we can question just how 'dependent' the cultural economy is, and if it is emerging as a driver in its own right. I will argue that the gentrification literature suffers from a similar problem.

I want to direct us back to an earlier manifestation of what might be called gentrification in an earlier period. I want to highlight the lens through which it was viewed. Sharon Zukin's (1982) seminal work on 'loft living' has always had an uneasy relationship both with the global cities paradigm and the gentrification literature. The properties that she examined were previously industrial spaces. Zukin's work offered a particular insight into what would later be called, after Bourdieu (1979), 'habitus'. Zukin was writing before the translation of Bourdieu, and working more closely to a tradition of structural Marxism. Zukin's work on Loft Living was notable for many reasons; here, I want to point to the methodological import of recovering culture from the economic, an insight which can help with contemporary debates about gentrification and culture. Her focus on 'gentrification' concerned the cultural mores and aspirations as expressed through proximity and decoration of the converted lofts she found in Lower Manhattan. Of course, a parallel concern was a focus which has been codified as a second iteration of the gentrification literature, the embrace of culture (Lees, Slater and Wyly 2008); Zukin did this avant la lettre but in a way that was different from how culture was subsequently framed in the gentrification literature (see Lees 1994, on Zukin in the economic versus culture debate).

The standard reading of Zukin's work stresses cultural differentiation, and glosses over the fact that this was a form of economic revaluing (a rent gap existed for sure), and that the displacement was of manufacturing and warehousing activity; an activity that had already left: the buildings were empty. Readings of Zukin's work are often shorn of a sense of place and time, and context. We noted above in David Byrne's cri de coeur that the artists were being moved out of their lofts; by just the people that Zukin was writing about, and those that followed. The pioneers of the 'downtown scene' in what became SoHo (before it became a by-word for high-end consumption) were a group of artists that valued the cheap rents that allowed expansive studio space for 'space hungry' art forms: abstract art, dance, music and everything in between. Perhaps the best known, Andy Warhol, had his studio space, which he called 'The Factory' (Pratt 2012), creating a resonance through every such conversion to today. From artists such as Pollock to Anderson, to Maattu-Clark, Tharpp and Glass, and eventually to Byrne, the studio space was a breeding ground for new art forms (Yi 2011; Miller 2016).

The use of the term 'loft' was/is not original to these factory buildings; but is a nod to the original mid-19th-century Parisian Latin Quarter, popularised by Puccini in La Boheme; the loft or garret room was the cheap space at the top of a multi-dwelling house occupied by artists. Of course, this was the early usage of the term 'Bohemian' (to designate a style of living, and consumption) as well (Lloyd 2006). The gallery scene of SoHo in the 1970s, and its demi-secret, was part and parcel of the attraction for Zukin's loft dwellers. The irony is that the loft dwellers in New York City that Zukin wrote about were doing it on the cheap (they were not super-gentrifiers), indeed New York City was bankrupt, and property was cheap.

It is important to note that Neil Smith (Smith 1987, 1996) was writing about gentrification, from a Marxist point of view, at the same time, in the same city, narrating events a few blocks east. Smith's story was of the classic economic cycle of decline, refurbishment and revaluing in the residential area of Alphabet City. The point to be made is the development of particular analytical lenses. Whilst acknowledging the role of the state, Smith's interpretation put economics first, and characterised culture as dependent. Later interpretations sought to re-balance this. What got lost in the narrative were the artists, the very embodiment of the delicate relationship between the economic and the cultural. It became a neat fit to view artists as another class of the displaced.

Whilst the loft dwellers moved uptown, or to Brooklyn, the artists moved on too, as a later paper of Zukin's (Zukin and Braslow 2011) elaborates. However, it is important to note a further step many of these converted warehouse spaces progressed through: many (in San Francisco and London, as well as New York) became the site of new media companies (Pratt 2000; Jarvis and Pratt 2006; Pratt 2009), only later to become residential conversions. This serial displacement has significant impacts for the changing mix of creative industries, as well as their eventual eviction altogether. The history of Hoxton Square (half a mile north of Brick Lane) provides a neat empirical chronology – as we saw illustrated by Perry previously – of residential decline and vacancy, to artist studios, to new media offices, to nightclubs and restaurants, and finally to high-end residential. In the London case the life cycle shortened from that of New York's 25 years, to less than 15 years.

These cases illustrate the importance of examining the serial and progressive displacement of different users (within a legally restricted 'use class'); in this case, the change of economic character in the locale. This process challenges both the employment and the economic basis of the city. As noted above, the economic contribution of the new cultural economy to cities has changed in recent years. It is this new tension, and its economic implications – the over emphasis on the 'cultural' and the relative neglect of displacement of economic uses by high-end residential developments, that needs more attention (for indicative studies see Curran 2004, 2010; Hutton, Catungal et al. 2009; Yoon and Currid-Halkett 2014).

The normative view is to naturalise this process as one of growth and succession, and the attitudes that have been prevalent support this, namely that artists are expendable, or that new media workers, or artists, will move on and find another cheap space. A Marxian interpretation might simply be that the artists were used and exploited in the process of revaluing. However, there is nothing natural or inevitable about it. On the one hand, as we know from 'rent gap' theory there is the economic opportunity created by property speculation. On the other hand, there are individuals looking for environments in which to experiment and innovate. It seems remarkable in moral terms, but also economic terms, that the latter be quashed by the former. Would we apply such a logic to the financial services industries? Quite the opposite, in the case of financial services, cities fall over themselves to provide subsidised office buildings and residential accommodation, and even to the extent of creating new transport infrastructure. It is the argument of this chapter that this point of view needs revisiting. However, before doing that I want to plot out the fate of culture and the cultural economy in the post-industrial city.

21.3 PART II: CULTURE AND THE POST-INDUSTRIAL CITY

Global city formation has clearly intensified and projected gentrification studies into a new space; but as we have seen it also marks the re-entry of debates about artists and cultural workers. Despite the shifting theoretical focus from the systematic and universal global city paradigm to a more contextual approach (variously described as comparative, or planetary) a continuing question concerns the relationship of the cultural and the economic. Despite Zukin's (1982) inclusion of culture in a Marxist framework and Lees (1994) and Clark's (1994) wish to broach the economic-culture divide in gentrification studies, debates are still, more often than not, presented as separate issues, or focused on the role of cultural makers in gentrification. In this section, I interpret a shift in the linkage of culture and the city, one that has some (mostly unacknowledged) impacts on cultural workers; the impacts are manifest as displacement. I present three variants of linking culture and the city under conditions of post-industrial redevelopment: design-led development, cultural branding, and instrumental remediation. They are all characterised by state-led initiatives, and the subordinate position of culture in relation to large-scale infrastructure projects; showing how culture is viewed as instrumental in 're-valuing' land, and in generating consumption.

A perspective that I want to explore next concerns what is – for the most part – a state-led response to de-industrialisation: urban regeneration. The ravages of de-industrialisation and the decaying hearts of Euro-American cities were clearly a barrier to new development. If cities were to attract new people (to pay taxes and finance the city), new homes and jobs would have to be found; and moreover, appropriate buildings constructed to accommodate different economic activities. The old infrastructure was decayed and in disrepair, but it was also not suitable for modern uses. For the most part the city was given a boost by regeneration through state-led investment in mega-projects; but culture played and plays a subservient role in these plans.

21.3.1   Design-led Development

A notable feature of this redevelopment is the large-scale challenge of creative public space and public uses as well. The challenge was clear to all; this was not simple 'in-fill' development but whole-scale rebuilding. A theme that emerged was for cities to redevelop extensive land-uses such as port areas. A cultural shift was required that sought to celebrate 'waterfront development', for housing and retail, and sometimes offices. Due to the history of most rivers and ports in cities, development had literally 'turned its back' on the waterways (Brownill 2013). Any number of schemes sought to regenerate port facilities this way; and to develop riverside activities in the urban centre (Jones 1998).

The model of the entertainment or cultural anchor tenant for urban redevelopment has been a common one explored in the US to repopulate the inner city, a strategy referred to as the 'urban entertainment machine' (Lloyd and Clark 2001). This governance concept references the notion of the (mainly retail and hotel) 'growth machines' of many US cities whereby retail and entertainment capital dominate urban regeneration programmes (Molotch 1976). In many cases this economic control was supported by social control where police adopted aggressive positions with respect to behaviour that disrupted the 'clean' city image (Parenti 2000). Most clearly, action targeted the homeless, but it also impacted on other non-normative street practices.

The irony is that 'cleaning the streets' created a bland and 'culture-less' space. This was experienced most notably in massive urban regeneration projects such as that of London's Docklands. The short-term benefits to developers were seldom moderated by long-term responsibility for city building; simply, as in cases such as London, developers were given a free hand to develop buildings, but without the social responsibility for community, housing or public space. It took nearly 20 years for Canary Wharf to develop the aspects of urban conviviality that one might expect of a city. The grandiose nature of these developments and the master-planning style adopted neglected the social and the cultural; a point latterly acknowledged in a significant UK report (Rogers 1999) that highlighted the importance of mixed uses, and of a social agora, for good city planning and design (Imrie and Raco 2003). Not surprisingly, many precarious tenants of abandoned port facilities were artists, clinging onto gaps in the real estate market; they had to move on. It is notable that the 'needs' of artists and cultural workers were simply not part of the agenda in this phase of urban regeneration.

21.3.2 Cultural Branding

Culture, but not artists, did become a focus of regeneration in a different style of redevelopment. This was driven by an instrumentalism of competition between cities, whereby high-profile public buildings, usually contemporary art galleries, are used to 'pimp' a city's image. The classic example is the Guggenheim in Bilbao; striking architecture is used to create global visibility and to act as an anchor tenant for a redevelopment project. Moreover, contemporary art has a symbolic power projecting an old deindustrialised city to appear forward and culturally engaged. The strategy is based on place-branding, underpinned by the notion that in an increasingly homogenous global landscape differentiation can be achieved by culture (Evans 2003). Contemporary art is a particularly useful platform as it is new, and still being made, in contrast with classical art (and the galleries, and cities, which these new cities seek to compete with).

There has been much debate about the success and failures of hard branding, and the Guggenheim model (Plaza 2000); however, the position of local artists and creative workers is not part of this debate. On the one hand, there are many examples of artist communities and studios that were destroyed as part of such gallery redevelopment; on the other hand, the high-end apartments that accompany projects such as the Tate Modern exacerbate an already starkly polarised housing market (Dean et al. 2010). Either way, there is no space for artists. Along the lines of the 'urban entertainment machine', the designated audience are tourists and consumers, the city benefits from the number of bed-nights, and other generated income from visitors.

The singular project, usually a contemporary art gallery, is one variant of city branding; another is a more extensive approach pioneered by cities such as Glasgow. The European Capital of Culture was a project devised to circulate Europe to celebrate the cultural diversity, and history of the continent. Glasgow's contribution was to mobilise the designation to an extensive set of projects based on a re-branding of Glasgow, and an association of Glasgow with culture. Due to the perceived success of the Glasgow event, similar objectives have underpinned other candidate city strategies since (Palmer-Rae Associates 2004; Garcia, Melville et al. 2010; Lähdesmäki 2012). However, despite the more strategic perspective, and the more variegated art forms, as well as a stronger focus on participation, the more integrative Glasgow model still viewed culture as consumption, and not production (Garcia 2005).

21.3.3 Instrumental Remediation

A third variant of culture-city relationships in post-industrial regeneration concerns what are best referred to as mega-projects. Of course, the European Capital of Culture is a contender here; I want to differentiate the Glasgow case from some of the examples that followed based on a critical factor: land remediation. So far, the examples that have been discussed have predominantly concerned conversions, and rebuilding, and new developments on existing sites. For urban redevelopment, these are the 'low hanging fruit', the real problem concerns redeveloping sites on polluted land. The key point here is that the land value is in effect negative (due to the upfront investment in 'cleaning' the site before any development can take place) (Syms 1994). Culture has been part of an instrumental package to 'unlock' this land (often located close to the city centre).

A classic example was that of the Millennium Dome in London. The initial plan was that public remediation would be paid for by the 'celebratory' experience of the Dome (which was to be temporary), which would act as a marketing tent (literally, as it was a tent) for the site, the same model can be seen to underpin the Liverpool Garden Festival (Pratt 2010). Despite substantial criticisms of the perceived value for money (to the public purse) of such developments the model was used to create the London Olympic Park, the site of the 2012 Olympics. A temporary cultural event is a staging post for polluted land to be remediated, and then sold on to the market. The place for culture and the event is temporary, based solely on short-term consumption.

As will now be a familiar story, the London Olympic site development created significant displacement of a community of cultural producers (a few of whom are still hanging on in the Hackney Wick cultural quarter). Whilst Hackney Wick is now seen as London's next cultural growth zone, it was not part of the original plan. That original plan did have a cultural economy focus; the Olympic media complex was to be redeveloped as London's new media quarter (Foord 2013). However, the idea to relocate what is known as 'Silicon Roundabout', the new media community that had grown up around Hoxton and Old Street, proved to be a non-starter (Nathan, Vandore et al. 2012).

So, to add further irony the London Olympic site plan did include a focus on the creative economy; however, in making the plan, cultural workers were displaced and destabilised, and a temporary cultural project was mounted. The new development was proposed based on relocating creatives from one part of London to another. These projects are misguided due to a 'blindness' to the operation of the creative economy. Developers and planners do not see already existing cultural activity (or they do not value it). Moreover, there is a lack of appreciation of the extent to which cultural activities are embedded in a social, economic and cultural ecosystem that forms a co-dependent environment (Martins 2015). Constant relocation imperils such communities of practice; as well as ignoring the cultural embedding of creative activities in the city itself. It is to these issues that we turn in Part III of the chapter. Before that we explore the high-point of the culture-city (consumption) relationship: the creative class and the city.

This section has dwelt on UK examples for a reason; they have commonly been taken as 'best practice' for policy makers worldwide. Clearly, on one hand this is part and parcel of neo-liberal evangelism exemplified by 'fast policy' (Peck and Theodore 2015); on the other hand, policy making underpinned by a global city paradigm that is insensitive to local cultures and institutions (Pratt 2009). The following approach, based upon Florida's creative class thesis combines the worst of both approaches.

21.3.4   The Creative Class and the City

The debate, and policy movement, inspired by Florida's (2002) 'rise of the creative class' has become identified with the notion of the 'creative city'. Arguably, this is the worst iteration yet of the relationship between culture and the city for creative workers. Florida's argument boils down to the attraction of foreign direct investment to cities. The assumption being that if capital is mobile, then the unique selling point of a location will secure the investment, and hence jobs. Cities have long engaged in this process; their tools were first lowering costs: rent free periods, subsidised land, holding local wages down. In the era of globalisation, the multi-plant enterprise faced a problem of moving experienced staff around the world, and overcoming resistance from staff and their families on reloca-tion. City mayors realised that if they sold their cities as attractive to managers responsible for re-location decisions, they might win the game through a 'soft power' of welcoming green and clean environments, augmented by high culture and heritage attractions.

Florida's insight was taken from Daniel Bell's (1973) notion of the growth of a post-industrial economy, recognising that in the new economy the 'talent' was what mattered to companies. Florida developed this argument, suggesting the existence of a 'creative class', who are attracted to liberal, and contemporary cultural environments. Florida's key intervention was to suggest that the creative class were the critical human capital that would attract hi-tech, high-growth companies (reversing the traditional idea that labour would move to employers). Thus, by modelling themselves as a cultural class playground, workers would gravitate to cities, and then companies would seek them out, and want to be located there. Such an argument plays to the eternal weaknesses of politicians of self-promotion and short-term popularity, and a veneer of academic respectability.

There are two significant issues with the 'Creative City' argument. First, that the crea-tive class identified by Florida, are the workers of hi-tech, not the cultural industries; in fact, the argument is one about the consumption power of the creative class. The culture is instrumental, to provide a 'funky environment'. Second, the consequence that cities should privilege the creative class. That a city could decide that the creative class (already a privileged group) should be first in the queue for resource and support is challenging. Moreover, that the city should re-make its infrastructure and services to please this group sets some clear priorities. The knock-on effects are plain and apparent: that gentrification is legitimised and promoted as the motor process of urban regeneration; and, that the distributional balance of resource is skewed to the least needy, and to a sectional taste. The paradox, or rather stark contradiction is of a city, promoting itself as 'creative' whilst at the same time limiting access to culture, focusing on consumption, and not simply neglecting but actively undermining cultural production through a super-fuelled gentrification of commercial and residential properties (Pratt 2011a). Clear examples of the sort of forces that are unleashed and legitimised by such support for a creative class strategy are evidenced in many cities, but particularly starkly in San Francisco (Jarvis and Pratt 2006), Vancouver (Hutton 2008), Shenzhen (O'Connor and Liu 2014; see also Lees, Shin and López-Morales 2016, on 'creative cities' in the global south).

21.4   PART III: FINDING A PLACE FOR CULTURAL PRODUCTION IN THE CITY

It will be clear that the extant models of culture and the city do not have a place for the creative worker. The site is occupied by creative consumption, one where culture is used instrumentally to achieve a short-term economic benefit. In the meantime, it will actually displace and undermine cultural producers. Artists and cultural workers have been caught in a perfect storm of contradictions where they are noticed, but ignored; wanted, but then disposed of. The problem is twofold. First, that empirically the cultural economy has grown in many cities (and in the global economy), it challenges 'traditional' industries in terms of its economic strength, it carries additional cultural power as well. Second, and perhaps related to the first, our conceptual lenses need refocusing on culture and the cultural economy, not viewing them as dependent, or expendable, but as integral to the urban process. In this final part of the chapter I will outline why and how the creative economy, artists and cultural workers may be recognised as a central part of urban change.

21.4.1　Alternatives for Culture and the City

The need for creative cities, and creativity, is a common refrain from politicians. However, in practice what has been delivered either through policy, or simply urban redevelopment practices, undermines the possibility of a vibrant cultural and creative community. In part, as I have argued, this is because culture and creativity have been primarily conceived of through the lens of consumption, from museum and gallery visits to bars, restaurants and nightclubs. Culture is seen as a way to burnish the city's image. None more so than in the age of the Creative City where the edgy-contemporary arts consumerism is one more necessary environmental must-have to attract hi-tech investors in search of creative class knowledge workers. In this normality it is regarded as fine for artists to be regularly uprooted from their studios and pushed further out of the city. In fact, artists are now put in the (unwilling and unasked-for) role of the 'shock troops' of gentrification: troops that will be the first to suffer as economic growth in a community takes off. In short, the gentrification of artists has been normalised (Park 2016).

However, at the same time the value of urban cultural production has been transformed from that of primarily heritage and provision of consumption experiences to one of cultural production that produces both substantial economic and cultural value. The growth of cultural production has taken place despite the conditions. The normal pattern has been for artists to fight a running battle to simply hold their place in the city. Artists have been subject to the same, some might say more exaggerated, form of the rent gap as industrial properties have been re-developed and re-valued. To some extent, commentators have been blind to the experiences of artists as they occupied industrial spaces.

The strategies that artists have used to 'cling on' has been via collective 'self-provisioning'. A popular model to step off the rent gap escalator has been to remove the property from the market, to buy it; then to provide rent control for artists. These collectives, found in many cities, are predominantly run by and for artists. However, recent studies have highlighted the complex and nuanced responses of artists (Grodach, Foster et al. 2016; Borén and Young 2017); rather than being the unwitting cause or dupes of community erosion, artists may be at the forefront of community action (Gainza 2016). Other critics have pointed to the narrow social representation of artists and their role in the reproduction of male heteronormativity in 'community' development (McLean 2014). This range of perspectives underlines the inadequacy of, and the unitary and universal notions sustained in, the 'creative class' as a concept. Moreover, that the notion of the creative class is not a foundation for understanding the creative city in practice.

Artists have not been given respect as citizens. Not only have they suffered the usual challenges of displacement due to rental increases and redevelopment, but they have also been used, consciously or not, to popularise run-down areas. Policy makers and politicians, and many in the local community, and artists, seem to accept that this is 'how it is'.

Little attention has been paid until recently to artistic activity, how it is organised, and the importance of its social, economic and cultural embedding (Pratt 2017). Understanding this, and responding to it, would be a normal response to other sectors of economic development in a city. However, such a realisation has been slow to dawn with regard to the creative economy. Not-for-profit provision of studio space insulated from extreme rent reviews is one thing; however, there are other lessons to learn from these 'creative hubs', or 'art factories' (Pratt et al. 2016). Closer inspection reveals that they are not simply flexible co-working spaces, nor simply cheap. Instead their defining characteristic is the provision of a community of practice (Wenger 1998) associated with art forms, and commonly a support infrastructure of service provision (Virani and Pratt 2016). The latter is particularly important as most artists work individually, or in small groups, and the economics of service provision works against them. A variant of collective services that are often provided include training courses, business advice, and access to professional networks, and experience. This folds back into the former point: participation in a community of practice where skills and experience can be exchanged and discussed.

It is this realisation, that cultural work is a viable option in today's urban economy, that has latterly prompted city authorities to learn from, and acknowledge, what third sector agencies have been doing. This has required a conceptual shift away from the dependency of culture, and an exclusive focus on consumption. It is nothing short of recasting a 'new normal' for the city, one that includes cultural production as well as cultural consumption.

21.5 CONCLUSION

Arts and culture have a precarious position in the city. Until recently it is true to say that the artist was likely to be a victim of gentrification. Confusingly, cultural consumers – the creative class, hipsters – have been mistaken for artists and cultural producers, creating a bizarre perspective of the artist being both perpetrator and victim of gentrification. Whilst Zukin's work alerted us to the cultural dimensions of gentrification, the dominant focus in gentrification writings has concerned the implications for consumption and representation in relation to retailing, residential and regeneration projects more generally. This chapter has sought to bring equal attention to the relationship with cultural production. Recent studies reveal the complex and nuanced position of the creative economy in urbanisation; the change of emphasis to comparative and planetary work has led to a welcome attention being paid to the situated nature of development. In turn, this has also undermined the notion of the creative class as a valid, unified, or universal agent in contemporary urbanisation.

From a normative perspective, the artist is overlooked, and only manages to make a living at the margins – an ever-shifting margin in short life housing, and poorly maintained industrial buildings. The post-industrial city with its large-scale redevelopment of space, and of the working population, literally did not see a place for creative labour. As the cultural economy has grown – in cities, and across the world – this image of the artist and cultural worker has been challenged; it also troubles our conceptions of the position of the artist in the city. There is a dawning realisation that the cultural economy matters, and that artists and creatives need to have a place found for them in the 'new normal' city.

Instead of being forced to be nomadic and precarious, some policy makers are realising the value of the artistic and cultural economy being stabilised. Property provision models are being devised that give dignity to artists and do not see them as ways of simply boosting residential prices. More sophisticated understandings of how the cultural economy works, and what cultural practice and organisation looks like, and what its strengths and weakness might be are changing the ways that city authorities regard culture. The short-term and instrumental uses are not going to disappear overnight, but they are part of a change which could see an accommodation of the city to the artist. However, this viewpoint is still a minority perspective.

At the same time, we need to find a place for artists in the literature and debates about gentrification. For too long they have been marginalised, or excluded. Recent developments are a stimulus to reconceptualise and refine our insights. Can industrial and economic use changes be considered as gentrification, or must the term only apply in the case of residential to residential changes? I would argue that it can and should; in fact, the complex and multiple switching between building uses requires us to do so. So, this is perhaps a unique sub-class of gentrification, but one that is subject to similar processes. Moreover, discussion of artists and cultural practice should also challenge us to think about what role 'culture' plays in this picture. Analyses of cultural production have begun to challenge simple production/consumption binaries, culture–economy tensions, as well as culture as practice versus cultural as category. These are conceptual as well as practical issues that face both those concerned with gentrification and those concerned with cultural economy.

REFERENCES

Anholt, S. (2010) *Places: Identity, Image and Reputation*, Basingstoke: Palgrave Macmillan.
Atkinson, R. and Bridge, G. (2005) *Gentrification in a Global Context: The New Urban Colonialism*, London: Routledge.
Bell, D. (1973) *The Coming of Post-industrial Society*, New York: Basic Books.
Bianchini, F. and Parkinson, M. (1993) *Cultural Policy and Urban Regeneration: The West European Experience*, Manchester: Manchester University Press.
Borén, T. and Young, C. (2017) 'Artists and creative city policy: resistance, the mundane and engagement in Stockholm, Sweden', *City, Culture and Society*, 8(1), first published online 19 January.
Bourdieu, P. (1979) *Distinction: A Social Critique of the Judgement of Taste*, London: Routledge.
Brooks, D. (2000) *Bobos in Paradise: The New Upper Class and How They Got There*, New York; London: Simon & Schuster.
Brownill, S. (2013) 'Waterfront regeneration as a global phenomenon', in *The Routledge Companion to Urban Regeneration*, London: Routledge, pp. 45–55.
Buitrago Restrepo, F. and Duque Márquez, I. (2013) *The Orange Economy: An Infinite Opportunity*, Washington: Inter American Development Bank.
Butler, T. and Lees, L. (2006) 'Super-gentrification in Barnsbury, London: globalization and gentrifying global elites at the neighbourhood level', *Transactions of the Institute of British Geographers*, 31(4), 467–487.
Byrne, D. (2013) 'If the 1% stifles New York's creative talent, I'm out of here', *The Guardian*, London, 7 October, https://www.theguardian.com/commentisfree/2013/oct/07/new-york-1percent-stifles-creative-talent.
Castells, M. (1989) *The Informational City*, Oxford: Blackwell.
Clark, E. (1994) 'Towards a Copenhagen interpretation of gentrification', *Urban Studies*, 31(7), 1033–1042.
Curran, W. (2004) 'Gentrification and the nature of work: exploring the links in Williamsburg, Brooklyn', *Environment and Planning A*, 36(7), 1243–1258.
Curran, W. (2010) 'In defense of old industrial spaces: manufacturing, creativity and innovation in Williamsburg, Brooklyn', *International Journal of Urban and Regional Research*, 34(4), 871–885.
d'Ovidio, M. and Rodríguez Morató, A. (2017) 'Against the creative city: activism in the creative city: when cultural workers fight against creative city policy', *City, Culture and Society*, 8(1), first published online 19 January.
Dean, C., Donnellan, C. and Pratt, A. (2010) 'Tate Modern: pushing the limits of regeneration', *City, Culture and Society*, 1(2), 79–87.
Evans, G. (2003) 'Hard-branding the cultural city – from Prado to Prada', *International Journal of Urban and Regional Research*, 27(2), 417–440.
Florida, R. (2002) *The Rise of the Creative Class: And How it's Transforming Work, Leisure, Community and Everyday Life*, New York: Basic Books.

Florida, R. (2008) *Who's Your City?: How the Creative Economy is Making Where to Live the Most Important Decision of Your Life*, New York: Basic Books.

Foord, J. (2013) 'The new boomtown? Creative city to tech city in east London', *Cities*, 33, 51–60.

Freeman, A. (2010) *London's Creative Workforce: 2009 Update*, London: Greater London Authority.

Gainza, X. (2016) 'Culture-led neighbourhood transformations beyond the revitalisation/gentrification dichotomy', *Urban Studies*, first published online 11 July.

Garcia, B. (2005) 'Deconstructing the city of culture: the long-term cultural legacies of Glasgow 1990', *Urban Studies*, 42(5–6), 841–868.

Garcia, B., Melville, R. and Cox, T. (2010) 'Creating an impact: Liverpool's experience as European Capital of Culture', *Liverpool: University of Liverpool/Impacts*, 8.

Glass, R. (1964) *London: Aspects of Change*, London: MacGibbon & Kee.

Green, N. (1999) 'The space of change: artists in the East End 1968–1980', *Rising East*, 3(2), 20–37.

Grodach, C., Foster, N. and Murdoch, J. (2016) 'Gentrification, displacement and the arts: untangling the relationship between arts industries and place change', *Urban Studies*, published online 6 December.

Hubbard, P. (2016) 'Hipsters on our high streets: consuming the gentrification frontier', *Sociological Research Online*, 21(3), 1.

Hutton, T. (2008) *The New Economy of the Inner City: Restructuring, Regeneration and Dislocation in the Twenty-first-century Metropolis*, Abingdon: Routledge.

Hutton, T. (2015) *Cities and the Cultural Economy*, London: Routledge.

Hutton, T., Catungal, J., Leslie, D. and Hii, Y. (2009) 'Geographies of displacement in the creative city: the case of Liberty Village, Toronto', *Urban Studies*, 46(5–6), 1095–1114.

Imrie, R. and Raco, M. (2003) 'Community and the changing nature of urban policy', in Imrie, R. and Raco, M. (eds) *Urban Renaissance? New Labour, Community and Urban Policy*, Bristol: Policy Press, pp. 3–36.

Jarvis, H. and Pratt, A. (2006) 'Bringing it all back home: the extensification and "overflowing" of work. The case of San Francisco's new media households', *Geoforum*, 37(3), 331–339.

Jones, A. (1998) 'Issues in waterfront regeneration: more sobering thoughts – a UK perspective', *Planning Practice and Research*, 13(4), 433–442.

Jung, T., Lee, J., Yap, M. and Ineson, E. (2015) 'The role of stakeholder collaboration in culture-led urban regeneration: a case study of the Gwangju project, Korea', *Cities*, 44, 29–39.

Khomami, N. and Halliday, J. (2015) 'Shoreditch Cereal Killer Cafe targeted in anti-gentrification protests', *The Guardian*, London 27 September, https://www.theguardian.com/uk-news/2015/sep/27/shoreditch-cereal-cafe-targeted-by-anti-gentrification-protesters.

Kim, J. (2016) 'Cultural entrepreneurs and urban regeneration in Itaewon, Seoul', *Cities*, 56, 132–140.

King, A. (1995) *Re-presenting the City: Ethnicity, Capital and Culture in the Twenty-first-century Metropolis*, Basingstoke: Macmillan.

Kong, L. (2012) 'Ambitions of a global city: arts, culture and creative economy in "Post-Crisis" Singapore', *International Journal of Cultural Policy*, 18(3), 279–294.

Lähdesmäki, T. (2012) 'Rhetoric of unity and cultural diversity in the making of European cultural identity', *International Journal of Cultural Policy*, 18(1), 59–75.

Lees, L. (1994) 'Rethinking gentrification: beyond the positions of economics or culture', *Progress in Human Geography*, 18(2), 137–150.

Lees, L. (2003) 'Super-gentrification: the case of Brooklyn Heights, New York City', *Urban Studies*, 40(12), 2487–2509.

Lees, L., Shin, H. and López-Morales, E. (2016) *Planetary Gentrification*, London: John Wiley & Sons.

Lees, L., Slater, T. and Wyly, E. (2013) *Gentrification*, London: Routledge.

Lloyd, R. (2006) *Neo-Bohemia: Art and Commerce in the Postindustrial City*, London: Routledge.

Lloyd, R. and Clark, T. (2001) 'The city as an entertainment machine', *Critical Perspectives on Urban Redevelopment*, 6(3), 357–378.

Mar, P. and Anderson, K. (2010) 'The creative assemblage: theorizing contemporary forms of arts-based collaboration', *Journal of Cultural Economy*, 3(1), 35–51.

Martins, J. (2015) 'The extended workplace in a creative cluster: exploring space(s) of digital work in Silicon Roundabout', *Journal of Urban Design*, 20(1), 125–145.

Mayor of London (2012) *World Cities Culture Report*, London: Mayor of London.

McLean, H. (2014) 'Digging into the creative city: a feminist critique', *Antipode*, 46(3), 669–690.

Miller, H. (2016) *Drop Dead: Performance in Crisis, 1970s New York*, Evanston: Northwestern University Press.

Molotch, H. (1976) 'The city as a growth machine: toward a political economy of place', *American Journal of Sociology*, 309–332.

Nathan, M., Vandore, E. and Whitehead, R. (2012) *A Tale of Tech City: The Future of Inner East London's Digital Economy*, London: Centre for Cities.

NESTA (2013) *A Manifesto for the Creative Economy*, London: NESTA.

Oakley, K. and Pratt, A. (2010) 'Brick Lane: community-driven innovation', in *Local Knowledge: Case Studies of Four Innovative Places*, NESTA. London: National Endowment for Science, Technology and the Arts, pp. 28–39.

O'Connor, J. and Liu, L. (2014) 'Shenzhen's OCT-LOFT: creative space in the City of Design', *City, Culture and Society*, 5(3), 131–138.

Palmer-Rae Associates (2004) *European Cities and Capitals of Culture*, Brussels: European Commission.

Parenti, C. (2000) *Policing the Theme Park City*, PhD, London School of Economics.

Park, S. (2016) 'Can we implant an artist community? A reflection on government-led cultural districts in Korea', *Cities*, 56, 172–179.

Peck, J. and Theodore, N. (2015) *Fast Policy*, Minneapolis: University of Minnesota Press.

Perry, G. (2014) *Playing to the Gallery: Helping Contemporary Art in its Struggle to be Understood*, Harmondsworth: Penguin.

Plaza, B. (2000) 'Evaluating the influence of a large cultural artifact in the attraction of tourism: the Guggenheim Museum Bilbao case', *Urban Affairs Review*, 36(2), 264–274.

Pratt, A. (2000) 'New media, the new economy and new spaces', *Geoforum*, 31(4), 425–436.

Pratt, A. (2007) 'The state of the cultural economy: the rise of the cultural economy and the challenges to cultural policy making', in Ribeiro, A. (ed) *The Urgency of Theory*, Manchester: Carcanet Press/Gulbenkin Foundation, pp. 166–190.

Pratt, A. (2009) 'Urban regeneration: from the arts "feel good" factor to the cultural economy. A case study of Hoxton, London', *Urban Studies*, 46(5–6), 1041–1061.

Pratt, A. (2010) 'Creative cities: tensions within and between social, cultural and economic development. A critical reading of the UK experience', *City, Culture and Society*, 1(1), 13–20.

Pratt, A. (2011a) 'The cultural contradictions of the creative city', *City, Culture and Society*, 2(3), 123–130.

Pratt, A. (2011b) 'The cultural economy and the global city', in Taylor, P., Derudder, B., Hoyler, M. and Witlox, F. (eds) *International Handbook of Globalization and World Cities*, Cheltenham: Edward Elgar, pp. 265–274.

Pratt, A. (2012) 'Factory, studio, loft: there goes the neighbourhood?', in Baum, M. and Christiaanse, K. (eds) *City as Loft: Adaptive Reuse as a Resource for Sustainable Development*, Zurich: gta Verlag, pp. 25–31.

Pratt, A. (2017) 'Innovation and the cultural economy', in Bathelt, H., Cohendet, P., Henn, S. and Simon, L. (eds) *The Elgar Companion to Innovation and Knowledge Creation: A Multi-disciplinary Approach*, Cheltenham: Edward Elgar, pp. 200–215.

Pratt, A., Dovey, J., Moreton, S., Virani, T., Merkel, J. and Lansdowne, J. (2016) *The Creative Hubs Report*, London: British Council.

Rogers, R. (1999) *Towards an Urban Rennaisance*, London: Spon.

Sassen, S. (2001) *The Global City: New York, London, Tokyo*, Princeton: Princeton University Press.

Smith, N. (1987) 'Gentrification and the rent gap', *Annals of the Association of American Geographers*, 77(3), 462–465.

Smith, N. (1996) *The New Urban Frontier: Gentrification and the Revanchist City*, London: Routledge.

Straw, W. (2001) 'Scenes and sensibilities', *Public*, 22–23, 245–257.

Syms, P. (1994) 'The funding of developments on derelict and contaminated sites', in Pratt, A. and Ball, R. (eds) *Industrial Property: Policy and Economic Development*, London: Routledge, pp. 63–82.

Virani, T. and Pratt, A. (2016) 'Intermediaries and the knowledge exchange process: the case of the creative industries and higher education', in Comunian, R. and Gilmore, A. (eds) *Beyond the Campus: Higher Education and the Creative Economy*, London: Routledge, pp. 41–58.

Wenger, E. (1998) *Communities of Practice: Learning, Meaning, and Identity*, Cambridge: Cambridge University Press.

Yi, L. (2011) *Laurie Anderson, Trisha Brown, Gordon Matta-Clark: Pioneers of the Downtown Scene, New York 1970s*, Munich: Prestel Art.

Yoon, H. and Currid-Halkett, E. (2014) 'Industrial gentrification in West Chelsea, New York: who survived and who did not? Empirical evidence from discrete-time survival analysis', *Urban Studies*, 52(1), 20–49.

Zukin, S. (1982) *Loft Living: Culture and Capital in Urban Change*, Baltimore: Johns Hopkins University Press.

Zukin, S. and Braslow, L. (2011) 'The life cycle of New York's creative districts: reflections on the unanticipated consequences of unplanned cultural zones', *City, Culture and Society*, 2(3), 131–140.

Zukin, S., Trujillo, V., Frase, P., Jackson, D., Recuber, T. and Walker, A. (2009) 'New retail capital and neighborhood change: boutiques and gentrification in New York City', *City & Community*, 8(1), 47–64.

22. Wilderness gentrification: moving 'off-the-beaten rural tracks'

Darren Smith, Martin Phillips and Chloe Kinton

22.1 INTRODUCTION

> You don't have to be Robinson Crusoe to live according to the moods of the weather, the arc of the sun and the changing seasons. There are people who prize solitude above worldly success, and who choose to live off-road, off-grid and off mains sewerage with only moors and mountains for company. (McGhie 2015; quoted in *Property and Finance*, The Telegraph)

Conceptually, the vast majority of scholarship on gentrification has investigated the definitional signifiers of the processes of this transformation, such as displacement and social class change, within highly visible, human built landscapes with residential populations (Lees et al. 2008, 2015, 2016). This is most obvious in the widespread focus on urban gentrification, but can also be seen in the much smaller field of rural gentrification studies. Across both urban and rural spaces, taken-for-granted housing and population markers of gentrified landscapes (Smith 2002a), interspersed with combinations of retail, educational, industrial, welfare, state, religious and other buildings (e.g. Bridge and Dowling 2002; Phillips 2002; Zukin et al. 2009; Hubbard 2017), appear as intrinsic features in the very diverse geographies of gentrification (Janoschka et al. 2014; Lees 2012, 2016). To some degree, this underpinning is reflected in the preponderance of gentrification scholarship in fittingly titled journals such as *Environment and Planning A, Housing Studies, Population, Space and Place*, and *Urban Studies*.

Yet, not only have some studies of urban gentrification emphasised how gentrification may have transformed open green spaces beyond buildings, including parks, public squares, landscaped verges and walkways (e.g. Mills 1988; Smith 1996; Lees 1998; Davidson and Lees 2005; Lees et al. 2016), but some studies have highlighted how rural gentrification might critically involve spaces other than those associated with buildings. Smith and Phillips (2001), for example, coined the phrase 'greentrification' to reflect their view that rural gentrification was being stimulated by 'the demand for, and perception of, "green" residential space'. Likewise, Phillips (2005, p. 1) argues for recognition that rural gentrification often occurs in what is seen as a 'space of nature', and that this contextualisation is 'arguably one of the most rural, and least urban, aspects of rural gentrification' (see also Bryson 2013). Murdoch (2003) develops similar arguments, albeit framed in the language of counterurbanisation rather than rural gentrification (although see Phillips 2010a for a discussion of the relationships between these concepts), suggesting that the 'primary cause' of migration to the countryside was a 'desire . . . to be immersed in rurality'. He adds that, drawing on the work of Bell (1994), 'this "immersion" has two aspects: firstly a social aspect . . . [a] wish to reside in a rural community; secondly, a natural aspect as counter-urbanisers seek to live within a particular kind of material environment . . . that includes traditional buildings, open space, green fields . . . [and] proximity to nature' (Murdoch 2003, p. 277). This work in effect highlights how some people seem to be attracted to live in, and in some cases gentrify, the countryside, because it appears to be a very humanised social environment, whilst others seek connections to non-human or more-than-human aspects of these spaces.

In Smith and Phillips (2001) these desired relations with the countryside become expressed through two distinct strands of rural gentrification in the Hebden Bridge district of West Yorkshire. On the one hand, there are rural gentrifiers who locate to the populated settlements of the river valley, in association with an aspiration to acquire a space where they can feel 'a sense of belonging to the local community' (ibid., p. 464), as well as one which exhibited a green pastoral landscape of 'working farms, country lanes, green fields and sheep' (ibid., p. 460). This group of gentrifiers, hence, seemed to be attracted both to the communal life of human settlements and to 'green' spaces which exhibited a high degree of human influence and even control, as well as the presence of more-than-human elements. By contrast, a second group of gentrifiers located to moor-top locations that were seemingly quite 'remote' from populated settlements, apparently valuing solitude and an environment that was seemingly far from controlled by human activity, being viewed and appreciated as a hard, hostile and 'wild' landscape (Smith 2002b).

Such contrasting valuations of space have been widely discerned, with Short (1991, p. xvi), for instance, identifying the urban, the rural and the wilderness as being highly significant 'environmental myths', by which he means representations of space that 'resonate across space and time, which are widely used and reproduced, which are broad enough to encompass diverse experiences yet deep enough to anchor these experiences in a continuous medium of meaning'. He further argues that these three myths encompass environments from the most humanly occupied 'built environments' (the urban) through to the least occupied and humanly transformed environments of nature (the wilderness), with the rural occupying the middle ground in the continuum.

Clearly a range of objections can be raised about these constructions of space. A series of urban studies, for example, have highlighted the presence of 'urban natures' and 'wild things' (e.g. Cronon 1991; Gandy 2002; Whatmore and Hinchcliffe 2003; Hinchcliffe et al. 2005), whilst other work has emphasised how human activity has conditioned spaces of wilderness (e.g. Denevan 1992; Cronon 1995; Phillips and Mighall 2000; Monbiot 2017). Having said this, these conceptions can be identified as being both 'widely used and reproduced', including within a wide range of studies of gentrification. The terms 'urban' and 'rural' are, for instance, frequently used gentrification adjectives,[1] although the former has been much more widely used and, indeed, as outlined in Phillips (2004), gentrification is often interpreted as an intrinsically urban phenomenon or process, even amongst advocates of studies of the 'geography of gentrification' (e.g. Ley 1996).

It can be argued that gentrification studies often enact 'urbanormativity' (Thomas et al. 2011) or 'metrocentricity' (Phillips and Smith 2018a), whereby urban space, or indeed particular sub-sets of it, such as the central parts of a selection of cities in the Global North, are taken, largely implicitly, as the 'normal' space of operation, while alternative

---

[1]   Lees et al. (2016) argue that the boundaries between rural and urban have become blurred as the former becomes incorporated within a planetary urban realm through urbanisation (see Phillips and Smith 2018a, b).

locations are 'othered' as spaces of absence or abnormal forms of gentrification. A range of 'other geographies of gentrification' (Phillips 2004) have been identified, including 'suburban' (Niedt 2006; Charmes and Keil 2015; Jones and Ley 2016), 'peri-urban' (Hudalah et al. 2015) and 'ex-urban' (Walker and Fortmann 2003; Sandberg and Wekerle 2010), as well as a series of studies from various parts of the globe that have used the term 'rural gentrification' (e.g. Phillips 1993, 1998, 2007, 2014; Perrenoud 2008; Solana-Solana 2010; Stockdale 2010; Nelson and Nelson 2010; Qian et al. 2013; Mamonova and Sutherland 2015).

There have also been studies of 'wilderness gentrification' (Darling 2005) and studies of gentrification in 'other' more or less closely associated spaces: places such as 'the Outback' or 'Bush' in Australia (Freeman and Cheyne 2008), 'the range' in North America (Travis 2007; Abrams and Gosnell 2012), forests (Brown 1995; Paquette and Domon 2001), coasts and estuaries (Smith 2007; Freeman and Cheyne 2008) and islands (Clark et al. 2007; Jackson 2005), presenting some notion of being at the margin of human influence. The study of many of these 'other geographies' of gentrification can be seen, to borrow the words of Slater (2004, p. 1191), to be very much 'only in its infancy'.

For this reason, along with Short's claim about the significance of the environmental myths of wilderness, this chapter will focus its attention on the 'other geographies' of rurality and, particularly, wilderness. The chapter will proceed by considering the geography of the studies of rural and wilderness gentrification, highlighting how the study of the former has included a strong focus of attention within the UK, whilst the study of wilderness gentrification has been more significant in other countries, particularly Canada and the USA, although often not described explicitly using the term 'wilderness'. The chapter will then explore the extent to which this 'geography of the concept of gentrification' (Phillips and Smith 2018a) might be seen to reflect the character of space within the UK, or whether there might be scope for utilising the notion of 'wilderness gentrification' in the UK. This will be done through an exploratory mapping of gentrification against a proxy of wilderness areas within England and Wales, using data from the Labour Force Survey (2011) and the UK Census (2011) to identify 'remote' areas that are relatively disconnected from large urban centres for commuting and employment, and which are also characterised by very low population densities. As such these areas could be viewed as locations that can be characterised as having both relatively low levels of human habitation and being relatively disconnected from areas that are densely populated by people. Having constructed a map that could be seen as providing a sense of the geographies of wilderness in England and Wales, the chapter then seeks to explore patterns of gentrification drawing upon a typology of rural gentrification created as part of a comparative study of rural gentrification in the UK, USA and France.[2] The chapter concludes by outlining some possible directions of travel for cross-national comparative studies of wilderness and rural gentrification.

[2] This cross-national research project is entitled 'International rural gentrification' or iRGENT and is funded by the Economic and Social Research Council [ES/L016702/1], as well as by the National Science Foundation (NSF) in the USA and the Agence Nationale de la Recherche (ANR) in France. For details see www.i-rgent.com.

22.2   STUDIES OF RURAL AND WILDERNESS GENTRIFICATION

An examination of scholarship that makes use of the term 'rural gentrification' reveals that it has unfolded with quite distinct geographical foci in different countries. Knowledge-construction of rural gentrification in the UK, for example, has tended to be fixed on the discernible built forms of villages (e.g. Phillips 2014, 2015; Stockdale 2010) or semi-rural small towns (e.g. Smith 1998; Smith and Holt 2005), often in close proximity to large urban centres. The work of Sutherland (2012) is a notable exception, with her work focusing on the gentrification of agricultural spaces and promoting the notion of 'agricultural gentrification' as distinct from rural gentrification. Although her work is not focused on England and Wales, she notes some parallels occurring elsewhere, most notably in the USA where work such as that by Friedberger (1996) has examined transformations in ranching (see also Travis 2007; Abrams et al. 2013; Harner and Benz 2013). Yet, not only can it be argued that agricultural spaces have long been viewed as a key constituent of cultural constructions of rurality – providing, for instance, a 'pastoral landscape' that simultaneously contains indicators of human influence and the presence of more-than-human actants such as plants and animals – but also that rurality clearly encompasses a fuller diversity of forms and landscapes than just the spaces of rural settlement and agriculture, many of which have not permeated very much into current discussions of rural gentrification.

Other spaces of rurality that might connect to gentrification include 'peri-urban' or 'exurban' or 'urban-rural fringe' and 'wilderness'. In countries such as France, the notion of the peri-urban is widely used, having been incorporated into formal spatial classification since 1996 (Le Jeannic 1996). Conceptually, the term peri-urban is seen to designate locations that are functionally connected to urban areas, yet are also in some way or another differentiated from urban areas, such as through the morphological balance of built-up and open spaces, or land uses that occur in the area, or, indeed, how people perceive these spaces (see Briquel and Colieard 2005). Practically, as outlined in Cavailhès et al. (2004), these areas were classified in France through a combination of indices of the extent of a contiguous 'built-up environment' and employment within this built-up area, with peri-urban areas identified as spaces functionally connected to urban areas through a commuting level of over 40 per cent of residents but differentiated from urban areas in terms of the extent of their built-up environment and the overall level of employment they provide. Cavailhès et al. also remark that this classification system exhibits parallels with spatial classifications established by the U.S. Office of Management and Budget (OMB), which identifies 'metropolitan', 'micropolitan' and 'non-metropolitan' counties on the basis of population concentration and whether areas are 'economically and socially connected . . . as measured through commuting flows' (Johnson and Shifferd 2016, p. 29). Similar measures are further utilised by the U.S. Department of Agriculture's Economic Research Service in some of its spatial classifications, and also underpin Johnson and Shifferd's attempt to create a composition classification capable of differentiating urban, suburban, exurban and rural areas. Within this classification, the notion of the exurban was used in a similar manner to the peri-urban, being defined as areas where over 25 per cent of the population commutes to a metropolitan core area.

These classifications clearly highlight how notions of the peri-urban and exurban emphasise relational connections with urban space, but it can be argued that rurality and wilderness imply some degree of differentiation and, indeed, separation from the urban. Murdoch and Pratt (1993, p. 417), for example, argued that 'community studies' in the UK during the middle-decades of the twentieth century quite clearly viewed rural communities as inhabiting spaces that 'lay outside the influence of modernity', although noticeably viewing them as coming under its influence. Wright (1992, p. 199) makes similar comments, exclaiming that these studies were 'as far flung as possible from urban centres'. Whilst her comments, and associated map of the geography of these early community studies (ibid., p. 200), stand in clear contrast to the geography of rural gentrification studies outlined in Phillips and Smith (2018a) – which, as already mentioned, shows a strong clustering around areas close to urban centres – they do exhibit parallels with studies that make use of the term rural gentrification in both France and North America. In relation to France, it is clear that mountainous areas figure prominently amongst the still quite small number of rural gentrification studies (e.g. see Cognard 2010, 2012; Perrenoud 2008; Richard et al. 2014). This is also evident in studies of rural gentrification in North America, not least in the studies of the 'Rocky Mountain West' (e.g. Gosnell and Travis 2005; Gosnell et al. 2007; Hines 2007, 2010a,b, 2012; Travis 2007).

As Short (1991) notes, mountainous areas have often figured strongly within enactments of wilderness, with the Rocky Mountains being frequently quite explicitly foregrounded in discussions of wilderness. These mountain ranges contain, for instance, many areas that are formally designated as 'wilderness areas' under the provisions of the 1964 'Wilderness Act', including a series of 'National Parks' and areas of 'National Forest'. Under the Act, such areas are defined as spaces where 'the earth and community of life are untrammeled' by people, and people are 'a visitor who does not remain' (Wilderness Act 1964, p. 891). As such, the Act clearly enacts a sense of the wilderness as relatively unoccupied and untransformed by people. Given this, and the suggestion made earlier that gentrification has often been centred on spaces of significant human occupation and construction, it might appear paradoxical that these North American studies of rural gentrification, and, according to Nelson et al. (2010) the actual instances of rural gentrification, are so focused on areas of wilderness.

At least three distinct responses to this paradox can be identified from existing literatures. First, it is important to recognise that the Rocky Mountain area does not totally fall within the designations of the Act nor, indeed, evidence the non-built-up character implied by the Act. Many of the studies of rural gentrification in this area are actually focused on metropolitan centres located within the region. Ghose's (2004, p. 529) study of rural gentrification is, for example, focused on Missoula, a location she describes as 'Montana's fastest growing city'. She adds that from the 1990s much of this growth occurred through 'low density living' in areas that were previously farmland and which afforded 'views of the mountains'. The process of gentrification in this locality was seen as rural not only in the sense that it occurred on formerly agricultural land and involved the formation of low density settlement, but also because it was very clearly connected by developers and residents to the formation of a 'rural lifestyle/country way of living' as well as a view on and access to, 'beautiful landscape, scenery and environment' (ibid., p. 532). However, the processes of gentrification in Missoula appear closely connected to urbanity, with not only the new houses being a physical extension to the existing urban area of the city, but also many of the incoming gentrifiers having moved from urban areas and quite clearly desiring 'significant urban amenities', albeit packaged through symbolisations of rurality and embedded 'in an attractive wilderness setting' (ibid., p. 533).

Ghose's work makes clear reference to the significance of wilderness to processes of gentrification in Missoula, albeit conjoined with facets of rurality and urbanity. A series of other studies of rural gentrification within the Rocky Mountain West have focused more exclusively on rurality, making little if any reference to wilderness. Nelson et al. (2010, p. 349), for instance, identify the focus of gentrification studies in this area, but describe it largely in terms of a more general tendency for concentration in 'more remote counties, those not adjacent to major metropolitan or micropolitan areas', and make no specific reference to the potential influence of wilderness in accounting for this. Admittedly, their primary focus is on detailing the 'macroscale' pattern of occurrence of rural gentrification and some of its consequences, but where they do seek to provide some account of the processes of formation of gentrification they often highlight connections with other transformations impacting rural areas, such as '[a]gricultural consolidation and the urban to rural shifts in manufacturing and services' (ibid., p. 351), as well as connections to the global economy and transformations in urban labour and finance markets (see Nelson and Nelson 2014). Such work can be seen to represent a second response to the paradox surrounding the presence of gentrification in areas of wilderness, where the significance of wilderness is largely removed from discussion.

A third response, however, can be seen in the work of people such as Hines (2007, 2010a,b, 2012) where wilderness figures prominently in his accounts of rural gentrification in the Rocky Mountain West. Hines (2012, p. 83) has examined rural gentrification through ethnographic research in and around the town of Livingston, Montana, which is described as being 'pressed hard against the base of the Absaroka-Beartooth Wilderness Area', with 'dramatic views of the northern end of the stunning Absaroka Mountain'. Similarly to Ghose (2004), Hines identifies the significance of urbanity and rurality within the motivations and everyday practices of in-coming gentrifiers, suggesting that the former revolve around social amenities and character of the built-environment, whilst the latter encompasses both the agricultural and wilderness / natural environments. He suggests that in relation to rurality, there was a spectrum of views running from 'native industrial viewpoints' held by long-established agriculturalists, who emphasised agricultural productivity and the 'control of wilderness' (ibid., p. 91), through to incoming gentrifiers seeking to produce a more post-industrial / consumption agricultural lifestyle (ibid., p. 88), and onto gentrifiers focused on producing and consuming experiences centred on 'the "natural" environment and engagement with native Montana wildlife' (ibid., p. 92). As Hines outlines, tensions often existed between adherents of different positions within the spectrum, an issue also revealed in the work of Abrams and Gosnell (2012) and Abrams et al. (2013).

Hines clearly emphasises the significance of wilderness within his accounts of rural gentrification, but the work of Darling (2005) can be viewed as presenting a fourth account in relation to wilderness and gentrification. Exploring gentrification within Adirondack Park in New York State, USA, Darling both frames the area as 'a swath of wilderness' (ibid., p. 1018) and the process of gentrification as being one of 'wilderness gentrification', to 'set it apart from both urban gentrification and the rural gentrification described in the UK literature' (ibid., p. 1021). Darling's work is quite distinctive in this regard, and whilst her work has been widely cited, her specific proposal that wilderness gentrification constitutes a distinct form of gentrification has not been followed up.

In part, this lack of engagement with the specifics of Darling's work may reflect its adoption of a 'production-side' approach centred on the formation and realization of so-called 'rent gaps'. As Darling herself notes, production-side explanations have had little take-up in studies of rural gentrification, which have often centred their accounts on determining the significance of various locational preferences. In explicit contrast to this, Darling seeks to develop a capital focused approach concerned with the mechanisms that 'draws capital toward one particular location as opposed to another' (ibid., p. 1030). Drawing on the arguments of Smith (1996) about the need to situate studies of gentrification in both local and wider contexts, Darling examines the dynamics of both localised property development decisions and broader capital flows. In relation to the former, Darling emphasises the focus on the production of 'residential space' within studies of urban gentrification and suggests that this is largely displaced in wilderness gentrification by a focus on the 'production of recreational nature' (ibid., p. 1022). What attracts gentrification within areas of wilderness is, so she argues, not the potential value of a building and its spatial proximity to major centres of employment, consumption and services such as education, but rather 'proximity to wilderness areas, and particularly lakefronts' (ibid.). At a broader scale, Darling draws attention to how areas of wilderness have come to be produced and maintained, arguing, for instance, that planning regulations that limited the scale of residential developments in the area acted to heighten the value of recreational nature by preventing residential construction that might be viewed as 'devouring the very resource that allows for maximum rent capitalization in the first place: wilderness' (ibid., p. 1029).

Darling suggests that the presence of wilderness can produce a distinct form of gentrification centred on recreational rather than residential space, and indeed in operation in areas where residential space remains of limited extent. The extent to which this conceptualisation can be applied to areas beyond the Adirondack Park might be questioned given the significance of residential and other urban built environments highlighted in studies of rural gentrification in wilderness areas by people such as Ghose and Hines. Darling also very clearly sets her analysis of wilderness gentrification apart from UK-based studies of rural gentrification. In the following sections, we wish to consider whether it might be possible to undertake a study of gentrification in wilderness areas in the UK. As part of this we also consider the extent to which such a study might require movement away from arguments advanced in studies of rural gentrification and / or whether Darling is correct in suggesting that, because 'rural places are not merely different from cities, they are different from each other' (ibid., p. 1030), the idea of 'an overarching, homogeneous "rural gentrification" [is] suspect' and there needs to be a move to adopt 'more refined and specific set of labels to indicate a variety of landscape-specific gentrification models' (ibid., p. 1015).

22.3   WILDERNESS GENTRIFICATION IN THE UK?

Wilderness is a widely contested and multi-faceted concept that is difficult to define (e.g. Carver and Fritz 2013), although, as we have argued above, there is a widespread consensus that wilderness encompasses an absence of human habitation and other human-related influences and impacts, alongside some notion of naturalness (see Nash [1968] 2014; Short 1991; Daniels 1993; Schama 1995, for wider discussions of conceptualisations of wilderness). Carver et al. (2002, pp. 24–25) contend that despite the view that 'true wilderness simply no longer exists in Britain', it is possible to construct a 'continuum of the most altered and accessible to the most natural and remote'. They construct a continuum from multi-criteria measures of: remoteness from population and access (road, rail and ferry), apparent naturalness (e.g. settlements, railway lines, roads, radio masts), and biophysical naturalness (land use and vegetation cover) (see also Saarinen 2015).

Representations of wilderness areas are commonly matched to a distinct set of rural landscapes, including: remote, wild moorlands (e.g. Exmoor, Dartmoor); exposed, high mountainous areas (e.g. Lake District, Snowdonia); low-lying marshlands and fenlands, (e.g. The Wash / Fens, Romney Marsh, Norfolk / Suffolk Broads); and desolate, shingle flat-lands (e.g. Dungeness). Such landscapes have often figured strongly in scholarship focused on representations of wilderness in the 'Romantic movement' and tourism (e.g. Squire 1988; Short 1991; Cloke and Perkins 2002), and the (re)production and consumption of National Parks and nature (e.g. Magnaghten and Urry 1998; Phillips and Mighall 2000; Tolia-Kelly 2007). Many of these spaces are widely viewed as places 'unspoilt' by human activity, and where wildlife and nature is perceived to survive and flourish (Hall and Page 2014).

Whilst it is possible to contest such claims – as illustrated by assertions that the exposed fells of the Lake District, for example, are far from natural, but rather are a landscape that has been produced through heavily subsidised, technologised and environmentally destructive pastoral agriculture (Monbiot 2017) – it is also plausible to contend that such 'zones of wilderness', where there is an absence of visible housing settlements and communities, are viewed by some individuals as the antithesis of conventional percep-tions of the built environment and population signifiers of gentrification (Smith 2013). Of course, it can also be contended that these so-called 'natural spaces' are, 'socially produced natures' rather than 'pristine' natures (see Demeritt 2002; Ginn and Demeritt 2008; Phillips 2010b; Olafsdottir and Runnström 2011).

Nevertheless, socio-cultural meanings of wilderness are (in)directly interwoven into material expressions of urban and rural gentrification, and the effects of physical and social constructions of wilderness cannot be under-stated. As already discussed, Smith and Phillips' (2001) analysis of rural gentrification in the Hebden Bridge district of West Yorkshire highlighted how gentrifiers were differentially attracted to village and remote moor top environments (see also Smith 2002b). The latter group of gentrifiers are of key relevance here, given that they were seemingly attracted to moor top locations that they commonly perceived as representing harsh, isolated and 'wild' open spaces, where there was a lack of a built environment and a neighbouring resident population. As such these gentrifiers seemed to seek an environment that was visually and experientially devoid of features of urbanity, in some contrast to the studies of the rural gentrification in the Rocky Mountain West, which as discussed earlier, frequently stressed physical and social connection to urban space. Separation from the urban was, however, far from complete for these Pennine moor top gentrifiers, the majority of whom were highly dependent on nearby urban centres for employment and social interaction. However, it did appear that a degree of anti-urbanism and a desire to locate within wilderness were of major importance to these gentrifiers, as expressed by comments relaying the appeal of a Northern England Pennine aesthetic of 'Brontesque wilderness' involving desolate moorland landscapes, frequent drizzle and grey clouds, isolation, solitude, and getting away from other people to find 'self'.

This reference to a Brontesque landscape suggests that migrational related assessments of place can be influenced by literary and other representations, and thereby highlights the need to consider place-specific processes of gentrification within wider socio-cultural spatial frames. It also points to the need to consider how representations might connect to the physical and material constituents of a locality: the presence of drizzle and grey clouds in the locality, the ability to walk without seeing another person or indeed building. Such material constituents of place afford particular representations and experiences, as outlined in Phillips' (2014) discussion of the 'gentrified nature' of a Leicestershire village, but attention needs to be paid to exploring how specific place forms connect to gentrification across a broader network of places and environments (Phillips et al. 2001), including many that might be encompassed within notions of wilderness, such as estuaries and marshlands (see Smith 2007).

In other urban and rural places it is likely that spaces of wilderness perceived to be 'on the-door-step' or in relative proximity and accessible, may be an important constituent of gentrification. In the North American context, for example, Duncan and Duncan (2004) have highlighted how notions of wilderness, alongside those of pastoralism and a New England village built environment, stimulated a series of middle class movements into Bedford Town and adjacent areas of countryside. This argument is also salient in England and Wales where there is evidence of some regional (McNaughton and Urry 1998) and sub-regional constructions of identity incorporating signifiers of wilderness, such as distinct parts of the Pennines in West Yorkshire promoted as *Bronte Country* (environs of Haworth) and *Last of the Summer Wine Country* (environs of Holmfirth). This is borne out in national media discourses over the past two decades (e.g. Pearson 2005; Lister-Kaye 2010; Cowen 2016), which have described some distinct rural locations, such as the Black Mountains (Smith 2015a), Dartmoor (Smith 2015c), the Lake District (Smith 2015b) and Wye Valley (Llewellyn 2017), as bastions of wilderness.

Dominant social and cultural representations of wilderness in England and Wales are closely tied to the geographic distribution of National Parks, in part no doubt reflecting the conjunction of these with ideas of wilderness within the North American origins of the National Park Movement (see Nash 1970; MacEwen and MacEwen 1998). Whilst in the UK, National Parks are not defined officially as areas of wilderness, it is also evident that their emergence owed much to the discourses and practices of wilderness embodied within the Romantic movement of poets and artists. For instance, not only is the poet William Wordsworth viewed as a leading exponent of the value of wilderness, but he is also seen by some commentators as having promoted the idea of the Lake District becoming a National Park (see McCormick 1992; Phillips and Mighall 2000; Hall 2002). Connections between wilderness and National Parks is also evident in more recent discourses and representations, clearly present, for example, in Phoebe Smith's (2015d) book, *Wilderness Weekends: Wild Adventures in Britain's Rugged Corners*, which highlights diverse rural places of wilderness within many of the UK National Parks (see also, for example, Wilderness Foundation UK, which aims to protect wilderness areas alongside addressing the requirements of human communities).

Perceptions and materialities of wilderness may both have an influence on wider gentrification processes in England and Wales. First, the lack of built settlement forms and the prominence of open spaces (of wilderness) may directly appeal in a functional way to those gentrifiers seeking residence in a location that has no / few neighbours, and hence offers solitude, isolation and escape from the conditions of metropolitan and provincial societies. Living close to wilderness may also appeal for a series of cross-cutting functional and perceptual reasons. For instance, residence may be sought in relatively close proximity to wilderness spaces to allow close access for leisure and recreational activities (e.g. rambling, climbing, cycling, hunting, photography, birdwatching). In the North American context, these practices are often termed 'amenity migration' (see Gosnell and Abrams 2011), although in the UK context, much less attention has been devoted to the significance of such environmental amenities to gentrification, despite such outdoor practices and pursuits being prominent across the UK.

At the same time, and as outlined in the opening quote of this chapter, leading actors in the real estate market and associated industries are increasingly promoting the recreational and residential values of wilderness in specific rural locations. These campaigns have the potential to maintain and exacerbate social change in rural places through permanent and temporary residence in rural places that have the social and cultural meanings of wilderness. This is typified by the rise of second home ownership in many National Park areas or other protected areas; an emotive issue which is not just a contemporary phenomenon (Shucksmith 2000). Gallent et al. (2003) and Gallent (2014), for instance, has shed light on how rural places are transformed through second home ownership in ways that have many parallels to processes of rural gentrification, including displacement, social class change, and transformations in local housing markets and services. Indeed, it is surprising that most scholarship on second home ownership has not more fully engaged with debates around rural gentrification (and vice versa), and, likewise, with studies of counterurbansiation which have examined wilderness (e.g. Halfacree 2009). Perhaps the topic of wilderness provides a useful nexus for the coalescence of often-discrete strands of research relating to rural places and the social and cultural meanings of wilderness.

22.4   IDENTIFYING AREAS OF WILDERNESS FOR STUDIES OF RURAL GENTRIFICATION IN THE UK

Despite the lack of discussion of wilderness within UK studies of rural gentrification, other studies of rural change in areas of wilderness such as research on the effects of planning and housing on local communities within National Park areas, have exposed findings that are often the mainstay of gentrification scholarship. These include the unfolding of exclusionary housing markets and a lack of affordable housing, as well as cultural transformations tied to the in-migration of higher income social groups. An exemplar here is the early work of Shucksmith (1980: 418) on the Lake District, which revealed that: 'Policies designed to serve the national interest can work to the disadvantage of local people and rural communities'. Similarly, in a study of the ecological value of the Lake District, Richard (2010) forged new understandings of the exclusionary effects of the appropriation of the Lake District for residential and recreational purposes by middle class in-migrants. Both of these studies illustrate the potential value of greater engagement by rural gentrification scholars with the wild(er) spaces of the UK. One key factor accounting for this lack of engagement may be the lack of a clear indicator of wilderness that is readily available and which would allow researchers to differentiate areas of wilderness from other types of rural space in the UK. It is, however, possible to make use of some existing spatial classifications, alongside data on commuting flows, to work towards such a classification.

The Rural and Urban Classification (RUC) is an official governmental classification of England and Wales Official Statistics used to distinguish rural and urban areas (see Bibby 2013). It differentiates urban from rural space, and presents an assessment of different intensities of rurality using the categories of Rural Town and Fringe; Rural Town and Fringe in a Sparse Setting; Rural Village in a Sparse Setting; Rural Hamlet and Isolated Dwellings; and Rural Hamlet and Isolated Dwellings in a Sparse Setting. As Figure 22.1

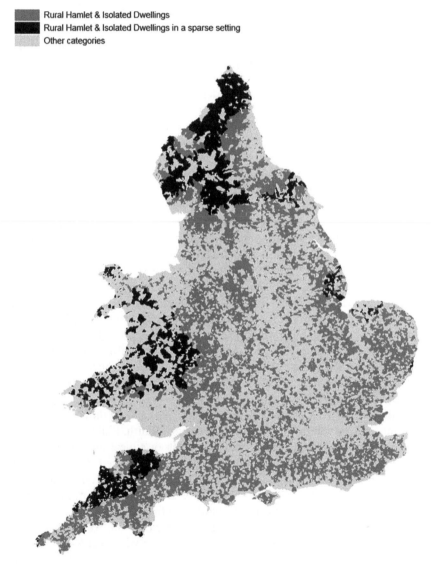

*Figure 22.1   Area-level Rural-Urban Classification (RUC) (2011) showing most remote
            rural areas*

shows, the latter category (Black) is mostly concentrated in Northumberland, the Lake District and the Yorkshire Dales, parts of the North York Moors, Lincolnshire, parts of West Norfolk, Mid Wales and Herefordshire/Shropshire, Pembrokeshire, the Brecon Beacons, and Exmoor/North Cornwall. These are clearly very different landscapes, ranging from the mountainous parts of the Lake District to the low-lying salt marshes of West Norfolk, and each potentially has different effects on expressions of rural gentrification. At the same time, some of the Rural Hamlet and Isolated Dwellings in a Sparse Setting areas will include environs that are not readily associated with the social and cultural meanings of wilderness, such as the productive agricultural landscapes of Shropshire. Moreover, using the 'rural sparse setting' categories of the RUC 2011 does not provide an effective representation of wilderness.

Instead, to provide a more indicative mapping of wilderness in England and Wales, we take our cue from Amin and Thrift's (2002) assertion that the vast majority of the UK is now urbanised, with most parts of the countryside interwoven into larger urban systems of commuting and the inter-dependence of city-regions (cr. Lees et al's, 2016 arguments). Following this logic, it is plausible that rural places with sparse populations and with the lowest incidence of (out)commuting into nearby larger urban centres are most likely to be subjectively perceived as being more detached, remote and isolated, and thus may signify a proxy measure of relative wilderness (see below). It also means that local residents in these remote rural locations are more likely to work within the locality, or from home in the locality of residence, and be less (physically) interdependent with urban places.

To identify such areas of very remote rural, we extracted data from the Labour Force Survey of total individual outward commuting flows (2011) from place of residence to workplace at Local Authority District (LAD) level. We then identified LADs (as defined by the Rural-Urban Classification 2011) that had relatively low levels of commuting to 147 'urban poles' (LADs with the highest number of commuters originating from a different LAD) in England and Wales. The result is shown in Figure 22.2, which indicates the distribution of these 'very remote rural' LADs (Black), characterised by less than 10% of total economically active population (based on 2011 UK census data) commuting to an urban pole and low population densities. Areas within Cornwall and Northumberland are excluded from our analysis due to the official amalgamation of smaller area units in 2009 (shown with hatched shading in Figure 22.2). This is a limitation of our analysis that is not possible to fix using the 2011 data.

Within remote rural LADs, we were able to spatially analyse different levels of rural gentrification, using a typology of rural gentrification (Smith, Phillips and Kinton 2017) based on the proportion of individuals with high levels of education credentials (a degree or above qualification), as a percentage of the total population aged 16–74, extracted from the 2011 UK Census. We focused on the 17,666 Outputs Areas (OAs) termed 'village' or 'hamlet and isolated dwellings' by the RUC 2011, excluding major/minor urban conurbation and town and fringe OAs classed as 'urban' from the analysis.

To represent the different geographies of rural gentrification, we use here an educational indicator, namely the percentage of the population with degree-level or above as our key indicator of rural gentrification. It is acknowledged that there are longstanding debates about the most effective way to identify and/or quantify gentrification processes and gentrified places, which have been explored using a gamut of demographic, social,

Urban Pole
Linked Rural (>40%)
Semi-Linked Rural (30%-39%)
Remote Rural (10%-29%)
Very Remote Rural (<10%)

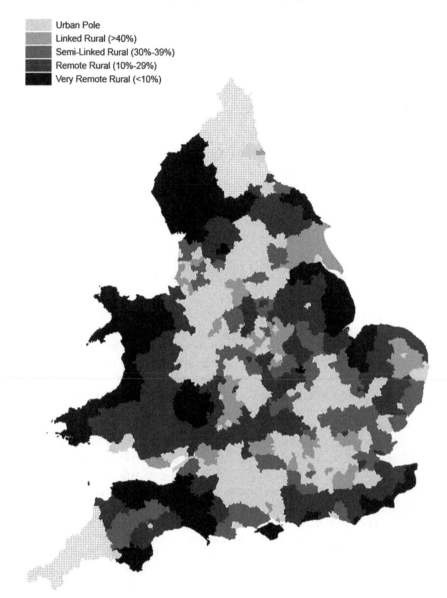

*Figure 22.2   Remote rural areas based on levels of out-commuting flows and relative
population density (2011)*

economic, cultural and environmental measures (e.g. Ley 1986, 1988). Our purpose in this
chapter is to create an indicative measure that seeks to capture gentrification as a process
that is reflective of high levels of education-spawned cultural capital and appropriate 'cultural competence' (Cloke et al., 1998). Further analysis of this indicative measure showed
very high correlation coefficients between education and social class/occupational status
for (non)gentrified OAs (see also Phillips 2011). We recognise that this is not the only or

best measure of gentrification, but rather should be viewed as, at best, only providing an 'indicative signifier' of the presence of probable gentrifier populations.

After calculating the rural mean of the usual resident population educated to degree-level or above (32.32%), OAs above the mean can then be divided at the 1st (44.58% and above), 3rd (40.64–44.57%), 5th (37.50–40.63%), 7th (34.84–37.49%), and 9th (32.32–34.83%) deciles based on this indicator. OAs below the mean are termed 'Other', signifying little or no gentrification (i.e. less than 32.32% of the population was highly qualified).

This method evenly distributes OAs in England and Wales across the gentrification categories. To distinguish between different intensities of probable gentrifier populations, we use a cheese-strength based metaphor. OAs are referred to as: vintage (1,782), extra mature (1,782), mature (1,782), medium (1,782), mild (1,782) and other (8,757), to represent the strength of gentrification at this low geographical resolution.

22.5   MAPPING RURAL GENTRIFICATION IN AREAS OF WILDERNESS IN ENGLAND AND WALES

During the past three decades, Phillips (1993, 2004, 2015) has consistently urged for more empirical studies of rural gentrification, noting that the focus on the rural has not kept pace with urban counterparts in gentrification scholarship. This may be one of the main reasons why there is a lack of attention to the relations between rural gentrification and wilderness in the UK, although as previously mentioned there have also been claims that the concept of wilderness has little relevance to the UK, which has at best only a handful of spaces where the term might be viewed as being applicable. An exemplar here is the European Wilderness Continuum Map produced by Carver et al. (2002) using remote sensing of land-use cover. This mapping identifies a handful of wild areas in Scotland, the Lake District and North Pennines in England, and Snowdonia in Wales (see also Carver and Fritz 2013). If we were to use this mapping of wild areas it would exclude many of the locations where we have already identified that wilderness appears to be of some significance in processes of gentrification, including the remote moor tops around Hebden Bridge. For these reasons, we feel that a definition of wilderness that creates a wider 'spatial lens' (Smith 2000b, p. 390) for studying wilderness gentrification is needed.

Accordingly, Figure 22.3a identifies 11 key areas of wilderness in England and Wales, using our indices of relatively low population density and low levels of commuting out of the area for employment.

It can be seen that, using this measure, the largest swathes of wilderness are found on the western side of England and Wales in: the English Lake District/Solway Coast and parts of the Yorkshire Dales/North Pennines; North and Mid/West Wales and Pembrokeshire; the Shropshire Hills; Exmoor/Quantock Hills and Dorset AONB; South Devon AONB (South of Dartmoor). Interestingly, Figure 22.3a also reveals relatively large areas of wilderness on the Eastern side (North York Moors; Lincolnshire Wolds; West Norfolk), and, to a lesser extent, in South-East England (Thanet, East Kent); Dungeness and parts of the Kent Downs; parts of the South Downs; and parts of the Isle of Wight.

It is notable that Hebden Bridge is not captured as an area of wilderness in Figure 22.3a.

Figure 22.3a   Areas of wilderness in England and Wales (2011)

This is a result of the spatial resolution of our analysis at the LAD level, with the wilderness of Hebden Bridge masked by the adjacent built-up areas of the Calder Valley LAD (in which Hebden Bridge is located). This suggests that our mapping of wilderness may not include some relatively smaller patches of wilderness that are obfuscated by analyses at the LAD level.

To specifically focus in on wilderness and rurality, Figure 22.3b maps rural OAs within the areas of wilderness as identified in Figure 22.3a. In other words, urban and urban-fringe OAs have been excluded. For instance, in the Lake District area, the urban settlements of Carlisle, Workington, Whitehaven, Barrow-in-Furness, Kendall, and Keswick are omitted from the areas of wilderness shown in Figure 22.3b.

Figure 22.4 shows the National Parks in England and Wales, to compare with Figure 22.3b. This reflects our earlier comments that, in the UK, wilderness is closely tied to the distribution of National Parks. It is important to note that the National Parks of the Brecon Beacons, Dartmoor, New Forest, South Downs, Peak District, the Broads, and Northumberland lie outside of the area of wilderness as identified by our measure. It is probable that this is a result of the relatively high levels of commuting from these rural places into nearby urban centres such as Cardiff/Swansea, Plymouth, Southampton/ Bournemouth, Brighton and Hove, Manchester/Sheffield, and Newcastle, respectively. This means that these areas have not been identified as wilderness using our methodology based on levels of commuting and population density. Of course, in these rural areas (not defined as wilderness), National Park status may act to convey social and cultural meanings of wilderness.

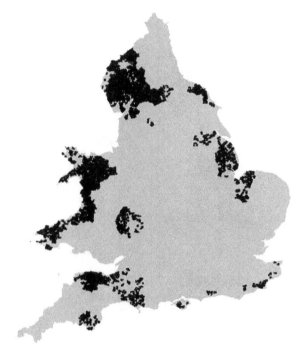

Figure 22.3b   Areas of wilderness by rural output areas in England and Wales (2011)

Figure 22.4   Designated National Park areas in England and Wales

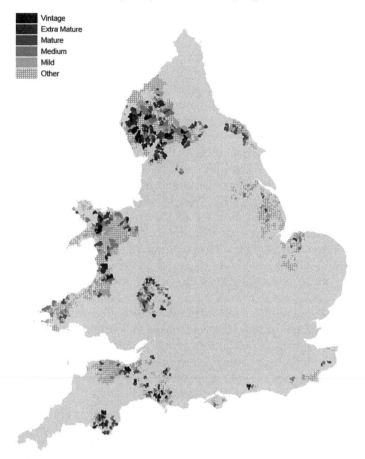

Figure 22.5   Rural gentrification in wilderness areas using cheese typology

It is also significant to note the presence of rural areas identified as wilderness, but which lie beyond the boundaries of a designated National Park. These include: northern parts of Cumbria near the Solway Coast AONB, West Wales (Bae Ceredigion), the Lincolnshire Wolds AONB, West Norfolk/The Wash National Nature Reserve, Shropshire Hills AONB, Dorset AONB and South Devon AONB, Isle of Wight AONB, Thanet (East Kent), Dungeness National Nature Reserve, and part of Kent Downs AONB. The majority of these rural areas are, however, 'protected' and 'managed' by designations such as Nature Reserves and AONBs, suggesting that these locations may have qualities associated with ideas of unspoilt landscape beauty and nature.

Figure 22.5 shows the distribution of rural gentrification within wilderness areas, using the cheese typology described in the previous section.

It is noteworthy that there are large swathes of non-gentrification (hatched shading) in the wilderness areas of the Lake District, Wales, Exmoor, North York Moors, Lincolnshire, West Norfolk and Dungeness. In part, this could be tied to the ways in which housing markets are highly regulated and managed within National Parks, AONBs and other protected designations (see Barker and Stockdale 2008). In essence, the apparent absence of rural gentrification in these wilderness areas could be a result of the lack of housing and/or zero-tolerance towards new developments or conversions of agricultural buildings. Equally, other influential factors here may include the continued presence of agricultural/forestry/fishing or other industrial workforces in some rural locations, or even perhaps the presence of gentrifier social groups that do not have high levels of education credentials. Phillips' (2010a) previous mapping of the petite-bourgoisie may be pertinent in these locations, and warrants further attention.

It is, however, also striking to acknowledge the relatively high concentration of vintage (Black) and extra mature (Darkest grey) gentrified rural OAs both within and beyond the designated National Parks, with the former often being concentrated towards the edges of the Parks. Areas such as the West Lake District, along the Menai Straits of North Wales, east of Aberystwyth, south of Dartmoor, within the Dorset AONB and in the Quantock Hills all appear to have significant concentrations of gentrifers, and are noteworthy given that they are all areas on the edges of designated National Parks, or away from National Park areas. In the areas bordering National Parks, it is clearly possible that the wilderness within the National Park areas may be influencing the rural gentrification processes in these areas. Here parallels might be made with the studies of Ghose (2004) and Hines (2012) discussed in the context of gentrification within locations close to areas of officially designated wilderness. This raises the question: is the rural gentrification of some rural places in close proximity to National Parks an unintentional consequence of National Park status? Further analysis is required to more fully address this, and associated questions about the possible effects of more relaxed planning controls outside of National Parks, which might, for instance, allow for the delivery of higher levels of new-build housing, and thus relatively lower housing costs, than are present within National Parks. This may allow more people to access these areas, when compared to the relatively higher cost areas of National Parks, and also increase pressure on marginal agriculture, which might also be impacted by fewer opportunities for farm diversification in areas beyond National Parks, and the relative higher number of second homes than within National Parks.

22.6   RURAL GENTRIFICATION IN CUMBRIA AND THE YORKSHIRE DALES

To illustrate the diverse geographies of wilderness gentrification in a rural context, we briefly focus on Cumbria (including the English Lake District) and, to a lesser degree, the Yorkshire Dales. Despite numerous media and historical discourses describing the gentrification of the Lake District, there is, surprisingly, limited academic study of gentrification in this location (although see Shucksmith 1980, 1981, 1991; Richard 2010). Nonetheless, other studies of the Lake District describe social, cultural and economic changes that point to gentrification processes (e.g. Paris 2009; Scott 2010). Indeed, the Lake District National Park Authority (2017) claim that there are serious issues of housing affordability and displacement of local people from the park, with a current house price to income ratio of 12:1. This is compounded by the long history of the production and consumption of second homes in the National Park (see, for example, Clark 1982).

Figure 22.6   Cumbria/Yorkshire Dales and rural gentrification using the cheese typology

Richard (2010) notes in his study of social change that large areas of the Lake District have been shaped by processes of rural gentrification, leading to the displacement of settled local residents.

Figure 22.6 shows the rural OAs of the Lake District and the cheese typology for 2011 Census data, and bears out the key findings of Richard (2010). It is evident that processes of rural gentrification are engrained throughout Cumbria and the Yorkshire Dales. In brief, five main clusters of rural gentrification can be identified in Figure 22.6; three of which would appear to be closely connected to the geographic location of lakes in the area (cf. Halseth 1998; Darling 2005, in North American contexts). First, there is a concentration of vintage and extra mature gentrified OAs in the South Lakes area close to Windermere and Coniston Water; in villages such as Torver, Grizedale, Hawkshead and Troutbeck. To the east, there is a concentration of vintage and extra mature gentrified

OAs close to Ennerdale Water, Crummock Water, Buttermere and Loweswater. To the north, gentrified rural OAs are dominated by mature and medium categories around Thirlmere, Ullswater and Haweswater. Towards the Yorkshire Dales and running in a south-north belt to the east of the M6 motorway and Kendal, there is a concentration of mature gentrified OAs, with some vintage OAs. Further east into the Yorkshire Dales, there is a combination of gentrified OAs in villages such as Kirby Lonsdale, Sedbergh, and Dent, perhaps fuelled by the presence of prestigious and high performing public schools (Smith and Higley 2013). Overall, it can be seen that patterns of rural gentrification in Cumbria and the Yorkshire Dales are highly uneven, a finding that finds echoes in work in other rural locations. Phillips (2005) in Norfolk and Phillips et al. (2008) in Leicestershire both, for example, highlight the presence of very localised differences in the level, and dynamics, of rural gentrification. In areas of the Lake District and Yorkshire Dales it is possible that mountainous areas or areas of moorland may mean that human habitation and the building of dwellings is not possible or economically feasible, or indeed they may be closed areas of private land-ownership and, in this sense, these spaces are not open to processes of rural gentrification. They may, however, be at the heart of rural gentrification processes in nearby gentrified areas, even perhaps forming a recreational asset along the lines identified by Darling, even though the Lake District and the Yorkshire Dales are far from spaces devoid of residential space.

22.7　CONCLUSION

Our main aim in this chapter has been to explore the links between rural gentrification and wilderness. We have reviewed existing studies of rural and wilderness gentrification, identifying how even in areas such as the Rocky Mountain West in North America where there has been a concentration of studies of rural gentrification in or close to areas of officially designated wilderness, the presence and significance of wilderness has often been neglected. An exception to this has been the work of Darling (2005) who has explicitly argued that wilderness provides the basis for its own strand of gentrification based on recreational as opposed to residential capital. Following on from this discussion of existing literatures on rural gentrification and wilderness, we have sought to explore its relevance to UK studies. We have highlighted how, conceptually, gentrification and wilderness may be seen as antithetical concepts, the former being associated with areas of humanly constructed built environments that act as housing for people, whilst the latter are viewed as spaces that show little or no trace of people and their buildings. But in the UK it is possible to see some interesting, if unacknowledged, connections between gentrification and wilderness. In addition to highlighting the recognition of 'wilderness' in studies of rural gentrification in, for example, Hebden Bridge (Smith and Phillips 2001; Smith 2002b), more historical connections might also be forged. Richard (2010), for example, notes how Wordsworth, renowned for espousing the virtues of a wilderness experience in his Romantic poetry, and also as discussed, identified with the emergence of a National Park movement in the UK, also made some references to social changes that could be interpreted as being many of the hallmarks of gentrification. In his *Guides to the Lakes* (Wordsworth [1810] 2004, p. 66), for instance, he wrote about the Lake District falling 'into the possession of Gentry', as a result of the arrival of 'wealthy purchasers, who . . . erect new mansions out of the ruins of the ancient cottages'.

The focus of this chapter has been more contemporary. Using a proxy measure of wilderness, and recognising the difficulties of mapping areas of wilderness, we have shown, using information derived from the 2011 Census and Labour Force Survey, that there are uneven and diverse geographies of gentrification in the wilderness areas of England and Wales. Our analysis has allowed a consideration of the outcomes of rural gentrification, although we have not explored in any depth the processes and dynamics of rural gentrification that mediate these patterns. We can speculate, however, that in some wilderness areas, inhospitable environments and a relative lack of housing supply, due to regulated and constrained housing delivery in protected rural areas, may mean that resident populations are relatively low. Suffice to say, there is not an extensive pre-existing housing stock to be gentrified, and/or in situ or potentially latent populations to displace. It is also possible that constraining structural conditions do not enable or spark new build developments or conversion of agricultural buildings to residential dwellings, such as some rigid planning regimes within National Park areas. In contrast, it appears that some adjacent areas in close proximity to protected areas of wilderness may be more fully influenced by processes of rural gentrification.

Of course, the issue of second homes will have a major bearing on processes of rural gentrification and, as outlined in the previous section, links between rural gentrification and second homes warrant urgent further attention. Likewise, more research is required to explore symbolic and experiential constructions of wilderness and how these cross-cut with the residential and migrational decision-making processes of gentrifiers. What may be perceived as wilderness (and rural) by one gentrifier may not be perceived as wilderness (or rural) by another gentrifier, even in the same place at the same time. Equally, there may be important local and regional differentials of wilderness influencing processes of rural (and indeed urban) gentrification, which may be shaped in important ways by influential media and institutional discourses, such as estate agents and developers, and through word-of-mouth in local lay discourses. We have sought in this chapter to provide a first manoeuvre to shed light on the geographies of wilderness gentrification in England and Wales, and draw more attention to the importance of other geographies of rural gentrification. Our discussion serves to demonstrate that wilderness gentrification warrants a fuller analysis by scholars of gentrification, and other fields of study such as counterurbanisation and second home ownership.

A useful springboard here may be to provide comparative discussions between studies of rural gentrification in wilderness areas of North America and the UK. For example, geographies of rural gentrification are likely to differ between North America and the UK due to the longer distances between large metropolitan systems and remote rural settlements in North America, when compared to the UK. Likewise, it may be valuable to transpose theoretical and conceptual ideas from North American scholarship to UK studies of rural gentrification in wilderness areas, and vice versa. For example, Darling (2005, p. 1030) notes that an important commonality between urban and wilderness gentrification is the 'fundamental assumption that capitalism operates the same regardless of what sort of landscape it is working upon'. Of course, there are likely to be dramatic differences between social and cultural representations of wilderness in North America and the UK, and the ways in which spaces of perceived wilderness are managed, regulated and controlled via policies and legislation. The transposition of Darling's findings, and the work of others scholars such as Hines (2012) and Nelson (2011), to the UK context should therefore be treated with some caution, but equally provide an exciting launch pad for more research on wilderness gentrification, such as questions about how wilderness is itself socially produced through processes of rural gentrification (and vice versa), and how some areas become concentrations of settlement and gentrification within a wider wilderness (such as Bowness-on-Windermere in the Lake District). What this engagement will demand is a fuller consideration of the salience of the term 'wilderness gentrification', or perhaps deeper acknowledgement of the wider gamut of geographies of rural gentrification. As Woods (2013) has highlighted, geographies of rurality encompass a fuller diversity of forms and landscapes than is often recognised, and many have not permeated very much into current discussions of rural gentrification.

This direction of travel for studies of rural and wilderness gentrification could also usefully weave in a fuller engagement with amenity migration scholarship from North America (e.g. Cadieux and Hurley 2011), to more fully understand the motives and outcomes of moving to a rural area for its perceived and/or physical wilderness. This is important given similar migration trends and processes are apparent in the UK (Brown et al. 2015), and may point to deeper structural forces fuelling and extending processes of rural gentrification. This is also timely with more households seeking to connect with nature and wilderness on a daily basis, as part of the quest to acquire greener, more sustainable lifestyles and living arrangements (Kondo et al. 2012).

REFERENCES

Abrams, J. and Gosnell, H. (2012) 'The politics of marginality in Wallowa County, Oregon: contesting the production of landscapes of consumption', *Journal of Rural Studies*, 28(1), 30–37.

Abrams, J., Bliss, J. and Gosnell, H. (2013) 'Reflexive gentrification of working lands in the American West: contesting the "middle landscape"', *Journal of Rural and Community Development*, 8(3), 144–158.

Amin, A. and Thrift, N. (2002) *Cities: Reimagining the Urban*, Bristol: Polity Press.

Barker, A. and Stockdale, A. (2008) 'Out of the wilderness? Achieving sustainable development within Scottish national parks', *Journal of Environmental Management*, 88(1), 181–193.

Bell, M. (1994) *Childerley: Nature and Morality in a Country Village*, Chicago: Chicago University Press.

Bibby, P. (2013) *Urban and Rural Area Definitions for Policy Purposes in England and Wales: Methodology (v1.0)*, London: Government Statistical Service.

Bridge, G. and Dowling, R. (2001) 'Microgeographies of retailing and gentrification', *Australian Geographer*, 32(1), 93–107.

Briquel, V. and Collieard, J. (2005) 'Diversity in the rural hinterlands of European cities', in Hoggart, K. (ed) *The City's Hinterland: Dynamism and Divergences in Europe's Peri-urban Territories*, Aldershot: Ashgate, pp. 19–40.

Brown, B. (1995) *In Timber Country: Working People's Stories of Environmental Conflict and Urban Flight*, Philadelphia: Temple University Press.

Brown, D., Champion, T., Coombes, M. and Wymer, C. (2015) 'The migration-commuting nexus in rural England, a longitudinal analysis', *Journal of Rural Studies*, 41, 118–128.

Bryson, J. (2013) 'The nature of gentrification', *Geography Compass*, 7(8), 578–587.

Cadieux, K. and Hurley, P. (2011) 'Amenity migration, exurbia, and emerging rural landscapes: global natural amenity as place and as process', *GeoJournal*, 76(4), 297–302.

Carver, S. and Fritz, S. (2013) 'Introduction', in Carver, S. and Fritz, S. (eds) *Mapping Wilderness: Concepts, Techniques and Applications*, London: Springer, pp. 1–16.

Carver, S., Evans, A. and Fritz, S. (2002) 'Wilderness attribute mapping in the United Kingdom', *International Journal of Wilderness*, 8(1), 24–29.

Cavailhés, J., Peeters, D., Sékeris, E., Thisse, J-F., Goffette-Nagot, F. and Schmitt, B. (2004) 'The periurban city: why to live between the suburbs and the countryside', *Regional Science and Urban Economics*, 34(6), 681–703.

Charmes, E. and Keil, R. (2015) 'The politics of post-suburban densification in Canada and France', *International Journal of Urban and Regional Research*, 39(3), 581–602.

Clark, E., Johnson, K., Lundholm, E. and Malmberg, G. (2007) 'Island gentrification and space wars', in Baldacchino, G. (ed) *A World of Islands: An Island Studies Reader*, Charlottetown: Institute of Island Studies, University of Prince Edward Island, pp. 483–512.

Clark, G. (1982) 'Housing policy in the Lake District', *Transactions of the Institute of British Geographers*, 1(1), 59–70.

Cloke, P. and Perkins, H. (2002) 'Commodification and adventure in New Zealand tourism', *Current Issues in Tourism*, 5(6), 521–549.

Cloke, P., Goodwin, M. and Milbourne, P. (1998) 'Inside looking out; outside looking in. Different experiences of cultural competence in rural lifestyles', in Boyle, P. and Halfacree, K. (eds) *Migration into Rural Areas. Theories and Issues*, Chichester: John Wiley & Sons, pp. 135–150.

Cognard, F. (2006) 'Le rôle des recompositions sociodémographiques dans les nouvelles dynamiques rurales: l'exemple du Diois', *Méditerranée: Revue géographique des pays méditerranéen*, 5–12.

Cowen, R. (2016) 'How to escape to the wild (and forget about modern life completely)', 19 July. Available: http://www.telegraph.co.uk/men/the-filter/how-to-escape-to-the-wild-and-forget-about-modern-life-completel/.

Cronon, W. (1991) *Nature's Metropolis*, New York: W.W. Norton.

Cronon, W. (1995) 'The trouble with wilderness; or, getting back to the wrong nature', in Cronon, W. (ed) *Uncommon Ground: Toward Reinventing Nature*, New York: W.W. Norton, pp. 69–90.

Daniels, S. (1993) *Fields of Vision: Landscape Imagery and National Identity in England and the United States*, Cambridge: Polity Press.

Darling, E. (2005) 'The city in the country: wilderness gentrification and the rent gap', *Environment and Planning A*, 37(6), 1015–1032.

Davidson, M. and Lees, L. (2005) 'New-build "gentrification" and London's riverside renaissance', *Environment and Planning A,* 37(7), 1165–1190.

Demeritt, D. (2002) 'What is the "social construction of nature"? A typology and sympathetic critique', *Progress in Human Geography*, 26(6), 767–790.

Denevan, W. (1992) 'The pristine myth: the landscape of the Americas in 1492', *Annals of the Association of American Geographers*, 82(3), 369–385.

Duncan, J. and Duncan, N. (2004) *Landscapes of Privilege: The Politics of the Aesthetic in an American Suburb*, London: Routledge.

Friedberger, M. (1996) 'Rural gentrification and livestock raising: Texas as a test case, 1940–95', *Rural History*, 7, 53–68.

Freeman, C. and Cheyne, C. (2008) 'Coasts for sale: gentrification in New Zealand', *Planning Theory and Practice*, 9(1), 33–56.

Gallent, N. (2014) 'The social value of second homes in rural communities', *Housing, Theory and Society*, 31(2), 174–191.

Gallent, N., Mace, A. and Tewdwr-Jones, M. (2003) 'Dispelling a myth? Second homes in rural Wales', *Area*, 35(3), 271–284.

Gandy, M. (2002) *Concrete and Clay: Reworking Nature in New York City*, Cambridge, MA: MIT Press.

Ghose, R. (2004) 'Big sky or big sprawl? Rural gentrification and the changing cultural landscape of Missoula, Montana', *Urban Geography*, 25(6), 528–549.

Ginn, F. and Demeritt, D. (2008) 'Nature: a contested concept', in Clifford, N., Holloway, S., Rice, S. and Valentine, G. (eds) *Key Concepts in Geography*, London: SAGE, pp. 300–311.

Gosnell, H. and Abrams, J. (2011) 'Amenity migration: diverse conceptualizations of drivers, socioeconomic dimensions, and emerging challenges', *GeoJournal*, 76(4), 303–322.

Gosnell, H. and Travis, W. (2005) 'Ranchland ownership dynamics in the Rocky Mountain West', *Rangeland Ecology Management,* 58(2), 191–198.

Gosnell, H., Haggerty, J. and Byorth, P. (2007) 'Ranch ownership change and new approaches to water resource management in southwestern Montana: implications for fisheries', *Journal of the American Water Resources Association,* 43(4), 990–1003.

Gosnell, H., Haggerty, J. and Travis, W. (2006) 'Ranchland ownership change in the Greater Yellowstone Ecosystem, 1990–2001: implications for conservation', *Society and Natural Resources,* 19(8), 743–758.

Halfacree, K. (2009) '"Glow worms show the path we have to tread": the counterurbanisation of Vashti Bunyan', *Social & Cultural Geography*, 10(7), 771–789.

Hall, C. (2002) 'The changing cultural geography of the frontier: National Parks and wilderness as frontier remnant', in Krakover, S. and Gradus, Y. (eds) *Tourism in Frontier Areas*, Lanham, Maryland: Lexington Books, pp. 283–298.

Hall, C. and Page, S. (2014) *The Geography of Tourism and Recreation: Environment, Place and Space*, London: Routledge.

Halseth, G. (1988) *Cottage Country in Transition: A Social Geography of Change and Contention in the Rural-Recreational Countryside*, Montreal: McGill-Queen's University Press.

Harner, J. and Benz, B. (2013) 'The growth of ranchettes in La Plata County, Colorado, 1988–2008', *Professional Geographer*, 65(2), 329–344.

Hinchliffe, S., Kearnes, M., Degen, M. and Whatmore, S. (2005) 'Urban wild things: a cosmopolitical experiment', *Environment and Planning D: Society and Space*, 23(5), 643–658.

Hines, J. (2007) 'The persistent frontier and the rural gentrification of the Rocky Mountain West', *Journal of the West*, 46(1), 63.

Hines, J. (2010a) 'Rural gentrification as permanent tourism: the creation of the "New" West Archipelago as postindustrial cultural space', *Environment and Planning D: Society and Space*, 28(3), 509–525.

Hines, J. (2010b) 'In pursuit of experience: the postindustrial gentrification of the rural American West', *Ethnography*, 11(2), 285–308.

Hines, J. (2012) 'The post-industrial regime of production/consumption and the rural gentrification of the New West Archipelago', *Antipode*, 44(1), 74–97.

Hubbard, P. (2017) *The Battle for the High Street*, London: Palgrave Macmillan UK.

Hudalah, D., Winarso, H. and Woltjer, J. (2015) 'Gentrifying the peri-urban: land use conflicts and institutional dynamics at the frontier of an Indonesian metropolis', *Urban Studies*, 53(3), 593–608.

Jackson, R. (2005) 'Bruny on the brink: governance, gentrification and tourism on an Australian island', *Island Studies Journal*, 1(2), 201–222.

Janoschka, M., Sequera, J. and Salinas, L. (2014) 'Gentrification in Spain and Latin America – a critical dialogue', *International Journal of Urban and Regional Research*, 38(4), 1234–1265.

Johnson, B. and Shifferd, J. (2016) 'Who lives where: a comprehensive population taxonomy of cities, suburbs, exurbs, and rural areas in the United States', *The Geographical Bulletin*, 57(1), 25–40.

Jones, C. and Ley, D. (2016) 'Transit-oriented development and gentrification along Metro Vancouver's low-income SkyTrain corridor', *Canadian Geographer*, 60(1), 9–22.

Kondo, M., Rivera, R. and Rullman, S. (2012) 'Protecting the idyll but not the environment: second homes, amenity migration and rural exclusion in Washington State', *Landscape and Urban Planning*, 106(2), 174–182.

Lake District National Park Authority (2017) Second Homes. Available at: http://www.lakedistrict.gov.uk/caringfor/policies/secondhomes-2.

Le Jeannic, T. (1996) 'Une nouvelle approche territoriale de la ville', *Économie et Statistique*, 294/295, 25–46.

Lees, L. (1998) 'Urban renaissance and the street: spaces of control and contestation', in Fyfe, N. (ed) *Images of the Street: Planning, Identity and Control in Public Space*, London: Routledge, pp. 231–247.

Lees, L. (2012) 'The geography of gentrification', *Progress in Human Geography*, 36(2), 144–171.

Lees, L. (2016) 'Gentrification, race, and ethnicity: towards a global research agenda?', *City & Community*, 15(3), 208–214.

Lees, L., Shin, H. and López-Morales, E. (eds) (2015) *Global Gentrifications: Uneven Development and Displacement*, Bristol: Policy Press.

Lees, L., Shin, H. and López-Morales, E. (2016) *Planetary Gentrification*, Cambridge: Polity Press.

Lees, L., Slater, T. and Wyly, E. (2008) *Gentrification*, London: Routledge.

Ley, D. (1986) 'Alternative explanations for inner city gentrification', *Annals of the Association of American Geographers*, 76(4), 521–535.

Ley, D. (1988) 'Social upgrading in six Canadian inner cities', *Canadian Geographer*, 32(1), 31–45.

Ley, D. (1996) *The New Middle Classes and the Remaking of the Central City*, Oxford: Oxford University Press.

Lister-Kaye, J. (2010) 'Why we need our wilderness', *The Telegraph*, 31 January. Available: http://www.telegraph.co.uk/personal-view/7112946/Why-we-need-our-wilderness.html.

Llewellyn, S. (2017) 'Why a weekend in Hay-on-Wye should be on your bucket list', *The Telegraph*, 4 April. Available at: http://www.telegraph.co.uk/travel/destinations/europe/united-kingdom/articles/hayfestival-how-to-get-tickets-advice-guide/.

MacEwen, A. and MacEwen, M. (1998) *Greenprints for the Countryside: The Story of Britain's National Parks*, London: Unwin Hyman.

MacNaghten, P. and Urry, J. (1998) *Contested Natures*, London: SAGE.

Mamonova, N. and Sutherland, L.-A. (2015) 'Rural gentrification in Russia: renegotiating identity, alternative food production and social tensions in the countryside', *Journal of Rural Studies*, 42, 154–165.

McCormick, J. (1992) *The Global Environmental Movement*, Chichester: John Wiley & Sons.

McGhie, C. (2015) 'How to live like a hermit in Britain's most remote homes', *The Telegraph*, 10 July. Available: http://www.telegraph.co.uk/finance/property/11731563/How-to-live-like-a-hermit-in-Britains-most-remote-homes.html.

Mills, C. (1988) 'Life on the upslope: the postmodern landscape of gentrification', *Environment and Planning D: Society and Space*, 6(2), 169–189.

Monbiot, G. (2017) 'The Lake District as a world heritage site? What a disaster that would be', *The Guardian*, 9 May. Available at: https://www.theguardian.com/commentisfree/2017/may/09/lake-district-world-heritage-site-george-monbiot.

Murdoch, J. (2003) 'Co-constructing the countryside: hybrid networks and the extensive self', in Cloke, P. (ed) *Country Visions*, London: Pearson Education, pp. 263–282.

Murdoch, J. and Pratt, A. (1993) 'Rural studies: modernism, postmodernism and the "post-rural"', *Journal of Rural Studies*, 9(4), 411–427.

Nash, R. ([1968] 2014) *Wilderness and the American Mind*, Yale: Yale University Press.

Nash, R. (1970) 'The American invention of National Parks', *American Quarterly*, 22(3), 726–735.

Nelson, L. and Nelson, P. (2010) 'The global rural: gentrification and linked migration in the rural USA', *Progress in Human Geography*, 35(4), 441–459.

Nelson, P. (2011) 'Commentary: special issue of GeoJournal on amenity migration, exurbia, and emerging rural landscapes', *GeoJournal*, 76(4), 445–446.

Nelson, P., Nelson, L. and Trautman, L. (2014) 'Linked migration and labor market flexibility in the rural amenity destinations in the United States', *Journal of Rural Studies*, 36, 121–136.

Nelson, P., Oberg, A. and Nelson, L. (2010) 'Rural gentrification and linked migration in the United States', *Journal of Rural Studies*, 26(4), 343–352.

Niedt, C. (2006) 'Gentrification and the grassroots: population support in the revanchist suburb', *Journal of Urban Affairs*, 28(2), 99–120.

Olafsdottir, R. and Runnström, M. (2011) 'How wild is Iceland? Wilderness quality with respect to nature-based tourism', *Tourism Geographies*, 13(2), 280–298.

Paquette, S. and Domon, G. (2001) 'Trends in rural landscape development and sociodemographic recomposition in southern Quebec (Canada)', *Landscape and Urban Planning*, 55(4), 215–238.

Paris, C. (2009) 'Re-positioning second homes within housing studies: household investment, gentrification, multiple residence, mobility and hyper-consumption', *Housing, Theory and Society*, 26(4), 292–310.

Pearson, H. (2005) 'Wilderness UK', *The Guardian*, 8 January. Available at: https://www.theguardian.com/travel/2005/jan/08/unitedkingdom.guardiansaturdaytraelsection1.

Perrenoud, M. (2008) 'Les artisans de la "gentrification rurale": trois manières d'être maçon dans les Hautes-Corbières', *Sociétés Contemporaine*, 71, 95–115.

Phillips, M. (1993) 'Rural gentrification and the processes of class colonisation', *Journal of Rural Studies*, 9, 123–140.

Phillips, M. (1998) 'Rural change: social perspectives', in Ilbery, B. (ed) *The Geography of Rural Change*, Harlow: Longman, pp. 31–54.

Phillips, M. (2002) 'The production, symbolisation and socialisation of gentrification', *Transactions of the Institute of British Geographers*, 27(3), 282–308.

Phillips, M. (2004) 'Other geographies of gentrification', *Progress in Human Geography*, 28(1), 5–30.

Phillips, M. (2005) 'Differential productions of rural gentrification', *Geoforum*, 36(4), 477–494.

Phillips, M. (2007) 'Changing class complexions in and on the British countryside', *Journal of Rural Studies*, 23, 283–304.

Phillips, M. (2010a) 'Counterurbanisation and rural gentrification', *Population, Space and Place*, 16(6), 539–558.

Phillips, M. (2010b) 'Rural gentrification and the built environment: exploring the connections', in Columbus, F. (ed) *Built Environment: Design, Management and Applications*, Hauppauge, New York: Nova Publishers, pp. 33–62.

Phillips, M. (2011) 'Material, cultural, moral and emotional inscriptions of class and gender', in Pini, B. and Leach, B. (eds) *Reshaping Gender and Class in Rural Spaces*, Aldershot: Ashgate, pp. 23–52.

Phillips, M. (2014) 'Baroque rurality in an English village', *Journal of Rural Studies*, 33, 56–70.

Phillips, M. (2015) 'Assets and affect in the study of social capital in rural communities', *Sociologia Ruralis*, 56(2), 220–247.

Phillips, M. and Mighall, T. (2000) *Society and Nature through Exploitation*, London: Harlow.

Phillips, M. and Smith, D. (2018a) 'Comparative approaches to gentrification: lessons from the rural', *Dialogues in Human Geography*, forthcoming.

Phillips, M. and Smith, D. (2018b) 'Comparative ruralism and opening new windows on gentrification studies', *Dialogues in Human Geography*, forthcoming.

Phillips, M., Fish, R. and Agg, J. (2001) 'Putting together ruralities', *Journal of Rural Studies*, 17, 1–27.

Phillips, M., Page, S. and Saratsi, E. (2008) 'Diversity, scale and green landscapes in the gentrification process', *Applied Geography*, 28(1), 54–76.

Qian, J., He, S. and Liu, L. (2013) 'Aestheticisation, rent-seeking, and rural gentrification amidst China's rapid urbanisation: the case of Xiaozhou village, Guangzhou', *Journal of Rural Studies*, 32, 331–345.

Richard, F. (2010) 'La gentrification des "espaces naturels" en Angleterre: après le front écologique, l'occupation?. L'exemple du Lake District et de ses environs, *L'Espace Politique*', *Revue en ligne de géographie politique et de géopolitique*, (9).

Richard, F., Dellier, J. and Tommasi, G. (2014) 'Migration, environment and rural gentrification in the Limousin mountains', *Revue de Géographie Alpine*, 102–3, 1–15.
Saarinen, J. (2016) 'Wilderness use, conservation and tourism: what do we protect and for and from whom?', *Tourism Geographies*, 18(1), 1–8.
Sandberg, L. and Wekerle, G. (2010) 'Reaping nature's dividends: the neoliberalization and gentrification of nature on the Oak Ridges moraine', *Journal of Environmental Policy and Planning*, 12(1), 41–57.
Schama, S. (1995) *Landscape and Memory*, London: Harper Collins.
Scott, A. (2010) 'The cultural economy of landscape and prospects for peripheral development in the twenty-first century: the case of the English Lake District', *European Planning Studies*, 18(10), 1567–1589.
Shucksmith, M. (1980) 'Local interests in a National Park', *Town and Country Planning*, 49(11), 418–421.
Shucksmith, M. (1981) *No Homes for Locals?*, Farnborough: Gower Press.
Shucksmith, M. (1991) 'Still no homes for locals? Affordable housing and planning controls in rural areas', in Champion, T. and Watkins, C. (eds) *People in the Countryside: Studies of Social Change in Rural Britain*, London: Paul Chapman.
Shucksmith, M. (2000) 'Endogenous development, social capital and social inclusion: perspectives from LEADER in the UK', *Sociologia Ruralis*, 40(2), 208–218.
Slater, T. (2004) 'North American gentrification? Revanchist and emancipatory perspectives explored', *Environment and Planning A*, 36(7), 1191–1213.
Smith, D. (1998) 'The "green" potential of West Yorkshire', *Regional Review*, 14(1), 6–7.
Smith, D. (2002a) 'Extending the temporal and spatial limits of gentrification: a research agenda for population geographers', *Population, Space and Place*, 8(6), 385–394.
Smith, D. (2002b) 'Rural gatekeepers and "greentried" Pennine rurality', *Journal of Social and Cultural Geography*, 3(4), 447–463.
Smith, D. (2007) 'The "buoyancy" of "other" geographies of gentrification', *Tijdschrift voor Economische en Sociale Geografie*, 98(1), 53–67.
Smith, D. (2013) 'What is rural gentrification?', *Planning Theory and Practice*, 12, 593–605.
Smith, D. and Higley, R. (2012) 'Circuits of education, rural gentrification, and family migration from the global city', *Journal of Rural Studies*, 28(1), 49–55.
Smith, D. and Holt, L. (2005) 'Lesbian migrants in the gentrified valley: other "geographies" of gentrification', *Journal of Rural Studies*, 21, 313–322.
Smith, D. and Phillips, D. (2001) 'Socio-cultural representations of greentrified Pennine rurality', *Journal of Rural Studies*, 17, 457–469.
Smith, D., Phillips, M. and Kinton, C. (2017) 'Geographies of rural gentrification: a relational social class approach', paper presented to the Annual Conference of Association of American Geographers, Boston, USA, 7 April.
Smith, N. (1996) *The New Urban Frontier*, London: Routledge.
Smith, P. (2015a) 'UK wilderness adventures: a walk on high in the Black Mountains, south Wales', *The Guardian*, 25 March. Available at: https://www.theguardian.com/travel/2015/mar/26/walking-camping-brecon-beacons-black-mountains-wales.
Smith, P. (2015b) 'UK wilderness adventures: discover a vanished world on Dartmoor', *The Guardian*, 2 April. Available at: https://www.theguardian.com/travel/2015/apr/02/walking-wild-camping-trips-dartmoor-devon.
Smith, P. (2015c) 'UK wilderness adventures: sleep in a cave in the Lake District', *The Guardian*, 21 March. Available at: https://www.theguardian.com/travel/2015/mar/21/sleep-in-cave-dove-crag-lake-district.
Smith, P. (2015d) *Wilderness Weekends: Wild Adventures in Britain's Rugged Corners (Bradt's Travel Guides)*, Chalfont St. Peters: Bradt Travel Guides.
Solana-Solana, M. (2010) 'Rural gentrification in Catalonia, Spain: a case study of migration, social change and conflicts in the Empordanet area', *Geoforum*, 41(3), 508–517.
Squire, S.J. (1998) *Cultural Discourses of Destinations, Gender and Tourism History in the Canadian Rockies. Destinations: Cultural Landscapes of Tourism*, Abingdon: Routledge.
Stockdale, A. (2010) 'The diverse geographies of rural gentrification in Scotland', *Journal of Rural Studies*, 26(1), 31–40.
Sutherland, L. (2012) 'Return of the gentleman farmer? Conceptualising gentrification in UK agriculture', *Journal of Rural Studies*, 28(4), 568–576.
Thomas, A., Lowe, B., Fulkerson, G. and Smith, P. (2011) *Critical Rural Theory: Structure, Space, Culture*, Lanham, Maryland: Lexington Books.
Tolia-Kelly, D. (2007) 'Fear in paradise: the affective registers of the English Lake District landscape re-visited', *The Senses and Society*, 2(3), 329–351.
Travis, W. (2007) *New Geographies of the American West*, Washington, D.C.: Island Press.
Walker, P. and Fortmann, L. (2003) 'Whose landscape? A political ecology of the "exurban" Sierra', *Cultural Geographies*, 10(4), 469–491.
Whatmore, S. and Hinchliffe, S. (2003) 'Living cities: making space for urban nature', *Soundings*, 22, 137–150.

Wilderness Act (1964) Public Law No. 88-577, Stat. 78.

Williams, A. (2007) *Therapeutic Landscapes*, London: John Wiley & Sons.

Woods, M. (2013) 'The elite countryside: shifting rural geographies of the transnational super-rich', in Hay, I. (ed) *The Geographies of the Super-Rich*, Cheltenham: Edward Elgar, pp. 123–136.

Wordsworth, W. ([1810] 2004) *Guide to the Lakes*, London: Francis Lincoln.

Wright, S. (1992) 'Rural community development: what sort of social change?', *Journal of Rural Studies*, 8(1), 15–28.

Zukin, S., Trujillo, V., Frase, P., Jackson, D., Recuber, T. and Walker, A. (2009) 'New retail capital and neighbourhood change: boutiques and gentrification in New York City', *City and Community*, 8(1), 47–64.

PART 5

LIVING AND RESISTING GENTRIFICATION

23. Resisting gentrification
Sandra Annunziata and Clara Rivas-Alonso

23.1 INTRODUCTION

Currently processes of urban destitution are gripping the vast majority of cities across the world. We believe that understanding the responses to these attacks on the most vulnerable holds the key to unlocking present and future struggles. This chapter challenges the conceptualization of resistance in gentrification theory and seeks to foster debate about the analytical framework for studying resistance to gentrification. We begin by discussing what resistance is and what we mean by resistance in the field of gentrification studies. We argue that we need to go beyond the current state of affairs in the literature given the acuteness of gentrification at the present time – a time characterized by economic breakdown and political upheaval, a global financial crisis, austerity measures, and a crisis of democracy.

Rather than assuming a given definition of what it means to resist gentrification, we seek to open up the notion of resistance to gentrification asking: which specific set of practices can be catalogued under the label of 'gentrification resistance' today? Under which circumstances does it overtly and covertly unfold? What if the 'appeal' and visibility of resistance is not that useful after all and invisibility is the best strategy to resist gentrification pressures? Moreover, could resistance to displacement be a reactionary concept? In other words, are we referring to the creation of alternatives or simply to oppositional, defensive practices?

International comparisons of gentrification have framed some of the regularities as the 'state-led class restructuring of urban space' (Lees et al. 2015: 443). However, can we also talk about global regularities and tactics in the way urban populations, both organized or individually, resist? As post-colonial conceptualizations challenge Anglo-Saxon hegemony in knowledge production, new geographies of gentrification contribute to the understanding of the global regularities of class restructuring processes intertwined with unresolved colonial histories and racial fault lines. As Mbembé and Nuttall point out, the question needs to be posed whilst complicating 'the center of gravity of traditional forms of analysis' (2004: 351). Thus we argue here that looking at different forms of resistances explicitly self-defined as anti-gentrification or implicitly addressing this issue (anti-speculation, anti-system, anti-privatization) can strengthen our collective repertoire and social imaginaries regarding the potential and limits of what we know (and do) to counter processes of gentrification. But in doing so we open up the tricky question of what counts (and what does not) as resistance to gentrification.

We start from the assumption that resistance to gentrification is a set of complex practices that should be pluralized and problematized in relation to its scope, its agents and its intentionality. We attempt to foster much-needed conversations across scales, going from the micro to the macro (and everything in between). Furthermore, we do so by focusing on both strengths and weaknesses, in order to understand the limits and potential of resistance to the acute and generalized phase of gentrification and its global dimension, acknowledging the fact that gentrification processes might have long taken place in other places under different labels (see Maloutas 2012; Janoschka and Sequera 2016).

In the following section we will frame the way resistance to gentrification and displacement is conceptualized in the gentrification literature, underlining what is missing and what has been less explored. In the first section, which draws on classical studies and political economy approaches, we will frame resistance as the right to stay put and as a conscious opposition to the structural forces that result in the current regimes of expulsion. We then go on to offer a classification of resistance practices, followed by an attempt to enrich the conceptualization of resistance: we problematize the way resistance has been conceptualized in gentrification studies drawing on post-structuralist theories, relational approaches, and other disciplines that have addressed its complexity.

Exploring the heterogeneity of practices that seek to counter displacement (in its direct, indirect, symbolic and exclusionary forms) has allowed us to argue that politically conscious, overtly oppositional, intentional and visible practices of resistance are not the only way to counteract gentrification-induced displacement. While interesting regularities and convergences among different practices of resistance are on the horizon, we argue that the field of resistances is also characterized by non-politicized, covert, unintentional, informal, and deliberately invisible practices of everyday life that draw on different perceptions of time and survival, the negotiation of ambiguity and mobilization of invisibility. We argue that the visibility of resistance and counter collective knowledge production, central in anti-gentrification practices, might not be that useful after all in spaces where informality, ambiguity and invisibility have become some of the best strategies through which to resist the assault of displacement.

23.2   THEORIZING RESISTANCE IN GENTRIFICATION STUDIES

Resistance is a recurrent theme in gentrification studies. Most critical gentrification scholars agree that after having explored processes of gentrification, their geographies, causes and effects, it is high time that we shift our attention to resistance (Lees et al. 2008). However, exploration of those strategies and tactics that seek to counter the violence of gentrification remains very limited. As Lees and Ferreri (2016) point out, through their direct involvement in resistance to state-led gentrification practices in London, '(r)esistance to gentrification still deserves renewed attention in gentrification studies and beyond' (p. 3).

Knowledge of gentrification resistance, however, benefits from going beyond the field of gentrification studies. Acknowledging that resistance can encompass everything from revolution to hairstyle, Hollander and Einwohner (2004) argue that practices of resistance have in common a system (or a target) they seek to oppose and they imply action (or a set of actions). More specifically in gentrification studies the most commonly defined practice of resistance is the Right to Stay Put. It is described by Hartman (1984) as a long life right of tenure for tenants. It has become a political slogan and a resistance practice; it implies recognition of the forces that produce displacement (e.g. Marcuse 1985a; Janoschka 2016);

forces induced by gentrification and for the production of gentrification.[1] It involves an action of opposition to the mode of urban development that generates displacement of the most vulnerable. In gentrification studies resistance has a very specific, social scientific, meaning: it is the practices of individuals and groups who attempt to stay put in the face of exclusionary, neoliberalizing forces. In this respect we can say that resistance to gentrification 'seeks to occupy, deploy and create alternative spatialities from those defined through oppression and exploitation' (Pile, in Rose 2002: 3). However, this is, we argue, a rather 'minimal definition' (ibid) of resistance as a 'common sense' reaction to the regimes of expulsion taking place both in the so-called global South and North.[2]

Under the current regimes of expulsion, practices that counter gentrification are also identity-based and have much more micro, less visible dimensions. As much as resistance to gentrification can be collective, politically organized and visible, it can also be highly heterogeneous, somehow contradictory and incoherent, reflecting the intimate conflicting feelings of individuals, deliberately invisible, unconscious and practised in solitude. We have to learn how to explore the different forms that resistance to gentrification takes, as well as the cultural politics of agency (Rankin 2009), and to navigate outside of what we see and can decipher as an anti-gentrification resistance if we are to enrich the notion. As Rankin (ibid) argues in regards to planning theory, gentrification theory can be informed by Scott's (1985) observation of the 'hidden transcripts' and the 'infra-politics' in reference to the everyday practices of resistance mobilized by peasants in South Asian rural areas. They are described as 'weapons of the weak', in the sense that they constitute the root of a collective social mobilization. In her reconceptualization of resistance, Hynes (2013) refers to Collins and Munro (2010: 550), and calls for a 'micro politics of everyday life' to suggest an exploration of resistance in between macro-political analyses of visible, collective struggles against structures of power (e.g. urban social movements and squatting practices) and micro-sociological analyses, which take seriously the smaller-scale dynamics of power and resistance as they affect individuals in the context of everyday life. In this sense we must consider that resistance to gentrification is intrinsically related to scale, and the possibility of jumping scales: from the body, to the home, to the neighbourhood up to the national and global (Smith 1992).

Assessments of valuable and practical alternatives that go beyond resistance as an oppositional (contradictory and paradoxical) practice have been, to date, a marginal part of gentrification studies. In fact, even if we use a 'strategic' concept with 'political' value (Lees et al. 2016), such as gentrification-induced displacement, we argue that we still lack understanding of resistance in gentrifying contexts, besides institutional measures or housing cooperatives (ibid: 221–224), radical policy incrementalism (see Gallaher's 2016 interpretation of condo conversion and right to buy as a practice of staying put in Washington DC) and the building of local strategic alliances (as in the Traditional Retail Markets Networks discussed in Dawson and Gonzales 2016). Alongside the now classic work of Chester Hartman (1984), anti-gentrification studies and progressive policies have

---

[1] This concept is borrowed from the idea of displacement by and for development explored by Penz et al. (2011). On the need to strengthen the nexus between development studies and gentrification studies see Lees et al. (2016).

[2] We say so-called as we follow Comaroff and Comaroff's (2012) remark (quoted in Roy 2016: 207) of the South being a 'relation, not a thing in and of itself'.

been developed in the Anglo-American context such as: Peter Marcuse's (1985b: 922) 'floating zone': 'a set of policies and procedures capable to reverse the negative effect of gentrification: provision and maintenance of decent, secure and affordable housing in stable and non-discriminatory neighbourhoods for all city residents'; the anti-growth machine movement and the preservation of a single occupancy hotel in the Tenderloin, San Francisco (Robinson 1995); and the battle for Tompkins Square Park in New York City (Smith 1996). These are cases that remain key reference points in the gentrification literature but they do not help us much when faced with a new, acute and predatory phase of capitalist accumulation in cities around the globe. As Lees and Ferreri (2016) argue, such classic US-centric studies must not remain dominant in a properly cosmopolitan gentrification studies.

A more multidisciplinary approach to resistance can be found in urban social movement theory. In fact, for urban social movement theorists, practices of resistance at the urban scale are often in relation to gentrification processes. According to Mayer (2013) anti-gentrification struggles are part of the fragmented, variegated, and deeply impacted by the neoliberal order, field of urban social movements, and stand against the commodi-fication of urban space, 'scandalizing' the new regime of accumulation. Activists today deal with a diverse set of practices: squatting, social centres and autonomous spaces, citizen organizations claiming the urban commons or spontaneous movements with a poetic perception of social reality (Petropoulou 2014) that can be grouped under the umbrella of 'the right to the city' (Mayer 2009, 2013). They encompass different 'forms of alliances across towns and across issues, between housing activists and artists, leftist groups and cultural workers, small business owners and the new precarious groups – as all of them feel threatened by contemporary forms of development entailing gentrification, mega projects, and displacement' (Mayer and Boudreau 2011: 281). They are overtly oppositional and clearly visible. Making the invisible and the unspoken dimension of injustice visible is one of the core issues of urban social movements that deliberately use anti-gentrification (and anti-systemic) discourses. In fact, visibility makes a collective claim easily recognizable and recognition is a fundamental component of resistance (Hollander and Einwohner 2004).

Besides these academic debates, we should also acknowledge that the most effective (and interesting) work on resistance to gentrification is not academic. It comes from activist-scholars who position themselves halfway between community engagement and academic reflection (Routledge and Derickson 2015). This body of work assumes the form of handbooks, blogs, passionate writing, documentaries/movies and artist-activist works. These types of material are accessible, easy to read, reduce complexity and clearly offer possible solutions. They are written for and with communities, and imply the participation of those directly affected by gentrification. The first handbook of this type was *Displacement, How to Fight It?* by Hartman et al. (1982). They argued that 'each variation of the basic profiteering assault on housing requires different sort of responses from anti-displacement groups' (1982: 28) and they provided a whole set of place-specific, cause-related and community-based ways to fight displacement. More recently, new anti-gentrification handbooks have been produced in relation to the distinctiveness of displacement in context. Among them the struggle against a new gentrification, that of council estates, as seen in *Staying Put: An Anti-Gentrification Handbook for Council Estates in London* (2014), the result of a collaboration between the London Tenants

Federation, gentrification scholar-activist Loretta Lees, Just Space and Southwark Notes Archive Group. In Spain, a passionate biographical account of the struggle against eviction for mortgage arrears *Vida Hipotecada* [Mortgaged Lives] written by Colau and Alemany (2012) as a result of the work of the *Plataforma de los Afectados por la Hipoteca* (PAH), can also be seen as an anti-displacement manifesto.

23.3   A CLASSIFICATION OF ANTI-GENTRIFICATION PRACTICES

While acknowledging that anti-gentrification practices must be contextualized, we also think that the existing anti-gentrification literature allows us to establish a set of regularities. We have classified the literature in Table 23.1 into the following categories: prevention, institution-based measures: e.g. fostering public housing policies, tenants protection, and alternative planning tools to prevent and mitigate displacement; mitigation and legal bricolage: e.g. delay, negotiation, compensation practices, anti-eviction, re-housing, buyout practices that can only postpone the problem or move it somewhere else; building alternatives: e.g. community planning, squats, occupations, protests and urban commons; counter narratives, building awareness and strategic mobilization of (collective) identities: e.g. collective constructions of sense of belonging and alternative narratives mobilized against mainstream discourses. We discuss each group referring to the literature listed in the table. Although we have tried to be as comprehensive as possible the table will no doubt have gaps, it is however a fair reflection of the kinds of resistances to gentrification happening around the world.

23.3.1   Prevention

A lot of the measures that prevent gentrification-induced displacement are directly dependent on land and housing regimes, namely public housing policies, tenants' protection and rent regulation. Publicly subsidized housing plays a crucial role in the prevention of gentrification. It is described as a 'barrier to gentrification' (Ley and Dobson 2008) and a fundamental part of spatial justice based on rights that have spatial implications (Brenner et al. 2011). The role played by housing policies as a barrier to gentrification was explored by Newman and Wyly (2006), who asked what the tipping point was in terms of low-income residents staying in a gentrifying neighbourhood. The decline of tenants' protection under neoliberal regimes is due to the erosion of low income housing stock as a collective asset (via demolition or privatization) and the weakening of regulations that protect tenants (such as the abolition of rent control, the introduction of express eviction measures and property-oriented taxation regimes). The critique of the demolition and privatization of public housing is the premise and the core of any anti-displacement discourse applicable also to the clearing of informal housing (Ascensao 2015; İslam and Sakızlıoğlu 2015). However, the success in banning privatization depends on the strength of solidarities among tenants. Their desire to become property owners or achieve acceptable compensation can become a divisive force.

Rent regulation, a fundamental anti-gentrification measure, is under threat or has been completely abandoned under certain neoliberal-oriented regimes. After decades of

Table 23.1   A classification of practices used to resist gentrification

Focus	Prevention, institution-based measures	Mitigation and legal bricolage: delay, negotiation, compensation	Building alternatives: community organization, community planning, squats, occupations, protests and urban commons	Enhancing visibility, counter narratives, building awareness and strategic mobilization of (collective) identities
Eviction *Housing privatization* *Building conversion* *Demolition*	*Publicly subsidized housing as a 'barrier to gentrification':* Vancouver: Ley and Dobson (2008); Buenos Aires: Rodriguez and Di Virgilio (2016) *Tenants protections, rent control and regulations:* New York: Newman and Wyly (2006); USA: Hartman (1984); Berlin: Holm, Grell and Bernt (eds) (2013), Connolly (2016) *Urban renewal without evictions:* Lima, Perù: Betancur (2014); Belgium: Uitermark and Loopmans (2013)	*Zoning regulations* (encouragement and discouragement zones): New York: Marcuse (1985) *Anti-eviction practices:* Spain: Colau and Alemany (2012); Rome, Athens, Madrid: Annunziata and Lees (2016); Rome: Mudu (2015), De Feliciantonio (2016) *Displacement Free Zones:* Park Slope, New York City: Lees et al. (2008: 250–255); USA: Kolodney (1991); Puerto Rico, Morales-Cruz (2012)	*Community organization, grassroots movements and alternative planning:* USA: Hartman, Keating and LeGates (1982), DeFilippis (2004); London Tenants Federation et al. (2014); Istanbul: Erman and Coşkun-Yıldar (2007); Caracas, Venezuela: Velásquez-Atehortúa (2014); Sweden: Rätt att bo kvar (n.d.)	

				Counter narratives of mainstream urban governance
	Building conversion regulations: Barcelona: Assemblea de Barris per un Turisme Sostenible (ABTS) (2016); Berlin: Holm, Brendt, Britta (2014) *Anti-privatization struggles*: London, Berlin, Amsterdam: Holm (2007); Berlin: Mayer (2013) *Single occupancy hotels*: San Francisco: Robinson (1995) *Street vendors' resistance*: Mexico City, Mexico: Betancur (2014), Crossa (2013)	*Resistance via legal action and legal struggle*: Puerto Rico: Morales-Cruz (2012); London: Lees and Ferreri (2016); Lima, Perù: Betancur (2014) *Resistance by tenants and tactics of negotiation*: Rome: Herzfeld (2009) *Court cases against master plans*: Santiago, Chile, in Lees, Shin and López-Morales (2016) *Compensation, in the case of condo conversion*: Washington DC: Gallaher (2015)	*Anti-gentrification protests*: Tompkins Square Park in New York City (see Smith 1996); Gezi Park, Istanbul: Gül and Cünük (2014); Accra, Ghana: Gillespie (2016) *Political housing squats*: European cities: Martinez and Cattaneo (2016); Europe: Squatting Collective (2015); Rome: Mudu (2015); Berlin: Holm and Kuhn (2011); New York: Maeckelbergh (2012); Amsterdam: Prujit (2013), Uitermark (2004) *Critical resilience and the reproduction of the commons*: London, Los Angeles, Sydney: DeVerteuil (2016); Athens: Stavrides (2016) *Informal occupation and land squatting*: Santiago: Casgrain and Janoschka (2013); South Africa: Cabannes, Yafai, and Johnson (2010); Lisbon: Ascensao (2015); India: Slum Dwellers International, McFarlane (2010)	*Blogs and media activism*: Berlin: GentrificationBlog; UK: Slater (2014) *Arts*: Mexico City: Crossa (2013); Lisbon: LefthandRotation; Berlin, Hamburg: Novy and Colomb (2013) '*visioning workshop' and alternative design competitions*: London, UK: Lees and Ferreri (2016); Barcelona: Portelli (2015)
Historical centre preservation *Urban renewal/ regeneration plans* *Retail changes* *Slum improvement*	*Community land trusts*: New York: Hartman, Keating and LeGates (1982); London: London Tenants Federation, Lees, Just Space and SNAG (2014) *Vacancy control, confiscation/acquisition of abandoned property*: New York: Hartman, Keating and LeGates (1982)	*Grassroots movements' legal controls over urban renewal policy*: San Francisco: Hartman (1974), Robinson (1995) *Environmental legal struggle*: Pearsall (2014)		

Table 23.1   (continued)

Focus	Prevention, institution-based measures	Mitigation and legal bricolage: delay, negotiation, compensation	Building alternatives: community planning, squats, occupations, protests and urban commons	Enhancing visibility, counter narratives, building awareness and strategic mobilization of (collective) identities
Environmental planning	*Anti-speculation ordinance:* San Francisco: Hartman (1974) *Land value extraction policies:* Puerto Rico: Lees, Shin and López-Morales (2016) *Retail resistance:* Mexico City: Lefthandrotation (2015), *Defend Traditional Retail Markets Networks*, London: Dawson and Gonzales (2016)		*Armed conflict:* Turkey (this chapter); South America: Janoschka and Sequera (2016)	*Antievictionmappingprojecj.or – Poetry:* Mexico and Greece: Petropoulou (2014) *Alternative culture and social centre:* Hamburg: Noeger (2012) *Mutual support for threatened groups (evicted, minorities, street vendors, specific guilds):* Spain: Colau and Alemany (2012), Crossa (2013) *Informal networks of support:* Jakarta, Dakar: Simone (2009) *Invisible forms of resistance (collective and individual):* South East Asia: Scott (1985); Egypt, Iran: Bayat (2000); Israel/Palestine: Yiftachel (2009)
Criminalization of informality and squatting				
Militarization of urban spaces				
Symbolic changes				
Otherization of minority groups				

housing deregulation, rent control, which brought housing law reforms, has been subject to revisionism (Arnott 1995). The first generation of rent control, the 'nominal rent freeze system' (ibid) has been substituted in some cases by a new, more flexible second generation of rent control described as 'highly beneficial' for tenants' protection (Lind 2001). This type of rent cap can be seen in cases such as Berlin, where low income tenants were protected in areas targeted by cautious urban renewal programmes and upgrading (Holm et al. 2013). The regulation of condo conversions into luxury apartments can also prevent gentrification to a great extent. For instance, the Berlin North-Neukölln Tenants' Alliance achieved the enforcement of a pre-existing anti-speculative measure, *milieuschutz* (social environmental protection), to ban the luxury conversion of historical and former low-income apartments in the area (Connolly 2016). Similar requests come from organizations advocating for the de-growth of tourism and regulation of building conversions for temporary and touristic uses (such as *Assemblea Barris Turisme Sostenible* [Assembly of Districts for Sustainable Tourism], n.d., in Barcelona).

In the case of redevelopment, rehabilitation and land use transformation, alternative community planning has proven effective for neighbourhood stability. The self-hab program proposed in New York City in the 1980s is still relevant for the new housing crisis. This practice sought the recovery and self-renovation of abandoned property, given to tenants' cooperatives by the city after a process of confiscation.[3] This type of practice has been linked to vacancy control guaranteed by a juridical system that implies that abandoned or empty property can be taken over by the city and converted into social housing. However, vacancy control is not implemented in all situations. For this reason, critical planning practices attempt to foster community engagement and participation as a strategy to mitigate top-down planning decisions before it negatively impacts residents (Taylor and Edwards 2016; Novy and Colomb 2013; Uitermark and Loopmans 2013). This type of work challenges the responsibility and reflexivity of planning professionals in the face of an urbanism that is reproducing injustice. Even if highly heterogeneous (see a comparison of anti-privatization movements in Europe by Holm 2007), critical planning practices advocate for alternative forms of urban development. They are oriented towards a long-term goal such as radical egalitarian access to the city as well as a more short-term set of claims such as the preservation of urban heritage of the built environment (Mayer 2013), banning renewal projects and asking for a more cautious type of intervention (see Holm and Kuhn 2011) or stopping eviction (see the case of Kotti and Co, in Berlin, in Mayer 2013). As for North America and London, practices of community organizing can inform the most appropriate forms of solidarity, collective ownership when desired (see DeFilippis 2004), as well as sustainable economy and alternative city plans.[4]

23.3.2 Delaying, Compensation and Re-housing

When preventative measures are not in place (the norm nowadays) resistance practices can easily take the form of compensation, re-housing and delaying strategies. One

---

[3] A similar scheme was introduced in Italy as a result of the claims of the housing squatting movement and became regulated by a regional law for Self-Rehab (*autorecupero*) in 1998.
[4] See for example 'Towards a community-led plan for London: policy directions and proposals' (2013), which was a proposal for the next London Plan by Just Space in London.

delaying strategy is the request for an eviction free zone (EFZ). This tool was described by Kolodney (1991: 513) as a 'legal bricolage in an era of political limited expectation'. An EFZ can be place-based, applied directly onto an entire neighbourhood, or people-based, helping vulnerable residents. It must be accompanied by a whole set of legal services, where lawyers work together with community groups on tenants' rights to delay or stop evictions. The core of an anti-eviction zone is a 'vigorous (and participated by the community) legal defence against eviction' (ibid: 518). EFZs have never properly existed; however, moratoria on anti-eviction practices were extensively implemented city-wide for vulnerable groups in Rome until the advent of the crisis which represented a real turning point for anti-eviction practices (Annunziata and Lees 2016). When the attempt to stop or delay eviction fails and eviction becomes unavoidable, resistance practices call for one-to-one replacement (from the previous home to a new home, for everyone). The re-housing process must consider a possible relocation near the previous home, to allow continuity in everyday life (such as school for children and other facilities regularly used by residents). This is for instance one of the core claims of the anti-eviction manifesto of the European Coalition for the Right to Housing (see https://housingnotprofit.org/en) and the claim of the housing movements in Rome: '*Ogni sfratto sarà una barricata*' [each eviction will be a barricade] (Mudu, in Martínez and Cattaneo 2016).

Recently Gallaher (2016) drawing on the case of Washington DC argued that the tenants' right to buy in cases of condo conversion and related forms of compensation can be seen as a way to enable residents to stay put. Explaining how challenging and contradictory the practices can be, she argues that compensation may result in a new opportunity in the life of indebted tenants. Drawing from Roy (2009), Karaman (2014: 290) has further complicated the picture by problematizing resistance in the context of a '"politics of compensation" that is simultaneously, and paradoxically, communitarian and market-centered'. However, considering the severity of displacement, the literature also considers compensation or buying someone out a very divisive practice which limits solidarity and undermines the possibility of staying put for the most fragile residents.

23.3.3 Critical-counter Narratives, Awareness Campaigns, Collective Identities

When the production of gentrification implies spatial, semantic and social cleansing to accommodate new uses and meanings (the subtlest and most pervasive form of displacement) resistance is very challenging. Exclusionary and symbolic displacement (see Blomley 2004; Janoschka 2016) permeates everyday life and calls for a different type of conceptualization and related forms of resistance. Here the production of critical counter-narratives and awareness campaigns which aim to delegitimize planning practices and rent extraction are crucial. Collective knowledge production has taken the form of open platforms, blogs, websites, public lectures, art and media work, all done with the specific goal of framing counter narratives, and/or a critical and ironic understanding of gentrification. A variety of methods have been used such as the artist interventions of the collective Left Hand Rotation (n.d): *Gentrificación no es un Nombre de Señora, Museo de los Desplazados, Ficción Inmobiliaria*, the Creative Charlois Control; the Swedish version of LTF et al's (2014) The Right to Stay Put, *Rätt att bo kvar* (n.d.), in council estates which used reggae to spread its message; Italian hip hop in the case of the lake struggle in Rome, *'IL LAGO CHE COMBATTE'* – *Assalti frontali & Il Muro del Canto* (2014);

Turkish hip hop denouncing Roma cleansing through so-called urban renewal (*Sulukuleli Roman Rap Grubu Tahribad-ı İsyan – TOKİ KAFALAR*, 2015); Berlin anti-tourist actions, 'Berlin Doesn't Love You', that seeks to build awareness of the pervasive multiple forms of gentrification happening in Berlin. A critical political economy approach regarding urban transformation in Berlin is at the core of the detailed Berlin Gentrification Blog (n.d.) edited by Andrej Holm, as well as systematic, prompt and full responses to the mainstream, acritical interpretation of housing unaffordability in the media.[5]

Another practice that builds awareness about the effects of gentrification is critical mapping and data analysis. The Anti-Eviction Mapping Project (n.d.) in the San Francisco Bay Area makes visible the nexus between urban displacement and more contemporary (self)entrepreneurial, touristic and high-tech related urban development. The eviction maps in Madrid (*Madrid Desahuciado* 2015) by VIC in collaboration with the *Plataforma de los Afectados por la Hipoteca* (PAH) show the effects of the debt-induced housing crisis in Madrid.

These works have in common an attempt to challenge consolidated social imaginaries and define a counter narrative to the hegemonic idea of urban living. Irony, creativity and rhetoric are used to counter the mainstream discourses and legitimacy surrounding the kind of urban development that implies financial burden and displacement for local residents. These practices of resistance, have however, been documented as internally contradictory, at risk of being hijacked by new forms of economic development such as 'the creative city' (Mayer 2013) or falling into the trap of the 'commodification of the culture of resistance' as documented by Noeger (2012: 157) in the case of anti-gentrification practices in Hamburg, which became incorporated into the processes of gentrification they originally meant to defend against.

Methods of urban mobilization and resistance draw, in some situations, on the strategic mobilization of (collective) identity and cultural practices. For example, in the case of *Ripensar Bon Pastor*, a collective in Barcelona who developed an engaged anthropology and considered the character and culture of the neighbourhood as an important tool for resistance. In this particular case, as can happen in other neighbourhoods with a strong historical (and political) identity, collective memory was mobilized in order to construct belonging in the present, thus rooting their lives and strengthening ties to their neighbourhood under threat (Portelli 2015). In other contexts, the strategic mobilization of collective identities includes the militarization of neighbourhoods (Janoschka and Sequera 2016), or the work of neighbourhood associations that organize struggles (or alliances) with gentrifying forces (e.g. Erman and Coşkun-Yıldar 2007). Practices of mobilization of identity that are not necessarily deemed overtly antagonist can easily escape epistemological exercises that attempt to recognize them as resistance. However, these could pave the way for further conceptualizations of innovative ways of escaping the physically and symbolically destructive character of gentrification.

---

[5] Among them see Tom Slater's (2014) response to the *Guardian* newspaper.

23.3.4   Organized and Informal Squatting

Squatting is considered the quintessential practice of staying put (Martínez and Cattaneo 2016). Social movement theorists have contributed extensively towards exploring the varieties and heterogeneity of squatting practices (Uitermark 2004; Mudu 2015). The 'political squatting movement' as a direct answer to housing and the loci of an alternative to capitalism is the assumption of the Squatting European Kollective (Martínez and Cattaneo 2016). However, we can say that today squatting does not necessarily relate to a consciously political and oppositional choice by individuals in search of a counter culture or alternative to capitalism. Deprivation-based squatting, one of the configurations of squatting described by Pruijt (2004), is back as a visible manifestation of a time characterized by multiple crises: economic breakdown and political upheaval, a global financial crisis connected to housing, austerity measures and the shrinkage of citizenship rights. McFarlane (2010) sees squatting as a global phenomenon and links it with squatted settlements and informal housing. In the context of the so-called Global South, organizations such as Slum Dwellers International and the achievement of legal title deeds through legalization of informality contribute to an 'entrepreneurial image of urban squatters as skilled and capable' (ibid: 772). These initiatives carry an anti-poverty discourse that can be seen as a right to stay put. However, even if informal settlements can be considered a form of do-it-yourself strategy, their legalization and inclusion in formal market dynamics carries the risk of rising land and housing prices 'to the point where the original inhabitants are priced out' (ibid: 771).

Besides the organized forms of squatting and the newly emerging anti-eviction platforms, we also find a large number of fragmented 'residents survival' tactics as documented by Herzfeld in Rome (2009). In some cases, they are capable to act as a bounded community. However, when it comes to displacement, social ties get broken and solidarity erodes, which has an intimate and irredeemable effect on displaced people. Contrary to the mobilization of visibility, irony and thought-provoking anti-gentrification practices, 'resident survival' remains largely invisible. We will argue in the following section that mobilizing invisibility rooted in everyday practices becomes a tactic of survival.

23.4   TOWARDS MORE INCLUSIVE GEOGRAPHIES OF RESISTANCE

As said earlier the above classification has its limits. It is dominated by the Anglo-Saxon conceptualizations of resistance within gentrification studies. It contains then, the 'shortcomings that both post-colonial and post-structuralist theory have identified' (Lees et al. 2015: 9), this cannot be ignored and it pushes us to consider the real complexity and variants of a given moment of resistance, something that might allow us to identify the opening up of possibilities (Cerulo 2009; Farías 2011; McFarlane 2011a). We recognize the need to go beyond the idea of a homogeneous hegemonic force, namely capitalism, in its globalized form (Roy 2011), as the main factor behind urban processes of destitution in order to account for the complexity and indeed possible successes of practices of resistance. In an attempt to respond to Roy's (2016) 'Who's afraid of postcolonial theory?' we recognize the urgent need to unpack understandings of resistance rooted in Western theorizations, not by simply choosing to focus on cases located in the so-called Global South, but by also trying to theorize away from the 'master narrative that is Europe' (2016: 205). As argued by Ley and Teo (2014) the epistemological absence of gentrification as a term to explain the phenomena does not necessarily imply the absence of the process itself; in the same vein, we argue that the absence of theorization of resistance to gentrification does not imply its absence either.

New and recently conceptualized types of gentrification continue to affect the everyday life of urban citizens. Moving away from a political economy approach in the study of gentrification, we find the micro-politics of everyday life to be a starting point in challenging the conceptualization of resistance in gentrification studies. We see everyday life as the 'quiet encroachment of the ordinary' (Bayat 2000: 545), the struggle of 'thousands of small movements in spaces of survival and stealth' (Yiftachel 2009: 250). The experience of the everyday is a breeding ground for non-normative ways of associating. In this field, Bebbington (2007) draws on Habermas to identify the links between mobilization and everyday practices, as the latter are being colonized by 'modern capitalism and welfare statism'. Merrifield (2013) advocates 'encounter' as an inspiration to conceive another way of political engagement. It is 'a more free-floating, dynamic, and relational militancy, to be sure, "horizontal" in its reach and organization' (p. xvii). Subsequently he presents us with a key question: 'How to ensure that this encounter in everyday life – this spontaneous lived moment – assumes a mutation of world-historical significance?' (Merrifield 2013: 92). Similarly, we ask if these practices can be seen as resistance to gentrification and whether they are in fact reactionary.

It is through these new critical openings within the literature that struggle and resistance in everyday practices of urban living might be understood better. In particular, the notion of urban assemblage as developed by Farías (2011) 'allows us to think about spatial formations as products that must be constantly defended, held together, maintained and repaired' (Farías 2011: 370); McFarlane (2011a) also sees in urban assemblage a key to unlock the complexity of becoming urban: 'Assemblage is a latent possibility of new politics and movements based on desire and becoming that can both emerge through and exceed capitalism' (p. 211). Urban assemblage theory thus compels us to seek the processes rather than the structures, radically opening up the meaning of urban resistance, which might translate into the different ways dwellers perform the 'right to be' (drawing from Merrifield 2013) or into 'everyday practices of emergence' as described by Ong (2011) when referring to the worlding of cities.

Considering this critique and the gaps identified in the literature we are opening up the notion of resistance to its (yet) non-politicized forms, its covert dimensions, to informality and invisibility. Besides the different types of anti-gentrification measures identified in the literature, we propose here four aspects, deeply rooted in the everyday urban experience, under which we could further analyse different practices of resistance: temporalities, negotiating ambiguity (and limits of solidarity), invisibility, and informality.

23.4.1 Temporalities

Different temporalities of practices of resistance depend on strategic positioning in respect to gentrification pressures. 'In dwelling the city, people draw upon previous experience or memories, and the multiple temporalities and rhythms of the city itself help to shape the possibilities of learning through dwelling' (McFarlane 2011b: 23). There are practices that seek a long-term solution for staying put or short-term steps for solving urgent need (such as re-housing of evictees or temporary shelter). They might be oriented towards the strategic reframing of the long-term strategic view for city development (such as counter-narratives) or be limited to the short-term improvement of a neighbourhood resulting in neighbourhood-based practices.

Time is also a crucial variable for understanding the dynamics of resistance, since it does not have the same value and is not perceived in the same way by those involved in the process. For a household under threat, time is a matter of survival. For the city administration, a financial organization, a real estate broker, it is just a matter of postponement of financial gains, a practice of power-relations. At the same time, how past and future are conceptualized within the implementation of gentrification projects is essential in order to understand the positions different actors take and the narratives they draw from. The memory of a completed project or a gentrified neighbourhood can be mobilized by those resisting in order to remind the public and institutions how these projects do not work for the benefit of all. At the same time, and once a project has started, agents act on their guesses of the different future outcomes of the gentrifying landscape: some will decide to organize themselves (more often than not, the more precarious the position the less they are likely to get involved); others will decide that the struggle is not for them, and will try to find an escape route (normally trying to find housing nearby, if affordable); other dwellers will actually act on the possibility of taking advantage of the changes. It is thus that aspirations, desires and conceptualizations of past and future have a direct impact on how dwellers decide to take different positions in the present. The different meanings of time stress the need to clearly understand different threats or fears, intentionality and positionality of the agents involved in the struggle against gentrification.

23.4.2   Negotiating Ambiguity

The need to be flexible in searching for alternatives sheds light on the limits of solidarity when dealing with material needs and the negotiation of ambiguity. The austerity and violent urbanizing practices which characterize the global financial crisis around the world result in highly visible solidarity in the face of displacement (see the growing anti-eviction platforms in Chicago, Spain, Ireland, to name a few). The real burden for the success of these resistance practices comes from a culturally rooted, internal contradiction within the anti-displacement movement. In a proprietary society anti-gentrification practices have to face a consolidated (and culturally rooted) preference for homeownership as a means of wealth, welfare and social reproduction. The landscape of resistance is full of contradictions as far as the challenge posed by homeownership and lack of tenure alternatives is not resolved. For instance, the collective struggle against the privatization of public housing in Rome can result in a de-facto anti-eviction zone or in negotiations with the institution for the most convenient sale price. Those willing to negotiate in this climate are mainly organized tenants willing to buy. However, negotiation can be contradictory when proprietary aspirations are prioritized against the need of tenants or other groups severely affected by housing vulnerability (those forced to pay prohibitive rent at market prices, unable to buy or access public housing due to a chronic shortage, already evicted from previous houses and living in temporary accommodation). There are notable exceptions, where homeownership concerns can become a force of further solidarity actions that include tenants and informal dwellers. In cases where informal housing is historically rooted, applying for and receiving homeownership certificates or regularization might be the main objective for the fulfilment of citizenship rights. And yet, this move works as a strategy to improve informal dwellers' position at the possible negotiating table, thus forming and strengthening a collective that cares for the neighbourhood as a whole, as much as their own personal homeownership situations.

Moreover, both negotiating with the local authorities whilst building an anti-institution narrative can go hand in hand. Local authorities might be the only point of information in regards to a possible urban renewal plan, and thus become a possible key ally in the struggle. This allows us to break down the idea of the state or institutions as homogeneous constructions (in fact, there are civil servants within the institutions that consider their work to serve and protect dwellers, whilst dealing with political interests, top-down questionable decisions and nepotism). This inherent complexity of the (corrupted) institutional apparatus can work both in favour of and against those affected residents. On the one hand, dwellers need to carry out a certain amount of research (with the help of city-wide voluntary organizations and activists) to improve their position. On the other hand, that same complexity also translates into sometimes institutional incompetence, which gives room for informed resistance to intervene and can lead to delays in the implementation of urban plans (when no one really knows exactly what is going on – especially if the legal framework changes rapidly). The ambiguity of the positions different actors take in regards to urban transformation depending on the circumstances and what is to be gained, are key in the processes.

23.4.3 Mobilizing Invisibility and Informal Networks

We would like to draw attention to a growing number of practices of resistance which do not fit the classification of formal/visible practices. Contrary to the mobilization of visibility, irony and thought-provoking anti-gentrification practices can remain invisible. Not everyone is willing to negotiate overtly with those responsible for their displacement. In these cases, we argue that people tend to find solutions informally and outside of institutional regimes, especially when they start failing them. The majority of practices of resistance are in fact outside the classic/institutional/normative approach in which progressive policies have been formulated. Invisibility and informality play a key role in those cases. McFarlane's (2012: 105) conceptualization of informality/formality is particularly helpful when addressing their possible politicization: 'They co-constitute and dissolve spaces, becoming politicized or depoliticized at different moments, and they both enable and restrict urban life.' Furthermore, Simone's (2004) account of informality and notion of 'people as infrastructure' is particularly relevant: 'These intersections, [. . .], have depended on the ability of residents to engage complex combinations of objects, spaces, persons, and practices. These conjunctions become an infrastructure – a platform providing for and reproducing life in the city' (2004: 408). Informality can be applied to ambiguous homeownership situations, whereby dwellers who have built their own houses mobilize this identity to organize themselves. Another way informality works is through networks whereby family and neighbours get together to support whoever is in need. These radical forms of solidarity could strategically mobilize (in)visibility (drawing on

Papadopoulos and Tsianos 2007) to hide from (or block) the relentless path of urban restructuring in its various forms. Remaining institutionally invisible is a key tool in order to stay put: if you become too visible, too noisy, you risk being stigmatized or excluded from a normative way of living.

We have created a working table (Figure 23.1) where we present what we have seen as practices of resistance to gentrification so far in the tension between visibility and invisibility/formality and informality. We argue that using the different conceptual threads described above as points of reference allows us to anchor highly diffuse and unstable concepts for detailed exploration. We hope this will trigger further conversations about different ways of resisting gentrifying forces.

23.5 CONCLUSION

We initially identified four sets of practices that have sought to mitigate gentrification from the gentrification literature, as summarized in Table 23.1. This body of work allows us to say that practices of resistance and possible alternatives can only be site-specific. If we see them all together they constitute an attempt to contextualize and define place-specific anti-displacement agendas and localized action plans as suggested by Lees et al. (2016: 224).

However, the achievements of these practices in the face of the acuteness assumed by gentrification at the current conjuncture are limited. In some cases, those limits are not only the lack of institutional attempts to prevent displacement but also internal contradictions within the resistance practices themselves. In order to problematize the way resistances have been conceptualized in gentrification studies to date we drew on post-structuralist theories and relational approaches. These angles have allowed us to see that politically conscious, overtly oppositional, intentional and visible practices of resistance are not the only way to counteract gentrification-induced displacement. We have argued that the field of resistances is also characterized by non-politicized, covert, unintentional, informal, and deliberately invisible practices of everyday life that draw on different perceptions of time and survival, negotiations of ambiguity and mobilization of invisibility.

We have witnessed the growth of collective practices aimed at amplifying the possibilities of a future where dwellers retain as much agency as possible within a landscape of urban displacement and dispossession. There are certain regularities in resistance practices that enrich our repertoire: informality mobilized whenever necessary, informal networks of support where precious knowledge is shared (that might include neighbours, acquaintances in local municipalities, practices of situated solidarity), and differences between homeowners and tenants' aspirations that at first might seem insolvable, but that finally might help organize a neighbourhood better against gentrification pressures.

In order to further understand what the possibilities are in the face of dispossession and eviction, we have tried to unpack the concept of resistance, unburdening it from more structural narratives and further incorporating all those aspects that enrich the concept ontologically. Resistance is far from a uni-dimensional, linear storyline of collective action: in fact, resistance happens at different levels of engagement and in constant relation to other processes (what today is resistance tomorrow can be compliance), from the forces it seeks to overcome to multi-scalar hegemonic fault lines. In this sense, the meaning of resistance needs to be constantly negotiated according to an ever-changing landscape of circumstances.

Negotiating ambivalences and ambiguities (or refusing to negotiate) with institutional and private actors demonstrates how resistance itself is a deeply complex concept, relative and adapted to the context precisely by those who carry it out, and consider themselves part of it. Further difficulties arise when individual everyday actions that allow dwellers to stay put, or to find other options in the face of brutal evictions, are not considered part of traditional forms of organized resistance. We have tried here to find a balance on what counts as formal anti-gentrification practices and individual, non-organized, (and sometimes) incoherent behaviour, whilst staying away from romanticizing the precarious lives of the resisting 'urban poor'.

REFERENCES

Annunziata, S. and Lees, L. (2016) 'Resisting austerity gentrification in Southern European cities', *Sociological Research Online*, 21 (3), np, [Online]. Available at: www.socresonline.org.uk/21/3/5.html (accessed 14 November 2016).

Arnott, R. (1995) 'Time for revisionism on rent control?', *The Journal of Economic Perspectives*, 9(1), 99–120.

Ascensao, E. (2015) 'Slum gentrification in Lisbon, Portugal. Displacement and the imagined future of an informal settlement', in Lees, L., Shin, H. and López-Morales, E. (eds) *Global Gentrifications: Uneven Development and Displacement*, Bristol: Policy Press..

Assemblea de Barris per un Turisme Sostenible (ABTS) (n.d.), [Online]. Available at: assembleabarris.wordpress.com (accessed 14 November 2016).

Bayat, A. (2000) 'From "Dangerous Classes" to "Quiet Rebels": politics of the Urban Subaltern in the Global South', *International Sociology*, 15(3), 533–557.

Bebbington, A. (2007) 'Social movements and the politicization of chronic poverty', *Development and Change*, 38, 793–818.

Betancur, J. (2014) 'Gentrification in Latin America: overview and critical analysis', *Urban Studies Research*, [Online]. DOI: http://dx.doi.org/10.1155/2014/986961 (accessed 30 November 2016).

Blomley, N. (2004) *Unsettling the City: Urban Land and the Politics of Property*, New York: Routledge.

Brenner, N., Marcuse, P. and Mayer, M. (2011) *Cities for People, Not for Profit: Critical Urban Theory and the Right to the City*, New York: Routledge.

Cabannes, Y., Yafai, S. and Johnson, C. (2010) *How People Face Evictions*, London: Development Planning Unit, University College London.

Casgrain, A. and Janoschka, M. (2013) 'Gentrificación y resistencia en las ciudades latinoamericanas El ejemplo de Santiago de Chile', *Andamios*, 10(22), 19–44.

Cerulo, K. (2009) 'Nonhumans in social interaction', *Annual Review of Sociology*, 35, 531–552.

Colau, A. and Alemany, A. (2012) 'Mortgaged lives. From the housing bubble to the right to housing', *Journal of Aesthetics & Protest Press*, [Online]. Available at: http://www.joaap.org/press/pah/mortgagedlives.pdf (accessed 14 November 2016).

Collins, R. and Munro, R. (2010) 'Exploring the sociological re-imagining of politics: a conversation', *Sociological Review*, 58(4), 548–562.

Connolly, K. (2016) '"No bling in the hood . . ." Does Berlin's anti-gentrification law really work?', *The Guardian*, 4 October, [Online]. Available at: www.theguardian.com/cities/2016/oct/04/does-berlin-anti-gentrification-law-really-work-neukolln (accessed 14 November 2016).

Crossa, V. (2013) 'Play for protest, protest for play: artisan and vendors' resistance to displacement in Mexico City', *Antipode*, 45(4), 826–843.

DeFilippis, J. (2004) *Unmaking Goliath: Community Control in the Face of Global Capital*, New York, NY: Routledge.

Di Feliciantonio, C. (2016) 'The reactions of neighbourhoods to the eviction of squatters in Rome: an account of the making of precarious investor subjects', *European Urban and Regional Studies*, first published on 8 August 2016 doi:10.1177/0969776416662110.

Erman, T. and Coşkun-Yıldar, M. (2007) 'Emergent local initiative and the city: the case of neighbourhood associations of the better-off classes in post-1990 urban Turkey', *Urban Studies*, 44(13), 2547–2566.

Farías, I. (2011) 'The politics of urban assemblages', *City*, 15(3–4), 365–374.

Gallaher, C. (2016) *The Politics of Staying Put, Condo Conversion and Tenant Right-to-Buy in Washington DC*, Philadelphia: Temple University Press.

Gentrification Blog (n.d.), [Online]. Available at gentrificationblog.wordpress.com (accessed 14 November 2016).

Gillespie, T. (2016) 'Accumulation by urban dispossession: struggles over urban space in Accra, Ghana', *Transactions of the Institute of British Geographers*, 41(1), 66–77.

Gül, M., Dee, J. and Cünük, C. (2014) 'Istanbul's Taksim Square and Gezi Park: the place of protest and the ideology of place', *Journal of Architecture and Urbanism*, 38(1), 63–72.

Hartman, C. (1984) 'The right to stay put', in Lees, L., Slater, T. and Wyly, E. (2010) (eds), *The Gentrification Reader*, New York: Routledge, pp. 531–541.

Hartman, C., Keating, D. and LeGates, R. (1982) *Displacement: How to Fight It*, Washington DC: National Housing Law Project.

Herzfeld, M. (2009) *Evicted from Eternity: The Restructuring of Modern Rome*, Chicago: University of Chicago Press.

Hollander, J. and Einwohner, R. (2004) 'Conceptualizing resistance', *Sociological Forum*, 19(4), 533–554.

Holm, A. (2007) 'Housing privatisation in London, Berlin and Amsterdam comparison of procedures, driving forces, and resistance', *PRESOM*, Newsletter 3, 1–9.

Holm, A., Grell, B. and Bernt, M. (eds) (2013) *The Berlin Reader. A Compendium on Urban Change and Activism*, Bielefeld: transcript-Verlag.

Holm, A. and Kuhn, A. (2011) 'Squatting and urban renewal: the interaction of squatter movements and strategies of urban restructuring in Berlin', *International Journal of Urban and Regional Research*, 35(3), 644–658.

Hynes, M. (2013) 'Reconceptualizing resistance: Sociology and the affective dimension of resistance', *The British Journal of Sociology*, 64(4), 559–577.

'IL LAGO CHE COMBATTE' – Assalti frontali & Il Muro del Canto (2014) YouTube video, added by Marcello Saurino, [Online]. Available at www.youtube.com/watch?v=Dcb_Thrq2P8 (accessed 14 November 2016).

İslam, T. and Sakızlıoğlu, B. (2015) 'The making of, and resistance to, state-led gentrification in Istanbul, Turkey', in Lees, L., Shin, H. and López-Morales, E. (eds), *Global Gentrifications: Uneven Development and Displacement*, Bristol: Policy Press, pp. 249–269.

Janoschka, M. (2016) 'Gentrification displacement dispossession: key urban processes within the Latin American context', *INVI*, 31(88), 17–58.

Janoschka, M. and Sequera, J. (2016) 'Gentrification in Latin America: addressing the politics of the geography of displacement', *Urban Geography*, 37(8), 1175–1194.

Just Space (2013) Towards a Community-Led Plan for London: Policy directions and proposals. [Online]. Available at: justspacelondon.files.wordpress.com/2013/09/just-space-a4-community-led-london-plan.pdf (accessed 14 November 2016).

Karaman, O. (2014) 'Resisting urban renewal in Istanbul', *Urban Geography*, 35(2), 290–310.

Kolodney, L. (1991) 'Eviction free zones: the economics of legal bricolage in the fight against displacement', *Fordham Urban Law Journal*, 18(3), 507–544.

Lees, L. and Ferreri, M. (2016) 'Resisting gentrification on its final frontiers: learning from the Heygate Estate in London (1974–2013)', *Cities*, 57, 14–24, [Online]. DOI: http://dx.doi.org/10.1016/j.cities.2015.12.005 (accessed 13 November 2016).

Lees, L., Shin, H. and López-Morales, E. (eds) (2015) *Global Gentrifications: Uneven Development and Displacement*, Bristol: Policy Press.

Lees, L., Shin, H. and López-Morales, E. (2016) *Planetary Gentrification*, Cambridge: Polity Press.

Lees, L., Slater, T. and Wyly, E. (2008) *Gentrification*, New York: Routledge.

Left Hand Rotation (n.d.) [Online]. Available at: http://www.lefthandrotation.com/home/index.htm (accessed 14 November 2016).

Ley, D. and Dobson, C. (2008) 'Are there limits to gentrification? The contexts of impeded gentrification in Vancouver', *Urban Studies*, 45(12), 2471–2498.

Ley, D. and Teo, S. (2014) 'Gentrification in Hong-Kong? Epistemology vs. ontology', *International Journal of Urban and Regional Research*, 38(4), 1286–1303.

Lind, H. (2001) 'Rent regulation: a conceptual comparative analysis', *International Journal of Housing Policy*, 1(1), 41–57.

London Tenants Federation, Lees L., Just Space and SNAG (2014) *Staying Put: An Anti-Gentrification Handbook for Council Estates in London*, [Online]. Available at: southwarknotes.files.wordpress.com/2014/06/staying-put-web-version-low.pdf (accessed 10 September 2016).

Madrid Desahuciado (2015) *viveroiniciativasciudadanas.net*, 10 March [Online]. Available at: viveroiniciativasciudadanas.net/2015/03/10/madrid-desahuciado (accessed 14 November 2016).

Maeckelbergh, M. (2012) 'Mobilizing to stay put: Housing struggles in New York City', *International Journal of Urban and Regional Research*, 36(4), 655–673.

Maloutas, T. (2012) 'Contextual diversity in gentrification research', *Critical Sociology*, 38(1), 33–48.

Marcuse, P. (1985a) 'Gentrification, abandonment and displacement: connection, causes and policy responses in New York City', *Journal of Urban and Contemporary Law*, 28(1–4), 195–240.

Marcuse, P. (1985b) 'To control gentrification: anti-displacement zoning and planning for stable residential districts', *New York University Review of Law & Social Change*, 13(4), 931–952.

Martínez, M. and Cattaneo, P. (eds) (2016) *The Squatters' Movement in Europe: Commons and Autonomy as Alternatives to Capitalism, Squatting Europe Kollective*, London: Pluto Press.

Mayer, M. (2009) 'The "right to the city" in the context of shifting mottos of urban social movements', *City*, 13(2), 262–374.

Mayer, M. (2013) 'First world urban activism: Beyond austerity urbanism and creative city politics', *City*, 71(1), 5–19.

Mayer, M. and Boudreau, J-A. (2011) 'Social movements in urban politics: trends in research and practice', in Mossberger, K., Clarke, S.E. and John, P. (eds), *Oxford Handbook on Urban Politics*, Oxford: Oxford University Press, pp. 273–291.

Mbembé, J.-A. and Nuttall, S. (2004) 'Writing the world from an African metropolis', *Public Culture*, 16(3), 347–372.

McFarlane, C. (2010) 'Squatting movement', in Hutchison, R. (ed), *Encyclopedia of Urban Studies*, Thousand Oaks, California: SAGE Publications, Inc, pp. 771–774.

McFarlane, C. (2011a) 'Assemblage and critical urbanism', *City*, 15(2), 204–224.

McFarlane, C. (2011b) *Learning the City: Knowledge and Translocal Assemblage*, Hoboken, NJ: Wiley-Blackwell.

McFarlane, C. (2012) 'Rethinking informality: politics, crisis, and the city', *Planning Theory & Practice*, 13(1), 89–108 [Online]: DOI: 10.1080/14649357.2012.649951 (accessed 15 September 2016).

Merrifield, A. (2013) *The Politics of the Encounter: Urban Theory and Protest Under Planetary Urbanisation*, Athens, GA: University of Georgia Press.

Morales-Cruz, M. (2012) *Lawyers and 'Social' Movements: A Story About the Puerto Rico 'Zero Evictions' Coalition* [Online]. Available at: www.law.yale.edu/documents/pdf/sela/SELA12_Morales-Cruz_CV_Eng_20 120508.pdf (accessed 30 November 2016)

Mudu, P. (2015) 'Housing and homelessness in contemporary Rome', in Clough Marinaro, I. and Thomassen. B. (eds), *Global Rome: Changing Faces of the Eternal City*, Bloomington IN: Indiana University Press, pp. 62–80.

Newman, K. and Wyly, E. (2006) 'The right to stay put, revisited: gentrification and resistance to displacement in New York City', *Urban Studies*, 43(1), 23–57.

Noeger, L. (2012) *Gentrification and Resistance*, Munich: Lit Verlag.

Novy, J. and Colomb, C. (2013) 'Struggling for the right to the (creative) city in Berlin and Hamburg: new urban social movements, new "spaces of hope"?', *International Journal of Urban and Regional Research*, 37(5), 1816–1838.

Ong, A. (2011) 'Introduction: Worlding cities, or the art of being global', in Roy, A. and Ong, A. (eds), *Worlding Cities: Asian Experiments and the Art of Being Global*, Malden, Oxford: Wiley-Blackwell, pp. 1–26.

Papadopoulos, D. and Tsianos, V. (2007) 'How to do sovereignty without people? The subjectless condition of postliberal power', *boundary 2*, 34(1), 135–172.

Pearsall, H. (2014) 'Superfund me: a study of resistance to gentrification in New York City', *Urban Studies*, 50(11), 2293–2310.

Penz, P., Drydyk, J. and Bose, P. (2011) *Displacement by Development. Ethics, Rights and Responsibility*, Cambridge: Cambridge University Press.

Petropoulou, C. (2014) 'Crisis, Right to the City movements and the question of spontaneity: Athens and Mexico City', *City*, 18(4–5), 563–572.

Portelli, S. (2015) *La ciudad horizontal. Urbanismo y resistencia en un barrio de casas baratas de Barcelona*, Barcelona: Ediciones Bellaterra.

Pruijt, H. (2004) 'Okupar en Europa' [Squatting in Europe], in Martínez Lopez, M. and Adell, R. (eds), *¿Dónde están las llaves? El movimiento okupa: prácticas y contextos sociales*, Madrid: La Catarata, pp. 35–60.

Rankin, K. (2009) 'Critical development studies and the praxis of planning', *City*, 13(2), 262–374.

Rätt att bo kvar (n.d.), [Online]. Available at: koloni.info/Ratt_att_bo_kvar_2016.pdf (accessed 14 November 2016).

Robinson, T. (1995) 'Gentrification and grassroots resistance in San Francisco's Tenderloin', *Urban Affairs Review*, 30, 483–513.

Rodríguez, M. and Di Virgilio, M. (2016) 'A city for all? Public policy and resistance to gentrification in the southern neighborhoods of Buenos Aires', *Urban Geography*, 37(8) [Online]. DOI:10.1080/02723638.2016.1 152844 (accessed 30 November 2016).

Rose, M. (2002) 'The seductions of resistance: power, politics, and a performative style of systems', *Environment and Planning D-Society & Space*, 20(4), 383–400.

Routledge, P. and Derickson, K. (2015) 'Situated solidarities and the practice of scholar activism', *Environment and Planning D: Society and Space*, 33(3), 391–407.

Roy, A. (2009) 'The 21st century metropolis: new geographies of theory', *Regional Studies*, 43(6), 819–830.

Roy, A. (2011) 'Slumdog cities: rethinking subaltern urbanism', *International Journal of Urban and Regional Research*, 35(2), 223–238.

Roy, A. (2016) 'Who's afraid of postcolonial theory?', *International Journal of Urban and Regional Research*, 40, 200–209.

Scott, J.C. (1985) *Weapons of the Weak: Everyday Forms of Peasant Resistance*, New Haven CT: Yale University Press.

Simone, A. (2004) 'People as infrastructure: intersecting fragments in Johannesburg', *Public Culture*, 16, 407–429.

Slater, T. (2014) 'There is nothing natural about gentrification', *Newleftproject.org*, 24 November [Online]. Available at: www.newleftproject.org/index.php/site/article_comments/there_is_nothing_natural_about_gent rification (accessed 14 November 2016).

Smith, N. (1992) 'Contours of a spatialized politics: homeless vehicles and the production of geographical scale', *Social Text*, 33, 54–81.

Smith, N. (1996) *The New Urban Frontier: Gentrification and the Revanchist City*, Routledge.

Stavrides, S. (2016) *Common Space: The City as Commons (In Common)*, London: Zed Books.

Sulukuleli Roman Rap Grubu Tahribad-ı İsyan – TOKİ KAFALAR (2015) YouTube video, added by Eşitlik Özgürlük Emek [Online]. Available at www.youtube.com/watch?v=wddJgQDslrE (accessed 14 November 2016).

Taylor, M. and Edwards, M. (2016) 'Just space economy and planning: opening up debates on London's economy through participating in strategic planning', in Beebejaun, Y. (ed), *The Participatory City*, Berlin: Jovis, pp. 76–86.

The Anti-Eviction Mapping Project (n.d.) [Online]. Available at: http://www.antievictionmappingproject.net/narratives.html (accessed 14 November 2016).

Uitermark, J. (2004) 'Framing urban injustices: the case of the Amsterdam squatter movement', *Space and Polity*, 8(2), 227–244.

Uitermark, J. and Loopmans, M. (2013) 'Urban renewal without displacement? Belgium's "housing contract experiment" and the risks of gentrification', *Journal of Housing and the Built Environment*, 28(1), 157–166.

Velásquez-Atehortúa, J. (2014) 'Barrio women's invited and invented spaces against urban elitisation in Chacao, Venezuela', *Antipode*, 46(3), 835–856.

Yiftachel, O. (2009) 'Critical theory and "gray space": Mobilization of the colonized', *City*, 13(2–3), 246–263.

24. Alternatives to gentrification: exploring urban community land trusts and urban ecovillage practices

Susannah Bunce

24.1 INTRODUCTION

In writing about alternatives to gentrification there lies a risk that suggestions for thinking beyond gentrification may be viewed as excessively optimistic remedies or stop-gap solutions to the now generalized challenges of gentrification and displacement. Discussions about alternatives to gentrification have been noticeably absent from the gentrification literature (Slater, 2009), most likely due to the reason above but also because debates have largely centred on defining gentrification and deliberations over how gentrification is produced and its social outcomes through eviction and displacement. Critical voices have actively challenged both scholarly and policy-led celebrations of gentrification (Lees, 2012; Davidson, 2015; Slater, 2009; Lees, Slater and Wyly, 2008; Smith, 2002) that, as Wyly (2015) notes, view gentrification as a process that cultivates positive revitalization for communities and cities or which temper and normalize gentrification by defining it as a natural and inevitable outcome of urbanization processes. Much of the critical work on gentrification has enacted consistent critiques of these normative definitions of gentrification in order to articulate and maintain strong, countering positions in academic discourse about gentrification. Yet, as Slater (2009) suggests in his analysis of the importance of planning scholar Peter Marcuse's research on gentrification and displacement, discussions in critical urban studies must attempt to reorient gentrification discourse towards social justice issues, specifically housing as a 'question of social justice', and foster a more radical, analytical path of questioning that reframes traditional understandings of property and its dominant forms of ownership and exchange (p. 307). This argument encourages the unfolding of scholarly critiques of gentrification but also widens space for the consideration and integration of scholar-activist and community-based activist perspectives and grounded work that seeks to challenge gentrification. Community-based organizations and resident activists are often on the front lines of addressing the roll-out of gentrification in cities and are left to enact the service and care work of tending to its outcomes and impacts on individuals and families, such as physical eviction from housing, free legal services, childcare, and programmes to find affordable housing alternatives. Such work has been well-documented in academic research that identifies the important role of community-based organizations in advocating for social justice and providing care work to communities that are facing complex problems caused by gentrification. Often, this literature has demonstrated how community-based strategies to resist gentrification pressures can include different practices that defy displacement or which encourage the community control of land and housing stock (Blomley, 2004; DeFillippis, 2004; Gibson-Graham, Cameron and Healy, 2013; Medoff and Sklar, 1999; Rameau, 2008; Robinson,

413

1996; London Tenants Federation, Lees, Just Space and Southwark Notes Archive Group, 2014). Recently, some urban community-based organizations have shaped explicit mandates to resist gentrification through street-level direct action protests and programs to highlight the struggles of low-income and often racialized communities facing eviction and displacement in light of rising housing prices, land privatization, increasing land values, and existing social surveillance and inequality in their neighbourhoods and cities, as well as the proposal of community-based alternatives (cf. Class War, 2015; Eviction Free San Francisco, 2016; Ontario Coalition Against Poverty, 2016; Serve the People/ Servir al Pueblo Los Angeles, 2016; Alternatives for Community and Development, 2015; Rose, n.d.; Seminary of the Street, n.d.).

My intention in this chapter is not to champion or prescribe certain models or practices as ideal types or as cure-alls for gentrification, but instead to explore current progressive community-based alternatives to housing provision and land ownership and stewardship as methods to challenge local scale gentrification processes and encourage community self-determination. Through the study of community land trusts and ecovillages in cities, this exploration demonstrates how individuals and communities, largely at the neighbourhood scale, can engage in alternative practices of everyday urban living and how these may act as aspirational spaces for community-based empowerment and for shaping new urban futures. While not all urban community land trusts and ecovillages identify their rationales and mandates as resisting gentrification, the work of these organizations inherently challenge dominant relations of production and consumption through the de-commodification of housing and land and by acting as collective, participatory spaces for cultivating social and environmental justice and change in everyday life. Largely located at the neighbourhood scale, urban community land trusts and ecovillages are discursive, material, and relational spaces for people to interact and share ideas about community-based problems and solutions as well as develop capacity to resist these problems (Bunce, 2016; Chitewere, 2010; Ergas, 2010; Litfin, 2014; Pickerill, 2016; Thompson, 2015). These practices relate to current scholarly discussion regarding commons and commoning as micro-scalar ways by which to resist practices of capital accumulation (Caffentzis and Federici, 2014; Federici, 2010; Susser and Tonnelat, 2013) in light of increasing dispossession in cities through privatized enclosures, evictions and displacement, and struggles over gaining rights to land and social spaces (Coulthard, 2014; Harvey, 2009, 2012). Community land trust organizations and ecovillage organizations that utilize a community land trust model intend to remove land from the speculative market for the purposes of capturing land value and prohibiting profit-making from the resale of land or building stock on the land (Aird, 2010; Davis, 2010; Crabtree, 2010, 2014; Sungu-Erylimaz and Greenstein, 2007). The removal of land and its enclosure by a community organization might suggest yet another act of modern enclosure through the private ownership of land by a community organization, the identification of its uses by a self-identified community, and, in the particular case of ecovillages, the intentional production of separate 'environmental islands' within cities. Yet, a focus on social and environmental land stewardship, the removal of land from property speculation, emphasis on de-commodifying land and building stock, and the collaborative and counter-normative work of these organizations suggests that they have more in keeping with notions of emancipatory commons and collective action (Bunce, 2016; Thompson, 2015) than modern practices of enclosure. Community land trust and ecovillage organizations advocate for community-based development, often with a 'development without displacement' agenda, and for equitable and representational governance structures in order to rectify conflicts and power imbalances in organizational dynamics and act as positive spaces for community engagement. I suggest that the strength of, and opportunities inherent in, community land trust and ecovillage organizations rests in their unique contributions to addressing urban socio-economic, environmental, and spatial issues and injustices at the neighbourhood level, and as hopeful places for the enactment of progressive and sometimes radical social and environmental change in cities. The following sections examine the East London Community Land Trust (ELCLT) urban community land trust organization in London, United Kingdom, and the Parkdale Neighbourhood Land Trust (PNLT) in Toronto, Canada, through a narrative of their organizational formation and development that also includes the challenges of acquiring community-owned land within two rapidly gentrifying neighbourhoods with similar characteristics. Urban ecovillage practices are explored through the example of the Los Angeles Ecovillage (LAEV), an ecovillage located in the downtown core of Los Angeles that has recently added a land trust component to its organizational structure in order to demarcate and preserve community land. The community land trust and ecovillage examples that are discussed in this chapter act as alternative intentional spaces within gentrifying and gentrified urban neighbourhoods yet also retain relational associations with surrounding communities and the wider city in order to mitigate isolationist dynamics, which make them progressive examples for how alternative communities situated within large, dense urban areas can be organized and enacted.

24.2   URBAN COMMUNITY LAND TRUSTS

Community land trusts (CLTs) can be defined as non-governmental, non-profit organizations that acquire donated or purchased land within a community area that is defined by the organization's members. The organization identifies uses for the land based upon collaborative engagement with local residents in order to best define community needs for the land. The most prominent use of CLT land has been for the provision of affordable housing for homeownership and lease, but more recent uses include social enterprises, community gardens, and urban farms (Yuen, 2014; Yuen and Rosenberg, 2013). Community land trusts hold in trust for the community and place legal restrictions on the future resale of the land and buildings as a way to maintain affordability and prevent profit making from increased land value and building prices. Building stock on the land can be owned by individuals that are connected to the CLT organization; however, the separation of land ownership from building stock on the land is embedded in a ground lease, created by the CLT, that delineates the organization as the landowner and prevents or mitigates future profit making upon the resale of housing by the owner and also ensures the limitation or absence of rental increases for buildings owned by the CLT. By holding title to land on an indefinite basis with the objective of maintaining land affordability, separating ownership of land from building infrastructure, and preventing profit making from resale through legal contracts, CLTs act as a land value capture mechanism and emphasize the long-term stewardship of affordable land and building stock for community purposes (Davis, 2010; Bunce, 2016; Bunce, Khimani, Sungu-Erylimaz and Earle, 2013; Crabtree, 2010, 2014; Davis, 2010; Gray, 2008; Meehan, 2014; Moore and McKee, 2012; Thompson, 2015).

Community land trusts have emerged over the past several decades in the United States, and more recently in Canada, Australia, and the United Kingdom, as well as in Kenya (Midheme and Mouleart, 2013). Their modern origins are based in organizing by African-American sharecroppers in the southern United States as part of the civil rights movement and as an act of resistance to the lack of available farming land for African-American tenant labourers (Curtin and Bocarsly, 2010; Davis, 2010). The first CLT, New Communities Inc., was located in rural Georgia, and proved successful for several years as a way for African-American farmers to collectively own land (Davis, 2010). The CLT model first developed in American cities in the early 1980s, with the first urban CLT being located in a low-income, primarily African-American, inner-city neighbourhood of Cincinnati, as a way to retain land for community purposes in light of public sector disinvestment (ibid, 2010). More broadly, urban CLTs have most frequently organized as community-based development and capacity building forums for local residents in order to enact community-led neighbourhood revitalization. This has been most readily apparent in low-income and racialized urban neighbourhoods with traditional patterns of public sector disinvestment alongside neglectful and/or absentee private landowners, and, in some contexts, as a concurrent anti-gentrification strategy in order to gain community control over land and combat land inflation (Davis, 2010; Medoff and Sklar, 1994). For example, the Dudley Street Neighborhood Initiative (DSNI), in the Roxbury neighbourhood of South Boston, formed as a community-based organization (CBO) in 1984 with the purpose of addressing social and environmental issues of property abandonment, arson fires, waste disposal on abandoned lots, and public sector neglect in a community with a large number of African-American and Hispanic residents (Holding Ground, 1996; Medoff and Sklar, 1994). After several years of social and environmental justice activism, Dudley Street Neighborhood Initiative (DSNI) formed Dudley Neighbors Inc. (DNI) as a community land trust organization. In 1988, DNI received a right to use the governmental and legal mechanism of eminent domain ('compulsory purchase' or 'expropriation') from the Boston Redevelopment Authority in order to legally expropriate and acquire title to privately owned, vacant land lots. In doing so, DNI became the first non-governmental, non-profit community organization in the United States to be granted permission to use eminent domain (Taylor, 1995). This allowed for land accruement within a 60-acre neighbourhood radius (Loh, 2015) to be held in trust by DNI. Since the 1980s, DNI has developed 225 affordable housing units, a community garden, children's playgrounds, and community office space for non-profit organizations, on land owned by DNI (Dudley Neighbors Inc., 2016). While the Dudley Street example provides a brief insight into how CLTs have been used in the context of American inner cities, I turn to the more recent use of the CLT model in gentrifying areas of Toronto and London. Both CLTs are interesting for their shared characteristics of being more recently formed social justice-oriented organizations with a focus on acquiring land and community benefits for low-income residents in light of gentrification pressures. Each CLT emphasizes participatory governance through a broad membership base and strong community engagement, in addition to the traditional CLT approach of a board of directors (Davis, 2010; Sungu-Erylimaz and Greenstein, 2007). In their work towards the acquisition of land for community-oriented amenities, both organizations have highlighted the role of CLTs in mitigating the effects of gentrification while at the same time raising awareness about the negative impacts of gentrification on neighbourhood diversity and vitality.

24.2.1   Parkdale Neighbourhood Land Trust, Toronto

The Parkdale neighbourhood, in the western downtown area of Toronto, has transformed from being a community largely constituted by low-income residents and social and commercial services geared towards these residents into a more gentrified area over the past two decades. Slater (2004) notes that gentrification in Parkdale started in the mid-1980s as property values rose in other central downtown neighbourhoods and middle-class professionals began to move into the neighbourhood with a focus on converting Victorian-era duplexes or triplexes into single family homes. The inexpensive cost of properties suggested that new gentrifiers bought housing with the intention 'that property values [in Parkdale] would eventually rise as the neighbourhood's profile rose, leading to handsome profits in years to come' (Slater, 2004, 312). The socially diverse components of Parkdale, as a residential place for new immigrants and refugees, artists in need of inexpensive housing and studio spaces, political activists, as well as out-patients from a nearby hospital for mental health and addiction treatment, have given the neighbourhood an eclectic character. This became an attractive feature for gentrification by artists and more progressively minded middle-class residents from the mid-1980s onwards (Slater, 2004). Additionally, Toronto's municipal government crafted and implemented regulatory enactments to mitigate the rental of multi-unit and single room occupancy housing as forms of inexpensive accommodation, which have limited the availability of affordable housing (Mazer and Rankin, 2011; Slater, 2004; Slater and Whitzman, 2006; Whitzman, 2009). Parkdale's gentrification has largely been impacted by what Zukin calls 'creeping gentrification' (Zukin, 1989), influenced by new-build, market-oriented residential and commercial districts such as the nearby Liberty Village (Catungal, Leslie and Hii, 2009) and already gentrified neighbourhoods located to the east of the neighbourhood and closer to Toronto's downtown core.

Gentrification within Parkdale has largely occurred in smaller residential areas in the north end of the neighbourhood, with the Sorauren and Roncesvalles Village areas now inhabited by professionalized, middle-to-high income families with accompanying support labour such as housekeepers, nannies, personal trainers, and home chefs. This has increasingly encroached upon the southern area of the neighbourhood, known as South Parkdale, where the majority of tower apartments with rental accommodation and other leased housing arrangements geared towards lower-income residents are located. In addition to gentrification pressures in Parkdale, the neighbourhood is considered to be one of the few remaining areas of downtown Toronto where new immigrants and refugees can access affordable housing and other settlement services (Logan and Murdie, 2016). Census data from the federal government demonstrates that 52% of Parkdale residents were born outside of Canada with 71% of the neighbourhood's recent newcomers arriving from countries in South Asia, in particular (Logan and Murdie, 2016, 100). Recently, a large community of Tibetan refugees has settled in South Parkdale (ibid, 2016) with a need for community-based and affordable settlement services and programs.

Within this context, the Parkdale Neighbourhood Land Trust (PNLT) formed through the 'Parkdale People's Economy' project, a research initiative that started in 2010 and was based at the Parkdale Activity-Recreation Centre (PARC), a community activity and social program centre located in South Parkdale. The project first developed as a collaborative research exercise between students in a University of Toronto urban planning course and PARC staff that studied the effects of gentrification on food security issues in Parkdale (Richer, Htoo, Kamizaki, Mallin, Goodmurphy, Akande and Molale, 2010). The study recommended, among other ideas, the establishment of a community land trust as a way to 'hold land in trust for the community of Parkdale, and rent it to community agencies, local businesses and residents for a variety of uses that meet the community's needs' (ibid, 2010, ii). The report identified five suggestions for the creation of a CLT that would focus more on commercial and other alternate uses instead of affordable housing: i) fostering a dialogue with a 'wide range of community members about the idea of using a CLT for protecting small businesses from gentrification, for leasing spaces to food-related program/projects' such as the West End Food Co-op; ii) establishing an inventory of vacant land and government owned land and identification of 'sympathetic allies' who would consider donating or selling their land at a below-market rate to a CLT organization; iii) creating a CLT non-profit organization with registered charitable status; iv) establishing a financial plan and seeking governmental and philanthropic funding; v) finding non-profit developers to construct or renovate buildings on CLT land (ibid, 2010, 30–31). The study was adopted by PARC in order to assess the feasibility of the recommendations, which included the hire of a staff person to further develop the project and the community land trust idea in particular.

Following a period of research on the CLT model and various CLT organizational governance structures and methods of land use, the initiative developed into the Parkdale Neighbourhood Land Trust and was incorporated as a non-profit, non-governmental organization in 2014. The organization also received funding from the Ontario Trillium Foundation, a granting foundation of the Ontario provincial government that funds non-profit and charitable projects, that aided the creation of a more comprehensive organizational governance structure with representation from local residents, community businesses, and NGOs, and specific committees focused on program planning, community engagement, fundraising, and research. The current mission of PNLT is as follows, 'through the community land trust model, PNLT will acquire land and use it to meet the needs of Parkdale by leasing it to non-profit partners who can provide affordable housing, furnish spaces for social enterprises and non-profit organizations, and offer urban agriculture and open space' (The Parkdale People's Economy Project, 2015b). While the initial report that informed the creation of PNLT explicitly acknowledged the negative impacts of gentrification in Parkdale and offered the CLT as a mitigating solution, recent communications of the PNLT have somewhat tempered that approach. Although PNLT still emphasizes social and environmental justice as pursuits of CLT development, the organization has stated that, 'Parkdale is changing rapidly. This change is not inherently good or bad, but it raises important questions about affordability, diversity, and community assets in Parkdale. How can we ensure that everyone, particularly those with fewer resources and lower income, benefit from these changes?' (The Parkdale People's Economy Project, 2016). The inclusion of a 'value free' interpretation of neighbourhood change suggests that PNLT is hoping to broaden and attract more diverse participants in CLT activities and does not want to be characterized as a radical and explicitly 'anti-gentrification' organization. However, the tempering of a critique of gentrification does open possible space for CLT participant co-optation. This may include increased participation in CLT activities by gentrifier residents who consider themselves to be socially and/or environmentally progressive and have influential networks due to their

Source: Tish Carnat.

Figure 24.1 Milky Way Garden, Parkdale, Toronto

social positioning and professional occupations, yet who do not genuinely share the same social equity and justice concerns and needs as low-income residents. Nonetheless, the official organizational values that PNLT articulate focus on equitable development for low-income and marginalized people, collective action and engagement, and 'land as commons', among others (PNLT Purpose Vision Values, 2015a).

PNLT is currently acquiring its first land parcel following a sale offer of a 'lower-than-market price' for a lot owned by a local family, who had originally purchased the land in 2001. The landowners had been unable to secure the required municipal infrastructure provisions in order to build a house on the lot (Porter, 2016). While negotiating municipal permissions, the landowners leased the site, of approximately 5,500 square feet, to a local publicly funded 'English as a Second Language' learning program for use as a community garden, called the 'Milky Way Garden' after the name of the laneway close to where it is situated. The learning program largely engages Tibetan refugees who develop language skills through social interactions in the garden while at the same time growing and harvesting produce for their personal use and to share (ibid, 2016). Through local fundraising and individual donations, PNLT will be purchasing the lot and embarking on a community planning process to identify additional uses for the site, including a possible food incubator and small block of affordable housing units.

Although the land being acquired by PNLT is fairly small, the processes of community engagement in securing that land have created a sense of achievement and collaboration among and between PNLT advocates, language students who use the garden, and other Parkdale community organizations in relation to PNLT's goal of common land ownership. In this way, it is not so much the quantity of land that is being acquired but, instead, the relational connections with community-based issues and problems and a shared engagement in decisions over the common ownership of land that defines the PNLT as an alternative community organization and space. While not acting as a solution to entirely halt neighbourhood or city-wide gentrification processes, it offers a new space in Parkdale, and in Toronto more broadly, for community-focused discussions about gentrification and the future of the Parkdale neighbourhood while at the same time meeting the needs of low-income and other marginalized residents.

24.2.2   East London Community Land Trust, London, United Kingdom

The East London Community Land Trust (ELCLT) was formed in 2007 as a charitable organization of London Citizens, a social justice NGO and a member of the larger Britain-wide Citizens UK activist network. The use of CLTs in British cities has increased over the past decade as a community-based development approach to revitalize marginalized urban neighbourhoods, as well as to mitigate the effects of gentrification, depending on the location. Community land trusts now exist in cities such as Leeds, Liverpool, and Bristol, in addition to London (Bunce, 2016; Moore and McKee, 2012; Thompson, 2015). The ELCLT was organized as a way to address gentrification impacts in the eastern boroughs of London as well as concomitant problems of a lack of new affordable housing and overcrowding in existing affordable housing (ELCLT, 2010). Gentrification has become increasingly prevalent in eastern London boroughs such as Hackney over the past decade (Butler, Hamnett and Ramsden, 2013; Butler and Hamnett, 2011) with evidence of growing social polarization based on income disparity and lack of affordable housing (New Policy Institute, 2015). These transitions are particularly problematic in boroughs of London that have traditionally served as receptor areas for the working class and immigrants to Britain (Glynn, 2005).

In 2008, through extensive community engagement with different organizations and residents' groups in east London, the ELCLT selected a former National Health Service (NHS) hospital location, St. Clement's Hospital in Mile End in the eastern borough of Tower Hamlets, as a potential acquisition site. The site had initially been identified through research conducted by students at Queen Mary University, in collaboration with local institutions such as the East London Mosque and the Central Foundation School for Girls. The site and buildings, consisting of 4.6 acres of land and approximately 11,000 square metres of building mass, had been originally sold by the NHS to the Homes and Communities Agency (HCA) in 2005 (London Citizens, 2010a,b). With emphasis on potential ownership of the property, ELCLT staff facilitated discussions between

2008–2010 about possible community-oriented uses for the site through open public meetings and dialogue with local NGOs and educational and faith-based institutions. These discussions were also intended to convince the HCA to donate or sell the land to the ELCLT at a lower than average value (East London Community Land Trust, London, United Kingdom, personal interview, 11 October 2010; East London Community Land Trust, National CLT Conference, Albuquerque, USA, personal interview, 10 November 2010).

The HCA embarked, instead, on an open bid tendering process, requesting proposals that included those from private developers. Following the devolution of the HCA's responsibilities to the Greater London Authority (GLA), the ELCLT was asked to submit a second proposal after having their initial proposal accepted. The organization's bid emphasized development partnerships, with the inclusion of a private housing developer, in the community-based ownership of land. The ELCLT was also emboldened by broader political support around the inclusion of a 'community trust arrangement' in the bid criteria outlines by the GLA (East London Community Land Trust, London, United Kingdom, personal interview, 14 July 2011). Sadly, the GLA's final decision, announced in 2012, did not accept the ELCLT's bid but instead selected a proposal by Galliford Try, a London-area residential developer that supported establishing a 'community trust' on the site. The GLA, following the selection, suggested that Galliford Try work with ELCLT organizers to initiate a community land trust arrangement in the eventual development (East London Community Land Trust, Toronto, Canada, personal interview, 26 May 2014; Kelly, 2012). Following these deliberations, an agreement was negotiated between the GLA and Galliford Try that requires the freehold of the St. Clement's site to be transferred to an unspecified 'community foundation' upon completion of the development with a caveat that Galliford Try develop 223 housing units with 35% of the units geared towards affordable rental or affordable homeownership (Greater London Authority, 2012). The final agreement states that the ELCLT will own and arrange the sale of approximately 21 of the built affordable units, while Peabody Trust, a London-based housing association, will manage the affordable rental units (ibid, 2012).

In keeping with the ELCLT's dedication to securing affordable housing for local residents, the ELCLT's affordable homes, now increased to 23 units and currently in the process of being sold, are being made available to Tower Hamlets residents who are unable to afford market rate housing and who are ELCLT members (London Community Land Trust, 2016). The units will cost approximately half of the average market rate for housing in Mile End (Right Move, 2016) and are priced at approximately £130,000 for a one bedroom unit and £235,000 for a three bedroom unit (London Community Land Trust, 2016). Eligibility for affordable housing will be measured against the average annual income of Tower Hamlets residents and each new owner will enter into a binding contract with the ELCLT that will significantly mitigate their ability to profit from any future resale of the housing unit (National CLT Network, East London CLT and Citizens UK, 2014; Smith, 2014). The final decision over the development of the site has resulted in less affordable units than was initially proposed in the ELCLT's first ownership and development bid. The decision also demonstrates that the GLA selected their preferred developer while at the same time drawing on support from the ELCLT for implementing a community land trust arrangement, yet with only limited control and involvement by the ELCLT. Despite the outcome, however, the ELCLT views the inclusion of a community trust arrangement and the ownership of affordable housing on the site as a success and demonstrative of their political campaigning for and community engagement around the idea of a CLT (Interview D, 2014). It is also understood as a victory for raising public awareness about the current problems of property ownership and localized gentrification and the need for the de-commodification of land and housing as a response (Smith, 2014). Additionally, the public attention on the St. Clement's site and the role of community land trusts in allowing for community assets and affordable housing has recently sparked recent CLT initiatives in other areas of London. The ELCLT has initiated a name change to 'London Community Land Trust' in order to better advocate for CLT development in all London boroughs (London CLT, 2016; National CLT Network, East London Community Land Trust and Citizens UK, 2014). Like the Parkdale Neighbourhood Land Trust, the success of the ELCLT and its role in community-based development and challenging gentrification lies not in the size or scope of their implementation of the community land trust model but rather in the enhancement of community and city-wide awareness and discussion about CLTs as an alternative to traditional property ownership practices and as a reaction to housing affordability problems caused by gentrification. While 23 affordable ownership homes seems like a small number given the necessity of affordable housing in east London, the use of the CLT approach in Tower Hamlets and the subsequent 'butterfly effect' of interest in CLT development across London suggests that there is emerging interest in, and need for, community-based control over property ownership and land stewardship. The ELCLT has also developed connections with broader networks of CLT organizations in the UK through their association with the National Community Land Trust Network, an NGO that provides technical and communications assistance to rural and urban CLTs in England and Wales (National Community Land Trust Network, 2016).

24.3   URBAN ECOVILLAGES

In a similar way to community land trusts, ecovillages or ecocommunities support collective decision making about land use and community assets. Ecovillaging, however, places an emphasis on shared concerns about the biophysical environment and environmental sustainability with the idea that ecovillage spaces provide respite from environmental problems and a forum for an alternative lifestyle that resists and challenges consumerist practices (Boyer, 2015; Ergas, 2010; Litfin, 2014). Pickerill (2016) writes that, 'living in eco-communities is about acknowledging the interdependency of humans with each other and nature, and practicing mutual care . . . In this context, eco-communities are understood to be part of a wider movement advocating communing; to produce, live off and through the commons' (p. 221). Ecovillages were first named by Robert Gilman, author of a policy report on intentional sustainable communities written in 1991 for the environmental charity, Gaia Trust. The use of the term 'ecovillage' was a way to comprehensively define emerging, self-determined, environmental communities that specifically focused on ecological planning and design and to differentiate these communities from other intentional settlements (Ergas, 2010). Increasingly, ecovillages have become relevant in cities as a way for individuals to develop a collective, ideological, and spatial identity that opposes contemporary urban production and consumption practices and allows for experimental lifestyle within cities rather than opposing urban contexts in favour of rural or wilderness locations (Boyer, 2015; Chitewere, 2010) that are considered to be more 'in nature' and 'off-grid'.

Rather than being insular communities, ecovillages have established inter-organizational connectivity through the formation of international on-line and educational networks. For example, the Global Ecovillage Network (GEN) is a United Nations Economic and Social Council affiliated NGO that connects over 400 ecovillages in urban and rural locations in Africa, North America, Latin America, Europe, and Asia, with additional regional network organizations (Global Ecovillage Network, 2014; Litfin, 2014). GEN Africa, for example, connects over 200 ecovillages across the continent and shares technical and educational resources (GEN Africa, 2014).

24.3.1 Eco-Yoff, Dakar, Senegal

Africa's first national-level ecovillage network, GENSEN, was developed in Senegal and links together 45 rural and urban ecovillages across the country. One particular urban ecovillage, Eco-Yoff, located in the northern section of Dakar and in close proximity to Senegal's primary airport, serves as a global model for urban ecovillaging due to its emphasis on poverty alleviation through social and environmental micro-enterprises. Eco-Yoff prohibits automobile use in the community, operates an environmental education centre that receives local and international 'ecovillagers' for ecovillage training workshops, and supports environmental practices such as waste water recycling, solar powered electricity, and planting vegetation as a measure against climate change impacts such as flooding (Birkeland, 2008; Gaia Education, 2016; GENSenegal, n.d.). Eco-Yoff organizers also list land speculation in the coastal neighbourhoods surrounding Yoff as a recent challenge (GENSenegal, n.d.). This relates to the occurrence of rising property values due to middle class gentrification and growing foreign investment in luxury vacation property development along Dakar's coastline and a recently estimated 256% increase in the city's property prices between 1994–2010 (Senegal National Statistics Agency in Global Property Guide, 2014). Eco-Yoff demonstrates how ecovillage practices in the global south are developing as community-based solutions to poverty, environmental problems, and new forms of land speculation and development. This is particularly important given the globalization of gentrification and the increasing occurrence of gentrification in major African cities (Lees, Shin and López-Morales, 2015, 2016; Simone, 2010; Simone and Abouhani, 2005).

The role of urban ecovillage organizations in addressing the impacts of gentrification is less explicit than with community land trusts but their significance rests in providing an alternative method of urban living that inherently opposes the production and consumerist practices of gentrification. Urban ecovillages must cope with the pressures and challenges of carving out an alternative space within broader political-economic contexts of urban development and growth, often in close spatial proximity to areas with rising property values. Ecovillages also have to address the everyday challenges of choosing subsistence living as a practice of resistance and sustainability within the pressures of larger urban consumerist society. In writing about the counter-normative characteristics of ecovillages, Ergas (2010) suggests that they 'confront ideological differences from a dominant culture that designates status in terms of material possessions that require the perpetual extraction of precious resources' (p. 35). In her ethnographic study of ecovillagers and their personal motivations for living in alternative intentional communities, she notes that, 'ecovillagers believe they live a critique. Their everyday actions deny consumerist ideologies and are political in a dominant culture that sets the consumerist context' (Ergas, 2010, 35–36). Certainly, common ecovillaging practices that are also prevalent in urban ecovillages, such as subsistence-oriented permaculture and small livestock farming, clothes making and other cottage industries, the construction of housing with renewable materials, and a reliance on reusable water and renewable energy sources, emphasize the internal use of material goods that are primarily produced through ecovillage labour, intended for community subsistence, and greatly differ from the everyday realities of urban living.

24.3.2 The Los Angeles Ecovillage, USA

The Los Angeles Ecovillage (LAEV) is a strong example of a culturally diverse eco-community that adheres to social and environmental justice principles and identifies as a distinct community but also has associations with surrounding communities and neighbourhoods. The community has also had to address pressures caused by gentrification in the downtown core of Los Angeles and the need to protect commonly held land in light of these issues. Litfin (2014), as part of her international ethnographic study of fourteen ecovillages, notes that the formation of LAEV was heavily influenced by a need for progressive, 'on the ground' social and environmental justice responses following the Los Angeles riots in 1992 (p. 30). The Los Angeles Ecovillage is located on two street blocks within the Wilshire Centre/Koreatown section of Los Angeles and has managed to develop and maintain its micro-scale focus, despite its location and pressures from surrounding central city developments and private landowners (Boyer, 2015). Boyer (2015) writes that the LAEV project was initiated through local NGO efforts to create a visionary 'neighbourhood of co-operatives' that would provide co-operative services and programs in one location. Between 1986 and 1991, the NGO focused on raising funds to acquire what was, at that time, inexpensive land with the intention of creating a social and environmental community that embraced communal practices. In 2007, LAEV residents formed the Beverly-Vermont Community Land Trust and transferred land ownership to the CLT, which arranged a 99-year lease with the ecovillage's co-operative association that manages the housing units. The use and integration of a community land trust into LAEV was a way to retain and protect long-term ownership and affordability of the land in light of increasing property development pressures, to place collective restrictions on land use, and prevent the future resale of ecovillage land and building infrastructure for profit (Beverly-Vermont Community Land Trust, 2016). The Los Angeles Ecovillage currently consists of 40 residents residing in three cooperative housing complexes on land owned by the CLT, with various environmental initiatives, such as a bicycle repair shop for ecovillage and Los Angeles residents, vegetable gardens and a large rain garden, permeable sidewalks to reduce stormwater flow, a bulk food cooperative that procures organic food from local farms, skills trading and currency free exchange, and artistic events such as Eco-Maya, which celebrates Mayan cultural history and is open to all Los Angeles residents (Boyer, 2015; Litfin, 2014; Los Angeles Ecovillage, 2016). The longevity of LAEV demonstrates a commitment to building an intentional community with strong organizational mechanisms such as the community land trust to retain land ownership as well as connections with surrounding neighbourhood residents and the wider city. The Los Angeles Ecovillage's more fluid and less insular approach to ecovillaging presents a model for how urban ecovillages might develop in gentrifying or already gentrified urban areas.

24.4   CONCLUSION

As alternative organizations and spaces, community land trusts and ecovillages strive to resist and challenge both the production and consumerist practices of gentrification in cities. I suggest that a strength of community land trusts and ecovillages lies in their ability to galvanize public attention towards and raise necessary discussions about community owned land as an alternative mode of property ownership. Although these organizations work at a small scale, their collective efforts are now becoming increasingly evident through emerging national and global networks of both community land trusts and ecovillages. Community land trusts, with their uniform focus on community-based land ownership and maintaining the long-term affordability of land through the creation of ground lease contracts, offer an alternative model that can be replicated in various urban locations. The practices of environmental subsistence found in urban ecovillages demonstrate an environmentally sound approach that inherently opposes consumerist practices and suggests new communal ways to reside in cities. Although challenges exist for both approaches with regard to how easily land can be acquired in areas with high property values, community land trusts and ecovillages offer emergent and important possibilities for countering social, economic, and environmental pressures caused by gentrification.

REFERENCES

Alternatives for Community and Development (2015) *Fighting Gentrification and Displacement* 19 August 2015. Available at: www.ace-ej.org/node/11641 (last accessed: 16 July 2016).

Beverly-Vermont Community Land Trust. Available at: laecovillage.org/community-land-trust (last accessed: 30 June 2016).

Birkeland, J. (2008) *Positive Development: From Vicious Circles to Virtuous Cycles through Built Environmental Design*, London: Earthscan.

Blomley, N. (2004) *Unsettling the City: Urban Land and the Politics of Property*, Abingdon: Routledge.

Boyer, R. (2015) 'Grassroots innovation for urban sustainability: comparing the diffusion pathways of three ecovillage projects', *Environment and Planning A*, 45, 320–337.

Bunce, S. (2016) 'Pursuing urban commons: politics and alliances in community land trust activism in east London', *Antipode*, 48(1), 134–150.

Bunce, S., Khimani, N., Sungu-Erylimaz, Y. and Earle, E. (2013) *Urban Community Land Trusts: Experiences from Canada, the United States, and Britain*. Available at:http://www.academia.edu/2584425/Urban_Community_Land_Trust_Handbook_2013_ (last accessed: 3 July 2016).

Butler, T. and Hamnett, C. (2011) *Ethnicity, Class and Aspiration: Understanding London's New East End*, Bristol: Policy Press.

Butler, T., Hamnett, C. and Ramsden, M. (2013) 'Gentrification, education and exclusionary displacement in east London', *International Journal of Urban and Regional Research*, 37(2), 556–575.

Caffentzis, G. and Federici, S. (2014) 'Commons against and beyond capitalism', *Community Development Journal*, 49(s.1), i92–i105.

Catungal, J., Leslie, D. and Hii, Y. (2009) 'Geographies of displacement in the creative city: the case of Liberty Village, Toronto', *Urban Studies*, 46(5/6), 1095–1114s.

Chitewere, T. (2010) 'Equity in sustainable communities: exploring tool from environmental justice and political ecology', *Natural Resources Journal*, 50(2), 315–339.

Class War (2015) *Poor Doors*. Available at: www.classwarparty.org.uk/category/poor-doors/ (last accessed: 30 June 2016).

Coulthard, G. (2014) *Red Skin, White Masks: Rejecting the Colonial Politics of Recognition*, Minneapolis: University of Minnesota Press.

Crabtree, L. (2010) 'Fertile ground for CLT development in Australia', in Davis, J.E. (ed) *The Community Land Trust Reader*, Cambridge, MA: Lincoln Institute of Land Policy, pp. 464–476.

Curtin, J. and Bocarsly, L. (2010) 'CLTs: a growing trend in affordable home ownership', in Davis, J.E. (ed) *The Community Land Trust Reader*, Cambridge, MA: Lincoln Institute of Land Policy, pp. 289–314.

Davidson, M. (2011) 'Critical commentary: gentrification in crisis: towards consensus or disagreement?', *Urban Studies*, 48(10), 1987–1996.

Davis, J.E. (ed) (2010) *The Community Land Trust Reader*, Cambridge, MA: Lincoln Institute of Land Policy.

DeFilippis, J. (2001) 'The myth of social capital in community development', *Housing Policy Debate*, 12(4), 781–806.

DeFilippis, J. (2004) *Unmaking Goliath: Community Control in the Face of Global Capital*, Abingdon: Routledge.

Dudley Neighbors Incorporated (n.d.) The Community Land Trust: Land Trust 101. Available at: http://www. dudleyneighbors.org/land-trust-101.html (last accessed: 10 July 2016).

Ergas, C. (2010) 'A model of sustainable living: collective identity in an urban ecovillage', *Organization and Environment*, 23(1), 32–54.

Eviction Free San Francisco (2010) Available at: evictionfreesf.org (last accessed: 30 June 2016).

Federici, S. (2010) 'Feminism and the politics of the commons', in Hughes, C., Peace, S. and Van Meter, T. (eds) *Uses of a Whirlwind: Movement, Movements, and Contemporary Radical Currents in the United States*, Oakland: AK Press, pp. 283–294.

Gaia Education (n.d.) *About Gaia Trust Ecovillages*. Available at: www.gaia.org/gaia/education/living/ (last accessed: 16 July 2016).

GEN Africa (n.d.) *Global Ecovillage Network Africa*. Available at: www.gen-africa.org/ (last accessed: 16 July 2016).

GEN Senegal (n.d.) *GENSEN: Global Ecovillage Network Senegal*. Available at: www.gensenegal.org/ (last accessed: 16 July 2016).

Gibson-Graham, J.K., Cameron, J. and Healy, S. (2013) *Take Back the Economy: An Ethical Guide for Transforming Our Communities*, Minneapolis MN: University of Minnesota Press.

Global Ecovillage Network (2014) *Connecting Communities for a Sustainable World*. Available at: www.gen. ecovillage.org/ (last accessed: 16 July 2016).

Global Property Guide (2014) Senegal's property boom continues, 27 December 2014. Available at: www. globalpropertyguide.com/Africa/Senegal (last accessed: 16 July 2016).

Glynn, S. (2005) 'East End immigrants and the battle for housing: a comparative study of political mobilization in the Jewish and Bengali communities', *Journal of Historical Geography*, 31, 528–545.

Gray, K. (2008) 'Community land trusts in the United States', *Journal of Community Practice*, 16(1), 65–78.

Greater London Authority (2012) Request for Mayoral Decision – MD1028, 16 July 2012 London, Greater London Authority.

Gujit, I. and Shah, M. (eds) (1998) *The Myth of Community: Gender Issues in Participatory Development*, London: Intermediate Technology Publications.

Harvey, D. (2009) 'The "new" imperialism: accumulation by dispossession', in Panitch, L. and Leys, C. (eds) *Social Register 2004: The New Imperial Challenge*, London: Merlin, pp. 63–87.

Harvey, D. (2012) *Rebel Cities: From the Right to the City to the Urban Revolution*, London: Verso.

Kelly, L. (2012) 'Community trust sparks move towards genuinely affordable housing in capital', *The Guardian* Monday 16 July 2012. Available at: https://www.theguardian.com/housing-network/2012/jul/16/london-community-land-trust-homes.

Lees, L., Shin, H. and López-Morales, E. (eds) (2015) *Global Gentrifications: Uneven Development and Displacement*, Bristol: Policy Press.

Lees, L., Shin, H. and López-Morales, E. (2016) *Planetary Gentrification*, Cambridge: Polity Press.

Lees, L., Slater, T. and Wyly, E. (2008) *Gentrification*, New York: Routledge.

Litfin, K. (2014) *Ecovillages: Lessons for Sustainable Community*, Cambridge: Polity Press.

Logan, J. and Murdie, R. (2016) 'Home in Canada? The settlement experiences of Tibetans in Parkdale, Toronto', *International Migration and Integration*, 17, 95–113.

Loh, P. (2015) 'How one Boston Neighborhood Stopped Gentrification in its Tracks', *Yes! Magazine* 28 January.

London Community Land Trust (2016) Available at: www.londonclt.org (last accessed: 3 July 2016).

London Tenants Federation, Lees, L., Just Space and Southwark Notes Archive Group (2014) *Staying Put: An Anti-Gentrification Handbook for Council Estates in London*. Available at: southwarknotes.files.wordpress. com/2014/06/staying-put-web-version-low.pdf.

Los Angeles Ecovillage (2016) Available at: http://laecovillage.org (last accessed: 3 July 2016).

Mazer, K. and Rankin, K. (2011) 'The social space of gentrification: the politics of neighborhood accessibility in Toronto's Downtown West', *Environment and Planning D*, 29(5), 822–839.

Medoff, P. and Sklar, H. (1999) *Streets of Hope: The Fall and Rise of an Urban Neighborhood*, Boston MA: South End Press.

Meehan, J. (2014) 'Reinventing real estate: the community land trust as a social invention in affordable housing', *Journal of Applied Social Science*, 8(2), 113–133.

Midheme, E. and Mouleart, F. (2013) 'Pushing back the frontiers of property: community land trusts and low-income housing in urban Kenya', *Land Use Policy*, 35, 73–84.

Moore, T. and McKee, K. (2012) 'Empowering local communities? An international review of community land trusts', *Housing Studies*, 27(2), 280–290.

National CLT Network, East London Community Land Trust, and Citizens UK (2014) *Evidence to the Review: Improving the Secondary Market for Affordable Homes*, London, National CLT Network.

National CLT Network (2016) Available at: www.communitylandtrusts.org.uk/ (last accessed: 16 June 2016).

Ontario Coalition Against Poverty (2016) *Homelessness/Housing*. Available at: update.ocap.ca/housing (last accessed: 30 June 2016).

Parkdale People's Economy Project (2015a) *Purpose Vision Values*. Available at: www.pnlt.ca/about/ (accessed: 16 June 2016).

Parkdale People's Economy Project (2015b) *Community Land Trust*. Available at: www.pnlt.ca/about/ (accessed: 16 June 2016).

Pickerill, J. (2016) *Eco-Homes: People, Place, and Politics*, London: Zed Books.

Porter, C. (2016) 'Activists' generosity blooms in Parkdale garden', *The Toronto Star* 27 May 2016.

Rameau, M. (2008) *Take Back the Land: Land, Gentrification, and the Umoja Village Shantytown*, Oakland, CA: AK Press.

Richer, C., Htoo, S., Kamizaki, K. et al. (2010) *Beyond Bread and Butter: Toward Food Security in a Changing Parkdale*. Available at: www.pchc.on.ca/assets/files/beyond%20bread%20and%20butter.pdf (last accessed: 8 June 2016).

Robinson, T. (1996) 'Inner-City innovator: the non-profit community development corporation', *Urban Studies*, 33(9), 1647–1670.

Rose, K. (n.d.) 'Combating gentrification through equitable development', *Re-imagine! Race, Poverty and the Environment*. Available at: www.reimaginerpe.org/node/919 (last accessed: 25 June 2016).

Seminary of the Street (n.d.) 'Meet us at the Corner of Love and Justice!'. Available at: www.seminaryofthestreet. org (last accessed: 25 June 2016).

Serve the People Los Angeles (2016). Available at: servethepeoplela.org (last accessed: 30 June 2016).

Simone, A. (2010) *City Life from Jakarta to Dakar: Movements at the Crossroads*, Abingdon: Routledge.

Simone, A. and Abouhani, A. (2005) *Urban Africa: Changing Contours of Survival in the City*, London: Zed Books.

Slater, T. (2004) 'Municipally managed gentrification in South Parkdale, Toronto', *Canadian Geographer*, 48(3), 303–325.

Slater, T. (2009) Missing Marcuse: On gentrification and displacement', *City*, 13(2–3), 292–311.

Smith, D. (2002) 'Rural gatekeepers: closing and opening up "access" to greentrified Pennine rurality', *Social and Cultural Geography*, 3, 445–461.

Smith, D. (2007) 'The "buoyancy" of "other" geographies of gentrification: going "back-to-the-water" and the commodification of marginality', *Tijdschrift voor Economische en Sociale Geografie*, 98(1), 53–67.

Smith, D. (2014) 'The half-price houses coming soon to east London', *The Guardian* 27 March 2014.

Sungu-Erylimaz, Y. and Greenstein, R. (2007) *A National Study of Community Land Trusts*, Cambridge, MA: Lincoln Institute of Land Policy.

Susser, I. and Tonnelat, S. (2013) 'Transformative cities: the three commons', *Focaal*, 66, 105–121.

Taylor, E. (1995) 'The Dudley Street Neighborhood Initiative and the power of eminent domain', *Boston College Law Review*, 35(5), 1061–1087.

Thompson, M. (2015) 'Between boundaries: from commoning and guerilla gardening to community land trust development in Liverpool', *Antipode*, 47(4), 1021–1042.

Whitzman, C. and Slater, T. (2006) 'Village ghetto land: myth, social conditions, and housing policy in Parkdale, Toronto, 1879–2000', *Urban Affairs Review*, 41(5), 673–696.

Wyly, E. (2015) 'Gentrification on the planetary urban frontier: the evolution of Turner's noosphere', *Urban Studies*, 52(14), 2515–2550.

Yuen, J. (2014) 'City farms on CLTs', *Land Lines*, April Issue Cambridge, MA: Lincoln Institute of Land Policy.

Yuen, J. and Rosenberg, G. (2013) 'Hanging on to the land', *Shelterforce: The Voice of Community Development* (February Issue).

Zukin, S. (1989) *Loft Living: Culture and Capital in Urban Change*, New Brunswick, NJ: Rutgers University Press.

25. Immigration and gentrification
Geoffrey DeVerteuil

25.1 INTRODUCTION

Immigration involves the 'deliberate crossing of nation-state borders', moving into a particular country rather than out, sometimes permanently but increasingly with (transnational) ties to the home country (Waters, 2009: 297; Boyle, 2009). This differs from migrants, who could be internal to the nation-state, region or even city, connecting to ideas of residential mobility. International immigration is presently one of the main generators of demographic change in cities, while gentrification is one of the main pathways of class-based restructuring and re-composition of urban space – yet the two have rarely been placed systematically alongside each other (but for localized examples see Betancur, 2002; Murdie and Teixeira, 2011; Stabrowski, 2014). In fact, 'immigration' does not even feature in the much-cited *Gentrification* compendium (Lees et al, 2008), despite Lees (2000) listing it as a future research issue, although it is implicit in certain case studies. But while immigration has been largely ignored, this is not the case with the sometimes-overlapping notion of 'race', defined as 'a social construction but, as such, has material consequences that can be matters of life and death' (Winders, 2009: 53). The intersections of 'race' and class-inflected gentrification are particularly prominent in the United States, such that Freeman (2006: 3) noted the 'Black inner city of America is surely a singular and unique phenomenon that demands its own perspective when considering gentrification' (see also Lees, 2016). The relationship between 'race' and gentrification has been well-covered, with a plethora of studies on the spectre of incoming White gentrifiers (and sometimes incumbent Black ones) displacing poorer residents in formerly disinvested African-American neighborhoods – such as Venice in Los Angeles (Deener, 2012), Capitol Hill in Washington DC (Hopkinson, 2012), Harlem in New York City (Freeman, 2006) and Bywater in New Orleans (Peck, 2006).

This gentrification-induced reversal of White flight from American cities to the suburbs, however, has likely drawn precious attention away from the relationship between gentrification and immigrants. Perhaps another reason why little has been written systematically on this relationship is the assumption that gentrification and immigration effectively repel each other in urban space – concentrated immigration forecloses gentrification by vexing higher-income groups, while increased gentrification pushes out immigrant enclaves (Ley, 2010; Vicino et al, 2011; Walks and Maaranen, 2008). But surely there is more empirical complexity than this, such that the relationship ought to be unpacked both conceptually but also geographically. More to the point, while 'race' is compelling precisely because of its stereotypically 'black and white' nature between downtrodden resident and incoming gentrifier, the relationship between immigrant and gentrifier is likely to be more multifaceted – do they meet, do they repel, do they overlap, do they work as one, do they polarize?

In this chapter, I propose a fivefold typology of immigrant-gentrification relationships, drawing on globe-spanning material that suggests various permutations: (1) immigrants as barriers to gentrification; (2) immigrants living side-by-side with gentrification, essentially a bubble model; (3) immigrants displaced by gentrification; (4) immigrants avoid gentrified areas a priori; and (5) immigrants are themselves gentrifiers, enclave-style. Throughout the description of the typology, I am conscious of Clerval's (2013) argument that immigrants and gentrifiers are not equal in their social and economic standing. To her, gentrifiers are doubly dominant in that they belong to the class and race in power, enabling them to effectively make their mark upon the neighbourhood and appropriate its symbols, rather than assimilating into local realities and long-held legacies as immigrants are expected to. Yet while many immigrants are clearly racialized and thus held to be subordinate, others are considered more 'ethnic', in terms of having shared culture and heritage, and without necessarily holding a lower racial category from the non-immigrant, so-called 'native' population and gentrifiers (Winders, 2009). This opens up the consideration that some immigrants may gentrify their own enclaves, and so I entertain in the last category the potential that the two groups can actually be the same. Given that the last category has hence largely been ignored, I will provide a case study of Koreatown (Los Angeles), using primary and secondary data to delve further into the dynamics of gentrification undertaken by first- and second-generation Korean immigrants in their original 'hub neighbourhood' (original point of entry, but also considered the cultural heart of the immigrant community) west of Downtown Los Angeles.

By taking immigrants seriously in their relationship to gentrification, this chapter is inspired by recent tendencies in gentrification theory that advance a more theoretically and empirically open approach, while building on the still-useful insights of three decades of the traditional political economy perspective. More specifically, gentrification has long been wedded to a narrow set of Western cities and plagued by insular (and polarizing) debates (e.g. Slater, 2006; Davidson, 2007; Lees et al, 2008; Wyly, 2015), especially in terms of causation but also with respect to consequences. Of late, there has been a concerted effort to link gentrification with more cosmopolitan and comparative stances, effectively connecting gentrification theory with more open-ended constructs (including planetary urbanization, comparative methods) and thereby decolonizing its once parochial touchstones (Wyly, 2015; Lees et al, 2015, 2016; Shin et al, 2016). This allows us to fully appreciate Atkinson and Bridge's (2005: 15) insight that 'gentrification provides a vital debate around which the analysis of globalization, international migration, and neighbourhood change are increasingly attached'. This more globalized stance (see also Davidson, 2007) further links to ideas of planetary gentrification, whose fundamental characteristics and 'global regularities' (Lees et al, 2015: 6) of class polarization, re-investment and displacement profuse across the Global North and the Global South, acting as a privileged gateway to understanding urban inequality writ large. In other words, seeing 'gentrification as a dimension of planetary urbanization' as much as 'gentrification in cities' (Wyly, 2015: 2515). If we are serious about committing to a globalized, cosmopolitan and comparative approach to gentrification, then surely one way forward is to consider its relationship with another potentially globe-spanning agent – the immigrant – which moves us beyond merely considering gentrification as a globally mobile policy strategy, anchored in global cities and articulated by cosmopolitan subjects (Davidson, 2007) to considering the extralocal and the 'elsewhere' beyond the 'usual suspects' (e.g. London, New York City, San Francisco, Sydney).

25.2   TYPOLOGY

In this age of rapid conceptual churn and flux within urban studies (DeVerteuil, 2016), it might seem quaint to use a typological approach to understand the idiosyncrasies of the immigrant-gentrification relationship. However, my proposed typology will prove useful in building up a 'geography of gentrification' (Lees, 2000), in which immigrant settlement patterns play an equally important role in the processes of gentrification, thereby capturing tensions that exist between the two dynamics of contemporary urban change. Furthermore, it is a geography focused not just on the top-tier global cities but also on less dynamic places where gentrification and immigration are only beginning to rub shoulders (Hwang, 2015).

Snow and Anderson (1993: 36) defined typologies as '. . . the process by which members of some empirical domain are categorized and ordered in terms of their similarities and differences . . . . The resulting classificatory scheme directs the observer's attention to certain aspects of the phenomenon under study'. I will focus on just a few critical dimensions that most encapsulate the relationship between gentrification and immigration at the neighbourhood scale, set within the larger metropolitan context: the degree and nature of spatial interactions between gentrification and immigration; the intra-urban dynamics that help structure those interactions; and the level of gentrification at the metropolitan scale. More specifically, while I focus on the spatial interactions at the neighbourhood scale, these cannot be divorced from (and are in fact in relation with) larger metropolitan processes, including the timing and extent of the overall gentrification and immigration patterns (and policies), the inertia and legacy of the built environment, and metropolitan dynamics in terms of centripetal or centrifugal tendencies of (re)investment.

My typology overlaps with (1) a locally specific yet globally crosscutting view of gentrification and immigration (Krijnen and Beukelaer, 2015), and (2) a comparative urbanism approach, open to different forms of gentrification based on very different urban cultures and systems (Ley and Teo, 2014). Most but certainly not all of the examples in Table 25.1 come from the Global North, which is inevitable given the greater focus on these cities as crucibles of both gentrification and international immigration (Ley, 2010). However, the majority of immigrants come from the Global South, which inherently mixes the two urban worlds up, and that some Global South cities do more than just produce migrants to the North – they also attract Global South migrants, to places such as Dubai, Johannesburg and Singapore (see also Benton-Short et al, 2005).

The proposed five categories of gentrification-immigration relationships build on previously established stage models in gentrification that incorporate both temporal and spatial sequences. Early models, such as that of Clay (1979), represented gentrification in an 'orderly temporal, sequential progress' (Lees et al, 2008: 34) from pioneer to established, while more recent models are less teleological and can follow myriad sequences, including gentrification stalling or even reversing itself, but increasingly underlining the squarely state-sponsored nature of gentrification (Lees et al, 2016). It is important to note that categories 2 through 4 are part of a sequence, one in which gentrification overspills onto immigrant settlements and eventually, given enough time, displaces them entirely from the inner city, to the point where immigrants will avoid these inner-city areas a priori. Yet there is nothing inevitable about this sequence, as neighbourhood gentrification can be postponed in any of these categories. However, categories 1 and 5 are outliers – the first

Table 25.1 Typology of the immigrant-gentrification relationship

RELATIONSHIP	METROPOLITAN CONTEXT: INTRA-URBAN DYNAMICS	METROPOLITAN CONTEXT: OVERALL LEVEL OF GENTRIFICATION	NEIGHBOURHOOD SPATIAL INTERACTIONS	NEIGHBOURHOOD EXAMPLES
CATEGORY 1: IMMIGRANTS AS BARRIER TO GENTRIFICATION	heavily immigrant	weak	no interactions	Paris – Goute d'Or; Buenos Aires – Once; Jo'burg – Hillbrow; Singapore – Little India
CATEGORY 2: IMMIGRANTS LIVE SIDE BY SIDE WITH GENTRIFICATION	gentrifying, strong center	gentrifying	The two groups live in geographical proximity yet socially tectonic (Butler, 2003)	London – Stoke Newington; Paris – 10th arrondissement
CATEGORY 3: IMMIGRANTS DISPLACED BY GENTRIFICATION	gentrifying, strong center	gentrifying	dwindling	New York – Chinatown; Panama City – Casco Viejo
CATEGORY 4: IMMIGRANTS AVOID GENTRIFIED AREAS A PRIORI	gentrified, strong center	very strong and established	no interactions	Toronto suburbs; New York City beyond Manhattan; Sydney suburbs; Vancouver suburbs
CATEGORY 5: IMMIGRANTS AS GENTRIFIERS	heavily immigrant, polycentric or weak center	weak	collapsed	Miami – Little Havana; Los Angeles – Koreatown

category speaks to a heavily immigrant inner city where barriers are many to potential gentrification, while the fifth category sees immigrants as the gentrifiers, working to upgrade their own enclaves. This model should not, however, be confused with other forms of upgrading via overseas investors, who do not follow the enclave model and invest in established areas of wealth, such as Russians in London.

25.2.1   Category 1: Immigrants as Barrier to Gentrification

In this first category, immigrants are a solid barrier to gentrification. I can begin to consider this 'thwarted gentrification' in the heavily immigrant areas of Paris such as the Goutte d'Or (Pattaroni et al, 2012; Clerval, 2013), which adjoins solidly immigrant suburbs. Clerval (2013) notes that two intertwined barriers to gentrification presented themselves in eastern arrondissements – a conspicuous concentration of social housing and a strong presence of immigrants (mostly African and North African), thereby linking a discredited and outdated built environment with a population held in suspicion, and representing the tip of much larger immigrant/social housing enclaves to the north and east of the city. For her, immigrants are the new working class in the city, subsuming the once much larger and decidedly native-born cluster in the east of Paris, une classe ouvrière et populaire, which had endured Hausmann's violent 19th-century displacements but could not survive the massive spatial dislocations in post-war France. The sheer domination of immigrants in these areas puts off gentrification, both symbolically in public spaces and materially in terms of the density of social housing and absentee landlords. Pattaroni et al (2012: 1236) concurred, proposing that 'even left-wing liberal gentrifiers – unable to anchor a satisfactory mode of living – are also leaving the Goutte d'Or', which links to the broader literature on barriers to gentrification that include a poor built environment, lack of amenities, unconventional public behaviour and a politics of resistance abetted by the state (Ley and Dobson, 2008; DeVerteuil, 2012). This can be extended to places such as Pico-Union to the immediate west of Downtown Los Angeles, where a solid wall of working poor immigrants from Mexico and Central America present a daunting barrier to even the hardiest of pioneer gentrifiers (DeVerteuil 2011, 2015; for Toronto see Walks and August, 2008, on how entrenched and stable immigrant communities, based in secure tenancy and deep-seated ties, hold back the tide of gentrification).

The Global South also has its fair share of heavily immigrant areas that thwart incipient gentrification. Here I can point to Johannesburg, where once White-only areas near the CBD, such as Hillbrow, have been sequentially disinvested and resettled by African immigrants in large numbers. What little gentrification there is in central Johannesburg has left this area untouched (Rogerson and Rogerson, 2014). In a similar example in Buenos Aires, where gentrification has taken hold to the south of the CBD (San Telmo, Boca), the heavily immigrant areas (e.g. Paraguayan, Bolivian) to the west, such as Once, have seen little in the way of upgrading (Herzer et al, 2015). Finally, Little India in Singapore has also seen little gentrification, its internal coherency protected by a high degree of ethnic concentration and solidarity (Chang, 2016).

25.2.2 Category 2: Immigrants Live Side by Side with Gentrification – Bubble Model

This bubble model was first proposed by May (1996) in Stoke Newington in north-east London, who found the routine of gentrified life was strictly demarcated, surrounded by immigrants but rarely encountering them in meaningful ways. In this account, social life was 'tectonic' (Butler, 2003), in that gentrifiers and immigrants lived spatially proximate yet socially separate existences. In his study of gentrification of Islington in London, Butler (2003: 2469) found newer gentrifiers were 'unwilling to invest social capital in the area and that their relationships are almost entirely with "people like us"', and this despite the fact that gentrifiers find many immigrant neighbourhoods initially interesting for their diversity. In effect, there is little actual mixing and social institutions remain segregated, especially education (see Clerval, 2013; Butler, 2003; Freeman, 2006).

Clerval (2013) describes a similarly tectonic relationship in the more mixed immigrant quartiers of Paris, where gentrifiers would feel more comfortable in the social mix while studiously avoiding sending their children to local schools (see also Clerval and Fleury, 2009). This state of affairs should not be surprising, given that gentrification is late in coming to Paris, thereby allowing gentrifiers to rub shoulders with longstanding immigrant communities, especially in eastern arrondissements such as the 10th. Another example may be given in central Madrid (Sequera and Janoschka, 2015), where non-European immigrants are a strong presence but not in sufficient numbers to have deterred an equally strong presence of gentrifiers, co-existing for the time being in the same 'exotic' space but worlds apart socially. Across the Atlantic, the Mission District in San Francisco was an example of scrupulous yet precarious co-existence between long-established Latino immigrants and newer White gentrifiers (Lees et al, 2008). When Castells (1983) used the Mission as an example of immigrant-based neighbourhood politics making demands on the city, the balance was massively in favour of Latinos; by 2000 this had begun to shift the other way as the dot.com boom promoted aggressive gentrification, a trend that has only accelerated by the 2010s (Pogash, 2015). In the Global South, the example of Istanbul is instructive: formerly stigmatized migrant areas used by the state to dump unwanted populations have produced an artificial rent gap that many are now keen to exploit in the name of profits, 'edginess' and 'creativity' (Sakizlioglu and Uitermark, 2014).

25.2.3 Category 3: Immigrants Displaced by Gentrification

In this category, immigrants are increasingly displaced by gentrifiers, the seeds of which are sown in the 'bubble' model by pioneer gentrifiers. This displacement can be physical through evictions, but also symbolic through the erosion of immigrant culture and commerce. This has been documented again in Paris (Clerval, 2013), but also in New York, where Vicino et al (2011: 399) note the almost complete absence of immigrant neighborhoods in Manhattan – only Washington Heights and Chinatown could still be defined as urban immigrant neighborhoods in the 2000s. Similarly, immigrant San Francisco clings on to only the Mission District and Chinatown, both of which are currently experiencing displacement pressures. Vicino et al (2011) demarcated these immigrant neighborhoods as Census tracts having a location quotient of 1.25 or greater in terms of the percent foreign-born population when compared to the overall metropolitan area.

This category suggests that the idea that immigrant hubs may well stimulate

gentrification, in terms of being treated more as exotically 'ethnic' rather than subordi-
nately racialized spaces, and thus enticing to monied outsiders. Inner-city Chinatowns
in a North American context present a particularly compelling example. Long ignored
as self-sustaining communities and born of imposed segregation and ghettoization,
Chinatowns are now targeted for displacement and whose exotic ethnic makeup is used
as a packaging for gentrification itself. Chinese make up less than half the population of
gentrified Chinatowns in Boston, New York and Philadelphia, and the proportion has
decreased since 1990 – proof of displacing gentrification as the White population gains
hold, while much of the Chinese immigrant population now move directly to suburban
Chinatowns – an issue taken up in the next category (Li et al, 2013). The same fate has
befallen certain Latino barrios in places such as Chicago and San Francisco (Lees et al,
2008). Betancur (2002) outlines the erosion of community fabric in Latino immigrant
neighborhoods in Chicago under the full weight of (incoming White) gentrification.
Toronto's Little Portugal presents a similar case of gentrification once rebuffed by
strong community ties but now increasingly dissipating (Murdie and Teixeira, 2011),
and a similar situation occurs in Greenpoint (Brooklyn), where the more recent Polish
immigrant areas are slowly being eroded by an 'ongoing and protracted transformation of lived space in the homes, communities, and neighborhoods being gentrified'
(Stabrowsky, 2014: 796).

In the Global South, examples include the revitalizing Casco Viejo in Panama City
(Sigler and Wachsmuth, 2016), where long-time migrant communities have been displaced
by transnational gentrifiers abetted by local developers. A similar state of affairs has
occurred in Zokak el-Blat in Beirut, where refugees from decades of civil war and foreign
occupations have been displaced by new-build gentrification (Krijnen and De Beukelaer,
2015). For all of these examples, the endgame becomes perhaps more clear – exclusionary
displacement will lead to entirely gentrified inner cities that push new (and priced out)
immigrants directly to suburbia. However, not all metropolitan areas inevitably suffer
this sequence – cities such as Montreal and Brussels (Van Criekingen and Decroly, 2003)
have seen cases of stalled gentrification that allow immigrants to maintain their central
location, at least for the time being.

25.2.4 Category 4: Immigrants Avoid Gentrified Areas A Priori

In these instances, immigrants avoid gentrified inner-city areas altogether, due to the
latter's pervasively gentrified nature, enabling an enforced (or incumbent) predilection
for suburban living. The example of Vancouver is instructive (Ley, 2010), where Chinese
migrants eschew inner-city Chinatown as well as gentrifying inner Vancouver (with the
exception of some new-build high-rise condos and areas of established wealth) to locate in
suburban enclaves – what Li (1998) deemed 'ethnoburbs' in the Los Angeles context (see
also Reckard and Khouri, 2014). In this case, Ley (2010: 15) explained that

> the older model of inner city sites of arrival and residence . . . is being bypassed. Today many
> immigrants enter and leave a city repeatedly by air, and for some of them proximity to the
> suburban airport is desirable. But the suburbs have other assets. Downtown and inner-city
> neighbourhoods in gateway cities have been increasingly claimed as the employment and hous-
> ing markets of global rangers engaged in private and public corporate activity, so that poorer
> immigrants are commonly displaced to the housing stock of cheaper suburbs, the new location

of industry, warehousing and routine service activities that have themselves re-located from the expensive post-industrial core.

For Vancouver, this means moving directly to suburban Richmond, especially for afflu-ent Chinese migrants (Ley, 2010), while avoiding the crowded and somewhat decrepit Chinatown, itself a hangover of a ghetto model of immigrant settlement. As Ley (2010: 148) again recounted, 'the marked preference for areas of detached single-family homes left a demand void in the major multi-family neighbourhoods of Vancouver's downtown and inner city. In this area of primarily apartment units, with gentrification as a key process, there was marked under-representation of new ethnic Chinese households . . .'. The same suburban dynamic could be applied to Los Angeles, where the vast majority of Chinese investment and immigration goes directly to the San Gabriel Valley – even as far back as 1992, when this area had 55% of all Chinese businesses in Los Angeles, compared to just 6% in the traditional, inner-city Chinatown (Light, 2002: 221).

Similar patterns of immigrant evacuation from the city are observable in places such as Sydney (Forrest and Dunn, 2007) and Toronto (Harris, 2014). Using data from the most populous metropolitan areas in Canada (Montreal, Toronto and Vancouver) between 1971 and 2001, Walks and Maaranen (2008) found increased gentrification led to decreased ethnic diversity and immigrant deconcentration. In Toronto, the vast majority of new incoming immigrants now move directly to the suburbs, especially the inner-ring ones built in the 1950s and 1960s and which constitute the main crucible of poverty in the metropolitan area (Harris, 2014). In Washington DC, virtually all immigrants avoid the inner city, the preserve of the long-established African-American community but also the core of White-influx gentrification where 67% of all urban tracts were considered gentrified in 2000 (Vicino et al, 2011).

25.2.5   Category 5: Immigrants as Gentrifiers

But what happens when immigrants are themselves the gentrifiers, re-investing in inner-city areas rather than the suburbs? The most obvious case is immigrant-gentrifiers grafting onto existing immigrant enclaves, usually constituting the original point of entry. So rather than the self-segregated inner-city enclave being gentrified by outsiders, as in the case of American Chinatowns, the enclave is upgraded by incoming (or even returning) co-ethnics, moving beyond the 'immigrant growth machine' model in which the enclave forms the basis for the ethnic economy (Lin, 1998; Light, 2002) and ethnic political platforms that make resource demands on the local state (Castells, 1983) to a full-blown process of re-investment, displacement and class polarization.

What is particularly interesting about this final category is that it seems to occur in cities with less obvious centrality, greater immigrant focus, and a shorter history of overspill (rather than amenity-driven) gentrification. Cities such as the American Sunbelt settlements of Los Angeles and Miami can be viewed as illustrative of this category. In these distinctly 20th-century cities, weak centrality mixed with advanced polycentrism and longstanding suburban investment have led to weak gentrification patterns overall, struc-tured more by proximity to natural amenities (especially coastal areas) than to a central business district, at least until recently. As such, places such as Miami and Los Angeles challenge the model of the spillover and strongly centralized, dominant-population characteristics of gentrification in New York and London. Locations in this new category also directly challenge Clerval's (2013) concept of gentrifiers as not only a different class but also a different race or ethnicity to the non-gentrifiers. While examples – Little Havana in Miami, and Koreatown in Los Angeles – can be seen as relatively rare, built up entirely through co-ethnic investment rather than mainstream sources (Keil, 1998; Light, 2002), they epitomize both the parochial, place-bound nature of gentrification and the cosmopolitan, place-spanning nature of immigration.

This participant, enclave model is intergenerational and transnational (see Feldman and Jolivet, 2014), moving beyond just incumbent stabilization of neglected ethnic areas, such as the 'Russification' of Brighton Beach (Brown and Wyly, 2000) or the 'Polonization' of Greenpoint, both in Brooklyn (Stabrowski, 2014) that may lay foundations for subsequent gentrification by that very group. For instance, Little Havana is being gentrified by returning Cuban immigrants who originally came to Miami in the 1950s and 1960s and their offspring, rather than through direct overseas investment from Cuba itself. As such, Little Havana experiences renewed investment that has little to do with incoming Whites (Feldman and Jolivet, 2014). Like Miami, the lack of obvious centrality to structure gentrification in Los Angeles means that it deviates from the Anglo-American model while advancing an alternatively polycentric one (DeVerteuil, 2011, 2012, 2015). And just as Los Angeles is an outlier to the usual model of gentrification, so too is Koreatown an emblematic and highly illustrative case of enclave-style gentrification, but not necessarily as a comparative yardstick, thus avoiding a new list of 'usual suspects'.

25.3   KOREATOWN CASE STUDY

Koreatown is a densely populated inner-city area to the west of Downtown Los Angeles. The area comprises over 150,000 people, of which approximately one-third are Korean set within a Latino majority population (US Census, 2010). Given this mix, Koreatown is held up to be an 'emblematic transnational space' (Lin, 1998: 313), yet its gentrification process has been decidedly localized, with first-generation immigrants comprising not only the gentrifiers but also residential and commercial investors. While the Korean population has never comprised the majority of Koreatown, their totals have grown gradually over time – in 1990, the Korean population was 31,700, and by 2010 it had grown to 41,426. And while commercial gentrification predated residential gentrification (Keil, 1998), recent new-builds along Wilshire Boulevard, which bisects Koreatown on its way to the wealthy Westside of Los Angeles, are harbingers of upgrading, displacement and social polarization.

In 2013 and 2014, and with the help of two Korean-speaking research assistants, I collected and analyzed 25 interviews with Korean immigrant gentrifiers in new-build condos in Koreatown, alongside 10 'key informant' interviews with developers, architects and community spokespersons (DeVerteuil et al, forthcoming). Questions focused on the following elements: residential history spanning both South Korea and Los Angeles; current living quarters; reasons for living in Koreatown; everyday spaces of encounter with others in Koreatown; and evidence of transnational movements back to South Korea. All those interviewed considered themselves both as immigrants and gentrifiers, enabling a perspective on how gentrification and immigration related to each other *through* and *in* the spaces of Koreatown. To bolster this qualitative approach, I also used real estate data (Data Quick, 2013) for the 2003–2013 period, which indicated that Koreatown as a whole saw median price increases of 25%, which is in between the City of Los Angeles (37%) and Los Angeles County (18%) increases, save for 90010 zip code which strictly follows Wilshire Boulevard, whose increase of 55% sets it apart. Not surprisingly, this was the only zip code with a Korean majority in Los Angeles, as well as the only one with significant new-build gentrification.

From the 35 interviews, the lineaments of an immigrant enclave model of gentrification in Koreatown emerged. The first of five elements of this model was the gentrification of the enclave that had been attracting immigrants and entrepreneurs since the 1980s. As one first-generation Korean immigrant-gentrifier noted,

> Koreans in Koreatown are reinvesting in Koreatown. So, Koreatown will only be more gentrified. . .Today's Koreatown is located in a central part of LA and it was established through the Koreans' diligence.

He went on to say that Koreatown is,

> very convenient for Koreans. I don't need to worry about speaking English. I don't feel lonely because I could easily meet other Koreans and talk to them. Moreover, I can access Korean food easily here. When I bought the condo, I was mostly motivated by those things.

As a second element, this enclave gentrification leans towards a new-build Asian model (Lees et al, 2016) but without the heavy-handed state intervention found in South Korea. Seoul is one of the world's densest and most expensive cities, and transnational Koreans touching down in Los Angeles are interesting in that they know little about the Anglo-American model of gentrification, which sets them apart from overseas Jews gentrifying areas in Tel Aviv (Gonen, 2015) or even diasporic Lebanese in Beirut (Krijnen and De Beuikelaer, 2015) who have learned about gentrification while living in places such as New York and Paris. Rather, the process takes cues from Korean-style gentrification, which is overwhelmingly new-build, high-rise and planned, urban renewal as gentrification rather than gradual upgrading:

> In comparison with Western cities, gentrification seems to have taken a somewhat different path in South Korea, which has seen real estate development being a central force in urban economic expansion over the last 30 years . . . I argue that these urban renewal projects, are in fact, a form of urban gentrification because they often involve the displacement of poor residents from their city neighbourhoods, for those tenants are unable to pay the increased rents or afford the pricey new housing (Ha, 2015: 165; see also Shin, 2008, 2009).

In this respect, gentrification goes hand in hand with state-led densification. Yet the role of the state in Koreatown is nowhere as overwhelming, not unsurprising given the relatively hands-off nature of neoliberal urban policy in Los Angeles. If anything, Koreatown has been ignored by the local government, whether during and in the immediate aftermath of the 1992 unrest that caused extensive damage, to the slowness in providing green space and effective policing. It is a different kind of state, in the words of a planner:

> Pushing out original residents by gentrification might be possible in Korea but it is impossible in America. America is a society where people respect each other. If we go to city hall, we can see

the development plan of the city over the span of 50 years. America's development clock moves slower than South Korea's. I acknowledge the changes but all changes by gentrification come to us slowly and not quickly.

Just the same, the Community Redevelopment Agency (CRA) and the Metropolitan Transportation Authority (MTA) both indirectly stimulated upgrading by pushing higher-density projects along Wilshire Boulevard, many of which have become beach-heads for gentrification. Ultimately however, it is the first-generation Koreans who arrived in LA in the 1980s that provide the impetus for gentrification. The main source of financing for the new-build gentrification has been largely Korean-American, rather than transnational capital emanating from Seoul.

Allied to this homegrown capital, a third key element to Koreatown gentrification has been the role of sharp crises, rather than the slow and gradual emergence of disinvestment and rent gaps. As a key informant noted,

> So even after the 1992 riot, a lot of people are wow, this community has been devastated, this community has been the end victim of something that maybe is a misunderstanding or something but anyways, the whole anger of the Latino community, from the black community was lashed out at Koreans; we just became the victims. But we're resilient people so we were able to build back,
> Interviewer: So do you feel that the area has changed. I know it's been 20 years since the riots, but particularly in the past 10 years based on your own knowledge if there is change?
> Yes. um. Initially it was Korean business owners that who wanted to invest back.
> Interviewer: What do you mean Korean business owners? Like from Korea or from here?
> No. no. no. Korean American. Korean American. The ones who lost their livelihoods. But they worked hard to rebuild, so, obviously it has to be rebuilt. Some were covered by the insurance, but you know insurance system stopped.

The fourth key element was the community rebuilding after 1992 that sowed the seeds for current gentrification, with first-generation empty-nester immigrants returning to Koreatown by the early 2010s. As one elderly gentrifier made clear,

> Many Koreans live here but many immigrants who are just starting off also live in Koreatown. Many Koreans live here until before their children are grown up. If their children grow up, they move out of Koreatown for their children's education and they return after they become older. This became a pattern. There are many ethnicities here and due to this Koreans think it has become a bad educational environment for their children. I've heard that many Korean parents don't want to send their children to school here where their children have to study with bad students in Koreatown.

Another elderly gentrifier put it similarly:

> First, Koreans left LA because it was dirty and dangerous. Because at the time Blacks and Hispanics made up half of the population. Koreans made up 20%. The Koreans who lived here were those Koreans who lived in rented apartments paying low rent. But now, they know that Koreatown has turned into a convenient place to live. As the business district grows and it has become cleaner, the people who lived in the suburbs, the old-timers, because of homesickness, they moved here. So older people who lived in single family homes in the suburbs will move to the city and will purchase homes within Koreatown and because there is a demand, they start building upscale condominiums. The reason they are building upscale condominiums is because older people want to live comfortably and want to live closer to Koreatown.

This 'residential loop' adds novelty to the usual gentrification model that takes for granted a permanently suburbanized American middle class. It also speaks to the relative lack of a suburban Koreatown in Los Angeles, unlike the Chinese with the San Gabriel Valley that can absorb incumbent (and transnational) re-investment. Finally, this speaks to a fifth element – that Koreatown has become cool, like other ethnic areas, but not yet attractive to incoming White gentrifiers, demonstrating that Koreatown has gone from dangerous to hip, in the words of this middle-aged gentrifier:

> But from what everyone told me and what I remember, Koreatown was like . . . it was considered a bad place to be. When I would meet people and they'd ask, 'Where do you live,' And I respond by saying, 'Koreatown,' They'd always respond by saying, 'Isn't that dangerous?' So I heard a lot of that but now it's different. Uhm, a lot of my friends or co-workers think Koreatown is really hip. So it's like changing where it's more of a hip place to be. People also think that rents aren't as cheap. So before, people would come to K-town for cheap rent. No longer. . .

But what of the experiences of the immigrant gentrifiers themselves, within this new enclave model? A key component seems to be the rejection of suburban living for the convenience and diversity of Koreatown. In their words:

> I am getting older and consider the conveniences as being most important for my life and Koreatown provides just that. My children are grown up and I don't need to worry about their education. Koreatown doesn't have good education system. My children live not too far from my current house. Without driving, I can access all Korean-related culture and entertainment here. Moreover, in my house I can watch all Korean TV programs without needing to buy any satellite dishes. I even don't need to pay extra fees to watch those channels in my house.

The seeking of diversity has led to a certain hybridity, a combination of Korean and American culture:

> There are many differences between Koreatown and my hometown such as culture, food, language, people, the way of thought and so on. Koreatown is not exactly 'Korea' or 'America' per se.

The experiences of immigrant-gentrifiers in Koreatown are therefore rooted in Los Angeles, and not necessarily transnational – as with Miami Cubans, there was little back-and-forth among actual gentrifiers, with fewer than 20% of the sample making even an annual trip back to Korea. The preference for ethnic diversity also resonated across the sample, and particular emphasis was placed on the fact that Koreatown was not mono-ethnic like Chinatown, even though ironically all the new-build condo towers were over 90% Korean:

> Various ethnicities lead to improving a city's value. Koreatown mustn't develop as Chinatown did. Other ethnicities except Chinese find it difficult to live in Chinatown. Diversity brings improvement to many things;

> I think that diversity is a positive thing for Koreatown. This is not Korea. If they want to stubbornly maintain that the sole ethnicity of the town is Korean and don't like living with others in Koreatown, then they have to go back to Korea.

The desire for diversity clashed with the fear that gentrification was already causing displacement, an uncomfortable notion at it implies that one immigrant population is displacing another (Sims, 2016), in this case Latinos:

I agree that gentrification is pushing out original residents. There were so many Latinos before around my current living area. However, I don't see Latinos as much now as I did before;

The undocumented population is gonna suffer the most. If I provide low-income housing I have to have documented citizens that have. . . you know, tax returns and they document the fact that they are low-wage earners and so. . . if. . . I go in and I'm displacing 37 families. . . what if 10 of them are undocumented. . . and they can't come back. . . you know? That's the biggest concern. . . the undocumented population who do need the low income housing. . . what happens to them?

25.4   CONCLUSIONS

Shin et al (2016: 456) noted that 'the gentrification literature has been overly occupied with the identification of particular forms of gentrification without paying adequate attention to how gentrification interacts with other urban processes'. In this chapter, I have connected gentrification with immigration, revealing a complex series of well-established and emerging relationships. The five-fold typology holds value as a heuristic tool, building on stage models of gentrification but also suggesting two outlier trajectories. Following on, the Koreatown case study stretched models of gentrification away from the traditional cohort of young professional adults so thoroughly studied in the 1980s and 1990s to include, most prominently, immigrants, but also: those over 50 years of age; empty nesters; and those re-investing in new-build condos in their own immigrant enclave. The gentrification of the Koreatown enclave showed components of both the imported Asian model (Shin et al, 2016) and North American models, a hybrid of new-build and segregation/displacement set within a largely hands-off local state. This shows at least partially the possibility of a new Asian model moving to the Global North, especially in more receptive cities such as Los Angeles where gentrification remains incipient.

While the last category of the typology has been fleshed out in some detail, the first four categories are rarely applied to cities of the Global South which are increasingly experiencing dimensions of gentrification that include class polarization, re-investment and displacement. Such a focus, using a comparative and decolonizing perspective, would surely move us beyond Global North models while also valorizing alternative understandings of incipient gentrification. Finally, and returning to notions of gentrification and 'race', in the Global North immigrants are usually a different 'race' than the mainstream population or that of gentrifiers – and so immigration needs to be brought into the conversation through place-spanning practices and globalization from below. Immigration adds to the complexity of race and gentrification, as some immigrants are racialized while other are not, translating into different positions vis-à-vis gentrification – stubborn in resistance, subordinate and displaced, or even in control. Indeed, the first four categories featured somewhat disparaged immigrants – stigmatized enough to produce a barrier to gentrification, or expendable enough to be displaced – while the fifth category places certain immigrants as dominant.

REFERENCES

Atkinson, R. and Bridge, G. (2005) *Gentrification in a Global Context: The New Urban Colonialism*, London: Routledge.

Benton-Short, L., Price, M. and Friedman, S. (2005) 'Globalization from below: the ranking of global immigrant cities', *International Journal of Urban and Regional Research*, 29(4), 945–959.

Betancur, J. (2002) 'The politics of gentrification: the case of West Town in Chicago', *Urban Affairs Review*, 37, 780–814.

Boyle, P. (2009) 'Migration', in Kitchin, R. and Thrift, N. (eds) *The International Encyclopedia of Human Geography*, London: Elsevier Press, pp. 96–107.

Brown, K. and Wyly, E. (2000) 'A new gentrification? A case study of the russification of Brighton Beach, New York', *The Geographical Bulletin*, 42(2), 94–105.

Butler, T. (2003) 'Living in the bubble: gentrification and its "others" in North London', *Urban Studies*, 40(12), 2469–2486.

Caldeira, T. (2000) *City of Walls: Crime, Segregation and Citizenship in Sao Paulo*, Berkeley, CA: University of California Press.

Castells, M. (1983) *The City and the Grassroots*, Berkeley and Los Angeles, CA: University of California Press.

Chang, T.C. (2016) '"New uses need old buildings": gentrification aesthetics and the arts in Singapore', *Urban Studies*, 53(3), 524–539.

Clerval, A. (2013) *Paris sans le people: La gentrification de la capitale* (Paris without the people: The gentrification of the capital), Paris: Découverte.

Clerval, A. and Fleury, A. (2009) 'Politiques urbaines et gentrification, une analyse a partir du cas de Paris', *L'Espace Politique*, 8, 33–46.

Data Quick Corporation (2013) Custom zip code report for zip codes 90004, 90005, 90006, 90010, 90020.

Davidson, M. (2007) 'Gentrification as global habitat: a process of class formation or corporate creation?', *Transactions of the Institute of British Geographers*, 32, 490–506.

Deener, A. (2012) *Venice: A Contested Bohemia in Los Angeles*, Chicago, IL: University of Chicago Press.

DeVerteuil, G. (2011) 'Survive but not thrive? Geographical strategies for avoiding absolute homelessness among immigrant communities', *Social and Cultural Geography*, 12(8), 929–945.

DeVerteuil, G. (2012) 'Resisting gentrification-induced displacement: advantages and disadvantages to "staying put" among non-profit social services in London and Los Angeles', *Area*, 44(2), 208–216.

DeVerteuil, G. (2015) *Resilience in the Post-Welfare Inner City: Voluntary Sector Geographies in London, Los Angeles and Sydney*, Bristol: Policy Press.

DeVerteuil, G. (2016) 'Pace and place: resilience in an age of urban and theoretical churn', *Geoforum*, 68, 69–72.

DeVerteuil, G., Yun, O. and Choi, C. (forthcoming) 'Between the cosmopolitan and the parochial: the immigrant gentrifier in Koreatown, Los Angeles', in *Social and Cultural Geography*, DOI http://www.tandfonline.com/doi/full/10.1080/14649365.2017.1347955#metrics-content.

Feldman, M. and Jolivet, V. (2014) 'Back to Little Havana: controlling gentrification in the heart of Cuban Miami', *International Journal of Urban and Regional Research*, 38(4), 1266–1285.

Forrest, J. and Dunn, K. (2007) 'Constructing racism in Sydney, Australia's largest EthniCity', *Urban Studies*, 44(4), 699–721.

Freeman, L. (2006) *There Goes the 'Hood: Views of Gentrification From the Ground Up*, Philadelphia, PA: Temple University Press.

Gonen, A. (2015) 'Widespread and diverse forms of gentrification in Israel', in Lees, L., Shin, H. and López-Morales, E. (eds) *Global Gentrifications: Uneven Development and Displacement*, Bristol: Policy Press, pp. 143–164.

Ha, S.K. (2015) 'The endogenous dynamics of urban renewal and gentrification in Seoul', in Lees, L., Shin, H. and López-Morales, E. (eds) *Global Gentrifications: Uneven Development and Displacement*, Bristol: Policy Press, pp. 165–180.

Harris, R. (2015) 'Using Toronto to explore three suburban stereotypes, and vice versa', *Environment and Planning A*, 47(1), 30–49.

Hilda, H., Di Virgilio, M. and Rodríguez, M. (2015) 'Gentrification in the city of Buenos Aires: global trends and local features', in Lees, L., Shin, H. and López-Morales, E. (eds) *Global Gentrifications: Uneven Development and Displacement*, Bristol: Policy Press, pp. 199–222.

Hwang, J. (2015) 'Gentrification in changing cities: immigration, new diversity, and racial inequality in neighborhood renewal', *The Annals of the American Academy of Political and Social Science*, 660(1), 319–340.

Keil, R. (1998) *Los Angeles*, London: Wiley.

Krijnen, M and de Beukelaer, C. (2015) 'Capital, state and conflict: the various drivers of diverse gentrification processes in Beirut, Lebanon', in Lees, L., Shin, H. and López-Morales, E. (eds) *Global Gentrifications: Uneven Development and Displacement*, Bristol: Policy Press, pp. 285–310.

Lees, L. (2000) 'A re-appraisal of gentrification: towards a "geography of gentrification"', *Progress in Human Geography*, 24(3), 389–408.

Lees, L. (2016) 'Gentrification, race and ethnicity: towards a global research agenda, *City and Community*, 15(3), 208–214.

Lees, L., Shin, H.B. and López-Morales, E. (2015) 'Introduction: "gentrification" – a global urban process?', in Lees, L., Shin, H. and López-Morales, E. (eds) *Global Gentrifications: Uneven Development and Displacement*, Bristol: Policy Press, pp. 1–18.

Lees, L., Shin, H.B. and López-Morales, E. (2016) *Planetary Gentrification*, Cambridge: Polity Press.

Lees, L., Slater, T. and Wyly, E. (2008) *Gentrification*, London: Routledge.

Ley, D. (2010) *Millionaire Migrants: Trans-Pacific Lines*, London: Wiley-Blackwell.

Ley, D. and Dobson, C. (2008) 'Are there limits to gentrification? The context of impeded gentrification in Vancouver', *Urban Studies*, 45(12), 2471–2498.

Ley, D. and Teo, S. (2014) 'Gentrification in Hong Kong? Epistemology vs. ontology', *International Journal of Urban and Regional Research*, 38(4), 1284–1303.

Li, B. (2013) *Chinatowns Then and Now*, New York, NY: Asian American Legal Defense and Education Fund.

Li, W. (1998) 'Anatomy of a new ethnic settlement: the Chinese ethnoburb in Los Angeles', *Urban Studies*, 35(3), 479–501.

Light, I. (2002) 'Immigrant place entrepreneurs in Los Angeles, 1970–1999', *International Journal of Urban and Regional Research*, 26, 215–228.

Lin, J. (1998) 'Globalization and the revalorizing of ethnic places in immigration gateway cities', *Urban Affairs Review*, 34, 313–339.

May, J. (1996) 'Globalization and the politics of place: place and identity in an inner London neighbourhood', *Transactions of the Institute of British Geographers*, 21, 194–215.

Murdie, R. and Teixeira, C. (2011) 'The impact of gentrification on ethnic neighborhoods in Toronto: a case study of Little Portugal', *Urban Studies*, 48(1), 61–83.

Nijman, J. (2007) 'Mumbai since liberalization: the space-economy of India's gateway city', in Shaw, A. (ed) *Indian Cities in Transition*, New Delhi: Orient Longman, pp. 238–259.

Pattaroni, L., Kaufman, V. and Thomas, M. (2012) 'The dynamics of multifaceted gentrification', *International Journal of Urban and Regional Research*, 36, 1223–1241.

Peck, J. (2006) 'Liberating the city: between New York and New Orleans', *Urban Geography*, 27(8), 681–713.

Pogash, C. (2015) 'Gentrification spreads an upheaval in San Francisco's Mission District', *New York Times* 22 May.

Reckard, S. and Khouri, A. (2014) 'Wealthy Chinese home buyers boost suburban LA housing markets', *Los Angeles Times* 24 March.

Rogerson, C. and Rogerson, J. (2015) 'Johannesburg 2030: the economic contours of a "linking global city"', *American Behavioral Scientist*, 59(3), 347–368.

Sakizlioglu, N. and Uitermark, J. (2014) 'The symbolic politics of gentrification: the restructuring of stigmatized neighborhoods in Amsterdam and Istanbul', *Environment and Planning A*, 46, 1369–1385.

Sequera, J. and Janoschka, M. (2015) 'Gentrification dispositifs in the historic centre of Madrid: a reconsideration of urban governmentality and state-led urban reconfiguration', in Lees, L., Shin, H. and López-Morales, E. (eds) *Global Gentrifications: Uneven Development and Displacement*, Bristol: Policy Press, pp. 375–393.

Shin, H.B. (2008) 'Living on the edge: financing post-displacement housing in urban redevelopment projects in Seoul', *Environment and Urbanization*, 20(2), 411–426.

Shin, H.B. (2009) 'Property-based redevelopment and gentrification: the case of Seoul, South Korea', *Geoforum*, 40(5), 906–917.

Shin, H.B., Lees, L. and López-Morales, E. (2016) 'Introduction: locating gentrification in the Global East', *Urban Studies*, 53, 455–470.

Sigler, T. and Wachsmuth, D. (2016) 'Transnational gentrification: globalisation and neighbourhood change in Panama's Casco Antiguo', *Urban Studies*, 53(4), 705–722.

Sims, R. (2016) 'More than gentrification: geographies of capitalist displacement in Los Angeles 1994–1999', *Urban Geography*, 37(1), 26–56.

Slater, T. (2006) 'The eviction of critical perspectives from gentrification research', *International Journal of Urban and Regional Research*, 30, 737–757.

Snow, D. and Anderson, L. (1993) *Down on Their Luck: A Study of Homeless Street People*, Berkeley, CA: University of California Press.

Stabrowski, F. (2014) 'New-build gentrification and the everyday displacement of Polish immigrant tenants in Greenpoint, Brooklyn', *Antipode*, 46(3), 794–815.

US Census (2010) Demographic profile of census tracts in Los Angeles County, Washington DC: US Census.

Van Criekingen, M. and Decroly, J. (2003) 'Revisiting the diversity of gentrification: neighbourhood renewal processes in Brussels and Montreal', *Urban Studies*, 40(12), 2451–2468.

Vicino, T., Hanlon, B. and Short, J. (2011) 'A typology of urban immigrant neighborhoods', *Urban Geography*, 32(3), 383–405.

Walks, A. and August, M. (2008) 'The factors inhibiting gentrification in areas with little non-market housing', *Urban Studies*, 45, 2594–2625.

Walks, A. and Maaranen, R. (2008) 'Gentrification, social mix, and social polarization', *Urban Geography*, 29(4), 293–326.

Winders, J. (2009) 'Race', in Kitchin, R. and Thrift, N. (eds) *The International Encyclopedia of Human Geography*, London: Elsevier Press, pp. 53–58.

Wyly, E. (2015) 'Gentrification on the planetary urban frontier: the evolution of Turner's noösphere', *Urban Studies*, 52(14), 2515–2550.

26. Property and planning law in England: facilitating and countering gentrification

Antonia Layard

'The rent of land, it may be thought, is frequently no more than a reasonable profit or interest for the stock laid out by the landlord upon its improvement. . . When the lease comes to be renewed, however, the landlord commonly demands the same augmentation of rent as if they had been all made by his own.' Adam Smith, *An Inquiry into the Nature and Causes of the Wealth of Nations*, Book 1, Chapter 11, Of the Rent of Land, 1776, 02

'. . . every letting agent should spare a kind thought for the memory of Margaret Thatcher – they owe her their livelihood.' *Martin & Co (2013)'*

26.1 INTRODUCTION

At the heart of gentrification is change. This includes the alteration of physical buildings, the emergence of new bars, the loss of established shops or community and social centres. It entails alterations in types of people who live in a neighbourhood, sometimes understood in terms of class or race and ethnicity, as well as in terms of appetites, preferences and social practices. Gentrification includes shifts in transportation systems, the introduction of private buses or cycling lanes. Gentrified locations are perceived as 'improved', and, perhaps 'less authentic'. As Glass (1964) famously wrote: '[o]nce this process of "gentrification" starts in a district it goes on rapidly until all or most of the original working class occupiers are displaced and the social character of the district is changed' (p. 139). And as Smith noted 30 years later: 'Gentrification is no longer about a narrow and quixotic oddity in the housing market but has become the leading residential edge of a much larger endeavour: the class remake of the central urban landscape' (Smith, 1996, 39). Gentrification is about place and networks (of people, capital and cultures) and the relationships between the two.

The causes of these changes are, of course, contested (production, consumption, or – probably – both [Lees et al, 2008]). Gentrification is produced by private actors but often in collaboration with public-private partnerships facilitating private development on public land both in residential contexts (including the 'regeneration' of council estates or retail-led urban regeneration). Networked effects, including tourism, university expansion, use of sexually orientated businesses or changes in the night-time economy, all bring 'outsiders' into gentrifying areas. There are continued arguments about whether these changes are positive, improving urban landscapes and local cultural offers, or negative, displacing long-standing residents in favour of wealthier, more articulate, privileged incomers.

All of these aspects of gentrification are legally co-produced. In particular, gentrification is produced by planning and property laws, specific to each jurisdiction, coupled with practices, implementation and the priorities of landowners. Gentrification decisions are co-produced by legal geography – the interaction of the social, the spatial and the legal (Blomley, 2004; Bennett and Layard, 2016). This is often observable in case studies, tracking change (including, Blomley, 2004; Hodkinson and Essen, 2015; Hubbard et al, 2009) as well as in the interaction of historical legacies, 'ghost jurisdictions' (Valverde, 2012; Freeman, 2017). Each legal framework, however, is jurisdiction-specific.

This chapter analyses both English residential and commercial legal provisions, which do not apply everywhere within the United Kingdom, let alone beyond. However, in explaining how gentrification can be facilitated by property and planning rules in England, we can identify where other researchers should look for legal rules and practices, overlaps and differences. Who owns property? What is the nature of that ownership freehold, leasehold or a licence? Is there security of tenure – can tenants – whether commercial or residential – choose to stay as long as they like? Are there restrictions on how or when rents can be raised? In new housing developments, who decides how much of the accommodation will be affordable, and what does affordable mean? These questions and legal details matter in gentrification studies. The more international collaborative projects investigate these questions, the better. With more legally inflected gentrification scholarship, we can understand how doctrinal provisions and legal practices facilitate change, as well as how jurisdictions might learn from each other to develop alternative provisions that could inhibit or slow down unwanted change.

26.2 RESIDENTIAL PROPERTY

Much has been written on residential displacement in gentrification including the vexed discussions of production and consumption and who or what gentrifiers are (Lees et al, 2008). One of the key markers of early gentrification by new residents in neighbourhoods has been the switch between leasehold and freehold, producing a tenurial transformation (Lees, 1994). As Glass (1964) described it in *Aspects of Change*: 'One by one, many of the working-class quarters of London have been invaded by the middle classes – upper and lower. Shabby, modest mews and cottages – two rooms up and two down – have been taken over, when their leases have expired, and have become elegant expensive residences' (p. 138). Tenants were replaced by owner occupiers in 1960s London and if, as Slater (2006) argues, we should focus on displacement 'from below', one way to do this is to understand how existing residents are evicted and how new residents are able to move into the locality in their place. Blomley's (2004) study of gentrification in Vancouver, for example, begins with the example of the Hotel California, where low income renters were evicted to make way for a more profitable hotel.

To explain how similar evictions, and a lack of security of tenure, exist in England as well, it is important to understand the distinction between freehold and leasehold property that is enshrined into English land law (section 1 of the Law of Property Act, 1925). Since 1925, the historically complex legal systems for governing property use and entitlement in England have been hugely simplified. As a result, while there are sophisticated debates about what property 'is' or should be (a bundle of rights, a numerus clausus (an irreducible core), informative, progressive or facilitative (for an overview, see Baron, 2010; Davies, 2007), the legal position about what rights of land law consist of in England is clearly prescribed. Landownership is either freehold or leasehold (there is no native title in England). The estate is not allodial (it does not consist of the soil itself); instead it is a metaphor for time (Gray and Gray, 2003). A freehold estate has no time limit. A leasehold estate is ownership of land with a time limit and it is subject to such conditions as the freeholder may impose in the lease (as well as statutory and common law provisions). While critics have argued that property should be different – encompassing 'a relational web of obligations, connections' (Blomley, 1997, 293) – the legally enshrined, dominant conception of property in England has remained largely immutable to such normative concerns.

While this legislative distinction between freehold and leasehold broadly explains the difference between owners and renters, there is no time limit to a lease in England and leases of up to 999 years are not uncommon and are often assumed to be equivalent to freehold (even though legally this is not the case). In England there is no equivalent to Australian strata title or Canadian condominiums and while 'commonhold' property is legally provided for (Commonhold and Leasehold Reform Act, 2002), this more collaborative property form has so far not taken off. Instead, both freeholders and long leaseholders are presumed to be owners of their estate, with similar powers to exclude. However, even with long leases, if no action is taken and no premium paid, the land 'reverts' to the freeholder at the end of the leaseholders' term (see generally, Gray and Gray, 2011; Cowan, 2011).

These two legal devices – freehold and leasehold – provide extraordinary security for one landowner (the freeholder) and possible vulnerability for another (the leaseholder), particularly in the case of private sector short leases (also known as tenancies). This vulnerability is of course a political choice. Jurisdictions where rent stabilisation and security of tenure is possible (notably in Germany, Austria and in cities including New York and Berlin) have made different legal and political choices (for Germany, see Urban, 2015a, and for a critique, see Deschermeier et al, 2016). These distinctive legal frameworks mean that a 'German lease' is quite different from an 'English lease'. Similarly, a 'social lease' in England is quite different from an assured shorthold tenancy (the default in the private sector), as this chapter will explain. Of course, an English landowner may agree a low rent with security of tenure with a tenant but there is no legal requirement that they do so. Similarly, rental terms are through practice – not legislation – generally for one year. In the absence of any 'ethical landlordism', legally implemented, political choices to regulate landlords lightly in England apply to leases. These rules are one reason for the housing market we have today.

Beginning then with private tenants – the most vulnerable residents – we need to turn to the 1988 Housing Act. This marked a turning point in English housing law for tenants in the private sector and it is the reason that Margaret Thatcher is thanked, on behalf of estate agents, at the head of the chapter. In particular, the 1988 Housing Act made two crucial alterations. First, it effectively abolished rent control for all new tenants. Broadly, rent control had been in place until 1965, while rent regulation existed from 1965 to 1988. From now on tenants would have to pay the market rent. If tenants could not afford this open market rent, they could apply for housing benefit to subsidise their occupation so that the landlord received the full market rent if landlords would rent to people in receipt of benefit ('No DSS' signs in windows or in instructions to letting agents became common devices) (see generally, Cowan, 2011; White and Lees, 2015). These costs are extraordinarily high. In 2014–15, around £27 billion was spent on housing benefit (ONS, 2016), with a broadly even split between local authority, housing association and private landlords receiving around 25%, 38% and 37% respectively (House of Commons Library, 2016a).

Second, the 1988 Act changed the rules on security of tenure so that landlords could grant either assured or assured shorthold tenancies. The assured shorthold tenancy (AST) became incredibly popular, and indeed the legal default in 1997 (after changes introduced by the 1996 Housing Act). An assured shorthold tenancy must be for a minimum of six months but after that time, the landlord can recover the property at the end of the term (conventionally, through estate agent and landlord practice, a year, although there is no legal maximum). The landlord can also recover the property for a variety of other grounds, including non-payment of rent for two months (Schedule 2, Housing Act 1988 as amended). Any tenancies from before the date of the 1988 Act came into force (in 1989) continued but all new tenants (unless they were on very low or very high rents or lived with their landlord), had far more precarious tenancies with the introduction of assured shortholds. While in 2014, the Government issued a model tenancy agreement with a three-year term, they noted that 'there is no legal requirement to use this particular agreement' (DCLG, 2014, 5). Similarly, in the 2017 Housing White Paper, the Government have proposed to 'make the private rented sector more family-friendly by taking steps to promote longer tenancies on new build rental homes' (DCLG, 2017a, para 4.35) but there is nothing legally binding here.

These two changes – a lack of restrictions on rent and almost no security of tenure – have been crucial to processes of gentrification in England. By far the most common private sector tenancy type today is an assured shorthold and in England in 2015–16 the private rented sector accounted for 4.5 million or 20% of households. This was up from approximately 10% of households throughout the 1980s and 1990s with the sector doubling in size from around 2002 and continuing to grow (DCLG, 2017b).

This matters for gentrification since, with no security of tenure for renters, and with no ability to 'remov[e] oneself from the vagaries of the private real estate market' (DeVerteuil, 2015), private tenants are at the mercy of landlords' decisions at the end of the lease. The quality of these living spaces is also often poor. The English Housing Survey found 28% of privately rented homes were 'non-decent' in 2015–16, far more than socially rented or owner occupied homes (DCLG, 2017b). And even when legal protections are enshrined (for example, the protections against retaliatory eviction in the 2015 Retaliatory Eviction and Deregulation Act), they are difficult to implement given the power dynamic between landlord and tenant. Specifically, in a gentrification context, it means that private sector tenants cannot resist eviction for very long if higher payers and more desirable tenants (however perceived) can be found. Recent research also indicates that it is, once again, increasingly widespread for landlords to refuse to let to tenants in receipt of housing benefit (which subsidises their rent) and that this is unlikely to amount to direct discrimination, since income and employment status are not protected characteristics under the Equality Act 2010 (House of Commons Library, 2016b).

This rental turnover is a new form of gentrification in England, since new tenants are quite different from first wave middle-class gentrifiers, buying the freeholds of their properties and becoming (landed) gentry (acquiring 'some version of the aristocratic country house' (Glass, 1964, 153)). Freeholders (and long leaseholders) have some protection against neighbourhood change. Private renters do not (however much they are paying). While in the United States, homeowners may pay increased property taxes in gentrified neighbourhoods (Smith and Williams, 1986) the opposite is true in England. Here, as council tax is based on local need, higher taxes are collected in poorer and older localities so that although council tax is constructed to be financially progressive, it is spatially regressive. For example, average Band D council tax in Westminster in central London is £680 a year, while in the North East of England the average is £1636 a year (HofC, 2016c). And even in the United States, with property taxes, there is evidence that gentrification hurts renters far more than homeowners (Martin and Beck, 2016).

The question then, is whether this rental insecurity, which is highlighted in gentrification studies, is particularly unusual. An alternative suggestion is that these inequities, as we see them, are a standard incident of the lease. This inability to stay put is an expression of housing precarity more generally, particularly in the private sector. The Housing Act 1988 applies to all locations. Rental 'churn' affects many locations, gentrifying or not, as Matthew Desmond's (2016) *Evicted*, set in the United States, so brilliantly illustrates. Indeed there is some suggestion that residential (leasehold) displacement is not exacerbated in gentrifying neighbourhoods (for American analyses, see Freeman, 2005, 2015, and Kleinhans and Kearns, 2013). Whether or not gentrification causes residential displacement, it is clear that rental insecurity is an ongoing concern, in many, many locations, frequently invisible to those in more secure housing settings.

In order to stop residential displacement whether as a consequence of gentrification or more generally, we might do one of two things. One option is to address the instruments that facilitate it, particularly the lease as constructed under the 1988 Housing Act. This would mean arguing for the introduction of some form of rent stabilisation in the private sector, so that rents are not determined by market forces alone. While public opinion in England appears increasingly to favour some form of rent control (Survation, 2014), Labour leaders, including Ed Milliband and Jeremy Corbyn, have been summarily critiqued for such suggestions ('with references to Venezuelan-style rent controls' quickly taken up by the press (*The Telegraph*, 2014). Rent regulation is not on the political agenda in England.

Some local authorities who have experienced resident change have attempted to go alone. Camden, in London, for example, commissioned research on rent stabilisation in 2014 and argued that 'Camden should positively enable longer-term tenancies with index-linked rent increases, voluntarily agreed by landlord and tenant, while at the same time improving transparency and contractual enforcement for both landlords and tenants across the sector' (Scanlon and Whitehead, 2014, 6). However, unlike in Berlin or New York where cities have constitutional powers to introduce restrictions on the rental market, in England rents are regulated nationally and local authorities do not have the constitutional powers to create their own land law rules. There is no constitutional basis for localised rent regulation.

Nevertheless, this idea of voluntary 'ethical renting' within the private sector can build on the understanding that leases are instruments that are only very lightly regulated and that as contracts as well as estates in land, landlords and tenants can agree their own terms. In the vast majority of private rental sector leases this will be a standard 12-month lease on relatively standard forms provided (for a fee) by estate agents or conveyancing solicitors. It may be possible to change the motivations of landlords (generally by changing who the landlords are) and landlords can of course introduce use of the three-year model tenancy for a 'reasonable' rent. This is their choice. A difference in practice is most obvious in the leases granted by (social) housing associations or local authorities (for council tenants) considered below. Any private landlord could also, however, grant a progressive (secure and for low rent) lease (although often this would mean that letting agent practices would have to become 'ethical' as well).

This is a particular possibility if community groups can buy property when prices are still (relatively) low. One such example is in Hastings, where White Rock Neighbourhood Ventures (WRNV) have bought Rock House in the White Rock area of Hastings to develop it as a 'co-habitation' space – co-housing, co-working, collaborative creative space. This is an explicit move: as Jess Steele, Director of WRNV, asks on the website: 'How can we capture the benefits of gentrification and control the downsides?' (Steele, 2014). Greater use of ethical leases, cooperative ventures or community land trusts, all offer the ability to provide long term housing security and so inhibit change and housing precarity (in DeVerteuil's (2015) term they can provide 'spatial resilience'). These are further tools, if, and this is a big if, the difficulties with land acquisition, finance and assumptions about expertise can be resolved (Field and Layard, 2016). If ownership can change to more benign freeholders, given a landowner's ability to set the agenda for the site, institutional resistance to gentrification can then take place.

What then of social housing? For local authority and housing association homes, different rules and practices apply. Although the leasehold mechanism is essentially the same (created still under section 1 of the 1925 legislation), there are different forms of tenancies, including secure, introductory or flexible for local authority housing, and secure, assured or starter tenancies in housing associations. There has been enormous political interference and new legislation in this field, so that social housing is for many seen as an 'ambulance service' rather than providing secure, affordable housing for life (Fitzpatrick and Pawson, 2012). The greatest change has been the shift from council housing to housing association provision through the 'arm's-length management' reforms, begun in the 1980s, and the creation of the social housing sector where different rules can apply (Cowan and McDermont, 2006). This has been a field of extraordinary change, most recently in the 2016 Housing and Planning Act. Social landlords are continually at odds – both with the Government and with one another – over 'who and what English social housing is for' (Fitzpatrick and Watts, 2016). Where they exist, however, secure tenancies remain by far the most protective tenancies and also generally include the right to buy (with generous discounts, facilitated particularly by Thatcher's 1980 Housing Act for tenants of local authorities and the Housing and Planning Act 2016 for tenants of housing associations). The most recent estimates, in 2015–16, found that 17% (3.9 million) of households lived in the social rented sector, compared with 20% (4.5 million) of households who were renting privately (DCLG, 2017b).

These numbers are, however, going down, largely as a consequence of the right to buy, reducing from 31% of households in the social sector in 1980 to 19% in 2000 (DCLG, 2016a). The primary reason for this reduction lies in right to buy discounts, the liberalisation of mortgage lending in the 1980s, and the introduction of 'buy-to-let' mortgages in the late 1990s (Crook and Kemp, 2011). With these developments, many private landlords bought council housing and former tenants often made substantial windfall profits. Estimates now suggest that between 30–40% of previously council owned properties are rented by private landlords (Murie 2016, 107) with many receiving housing benefit to subsidise the rent to market levels. This has significantly benefitted estate agents, as

Martin & Co (2016) point out in their tribute to Margaret Thatcher: 'All of this ex-council stock is now traded to the benefit of estate agents fees'. In practice, the right to buy has led to less stability and more rental churn, given private rental rules and practices, again facilitating gentrification. The English experience here echoes that in other jurisdictions as well, for example Sweden (Andersson and Turner, 2014).

Moreover, even within the much more stable and protective social housing sector that remains, there has been a growing concern in recent years about residential insecurity. Here, 'state-induced' or 'state produced' gentrification (Lees et al, 2008; Watt, 2009; Hodkinson and Essen, 2015) has seen the 'regeneration' of estates particularly in London. Often framed in the policy context of 'social mix' (Bridge et al, 2011), these initiatives have produced significant change both in material surroundings and in the identity of residents. For some time these sites of social housing – council owned housing estates – were barriers to gentrification (Butler and Robson, 2003). However, with limited local authority budgets and fantastically valuable urban freeholds, times have changed.

One notable instance of state-induced gentrification has been at the Heygate Estate in London (Lees, 2014a; Lees and Ferreri, 2016). Here, in 2010, the Labour run Southwark Council sold the 25-acre Heygate Estate for £50 million to Australian developers, Lendlease. Although overage provisions – where payments may become payable by Lendlease to Southwark, once particular profit margins have been met – were reportedly included in the agreement, this is only for the sale of the units. The site, first by land transfer to Lendlease, then by sale to private owners or landlords, has moved from public to private, and – for tenants – from social to private renting so that rent limits and extended security of tenure will no longer apply. The freedom of the Local Authority landlord to sell or regenerate as they see fit was illustrated by Southwark's initial decision to sell the land on which the adjacent Aylesbury Estate was built (see Lees, 2014b). The council justified this by arguing that the decision arose from concerns about 'commercial, legal and procurement risks' in using the Homes and Communities Agency's Developer Panel (Dentons, 2010). Although it has not yet been sold, the language illustrates that this was – and remains – a choice for Southwark to make (and one upheld by central Government) as the freehold owner of land, rather than redeveloping the site themselves.

These 'regenerated' council housing estates have become sites of resistance, particularly when they are also sites of diversity (Lees, 2014a; Lees and Ferreri, 2016). Activists have recourse to public law remedies that are not available to private renters as the landlords are public bodies. Extra procedural requirements apply, including access to information under the Freedom of Information Act 2000 as well as the Environmental Information Regulations 2004, which (broadly) apply to public authorities rather than private bodies. The greatest potential for resistance lies – perhaps ironically – in those residents on council estates who have either exercised their right to buy their property or have bought on from a previous council tenant who exercised their right to buy. For these residents, human rights (notably Article 8, the right to family life, of the European Convention on Human Rights [ECHR], and Article 1, the right to peaceful enjoyment of possessions, of Protocol 1 to the ECHR) can be raised to require either procedural or substantive changes by landowners. As the redevelopment of the Heygate Estate illustrates, even if individual estates cannot be saved, activism creates vital spaces for discussion (Lees and Ferreri, 2016).

While often legal resistance does little more than delay the process, it can create discursive space to bring gentrification arguments out into the open. On the Aylesbury Estate, for example, the decision to confirm the compulsory purchase of the long leaseholders and freeholders (under right to buy) was not confirmed by either the Government Inspector or the Secretary of State in 2016 (see Hubbard and Lees, 2018). Their justification for refusing the compulsory purchase order of the long leasehold properties included possible breaches of human rights, a failure to carry out an Equality Impact Assessment as well as the Public Sector Equality Duty (under section 149 of the Equality Act 2010). The decision found that particularly elderly and black and ethnic minority residents might find their cultural life 'likely to be disproportionately affected' by the compulsory purchase order and that this could lead to 'dislocation from their cultural heritage for some residents' (paragraphs 21 and 29, DCLG, 2016b). This decision was undoubtedly influenced by broader decisions, including that about the Heygate Estate.

This refusal to confirm the compulsory purchase of the long leaseholders' homes was a victory for Aylesbury activists (Lees, 2016). It also followed more encouraging litigation in Shepherd's Bush where a compulsory purchase order of a market was opposed by tenants (*Horada v Sec of State*, [2016] EWCA Civ 169). In creating discursive spaces, in delaying the processes, activist litigation can be felt to be having an effect. At the time of writing – early 2017 – a judicial review of the Secretary of State's refusal to confirm the compulsory purchase order at the Aylesbury Estate, brought by Southwark, the local authority wanting to redevelop, is pending. When it is heard, the court can decide to uphold the Secretary of State's refusal or, alternatively, require the compulsory purchase order to be made. Litigation has brought delay to the developers and could act as an incentive for Southwark to negotiate a better deal with the remaining leaseholders. Despite the difficulties in bringing any public-interest litigation in England, often as a consequence of costs and the limited remit of judicial review, these interventions matter even if ultimately they cannot limit the rights of landowners to do as they wish with the land. They create discursive spaces.

For while such legal activism is unlikely to stop some regeneration on these individual sites, the growing concern has led to governmental oversight and identification of 'best practice' (as in the 2016 *Estate Regeneration National Strategy*) (DCLG, 2016c). Such initiatives could lead to other local authorities thinking long and hard about simple land transfer models, where they sell land to (potentially) the highest bidder. Activism – especially when it involves costly legal bills – can create discursive spaces for discussion (what moral right did the Labour leader of Southwark Council have to strike the deal with Lendlease in respect of the Heygate Estate?), as well as preventing some of the reproduction of building practices (which have been so evident in the retail context – Layard, 2010). Property practices – drawing on standard form contracts and assumptions about (confidential) commerciality – can be disrupted through such interruptions.

The fight for English council estates is so important then, because being a resident on a publicly owned piece of land brings expectations (and some – albeit limited – rights) in respect of consultation, equality and human rights. These rights only exist where the landowner is a public authority. This is true both for long leaseholders who have exercised their right to buy (as on the Aylesbury Estate), as for short leaseholders (in the Cressingham Garden litigation, where one case was won (*R (on the application of*

Bokrosova) v Lambeth LBC [2015] EWHC 3386) and one lost (*R (on the application of Plant) v Lambeth LBC* [2016] EWHC 3324 (Admin)). Public law objectives on consultation are (in the words of the Supreme Court) 'to ensure not merely procedural fairness in the treatment of persons whose legally protected interests may be adversely affected, but also to ensure public participation in the local authority's decision-making process' (*R (on the application of Moseley) v London Borough of Haringey* [2014] UKSC 56, paragraph 38). These legal disputes are largely procedural as a consequence of the limitations of judicial review where courts cannot substitute their substantive judgment for that of the decision-makers. Nevertheless, the rights create discursive spaces for resistance and change, enabling discussion around gentrification to take place in ways that do not exist in private sector housing.

26.2.1   New Builds and Affordable Housing

What then of new developments and new affordable housing? Could these be used to counter gentrification? Certainly, the construction of affordable housing – often a bulwark of resistance to gentrification – has fallen dramatically; in 2016, to 32,100 homes in England. There has been a reduction of 52% from 2015/2016, bringing us back to levels last seen in 1991/1992 (DCLG, 2016d). This fall is despite an overall rise of 6% in house building completions this year, with 139,030 houses built (DCLG, 2016e) as well as an extraordinary release (mostly sale) of public land for housebuilding. One reason for this decline is that 84% of new housing is currently provided by the private sector (with 14% by housing associations and only 1% by local authorities). As in other jurisdictions (see Australia, for example (Van den Nouwelant et al., 2014)), planning is a central process through which new affordable homes are created. Yet in England, while private developers can be made subject to section 106 obligations to provide affordable housing when granted planning permission, these are declining and even when they are built, are not necessarily affordable, given revised rules on what 'affordable' means. For instance, over 12,000 affordable homes were built via section 106 obligations in 2015–16, the vast majority of which (about 8,500) were for affordable rent (80% of market prices), affordable home ownership, or shared ownership (DCLG, 2016d).

One reason affordable homes are not being built is that while planning permission for new developments must still be obtained (under sections 55 and 57 of the Town and Country Planning Act 1990 – the TCPA), and while this must be in accordance with the development plan (section 70(2) of the TCPA), there is a particularly controversial change in paragraph 14 of the National Planning Policy Framework (NPPF) (DCLG, 2012a). This introduces a presumption in favour of sustainable development, as well as paragraphs 47 and 49, which use five-year supplies of housing as mechanisms to either decide in line with, or effectively override, the local plan (this is a matter of extraordinary legal controversy at the moment, awaiting the decision of the Supreme Court in the *Hopkins Homes* litigation). The extent of legal technicality here, highlights the irony that the NPPF was introduced to simplify planning procedures and reduce red tape. It came about when the government accepted the critique that 'planning is the problem', preventing the development of new homes (even though the Local Government Association (LGA) identified 475,000 homes in England which have been given planning permission but which are yet to be built (LGA, 2016)).

Of course, we need more housing, and new developments can be welcome. However, the difficulty here, and the facilitation of gentrification, comes from the 'dark art' of viability, which was also introduced in the 2012 NPPF. This requires that in order to 'ensure viability, the costs of any requirements likely to be applied to development, such as requirements for affordable housing, standards, infrastructure contributions or other requirements, should, when taking account of the normal cost of development and mitigation, provide competitive returns to a willing land owner and willing developer to enable the development to be deliverable' (NPPF, paragraph 173). What this has meant in practice is that when developers apply for planning permission for a new housing development, they are now less likely to enter into a section 106 agreement in order to obtain their planning consent. This is both facilitated (via the presumption in paragraph 14 of the NPPF) and undercut by viability. For rather than pay for or provide new affordable housing as their 'planning obligation', developers can, often by relying on consultant surveyors, argue that if affordable housing is required it will make the development 'unviable'. The local authority often has little option but to grant planning permission even if no, or little, affordable housing is provided.

Sometimes a local authority might argue vehemently against the developers' calculations (which are often based on assumptions as to profitability). The cost of any planning appeal, or subsequent litigation, particularly at a time of severe local authority budget cuts in response to austerity politics, does, however, limit the space for dissent. And yet, there are some local authorities that are using the legal mechanisms at their disposal to resist. The London Borough of Islington has been particularly effective here. In its recent Supplementary Planning Document, Islington has set out its expectations on viability and appraisals, with a particular commitment to transparency, stating that: 'The council considers that information submitted as a part of, and in support of a viability assessment should be treated transparently and be available for wider scrutiny. In submitting information, applicants do so in the knowledge that this will be made publically available alongside other application documents' (Islington, 2016, 46). Alongside recent decisions assisting local authorities (including *Greenwich RLBC v Information Commissioner*, 2015 EA/2014/0122), this marks an effort by progressive public actors to ensure that at the very least the information on which to assess viability and argue for more affordable housing is in the public domain. These are occasional bright spots in the extraordinary facilitation of private sector development producing homes primarily at market prices.

What all this means for gentrification is that new developments can be proposed, often regenerating mixed use, industrial or even former residential sites, but planning officers and local councillors can impose increasingly fewer requirements to provide affordable housing. Legal provisions on planning, particularly since the introduction of the 2012 NPPF, have facilitated regeneration and housebuilding. However, with no mechanisms in place to control rents or prices, poorer residents are often excluded. When this is coupled with limits on welfare payments, and the introduction of universal benefit, it can lead to widespread social reorganisation, largely through housing (Hamnett, 2014) and framings of 'affordable rent'. Even Boris Johnson, then Mayor of London, argued in 2012 that this amounted to 'social cleansing' (Lees, 2014a). Apparently neutral, technical provisions can have enormous social and spatial effects.

What then can be done? Are there solutions that can be legally implemented other than a return to more progressive planning ways? The most effective way is to take a more robust approach to viability assessments – limiting profitability – perhaps through the standardised models that are now being proposed for London. The provision of affordable housing through planning obligations (section 106 obligations) has declined rapidly as profitability (viability) has become central to decision-making in planning. This can be reformed as some local authorities – notably Islington in North London – are demonstrating (Islington, 2016). London, as a whole, is also investigating how to implement a standardised viability methodology to address these problems (Mayor for London, 2016). The 2017 Housing White Paper (2017a) is, however, notably silent on the need for a standardised viability methodology.

Another way is to change what we require planning permission for, for example short-term lettings. In England, planning rules have been 'relaxed' to facilitate Airbnb despite the gentrification changes this can bring. Since the 2015 Deregulation Act, owners in London can rent their homes for up to 90 days, removing the requirement in the Greater London Council (General Powers) Act 1973 for planning permission if residential premises were to be used for temporary sleeping accommodation for less than 90 consecutive nights. While there are interventions by landlords, including London local authorities who remain the freeholders for flats purchased as 'right to buy', against tenants letting properties through Airbnb (for example, see *Nemcova v Fairfield Rents Ltd* [2016] UKUT 303), this relaxation in planning rules comes at exactly the same time as other cities, including Barcelona, Dublin and Berlin (Novy and Colomb, 2016; for Lisbon, see Gant 2016), have introduced regulations to restrict short lets. In Dublin, for example, planning permission may now be required with Airbnb where it is recognised as a potentially commercial practice and a business use of space. Constraints on leases or within regulation can quite easily be introduced, should political actors desire them (Vice, 2016). So far, however, national decision-makers have facilitated Airbnb, leaving it to individual landlords to impose restraints if the properties are held on a lease.

Another suggestion is to enrol materiality. This was illustrated early on in gentrification studies of the 'break up' of houses into flats from the 1960s to 1980s in London (Hamnett and Randolph, 1986). If sub-division is possible, gentrification is materially facilitated. If it is not – as for example in some post-Soviet buildings – the physical and financial commodification are more difficult to combine to produce a change of ownership (whether freehold or leasehold). In these instances there are material restraints on gentrification. Of course, these can be overcome by large-scale regeneration projects. This is most evident in the destruction of council estates (including the Heygate and Aylesbury Estates in the Elephant and Castle in London) where the land values are so high that the rent gap provides huge incentives for redevelopment (Lees, 2014a,b; Watt and Minton, 2016). In the regeneration of council housing estates an extraordinary amount of attention has been paid to the – apparently – poor design and quality of these estates. In England, materiality has often (for example, at both the Heygate and Aylesbury Estates) been enrolled to argue for gentrification, not against it. Architects have been criticised for outdated, often 1960s designs, while a lack of property maintenance has led to undesirable living conditions (particularly once decanting processes have been undertaken and only a few leaseholders remain). This lack of care justifies 'regeneration' with its physical, social and spatial consequences.

Materiality can however be protected. This is illustrated by Berlin's *Milieuschutz*, which uses legal restrictions to enrol material conditions as a mechanism to resist change

(Karow-Kluge and Schmitt, 2014; Holm, 2014). In Berlin, there is some anecdotal evidence that landlords are being refused permission to install marble ceilings, second bathrooms or lifts in five-storey apartment blocks. Framed as restrictions on taste, these material restrictions, legally implemented, can inhibit building change and so inhibit their market value (for rent or sale), making them more affordable for existing residents. It is plausible that in England, too, conservation, listing or any planning measures might be used to inhibit gentrification. Throughout the 1960s and 1970s, there is widespread evidence that preservation of heritage was used as a pro-gentrification strategy, requiring particular maintenance procedures and costly permissions. Might there be scope to extend listing beyond historically significant sites and aesthetically pleasing fabrics to 'landmark' or protect authentic places as conservation areas today? We know that design is crucial in attracting wealthier residents – and gentrification – whether as a result of conservation restrictions or apartments produced for wealthy international buyers. Material conditions might constitute part of a 'right to community' if this can be developed from the decision letter refusing to confirm the compulsory purchase orders on the Aylesbury Estate in 2016. In particular, there is potential here for minority narratives (given equality duties) to find protective legal form (as the Pueblito Paisa dispute, discussed below, illustrates).

One further planning initiative may also offer further hope. Throughout areas of outstanding beauty, including rural and coastal areas, 'locals' are being priced out by incomers, notably second homeowners who rarely use properties throughout the year. The effect has been that in Cornwall, the Yorkshire Dales and the Lake District, for example, coastal and rural locations have seen such house price inflation that residents without rental security or children of longstanding residents can no longer afford to own or rent locally. One local response has been to attempt to introduce planning rules that limit the construction of new properties that can be used as second homes. Instead houses are given planning permission only if they are to be used as primary residences (with provision within enforcement made for exceptional circumstances). Long desired, these changes have come through neighbourhood planning initiatives (introduced alongside the Localism Act of 2011). They have also been (in the case of St Ives, in Cornwall) upheld in court (in *R (RLT Built Environment Ltd) v Cornwall Council* [2016] EWHC 2817 (Admin)).

Neighbourhood planning might then be an ally in resisting gentrification. Certainly, minority perspectives have not always been incorporated in neighbourhood planning and some see the process as backward-looking and nostalgic, raising questions about the 'attempts to mobilize the affective and morally charged language of the local' (Tait and Inch, 2016, 174). However, there is a localism of hope that engages with differentiated civic capacities within and between communities. Wills (2016, 4) has argued persuasively for optimism, noting the difficulties and yet suggesting that as 'the shift towards localist statecraft exposes the limits of our dominant paradigms for thinking about politics and its geography, as well as the weakness of our institutional infrastructure, there is an opportunity to revisit questions about the importance of place'. Neighbourhood planning could be used progressively to plan for stable and sustainable communities, which indeed are the aims of many participants.

Legal mechanisms might then be developed to try to protect distinctive places (a further example might be the terroirs that are used as geographic indications to protect food producers, including champagne and prosciutto di Parma (Raustiala and Munzer,

2007)). We might imagine ways – by drawing maps and attaching protections as both neighbourhood planning and geographic indications do – to protect cultural patterns of consumption or local practices as efforts to inhibit gentrification. We could investigate the potential of using provisions analogous to these on second homes to inhibit 'buy to leave' of new build residential properties in high value urban areas (or even second homes in the City of London, the authority with by far the highest proportion in England (at 28.5%, compared with Cornwall's 5.4% (Estate Agent Today, 2016). Strikingly, there are no nationally compiled figures and – as with 'buy to leave' – researchers are heavily reliant on estate agents for information). It might – as with Airbnb regulation in Berlin, Barcelona and New York – involve some neighbourly investigation for enforcement. There may or may not be some distaste for that. As a legal mechanism, however, as these cities have demonstrated, such provisions can be drafted.

Of course, this is not straightforward. Tastes and practices change. Identifying 'locals' in restrictive ways (were your parents or your grandparents born here?) is exclusionary. There is a tension within gentrification studies between place and networks (including of immigration and globalisation). At the outset, Glass (1964) acknowledged this, writing that London is 'too vast, too complex, too contrary and too moody to become entirely familiar' (p. 133). We might, however, think about how to develop such ideas to create legal mechanisms to protect place and existing residents. Or we might adopt everyday acts of resistance from Cornish locals who (allegedly) might put a mackerel through the letterbox of a rarely used second home.

26.3　COMMERCIAL PROPERTY

Some of the most noted signs, or signifiers, of gentrification, are the emergence of hipster bars, artisanal pizza restaurants and estate agents in established – but not necessarily financially thriving – shopping streets. Zukin (2011) has argued that we need to acknowledge 'the entrepreneurial role of newcomers who open businesses in the district – art galleries, performance spaces, restaurants, boutiques, and bars – that not only provide spaces of consumption for residents and visitors to develop a lifestyle, but also provide visible opportunities for neighbourhoods to develop a new place identity' (p. 163). Such claims about place identity are not uncontroversial (Slater, 2006) but are facilitated by two legal mechanisms: (1) the construction of commercial leases; and (2) the granting of planning permissions and other licences for change of use. Current rules facilitate change – and so allow gentrification – while new rules might be envisaged to restrict change, better enabling existing retailers and businesses to stay put. While both leases and planning are crucial in commercial gentrification practices, for reasons of space, only leases will be considered here. For it is once again the lack of security of tenure and the decision-making power that so often remains with the freeholder that becomes the facilitator of change. This chapter will now review how leases operate to facilitate gentrification, contributing to growing debates on retail gentrification, which – as Hubbard (2017, 2) notes – 'remains poorly theorized as a form of gentrification'.

As a device to enable land ownership and use, leases have been used for hundreds of years, particularly as a mechanism to facilitate mortgage lending and in agricultural contexts, as already discussed, and these will be the focus of this section. For in the English commercial context, long leases are often used for major redevelopment, combined with public leasing of land, including 999-year leases for the construction of the Royal Albert Hall (Kelsey, 2001), as well as for Liverpool Football Club at Anfield in 2006. Long leases for 250 years are also common in retail-led regeneration (Layard, 2010). Such very long leases are close to freehold in respect of term (who knows what a site will look like 250 or 999 years from today?), and the agreements of the lease, even when the freeholder is a public body, are generally confidential. These long leases give extraordinary stability to developers, be they for commercial or philanthropic reasons.

Elsewhere, however, the average length of commercial leases is between six and seven years (BPF, 2015). Start-ups, in particular, will often only be offered a short lease or indeed they may choose one, particularly if the agreement does not have a break clause (giving either the tenant or landlord the ability to serve notice during the term of the lease). While shorter leases give businesses greater flexibility – if the business does not flourish, they will not be contractually obligated to pay rent for a long period – it also means that the rent can be increased more quickly when a new lease is negotiated at the end of the term.

This matters for gentrification since, while a freehold owner can use their property as they wish for as long as they wish, a leaseholder cannot. The ability to end a lease at the end of a fixed term (termination) or to vary its conditions (particularly, how much rent is payable) are part of the contractual relationship between landlord and tenant. At the end of the lease any increase in value – with any improvements made by the tenant, to the land, the property or the neighbourhood – accrue to the landlord. And while a lease is an estate, and so something to be owned within property law, it is also a contract, with terms to be negotiated. Although such negotiations must take place in the shadow of the law, historically the law of England and Wales has largely left the parties free to negotiate the initial form of a commercial lease.

The most contentious aspect of commercial leases has been the amount of rent payable. In England there are no restrictions and market forces determine the level. An initial rent will be agreed between landlord and tenant when a lease is first negotiated. The tenancy agreement may provide for rent increases or reviews during the term, but if it does not, the initial rent will normally apply for the full length of the tenancy. Rent review clauses can be inserted into commercial leases to provide a mechanism through which the landlord and tenants can agree rises in rent over the course of the tenancy. In times of recession there has been considerable concern about the use of 'upwards only' rent review clauses, so that even if the value of the capital property goes down, the rent is still required to go up. This matters because if the parties cannot agree a new rent under a rent review clause, costly arbitration or expert valuation procedures are used to resolve the disagreement. Mary Portas has been especially critical, recommending alternative lease structures for smaller businesses, in particular, including a turnover based rent, which gives 'landlords a stake in the success of the tenant's business' (Portas, 2011, 35).

This lack of restrictions on rent means that security of tenure for commercial tenants is limited. For while the Landlord and Tenant Act 1954 confers a statutory right of renewal on occupying business tenants (section 24), a landlord can still seek the end of the lease (section 25) if s/he can make out either disrepair, persistent delay in paying rent, breach of other obligation, offer of alternative accommodation, premises substantially more valuable as a whole, demolition or reconstruction or landlord's own occupation (section

30). More significantly still, the 1954 Act does not provide for any degree of rent regulation. Even if a tenant can renew his/her lease, 'the rent is to be that which the holding might reasonably be expected to be let in the open market by a willing lessor and lessee, disregarding the effect of the occupation of the tenant, any goodwill of the business and certain tenant's improvements' (section 34).

The effects of these provisions are vividly demonstrated by the experience of the Kaff Bar in Brixton in London, a thriving local business. As Steven Ross, manager of the Kaff Bar explains, after being served with a section 25 notice not to renew their short-term lease on the basis of alleged landlord's own occupation:

> [W]e finally received some proper dialogue from the other side. This was to now offer us a renewal on our lease. We expected a rise in the rent and were prepared, but not for over treble the amount we are currently paying!!! As you can imagine, we weren't best pleased with this so we have tried to challenge this since and tried to arrange a meeting to discuss terms of negotiation. However, with recent events and news about other properties and the future of Brixton in general I sat down and proceeded to do the sums to see if realistically we could stay. The short answer again is, no! (quoted in Urban, 2015b).

The use of these legal provisions, and the decisions of the landlord (the freeholder), led to the closure of this popular Brixton bar.

In gentrifying neighbourhoods, a lack of security of tenure coupled with rents pinned to the open market facilitates change. It produces steep rent hikes with no protection for existing tenants when their lease term expires or the landlord decides to evict under the terms of the lease. This is as true in Shoreditch in London as in Harlem in New York City. The tenant may well have put in effort to bring about positive transformations yet they will not share in the benefits at the end of any lease. For, as Adam Smith's quotation at the start of this chapter makes clear, it is the freeholder – the landlord – who benefits in increases in value in the land. And so in 2016, Dip & Flip, selling 'gourmet burgers and hot meat sandwiches topped with gravy in a simple-yet-stylish dining room' opened up in the Kaff Bar's old site, presumably (because these facts are commercially confidential) paying a higher rent.

How could we reform the law on commercial leases to inhibit gentrification? The Kaff Bar's story is one that is told over and again in gentrifying neighbourhoods. Local shops and businesses are displaced, replaced with new users, be they commercial or residential, producing higher profits to landlords (either in rents or, if the landlord 'cashes in' on rising land values, in capital receipts). While residential rent control is regularly discussed, commercial rent control is much less common. It was briefly introduced in Albany, New York, in 1948, existed in New York City (with measures for decontrol) from 1945 to 1963, and most comprehensively was introduced in Elmwood in Berkeley, California, in 1982, providing commercial rent stabilisation for a small shopping district of 84 stores (Keating, 1985). Zukin identifies the expiry of 'rent-control-type laws' as one reason for the rise of 'loft living' in New York City after the 1960s (1989, 52).

In England, however, there are no calls for commercial rent control. The 1954 Act gives security of tenure but no guarantees as to rent. In the absence of any prospective changes to commercial leases, another alternative is to work with landlords for positive change. Alive to the difficulties, the Royal Institute of Chartered Surveyors has developed a specimen lease for five years with no rent review (RICS, 2016). There is a lease code, setting out desirable provisions from the government's point of view, which landlords *may* follow. Very little of this has been legally transcribed and leases remain instruments that reflect the power dynamics (or market conditions, if you prefer) between landlord and tenant. Freeholders may often be non-resident. 'Shell' companies are created to be the freehold owners of land, sometimes registered abroad for tax reasons, making it difficult for individual tenants to deal with landlords directly, engaging instead with managing agents.

Again there is a role here for 'ethical landlordism', in the use of meanwhile leases, another legal mechanism to facilitate change. Lauded in DCLG's 2009 Report *Looking After Our Town Centres* and widely heralded as productive for high streets, entrepreneurs and charities as well as for landlords (minimising the payment of business rates and utilities while properties are empty, having the security of active occupation and showcasing possible future use), meanwhile leases are short-term by design. They facilitate (productive) change. Yet while the recent governments have worked collaboratively to develop guidance and a specimen lease for pop up shops (DCLG, 2012b), in practice, landlords require legal arrangements to be overseen and checked by a solicitor and/or surveyor (if alterations are to be made) of the landlords' choice and at the pop up tenants' cost. Although charities are advantaged here, as they can occupy otherwise empty premises and claim rate relief (they pay only 20%) often in exchange for 'tax-deductible donations' from landlords, for non-charitable entrepreneurs, turnover can be fast, with the costs almost always borne primarily by the tenant.

Encouraging philanthropic commercial landlordism for meanwhile or standard commercial leases might then be an avenue for productive resistance to gentrification whilst still facilitating change. If we can do little to change the law, we can change legal and commercial practice. Examples of good practice using leases without transferring the freehold for community benefit abound (CABE, 2008, 2010; DCLG, 2012b). Such developments can be perceived as gentrification but if sensitively implemented, they can provide genuine local benefits. However, in recent years, the impacts of austerity politics and the perceived need for local authorities to sell 'spare' sites to balance their books, coupled with a growing emphasis on using public land 'efficiently' (HM Treasury, 2013), has reduced opportunities for meaningful, community-led engagement with local authority landowners who often engaged productively in these schemes. We may need to look to greater community and private philanthropic landlordism in future, changing cultures rather than legal provisions, if we are to create brakes to slow down the constant change and rent increases facilitated by commercial leases. That of course requires access to land, which is of course becoming ever more expensive.

One last way in which legal rules on commercial property can facilitate gentrification is to note both the legal reproduction (the same agreements and the same legal mechanisms) are accompanied by materials and designs, which are also reproduced from site to site. As Anna Minton has noted:

> Take the Westfield shopping centre in Stratford City – you don't even need to know you're in Stratford. You've come by tube or you've come straight in on the motorway, which has taken you into the car park. You can go shopping. But if you make the effort to look across the road from the top of the entrance staircase, and you look down over the gyratory system, you've got this run-down 1970s mall, which is where local people go (quoted in Imrie and Lees, 2014, 35).

Gentrification is a profoundly material practice. Where once it consisted of the introduction of 'a cultural sensibility and refinement that transcended the post-war suburban ethos of conformity and kitsch' (Zukin, 1993, 192) or quiche Lorraines and Habitat furniture (Moran, 2007), it now takes physical form through architectural practices, using repeated consignments of materials. There is an emphasis on 'authenticity' (for micro-breweries or local bread, see Hubbard 2017) as well as large scale reproduction of new shopping centres that are materially reproduced with very little connection to place (for examples, see Hammersons 2016 Annual Report, with centres in England, expanding into France and Spain as well). Both the reproduced and the 'authentic' can be understood as gentrification. Similarly, as Smith and Williams (1986) note, the residential and the commercial are frequently interlinked in major construction projects; for example, in the redevelopment of urban waterfronts, industrial rezoning, or the rise of hotel, office or retail districts. These large projects could incorporate cultural and place-based planning restraints within the redevelopments but generally do not.

Such cultural and material choices are profoundly positional. With individual (though networked), early, gentrifiers these choices were noticeable but had little legal force. This became quite different when urban and historic conservation initiatives began to focus on the fabric of buildings and their curtilages. Conservation areas were introduced in 1967, with early gentrifiers often using their mechanisms to inhibit change or require costly renovation practices (Lees et al, 2008). These days, conservation areas are designated areas of special architectural or historic interest, 'the character or appearance of which it is desirable to preserve or enhance' (section 69(1) and section 69(2) of the Planning (Listed Buildings and Conservation Areas) Act 1990). The regulatory provisions can see off change, particularly in terms of the built fabric of a place. Yet they are invariably focused on historical artefacts and sites and reflect the conservation preferences of majority cultures.

This is also true of listed buildings. This began in England, post-war, in 1947, building on the Victorians' 1882 Ancient Monuments Protection Act. The system acknowledged a focus on the historic built environment and today buildings can be listed, and so protected, if they have architectural or historic interest that is longstanding (today these criteria are in section 1(3) of the Planning (Listed Buildings and Conservation Areas) Act 1990). If buildings are not aesthetically pleasing, they might still be listed, but only if they are 'important for reasons of technological innovation, or as illustrating particular aspects of social or economic history' (DCMS, 2010, 4) not because of their use today. As this illustrates, interpretations of which cultures we should protect and admire are inevitably subjective, privileging one set of cultural practices and preferences over those of others. Shaw is explicit about this: in writing of Sydney, she notes that: 'as desires for heritage develop and consolidate with gentrification, and become more inclusive of difference, migrant and indigenous heritages continue to remain outside the heritage orbit' (2005, 59).

The difficulties in protecting minority heritage has been achingly clear in the battle to maintain Pueblito Paisa, an indoor market in Seven Sisters in London (at Wards Corner). The market provides a spatial and social focus for Latin American cultures in its shops, cafes, restaurants, and barbers shops, on a site where 64% of the 36 units are occupied by traders either from Latin America or who are Spanish speaking. Earmarked as part of a major regeneration project, Haringey Borough Council granted planning permission for the demolition of existing buildings and erection of mixed-use developments instead. Initially protestors were able to succeed in their claim that the council had infringed the

Race Relations Act 1976 (as amended) in failing to pay due regard to the need to 'promote equality of opportunity and good relations between persons of different racial groups' as required by section 71. This finding was even upheld by the Court of Appeal (*R (on the application of Janet Harris) v London Borough of Haringey* [2010] EWCA Civ 70).

Nevertheless, at Pueblito Paisa, once the procedural steps had been observed, the plans for the proposed regeneration continued. These included a compulsory purchase order to assemble the land for the project, which was submitted to the Secretary of State (who needs to approve it) in September 2016. At the time of writing the battle at Pueblito Paisa continues, the United Nations even getting involved, but the legal mechanisms to facilitate change (including the compulsory purchase of leases, as well as planning) are well underway. They have, however, created a discursive space.

26.4 CONCLUSION

This chapter has argued that legal mechanisms and practices facilitate – and can be used to resist – the changes that lie at the heart of gentrification. It is the first step in a larger project that must be collaborative (see Lees, Shin and López-Morales, 2016, on international collaboration in gentrification studies), to collate the legal provisions and practices that are used to facilitate and resist gentrification around the world. Within gentrification studies we often focus on the same questions: unaffordable housing, retail conglomerates, internationally focused developers, minority cultural preservation or Airbnb. Comparative legal solutions, collected with sufficient detail, can provide a valuable resource to show sympathetic public officials, be they (Shadow) Secretaries of State, mayors or councillors, that legal changes can be crafted to effect resistance, to limit change and strengthen rights to stay put. These might include voluntary rent controls, planning restrictions whether on viability, and transparency or neighbourhood restrictions on secondary residences. Reforms might include material restrictions (akin to Berlin's *Milieuschutz*) or a concerted effort to keep land ownership in public or communal hands wherever possible (for example, Rock House above).

There are significant constitutional differences. Legally, London cannot, for example, regulate its housing or land use rules in the way that Berlin, New York or Barcelona can. England is a country where land use is primarily regulated at the national scale (increasingly presuming or automatically granting permission and so giving the decision-making power to individual developers instead). There is nothing in this chapter about Wales, let alone Scotland or Northern Ireland. Devolution has profound legal and practical effects. However, localised practices can change, particularly if arguments can be made that (for example) residential or commercial rent control or planning restrictions have facilitated 'authenticity' in highly regarded cities elsewhere.

Being alive to legal differences matters if we are to seek solutions. We need to acknowledge the possibilities and some apparent limits of change. Even in Vancouver, with a mayor deeply concerned with housing affordability and displacement, the introduction of a 15% tax on non-national property purchases is now subject to the approval of British Columbia Supreme Court, which will rule on a class-action suit from prospective foreign buyers. And yet, if we know where the legal difficulties lie, we can investigate whether there are soft spots, where can we challenge, what can we push? This is one purpose of legal work in gentrification studies.

Another key focus for legally aware comparative gentrification research is to identify land ownership. As this chapter has illustrated, the landowner, either the freeholder or a (very) long leaseholder, has extraordinary power to set the agenda for their land and determine the look, feel, taste and smell of a city. In England, within the private sector, landowners can then sell or rent land to the highest bidder and even when land is publicly owned (for example by a local authority) the rules on land ownership, or how to buy and sell or rent, remain broadly the same as for private owners (though there are human rights implications, some public law rules and possible requirements to consult) (Layard, 2016). More importantly, even though public landowners can act very quickly in redeveloping or gentrifying sites, procedural remedies can create space for discursive arguments about how public landowners should behave, drawing on histories and practices that are often site-specific. Public landowners are not necessarily more philanthropic or socially minded – as activists throughout London know well – but they can be open to debates about equality and access. It is this scope for different property practices that can be identified and developed through legal and political activism but first we need to keep asking: 'who owns the land?' Can we see any contracts? Concepts of property and contract, public and private, emerge throughout international practices of regeneration, often replicated even if they are almost always jurisdictionally distinctive.

To continue to internationalise gentrification studies then, we must consider the legal. Jurisdictions differ but broad concepts – freeholds, leases, human rights, participation rights and forms of judicial review – are similar. The details matter: a German lease with security of tenure and regulated rents is a very different creature from an English assured shorthold tenancy. To identify how legal mechanisms and practices are facilitating – and can resist – gentrification, scholars need to engage in the details of legal research.

Analysts of global gentrification studies have noted the 'trajectory' of gentrification beyond the usual suspects of 'London, New York etc.' (Lees, Shin and López-Morales, 2016). There will be many reasons for the extension of gentrification practices (economic, political, cultural), yet the mechanisms used will often be similar. The use of the lease – particularly when there is no or limited rent regulation or security of tenure – is a key instrument in facilitating gentrification. Planning permission may be required for a new development or change of use but if regulations do not impose requirements for affordable housing or retail, the planning system may facilitate – rather than prevent – gentrification. There is growing evidence that Anglo-American conceptual hegemony is being used – in primarily capitalist land use decisions – to produce gentrification across the globe (Lees, Shin, López-Morales, 2016). This chapter suggests that these shared concepts and practices are often legal – freeholds, leases and licences as well as planning permissions – facilitate the replication of gentrification. The relative ease with which this can occur is illustrated by public sector projects, often in the name of regeneration (for example, as discussed here on the Heygate and Aylesbury housing estates). As this chapter has discussed, there are only limited procedural legal safeguards. Conversely, however, while private sector developers may operate more slowly they are under far less public scrutiny and can enrol greater claims (both legal as well as rhetorical) of commercial confidentiality.

Asking legal questions is crucial to understanding how gentrification happens wherever it is taking place. It is so often the same legal mechanisms – leases, licences, planning permissions – as well as key legal absences – rent regulation, security of tenure or compulsory financial contributions to communities – that facilitate gentrification. Western concepts of property and land use have travelled extraordinarily well (Davies, 2007). As comparative gentrification studies illustrate, there are different ways of *doing* property and regeneration (including ethical landlordism, rent controls, security of tenure, state-led construction of affordable housing, community public spaces, social retail ventures, to name just a few) and we need to identify and publicise these. Roy (2009) has called for 'a more contoured knowledge' of cities and this applies to legal knowledge as well. We can – and should – look for legal concepts that act as alternatives to the standard Western incidents of property and planning practices to inform calls for change. As Lees, Shin and López-Morales (2016, 226) argue: 'We need to unpick "the planet's gentrified mind", we need to be counter-cultural again, to find radical ways and insights, to operate outside social assumptions, to generate social and urban change through contestation and the presentation of realistic alternatives'. Legal analysis will be crucial in this task.

ACKNOWLEDGEMENT

This chapter has benefitted greatly from the insightful comments by Loretta Lees, David Cowan and Ed Burtonshaw-Gunn.

REFERENCES

Andersson, R. and Turner, L. (2014) 'Segregation, gentrification, and residualisation: from public housing to market-driven housing allocation in inner city Stockholm', *International Journal of Housing Policy*, 14(1), 3–29.
Baron, J. (2010) 'The contested commitments of property', *Hastings Law Journal*, 61(4), 917–967.
Bennett, L. and Layard, A. (2015) 'Legal geography: becoming spatial detectives', *Geography Compass*, 9(7), 406–422.
Blomley, N. (1997) 'The properties of space: history, geography, and gentrification', *Urban Geography*, 18(4), 286–295.
Blomley, N. (2004) *Unsettling the City: Urban Land and the Politics of Property*, New York: Routledge.
BPF (2015) Available at: http://www.bpf.org.uk/media/press-releases/commercial-property-lease-lengths-hit-eight-year-high-occupier-confidence.
Bridge, G., Butler, T. and Lees, L. (eds) (2011) *Mixed Communities: Gentrification by Stealth?*, Bristol: Policy Press.
Butler, T. and Robson, G. (2003) 'Plotting the middle classes: gentrification and circuits of education in London', *Housing Studies*, 18(1), 5–28.
CABE (2008) *Public Space Lessons Land in Limbo: Making the Best Use of Vacant Urban Spaces.* Available at: http://webarchive.nationalarchives.gov.uk/20110118153133/http://www.cabe.org.uk/files/land-in-limbo.pdf.
CABE (2010) *Community-led Spaces: A Guide for Local Authorities and Community Groups.* Available at: http://www.neighbourhoodsgreen.org.uk/resources/community-led-spaces.
Cowan, D. (2011) *Housing Law and Policy*, Cambridge: Cambridge University Press.
Cowan, D. and McDermont, M. (2006) *Regulating Social Housing: Governing Decline*, Routledge-Cavendish.
Crook, T. and Kemp, P. (2011) *Transforming Private Landlords: Housing, Markets and Public Policy* (Vol. 43), John Wiley & Sons.
Davies, M. (2007) *Property: Meanings, Histories, Theories*, London: Routledge.
DCLG (2009) *Planning for Town Centres.* Available at: https://www.gov.uk/government/uploads/system/uploads/attachment_data/file/7781/towncentresguide.pdf.
DCLG (2012a) *National Planning Policy Framework.* Available at: https://www.gov.uk/government/publications/national-planning-policy-framework--2.
DCLG (2012b) Meanwhile Lease and Guidance. Available at: https://www.gov.uk/government/uploads/system/uploads/attachment_data/file/230037/Meanwhile_use_lease_and_guidance.pdf.
DCLG (2014) (updated 2016). Model Agreement for an Assured Shorthold Tenancy and Accompanying

Guidance. Available at: https://www.gov.uk/government/publications/model-agreement-for-a-shorthold-as sured-tenancy.

DCLG (2016a) Affordable housing supply: April 2015 to March 2016 England. Available at: https://www.gov. uk/government/statistics/affordable-housing-supply-in-england-2015-to-2016.

DCLG (2016b) Decision letter, compulsory purchase, Aylesbury Estate. Available at: http://35percent.org/img/ Decision_Letter_Final.pdf.

DCLG (2016c) Estate regeneration national strategy. Available at: https://www.gov.uk/guidance/estate-reg eneration-national-strategy.

DCLG (2016d) House building: June Quarter 2016, England. Available at: https://www.gov.uk/government/ uploads/system/uploads/attachment_data/file/639725/House_Building_Release_June_Qtr_2017.pdf.

DCLG (2016e) English housing survey 2014–2015: Headline report. Available at: https://www.gov.uk/governm ent/statistics/english-housing-survey-2014-to-2015-headline-report.

DCLG (2017a) Housing White Paper: *Fixing our broken housing market.* Available at: https://www.gov.uk/ government/publications/fixing-our-broken-housing-market.

DCLG (2017b) English housing survey 2015 to 2016: Headline report. Available at: https://www.gov.uk/ government/statistics/english-housing-survey-2015-to-2016-headline-report.

DCMS (2010) Principles of selection for listing buildings. Available at: https://www.gov.uk/government/uplo ads/system/uploads/attachment_data/file/137695/Principles_Selection_Listing_1_.pdf.

Dentons (2010) Future of London: Policy in Focus November 2010 Partnership Building: The key to housing delivery in the new policy landscape by Anita Rivera. Available at: http://documents.lexology.com/a0f02e3f- 980e-4d91-b586-cedd845b631f.pdf.

Deschermeier, P., Haas, H., Hude, M. and Voigtländer, M. (2016) 'A first analysis of the new German rent regulation', *International Journal of Housing Policy*, 16(3), 293–315.

Desmond, M. (2016) *Evicted: Poverty and Profit in the American City*, New York: Crown Publishing.

DeVerteuil, G. (2015) *Resilience in the Post-welfare Inner City: Voluntary Sector Geographies in London, Los Angeles and Sydney*, Bristol: Policy Press.

Estate Agents Today (2016) *Highest Number of Second Homes is in London not Tourist Hotspots.* [Online] accessed 5 May 2017. Available at: https://www.estateagenttoday.co.uk/breaking-news/2016/9/highest-numb er-of-second-homes-is-in-london-not-tourist-hotspots.

Field, M. and Layard, A. (2017) 'Locating community-led housing within neighbourhood plans as a response to England's housing needs', *Public Money & Management*, 37(2), 105–112.

Fitzpatrick, S. and Pawson, H. (2014) 'Ending security of tenure for social renters: transitioning to "ambulance service" social housing?', *Housing Studies*, 29(5), 597–615.

Fitzpatrick, S. and Watts, B. (2017) 'Competing visions: security of tenure and the welfarisation of English social housing', *Housing Studies*, 1–18. DOI: 10.1080/02673037.2017.12919.

Freeman, L. (2005) 'Displacement or succession? Residential mobility in gentrifying neighborhoods', *Urban Affairs Review*, 40(4), 463–491.

Freeman, L. (2017) 'Governed through ghost jurisdictions: municipal law, inner suburbs and rooming houses', *International Journal of Urban and Regional Research*, 41(2), 298–317.

Freeman, L., Cassola, A. and Cai, T. (2015) 'Displacement and gentrification in England and Wales: a quasi-experimental approach', *Urban Studies*, 53(13), 2797–2814.

Gant, A.C. (2016) 'Holiday rentals: the new gentrification battlefront', *Sociological Research Online*, 21(3), 10.

Glass, R. (1964 [1989]) *Clichés of Urban Doom and Other Essays*, Blackwell.

Goldstein, B. (2017) *The Roots of Urban Renaissance: Gentrification and the Struggle over Harlem*, Harvard University Press.

Gray, K. and Gray, S. (2003) 'The rhetoric of reality', in Getzler, J. (ed) *Rationalizing Property, Equity and Trusts: Essays in Honour of Edward Burn*, London: Butterworths, pp. 204–280.

Gray, K. and Gray, S. (2011) *Land Law*, Oxford: Oxford University Press.

Hamnett, C. (2014) 'Shrinking the welfare state: the structure, geography and impact of British government benefit cuts', *Transactions of the Institute of British Geographers*, 39(4), 490–503.

Hamnett, C. and Randolph, B. (1986) 'Tenurial transformation and the flat break-up market in London: the British condo experience', in Smith, N. and Williams, P. (eds) *Gentrification of the City*, London: Allen and Unwin, pp. 121–152.

HM Treasury *Managing Public Money*, A4 15.7 2013, amended 2015.

Hodkinson, S. and Essen, C. (2015) 'Grounding accumulation by dispossession in everyday life: the unjust geographies of urban regeneration under the private finance initiative', *International Journal of Law in the Built Environment*, 7(1), 72–91.

Holm, A. (2014) Wiederkehr der Wohnungsfrage. *Aus Politik und Zeitgeschichte*, 64, 20–21.

House of Commons Library (2016a) Briefing Paper No. 05638, 29 December 2016

House of Commons Library (2016b) Can private landlords refuse to let to Housing Benefit claimants? Briefing Paper No. 7008, 1 November 2016.

House of Commons Library (2016c) Council tax in England, Wales and Scotland: Social Indicators page, 11 November 2016.

Housing Benefit measures announced since 2010.

Hubbard, P., (2017) 'Introduction: gentrification and retail change', in Hubbard, P. *The Battle for the High Street: Retail Gentrification, Class and Disgust*, Palgrave Macmillan, 1–13.

Hubbard, P. and Lees, L. (2018) 'The right to community: legal geographies of resistance on London's final gentrification frontier', *City*, 21 December 2017.

Hubbard, P., Matthews, R. and Scoular, J. (2009) 'Legal geographies – controlling sexually oriented businesses: law, licensing, and the geographies of a controversial land use', *Urban Geography*, 30(2), 185–205.

Imrie, R. and Lees, L. (eds) (2014) *Sustainable London? The Future of a Global City*, Bristol: Policy Press.

Imrie, R., Lees, L. and Raco, M. (eds) (2009) *Regenerating London: Governance, Sustainability and Community in a Global City*, London: Routledge.

Islington (2016) *Development Viability Supplementary Planning Document January 2016*. Available at: https://www.islington.gov.uk//~/media/sharepoint-lists/public-records/planningandbuildingcontrol/publicity/public consultation/20152016/20160122developmentviabilityspdadoptedjan2016.

Karow-Kluge, D. and Schmitt, G. (2014) Gentrification neu denken–Wer ist beteiligt an Aufwertung und Verdrän-gung in städtischen Quartieren?. Available at: http://www.buergergesellschaft.de/fileadmin/pdf/gas tbeitrag_karow-kluge_schmitt_140704.pdf.

Keating Dennis, W. (1985) 'The Elmwood experiment: the use of commercial rent stabilization to preserve a diverse neighborhood shopping district', *Washington University Journal of Urban and Contemporary Law*, 28, 107.

Kelsey, P. (2001) 'Albert's new look', *History Today*, May, 51(5), 2.

Kleinhans, R. and Kearns, A. (2013) 'Neighbourhood restructuring and residential relocation: towards a balanced perspective on relocation processes and outcomes', *Housing Studies*, 28(2), 163–176.

Layard, A. (2010) 'Shopping in the public realm: a law of place', *Journal of Law and Society*, 37(3), 412–441.

Layard, A. (2016) 'Public space: property, lines, interruptions', *Journal of Law, Property and Society*, 2, i.

Lees, L. (1994) 'Gentrification in London and New York: an Atlantic gap?', *Housing Studies*, 9(2), 199–217.

Lees, L. (2014a) 'The death of sustainable communities in London?', in Imrie, R. and Lees, L. (eds) *Sustainable London? The Future of a Global City*, Bristol: Policy Press, pp. 149–172.

Lees, L. (2014b) 'The urban injustices of New Labour's "new urban renewal": the case of the Aylesbury Estate in London', *Antipode*, 46(4), 921–947.

Lees, L. (2016) 'Cameron's "sink estate" strategy comes at a human cost', *The Conversation*. Available at: https://theconversation.com/camerons-sink-estate-strategy-comes-at-a-human-cost-53358.

Lees, L. and Ferreri, M. (2016) 'Resisting gentrification on its final frontiers: lessons from the Heygate Estate in London (1974–2013)', *Cities*, 57, 14–24.

Lees, L., Shin, H. and López-Morales, E. (eds) (2015) *Global Gentrifications: Uneven Development and Displacement*, Bristol: Policy Press.

Lees, L., Shin, H. and López-Morales, E. (2016) *Planetary Gentrification*, Cambridge: Polity Press.

Lees, L., Slater, T. and Wyly, E. (2008) *Gentrification*, New York: Routledge.

LGA (2016) Local Government Association *Responses to the Housing and Planning Bill, House of Lords, Report Stage.*

Martin & Co (2016) [Online] accessed on 5 April 2017. Available at: https://www.martinco.com/estate-agents-and-letting-agents/branch/grantham/news/margaret_thatcher__her_role_in_shaping_the_modern_housing_market-7799.

Martin, I. and Beck, K. (2016) 'Gentrification, property tax limitation, and displacement', *Urban Affairs Review*, DOI: 10.1177/1078087416666959.

Mayor for London (2016) Homes for Londoners: Draft Affordable Housing and Viability Supplementary Planning Guidance 2016.

Moran, J. (2007) 'Early cultures of gentrification in London, 1955–1980', *Journal of Urban History*, 34(1), 101–121.

Murie, A. (2016) *The Right to Buy?: Selling Off Public and Social Housing*, Bristol: Policy Press.

Novy, J. and Colomb, C. (2016) 'Urban tourism and its discontents: an introduction', in Colomb, C. and Novy, J. (eds) *Protest and Resistance in the Tourist City*, Routledge, pp. 1–30.

Portas, M. (2011) *The Portas Review: An Independent Review into the Future of our High Streets*, Department for Business, Innovation and Skills.

Raustiala, K. and Munzer, S. (2007) 'The global struggle over geographic indications', *European Journal of International Law*, 18, 337–365.

RICS *Small Business Retail Lease*. Available at: http://www.rics.org/uk/knowledge/small-business-hub/property-in-business/small-business-retail-lease/.

Roy, A. (2009) 'The 21st century metropolis: new geographies of theory', *Regional Studies*, 43(6), 819–830.

Scanlon, K. and Whitehead, C. (2014) 'Rent stabilisation: principles and international experience', London Borough of Camden. Available at: http://www.lse.ac.uk/geographyAndEnvironment/research/london/pdf/Rent-Stabilisation-report- 2014.pdf.

Shaw, K. (2008) 'Gentrification: what it is, why it is, and what can be done about it?', *Geography Compass*, 2(5), 1697–1728.

Slater, T. (2006) 'The eviction of critical perspectives from gentrification research', *International Journal of Urban and Regional Research*, 30(4), 737–757.

Smith, N. (1996) *The New Urban Frontier: Gentrification and the Revanchist City*, New York: Routledge.

Smith, N. and Williams, P. (eds) (1986) *Gentrification of the City*, Allen and Unwin.

Steele, J. *Capturing Developers*. Available at: https://jesssteele.wordpress.com/page/2/.

Survation (2014) *Rent Controls Survey, 23/12/2014* Prepared on behalf of Generation Rent. Available at: http://survation.com/wp-content/uploads/2014/12/Rent-Controls-Survey-Cover-Sheet_merged.pdf.

Tait, M. and Inch, A. (2016) 'Putting localism in place: conservative images of the good community and the contradictions of planning reform in England', *Planning Practice & Research*, 31(2), 174–194.

The Telegraph (2014) 'Labour "rent controls" policy begins to unravel, critics claim', 1 May.

Urban, F. (2015a) 'Germany, country of tenants', *Built Environment*, 41(2), 183–195.

Urban, F. (2015b) 'The end of Brixton Kaff: A diary from the front line of gentrification', Brixton Buzz website. Available at: http://www.brixtonbuzz.com/2015/06/the-end-of-brixton-kaff-a-diary-from-the-front-line-of-gentrification/.

Valverde, M. (2012) *Everyday Law on the Street: City Governance in an Age of Diversity*, Chicago, IL, and London: University of Chicago Press.

Van den Nouwelant, R., Davison, G., Gurran, N., Pinnegar, S. and Randolph, B. (2014) 'Delivering affordable housing through the planning system in urban renewal contexts: converging government roles in Queensland, South Australia and New South Wales', *Australian Planner*, 52(2), 77–89.

Vice (2016) *How Full-Time Airbnb Landlords Are Making the Housing Crisis Even Worse*. Available at: https://www.vice.com/en_uk/article/zng743/airbnb-london-rentals-housing-deregulation-act.

Watt, P. (2009) 'Social housing and regeneration in London', in Imrie, R., Lees, L. and Raco, M. (eds) *Regenerating London: Governance, Sustainability and Community in a Global City*, Routledge, pp. 212–235.

Watt, P. and Minton, A. (2016) 'London's housing crisis and its activisms: introduction', *City*, 20(2), 204–221.

White, H. and Lees, L. (2015) 'Report for Housing Bill, Why we Can't Afford to Lose it: local authority housing in London protects the poor from homelessness', submitted as Evidence. Available at: http://ch1889.org/wp-content/uploads/2015/11/Canweaffordtolosethem-FC2.pdf.

Wills, J. (2016) *Locating Localism: Statecraft, Citizenship and Democracy*, Bristol: Policy Press.

Zukin, S. (1989) *Loft Living: Culture and Capital in Urban Change*, Rutgers University Press.

Zukin, S. (1993) *Landscapes of Power: From Detroit to Disney World*, University of California Press.

Zukin, S. (2011) 'Reconstructing the authenticity of place', *Theory and Society*, 40(2), 161–165.

Legislation

Commonhold and Leasehold Reform Act, 2002
Deregulation Act, 2015
Environmental Information Regulations, 2004
European Convention on Human Rights, 1950
Freedom of Information Act, 2000
Housing Act, 1988
Housing and Planning Act, 2016
Law of Property Act, 1925
Localism Act, 2011
Retaliatory Eviction and Deregulation Act, 2015

Cases

Greenwich RLBC v Information Commissioner, 2015 EA/2014/0122
Horada v Sec of State [2016] EWCA Civ 169
R (on the application of Bokrosova) v Lambeth LBC [2015] EWHC 3386
R (on the application of Plant) v Lambeth LBC [2016] EWHC 3324 (Admin)
R (on the application of Janet Harris) v London Borough of Haringey [2010] EWCA Civ 70
R (on the application of Moseley) v London Borough of Haringey [2014] UKSC 56
R (RLT Built Environment Ltd) v Cornwall Council [2016] EWHC 2817 (Admin)

27. Self renovating neighbourhoods as an alternative to gentrification or decline
Jess Steele

27.1 FALSE CHOICE URBANISM

> Perhaps a key victory for opponents of gentrification would be to find ways to communicate more effectively that either unliveable disinvestment and decay or reinvestment and displacement is actually a false choice for low-income communities (DeFilippis 2004: 89).

Although long challenged by critical geographers, 'false choice urbanism', the poisonous offer to neighbourhoods of gentrification or decline, has become 'common sense' both in the urban regeneration field and more widely. There are two reasons why this a 'false' choice. The binary does not hold under scrutiny, and the TINA (There Is No Alternative) hegemony both misses current realities and constrains future possibilities. First, the binary choice that continues to be promoted by policy-makers, politicians, media and most commentators, has long been questioned by academic authors. Whether using empirically grounded approaches or more abstract theorising, critical geographers have shown these 'options' as two sides of the same coin (Lees and Demeritt 1998), intertwined (Slater 2014), or indeed as a continuum, the peaks and troughs of a wave, the flow of capital into and out of areas (Smith 1982).

Drawing on Marxist dialectics, Neil Smith's body of work on uneven development pictures gentrification and disinvestment as the hills and the valleys of capitalist money flow. Capitalism requires the destruction of value in order to create gaps (Smith 1979); the money to be made is always in differentials. Smith saw reinvestment and disinvestment as intimately linked in the 'locational seesaw' of capitalism stalking ground rents:

> the successive development, underdevelopment, and redevelopment of given areas as capital jumps from one place to another, then back again, both creating and destroying its own opportunities for development (Smith 1982: 151).

Marcuse (1985) also explored this intimate relationship, the 'vicious circle' in which 'while neither process causes the other, each is part of a single pattern and accentuates the other' (1985: 197). More empirically, Lees has shown in her work on the Aylesbury Estate (2014) how disinvestment opens the door for reinvestment.

Both gentrification and abandonment lead to displacement and remind us of the social justice question at the heart of the study of urban change. If we are to argue that there is an alternative, we need to show how such an alternative can mitigate displacement on all levels.

Marcuse identified four types of displacement. The most obvious and most measured is direct last-resident displacement – people pushed out directly through physical 'winkling', reinforced dereliction, or economic 'price-hike' mechanisms. Freeman (2005) and Vigdor

(2010) argued that this direct displacement is lower than anticipated. However, Newman and Wyly (2006) showed that the data used, for example by Freeman and Braconi (2004), had systemic flaws when implemented for that purpose. Yet despite major methodological shortcomings and lack of nuance,

> the 'new evidence' rapidly jumped out of the scholarly cloister to influence policy debates that have been ripped out of context. . .[and] to dismiss concerns about [policies and strategies] designed to break up the concentrated poverty that has been taken as the shorthand explanation for all that ails the disinvested inner city (Newman and Wyly 2006: 25).

Marcuse's other types of displacement are also important when considering alternatives to the false choice. One group Marcuse called 'direct chain': those previously forced to leave by abandonment, demolition or redevelopment. There is another crucial field of people who are greyed-out spectres in the spreadsheets of Decision Makers: those people who might have but will not move in in future because of gentrification or abandonment. These people who will go somewhere else instead are the unresearched and unresearchable but they matter in the theory because the 'real' place will be really different due to their absence. Marcuse's other innovation was displacement pressure: the overwhelming sense of change due to gentrification or abandonment. While Marc Fried's work in the 1960s made visible the grief that many displaced people feel, Caitlin Cahill's (2006) research with young women experiencing cultural dislocation even while they stayed in the Lower East Side voiced their 'viscerally local and intensely personal' experience of 'both a social betrayal and a public assault on their subjectivities'. Atkinson (2015) has shown a similar experience for 'symbolic' displacees in Sydney and Melbourne, stressing that alongside actual physical dislocation for some, there is for others still residing in the neighbourhood a 'symbolic violence that they locate in a changing built environment and a shifting social physiognomy that impinges and threatens the viability of their tenure of these places' (Atkinson 2015: 373). He describes an 'incumbent unanchoring' or 'unhoming' that occurs whether or not people are actually forced to move away.

The long process of gentrification in a still-disinvested place such as the Lower East Side is experienced as a deepening of inequalities (Cahill 2006: 345). The neoliberal framing of poor people as problems to be pushed out of the 'circle of deservingness' is essential in order to secure public consent for the inevitable social costs of 'upscaling' the neighbourhood (ibid). This becomes even clearer in the 'mixed communities' programmes of 'gentrification by stealth' (Bridge, Butler and Lees 2012) in which the public is invited to collude in the common sense urbanism that any kind of gentrification is better than 'nothing' and that they will somehow be included in this 'mixing', which of course is rarely the case. Slater (2006, 2009, 2014) has been providing a running commentary on this link between gentrification and disinvestment. He concludes:

> Gentrification and 'decline'; embourgeoisement and 'concentrated poverty', regeneration and decay – these are not opposites, alternatives or choices, but rather tensions and contradictions in the overall system of capital circulation, amplified and aggravated by the current crisis (Slater 2014).

Slater quotes *New York* magazine (February 2014):

> Economic flows can be reversed with stunning speed: gentrification can nudge a neighborhood up the slope; decline can roll it off a cliff. Somewhere along that trajectory of change is a sweet

spot, a mixed and humming street that is not quite settled or sanitized, where Old Guard and new arrivals coexist in equilibrium. The game is to make it last.

Slater slams this 'game' that sets the urbanist's holy grail on the middle ground between 'up the slope' and 'decline', and argues that we need to overcome the

> tenacious and constrictive dualism of 'prosperity' (gentrification) or 'blight' (disinvestment) by showing how the two are fundamentally intertwined in a wider process of capitalist urbanisation and uneven development that creates profit and class privilege for some whilst stripping many of the human need of shelter. . . . Despite many attempts to sugar-coat it and celebrate it, gentrification, both as term and process, has always been about class struggle (Slater 2014: 519).

But, along with most of the scholars and activists arguing for 'the right to stay put' (Hartman 1984; Newman and Wyly 2006; Lees 2014), this may gird the loins of resistance but it fails to go beyond critical analysis and illuminate what might be possible instead.

27.2   ALTERNATIVES?

Kearns and Parkinson (2001), at the height of 'neighbourhood renewal' in the UK, captured the false choice in one paragraph. They argued Putman's (1995) point that bonding capital creates in-group loyalty but out-group antagonism. And then offered that, on the other hand, for some 'aspiring groups with sufficient resources', the neighbourhood can become the focal point for a 'coordinated action to create a self-conscious class habitus through processes of gentrification. The neighbourhood can then be the hero or villain of the piece' (p.2107). But they do not consider an alternative – that there could be coordinated action to create a cross-class, difference-embracing, open, collaborative process in good faith to self-renovate, to make our own neighbourhoods better for us and for others without that being a class-driven aspiration. In which case the neighbourhood is neither hero nor villain, but nursemaid and cradle and outcome, both parent and offspring of the revolution.

With that in mind, the second, and more urgent, reason to challenge this 'false choice' is that it is wrong both factually and ethically to claim there is no alternative to staying on the locational seesaw, only a question of how to be at the top end. Genuine alternatives are both imaginable and emerging and the TINA hegemony is itself the biggest barrier to their realisation. As David Harvey wrote in 2000 'how come is it that we are so persuaded that "there is no alternative"?' (p.155). Eric Clark asks: can gentrification be avoided? And answers:

> Yes, but resistance against gentrification involves a struggle for power over the entry of other entities and events into time-space: not only blocking gentrification, but creating alternative regimes for development (Clark 2010).

Clark stresses the three problems that must be overcome in the development of alternatives: the commodification of space, polarised power relations, and the 'dominance of vision over sight, characteristic of "the vagrant sovereign"' (Berry 1982). At the end of their 2008 text *Gentrification*, Lees, Slater and Wyly offered up the decommodification of housing as the way out, but they did not elaborate. Achtenberg and Marcuse had made a clarion call for a genuine alternative in 1986, arguing there was:

> an opportunity to develop a broad-based progressive housing movement that can unite low-and moderate-income tenants and homeowners around their common interest in decent, affordable housing and adequate neighbourhoods. . . a program that can alter the terms of existing public debate on housing and its role in our economic and social system, and that demonstrates how people's legitimate housing needs can be met through an alternative approach (1986: 475).

Such a programme would require social ownership of housing, social production of housing supply, public control of housing finance capital, social control of land, resident control of neighbourhoods, affirmative action and housing choice, and equitable resource allocation. It would 'limit the role of profit from decisions affecting housing, substituting instead the basic principle of socially determined need' (p.476).

Newman and Wyly posed the 'central dilemma' as the conflict between 'the use-values of neighbourhood and home versus the exchange values of real estate as a vehicle for capital accumulation' (2006: 31). A turbulent decade later, Marcuse and Madden restated it as 'a conflict between housing as lived, social space and housing as an instrument for profitmaking' (2016: 4). They also make clear that the so-called 'housing crisis' is in no sense novel for working-class and poor communities: 'for the oppressed, housing is always in crisis' (p. 10). Since capitalist market practices facilitate disinvestment in order to create opportunities for reinvestment, exploiting commodified housing regardless of the impact on access to its use-value, a key element of any alternative must be to take property out of that market. This has become known as the decommodification of housing.

A significant thread of this process has been underway for several decades in the cooperative housing and community land trust (CLT) movement (which The London Tenants Federation, Lees, Just Space and SNAG, 2014, put on the table as alternatives). John E Davis tells a lovely story about 'the sweet old lady' describing her community land trust which is involved in both urban agriculture and affordable housing: 'What we are really about is land reform, dear, but we hide behind the tomatoes'. Everything that CLTs do is focused on locality, yet they are also part of a global practical and philosophical programme of change. They are clearly trying to 'tether capital to place' (DeFilippis 2004); they are 'the developer that doesn't go away' (Davis 2015); they focus on stewardship in perpetuity; and they trade the chance to speculate for the prize of permanently affordable housing.

Alongside decommodification, the other literature to offer a jumping-off point in developing alternatives is the study of the urban commons. John Emmeus Davis, who has a long history of involvement in the CLT movement and has been instrumental in spreading the message more widely, complains that:

> far less creativity has gone into thinking about land than is regularly devoted to thinking about labor and capital. . . New ways of owning, controlling or utilizing land for the improvement of distressed places and for the empowerment of the people who live there are rarely considered – or summarily rejected as too difficult to do (2015: 1).

He contrasts this not only against the creative approaches of the community development sector to work (training, cooperative enterprise and employee ownership) and money (micro-lending, benefit maximisation) but also against the hyper-creative ways that commercial players find to arrange and allocate the rights, responsibilities, risks and rewards of land.

Yet there are limitations with both these literatures. While decommodification focuses almost entirely on housing rather than other parts of the built and social environment, urban commons focuses primarily on recognised shared public realm – the collective resource of local streets, parks, public spaces and a variety of shared neighbourhood amenities. Neither literature considers derelict privately held assets, often much loved but in delinquent ownership and highly problematic for local communities. Since each literature takes a different part of the built environment as focus, neither of them sees the neighbourhood holistically. And although both make a nuanced attempt to intertwine land and people in their specifics (people live in houses; people participate in and sometimes try to manage the public realm), I would argue that they do not make enough connection between *people*, *place* and *power*.

Moreover, both literatures focus heavily on ownership and governance. Despite the fundamental importance of those, I believe that building the alternative is not all about either ownership or governance; it is about who does it (SELF), the way they do it (RENOVATING) and the scale and target of their ambition (NEIGHBOURHOODS).

27.3 THE SRN ALTERNATIVE

I like to picture the country as a huge piece of fabric, fantastically varied, sparkly in places, folded and torn in others, some bright colours, some distinctive patterns, some threadbare patches. This fabric is both physical and social. . . and we don't have the option of going to the shop for a new one. Instead it must constantly be darned, stitched, carefully patched up. So who is the Great Seamstress? No-one! As with the Wizard of Oz, no-one else can make this happen. As citizens and communities, we have to do it for ourselves, right down there in among the stitches and the holes. And once you look closely enough, you realise that there is an enormous wealth of resource at that fine-grain level (Steele, 'Connected Society' Talk to Labour Party Policy Review, 28 November 2012).

I am currently researching this fine-grain renovation in four case study neighbourhoods – two in Hastings, two in Liverpool – using the theoretical framework of SELF / RENOVATING / NEIGHBOURHOODS.

27.3.1 Self (the subject)

The concept of self in SRN has to be collective and relational. This is not individual DIY to add value to a personal asset base. It is collaborative action for common and mutual good. For the purposes of SRN, the collective self must have a strong sense of agency. Bandura has shown exhaustively (1986, 1995, 1997) how important self-efficacy is to both agency and outcome. 'People's beliefs in their efficacy affect almost everything they do: how they think, motivate themselves, feel, and behave' (p.19). This is particularly relevant where the self does not control the resources required to undertake the renovation. It is all too easy to fall back on proxy control, abdicating power to those perceived as more efficacious. The 'price of proxy control is a vulnerable security that rests on

OUTCOME EXPECTANCIES

		−	+
EFFICACY BELIEFS	**+**	Protest Grievance Social activism Milieu change	Productive engagement Aspiration Personal satisfaction
	−	Resignation Apathy	Self-devaluation Despondency

Source: Bandura 1997: 20.

Figure 27.1   Efficacy beliefs

the competence, power and favours of others' (p.17), a dependence that further reduces opportunities to build skills.

People in poor neighbourhoods have been cast in subordinate roles and given stigmatising labels: 'the more the efficacy beliefs are dismissed, the greater is the performance debilitation' (p.18). The territorial stigmatisation (Wacquant et al 2014) is acute, particularly in Granby (Liverpool) and Ore Valley (Hastings) where people and place have been demonised as simultaneously incapable and dangerous. People in my case study areas have spent a lot of time in the unsatisfactory lower and left spaces of Bandura's matrix (see Figure 27.1).

Yet I chose these areas precisely because they are demonstrating a break with the imposed narratives, they are effectively contesting established perceptions and mobilising new stories about themselves (Lowndes, forthcoming). In doing so they draw on long and varied traditions of collective action from squatting and riots, to mutual saving and networked child-rearing, to make their way, tentatively, into the top right corner of Bandura's table.

SRN is invested in 'the people who will participate' in creating diverse economies (Gibson-Graham 2014). Perhaps they have been lying in wait beneath the burden of the previously available 'choices' of gentrification and decline, awaiting an opportunity to choose differently. Their acts count as economic because they relate to material survival 'including, to name just some, trust, care, sharing, reciprocity, cooperation, coercion, bondage, thrift, guilt, love, equity, self-exploitation, solidarity, distributive justice, stewardship, spiritual connection, and environmental and social justice' (Gibson-Graham 2014: S151).

How do the people of these urban neighbourhoods work together and rebuild their common resource pool of efficacy that will generate change? Collective efficacy is 'not simply the sum of the efficacy beliefs of individuals. Rather it is an emergent group-level attribute' (Bandura 1997: 7). It is built through the hard slog of cooperation, which Richard Sennett describes as a craft requiring dialogic skills and 'an earned experience rather than just thoughtless sharing' (Sennett 2012: 13). He also believes, following Amartya Sen and Martha Nussbaum (1993), that 'people's capacities for cooperation are far greater and more complex than institutions allow them to be' (Sennett 2012: 29).

Rose (1984) and Brown-Saracino (2004) both urge us to remember that the variety of social actors in a locality are distinguished by perspectival positions as well as material hierarchy. Rose described the early in-movers to poor neighbourhoods as 'marginal gentrifiers', often women, LGBT and other minorities who do not move to 'gentrify' the inner city because they cannot afford the suburbs but because they could not carry on their lifestyle 'out there'. She warned that we 'should not assume all gentrifiers have the same class positions as each other and that they are "structurally" polarised from the displaced' (p.67) and instead argued that there could be common cause between pre-gentrification residents and initial in-movers. Presciently, she suggested they could 'work together to develop housing alternatives that would provide them with the same "ontological security" as homeownership, but without upward redistributions of wealth and compatible with, or even dovetailing with, the needs of low-income tenants' (p.65). It is a defining feature of these marginal incomers that they soon become embedded in the neighbourhood, making use of its existing markets and facilities, mingling with the incumbent population while also developing specific services to fill any gaps in meeting their own needs. I find Brown-Saracino's concept of 'social preservationist' useful. While gentrifiers may seek to preserve 'aesthetic vestiges of the neighbourhood's past', social preservationists aim to preserve actual authentic residents, and the potential for similar residents to live there in future. They are therefore vehemently anti-displacement in all forms and particularly attuned to displacement pressure – the foreboding sense of exclusionary change.

Are Brown-Saracino and Rose talking about the same kinds of people? Are Rose's 'marginal gentrifiers' social preservationists, or are they just looking for a place that is affordable and tolerant? Perhaps they become social preservationists when they realise that their affordable, tolerant, diverse places are under threat from affluent gentrifiers? The boundaries are not clear-cut for specific individuals, Brown-Saracino argues that gentrifiers and social preservationists may not be culturally or demographically distinct but they are ideologically different:

> Gentrifiers seek to tame the 'frontier', while social preservationists work to preserve the wilderness, including its inhabitants, despite their own ability to invest in and benefit from 'improvements' or revitalization (Brown-Saracino 2004: 136).

The 'frontier' meme plays out in various typologies, which could be labelled colonialists, salvationists, and the symbolic consumers of diversity (Butler and Robson 2001). There are those who come to settle our spaces and exploit our resources. There are those who come to save us, to unleash hidden potential and 'transform once-grim neighbourhoods'.[1] And there are those that come to package up 'alternative culture' for sale to the millennial mainstream. Hostile to all of these, social preservationists doggedly seek to protect the 'wilderness', while painfully aware of the impacts of their own relative privilege and 'the risk of gentrification and displacement wrought by their very presence' (Brown-Saracino 2004: 152). Whatever they come for, those newcomers that join the neighbourhood, as

---

[1] 'Transform once-grim Deptford' was a phrase used by the developer of Broadway Fields in Deptford in c.2002.

distinct from the absent forces that continue to shape it, become part of it and will experience first-hand, alongside those previous residents that are able to stay, the crashing waves of uneven geographic development. They will have varied ability to withstand or actively gain from these pressures and therefore varied responses. Following Rose and Brown-Saracino's notion that some incomers and incumbents may share collective interests and could create alliances, I think there are alternatives for them to explore together.

Tim Butler's 1995 description of the gentrification of Hackney as 'gentle and understated' appears quite shocking in 2017! I would argue there were many missed opportunities in those early years for incumbents and the first-wave incomers to become the collective self by choosing to work together to create decommodified spaces that may have stopped some of the violence and destructiveness of later waves. It may be 'too late for Hackney'; there may still be time for Hastings.

Are there attributes that encourage or hinder self-renovating neighbourhoods? Without reprising the endless arguments about leadership, it is worth noting the community organising concept that 'leadership is an action many can take, not a position that only a few can hold' (Schmitz 2012: xviii). This is a commitment to create multiple opportunities for people to take up leadership roles and support for them to practise leadership behaviour. But leadership is not the only attribute required for SRN. In 2012 I identified key roles in the 21st-century world of DIY regen for 'the three grassroots virtues of thrift, impatience and sociability' and have begun to test these in the case study interviews of self-renovating neighbourhoods in practice.

27.3.2   Renovating (the verb)

Renovating is the verb in the clause – the doing word that makes the difference. I deliberately choose the word 'renovating', not in the sense of refurbishing individual old properties (although that is part of the task) but to conjure up the idea of mending, weaving together, darning the threadbare patches of the physical, social, cultural and economic fabric. This can include new build on brownfield sites where that new build process is initiated and driven by local people in order to renovate the neighbourhood. This is not to ignore the differences between traditional gentrification, in which the sweat equity of individuals upgrades specific individually owned properties, and large scale new-build gentrification coordinated by corporate developers and governments. That difference is important, not least because the gentrification aesthetic becomes a commodity produced by the developer and purchased by the resident who is buying or renting a lifestyle rather than creating one (Hackworth and Smith 2001; Davidson and Lees 2005). However, my argument is that there is a more significant difference between collective DIY regeneration that renovates the neighbourhood and corporate/state 'renewal' that (in)tends to destroy it.

The 'verb' must capture everything that needs doing to make and maintain a self renovating neighbourhood, from achieving control over land to planning and funding, from design and building to ongoing decision-making and the production and protection of communal wealth.

In order to do any kind of renovation, neighbourhoods must enact property (Blomley 2004) – they must acquire the rights to make change in the face of a hegemonic ownership model that excludes all but the proprietor from doing so. This will usually mean taking the land/buildings into collective ownership, although it could also involve shifting the relative rights of users and owners or coming to arrangements with owners that incentivise the collective benefit. Delinquent ownership is a major barrier. As Katrina Brown (2007: 507) describes, 'processes at the nexus of property, morality and materiality shape how "justice" is practised.'

Self-renovation is not a task-and-finish mission but a habitual process of ongoing stewardship, development and management. Here the focus is on local governance (Richardson 2008; Durose, Greasley and Richardson 2009), autonomous geographies (Pickerill and Chatterton 2006; DeFilippis 2004), urban commoning in which shared and porous urban spaces become 'not only the setting but also the means to collectively experiment with possible alternative forms of social organisation' (Stavrides 2016; Ostrom 1990), and what I choose to call 'neighbourhood housework' (caring, cleaning, nurturing, solidarity). Here users and uses come to the forefront, along with judgements about 'highest and best use' that could be radically different from those that drive the locational seesaw of uneven capitalist development.

Renovating of course requires construction labour and professionals. Robert Tressell was a painter and decorator in Hastings where he wrote and set his famous book *The Ragged Trousered Philanthropists* (2014). He died in Liverpool and both communities are rediscovering his renewed relevance a century later. He inspires me to think about new ways to create new kinds of non-exploitative, mutually obligated contractual relationships between client neighbourhoods, and the construction professionals and labour they need to create a self-determined alternative to gentrification or decline.

27.3.3   Neighbourhoods (the object)

Neighbourhoods are the object, the thing that is done to. I choose the geographic scale of neighbourhoods because I think they are so potentially powerful, and underestimated as a site for social good. Neighbourhoods are produced through processes of uneven development, capital mobility, changing patterns of ownership and governance, contested definitions of community. But they are constructed, as people are, through organic not mechanical processes. This is a process of everyday making, responding and remaking in which the relationships between personal and spatial identities are mutually and iteratively constitutive (Fincher and Jacobs 1998; Jackson and Butler 2015). *Places are peopled and people are placed* is a simple way to state this complex relationship, but with enough force to hint at Adrienne Rich's (1986) 'politics of location' which is a politics of rootedness, in our bodies, in our places, in 'the ground we're coming from' (p.34).

The n-word (*neighbourhood*) is complex, multivalent, almost as rich as the c-word (*community*). It brings to mind Heidegger's idea of 'dwelling in nearness'. Casey (1997) argues that such 'nearness' brings about neighbourhood rather than the other way round. However, shared space alone is not enough; there are increasing numbers of sterilised, privatised spaces that we are allowed in only as long as we show our faces and bring our wallets. They are not neighbourhoods.

Neighbourhood is a web of relationships but it is also a fine-grain physical collection of functioning spaces and buildings; beyond housing it may include the school, the pub, a set of shops, green space, play areas, roads, signs, rubbish bins, public conveniences, spaces for leisure, culture and politics, derelict buildings, abandoned spaces. It is the 'reservoir of resources. . . a "shaper" of who we are, both as defined by ourselves and by others' (Kearns and Parkinson 2001: 2109). Galster (2001) describes the neighbourhood as a 'bundle of spatially based attributes' making up a 'complex commodity' which competes with others in a marketised situation. He warns that it is a risky business choosing a neighbourhood because market mechanisms do not cope well with these highly idiosyncratic characteristics. He shows how consumers of neighbourhood (households, business people, property owners and local government) are also its producers, but within this overall multifaceted picture he gives, in my view, unwarranted primacy to 'external forces reverberating through the metropolitan housing market', stating that 'the prime origins of a particular neighbourhood changing are located outside that neighbourhood'.

My argument is based on the potential for constructive resistance to these 'externally induced' changes. I want to see a process of locality construction and maintenance – physical, socio-economic, semiotic – that is actively and purposively led by local people whose power and legitimacy lies in their willingness to take on the neighbourhood housework for the common and collective good. This is a daunting challenge – it needs to find ways to change everything: from 'tethering capital to place' (DeFillipis 2004), to developing a new social contract of rights and responsibilities around the 'moralities of land' (Blomley 2004), from building collective efficacy (Bandura 1997) to tackling 'vagrant sovereigns' (Berry 1982). And it needs to recognise the bewildering specificities of places everywhere, so that even within the same legal and political jurisdiction there will be no easy generalisability or replicability. While there is much to share between the UK and US contexts, for example, the political tools for neighbourhood action in the US are very different because of the direct link between property and the local tax base.

There are two standard 'neighbourhood' literatures to consider. The intricacies of the 'neighbourhood effects' literature are neatly tackled by the fact that, whether we can prove or explain the impact of the neighbourhood on outcomes for individuals, there are undoubtedly 'spatially ordered outcomes of local communities' (Timberlake 2013).

> In a kind of self-fulfilling prophecy, neighbourhoods have effects in part because people and institutions act *as if* neighbourhoods matter, further reinforcing the reproduction of inequality by place (Sampson 2014).

Neighbourhood dynamics is a complex and contested field (Manley 2013) but that does not stop the neighbourhood being important as a site for social change. In the practitioner world, fed by academics such as Florida (2004) and Landry (2000), 'place-making' is almost invariably boosterist and uncritical of gentrification and the role of capital. Whereas Harvey's (1996) concept of place-making as the carving out of 'temporary permanences' from space and Massey's (2005) temporary constellations, place/bundles and place-framing offer a richer seam. Pierce et al (2011) draw on these to conceptualise relational place-making as the dynamic, multi-scalar and flexible interplay of place, networks and politics. This can guide empirical research into the conflicts and commonalities between the place-frames of actors and institutions in specific case study neighbourhoods.

27.4 DISRUPTION

Can DIY regen and mission-driven ownership be disruptive of capitalist and statist forces at the neighbourhood scale? What happens if the neighbourhoods join up? Can they overcome the limits of 'folk politics' (Srnicek and Williams 2015)? Could neighbourhood action 'in, against and beyond life under capitalism' be *both* parochially prefigurative and also more widely disruptive by 'weaving together cracks that can purposefully crack the capitalist system' (Chatterton 2016: 411)? Both elements are challenging. Any given example can teach us lessons about potential futures but the localised action-effort required to genuinely prefigure a better future is significant and sustained. We ask people in the movement to be bi-focal – both do this fine-grain work in your own place and also be part of a 'diffuse and networked spatiality, where non-contiguous projects, ideas and people are strongly connected through counter-topographical networks (Katz 2001) that create islands of post-capitalist commons' (Chatterton 2016: 411). This has implications for 'scaling up' – not through traditional scaling or replication but via rhizomatic structures (Deleuze and Guattari 1987) and networked micro politics (Scott-Cato and Hillier 2011).

My interest is in the (re)politicisation of neighbourhood/locality, despite the dangers (Keith 2005). While the geography of gentrification may be moving towards a planetary scale (Lees, Shin and López-Morales 2016), I argue for taking neighbourhood more seriously as a site for social good and economic opportunity, both empirically right now and normatively for the future. My inspiration came from reflecting on two 'accidental transformations' in South East London (Steele 1993) – the purchase and renovation of Upper Brockley by well-networked West Indian families in the 1960s and the handover of Crossfield Estate to students and young social workers, teachers and musicians in the 1970s. In each of these cases the physicality of private and public spaces and the perception/reputation/valuing of the place was transformed. Not driven by policy or official intervention (unlike the multiple but far less impactful regeneration initiatives that the area was subjected to in subsequent decades), instead they were the expression of the clear self-interest of groups of local people. There are other examples of these accidental transformations: artist-led cultural quarters that transform area reputations; music studios that provide hubs of employment, entertainment and a strong sense of family; seaside towns that drag themselves out of the bottle and into the guide books; family squatting groups that took over whole streets of condemned housing and paid rent into the pot to DIY some more life into them; self-build groups that get an amazing buzz from being in physical control of their housing destiny. They usually begin with the relatively extreme affordability of space and with people who have the strength of will or peculiar circumstance to avoid the dead hand that keeps most from participating directly in neighbourhood change. But there are too few of these stories; they are often snuffed out by economics and politics, both micro and macro; and it is very rare indeed that the value uplift they create is captured and reinvested.

Pratt (2009) shows that as long as cultural regeneration policy takes the approach 'light the blue touch paper and retire' the cultural industries will briefly 'shine and burn'; out of their ashes comes residential development and then the expulsion of the creatives from the place they have lit so brightly for the advertisements. He extends the metaphor to argue that 'cities are wasting. . . one of the most dynamic industries as "starter fuel" for property development' (2009: 1043), neglecting the more substantial economic and cultural impact such industries could have. I would make a similar case in relation to the other kinds of self-renovators eulogised in my previous paragraph. The huge energy they contribute to neighbourhood improvement is but starter fuel for exclusionary price rises, unless and until, first, we begin to value both community and culture as 'higher and better uses' in their own right and, second, take action to enact ownership so that the collective self that renovates the neighbourhood can control at least some of the terms. Pratt highlights 'culture as production rather than ornament' (2009: 1044); I want to argue for neighbourhood renovation as a productive process for local people, not a consumable product for non-local profiteers.

To achieve this, self-renovating neighbourhoods will need to innovate organisationally and understand the recursive formation of production and consumption *in situ* (Pratt 2009: 1056). Joshua Compston, with his Factual Nonsense gallery in Hoxton in 1992, sought to 'exploit and eventually explode the gap between art, advertising and entertainment, high street retailing and real estate development' (Stallabrass 1999: 185). In 2016 one visitor called the self-renovating work in Hastings 'extreme shop-fitting'. SRN groups must operate in and eventually close the gap between community empowerment, cultural enterprise, the darning of the built fabric and the all-important achievement of real property, in order to tether (economic, social and cultural) capital to place and avoid the role of handmaiden to the speculators.

27.5   PRELIMINARY CONCLUSIONS

'The price of a successful attack is a constructive alternative' (Alinsky 1971: 126). Resistance will never be enough without creating 'alternative regimes for development'. Self renovating neighbourhoods offer an emerging model of high-impact collective action, a kind of 'insurgent regeneration' which is 'concretely reshaping the spaces of exclusion' and in the process expanding the notion and practice of citizenship (De Caldi and Frediani 2016). In crafting a constructive alternative to the false choice between gentrification and decline, the SRN process and its leaders must negotiate a path between the 'unruly and transgressive practices' (ibid) that build community and notionally compliant behaviours in order to enact property for the common good within the dominant ownership model. As this book shows, the need for alternatives to gentrification (and indeed decline) is more urgent than ever, given how this socially unjust process has progressed through time and space.

REFERENCES

Achtenberg, E. and Marcuse, P. (1986) 'Toward the decommodification of housing', in Bratt, R., Hartman, C. and Meyerson, A. (eds) *Critical Perspectives on Housing*, Philadelphia, PA: Temple University Press.
Alinsky, S. (1971) *Rules for Radicals: A Practical Primer for Realistic Radicals*, New York: Random House.
Atkinson, R. (2015) 'Losing one's place: narratives of neighbourhood change, market injustice and symbolic displacement', *Housing, Theory and Society*, 32(4), 373–388.
Bandura, A. (1997) *Self-efficacy: The Exercise of Control*, Macmillan.
Berry, W. (1982) *The Gift of Good Land: Further Essays Cultural and Agricultural*, San Francisco, CA: North Point Press.
Blomley, N. (2004) *Unsettling the City: Urban Land and the Politics of Property*, New York; London: Routledge.
Bridge, G., Butler, T. and Lees, L. (2012) *Mixed Communities: Gentrification by Stealth?*, Bristol: Policy Press.

Brown, K. (2007) 'Understanding the materialities and moralities of property: reworking collective claims to land', *Transactions of the Institute of British Geographers*, 32(4), 507–522.

Brown-Saracino, J. (2004) 'Social preservationists and the quest for authentic community', *City & Community*, 3(2), 135–156.

Cahill, C. (2006) '"At risk"? The fed up honeys re-present the gentrification of the Lower East Side', *Women's Studies Quarterly*, 34(1/2), 334–363.

Chatterton, P. (2016) 'Building transitions to post-capitalist urban commons', *Transactions of the Institute of British Geographers*, 41(4), 403–415.

Clark, E. (ed) (2010) *Advanced Course on the Analysis of Environmental Conflicts and Justice*, Universitat Autònoma de Barcelona: Powerpoint Slideshare.

Clark, E. (2011) 'Housing and real estate ("Gentrification; A neighborhood that never changes: gentrification, social preservation, and the search for authenticity") (Book review)', *Journal of the American Planning Association*, 77(2), 190–191.

Conn, E. (2011) 'Community engagement in the social eco-system dance', *Third Sector Research Centre Discussion Paper*.

Davidson, M. and Lees, L. (2005) 'New-build "gentrification" and London's riverside renaissance', *Environment and Planning A*, 37(7), 1165–1190.

Davis, J. (2010) *The Community Land Trust Reader*, Lincoln Institute of Land Policy.

Davis, J. (2015) 'Common ground: Community-led development on community-owned land'. Available at: http://www.cltroots.org/archives/3231 (accessed: 31 March 2017).

De Carli, B. and Frediani, A. (2016) 'Insurgent regeneration: spatial practices of citizenship in the rehabilitation of inner-city São Paulo', *GeoHumanities*, 2(2), 331–353.

Defilippis, J. (2004) *Unmaking Goliath: Community Control in the Face of Global Capital*, Routledge.

Deleuze, G. and Guattari, F. (1987) 'Introduction: rhizome', in *A Thousand Plateaus: Capitalism and Schizophrenia*, Minneapolis: University of Minnesota Press, pp. 3–25.

Durose, C., Greasley, S. and Richardson, L. (2009) *Changing Local Governance, Changing Citizens*, Bristol: Policy Press.

Fincher, R. and Jacobs, J. (1998) *Cities of Difference*, Guilford Press.

Florida, R. (2004) *The Rise of the Creative Class and how it's Transforming Work, Leisure, Community and Everyday Life*, New York: Basic Books.

Freeman, L. (2005) 'Displacement or succession? Residential mobility in gentrifying neighbourhoods', *Urban Affairs Review*, 40(4), 463–491.

Freeman, L. and Braconi, F. (2004) 'Gentrification and displacement New York City in the 1990s', *Journal of the American Planning Association*, 70(1), 39–52.

Fried, M. (1963) 'Grieving for a lost Home', in L. Duhl (ed) *The Urban Condition*, New York: Basic Books.

Galster, G. (2001) 'On the nature of neighbourhood', *Urban Studies*, 38(12), 2111–2124.

Gibson-Graham, J. (2014) 'Rethinking the economy with thick description and weak theory', *Current Anthropology*, 55(S9), S153.

Hackworth, J. and Smith, N. (2001) 'The changing state of gentrification', *Tijdschrift voor economische en sociale geografie*, 92(4), 464–477.

Hartman, C. (1984). 'Right to stay put', in Geisler C. and Popper F. (eds) *Land Reform, American Style*, Totowa, NJ: Rowman & Allanheld.

Harvey, D. (2000) *Spaces of Hope*, California: University of California Press.

Harvey, D. (1996) *Justice, Nature and the Geography of Difference*, Cambridge, MA; London: Blackwell Publishers.

Jackson, E. and Butler, T. (2015) 'Revisiting "social tectonics": the middle classes and social mix in gentrifying neighbourhoods', *Urban Studies*, 52(13), 2349–2365.

Kearns, A. and Parkinson, M. (2001) 'The significance of neighbourhood', *Urban Studies*, 38(12), 2103–2110.

Keating, W., Hartman, C., LeGates, R. and Turner, S. (1982) *Displacement: How to Fight it*, Berkeley, CA: National Housing Law Project.

Keith, M. (2005) *After the Cosmopolitan? Multicultural Cities and the Future of Racism*, London: Routledge.

Landry, C. (2000) *The Creative City: A Toolkit for Urban Innovators*, Stroud, UK: Earthscan Publications.

Lees, L. (2014) 'The urban injustices of New Labour's "New Urban Renewal": The case of the Aylesbury Estate in London', *Antipode*, 46(4), 921–947.

Lees, L. and Demeritt, D. (1998) 'Envisioning "The Livable City": The Interplay of "Sin City" and "Sim City" in Vancouver's Planning Discourse', *Urban Geography*, 19(4), 332–359.

Lees, L., Shin, H. and López-Morales, E. (2016) *Planetary Gentrification*, Cambridge: Polity Press.

Lees, L., Slater, T. and Wyly, E. (2008) *Gentrification*, New York: Routledge.

Ley, D. (1996) *The New Middle Class and the Remaking of the Central City*, Oxford: Oxford University Press.

Lowndes, V. (forthcoming) 'Narrative and storytelling', in Stoker, G. and Evans, E. (eds) *Methods that Matter: Social Science and Evidence-based Policymaking*, Bristol: Policy Press.

Manley, D. (2013) *Neighbourhood Effects or Neighbourhood Based Problems? A Policy Context*, Dordrecht; New York: Springer.

Marcuse, P. and Madden, D. (2016) *In Defense of Housing: The Politics of Crisis*, Verso Books.

Marcuse, P. (1985) 'Gentrification, abandonment, and displacement: connections, causes, and policy responses in New York City', *Washington University Journal of Urban and Contemporary Law*, 28, 195–240.

Massey, D. (2005) *For Space*, California: Thousand Oaks.

Newman, K. and Wyly, E. (2006) 'The right to stay put, revisited: gentrification and resistance to displacement in New York City', *Urban Studies*, 43(1), 23–57.

Nussbaum, M. and Sen, A. (1993) *The Quality of Life*, Oxford: Oxford University Press.

Ostrom, E. (1990) *Governing the Commons: The Evolution of Institutions for Collective Action*, Cambridge: Cambridge University Press.

Pickerill, J. and Chatterton, P. (2006) 'Notes towards autonomous geographies: creation, resistance and self-management as survival tactics', *Progress in Human Geography*, 30(6), 730–746.

Pierce, J., Martin, D. and Murphy, J. (2011) 'Relational place-making: the networked politics of place', *Transactions of the Institute of British Geographers*, 36(1), 54–70.

Pratt, A. (2009) 'Urban regeneration: from the arts "feel good" factor to the cultural economy: A case study of Hoxton, London', *Urban Studies*, 46(5–6), 1041–1061.

Putnam, R. (1995) 'Bowling alone: America's declining social capital', *Journal of Democracy*, 6(1), 65–78.

Rich, A. (1984) 'Notes towards a politics of location', in Lewis, R. and Mills, S. (eds) *Feminist Postcolonial Theory: A Reader*, Edinburgh: Edinburgh University Press, pp. 29–42.

Richardson, L. (2008) *DIY Community action: Neighbourhood Problems and Community Self-help*, Bristol: Policy Press.

Rose, D. (1984) 'Rethinking gentrification: beyond the uneven development of Marxist urban theory', *Environment and Planning D: Society and Space*, 2(1), 47–74.

Sampson, R. (2014) 'Inequality from the top down and bottom up: towards a revised Wacquant', *Ethnic and Racial Studies*, 37(10), 1732–1738.

Schmitz, P. (2011) *Everyone Leads: Building Leadership from the Community Up*, John Wiley & Sons.

Scott-Cato, M. and Hillier, J. (2010) 'How could we study climate-related social innovation? Applying Deleuzean philosophy to transition towns', *Environmental Politics*, 19(6), 869–887.

Sennett, R. (2012) *Together: The Rituals, Pleasures and Politics of Cooperation*, Yale University Press.

Slater, T. (2006) 'The eviction of critical perspectives from gentrification research', *International Journal of Urban and Regional Research*, 30(4), 737–757.

Slater, T. (2009) 'Missing Marcuse: on gentrification and displacement', *City*, 13(2–3), 292–311.

Slater, T. (2014) 'Unravelling false choice urbanism', *City*, 18(4–5), 517–524.

Smith, N. (1979) 'Toward a theory of gentrification: a back to the city movement by capital, not people', *Journal of the American Planning Association*, 45(4), 538–548.

Smith, N. (1982) 'Gentrification and uneven development', *Economic Geography*, 58(2), 139–155.

Srnicek, N. and Williams, A. (2015) *Inventing the Future: Postcapitalism and a World Without Work*, London: Verso Books.

Stallabrass, J. (1999) *High Art Lite*, London: Verso Books.

Stavrides, S. (2015) 'Common space as threshold space: urban commoning in struggles to re-appropriate public space', *Footprint*, 9(1), 9–19.

Steele, J. (1993) *Turning the Tide: The History of Everyday Deptford*, Deptford Forum Publishing.

Steele, J. (2012) 'Self-renovating neighbourhoods: unlocking resources for the new regeneration', *Journal of Urban Regeneration and Renewal*, 6(1), 53–65.

The London Tenants Federation, Lees, L., Just Space and SNAG (2014) *Staying Put: An Anti-Gentrification Handbook for Council Estates in London*.

Timberlake, J. (2013) 'Great American city: Chicago and the enduring neighborhood effect by Robert J. Sampson', *Journal of Urban Affairs*, 35(3), 385–387.

Tressell, R. (2014) *The Ragged Trousered Philanthropists*, Hastings Borough Council.

Vigdor, J. (2010) 'Is urban decay bad? Is urban revitalization bad too?', *Journal of Urban Economics*, 68(3), 277–289.

Wacquant, L., Slater, T. and Pereira, V. (2014) 'Territorial stigmatization in action', *Environment and Planning A*, 46(6), 1270–1280.

Index